For this second, annual volume of housing literature, the editors have selected twenty-nine major articles in such traditional fields as land economics, construction, mortgage finance, and community development as well as multidisciplinary studies of housing by political scientists, social psychologists, sociologists, and social anthropologists. As *Choice* commented on the first volume of this series, "The majority of the selections would not be too technical for a serious undergraduate (and) a library building a collection in current social problems should certainly include this series."

The book is organized in six parts:

I. Current Trends in Housing
II. Inner-City Housing
III. Economic Analysis and Housing Markets
IV. Race and Housing
V. Housing Finance
VI. Policy Considerations

HOUSING

Also edited by George Sternlieb:
HOUSING, 1970-1971, An AMS Anthology

Also by Virginia Paulus:
HOUSING: A BIBLIOGRAPHY, 1960-1972

HOUSING

1971 - 1972

An AMS Anthology

edited by

George Sternlieb

Director of the Center for Urban Policy Research

Rutgers University

and

Virginia Paulus

Center for Urban Policy Research

Rutgers University

AMS PRESS
NEW YORK

Library of Congress Catalog Card Number: 73-8098

International Standard Book Number:
Buckram bound   0-404-10402-9
Paper-bound   0-404-10452-5

Manufactured in the United States of America

TABLE OF CONTENTS

II. INNER-CITY HOUSING

III. ECONOMIC ANALYSIS AND HOUSING MARKETS

IV. RACE AND HOUSING

V. HOUSING FINANCE

VI. POLICY CONSIDERATIONS

ACKNOWLEDGMENTS

Acknowledgment is made to the authors and publishers below who have granted permission to reprint material and who reserve all rights in the articles appearing in this anthology.

Board of Governors, Federal Reserve System, "Ways to Moderate Fluctuations in the Construction of Housing," *Federal Reserve Bulletin*, March, 1972, pp. 215-225.

Craig, "The Dayton Area's 'Fair Share' Housing Plan Enters the Implementation Phase," *City*, Volume 6, January-February 1972, pp. 50-56.

DeSalvo, "A Methodology for Evaluating Housing Programs," *Journal of Regional Science*, Volume 11, 1971, pp. 173-185.

Downs, A., "Are Subsidies the Best Answer for Housing Low and Moderate Income Households?" *The Urban Lawyer*, Volume 4, No. 3, pp. 405-416.

Downs, J., "Demand and Market for Housing," *The Appraisal Journal*, January 1972, pp. 103-113.

Grebler, "The 'New System' of Residential Mortgage Finance," *The Mortgage Banker*, Volume 32, February 1972, pp. 4-24.

Hayes and Harlan, "Caveat Emptor in Real Estate Equities," *Harvard Business Review*, March-April 1972.

Heinberg and Sunley, "Tax Incentives for Rehabilitating Rental Housing," *Proceedings of the American Real Estate and Urban Economics Association*, Volume 6, 1971, pp. 197-218.

Hirshon, "The Interrelationship between Exclusionary Zoning and Exclusionary Subdivision Control," *Journal of Law Reform*, Winter, 1972, pp. 351-360.

Kain and Quigley, "Housing Market Discrimination, Homeownership, and Savings Behavior," *American Economic Review*, Volume LXII, June 1972, pp. 263-277.

Korobow and Gelson, "Real Estate Investment Trusts," *Monthly Review*, Federal Reserve Bank of New York, August 1971, Vol. 53, No. 8, pp. 188-195.

Kristof, "Federal Housing Policies," *Land Economics*, Volume 48, November 1972, pp. 309-320. Copyright © 1972 The Regents of the University of Wisconsin Systems.

Lapham, "Do Blacks Pay More for Housing?" *Journal of Political Economy*, November-December 1971, pp. 1244-1257.

Lazerow, "Discriminatory Zoning," *American University Law Review*, Volume 21, No. 1, pp. 157-183.

McAllister, Kaiser, and Butler, "Residential Mobility of Blacks and Whites," *American Journal of Sociology*, Volume 77, No. 3, pp. 445-456.

Murasky, "*James v. Valtierra*" *University of Chicago Law Review*, Fall, 1971, pp. 115-142.

Muth, "The Derived Demand for Urban Residential Land," *Urban Studies*, October 1971, pp. 243-254.

Nachbauer, "Empty Houses," *Howard Law Journal*, Volume 17, 1971, pp. 3-68.

Olsen, "An Econometric Analysis of Rent Control," *Journal of Political Economy*, November-December 1972, pp. 1081-1100.

Schulkin, "Real Estate Investment Trusts in an Era of Innovation," *Real Estate Review*, Fall 1972, pp. 48-58.

Shiefman, Werba, and Associates, "The Mobile Home Market," *The Appraisal Journal*, July 1972, pp. 391-411. The editors are particularly grateful to John Walbridge and the American Institute of Real Estate Appraisers for permission to reprint this article.

Sternlieb, "Death of the American Dream House," *Trans-action*, February 1972, pp. 39-42.

Sternlieb, Burchell, and Hughes, "Ticking Time Bomb," *Real Estate Review*, Spring 1972, pp. 34-40.

Syron, "The Hard Economics of Ghetto Fire Insurance," *New England Economic Review*, March-April 1972, pp. 2-11.

Welfeld, "That 'Housing Problem'" *The Public Interest*, No. 27, Spring 1972, pp. 78-95. Copyright © National Affairs Inc., 1972.

INTRODUCTION

The warm reception accorded the first volume of our housing anthology has encouraged us to publish this second collection of readings.

The subject of housing has generated considerable interest because its component elements—residential location, costs and amenities, subsidies and governmental intervention—represent in microcosm the enormously complex web we call society. But aside from its usefulness as an analogue for broader concerns, housing is of major interest in and of itself. As one of the largest single industries in the United States, it produced, in 1973 alone, approximately 2.4 million conventional housing units, plus an additional 600,000 so-called mobile homes—an output nearly double the average of the last decade.

Yet despite the industry's obvious vigor, its future promises to be anything but smooth. Ecologists and environmentalists are raising louder and more insistent demands for restrictions upon land use. The principle of growth for its own sake, which has until recently gone largely unchallenged, is now open to sharp attack. Critics raise questions of support levels, of noise and air pollution, of sewage facilities and water availability not merely as they impinge upon a given development but rather as they affect gross patterns of growth. In state after state, the land user is now accountable not only to local zoning boards or variance groups, but also to the formal strictures of a land use impact statement and to the manifold requirements of the Environmental Protection Agency and similar organizations.

The industry's operations will be further circumscribed by the rigors imposed by the energy crisis and the tightening national budget. The age of affluence may well be drawing to a close. And its demise could mean the end of the steady, dependable dollar, so essential to long-term, low-interest conventional borrowing.

Concurrent with these mounting pressures upon the industry is a shift in societal priorities. The central city, whose needs and problems have for so long been dominant, has gradually been assuming a secondary position. Gone is the zeal that fostered such programs as urban renewal, stepped-up code enforcement, model cities and the welter of housing rehabilitation efforts. In its place, all too frequently, is sullen resignation.

The downgraded emphasis upon the city is clearly evidenced in the extensive literature we explored in preparing this anthology. Periodicals, government reports, agency statements, all mirror the changing focus. As suburban zoning, land use and development assume stage center, the plight of the central city is reduced to a matter of historical import. Accounts of the hard, practical problems of urban life are notably lacking, relegated to dismal recitals of FHA foreclosures, central city lending problems and the like.

Accompanying the reordered priorities is a vague, generalized sense of unease. In the midst of America's most productive housing year (housing starts were more than double the level of new household formation) lurks the spectre of economic decline. One barometer of the national temper is the erratic motion of interest rates—the credit crunch of 1969 became the credit vise of '72-'73. Conventional interest rates have assumed the pattern of a one-way ratchet, with sudden leaps followed by a return to a base level that is always one notch ahead of its predecessor.

This nation's continuing provision of inexpensive housing hinges increasingly upon both the costs of infrastructure and the carrying costs of capital. But future governmental intervention in these areas in the form of federal interest subsidy programs has been severely threatened by the tremendous cost of providing such subsidies and by the mixed record of these programs as reflected in the growing number of central city foreclosures.

The controversy over central city improvement versus opening up the suburbs continues unabated. From the numerous writings on these two disparate approaches, we have chosen to include specific accounts describing increasing state intervention and analyzing the pros and cons of revenue sharing.

We have divided the readings into the following six sections:

I. *Current Trends in Housing*

This section, representing a sample of key literature on subsidies and alternatives, begins with a major descriptive effort of federal housing subsidies. It is followed by material on the distribution of subsidies, their efficacy and on some alternative approaches successfully implemented in Europe. Also included in this section are articles on zoning (particularly on exclusionary zoning), and on alternative land use controls.

II. *Inner City Housing*

From the relative dearth of literature on housing in the central cities, we have culled writings on the abandonment phenomenon, which increasingly menaces the core areas of older cities. Complementing these accounts is an article on the problems created by fires in abandoned structures. We have also included material on the economic hardships that beset various rehabilitation efforts.

III. *Economic Analysis in Housing Markets*

The information contained in this section should prove a valuable supplement to the tool kit of the professional houser. The wealth of materials available made our choice difficult indeed. What is most evident here is the sophistication of the analytical methods employed, whether their focus was upon housing programs, the mobile home market or an econometric study of rent control. Their nuts-and-bolts approach as much as their subject areas should be useful to planner and houser alike.

IV. *Race and Housing*

The vast range of literature available on this subject is increasingly characterized by rigorous analysis and has less recourse to pejoratives and moral imperatives. This trend toward quantitative fact-finding should help establish a more solid empirical base upon which to formulate moral decisions. Especially crucial in this sphere are the articles we have included on home ownership, savings and wealth among blacks and whites.

V. *Housing Finance*

The variety of new instrumentalities for financing real estate defies description. Yet despite the abundant materials available to us, we found surprisingly few analyses of the long-range housing outlook.

VI. *Policy Considerations*

In this lamentably brief section, we have grouped a number of key articles describing divergent attempts to bridge the gap between income and runaway housing costs. They focus variously upon efforts to minimize startup costs by reducing fluctuations in actual construction, to produce housing at the top so as to enhance filtering mechanisms, and to provide tax incentives for generating or preserving housing approaches. The final article raises important questions about the future adequacy of some of these measures.

—George Sternlieb
Virginia Paulus

I.

CURRENT TRENDS
IN HOUSING

FEDERAL HOUSING SUBSIDIES

By Henry Aaron

This paper describes the major Federal housing programs and presents estimates for selected recent years of the benefits they generate for families in various income brackets. The paper then suggests an alternative system of housing subsidies through allowances based on income and net worth and on local housing costs.

The major existing programs include:

Special tax benefits for homeowners.

FHA mortgage insurance and VA loan guarantees.

Low rent public housing.

Homeownership and rental assistance.

Rent supplements.

Below market interest rate loans.

Insured loans of the Farmers Home Administration.

Each of these programs reduces the cost of housing for selected economic groups. Overwhelmingly the largest housing subsidy is favorable tax treatment of homeowners which in 1966 left homeowners with about $7 billion more indisposable income than they would have had if they were treated like other property owners. This estimate ignores tax savings arising from the excess of allowed over true depreciation on rental housing and from other tax provisions. Income tax savings to homeowners are more than 10 times as large as benefits under the next largest program, low rent public housing. These benefits accrue largely to middle- and upper-income households, 64 percent to households with 1966 incomes of $10,000 or more, 36 percent to households with incomes of $15,000 per year or more.

Low rent public housing produced $510 million in benefits in 1966, 86 percent of which accured to families with incomes of $5,000 per year or less. Benefits from public housing have risen substantially since 1966 as the number of units under management has increased and general rent levels have risen.

Benefits from the newer rent supplement program also accrue primarily to low-income households. Total rent supplement payments are projected to rise from $21 million in 1970 to $91 million in 1972. According to present plans this program will remain much smaller than low rent public housing.

Homeownership and rental assistance, however, are projected eventually to surpass low rent public housing in size. The national housing goal projects 2.7 million units under these programs. Benefits will reach $299 and $151 million, respectively, in 1972. These programs primarily serve lower middle income households with incomes of $4,000 to $7,000 per year. The superseded below-market interest rate loan program also reached families in these income brackets, as does the system of Government loans administered by the Farmers Home Administration, principally for households in thinly settled areas.

The operations of the Federal Housing Administration and the Veterans' Administration in protecting lenders against default by borrowers generated measurable subsidies of about $141 million in 1966. In addition, the operations of these agencies have probably helped spur a revolution in home financing procedures. The measurable subsidies arise because these agencies do not charge each borrower (or lender) the actuarial cost of default protection which the agencies provide. The benefits accrued primarily to lower middle income families.

Important faults with existing housing programs include:

Inequities.—Most benefits accrue to middle and upper middle income families. Since not all families eligible for assistance on the basis of income receive, jealousy and resentment are growing.

Cost.—Existing subsidies plus housing expenditures required of subsidized households exceed greatly the amount the Bureau of Labor Statistics (BLS) estimates is necessary to buy standard housing in a "low cost" budget.

Rigidity.—Subsidies are tied to units under existing programs, so that an assisted household loses benefits if it moves. This characteristic reduces mobility and consumer choice of the assisted household.

An alternative housing subsidy program, the Housing Assistance Plan, is described that is free of these faults. A nationwide program costing $3.2 to $6.2 billion could provide housing assistance to all households sufficient to enable them to match housing outlays called for by the BLS "low cost" budget. These estimates would be substantially reduced if welfare reform were enacted.

The Federal Government undertakes numerous programs directly to improve the quality of housing in the United States. Some of these programs provide subsidies to encourage the construction, rehabilitation, and purchase of housing. During the late 1960's these programs brought benefits to selected households worth about $8 billion. Since then a number of these programs have expanded rapidly and benefits now exceed $10 billion. The value of these subsidies will continue to grow rapidly.

Subsidies of this magnitude deserve careful scrutiny. Housing subsidies, however, largely escape even periodic review by either the legislative or executive branches because the major subsidies arise through provisions of the Internal Revenue Code which concern only tax lawyers and some economists. Other programs, such as mortgage insurance administered by the Federal Housing Administration, operate under authorizations requiring infrequent renewal and generate no budget expenditures although they produce substantial benefits. Still other programs, such as homeownership and rental assistance or rent supplements, are subject to the normal budget cycle.

Three questions confront anyone interested in evaluating housing subsidy programs:

1. What service does each program provide?
2. Who benefits from these services?
3. How efficiently are these services provided?

This paper deals primarily with the first two questions although references to efficiency are scattered throughout. Part I describes the major housing subsidy programs. Part II summarizes the distribution of benefits under each program. Part III examines certain serious problems endemic to all existing housing subsidy programs. Part IV suggests an alternative approach to housing subsidies—housing allowances—discusses issues in the design of such a program, and presents estimates of the budgetary cost and regional distribution of an illustrative system of housing allowances.

I. MAJOR HOUSING SUBSIDY PROGRAMS

The major programs which generate housing subsidies are income tax treatment of homeowners, low-rent public housing, homeownership and rental assistance, rent supplements, below market interest rate loans on multifamily housing, Veterans' Administration guaranteed loans and Federal Housing Administration mortgage insurance, and Farmers Home Administration insured home loans.

A number of other programs that generate subsidies are not discussed here because they are much smaller in size than those listed.(1)

Also not discussed are many housing programs which do not provide subsidies in the usual sense, but which improve the operational efficiency of certain housing markets. In so doing they permit certain buyers and sellers who would not otherwise come to terms to complete a mutually beneficial transaction. For example, the Federal National Mortgage Association (FNMA), for many years a Government-controlled corporation, creates a secondary market for federally insured and guaranteed mortgages. Although the secondary market operations in recent years have provided no subsidies—in the sense that FNMA consistently bought mortgages for more or sold them for less than the market price—these operations presumably both increased the willingness of financial intermediaries to make home loans and improved the terms on which borrowers could obtain them.(2) Various other programs facilitate mutually beneficial transactions, but since their operations result in no expenditure or dissipation of capital, they are not discussed further.

INCOME TAX TREATMENT OF HOMEOWNERS(3)

The murky provisions of the Internal Revenue Code contain the most important housing programs currently administered by the Federal Government.

One program cost the Treasury $7 billion in 1966, and may well cost it $10 billion today. It subsidizes nearly every homeowner in the United States. Other tax programs provide $270 million in additional benefits to most renters. Despite their cost and pervasiveness, these programs receive negligible scrutiny within Government and, except for occasional academic analysis, almost none from outside the Government.

TABLE 1.—PERSONAL TAX LIABILITIES OF RENTER AND HOMEOWNER WITH EQUIVALENT EARNINGS, ASSETS, AND EXPENSES [1]

Item	Renter	Homeowner
Income:		
Earnings	$15,000	$15,000
From assets of $37,500:		
Interest (at 4 percent)	1,500	900
Imputed net rent on $15,000 equity in house		(600)
Money income	16,500	15,900
Housing cost:[2]		
Money expenditure	3,750	3,150
Imputed net rent		(600)
Residual money income	12,750	12,750
Taxable income:		
Money income	16,500	15,900
Less standard deductions and personal exemptions	5,000	5,000
Less mortgage interest and property taxes		2,100
Total	11,500	8,800
Tax liability	2,150	1,556

[1] Based on 1972 tax rates for a 4-person household with no members age 65 or over. Renter claims standard deduction of $2,000 and personal exemptions of $3,000; homeowner itemizes and claims as deductions $2,100 in mortgage interest and property taxes, $2,000 in other deductions, and personal exemptions of $3,000.

[2] Real housing costs are 25 percent of earnings for both renter and owner. Costs of homeownership include $601 net imputed rent, $1,350 in mortgage interest (6 percent on a $22,500 mortgage), $750 in property taxes, and $1,050 for maintenance and depreciation.

Source: Adapted from Richard Goode, "Imputed Rent of Owner-Occupied Dwellings Under the Income Tax," Journal of Finance, vol. 15 (December 1960), pp. 505—506.

The personal income tax encourages taxpayers to buy rather than rent housing by making the tax bill of homeowners smaller than that of renters in otherwise identical circumstances. Table 1 shows the tax liability of a renter and owner, both of whom earn $15,000 per year, occupy similar housing with a market value of $3,750 per year, and have $37,500 in assets. All assets of the renter yield taxable income. The homeowner holds $15,000 of his assets as equity in his home. He receives no cash income from his home, but he could have invested in the same asset as the renter and earned $600, or he could have rented the house to some other family for $3,750 which would have netted him $600, after he had paid $3,150 in housing expenses. Actually, the homeowner is playing two separable roles; he is a tenant who pays imputed rent to the landlord, and he is a real estate investor who receives imputed rental income from his tenant. Since the same person plays both roles, no cash changes hands.

A neutral tax system regarding homeownership would levy the same tax on the owner and renter described in table 1. In fact, the U.S. personal income tax collects $594 more from the renter than from the homeowner. Three aspects of the Internal Revenue Code explain this differential. If the homeowner were taxed like other investors, he would have to report as gross income the rent (R_G) he could have obtained had he rented the house to another person—$3,750 in table 1. He would be allowed deductions for maintenance expense (M), depreciation (D), mortgage interest (I), and property taxes (T) as expenses incurred in earning income. The difference, or net rent (R_N), would be taxable income. Symbolically, $R_N = R_G - (M+D+I+T)$. In fact, the homeowner need not report imputed net rent (R_N) as income, but he may deduct mortgage interest and property taxes $(I+T)$. Current tax treatment thus understates taxable income of homeowners relative to income of other asset holders by (R_N+I+T). In table 1, this understatement, $2,700, explains the difference between tax liabilities of owner and renter.

Homeowners paid $7 billion less in taxes in 1966 than they would have paid had they been taxed according to the same rules applicable to investors in other assets. This amount is 16.7 percent of the $42 billion collected from homeowners under the personal income tax in 1966. The change in the 1966 tax liabilities of homeowners under three alternative sets of rules can be seen in Table 2.

TABLE 2.—*Increase in tax revenues under 3 alternative laws compared with 1966 income tax provisions*

[In billions of dollars]

	Change in tax
Disallow deductions for property tax and mortgage interest	2.9
Include imputed rent in taxable income	4.0
Include net imputed rent and disallow deductions	[1] 7.0

[1] The revenue effect of this law exceeds the sum of the other 2 laws separately because some taxpayers become subject to higher marginal brackets when all changes are made simultaneously than they are subject to when each change is made independently.

Source: Author's estimates.

The distribution of these tax savings by income class is shown in table 5.

By 1971 the tax saving from deductibility of mortgage interest and property taxes had risen to $5.7 billion according to Treasury Department estimates. While comparable estimates of the revenue effect in 1971 of excluding net imputed rent are unavailable, they probably exceed the $4 billion of 1966. The combined tax saving to homeowners in 1971 almost certainly exceeded $10 billion.

LOW-RENT PUBLIC HOUSING

On June 30, 1969, 2.6 million Americans lived in 785,000 federally supported low-rent public housing units. By July 1972, 1,065,000 units will be available for occupancy. The number of public housing residents is about one-tenth of the number of people officially counted as poor, but not all public housing residents are poor. Federal, State, and local governments have been cooperating in the construction of low-rent public housing units for more than three decades. A few State and municipal governments have built additional public housing without Federal aid. Low-rent public housing is the major federally supported program intended solely for low-income Americans.

Over the years public housing has acquired a vile image—high-rise concrete monoliths in great impersonal cities, cut off from surrounding neighborhoods by grass or cement deserts best avoided after dark, inhabited by large, mostly black families, exhibiting the full range of social and economic difficulties. This image suggests that any benefits inhabitants derive from physical housing amenities are offset by the squalid environment.

In contrast, actual and prospective tenants seem to regard public housing as a better buy than alternative housing available to them on the free market. Most projects have extremely low vacancy rates and long waiting lists for admission.(4) The bad image of public housing contrasts also with the extremely heterogeneous architecture, tenant population, management efficiency, availability of social services, and other amenities.(5) Despite its unfavorable image and political opposition that threatened the program with extinction, public housing construction has been accelerated in recent years.

Public housing redistributes real incomes in two different ways.(6)

First, tenants buy housing services at a "bargain" and their real incomes thus increase.

Second, public housing alters real incomes of owners and tenants of other housing. As former occupants of free market housing become public housing tenants, some unsubsidized housing is vacated. In addition, local housing authorities build housing that would not otherwise be built. On the other hand, they often raze some private housing to clear sites for public housing. Rehabilitation generally reduces the number of units per building. Since doubling up and overcrowding are prohibited in public housing, an increase in public units may increase the number of households seeking housing.(7) If public housing reduces demand for unsubsidized housing more than it reduces supply, rents paid for low-cost, but unsubsidized, housing will tend to be somewhat lower than they would have been in the absence of public housing, at least until the unsubsidized housing stock adjusts to the advent of public housing. During this period, real incomes of tenants in unsubsidized housing will tend to be higher and incomes of owners will tend to be lower than they would have been in the absence of public housing. In addition, public housing will probably raise construction—more public housing construction, partially offset by some drop in unsubsidized construction. As a result, the demand for different factors of production will probably shift.(8)

Construction costs may rise, thus increasing the supply price of unsubsidized housing services. Moreover, public housing as a new competitor for expenditures on housing services may alter the prices people are willing to pay for unsubsidized housing thereby affecting unsubsidized rents.

Untangling these rather complex interrelationships would be hard enough if housing markets functioned without important lags or imperfections. The prevalence of racial discrimination, zoning restrictions, and other imperfections makes it completely impossible. Accordingly, estimates of the distribution of benefits from public housing will refer to benefits for tenants only. In addition, the improvement in housing conditions and living standards of public housing tenants may bring benefits to other members of society.

Public housing tenants enjoy a better standard of living than they would enjoy if they lived in ordinary housing. In order to bring these benefits to tenants, and to provide the larger community with whatever broader improvements public housing produces, the Federal Government incurs certain costs and municipal governments forego some property tax revenues. To measure the benefits to tenants, it would be desirable to know what they think the subsidy is worth. Unfortunately, such data are unobtainable.

The estimates presented below are based on the assumption that the total benefit from public housing equals the difference between public housing rents and rents on equivalent unsubsidized units. The estimates also presume that all benefits accrue to public housing tenants. This assumption is strong and highly unrealistic because improved housing may bring social benefits.

The difference between rents charged public housing tenants and rents charged privately for equivalent housing totaled $510 million in 1966. Table 5 shows the distribution of benefits by income bracket. More than half of estimated benefits accrued to households with incomes of $3,000 per year or less, 86 percent to households with incomes of $5,000 per year or less.

Public housing is clearly aimed at low-income households. The large proportion of benefits going to low-income families arises from admissions policies alone, as benefits per family vary little among income brackets.

HOMEOWNERSHIP AND RENTAL ASSISTANCE

Congress enacted homeownership and rental assistance (sec. 235 and 236 of the National Housing Act) in 1968, to help in the construction of 6 million federally assisted housing units as called for by the national housing goal.

The homeownership assistance program (sec. 235) requires homeowners to pay at least one-fifth of their adjusted income for mortgage amortization as a condition for assistance; the adjustment consists in deducting 5 percent of gross income in lieu of social security and $300 for each minor child from income. If the homeowner's payment is less than amortization, the Department of Housing and Urban Development pays the lender the difference. HUD's subsidy may not exceed the difference between amortization over 30 years at market rates and amortization at 1 percent interest. In 1968 when the program was enacted and mortgage interest rates were about 6½ percent, plus one-half percent insurance premium, the maximum subsidy was about 50 percent of mortgage payments. By 1970 with FHA rates at 8½ percent, the maximum subsidy was about 60 percent. For a family of five or more persons in a high-cost area with a $24,000 mortgage, the largest allowed under the program, the subsidy would be more than $117 a month. The rental assistance program (sec. 236) requires renters to pay one-fourth of adjusted income as rent. HUD pays the difference between this sum and fair market rents or the difference between amortization over 40 years at market interest rates and amortization at 1 percent, whichever is less. Since market rents include maintenance costs, taxes, vacancy allowances, and depreciation, the maximum subsidy at time of enactment was an estimated 35 percent. By 1970, when interest rates on FHA mortgages including insurance premiums had risen to 9 percent, the maximum subsidy had risen to 44 percent of market rents.

Only limited information is available on recipients of homeownership and rental assistance (see table 3). Most owners under section 235 have annual incomes in the $4,000-$7,000 range. Most tenants in 236 projects have slightly lower incomes—in the $3,000—$7,000 range. However, the larger family size in 235 units more than offsets the small amount of extra income.

Housing under sections 235 and 236 is too costly for very low-income households, unless they are renters who also qualify for rent supplement payments. Up to 20 percent of the units in any 236 project may be occupied by tenants who also receive rent supplements. The annual Federal payments under sections 235 and 236 are projected to reach $299 million and $151.4 million respectively by fiscal year 1972 and to rise rapidly thereafter. Unfortunately,

TABLE 3.—DISTRIBUTION OF TENANTS IN HOMEOWNER AND RENTAL ASSISTANCE PROGRAMS, BY INCOME AND OTHER CHARACTERISTICS, VARIOUS DATES, 1968-71

	Percentage of all tenants in program			
Characteristic	Below-market-interest-rate loans (1968)	Rent supplements (1969)	Home-ownership assistance (1971)	Rental assistance (1970)
Income bracket:				
Under $1,000	0.3	7.7		
$1,000 to $1,999	2.5	41.1		
$2,000 to $2,999	4.7	27.3	[1] 1.1	[1] 10.7
$3,000 to $3,999	10.1	17.0	4.2	13.5
$4,000 to $4,999	17.0	5.7	15.2	23.5
$5,000 to $5,999	22.6	1.2	25.7	25.6
$6,000 to $6,999	21.6	[2] .1	25.0	17.6
$7,000 to $7,999	12.5		16.8	6.6
$8,000 to $8,999	5.3		7.7	.1.9
$9,000 to $9,999	1.9		2.8	.4
$10,000 and over	1.5		1.5	.2
Age of head:				
Under 20	NA	3.0	2.7	7.5
20 to 29	NA	26.0	50.1	61.7
30 to 39	NA	14.5	29.2	14.1
40 to 49	NA	7.4	11.8	6.3
50 and over	NA	[3] 49.1	6.2	10.4
Family size:				
1 person	9.5	32.8	.2	13.6
2 persons	30.3	13.4	10.7	24.9
3 persons	29.4	15.4	24.9	31.6
4 persons	17.3	13.3	21.2	17.2
5 persons	8.2	12.5	17.2	7.9
6 or more persons	5.1	12.5	25.8	4.9
Monthly mortgage payment or rent:				
Under $40		32.9	.2	NA
$40 to $49		25.8	.2	NA
$50 to $59		14.2	1.9	NA
$60 to $69		10.3	6.9	NA
$70 to $79	[4] 3.8	10.6	16.1	NA
$80 to $89	10.2	3.4	22.7	NA
$90 to $99	12.8	1.9	20.0	NA
$100 to $109	14.6	[5] .9	13.9	NA
$110 to $119	18.9		9.2	NA
$120 to $129	17.2		5.1	NA
$130 to $139	11.1		2.0	NA
$140 to $159	9.0		[6] 1.2	NA
$160 and over	2.4			NA
Subsidy per month:				
Under $20	NA		.4	NA
$20 to $29	NA		.5	NA
$30 to $39	NA		1.3	NA
$40 to $49	NA	[7] 10.5	3.0	NA
$50 to $59	NA	6.3	6.5	NA
$60 to $69	NA	13.8	13.5	NA
$70 to $79	NA	16.2	23.8	NA
$80 to $89	NA	17.2	29.3	NA
$90 and over	NA	36.1	21.7	NA

NA—Not available.
[1] Less than $3,000.
[2] $6,000 and over.
[3] Those 60 and over accounted for 43.2 percent.
[4] Less than $80.
[5] $100 and over.
[6] $140 and over.
[7] Less than $50.

Sources: For below-market-interest-rate loan program, U.S. Department of Housing and Urban Development (HUD), Federal Housing Administration (FHA), Division of Research and Statistics, machine tabulations, May 25, 1970. For rent supplement program, derived from HUD, "Report of Rent Supplement Tenant Characteristics," with data for June to December 1969 (processed), and "Rent Supplement Tenant Characteristics," with data for May 31, 1969 (processed). For homeownership program, 1971 Housing and Urban Development Legislation, Hearings before the Subcommittee on Housing and Urban Affairs of the Senate Committee on Banking, Housing and Urban Affairs, 92 Cong. 1 sess. (1971), pt. 1, pp. 13-16, 27. For rental assistance program, HUD, Housing Management, Statistics Branch, unpublished tabulations, Feb. 8, 1971, and April 2, 1971. Percentages are rounded and may not add to 100.

data on subsidy payments or average mortgage amount by income class or other relevant categories are not available, so that the distributional effects of homeownership assistance cannot be measured. Moreover, recent reports of corruption suggest that some portion of these Federal outlays may benefit not the occupant, but builders, land owners, agents, and other middlemen.

RENT SUPPLEMENTS

The rent supplement program works as follows: A nonprofit or limited dividend corporation or a cooperative contracts with the Department of Housing and Urban Development to make rent supplement payments. The contract stipulates the maximum payments per year which HUD may be required to make. The contract authority refers to this maximum liability. Contract authority, therefore, gives rise to maximum Federal payments of this amount in each of 40 years for which the contracts run. Having secured this commitment, the housing developer then begins construction. Rent supplement payments start only after units are completed and occupied. Since some tenants pay more than the minimum 30 percent of market rents required of all tenants, actual rent supplement payments are less than the contracted maximum on some units. HUD estimates that over the 40-year estimated life of rent supplement projects, actual payments authorized from 1967 through 1971 will be about 83 percent of the maximum obligation.(9) Rent supplement housing may be financed in several ways. Rent supplements may be provided in combination with interest subsidies under a housing program for the elderly and handicapped (sec. 202), housing for lower income families (sec. 236) or sec. 221(d)(3) below market interest rate projects, or on State-aided projects.

Families on whose behalf rent supplements are paid have lower incomes but are smaller than those living in low-rent public housing. Rent supplement payments amount to nearly two-thirds of market rents on assisted units. Unfortunately, it is not possible with available data to compute the distribution of benefits from rent supplement payments. To do so it would be necessary to know the rent supplement payments made on behalf of each income bracket or other relevant classification. This information is not now available. The annual benefits under rent supplements approximately equal Government expenditures on the program, $91 million in fiscal year 1972. The present value of benefits over an estimated 40-year project life to tenants in 22,000 rent supplement units estimated to be completed during fiscal year 1971 was approximately $1.2 billion or about $14,338 per unit.(10)

BELOW MARKET INTEREST RATE LOANS ON MULTIFAMILY HOUSING

In 1961 Congress authorized loans at low-interest rates to nonprofit or limited dividend corporations or cooperatives for the construction of modest housing for lower middle-income households. By the end of fiscal year 1970, 131,000 units had been completed under this program, named 221 (d)(3) BMIR after its section number in the National Housing Act and the "below market interest rates" charged. This program never worked quite as intended. It was plagued by administrative delays; the myth grew up that it assisted households with higher incomes than Congress or the administration originally intended; the coup de grace came from reforms in budgetary accounting which increased the apparent current cost of the program. As a result the program was superseded by rental assistance under section 236 of the National Housing Act and by rent supplements. Units constructed under this program continue to be occupied, however, at rents below those which would have been feasible if the units were financed at market interest rates.

This is the way the program operated. Under the 221 (d)(3) BMIR program qualified builders could obtain loans at 3-percent interest from banks and other lenders.(11) Lenders made such loans only because the Government National Mortgage Association(12) immediately purchased the mortgage at par. Under this arrangement, FNMA was the real lender, the bank merely a middleman or broker.

The reduction in cost from such loans clearly depends on the rate at which the developer otherwise would have to borrow. With market interest rates at 6.5 percent, a 3-percent loan makes possible an estimated 27 percent reduction in rents.(13) With market interest rates at 9 percent, a rate prevailing during the later years of the program, a rent reduction of 37 percent is possible. The rental saving in 1970 from this program totaled an estimated $28 million. The breakdown of benefits by income class is shown in table 5. Somewhat more than half of all benefits accrued to whites, about two-fifths to blacks and small amounts to other groups. The characteristics of tenants are shown in table 3.

MORTGAGE INSURANCE AND LOAN GUARANTEES

The Federal Housing Administration (FHA) insures mortgages on single and multifamily housing. By far the largest of these programs concerns purchases of single family housing without Federal subsidy and occurs under section 203 of the National Housing Act. FHA insures lenders against most losses should borrowers default on payments. In return FHA charges borrowers an insurance premium equal to 0.5 percent of the unpaid mortgage balance. Ostensibly this program is financially balanced, with insurance premiums projected to cover claims.

The Veterans' Administration (VA) runs a similar program for veterans. VA guarantees lenders against the loss from default and foreclosure up to a stipulated fraction of the loan or a specified maximum loss. In 1971 the guarantee was limited to $12,500 or 60 percent of the mortgage, whichever is less. Unlike FHA, VA charges nothing for this service beyond a one-time fee of 0.5 percent of the home loan imposed on veterans eligible because of service after 1955.

The major consequence of these two programs has been to facilitate a revolution in home financing. During the 1920's and 1930's lending institutions typically required a downpayment of one-third to one-half of the purchase price and would not lend for 20, 30, or 40 years. Mortgage insurance and loan guarantees encouraged financial intermediaries to lend more and for longer terms. The result was smaller down payments and longer repayment periods, not only on Government insured and guaranteed loans, but on conventional mortgages as well. Because they do not need cash, many families can buy a house who would not have been able to do so under more stringent terms of the past. A large part of the liberalization in home mortgage terms might have occurred even if mortgage insurance and loan guarantees had not existed. The receding fear of economic depression might have encouraged lenders to make longer term loans than they did previously. But it seems likely that some significant part of easier home mortgage terms was due to the prodding of these two Federal programs.

By facilitating institutional changes these programs have brought substantial benefits to those families who wanted to buy houses and were enabled to do so. These institutional changes do not constitute subsidies in the usual sense.

In addition, however, both of these programs redistribute income. On the assumption that FHA mortgage insurance is financially balanced, some redistribution occurs within the program because borrowers pay the same premium for mortgage insurance but do not generate the same risk of loss from default or foreclosure. Loans made to low-income households on the average are riskier than loans to high-income households. Mortgages equal to a high fraction of the appraised value of the property which secures them are riskier than mortgages equal to a low fraction of property value. On the assumption that FHA mortgage insurance is financially balanced, it tends to redistribute income from high-income borrowers and from those whose mortgages carry a low ratio of loan to value, to low-income borrowers and to those whose mortgages carry a high ratio of loan to value. If FHA mortgage insurance is underfinanced—in the sense that losses over the long run exceed premium income—then FHA borrowers are receiving implicit transfers or subsidies from other taxpayers equal to the overall longrun deficit in the FHA fund.

VA loan guarantees distribute income from nonveterans and veterans who do not buy homes to veterans who buy homes. They do so because VA incurs certain expenses through its guarantees which must be met out of other VA funds or from general revenues. The aggregate benefits to borrowers who received VA loan guarantees in 1966 was approximately $141 million.

The combined benefits of VA loan guarantees and the redistribution which occurs among FHA borrowers is shown in Table 5, broken down by income class.

FmHA LOANS TO LOW- TO MODERATE-INCOME HOUSEHOLDS

The Farmers Home Administration (FmHA) runs one of the Federal Government's largest, but least noticed, housing programs. Between 1967 and 1972, FmHA will have provided more than $4.5 billion in loans and grants for the purchase, rehabilitation, or construction of new or existing housing. The largest of the several programs FmHA administers is a system of loans to low- and moderate-income households in rural areas. Despite the magnitude of FmHA's housing activities, discussion of Federal housing policy seldom accords them attention in proportion to their size, and it frequently ignores them entirely.

Large-scale housing assistance for farmers began with the Housing Act of 1949. In 1961 legislation made the nonfarmer eligible for FmHA housing assistance if he 1. owned real estate in rural areas, 2. lacked sufficient resources "to provide the necessary housing and buildings on his own account," and 3. was unable to obtain credit "from other sources upon terms and conditions which he could reasonably be expected to fulfill."(14) Some owners of properties within standard metropolitan statistical areas and some wealthy and high-income families have received loans. The great majority of loans, however, are made to households located in small towns or in open country and with modest incomes and wealth. Relatively few households with very low incomes have received loans. Fewer than one loan in 10 is made to farmers (see table 4).(15) FmHA is a "lender of last resort," since applicants must show that they cannot obtain credit elsewhere at fair terms. Since FmHA charges less than market rates and lacks sufficient funds to satisfy all rural credit demands, however, some significant discretion remains with the FmHA loan officer.

After it makes a loan, FmHA may either 1. retain the loan in its portfolio or 2. guarantee payment of principle and interest and sell the guaranteed loan to private lenders. In the former case, the loan is called a direct loan; in the latter case, an insured loan. Whether or nor FmHA insures and sells a loan does not affect the borrower in the slightest. The amount he can borrow, his repayment period, and the interest rate he must pay are all decided beforehand. The economic impact of direct and insured loans is identical.

In addition, FmHA administers the Federal Housing Administration's section 235 homeownership assistance; it placed 2,382 such loans in fiscal year 1970 in rural areas. FmHA also administers "interest credit assistance" on both single family housing and rental projects and two forms of rental assistance, one resembling the Federal Housing Administration's 221 (d)(3) below market interest rate program, the other resembling section 236, rental assistance.

Borrowers receive two kinds of benefits from FmHA's home mortgage programs. First, FmHA provides home mortgage credit in some communities where private lenders do not operate. Other lenders adhere to lending procedures of the 1920's and earlier—short-term, large downpayment, renewable loans. Without FmHA some borrowers, low- and high-risk alike, would obtain no credit, or would be offered it on such onerous terms that some transactions would be prevented. Second, FmHA borrowers receive a subsidy when they get a loan. Most FmHA borrowers have paid less than commercial interest rates in

TABLE 4.—DISTRIBUTION OF BORROWERS UNDER FMHA LOAN PROGRAM, BY INCOME AND OTHER CHARACTERISTICS, 1969

[In percent]

Characteristic	Distribution	Characteristic	Distribution
Income (dollars):		Net worth (dollars):	
Under 3,000	5.8	Under 5,000	82.9
3,000 to 3,999	8.0	5,000 to 9,999	12.0
4,000 to 4,999	12.7	10,000 to 14,999	2.3
5,000 to 5,999	20.4	15,000 to 49,999	2.1
6,000 to 6,999	24.7	50,000 to 74,999	.6
7,000 to 7,999	17.2	75,000 and over	0
8,000 to 8,999	5.2	Region:[1]	
9,000 to 9,999	2.4	Southeast	56.4
10,000 and over	3.6	Northeast	15.4
Residence:		West	7.4
Farm	6.6	Central	20.8
Open country	48.4	Age of family head:	
Place under 1,000 population	16.6	Under 30	39.3
Place of 1,000 to 2,499 population	15.2	30 to 39	29.2
Place of 2,500 to 5,500 population	13.2	40 to 49	17.0
		50 to 59	8.7
		60 and over	5.8

[1] Distribution is for 1968.

Source: Department of Agriculture (USDA), Farmers Home Administration (FmHA), tabulations, April 1970. The program coverage of the tabulations varies slightly among the characteristics presented.

most recent years.

The estimates of benefits to FmHA borrowers rest on the presumption that those households could have obtained credit from private sources at the yield of Federal Housing Administration mortgages. This assumption, if anything understates benefits to FmHA borrowers. Private lenders almost certainly would have charged FmHA borrowers more than they charged conventional mortgagers, much more if one accepts FmHA's claim that credit would be unavailable to its borrowers at reasonable rates.

The first year benefits under insured loans to low- to moderate-income households who secured FmHA loans in 1969 and 1968 totaled $10.8 million and $7.4 million, respectively. The present value of interest savings to these FmHA borrowers over the life of their loans was far larger, $123 million and $92 million, respectively. For fiscal year 1970, the present value of benefits rose to an estimated $188 million, based on the $729 million in loans reported in the 1972 budget, a yield on FHA mortgages of 9.20 percent (including 0.5 percent insurance premium) and on FmHA interest charge of 6¼ percent.

Borrowers under other FmHA programs also receive implicit subsidies, but these are small by comparison with those under section 502 and are not included in the foregoing estimates.

II. DISTRIBUTION OF HOUSING SUBSIDIES

The distribution of implicit and explicit housing subsidies is shown in table 5. The table is divided into five parts. The top part shows the distribution of

TABLE 5.—DISTRIBUTION OF BENEFITS FROM FEDERAL HOUSING POLICIES

[Millions of dollars]

Income bracket [1]	Subsidy provided by—							
	Income tax laws, 1966 [2]	FHA and VA programs, 1966 [2]	Public housing, 1965 [2]	Below-market-interest-rate loans, 1970 [3]	Home-ownership assistance, 1972 [4]	Rental assistance, 1972 [4]	Rent supplements, 1972 [4]	Rural housing loans, 1969 [5]
Under $1,000	253	5	27	(6)				(6)
$1,000 to $2,000			138	1				
$2,000 to $3,000			128	1				
$3,000 to $4,000	328	22	91	3				1
$4,000 to $5,000			57	5				1
$5,000 to $6,000	544	36	38	6				2
$6,000 to $7,000		34		6				3
$7,000 to $8,000	1,359	24	30	4				2
$8,000 to $9,000		14		2				1
$9,000 to $10,000				1				(6)
$10,000 to $15,000	1,986	5	2	(6)				(6)
$15,000 to $25,000	1,256							
$25,000 to $50,000	770							
$50,000 to $100,000	318							
Over $100,000	169							
Total, annual benefits	6,982	(7)	510	28	299	151	91	11
Present value of benefits	(7)	141	(7)	94	[8]2,078	[8]1,172	[8]1,185	123

[1] Definitions of income vary slightly from one program to another.
[2] Median family income was $7,500 (U.S. Bureau of the Census, Current Population Reports, Series P-60, No. 75, "Income in 1969 of Families and Persons in the United States" 1970).
[3] Median family income was $8,632 (ibid.).
[4] Benefits by income brackets were not estimated; total benefits indicated are estimated Federal program costs as reported in the Budget of the United States Government, 1972; Appendix, p. 521.
[5] Median family income outside metropolitan areas was $7,982 (ibid.).
[6] Less than $500,000.
[7] Not estimated.
[8] Calculated from requested budget authority for 1972 (see note d) and data in table 8-3 in Shelter and Subsidies: Who Benefits from Federal Housing Policies, Brookings Institution, 1972.

benefits by income bracket where such calculations were feasible. Then the table indicates the annual flow of benefits from the program to all beneficiaries under the program.(16) Next, the table shows the present value of benefits—the value of the stream of benefits initiated in the indicated year discounted at the then prevailing market rate of interest.

Overwhelmingly the largest housing subsidy is favorable tax treatment of homeowners which, in 1966, left homeowners with about $7 billion more in disposable income than they would have had if they were treated like other property owners. The $7 billion estimate understates the housing subsidies awarded by the tax system, since it excludes tax savings arising from accelerated depreciation on rented housing and other items. Income tax savings to homeowners are more than 10 times as large as benefits under the next largest program, low-rent public housing. These tax savings accrue largely to households with comfortable incomes. Only 8 percent of this subsidy accrues to taxpayers with incomes of less than $5,000, while 84 percent of all benefits to taxpayers with incomes of $7,000 per year or more, 64 percent to taxpayers with incomes of $10,000 per year or more, and 36 percent to households with incomes of $15,000 per year or more. Indeed, yearly tax savings to households with incomes of $50,000 per year or more are nearly as great as annual benefits under low-rent public housing and larger than annual benefits under any other housing program. These implicit tax subsidies are inequitable and as instruments for improving housing quality they are defensible only if it is a national goal to encourage the relatively well-to-do to buy even better housing than they would buy in the absence of such subsidies. Despite the high cost, inequity, and inefficiency of this accident of tax history, there is little prospect that this aspect of the tax code will be reformed in the near future.

Low-rent public housing is the major housing program aimed at low income Americans, and it lands squarely on target. While the very poorest may not be able to afford even low-rent public housing, the typical public housing tenant has very modest means. More than 86 percent of the $510 million in benefits in 1966 from that program accrued to families with incomes under $5,000. Benefits from public housing have risen substantially since 1966 as the number of units under management has increased and general rent levels have risen. Benefits from the newer rent supplement program also accrue primarily to low income households. Total rent supplement payments are projected to rise from $21 million in 1970 to $91 million in 1972, and to rise continuously thereafter, but according to present plans, this program will remain much smaller than low-rent public housing.

Homeownership and rental assistance are projected to grow more rapidly than low-rent public housing, a distinctly bullish assumption in light of the failure of past projections of growth in housing programs and of recently reported corruption and administrative problems. The national housing goal projects the construction of 2.7 million units under homeownership and rental assistance. These programs concentrate on lower middle income households with annual incomes of $4,000–$7,000. The 221 (d)(3) below market interest rate program, predecessor to rental assistance, generated approximately $27 million in benefits in 1968, the most recent year for which data are available. Most of the benefits under this program accrue to relatively small households with incomes of $4,000–$7,000 per year.

Residents of rural areas and small towns whose access to conventional credit sources is limited may obtain loans from the Farmers Home Administration (FmHA) at subsidized interest rates. This program also reaches households in the $4,000–$7,000 income range. It provided approximately $11 million in benefits in 1969, the latest year for which data are available. The President has requested authority for expanded lending activity by FmHA.

The operations of the Federal Housing Administration and the Veterans' Administration in protecting lenders against default by borrowers provided measurable subsidies of about $141 million in 1966. In addition, the operations of these agencies have probably helped spur a revolution in home financing procedures. The measurable subsidies arise because these agencies do not charge each borrower (or lender) the actuarial cost of default protection which the agencies provide. The amount of these subsidies was modest in 1966; even if they were much greater in other recent years, these actuarial subsidies cannot have been large. They accrued primarily to lower middle income families.

FHA and VA regulations may also have contributed to the relaxation of terms on home mortgages by lenders in general. Even if FHA and VA "caused" only a small part of this relaxation—in the sense that most of it might have occurred even in their absence—these benefits would dwarf those indicated above. Part of the benefits FHA and VA produce by making homeownership more accessible are tax benefits already included in another calculation. Part of the benefits arise from the improved operation of the home mortgage market as a result of which families who simply prefer homeownership (and would do so without tax benefits) can secure unsubsidized mortgage terms that make homeownership possible. While it is not possible to estimate the size of these benefits, they are almost certainly vastly larger than the subsidy benefits from FHA-VA programs shown in table 5.

III. THE EQUITY OF EXISTING HOUSING PROGRAMS

Should the Federal Government continue its present housing policies? If not, how should it deal with America's housing problems? Answers to these questions require a knowledge of the way housing markets work or fail to work, an understanding of how existing policies affect housing markets and whom they benefit, and judgments about which problems are most important.

Among the basic questions every country faces in designing a housing policy are whether the Government should concern itself with new or existing housing, or both; what kind of standards—if any—it should set for the quality of housing; whether policies should be directed at demand or supply, or both; whether subsidies should be channeled directly to the poor or to other income groups in the expectation that filtering will carry benefits to the poor; whether policies should be operated within the competitive housing market or independently of it; whether they should be designed to improve competition in housing markets; and whether they should be designed to affect housing services alone or the full range of residential services collectively.

The answers a country gives to such questions represent its housing strategy. Its strategy helps determine the cost of its housing policy, the distribution of income, the cleanliness, safety, and design of cities, the importance of markets, and other important political and economic conditions. Its answers will be affected by the level, distribution, and rate of growth of per capita income; the rate of population growth; migration; and construction costs. Rich countries can choose high mandatory housing standards and large subsidies that poor countries could not afford. How income is distributed affects the character of housing and the dispersion of political power. A rapidly growing or migrating population must make a considerable investment in new housing just to maintain standards and prevent overcrowding.

Even after a housing strategy has been adopted, many important tactical issues will remain. For example, should subsidies be provided directly to occupants or indirectly through construction subsidies, tax incentives, or various credit market devices? Should reliance be placed on statutory prohibitions and requirements or on incentives? Although the selection of a housing strategy does not settle such tactical questions, it is the basis decision, the expression of the goals a nation sets for itself.

Among the housing strategies the United States might plausibly adopt are the three sketched by Anthony Downs:

> *Filtering strategies.*—Involve strict enforcement of high or moderate quality standards for all new construction, and either (a) no public housing subsidies at all or (b) public subsidies focused mainly on middle-income or high-income households. Thus, nearly all new housing units are occupied by non-poor households. Poor households receive decent units through filtering down of older units from high income households.
> *Low-income subsidy strategies.*—Also involve strict enforcement of high or moderate quality standards (usually the latter) for all new construction, but include large scale public housing subsidies allocated directly to low-income households. High standard versions require either larger total public subsidies or reach fewer poor households than moderate standard versions. The latter are better able to use the economies of mass produced or industrialized housing.
> *Minimal standard strategies.*—Involve only partial enforcement of any housing quality standards in urban areas, primarily in existing good quality neighborhoods. A great deal of the new construction under such strategies consists of zero standard units built by their occupants. Any housing subsidies employed can be either concentrated on the poor or spread over all income groups.(17)

A country's choice of strategy should reflect the rationale of its housing policy.(18) If that rationale favors a weak and vague housing policy—no more perhaps than removal of discriminatory and monopolistic practices—the "minimal standards" strategy is appropriate. Under such a position bad housing would be seen as a problem of low income; low income, but not bad housing, might be a matter of collective concern. No construction standards should be imposed, for the market should generate the kinds and amounts of housing people demand. The zero standards approach assumes that in a country as rich as the United States few shacks or hovels would be built and few would persist because nearly everyone would demand housing consistent with his income and taste and would get it. Some construction might be far below standards now permitted, but it would satisfy the demand for housing by consumers who feel such housing best satisfies their needs. A few hovels and shacks might continue to exist for the destitute few who could not afford anything better.

The minimal-standards position is not inconsistent with radical income redistribution to aid the poor, and even with complete income equality. It presumes that the market reliably reflects individual tastes and it downgrades the importance of nonmarket social and economic interaction, but it does not necessarily involve passive acceptance of poverty. An advocate of both zero housing standards and major income redistribution might rationally foresake zero housing standards if the prospects for direct redistribution of income were poorer than for indirect redistribution through housing policy.

The choice on economic grounds between filtering and low income subsidy strategies hinges on which of the various reasons for Government actions in the housing market seem most compelling. If market imperfections, social costs of bad housing, racial discrimination, and other types of market failures are most often associated with housing inhabited by the poor, a low income subsidy strategy would be indicated. If such imperfections occur throughout the housing market, a filtering strategy, or some hybrid filtering—low income subsidy strategy—would be called for.

The simple laws of division decree that with a given sum of money, more families can be helped under a filtering strategy than under a low income subsidy strategy.

> The amount of subsidy per household needed to close the gap between a household's own ability to pay and the cost of a new decent unit is larger, the lower the household's income. Therefore, any given sized public housing subsidy can generate more new production of decent units if concentrated upon middle-income and upper-income groups than if concentrated upon the poorest groups. True, the frictions of the housing market mean that the immediate impact of such larger outputs upon the poorest households will be far less than a lower total output directly distributed to them. Yet focusing housing subsidies upon middle-income groups . . . enables the Government to assist more households per million dollars of subsidy, and therefore may be considered *politically* more efficient than direct housing aid to the poor.(19)

The crucial question is how serious the frictions are that defer the benefits of filtering for the poorest households. If filtering proceeds smoothly and quickly, the costs of delay may pale before the political gain of securing support from other income groups. If filtering works sluggishly, or if certain segments of the housing market remain largely unaffected, then a dilemma may exist between politically feasible programs that help least those who need help most and programs of direct aid for the poor around which no consensus can be formed.

At no time has Congress or the President publicly attempted to develop a housing strategy. Instead, legislation has been proposed, debated, amended, and enacted piece by piece. Despite this lack of neatness, the record indicates that the United States rather consistently has pursued a filtering strategy.

The pattern of benefits from housing programs, summarized in table 5, may be criticized on at least three grounds.

First, existing housing programs provide more direct assistance to middle and upper income households than to low and lower middle income households, although bad housing is not primarily an affliction of the well-to-do. Moreover, all housing programs intended for low and lower middle income households provide large amounts of help to a small fraction of eligible households and no direct help at all to all the rest.

Second, housing assistance is provided primarily in connection with newly constructed units. As a result, the sum of the subsidy per unit and housing expenditures by assisted households much exceeds the cost of standard housing as estimated by the Bureau of Labor Statistics in its "low cost" budget.

Third, housing assistance is linked to particular structures rather than to households. As a result, an assisted family cannot choose freely among vacant units and risks loss of benefits if it moves from an assisted unit. These features inhibit mobility and consumer choice.

Whether to help the poor directly or to help the nonpoor and hope the poor benefit is indeed a difficult choice. However, other circumstances have assured that even direct aid to middle-income families reaches only a fraction of eligible households. Although housing programs described here absorbed over $8 billion in Federal resources in 1966 and absorb far more today, most benefits drain away unsupervised through income tax benefits to homeowners. Given the resulting expenditure limitations on other housing subsidy programs and average benefits per recipient, there is simply not enough money to provide assistance for all who are eligible on the basis of income. The most straightforward courses would be to increase expenditure limitations and accommodate all eligible families within a set number of years. Unfortunately, this course raises another problem. As a practical matter, assistance is linked to new construction and assisted construction cannot be extended much beyond currently projected levels. The Department of Housing and Urban Development recognized this limit when it rejected as infeasible the construction of 6 million assisted units in 5 rather than 10 years under the national housing goal. Either residential construction activity would have ballooned to unsustainable levels or unassisted construction would have been squeezed to intolerably low levels.

The linkage between most overt subsidies and new housing units creates another equity issue. A household ineligible for subsidies on the basis of income may have poorer neighbors living in better subsidized housing than it can afford. This situation creates resentment and political resistance to housing assistance.(20)

The linkage between subsidies and new construction also makes the cost of housing assistance higher than the cost of housing families in socially acceptable existing housing. Housing assistance under the newest subsidy programs (homeownership and rental assistance) has run at about $1,000 per household per year. In addition, households must pay 20-25 percent of income toward housing costs. According to the Bureau of Labor Statistics, the cost of shelter within its low cost budget in 1967 was $1,013. Median housing costs under homeownership assistance were $1,608 in 1969(21) It is clear that the Government paid a considerable premium to house assisted families predominantly in new units.

One reason for linking housing subsidies with new construction was a fear that subsidies alone would drive up the price of housing available to the poor. This concern reflects an implicit assumption that subsidy recipients will be unable to choose new neighborhoods or different residences, that existing landlords can jack up rents with impunity, and that little effective competition exists in the housing market.

Housing subsidies and new construction were linked in addition, because policymakers hoped to provide improved housing for some groups without causing other groups to be housed less well. The increased demand for housing would be met by new units, not by units captured from other households. Most evidence, however, suggests that the housing stock a nation will support depends on such factors as the number of households, income, and the price of housing relative to other goods; residential construction, in turn, depends on household formation, changes in income, changes in the relative price of housing, and credit market conditions. Federal subsidies may cause a temporary increase in residential construction or influence the kind of units built, but there is no evidence that linking subsidies to new construction results permanently in a larger housing stock than would exist if housing subsidies alone were provided. Federal subsidies reduce the amount of bad housing since they place at the disposal of households too poor to support adequate housing from their own income enough resources to demand adequate housing. This objective is achieved, however, at greater cost than would be necessary if existing, rather than new, housing were used.

IV. ALTERNATIVE HOUSING STRATEGY AND TACTICS

The existing system of housing subsidies is inequitable and excessively costly. It aids a minority of lower middle-income families and a miniscule few among the poor. Those not directly aided may gain through filtering, but the benefits are probably random and irregular. The quality of housing for the eligible few may be superior to that of more comfortable neighbors. The limitation of most subsidies to new units results in high costs per households served.

Recognition of the inequities and excessive cost of subsidy programs has led many analysts to recommend a general subsidy payable to all (or nearly all) households with incomes below stipulated levels.(22) Although housing allowance plans differ in major respects, all would provide eligible households with cash or special certificates to defray part of the cost of new or existing housing selected by the recipients. The Department of Housing and Urban Development has announced plans to support a variety of experimental housing allowance plans.(23)

Answers to a number of policy questions would shape the precise character of the housing assistance plan.(24)

Should benefits be paid in cash or rent certificates? Recipients would be free to spend cash benefits on goods other than housing, and the assistance might add no more to housing expenditures than would general cash assistance. Administrative costs, however, would be minimized since there would be no need to verify the uses to which the benefits were put. Payments tied to actual housing outlays—in the form of rent certificates or mortgage payment coupons, or as the exact difference between housing costs and some fraction of income—would encourage households to spend more on housing than they would if benefits were unrestricted. Efforts to tie payments to housing expenditures would raise administrative costs since it would be necessary to verify rents paid (a difficult task since tenants and landlords would have incentives to collude) or to make sure that a black market for certificates or coupons did not arise.(25) Moreover, introduction of large tied housing subsidies might drive up the price of housing without improving quality commensurately; coupons or certificates would be "funny money," applicable to housing but nothing else. If the housing market were competitive, property owners would bid for tenants (or buyers) by improving housing quality.

Should housing benefits be combined with requirements that private landlords or homeowners upgrade low quality housing? The Government could undertake a vigorous program of code enforcement. Or benefits could be withheld from households residing in units that do not meet minimum standards. Deficient units would either become vacant or their owners would be subject to fines. Presumably, standards would be set at a level that could be supported and maintained from housing allowance payments. Direct efforts to control housing quality are especially attractive to those who fear that landlords would simply raise rents if large tied housing subsidies were paid. Past governmental efforts effectively and honestly to administer a program of code enforcement of some other measure to upgrade housing quality by fiat have failed repeatedly, perhaps because tenants were not able to pay enough to support housing at code standards.(26)

Who should be eligible for benefits? The plan might be limited to renters, on the assumption that homeowners must be less needy since they could amass a downpayment and undertake a commitment to monthly mortgage payments. The plan might include homeowners, but only if they are making monthly mortgage payments. Households who owned their residence free-and-clear might be excluded on the theory that any benefits to them would necessarily support consumption of goods other than housing. Single persons or couples under 65 years old might be excluded on the grounds that resources should be concentrated on the aged and families with children. While limitations based on other criteria than measurable need dilute equity, limited resources might compel policy makers to curtail eligibility. Ideally such limitations should not be based on criteria subject to control by potential beneficiaries; for example, a household that owned its residence free-and-clear could easily mortgage its house if the making of mortgage payments were a condition for benefits.

TABLE 6.—PROJECTED ANNUAL COST AND NUMBER OF BENEFICIARIES UNDER HOUSING ASSISTANCE PLAN, BY COVERAGE AND HOUSING COSTS, 1967

Coverage	Cost of plan (billions of dollars)		Number of beneficiaries (millions of households)	
	Stable housing costs	Housing costs rise 10 percent	Stable housing costs	Housing costs rise 10 percent
Universal	4.9	6.2	12.3	14.1
All families and all persons 65 and over	3.7	4.8	8.2	9.7
Families with children and all persons 65 and over	3.2	4.1	6.8	8.0
All families and all persons 65 and over, except home-owners without mortgages	3.2	4.1	6.9	8.0

Source: Author's estimates.

26 There is no doubt that some slumlords exploit tenants and earn unconscionable profits. This behavior cannot explain the large and increasing number of abandoned units in major cities. See Michael A. Stegman, "Slum Housing: Cash Flow, Maintenance and Management" in Stephen D. Messner (ed.), *Proceedings, American Real Estate and Urban Economics Association, 1969*, vol. 4 (1970), pp. 231–52; and George Sternlieb, *The Tenement Landlord* (Rutgers University Press, 1969).

Tables 6 and 7 contain estimates of the costs of several variations of the housing assistance plan, an illustrative housing allowance system. Each household is presumed to spend one-fourth of adjusted income (the sum of income from all sources and one-fifth of net worth) on housing. Housing costs are set equal to shelter costs reported in the low-cost budget for a family of four estimated by the Bureau of Labor Statistics for spring 1967. Benefits are equal to the difference between these two amounts.(27) Since BLS estimates of housing costs vary from one region to another, the amount of the subsidy would also vary. For example, in San Francisco the BLS rental was set at $1,519 for a family of four, and in Austin, Tex., at $1,056;(28) a family with an income of $3,000 and no net worth would receive $769 per year in San Francisco and $306 in Austin. Table 6 presents estimates of the costs of benefits (exclusive of administrative costs) under a universal coverage plan and three limited coverage plans. Because the cost of a housing assistance plan and the number of households it reaches are quite sensitive to the behavior of housing costs, one set of estimates is based on rental costs unaffected by benefits and another on a 10-percent rise in rents. If housing allowances raise rental costs 10 percent, payments to recipients rise roughly 25 percent and the number of households eligible for assistance 15 percent. Exclusion of single people under age 65 from the benefits reduces the cost by more than one-third. Narrowing eligibility further, either by excluding childless couples under 65 or by excluding homeowners without mortgages, reduces the size of benefits and the number of beneficiaries modestly. Other changes in the housing assistance plan would increase costs. For example, if households were presumed to spend less than one-fourth of adjusted income or if a small amount of net worth were disregarded in computing adjusted income, the number of beneficiaries and their payments would go up.

The distribution of benefits and beneficiaries by region and income bracket for a universal plan under which housing costs remain stable is shown in table 7. The South receives benefits for a larger percentage of households and in a larger total amount than any other region. The fact that incomes in the South are lower than in other regions explains both results. Most payments go to households living in central cities or in rural areas. Roughly one-fourth of households in these areas would receive housing allowances. Exclusion of households only eligible for small benefits, say, under $100 per year, would lower the number of beneficiaries by 1.8 million but would cut benefits only $89 million. Such a limitation might be justified on administrative grounds.

The administrative costs of a loosely administered Housing Assistance Plan—spot income verification and untied benefits, for example—might be as low as $15—20 per household, the cost of administering veterans' benefits, or $70—$95 million in the aggregate.(29) For a tightly administered plan—detailed applications, universal income checks, and tied benefits, for example—annual administrative costs might run as high as $100—$130 per household, the administrative cost per case under public assistance, or $500—$600 million in the aggregate. Tight administration would reduce benefits by uncovering some cheating and by discouraging applications from some eligible applicants who dislike obtrusive investigations. Besides administrative outlays, program costs should include the costs of code enforcement or of other direct efforts to raise housing quality.

TABLE 7.—PROJECTED DISTRIBUTION OF ANNUAL BENEFITS AND OF BENEFICIARIES UNDER A UNIVERSAL HOUSING ASSISTANCE PLAN, BY INCOME BRACKET, REGION, AND RESIDENCE, 1967

| Income bracket | Total | Census region | | | | Residence | | | | Incidence (average annual benefit) |
| | | Northeast | North-central | South | West | Standard metropolitan statistical area | | Other urban | Rural | |
						Central city	Outside central city			
Benefits (millions):										
Under $1,000	$1,459	$279	$367	$561	$252	$532	$256	$208	$462	$550
$1,000 to $1,999	1,338	232	347	602	208	555	247	185	402	381
$2,000 to $2,999	863	130	215	385	133	339	159	100	266	373
$3,000 to $3,999	621	95	168	229	130	251	148	64	159	408
$4,000 to $4,999	339	59	94	116	70	138	89	39	74	304
$5,000 to $7,499	209	27	75	57	49	97	58	26	28	202
Total	4,880	822	1,126	1,949	842	1,911	955	622	1,391	397
Beneficiaries (millions of households):										
Under $1,000	2.7	0.5	0.7	1.1	0.4	1.0	0.4	0.4	0.8	1 (82.3)
$1,000 to $1,999	3.6	0.8	0.9	1.4	0.6	1.5	0.6	0.6	1.0	1 (67.8)
$2,000 to $2,999	2.3	0.4	0.5	0.9	0.4	0.9	0.4	0.4	0.6	1 (47.2)
$3,000 to $3,999	1.5	0.3	0.3	0.6	0.3	0.6	0.4	0.2	0.4	1 (32.2)
$4,000 to $4,999	1.1	0.2	0.3	0.4	0.2	0.4	0.3	0.1	0.3	1 (24.7)
$5,000 to $7,499	1.0	0.2	0.3	0.3	0.2	0.4	0.3	0.1	0.2	1 (8.1)
Total	12.3	2.4	3.1	4.7	2.1	4.7	2.4	1.8	3.3	1 (19.9)
Percent of population receiving benefits	19.9	15.5	17.4	26.3	19.7	23.3	11.9	21.2	26.4	

1 Percent of population receiving benefits.

Initially, benefits probably should not be tied to housing outlays. To do so would run the risk that benefits would be eroded by increased housing costs. Such risks might be reduced if benefits were gradually tied to housing expenditures,(30) and particularly if independent actions to upgrade housing quality were undertaken.

The housing assistance plan is a possible substitute for direct subsidy programs such as homeownership and rental assistance, rent supplements, low rent public housing, below-market-interest-rate loans, and Farmers Home Administration loans to low to moderate income households. It is not a substitute for programs such as mortgage insurance and loan guarantees, secondary market operations, or Federal Home Loan Bank advances to members that influence the markets for mortgage credit. Nor is it designed to satisfy those who feel that the supply of housing for the poor is unresponsive to market forces and that governmental efforts to raise the supply of such housing are required to prevent subsidies from raising costs rather than quality. Housing markets seem to contain certain rigidities, notably those based on racial discrimination, that are not present in other markets; however, housing quality, in the narrow sense of better structures, has improved as income and wealth have increased. If the poor had adequate income to demand acceptable housing, if monetary conditions assured a plentiful supply of housing in the aggregate, and if laws against discrimination were vigorously enforced, the market for housing would probably respond by providing adequate housing for all. These conditions have never been fully satisfied. In their absence, special measures to channel adequate units to recipients of subsidies may be necessary.

The housing assistance plan would complement a more comprehensive system of income supplements to poor households. Living costs vary from one region to another principally because of variations in housing costs. Yet no national system of income supplements has provided for variations in support levels based on living costs because Congress, it is thought, would not accept such a plan. Housing benefits paid in addition to a general system of income support would meet this problem by removing housing from the needs the basic system would have to support.

LIMITS OF THE PLAN

The housing assistance plan, like the less equitable programs it might replace, does not squarely meet the bad housing problem. It enables all households with incomes below stipulated levels to demand a larger quantity of housing services than they can now afford. If housing markets are even sluggishly responsive to demand, the quality of housing services for assisted households will improve as low quality units are upgraded or removed from the housing stock and as units presently occupied by nonrecipients filter to beneficiaries of the program. But housing services are only one element of residential services, and inadequate housing services are only one element of the bad housing problem. Housing subsidies alone can do nothing, of course, to improve schools, to reduce crime rates, to make neighborhoods cleaner, or to improve transportation. These residential services depend on private behavior or on other public programs, largely under the control of State and local governments. Good schools and safe and convenient neighborhoods will always command a premium.

Since the essence of an equitable program of housing assistance lies precisely in the fact that all poor households are assisted *but not made better off than unassisted households*, recipients of housing benefits will continue to be least able to pay the premium for residential services. Even an equitable housing assistance plan will leave most aspects of the bad housing problem untouched. Though the housing assistance plan may lead to better housing structures, it is very far from a panacea for squalid neighborhoods.

NOTES

(1) For a listing of most housing subsidy programs, see Henry J. Aaron, Shelters and Subsidies: Who Benefits From Federal Housing Policies? App. A, "Characteristics of Selected Federal Housing Programs" (Brookings Institution, 1972).

(2) Dwight M. Jaffee casts considerable doubt on the durability of these effects in "An Econometric Model of the Mortgage Market: Estimation and Simulation" (Apr. 1, 1970; processed).

(3) For a full discussion of the impact of income tax provisions on homeowners see Henry J. Aaron, "Income Taxes and Housing," American Economic Review, vol. 60, No. 5 (December 1970), pp. 789-806; reprinted as Brookings Institution, reprint No. 193.

(4) Waiting lists exceeded vacancies in public housing in 47 of the 49 largest cities with public housing programs in November 1967. Waiting lists were more than 10 times larger than the number of vacancies in 32 of those cities. "Building the American City," report of the U.S. National Commission on Urban Problems, H. Doc. 91–31, 91st Cong., 1st sess. (1969), p. 131. The vacancy rate for all public housing units on June 30, 1969, was 2.2 percent: it was 1.5 percent or less in 18 States including New York, California, and Illinois. U.S. Department of Housing and Urban Development, "1969 HUD Statistical Yearbook," Washington, p. 204.

(5) See George Schermer Associates, "More than Shelter: Social Needs in Low- and Moderate-Income Housing," Research Report 8; prepared for the National Commission on Urban Problems (U.S. Government Printing Office, 1968). This report evaluates specific public housing programs in various cities, thinly disguised by pseudonyms made transparent by complementary information, for example, Chicago (alias Babylon, population 3,550,000), Detroit (alias Carsington, population 1,630,000).

(6) Previous estimates of the subsidy value of public housing include Robert L. Bish, "Public Housing: the Magnitude and Distribution of Direct Benefits and Effects on Housing Consumption," Journal of Regional Science, vol. 9 (December 1969), pp. 425-38; James Prescott, "Rental Formation in Federally Sponsored Public Housing: A Normative Analysis," unpublished Ph.D. dissertation, Harvard University, 1964. Eugene Smolensky, "Public Housing or Income Supplements: The Economics of Housing for the Poor," Journal of the American Institute of Planners, vol. 34 (March 1968), pp. 94-104; Edgar O. Olsen, "A Welfare Economic Evaluation of Public Housing" (Rice University, Ph;D. dissertation: processed); Eugene Smolensky and J. Douglas Gomery, "The Redistributive Effects of the Public Housing Program in 1965" (processed).

(7) The balance between supply of and demand for unsubsidized housing

would not change if (a) all public housing consisted of converted rather than new units and if public housing tenants were required to consume exactly the same quantity of housing services as they had consumed before or (b) public housing consisted of new construction only to the extent that consumption of housing services by public housing tenants was allowed to exceed what it had been before such tenancy.

(8) See Henry J. Aaron, Shelter and Subsidies: Who Benefits From Federal Housing Policies, ch. IV, "Housing Policies and Income Distribution" (Brookings Institution, 1972).

(9) Independent Offices and Department of Housing and Urban Development Appropriations for 1971, hearings before a subcommittee of the House Committee on Appropriations, 91 Cong., 2nd sess. (1970), pt. 3. pp. 654-55. The estimates do not discount payments to present value. If discounted, actual payments would be a higher fraction of maximum payments because tenant incomes are assumed to increase more rapidly than operating costs.

(10) This estimate presumes annual 1st year payments of $1,000 per unit (above the 1967-70 average and below the 1971 average for units begun under contract authority for those years), that over 40 years actual payments have a present discounted value equal to 90 percent of what they would be if all annual payments were $1,000, and that the appropriate discount rate is 8 percent.

(11) The original rate of 3-1/8 percent was increased to 3-3/8 percent for fiscal year 1964, to 3-7/8 percent effective July 1, 1964, and modified in 1965 to not exceed 3 percent.

(12) The Federal National Mortgage Association before 1968.

(13) George von Furstenberg and Howard R. Moskof, "Federally Assisted Rental Housing Programs: Which Income Groups Have They Served or Whom Can They Be Expected to Serve?" in The Report of the President's Committee on Urban Housing; Technical Studies (U.S. Government Printing Office, 1967), vol. 1, p. 153. These estimates are based on a comparison of average costs per unit under section 665 (d)(3) BMIR and those under the basic unsubsidized multifamily housing program, section 207. The estimates include allowances for other fees and for vacancies.

(14) Housing Act of 1949, title V, sec. 501(c), as amended.

(15) As indicated in the notes to table 7, cross tabulation of FmHA borrowers refer to different subsets of all FHA borrowers.

(16) The stream of benefits under Farmers Home Administration insured loans and Veterans' Administration insured loans are assumed to vest in the borrower when he obtains the loan. Accordingly, the annual flow of benefits and the present value of benefits both refer to the cohort of borrowers who obtained credit in the indicated year.

(17) "Housing the Urban Poor: The Economics of Various Strategies," American Economic Review, vol. 59 (Setoember 1969), p. 649.

(18) Many reasons can be advanced for adopting policies that interfere with the free operation of the housing market. In regrettably few areas does hard evidence suggest specific remedies, but in a disquietingly large number a widespread consensus supports collective action. See Shelter and Subsidies; Who Benefits from Federal Housing Policies, Brookings, 1972, chap. 1, "Rationale For a Housing Policy."

(19) Downs, "Housing the Urban Poor," pp. 647-48. Emphasis added.

(20) As one man wrote to his senator: "One thing struck my eye today. An ad for new houses in the $17,000 class being offered to low-income families for $200 down and $100 a month. This made possible by Government subsidy. In the meantime, my wife and I both work to make payments on our 30-year home of $136 a month and support our family without aid of the Government. Can you explain to me why I should be taxed to help someone else buy a home that I myself could not afford to live in?" Statement of Carl L. Curtis in "Housing and Urban Development Legislation of 1970," hearings before the Subcommittee on Housing and Urban Affairs of the Senate Committee on Banking and Currency, 91st Cong., second sess. (1970), p. 706.

(21) Median subsidy was $54 per month; median payment by mortgagor was $80 per month. The median of the sum of two series is not necessarily the sum of the two medians, but it is assumed here that median housing costs are $134 per month ($54+$80) and that annual costs are therefore $1,608.

(22) See Edwin Kuh, "A Basis for Welfare Reform," Public Interest, No. 15 (Spring 1969), pp. 112-17; William D. Nordhaus, "Tax Incentives for Low Income Housing," in National Tax Association, Proceedings of the Sixty-First Annual Conference on Taxation (1968), pp. 396-414; Eugene Smolensky, "Public Housing or Income Supplements—The Economics of Housing for the Poor," Journal of the American Institute of Planners, Vol. 34 (March 1968), pp. 94-101; Frank de Leeuw, Sam H. Leaman, and Helen Blank, "The Design of a Housing Allowance," Working Papers 112-25 (Urban Institute, Oct. 6, 1970; processed).

(23) See Jack Rosenthal, "HUD To Give Poor Funds for Homes," New York Times, Dec. 19, 1971.

(24) This discussion leans heavily on de Leeuw, Leaman, and Blank, "The Design of a Housing Allowance."

(25) See Gordon Tullock, "Subsidized Housing in a Competitive Market: Comment," and Edgar O. Olsen, "Subsidized Housing in a Competitive Market: Reply," American Economic Review, Vol. 61 (March 1971), pp. 218-19 and 220-28.

(26) There is no doubt that some slumlords exploit tenants and earn unconscionable profits. This behavior cannot explain the large and increasing number of abandoned units in major cities. See Michael A. Stegman, "Slum Housing: Cash Flow, Maintenance and Management" in Stephen D. Messner (ed.), Proceedings, American Real Estate and Urban Economics Association, 1969, vol. 4 (1970), pp. 231-52; and George Sternlieb, The Tenement Landlord (Rutgers University Press, 1969).

(27) Estimates are based on income including public assistance and other welfare programs reported for 1967. Welfare reform would substantially reduce these estimates.

(28) Bureau of Labor Statistics, Three Standards of Living, p. 25.

(29) Sam H. Leaman, "Estimated Administrative Cost of a National Housing Allowance," Working Paper 112-17 (Urban Institute, May 13, 1970; revised, May 22, 1970; processed), pp. 4-5.

(30) For example, a houshold with a $1,600 income per year and basic housing costs of $1,200 per year would be expected to spend $400 of its own resources on housing and would be eligible for $800 in benefits. During the first year the household might receive $800 in cash, during the second year $500 in

cash and $300 in housing certificates, and during the third year $200 in cash and $600 in certificates; during the fourth year it might receive $900 in certificates for which it would pay $100, and during the fifth year $1,200 in certificates for which it would pay $400 in cash.

THE DISTRIBUTION OF FEDERALLY
ASSISTED RENTAL HOUSING SERVICES
BY REGIONS AND STATES

By George M. von Furstenberg

It is argued that in all housing markets containing a significant number of low-income families at least some federally assisted rental housing should be supplied to supplement the private market and to provide for income transfers. The more that assisted housing is offered in one locality to the neglect of any other, the lower the marginal net benefits which may be expected. In spite of this, the variation in service levels is very large. For instance, in Utah, Wyoming, and Idaho there are only five assisted units for every 1,000 low-income households, while in Connecticut, Nevada, and the District of Columbia there are 120 per 1,000. The distribution of the existing stock of assisted housing across the Nation thus appears to be seriously unbalanced in relation to current needs.

INTRODUCTION AND PREMISE

The major assisted rental housing programs of the Federal Government fall into two classes. Public housing and rent supplement projects serve primarily low-income families, 50 percent of whom had total annual incomes of less than $3,000 in 1969-70. Families with median incomes of $5,000 to $6,000 are the intended beneficiaries of moderate income housing. This includes both the section 221(d)(3) below market interest rate (BMIR) program, involving up to 100 percent mortgage financing at 3 percent interest, and the more recent section 236 program in which interest costs are lowered further to 1 percent. In spite of the differences in tenant incomes, it has been estimated that annual subsidies of between $600 and $900 per household will be required under all programs, on the average over the life of the projects,(1) provided the existing section 221(d)(3)

BMIR projects will eventually all be converted to section 236 status.

Although income redistribution has been identified as the primary objective common to all of these heavily subsidized rental programs,(2) assisted housing services are supplied unevenly to different groups of eligibles. Interprogram differences in the demographic composition of tenants, for instance by age, race or size of family, have already been commented upon elsewhere.(3) However, inequalities in the geographic coverage of each program, and of all programs combined in relation to need, have hitherto received very little attention.

It can be argued that in all housing markets containing a significant number of low-income families, at least some federally assisted rental housing should be supplied both to supplement the private market and to serve as vehicles for income transfers. Some low-income families in any size class may desperately need housing assistance and have the greatest preference for—the least aversion to—living in the kinds of projects to which it is tied. On the other hand, the more assisted housing is offered in one locality to the neglect of any other, the lower the marginal net benefits which may be expected to result. For in that case, the program might reach well down the hierarchy of needs in one area, while in another, even the most pressing needs go unanswered. Hence, spatial balance in the distribution of housing assistance is not only of political interest as a matter of regional equity in the federal system, but it may also involve important dimensions of program efficiency.

II. THE RECORD OF ASSISTED HOUSING PRODUCTION

As of September 30, 1969, just over 900,000 households were living in federally assisted rental housing under the main subsidized programs. Public housing, which goes back to 1937 but now includes projects acquired through leasing and Turnkey methods, accounted for 78 percent of the total, while the 3 percent BMIR mortgage insurance program authorized in 1961 accounted for 18 percent. The newer rent supplement and section 236 programs, dating from 1965 and 1968 respectively, each contributed around 2 percent of the total volume. Under the last two programs, rents remaining to be charged to tenants are reduced to 25 percent of family income, but no less than 30 percent of full-cost rent or costs remaining after mortgage financing at 1 percent interest, respectively.

The number of units occupied under each of these programs in the 50 States and the District of Columbia is shown in table 1. While it is interesting to observe, for instance, that no rent supplement units at all had been provided in some small, generally Northern States, this table of the absolute numbers supplied is used mainly as an input for later tabulations involving comparison with needs. Since housing assistance is not strictly limited to low-income urban populations,(4) several definitions of the main group of eligibles must be tried to establish the fractions actually being reached in any State (columns 3 and 6 of table 2). We can then test how sensitive the ranking of states by relative service levels is to variations in the definition of the target group.

Column 4 of table 2 presents indexes of the provision of federally assisted rental units in relation to the interstate distribution of males at least 14 years of age and with some income of less than $2,000. Such males are regarded as potential heads of household. For column 7, families and unrelated individuals

TABLE 1.—FEDERALLY ASSISTED UNITS UNDER THE MAIN RENTAL HOUSING PROGRAMS: UNITS OCCUPIED AS OF SEPT. 30, 1969, BY STATES[1]

	Public housing	Rent supplements sec. 221(d)(3) MR	Sec. 221(d)(3) BMIR[2]	Sec. 236	Total
	(1)	(2)	(3)	(4)	(5)
Alabama	29,214	90	638		29,942
Arizona	3,468	86	615	70	4,239
Arkansas	7,789	528	644		8,961
California	40,883	895	13,064	2,541	57,383
Colorado	4,371	308	702		5,381
Connecticut	13,118	6	7,534		20,658
Delaware	1,909		253		2,162
Florida	22,007	2,159	1,760	470	26,396
Georgia	37,616	108	3,929	102	41,755
Idaho	336		32		368
Illinois	54,448		15,298	219	69,965
Indiana	8,479	70	8,475	2,453	19,477
Iowa	902	352	382	347	1,983
Kansas	1,778	550	2,505	149	4,982
Kentucky	15,516	12	1,099	573	17,200
Louisiana	19,521	726	2,159	62	22,468
Maine	657		471		1,128
Maryland	12,838	150	5,337	713	19,038
Massachusetts	25,403	772	13,146		39,321
Michigan	15,552	525	12,674	1,402	30,153
Minnesota	9,750	121	1,518	22	11,411
Mississippi	6,189	252	344		6,785
Missouri	12,053	118	5,689		17,860
Montana	1,007	60	73		1,140
Nebraska	5,497	40	844	120	6,501
Nevada	2,176	100	772		3,048
New Hampshire	1,970			150	2,120
New Jersey	38,138	309	5,911		44,358
New Mexico	2,070	645	694	140	3,549
New York	89,593	568	11,141	134	101,436
North Carolina	17,735	144	2,176	400	20,455
North Dakota	755		44		799
Ohio	30,280	1,098	3,952	1,106	36,436
Oklahoma	3,004	196	2,023	481	5,704
Oregon	4,313	304	536	92	5,245
Pennsylvania	51,730	131	3,652	238	55,751
Rhode Island	6,317	94	1,204	40	7,655
South Carolina	6,777	384	572	688	8,421
South Dakota	785	198	50		1,033
Tennessee	25,542	2,014	2,252	219	30,027
Texas	37,175	2,809	11,351	2,802	54,137
Utah	30	45			75
Vermont	330		336		666
Virginia	13,669	125	2,997	276	17,067
Washington	9,244	1,107	2,084	1,334	13,769
West Virginia	2,791				2,791
Wisconsin	6,448	163	1,007	104	7,722
Wyoming	55	60			115
District of Columbia	10,321	66	3,399		13,786
Alaska	620		56		676
Hawaii	3,502		1,859	126	5,487
Total	715,671	18,488	157,253	17,573	908,985

[1] The source for col. 1 was USHA run 223.0, table 7, "Units Occupied by Tenants or Project Employees Required to Live in Public Housing as of Sept. 30, 1969." The distribution in col. 2 gives insured rent supplement projects with units under payment as of the same date. Units in projects with insurance in force as of Mar. 31, 1970 and Feb. 28, 1970 are given in cols. 3 and 4, respectively. Sources for cols. 2 through 4 were the "02" reports of HUD, specifically, 302, 2102, and 3602.
[2] BMIR signifies below-market interest rate financing at 3 percent in contrast to the rent supplement program under the same section which involves market rate (MR) insured mortgage financing.

living in urban areas and having a total annual income of less than $4,000 in 1959 are used to define the need base. In either case, the definition of the indexes is simple. A number of 150, for instance, means that service levels in relation to needs were 50 percent higher in a particular State, than on the average for the Nation. Put differently, a low-income household in that State is 50 percent more likely to receive housing assistance than the typical low-income household in the United States as a whole.

The latest income distributions available in this detail can be computed only from the 1960 census and some risk is involved in assuming that they have remained sufficiently constant over time to establish the need distributions relevant to the stock of assisted housing existing in 1969. Also, no adjustment for equivalence—the different incomes required by families of varying size and in different places to support some equally low standard of living—is attempted. Furthermore, the choice of appropriate income cutoffs is inevitably somewhat arbitrary though it must be kept in mind that 1959 incomes of $4,000 would correspond to more than $5,500 in 1970, on account of inflation alone.

Not surprisingly, the consistency of the manifestations of poverty or low-income status is such that a disproportionately large share of poor persons in any State also implies a disproportion of poor families. Little variation in the interstate distribution of low-income households is observed if the poverty threshold is varied in either direction. The coefficient of rank correlation between the order of States by the index of assisted housing provision in relation to low-income males (column 5 of table 2) on the one hand, and in relation to urban families and unrelated individuals (column 8) on the other, for example, is 0.87 with standard error of 0.14. A coefficient of 1 would indicate perfect consistency between the rankings while zero would suggest the absence of any correlation. Hence we do not believe that our results are overly sensitive to variations in definitions and concepts within the relevant range.

To assess the degree of balance in the distribution of supply over States, we check the service level indexes just described for deviations from 100. An index above 100 indicates relative oversupply of assisted rental units while an index below 100 signifies undersupply in relation to the average frequency of housing assistance for all low-income population units—however defined—nationwide.

There are several reasons why "imbalance" as evidenced by the chosen criterion may be perfectly desirable. For instance, if the price of rental housing services relative to that of other "necessities" is unusually low in any particular area, the case for Federal assistance and additions to supply is correspondingly weak. We doubt, however, that variations in excess demand are nearly as wide and policy-significant over areas as large as States or regions, as they would be for individual locations. Intraregional variations are likely to be much greater than interregional variations, though some persistent differences in regional vacancy rates remain.(5)

One might, however, welcome another deviation from an allocation strictly in proportion to the number of low-income households in any State. With the data already assembled we can easily test for the presence of such a deviation. It can be argued that if the percentage of households with low incomes is exceptionally small in any State, filtering is much more likely to produce an adequate supply for them since there is more housing to filter down and fewer low-income households to filter to. In addition, certain external costs imposed by the poor

TABLE 2.—DISTRIBUTION OF FEDERALLY ASSISTED RENTAL HOUSING IN RELATION TO THE NEEDS OF LOW-INCOME PERSONS OR FAMILIES, BY STATES

	Concentration index[1] of low-income males (rank from lowest poverty concentration)		Federally assisted rental units in relation to distribution of low-income males			Federally assisted rental units in relation to urban families and unrelated individuals		
	Index	Rank[2]	Percent assisted	Service index	Rank (lowest relative frequency)	Percent assisted	Service index	Rank (lowest relative frequency)
	(1)	(2)	(3)	(4)	(5)	(6)	(7)	(8)
Alabama	140	43.5	8.28	134	40.0	10.83	191	49.0
Arizona	87	12.5	3.92	64	22.0	3.58	64	17.0
Arkansas	174	50.0	3.54	58	17.5	5.93	105	33.0
California	79	7.0	5.09	83	29.0	3.47	61	15.0
Colorado	95	19.0	3.70	60	19.0	3.13	55	14.0
Connecticut	67	3.0	14.02	227	49.0	10.63	186	48.0
Delaware	73	6.0	7.14	114	36.5	7.28	126	38.0
Florida	100	23.0	5.71	92	31.0	3.99	70	18.0
Georgia	127	39.0	9.68	157	42.0	12.24	215	50.0
Idaho	111	26.0	.62	10	3.0	.87	15	3.0
Illinois	83	10.0	10.51	170	45.0	7.86	139	40.0
Indiana	91	14.5	5.78	93	33.0	5.52	97	29.0
Iowa	125	37.5	.78	13	4.0	.94	17	4.0
Kansas	116	30.0	2.54	41	14.0	2.79	50	12.5
Kentucky	149	47.0	4.89	79	27.0	8.31	147	42.0
Louisiana	117	31.5	7.01	114	36.5	6.87	121	36.0
Maine	133	40.0	1.19	19	5.0	1.44	24	5.0
Maryland	75	4.0	9.27	150	41.0	8.44	148	43.0
Massachusetts	87	12.5	11.33	183	47.0	7.44	132	39.0
Michigan	83	10.0	5.66	92	31.0	5.20	92	26.5
Minnesota	112	27.0	3.78	61	20.0	4.48	79	22.0
Mississippi	182	51.0	2.16	35	11.0	4.27	76	19.5
Missouri	122	36.0	4.32	70	24.0	4.32	76	19.5
Montana	121	34.5	1.88	32	10.0	2.43	45	8.5
Nebraska	125	37.5	4.91	80	28.0	6.01	107	34.0
Nevada	59	1.0	15.47	262	50.0	13.85	243	51.0
New Hampshire	92	16.5	4.41	70	24.0	4.39	77	21.0
New Jersey	65	2.0	13.04	211	48.0	8.65	153	44.0
New Mexico	104	24.5	4.73	76	26.0	5.27	93	28.0
New York	77	5.0	9.90	161	43.0	5.79	102	32.0
North Carolina	140	43.5	3.84	62	21.0	6.67	118	35.0
North Dakota	153	48.0	1.17	20	6.0	2.50	45	8.5
Ohio	82	8.0	5.66	92	31.0	4.66	82	23.0
Oklahoma	134	41.5	2.28	37	12.0	2.38	42	6.5
Oregon	99	21.5	3.55	58	17.5	3.52	62	16.0
Pennsylvania	91	14.5	7.10	115	38.0	5.57	98	30.0
Rhode Island	104	24.5	11.05	179	46.0	6.97	124	37.0
South Carolina	141	45.0	3.03	49	16.0	5.03	89	24.0
South Dakota	158	49.0	1.35	21	7.0	2.49	42	6.5
Tennessee	144	46.0	7.20	117	39.0	9.75	172	45.0
Texas	114	29.0	5.82	94	34.5	5.19	92	26.5
Utah	83	10.0	.12	2	1.0	.11	2	1.0
Vermont	118	33.0	1.73	27	9.0	2.72	47	10.0
Virginia	117	31.5	4.29	70	24.0	5.14	91	25.0
Washington	96	20.0	5.81	94	34.5	5.62	99	31.0
West Virginia	134	41.5	1.57	26	8.0	2.70	48	11.0
Wisconsin	99	21.5	2.52	41	14.0	2.81	50	12.5
Wyoming	113	28.0	.45	6	2.0	.55	8	2.0
District of Columbia	93	18.0	25.30	408	51.0	10.21	180	46.0
Alaska	121	34.5	2.62	41	14.0	9.14	140	41.0
Hawaii	92	16.5	10.26	169	44.0	10.20	185	47.0
Total average	100	....	6.17	100	....	5.66	100	....

[1] The proverty concentration index is derived by dividing the fraction of all U.S. low-income males living in any State by that State's share of the national population, and multiplying by 100. An index number above 100 indicates above-average frequency of poverty.

[2] Ranked are 51 units, or the 50 States and the District of Columbia. The ranking is from the lowest incidence of poverty in col. 2 and from the lowest relative frequency of housing assistance in cols. 5 and 8.

on each other and on the rest of society may be expected to increase more than in proportion to their population share in any area. Much current thinking on shrinking local tax bases, "tipping points," and the breakdown of municipal services and school systems depends on such notions.(6) Within HUD, the popularity of "open communities planning" and the fostering of socioeconomic and, correlated therewith, racial mix reveals a similar conviction.

Accepting the premise, we postulated that the percentage of the low-income population served should be higher in relation to the average service ratio with index 100, the greater the share of poor persons in the total population of any State. Unfortunately this normative expectation was defeated decisively with the coefficient of rank correlation (r) between the orderings in column 2 and 5 of table 2 significantly negative (−0.53), rather than positive. Doubling the percentage of low-income persons in a State does not cause the supply of assisted rental housing to double, let alone more than double as we had hoped. Instead, it appears to affect the supply of assisted housing hardly at all.(7) In relation to need, our index of Federal housing provision is thus about halved as the low-income population share (the denominator) doubles, thereby accounting for the negative correlation between the two sets of rankings.

While there are wide and as yet unexplained variations, proportionality to the simple head count of population comes closest to defining the rule of the distributive calculus. As a result, most low-income States are undersupplied in relation to need while high-income States are oversupplied. Specifically, the States of Connecticut and Nevada and the District of Columbia, whose average rank in the distribution of low-income concentration indexes (column 1) is 7 (the seventh richest), had over twice as many federally assisted rental units in relation to need as are supplied on the average for the Nation. On the other hand, taking the mean of the indexes in columns 4 and 7, the frequency of housing assistance is found to be less than half of the national level in the States of Idaho, Iowa, Kansas, Maine, Montana, Oklahoma, the Dakotas, Utah, Vermont, West Virginia, Wisconsin, and Wyoming. Their average rank of 34 placed them way down in the distribution of the 51 "States" from the lowest to the highest concentration of low-income persons.

Let us accept the rough rule inferred from the historical distribution of assisted housing production for the moment and grant that the relevant need distribution is established not on the basis of the low-income population of States, but on the basis of their total population irrespective of income. Even under these conditions, significant differences still remain as shown in the last column of table 3. New England States (HUD Region 1, Boston), for instance, would have a service level index of over 130 in 1969, while northern Mountain States (HUD Region 8, Denver) would have an index of less than 40. If both need criteria agrée in the identification of regions which have experienced relative oversupply or undersupply, a de minimis case for corrective action may have been made in any man's book.

On balance, both service level indexes in table 3 decrease from East to West, but there is no systematic division between North and South. If the comparison is based on only those urban families and unrelated individuals who are defined as poor by referring to a single national poverty threshold (in 1960), income deficiencies in the South are exaggerated compared to those in the high-cost Northeast and West.(8) The South would be somewhat better supplied than appears from table 3, but then it also contains a disproportionately large share of all substandard housing units. The East-West differential would remain largely intact(9) if an adjustment were made for income equivalence.

TABLE 3.—THE SUPPLY OF FEDERALLY ASSISTED RENTAL HOUSING UNITS COMPARED TO THE DISTRIBUTION OF LOW-INCOME URBAN HOUSEHOLDS OR THE TOTAL POPULATION, BY HUD REGIONS [1]

New HUD region [2]	Index of provision of federally assisted rental housing in 1969 in relation to the distribution of low-income urban families and unrelated individuals in 1960		Index of provision of federally assisted rental housing in relation to the distribution of population in 1969	
	Index	(1) Percent	Index	(2) Percent
(1) Boston	128	7.86–6.12	138	7.86–5.71
(2) New York	114	16.04–14.12	127	16.04–12.61
(3) Philadelphia	107	12.16–11.39	105	12.16–11.59
(4) Atlanta	132	19.90–15.13	126	19.90–15.85
(5) Chicago	99	19.28–19.52	89	19.28–21.59
(6) Fort Worth	92	10.44–11.39	103	10.44–10.14
(7) Kansas City	61	3.45–5.67	62	3.45–5.55
(8) Denver	40	.94–2.37	35	.94–2.69
(9) San Francisco	67	7.73–11.53	70	7.73–11.08
(10) Seattle	80	2.20–2.76	69	2.20–3.19
Total	100	100–100	100	100–100

[1] The regional distributions are derived by summing over the States belonging to each region. (Sources: U.S. Census of Population: 1960, General Social and Economic Characteristics, State Reports PC(1)–2C to PC(1)–52C, and U.S. Bureau of the Census, Current Population Reports, Series P–25, No. 436.) The percentage of assisted housing in each region is then divided either by the percentage of all low-income urban households in that region (col. 1 above) or by the percentage of the total U.S. population living there (col. 2). The resulting quotient is converted to index form by multiplying by 100.
[2] Region 1 consists of New England with the States: Connecticut, Maine, Massachusetts, New Hampshire, Rhode Island, and Vermont all contained in census region Northeast. Region 2 consists of New Jersey, and New York, which form part part of the Middle Atlantic region of the Northeast. Puerto Rico and the Virgin Islands are excluded above. Region 3 contains Delaware, District of Columbia, Maryland, Pennsylvania, Virginia, and West Virginia, which, except for Pennsylvania, form the northeastern part of census region South. Region 4 embraces Alabama, Florida, Georgia, Kentucky, Mississippi, North Carolina, South Carolina, and Tennessee, all in the South. Region 5 includes Illinois, Indiana, Michigan, Minnesota, Ohio, and Wisconsin, all in North Central. Region 6 consists of Arkansas, Louisiana, New Mexico, Oklahoma, and Texas, all South except for New Mexico. Region 7 covers Iowa, Kansas, Missouri, and Nebraska, which form the western part of North Central. Region 8, with Colorado, Montana, North Dakota, South Dakota, Utah, and Wyoming, follows on with all except the Dakotas already in the West. Region 9 contains Arizona, California, Hawaii, and Nevada. Guam is excluded from our figures. Region 10 includes Alaska, Idaho, Oregon, and Washington—like region 9, all in the West.

III. REGIONAL DIFFERENCES IN PROGRAM IMPACT

Having considered the regional distribution of federally assisted rental housing units for all programs combined, we turn to a program-by-program investigation. From table 4 it appears that regional biases differ substantially. Public housing, which of course accounts for the bulk of all assisted units and thus dominates the totals, is concentrated in the Northeast but underrepresented in the West and South. The rent supplement program has precisely the opposite incidence with comparatively heavy concentrations in the South and West and undersupply in the Northeast. The BMIR and section 236 programs have both been unusually productive in the north-central region, but they are underrepresented relative to the needs in the South. Disproportionately many BMIR projects have also been built in the Northeast. Since up-to-date regional distributions of low-income families, derived by using 125 percent of the relevant poverty thresholds, could be used to define the need base in this comparison, problems of income equivalence and the intertemporal stability of poverty distributions do not arise.

One of the historical reasons for the basic East-West split in public housing is perhaps obvious. the eastern housing stock tends to be older and is thus more likely to be underequipped or dilapidated, although the South has the major share of all substandard housing units. In the past, when public housing was

TABLE 4.—THE PROVISION OF FEDERALLY ASSISTED RENTAL HOUSING UNITS UNDER THE MAIN PROGRAMS IN 1969 COMPARED TO THE DISTRIBUTION OF LOW-INCOME FAMILIES IN 1968, BY CENSUS REGIONS [1]

Region	Low-income families, percent	Public housing, percent	Index of distribution	Rent supplement 221(d)(3) MR, percent [2]	Index of distribution	221(d)(3) BMIR, percent	Index of distribution	Sec. 236, percent	Index of distribution	Total, percent	Index of distribution
	(1)	(2)	(3)=(2)/(1)	(4)	(5)=(4)/(1)	(6)	(7)=(6)/(1)	(8)	(9)=(8)/(1)	(10)	(11)=(10)/(1)
Northeast	19.4	31.8	164	10.2	53	27.6	142	3.2	16	30.0	155
North Central	22.1	20.5	93	17.5	79	33.4	151	33.7	152	22.9	104
South	45.3	37.7	83	52.8	117	26.0	57	38.6	85	36.0	79
West	13.2	10.0	76	19.5	148	13.0	98	24.5	186	11.1	84
Total	100.0	100.0	100	100.0	100	100.0	100	100.0	100	100.0	100

[1] The census regions are defined in the notes to the preceding table. The distribution of low-income families by region (col. 1) is obtained from "Manpower Report of the (U.S.) President" (March 1970) p. 127. The low-income cutoffs used in that source are 25 percent above the poverty thresholds. The weighted averages of the latter were for 1 to 7 or more person households $1,742, $2,242, $2,754, $3,531, $4,158, $4,664, and $5,722, respectively (1968). Cols. 2, 4, 6, 8, and 10, giving the regional distribution of federally assisted housing units under various programs, are derived from table 1. By relating to the distribution of needy families in col. 1, the indexes in columns 3, 5, 7, 9, and 11 are then derived. An index of 100 indicates correspondence between the population and assisted housing shares of any region, while an index of 200 would show that low-income families in a particular region are twice as heavily supplied as the average for the Nation (=100) indicates.

[2] The distribution of substandard housing units in 1968 was quite similar to that of rent supplement (apartment) units. For the 4 census regions, the breakdown was 12.9 percent, 25.8 percent, 53.3 percent, and 8.0 percent, respectively, indicating a greater frequency of substandard than of rent-supplement units in North Central and a lesser frequency in the West, with almost precise correspondence in the Northeast and South. Since rural housing is much more likely to be substandard than urban housing and more important in the South, not too much weight should be given to the similarity in these not strictly comparable distributions. See U.S. Bureau of the Census, "Current Housing Reports, Housing Characteristics," series H121, No. 17 (Washington 1970), p. 6.

most frequently built in the wake of slum clearance or removal of substandard units, projects were therefore concentrated in the Northeast and Southeast. Remnants of pioneer spirit of "the new conservatism" in the West may also be cited but hardly qualify as adequate explanations. There is ,however, tangible evidence of opposition to public housing in several Western States. For instance, until March 26, 1969, the legislature of Utah did not see fit to have a Housing Authorities Act enabling public housing to be built. Similarly, around 1950, Californians passed a constitutional amendment stipulating that low-rent public housing could not be built in any locality unless first approved by local referendum.

There are more compelling physical causes of the uniquely Southern and Southwestern orientation of the rent supplement program. Basic economic rent limits per apartment have been figured so tightly and the 25 percent maximum adjustment for high-cost areas has been so inadequate as to make the program inoperative in all but the lowest-cost locations. In 1967, for instance, it was estimated that the resulting total development cost limits for one- and two-bedroom apartments in Detroit, even with the maximum 25-percent adjustment, are still more than 20-percent below the equivalent limits implied by dwelling construction room cost constraints in public housing.(10) Not surprisingly, therefore, not a single rent supplement project has hitherto been completed in the Detroit area. For these reasons, the Kaiser committee stated bluntly that construction cost restrictions would have prevented any large volume outside the South and Southwest even if the program had been more adequately funded.(11) Since families moving out of substandard units are one of the few groups eligible for rent supplements, the distribution of substandard housing may also have influenced that of rent supplement units, as suggested in table 4.

The explanations which can be advanced to explain the North Central and Northeastern bias in the BMIR program are highly tentative. The volume produced under section 236 has as yet been insufficient to allow firm inferences, but first indications are that the regional distribution of BMIR projects will be replicated. Urban renewal activity is heavily concentrated in North Central and Northeast, with the new HUD regions 1, 2, and 5 having received almost 50 percent out of a total of $7 billion in project grants approved by the end of 1968. Hence, one hypothesis might be that the BMIR distribution has simply followed that of urban renewal. However, since only 23 percent of all BMIR projects are constructed in urban renewal areas, this factor cannot account for much of the difference in the regional impact of the program. Another partial explanation may be that builders and limited-dividend sponsors in the South and West have found BMIR projects less attractive because the cost of capital, and with it both effective mortgage interest rates and the required return on equity, are typically higher there than in the rest of the Nation.(12) Almost 42 percent of all BMIR projects are undertaken by limited-dividend sponsors and the regulations applied to them are uniform with no allowance for regional differences in profit requirements.

IV SUMMARY OF FINDINGS

On the average for the Nation, there are about six units of assisted rental housing available for every 100 low-income households. However, in States like Utah, Wyoming, and Idaho, there would be only one-half per 100. By contrast, in

Connecticut, Nevada, and the District of Columbia, at least 12 units per 100 households are available, or around 25 times as many as in the least supplied States. Hence, the probability of a low-income family receiving Federal housing assistance varies drastically from State to State. In general, the richer the State, the more assisted housing units are provided for its (relatively fewer) low-income families, and the poorer the State, the worse the odds.

Combining the States into either HUD or Census regions shows that there is a systematic undersupply in the West and oversupply in relation to the needs of the East. The middle tier of States, from the Great Lakes to the Gulf, is about average.

Given this aggregate outcome, regional biases still differ among the various rental programs with the inverse relation between public housing and rent supplement units and the concentration of BMIR units in the North Central region being the most remarkable. While public housing is heavily concentrated in the Northeast, the rent supplement program is serving primarily the South and Southwest. Several hypotheses were advanced about what might account for the differences in the geographical coverage of these programs. Suffice it here to note that as long as the biases specific to each program remain, changes in the relative importance of programs will also affect the regional incidence of housing assistance benefits in a manner which should be anticipated in policy planning.

V. POLICY CONSIDERATIONS

For reasons of both equity and efficiency, it seems imperative that the spatial distribution of housing assistance be made to mirror the distribution of low-income families much more closely. The probability of a low-income family receiving housing assistance should not depend critically on where it lives. The distribution of substandard housing units may perhaps be used as a secondary criterion in funding, since its adoption would serve, in effect, to give added weight to heavy concentrations of low-income households. Since any adjustment in the existing housing stock—now seriously unbalanced in relation to needs—can only be achieved gradually, a long-term plan is required first to compensate for past "mistakes" and then to maintain a better balance between changing needs and long-lived stocks. On the part of HUD, this requires active management of the spatial distribution of the annual additions to supply, and redirection rather than passive reliance on applications backlogs, past funding and performance, and "local interest."

NOTES

(1) These estimates were prepared under Sol Ackerman, until recently with the U.S. Department of Housing and Urban Development (HUD). Subsidy costs per apartment were higher in 1970, partly because most of the projects were still fairly new and because interest rates were unusually high during that year.

(2) In the program memorandum of HUD, income redistribution has long been identified as the principal objective in the assisted programs, while the declared function of those programs not involving major planned subsidies is to supplement the private market. See William B. Ross, "A Proposed Methodology for Comparing Federally Assisted Housing Programs," American Economic Review, Papers and Proceedings (May 1967), pp. 91–100.

(3) See, for instance, Walter Smart, et al., The Large Poor Family—A Housing Gap, research report No. 4, the National Commission on Urban Problems (Washington, 1968). Also see the author's "The Impact of Rent Forumlas and Eligibility Standards in Federally Assisted Housing on Families of Different Size." in Report of the President's Committee on Urban Housing, Technical Studies, vol. 1: Housing Needs and Federal Housing Programs (Washington, 1968), pp. 103-112.

(4) For instance, by 1970, 1,805 units of assisted housing were available for occupancy on Indian reservations in region 8, while 1,260 units were available in region 6. HUD region 8 (Denver) includes Montana and the Dakotas, while region 6 (Fort Worth) contains Oklahoma and New Mexico. "Indian housing" is included in the respective program totals, often low-rent public housing—Turnkey III.

(5) These differences seem to have narrowed in recent years. For instance, in 1964, rental vacancy rates in the Northeast, North Central, South, and West were 4.7, 7.3, 8.2, and 10.5 percent, respectively. Corresponding preliminary estimates for 1970 are 2.7, 5.6, 6.4, and 5.4 percent. It should be noted that differences in vacancy rates do not necessarily allow one to infer equivalent differences in excess supply, since normal (equilibrium) vacancy rates must be expected to be higher in regions with greater gross and net rates of population movement.

(6) Cf. Jay W. Forrester, Urban Dynamics (Cambridge, Mass.: MIT Press, 1969), "passim," especially pp. 65-101.

(7) This conclusion cannot fully be substantiated with rank correlation analysis alone. Rather, it is based on an ordinary least squares regression of the service level index (SLI) in column 4 on the poverty concentration index (PCI) in column 1 of table 2. With the standard error in parentheses, the results were: SLI=240-1.339 (0.335) PCI, r=-0.50, F—Value=16, S_e=66, n=51. A distribution strictly in proportion to population implies that a one point increase in PCI reduces SLI by about the same amount. In fact, the absolute value of the coefficient of PCI is even greater than unity, though not significantly so.

(8) Equivalence indexes for the measurement of poverty have been estimated for the Northeast, North Central, South, and West for places of varying size. For cities with over one million inhabitants they were in order, 1.500, 1.275, 1.050, and 1.200 while for cities with under one-quarter of a million they were 1.125, 0.975, 0.900, and 1.050, respectively. In 1966, application of the implied cost-of-living adjustment to the regions from the Northeast to West would have changed the distribution of the poor (by headcount), as follows: instead of 15.6, 23.3, 49.9, and 11.2 percent one would get 21.9, 23,7, 42, and 12.4 percent. In other words, the South now appears relatively less poor while the Northeast appears less rich. On the other hand, the share of the poor in the west and north-central regions changes little. See Harold W. Watts, "The Measurement of Poverty—An Exploratory Exervise," mimeo.

(9) The largest States in both the Northeast and the West have housing programs which are to some extent substitutable for the Federal programs here discussed. Under California's Cal-Vet program, around $2 billion has been lent at low interest rates to veterans for the purpose of buying homes (or farms). Under New York's Mitchell-Lama program, about 40,000 rental units have been completed to dated in New York City alone. Both programs aim at families in

the middle income range, although the veterans tend to haave low measured incomes for a year or two after discharge.

(10) See the author's paper with Howard R. Moskof, "Federally Assisted Rental Housing Programs," in "Technical Studies," vol. 1 (a supplement to report cited in the next footnote), p. 154 (note to table 5).

(11) "A Decent Home," Report of the President's Committee on Urban Housing (Washington 1968), pp. 64-65.

(12) For documentation see the author's article, "Interstate Differences in Mortgage Lending Risks: An Analysis of the Causes," Journal of Financial and Quantitative Analysis (June 1970), pp. 229-47.

ARE SUBSIDIES THE BEST ANSWER FOR HOUSING LOW AND MODERATE INCOME HOUSEHOLDS?

Anthony Downs

Direct federal housing subsidies are becoming an increasingly important stimulus to United States housing production. Since most economists believe high-level housing production will be vital to United States prosperity during the 1970's, such subsidies may play a key role in the larger economy. Moreover, they may even exert a significant influence on the socio-economic character of future urban neighborhoods. Yet, most Americans, including many housing officials, do not understand some of the most important impacts of both the size and particular forms of housing subsidies. For example, few people realize that shifting from present subsidies that help households pay their mortgage interest to a housing allowance might greatly alter the future spatial distribution of low and moderate income households in urban areas. This article seeks to clarify some of these little-understood aspects of housing subsidies, and to provide a brief view of an overall perspective from which they can be evaluated.

THE CURRENT EXTENT OF DIRECT HOUSING SUBSIDIES

In 1971, about 550,000 new housing units will receive some assistance from one or more of the many direct federal housing subsidy programs. This is not only an all-time high, but also represents over a ninefold increase from the average level of about 60,000 directly subsidized units per year that prevailed during most of the mid-1960's. Moreover, the share of directly subsidized units in total starts has also risen sharply. It was only about three percent in the mid-1960's, but will be over 20 percent in 1971. This is true even though total housing production in 1971 will be the greatest in United States history, with close to 2.5 million new units built—about 20 percent more than the previous record set in 1950. If mobile homes are excluded from consideration, then subsidized units comprise about one out of every four of the 2.05 million conventional units created in 1971.

Ironically, the Department of Housing and Urban Development (HUD) has become alarmed at its own remarkable success in expanding direct federal housing subsidies since the Housing and Urban Development Act of 1968. The rising costs of these subsidies—now about $1.4 billion per year—plus the huge long-term funding commitment they contain—which might reach over $5.0 billion per year by 1978—have caused HUD Secretary George Romney to propose a complete re-examination of the nature and size of existing direct housing subsidy programs. HUD is seriously considering substituting some form of housing allowance for the interest-rate subsidies that dominate present programs. This could both reduce the amount of subsidy required per household aided, and encourage greater use of older existing housing by the poor, rather than far costlier new units. The possibility that such a major shift might occur makes it crucial for those concerned to understand all of its potential implications.

THE NATURE AND "NEED" FOR DIRECT HOUSING SUBSIDIES

A housing subsidy is any form of financial assistance provided by a government to a household to help pay the cost of its housing. In theory, a household "needs" any particular form of subsidy only when its income is so low that it is suffering from "poverty" concerning the aspect of life covered by that subsidy. "Poverty" in turn means the household experiences a "subsidy gap" between that fraction of its income which society believes it should "normally" devote to the particular aspect of life concerned, and the cost of enjoying the socially-defined minimally-acceptable standard of living concerning that aspect of life. The "normal share" of income which society has traditionally defined as appropriate for housing is about 25 percent. Thus, the size of the housing "subsidy gap" for a household is measured as the amount by which 25 percent of its income falls short of paying the cost of occupying housing of a "minimally acceptable" size and quality for that size household.

Several things about this definition should be emphasized. *Anything which raises the income of a household with a subsidy gap reduces the size of the gap,* if other things remain the same. Hence all income support programs—such as the welfare program—are intimately bound up with the issue of housing subsidies. In effect, every housing subsidy is a restricted form of income support, and every income support is in part a housing subsidy. Also, *anything which changes the quality level which society regards as "minimally acceptable" influences the size of the subsidy gap for all households.* It, therefore, affects the number of households who theoretically "need" subsidies, and the size of subsidy required for each. Over the long run, this "minimally acceptable" quality level keeps rising with the success of our economic system in raising general living standards. For example, the size of the *average* single-family house built in the United States rose from 983 square feet in 1950 to 1,650 square feet in 1968—an increase of over 67 percent in eighteen years. Therefore, the very success of our economy creates ever-larger "needs" to subsidize those who have fallen behind economically, and keeps raising that per-household cost of enabling them to "catch-up" with "normal" households. Furthermore, *anything which changes the cost of producing any given quality level of housing—either up or down—also influences the size of the subsidy gap.* There is a widespread belief that this gap can be greatly reduced, or even eliminated, by large-scale industrialized production of housing at much lower costs than now prevail. In my opinion, this belief is mainly a myth. In fact, housing production costs have steadily risen over time, and seem likely to keep on doing so in the future.

From the above analysis *we can immediately conclude that some form of direct housing subsidy would be required to eliminate, or even significantly reduce, the housing subsidy gap now experienced by millions of United States households.* No one knows exactly how many households have such a gap, but it is certainly larger than the number of households considered "poor" by the official government definition. As of 1970, about 25 million Americans—or 13 percent of the entire nation—were officially considered to be poor. Moreover, close to half of them were not able to earn their way out of poverty by working because they were either too old, or disabled, or young children, or mothers who had to care for young children. Another one-fourth of the poor were in households with an employed breadwinner who earned such low wages they were still considered in poverty. Thus, around nine percent of the United States population seems to be in an almost permanent state of having "fallen behind" the average standard of living so far as to qualify as "needing" housing subsidies if they are ever to close their housing gap. In reality, the "need" for housing subsidies as defined above is probably much larger than even this estimate.

OUR UNWILLINGNESS TO MEET THIS "NEED" FULLY

Realistically, there is almost no chance whatever that the federal government will raise housing subsidies high enough to fully close this total housing subsidy gap in the foreseeable future. The cost would be too great to receive congressional support. One indication of this is that Congress has so far been unwilling to appropriate enough money to close the food subsidy gap in the United States. Yet that gap is much smaller in dollars than the housing subsidy gap, and food is clearly more important to life than housing. The food subsidy gap is the basis for our official government definition of poverty. A household is officially considered to be poor if 33 percent of its income (the fraction that society believes it "should be able to afford" for food) falls short of the cost of a bare subsistence diet which the Department of Agriculture has defined as "minimally acceptable." At present, the cost of such a diet for a household of four is around $1,300 per year—or 30¢ per meal per person. Hence any such household with an income below about $3,900 per year is considered poor, because 33 percent of its income will not pay for that diet.

In theory, an exactly analogous approach could be used to compute a "poverty level income" based upon housing instead of food. However, no one knows precisely how much the "minimally acceptable" quality of housing costs, because it is hard to define quality in housing, and housing costs vary immensely in different parts of the country. Nevertheless, I believe it is accurate to assume that a housing unit of "minimally acceptable" quality for a four-person household costs *at least* $90 per month on the average, or $1,080 per year. Since a household "ought to" spend about 25 percent of its income on housing, it must have an income of $4,320 per year to be above the "poverty level" computed in relation to housing. This income is 11 percent higher than the "poverty level" computed in relation to food—as the government now computes it. Hence there are more "housing poor" people in the United States than "food poor" people. Moreover, the cost of removing everyone from "housing poverty" is higher than the cost of removing everyone from "food poverty." Yet, Congress has been unwilling to pay anywhere near the cost of eliminating "food poverty" in the United States. Even the proposed Family Assistance Plan would raise incomes of all four-person households to about $2,400, or less than two-thirds of the officially "food poverty level" incomes for such households. If Congress believes ending "food poverty" is too expensive, it will surely be unwilling to make housing subsidies large enough to end "housing poverty." Furthermore, Congress is unwilling to focus all of the housing subsidies it now provides upon aiding relatively poor households who "need" housing subsidies. Rather, it continues to provide very large *indirect* housing subsidies to middle income and upper income homeowning households by allowing them to deduct their property taxes and mortgage interest from their federally taxable incomes. The resulting tax savings are really disguised housing subsidies that probably amount to around $4 billion per year. Yet they are received mainly by households which have no "need" for housing subsidies as defined above; that is, they are not suffering from "housing poverty." Other indirect housing subsidies are provided to occupants of rental housing built by developers and investors motivated by special tax-shelter advantages that make them willing to accept very low rates of return on their investments. This reduces the rents of such relatively new housing somewhat, aiding mainly households with incomes above the national median—and hence well above the "housing poverty level." This allocation of major *indirect* housing subsidies to relatively high-income households is really a key part of the basic "trickle-down" process of urban development explained further below.

HOW THE "TRICKLE-DOWN" PROCESS WORKS

The main process for providing housing to low and moderate income households in the United States is now, and has always been, the "trickle-down" process, or "filtering" system. This process shapes the entire structure of urban development in our country; hence, understanding it is a key prerequisite to understanding how various housing subsidies would affect urban development.

In this process, relatively high quality standards of size and construction are enforced for all newly built housing units. Hence only people in the upper half of the income distribution can afford to live in brand new units (except mobile homes). New units are built mainly on vacant land around the edges of metropolitan areas, because the rate of return on private investment there is higher than either in older central city areas, or far-out "new cities."

In the United States, households who can afford only relatively low quality housing are not allowed to build *new* low quality housing units as they do in most of the rest of the world. Such new low quality units can be seen in the suburbs of most of the world's largest cities outside the United States and Western Europe. They are usually called shacks or barrios, and are often built by the poor households who live in them. But poor households in the United States must live in *old* low quality units if they cannot afford high quality housing. These old low quality units are allowed to exist because of our double standard regarding the housing quality we permit in different areas. Low quality housing, whether new or old, is illegal everywhere in the United States. But whereas this legal standard is rigorously enforced in new-growth areas and most suburbs, it is deliberately ignored in enormous portions of older central cities and close-in suburbs. This dual standard of law enforcement restricts the supply of older and deteriorated housing—hence relatively inexpensive units—to those more centrally located neighborhoods. Poor households therefore tend to become concentrated in such neighborhoods, and rarely live in new-growth portions of the suburbs.

Realistically, the existence of different housing quality standards for the nonpoor and the poor is probably inevitable because of their great differences in economic capability. But there is no inherent reason why housing of different qualities must be spatially segregated as drastically as in the United States. Even in the poorest nations, the wealthy, the middle-class, and the poor tend to live in different neighborhoods. But all three types of neighborhoods are found both in the older centers of cities and in the new suburbs. Hence there is no massive exclusion of the poor from huge outlying suburban rings as in the United States—the very rings where new growth and new jobs are being created most dynamically. Yet, such exclusion is an inherent result of the way our housing "trickles down" through the income distribution. Relatively affluent households occupy housing when it is brand new and still on the edge of urban development. But as even newer and more modern units are built farther out, the original occupants move on and are replaced by middle income households moving up from still older housing. This gradual downward movement of housing units through the income distribution continues as the neighborhood ages, unless it is near some outstanding amenity (like a lakefront, park or university) that keeps high income households in the area. Finally, relatively poor households move in who cannot afford to pay the ever-rising maintenance costs of the then-aged housing. The area soon deteriorates markedly and becomes a "slum." This entire life cycle from new affluent neighborhood to aged slum condition may take anywhere from thirty to sixty years.

EVALUATING THE RESULTS OF THIS PROCESS

Economically, this process is remarkably efficient. It very neatly matches up the quality and cost of housing with the income levels of households. Each household lives in the type of housing it can afford out of its own income. Also, households at each income level live in relatively homogeneous neighborhoods (in terms of both incomes and housing quality) with other households of similar economic capabilities, because we differentially enforce housing quality standards to insure such homogeneity. They are rigorously enforced in new neighborhoods, moderately enforced in middle-aged neighborhoods, and largely ignored in slums. Moreover, all housing in the system is being used to its "maximum economic capability" at any given moment, and each household can find a neighborhood with a housing quality level suited to its income.

From the viewpoint of the wealthiest households, this system is great. It allows them to live in homogeneously high quality neighborhoods without having to grapple with any of the problems caused by poor residents. For middle income households, the "trickle-down" system is also beneficial. They can find areas where others like themselves predominate—also free from any problems of extreme poverty. Together, these two groups make up the vast majority of American households. Hence the system serves the majority of Americans quite well.

But for many of the urban poor, the "trickle-down" process is a disaster. It compels the poorest and often least competent households to live concentrated together in the worst quality housing in society. This concentration has a "critical mass" effect which multiplies the negative impacts of poverty. It creates an entire neighborhood environment dominated by poverty conditions and by certain types of social pathologies most intensively associated with poverty (although found among all income groups to some degree). The results are "crisis ghetto" areas marked by high rates of crime, vandalism, broken families, delinquencies, drug addiction, dilapidated housing, and poor quality education. These areas are found mainly in central cities and some close-in suburbs, because they have the oldest housing where the poorest people concentrate. As a result, many central cities and some older suburbs have become burdened with the highest economic and social costs in all of our urban areas.

Although "crisis ghettos" of this type are small realtive to the nation's total population, they are absolutely very large in some big cities. For example, in Cook County, Illinois, there were 512,000 people on welfare in April, 1971. Over 100,000 of these poor people were in households containing only one adult but six or more children. It is difficult for one adult to exercise effective control over six or more children under the best of circumstances. When the circumstances involve extreme poverty and deteriorated neighborhood conditions, it is almost certain that a sizable fraction of such households will experience some of the pathological behavior patterns described above. And compelling thousands of such households to live concentrated together in the worst quality housing in urban areas causes a reverberation of such pathologies which greatly magnifies their total ill effects. I believe this spatial concentration of poverty at the bottom of the "trickle-down" process is one of the most crucial causes of many key economic and social problems now being experienced by large central cities throughout the nation.

Thus, viewed as a whole, the "trickle-down" process is an ingenious arrangement through which the major social costs of creating wonderful neighborhood environments for the wealthy, and fine ones for the middle-class, are loaded onto the poorest households who are least capable of bearing such burdens. In fact, by compelling the poor to live concentrated together, this process magnifies the burdens which poverty itself would generate if the poor were spread out in many more neighborhoods. I recognize that many of the undesirable conditions in "crisis ghettos" are caused by the behavior of some of the poor themselves. Yet the majority of the poor residents there do not engage in such behavior. They are just as appalled by its consequences as those more affluent Americans who have fled elsewhere and erected legal barriers to keep millions of decent but poor households from sharing in the higher quality environments they enjoy.

Most of the middle income and upper income households who are so well served by the "trickle-down" process of urban development in the United States do not realize the cruelly exploitative costs it imposes upon the poor at the bottom of the heap. They live spatially isolated from the areas impacted by those costs, so they experience them only through an occasional television documentary. Their distance from this harsh reality also allows them to indulge in the morally complacent and false process of blaming the conditions in slums and ghettos solely upon their residents. This self-justifying attitude ignores the fact that many of these conditions arise because of the very concentration of the poorest households together, which in turn is an inexorable result of their deliberate exclusion from areas where higher income families live.

In my opinion, any social arrangement which benefits the relatively wealthy and the middle-class at the expense of creating large costs which it then loads onto the very poor is a gross injustice which cries out for redress. Yet, that is precisely the case regarding the entire "trickle-down" process that dominates urban development in the United States. And this situation is by no means a "natural" result of "free market forces." On the contrary, it is created, sustained, and furthered by public policies and laws which prevent free markets from operating in order to protect the vested interests of the urban majority at a terrible cost to the poor, who constitute a relative minority in our society.

THE LIKELY IMPACT OF VARIOUS HOUSING SUBSIDIES

The highly undesirable conditions at the bottom of the "trickle-down" process cannot be eliminated by providing better physical dwelling units for the poor through housing subsidies as long as the poorest households are still concentrated together in neighborhoods they dominate. This conclusion is vividly proven by widespread experiences in public housing projects across the country. In fact, it is a delusion to view the "housing problems" of the poor as mainly caused by their financial needs for subsidies to pay for physically better dwelling units. Equally important to solving those "housing problems" is the improvement of neighborhood quality by counteracting the effects of massing so many poor households together.

In my opinion, some type of dispersal of many poor households, on a purely voluntary basis, to areas where other poor people are not locally dominant is essential to any long-run amelioration of "crisis ghetto" conditions in our big cities. This does not imply a sudden massive exodus of all or even a large fraction of the urban poor from their present central city enclaves to an even scattering across every metropolitan area. But it does imply a greatly increased out-flow of such residents from central city neighborhoods to suburban areas that are now closed to them. This includes providing opportunities for low and moderate income households to live in suburban new-growth areas being built now, or to be built in the future. That in turn means federal housing subsidy programs that allow such households to occupy brand new housing units—even though the per household cost of subsidizing such occupancy is much higher than the per unit cost of helping them move to better quality existing housing. If we do not provide big enough per unit housing subsidies to help at least some low and moderate income households live in new-growth areas, we will simply perpetuate the process of exclusion which has helped create our present big-city slums.

This need to achieve at least some economic integration in new-growth suburban (and central city) areas has a direct bearing upon the particular form of housing subsidies the federal government should use. Theoretically, shifting from subsidizing mortgage interest rates (as in the present HUD Section 235 and 236 programs) to providing a housing allowance (as has frequently been proposed recently) would not influence our ability to achieve economic integration in new-growth areas. In fact, a housing allowance, if it were large enough per household, would allow a poor family to move directly into a new suburban area simply by buying or renting a home there. No suburban community could exclude poor households by using restrictive zoning laws, or by denying builders permits to build low cost or subsidized units, or by using any of the other tactics now employed to prevent entry of low and moderate income housing into new-growth areas.

Hence, the housing allowance at first appears to be a better mechanism for achieving economic integration in the suburbs than the present interest-rate subsidy programs. However, I do not think it would be nearly as good a mechanism in practice. According to proponents of the housing allowance form of subsidy, its main advantages over present interest rate subsidies are:

It would be more equitable because it would aid all households who were eligible, not just a small fraction of them;

It would be more efficient because most of its recipients would occupy older existing housing rather than much more expensive brand new housing, and that results in a lower subsidy cost per household served;

It would not commit Congress in advance to high annual levels of subsidy expenditure because the amount spent could be varied annually—unlike long-term interest commitments tied to mortgages; and

It would not necessarily be tied to 40-year mortgages with their high ratios of interest cost to initial construction cost.

But nearly all these advantages presume that the amount of subsidy per household aided would be far too small to permit any low and moderate income households to occupy brand new housing units. If Congress really tried to achieve "equity" by providing some type of housing allowance to all the millions of households that would be eligible, it would be under great pressure to hold total program costs down by keeping the per household amount quite small—just as it does in the existing welfare program and the proposed Family Allowance Program. Consequently, households receiving the allowance would use it to bid for existing older housing units better in quality than those they already occupy. This would in effect speed up and improve the "trickle-down" process by giving poor households enough money to maintain the older housing stock in better condition than at present. But it would not allow any low and moderate income households to move into suburban new-growth areas, where all housing is new and, therefore, relatively expensive. Nor would the housing allowance cause much decline in the spatial concentration of the poorest households in the worst housing stock that now prevails—even if the *absolute quality* of the worst housing improved over time. Hence, in reality, a housing allowance would be ineffective at changing the present adverse social impacts of the "trickle-down" process. In contrast, present interest-rate subsidies can do so as long as the units they create are at least partly located in suburban new-growth areas.

The above decision is hardly a complete analysis of the relative advantages and disadvantages of either housing allowances or present interest-rate subsidies.

But it illustrates the importance of taking into account the likely impact of every form of housing subsidy upon the spatial distribution of low and moderate income households in urban areas. It is vital to consider this impact in designing the nation's overall housing subsidy policy. That policy should be aimed in part at counteracting the immense injustice of the present forced concentration of the poor in deteriorating central city slum neighborhoods. President Nixon has said that his Administration "will not seek to impose economic integration upon an existing local jurisdiction." But I believe it is far more unjust to impose economic concentration of poverty upon those least able to bear its costs than to impose some economic integration upon middle income and upper income suburbanites with far greater capabilities for bearing the resulting costs. It is unfortunate that our historic policy has been to compel economic concentration of the poor together, and to block economic integration both through legal barriers like zoning rules and building codes and through use of indirect housing subsidies that help the more affluent occupy brand new housing. Now that we have developed and started to use interest-rate subsidies capable of helping to counteract this historic injustice, we should carefully weigh all the consequences before deciding to shift to some other form of subsidy like a housing allowance.

POSSIBLE OBJECTIVES OF HOUSING SUBSIDIES

The above discussion raises the question: What are the real objectives of housing subsidies? The answer might seem obvious: To help people in poor quality dwellings improve their housing conditions. But this is by no means the only objective which our present housing subsidies are designed to achieve—as is clear from our provision of *indirect* housing subsidies more to the wealthy and the middle-class than to the poor. In fact, there are at least seven different objectives for housing subsidies. Each has specific implications for the particular form of subsidy best designed to achieve it. These objectives and some brief comments on each are as follows:

> *Making the poor generally better off—not just in regard to housing.* I believe this objective is probably best accomplished through some form of general income maintenance rather than by aid specifically directed at housing.
> *Improving the housing conditions of the poor, regardless of their general level of welfare.* The housing conditions of the poor are influenced by the entire quality of life in their neighborhoods, not just by the nature of the physical structures they occupy. Hence, achieving this objective implies improving the neighborhood environments of the poor, as well as their dwelling units.
> *Promoting home ownership generally, without regard to the incomes of the households concerned.* This objective has been well served by indirect housing subsidies like the deductibility from taxable income of mortgage interest and local property taxes, and federal mortgage loan insurance for homeowners.
> *Stimulating the total number of housing starts as an aid to the building industry.* This objective has long played an important role in creating political support among builders for housing legislation.

Stabilizing the output of the building industry by helping it counteract cyclical variations in the availability of mortgage credit. This objective has been pursued through the creation of several publicly run vehicles to pump credit into housing markets. They include the Federal National Mortgage Association, the Government National Mortgage Association, and the Federal Home Loan Bank and its new secondary mortgage finance subsidiary.

Helping central cities counteract the deterioration of older areas by providing their residents with more funds available for housing maintenance. This is already being done indirectly through welfare programs that pay rents for the poor, and could be further accomplished through housing allowances.

Opening up more opportunities for low and moderate income households to live in suburban new-growth areas. This would provide such households with better access to new jobs, good schools and better quality environments than they now have available to them. It is also consistent with aiding central cities.

In designing a national housing subsidy, or any combination of particular subsidies, without relating it to *all* of these objectives, since it is likely to serve specific objectives very differently. Thus, our choice of different forms of housing subsidy is certainly not just a matter of assessing the cost-effectiveness of each in improving the physical dwellings of the poor. In addition, each has crucial spatial and other nonfinancial implications. In fact, the particular mixture of housing subsidies we finally adopt will affect the future social, economic, and racial composition of our urban neighborhoods, and their spatial relations to each other. In short, this choice has profound implications for the very nature of our society in many of its most significant dimensions.

OUR NEED FOR A MIXTURE OF DIFFERENT SUBSIDIES

My own view is that we need a mixture of different kinds of housing-related subsidies to serve several of the objectives set forth above. We should subsidize a significant number of brand new units for low and moderate income households, in spite of the high per household cost of doing so, in order to achieve some economic integration in suburban new-growth areas. But we also need a larger scale income maintenance program—perhaps including a housing allowance—to help the majority of poorer citizens move into better quality existing housing units. Furthermore, we probably need several other types of subsidies, such as continued pumping of federal credit into housing markets through special institutions for that purpose. No one form of housing subsidy can do all that needs to be done.

CONCLUSION

In summary, housing subsidies are the only way to help low and moderate income households who live in poor quality housing, or pay abnormally high fractions of their income for housing, to upgrade their housing to the standards we define as "minimal" in quality and "normal" in cost as a fraction of income.

However, Americans as a whole are almost certainly not willing to achieve these objectives completely. Middle income and upper income groups would have to pay a much bigger total housing subsidy to the poor than they are now willing to bear. Even the particular forms of housing subsidies we choose will depend in part upon how fully the middle and upper income majority in America wishes to confront and deal effectively with the causes of urban poverty. It appears to me that any effective attack on those causes must involve the sharing by many middle and upper income suburban households of their job opportunities, their schools, and their neighborhoods with a significant number of those poor households who are now excluded from these benefits. At present, I believe most Americans do not want to live near or share their schools or neighborhoods with the poor, regardless of race.

In short, we do not want to provide equality of opportunity to our fellow citizens if that requires us to share our everyday lives with them. Apparently, we believe that would be pushing the concept of "human brotherhood" too far. Until we alter that attitude, I must agree with that native American philosopher, Pogo, that, concerning the ultimate issue of housing for the urban poor, "We have met the enemy, and he is us."

THAT "HOUSING PROBLEM"—
THE AMERICAN VS.
THE EUROPEAN EXPERIENCE

Irving Welfeld

Begin at the beginning: There is housing *production* and there is housing *assistance*. They are two different things—and if you forget they are different, you are in trouble.

The focus of housing *production* is the creation of a new dwelling unit; its prime justification and purpose is the community's need for additional dwellings. The focus of housing *assistance* is the need of some citizens for a subsidy if they are to be able to afford decent housing, old or new; its prime justification and purpose is the community's sense of obligation to provide these citizens with suitable accommodations. In Europe, a clear distinction is drawn between housing production and housing assistance. Since 1937, the basic American approach has been to combine the production and assistance function in a single program. Thus, public housing(1)—the sole housing-subsidy vehicle until the 1960's—attempted to solve the nation's housing shortage, while meeting the needs of the ill-housed, by subsidizing the production of new housing units for the poor. The troubles that public housing has run into give us good reason to look at the European experience and see what we can learn from it.

True, since the late 1940's, America has made great strides in overcoming its housing shortage. The 1970 census found that of over 63 million housing units in the United States, fewer than four million lacked a full complement of plumbing facilities and fewer than one and a half million units were overcrowded (using as a standard more than one and a half persons per room). But, alas, the cause of this improvement was but minimally related to direct government support of housing for low-income families. Public housing completions during the 1948-1967 period were less than 475,000. Public and publicly-assisted housing accounted for less than two percent of the 30 million starts in the 20 years between 1948 and 1968. Indeed, the net effect of government action on the housing stock in the 1950's and 1960's was negative—demolitions of housing by public action destroying more units than were built.

By the end of the 1950's a consensus had emerged that public housing was incapable of solving the housing problems of the poor. This can be seen from a remarkable document published in 1960 by the Housing and Home Finance Agency (the predecessor of the Department of Housing and Urban Development), the agency responsible for administering the program. The document, like the Biblical book of *Lamentations*, is a veritable catalogue of woes. More than a decade before Forest Hills came to be associated with public housing's quandary rather than with championship tennis, public housing's defects included 1. poorly located sites, 2. economic and racial segregation, 3. poor design, and 4. high development cost. Some criticized public housing for having income limits that were too low, others for having income limits that were too high. While some called for ending the program, others criticized it as being inadequate. Support of public housing (even in someone else's neighborhood) had broken down as a litmus paper test to distinguish liberals from conservatives. The whole program was a muddle.

MOBILIZING THE PRIVATE SECTOR—THE 1960's

Given the success of private enterprise in meeting the needs of middle-income and upper-income households, it seemed obvious (or at least plausible) that what was missing in America was subsidized private production for the low-income market. This idea mobilized traditionally conservative housing industry groups in support of a liberal housing program. The 1960's therefore saw, not only a succession of programs in which public subsidies to private enterprise became the vehicle of housing production for the poor, but also increasing "privatization" of public housing through the various "turnkey" programs, which provide roles for the private sector ranging from site assembly and development to management and ownership.

The 1960's also witnessed attempts to provide housing subsidies to families with incomes that could be classified as "moderate" and "lower," as opposed to the "low-income" households served by public housing. The original rent supplement proposal in 1965 sought to serve an income group that could not purchase standard housing for 20 percent of their income, but which was nevertheless above the public housing admission limits. The thrust of the proposal was the creation of a program that might rapidly increase the supply of standard housing at not too great a cost to the Treasury. The program also introduced the concept of a tenant subsidy which varied according to need. This was not only judged more equitable but was also consistent with budgetary concerns, since (a) a full subsidy would not be used in cases where a partial one would do, and (b) if a tenant's income rose, the program's cost would be reduced (or the program could be expanded at no extra cost). Such a graded subsidy scheme also made unnecessary the eviction of families whose incomes had risen above the point of need, thus (a) encouraging economic integration in subsidized housing and (b) eliminating one of the major sore points of public housing—the disincentive to economic advancement produced by a program in which eviction is the mark of economic success.

The 1965 program ran into a great deal of legislative flak from both the left and right flanks. From the left came the argument that the program was unjustified, since there were still vast unmet needs of lower-income families. So the income limits were pushed down to public housing levels—and the program became enmeshed in all of the dilemmas it was supposed to resolve. True, the program enlisted private enterprise, but the introduction of new players did not change the rules of the game. The limitations imposed by Congress were just as successful in shackling private enterprise as they had been in shackling public enterprise.

In 1968, however, the story was very much different. Then, the Johnson Administration's interest-subsidy proposals were enacted in a fit of exuberance by a Congress that was in a state of innocence with regard to the mechanics of mortgage financing. These new programs, section 235 and section 236, have indeed unleashed private enterprise. The *homeownership subsidy program* (section 235)(2) resulted in 116,000 starts in 1970 and approximately 150,000 starts in 1971. The *rental subsidy program* (section 236)(3) reached 105,000 starts in 1970 and 130,000 starts in 1971. This achievement does not reflect—nor has it caused—a major shift in legislative opinion. It was all an accident. Ironically, it resulted from determined opposition in Congress to high levels of production for precisely the group the program is so successfully serving! A closer look at the legislative history and financial operation of the section 236 program illustrates the point.

THE MISCONCEPTIONS OF THE LAWMAKERS

As in 1965, the Administration set out in 1968 to obtain a high-volume program. The main features of the proposal were an interest-differential payment to the lender (in order to permit the owner to pay only a one percent interest rate), and income limits close to the local median. In response to a query as to why lower income limits weren't used, Secretary Weaver answered:

> By having the more liberal upper limits, you have the possibility of getting a greater volume quicker and also of providing relatively small subsidies to those who need less help but still need some help in order to obtain decent housing.

But Congress did not really like this idea at all. The Liberals deplored such high income limits; the conservatives deplored the subsidies. The liberal-dominated Senate cut the income limits to 70 percent of local median income, for 80 percent of the funds. The remaining 20 percent of the funds could be provided for families that exceeded these limits. It simultaneously allowed a $300 deduction for each minor child. Republican Senators were critical, with Senators Bennett, Tower and Hickenlooper stating: "To allow that 46 percent, or, almost half, of our nation's families must be supported by their government, to say nothing of 70 percent, is certainly not acceptable in our opinion."

To assure that the households affected were genuinely interested in housing, and not merely taking advantage of a good thing, the permissible rent/income ratio under section 236 was raised by the House from 20 to 25 percent. The 25 percent figure was plucked from the air. The U.S. Census for 1960 indicated that 80 percent of families in the $4,000-$4,999 range have a gross rent-to-income ratio of less than 25 percent, and in the $6,000-$6,999 range, 83 percent of the households pay less than 20 percent. The rationale for the 25 percent ratio was given in the following colloquy involving Rep. Brock, the author of the House amendment (who had unsuccessfully attempted to impose a 25 percent ratio in the home-ownership program):

> Mr. Eckhardt: If the . . . first amendment had been passed, would he offer this amendment at 30 percent . . . ?
> Mr. Brock: I think that probably I would and maybe 40 percent. . . . I honestly hope we could reduce this program. . . .

The more conservative House was also not satisfied by the rollback of the regular income limits to 70 percent of median income, and cut back (they thought) the maximum permissible income even farther—to a figure representing 130 percent of the income that would make one eligible for local public housing administration. A Senate-House Conference Committee finally settled on a 135 percent figure.

The use of income limits based on public housing eligibility did not result, as will be seen, in a program that serves, in the words of Rep. Reuss, "paupers plus 30 percent." Neither did it, in the words of Rep. Barrett, "cripple the program." The main result of this arcane game of income limits and rent/income ratios, contrary to *everyone's* expectations, was to prime the program for production and to price the poor right out of the program.

THE WONDERFUL WORLD OF FHA MORTGAGE FINANCE

The secret of section 236's production success lies in the key elements that had to be considered in calculating a mortgage based on debt service. These elements were the interest rate, the income limits, and the rent/income ratio.

The one percent interest rate means that a small amount of net rental income can support a large mortgage. The problem is how to generate that small amount of net income from a project geared to a lower-income segment of the population. The first step is to estimate low on future operating expenses. If Congressmen are attuned to the voice of their constituents, government employees are attuned to the voice of Congress. The latter had proclaimed that the name of the game was a production when, in 1968, it set a goal of six million subsidized units for the decade. Since, in any event, future operating expenses are "guesstimates," the developer invariably guessed low and received the benefit of the doubt.

In the case of the gross income of the tenants, not only was the voice of Congress heard but the written law could be read. The use of a 25 percent rent/income ratio in the law squeezes more income out of poor prospective tenants. But, most surprising, the prospective and permissible tenants under the law turned out not to be that poor. The "lower"-income levels of the section 236 program—135 percent of the income limits for public housing admission—are surprisingly high. Translated into specific income limits for specific localities, the results are quite liberal. The table below sets forth the permissible income limits, under section 236, in representative areas of the country before and after adjustment (addition of $300 per child and dividing by 95 percent), for a family of four. It illustrates how close the regular section 236 adjusted limits are to the median income limits in the various localities.

LOCALITY	MEDIAN INCOME LIMIT	SECTION 236 UNADJUSTED LIMIT	SECTION 236 ADJUSTED LIMIT	PERCENT OF MEDIAN
Concord, N.H.	9,050	7,020	8,020	89
Boston	9,600	7,695	8,730	90
Brockton, Mass. . . .	8,500	6,955	7,950	94
New Orleans	8,200	6,480	7,460	91
San Antonio	7,300	6,345	7,310	100
Dallas	7,950	5,670	6,600	83
Seattle	8,850	7,155	8,060	90

This miscalculation of Congress as to who would be eligible for rental subsidy under section 236 has turned out to be a boon for developers. After all, the key obstacle to the production of new subsidized housing is, frequently, neighborhood opposition. "Subsidized housing" conjures up the specter of a drab and dreary public housing project, and homeowners adjacent to the project immediately see the loss of their most precious possession—the equity in their house. The best possible defense of HUD and the developer is to prove to the neighbors that the units, although labeled "lower-income housing" are in fact nothing of the sort. This proof they were now able to offer.

Profit is also known to be a motive in the activities of private entrepreneurs. All the cards are stacked in favor of higher-cost units. There is little difference in time and talent (the developer's most precious commodities) in developing a 100-unit project with a per-unit cost of $16,000 rather than $14,000. Moreover: 1. If the mortgager is also a builder, the size of his fee is directly related to the size of his mortgage; 2. The size of his permitted equity return is also directly dependent on the cost of the project; 3. The value of the project on the "depreciation-deduction sales market" varies directly with the size of the mortgage; and 4. The management fee, in the usual case, is directly related to the project's *gross* income (i.e., before deducting operating and capital expenses) and, therefore, to the size of the mortgage. Of course, higher costs and rents may reduce the number of aspiring tenants. This factor is severely diluted, however, by the subsidy, which results in an approximately 34 percent discount from the otherwise economic rent of the unit. And just as the market constraints are diluted by the subsidy, the usual HUD constraints are diluted by the nature of the subsidy payment. A $1,000 increase in cost results in only a few-dollar increase in the monthly subsidy per tenant. The increase in cost need not even result in increased expense to the government if the project can draw higher-income (and, therefore, higher-rent paying) tenants.

The increased initial costs can also be justified on the basis of improving the economic soundness of the project. The mortgage that is insured is to be amortized over 40 years. If economic obsolescence is not to come many years prior to physical obsolescence, the building should contain many features that are considered "luxuries" today but which will be considered "necessities" tomorrow.

The consequence of this exotic brew of legislative unawareness, legal sleight of hand (in defining income limits), haphazard patterns of local public housing income limits, financial leveraging, and tax shelter economics was a fountain of profits that attracted producers and investors like flies to honey. A lot of housing began to be built.

IT'S BEGINNING TO LOOK LIKE EUROPE (IN THE 1950's)

The present interest-rate subsidies in many ways resemble the classical European housing production programs. In Europe during the 1950's, the governmental programs usually involved deep, long-term subsidies to the non-poor. In addition, the subsidized programs accounted for a large percentage of total construction. In Sweden and France, over 90 percent of new construction was and still is subsidized. In the Netherlands, the figure is 80 percent. In England, all non-luxury, rental housing is subsidized by the government. The only exception to the rule is Switzerland, which in 1960 had no subsidized housing. The unique situation in Switzerland is partly explained by the very low interest rates that prevail in a nation of bankers and first mortgages that do not require any payments of principal.

With a high percentage of new construction being subsidized for a long term, the housing stock grows arithmetically while budget costs increase geometrically. Although in most cases, the incomes of the housed families rose substantially over time, the standard European housing production approach did not have graded rents and did not allow the system to recapture a portion of the subsidies.

In the longer run, however, these subsidies produced an absurd situation. As rent (or on a means test prior to receipt of a production subsidy). Government officials were not only faced with a housing shortage, but also with rent control. As a result of rent control, the very households that could most afford a new unit were already living in low-priced units. The need was to entice these households, who had a low rent/income ratio, into new units. The imposition of a high rent/income ratio or high income limits would have been counterproductive, in both a figurative and literal sense.

In the loner run, however, these subsidies produced an absurd situation. As long as a housing shortage continued, the government was compelled to attract households into new units. With increasing interest rates and rising construction costs, the government discovered that only the higher-income households could afford the new subsidized units. However, these families were already living in comfortable, older, rent-controlled, and subsidized units—usually with ample space, since their needs had shrunk with time. On the other hand, poorer young families, who could not afford new units, and were effectively barred from the older subsidized units, were often left out in the cold. The result of the policy was, in the words of the late Charles Abrams, "free enterprise for the poor and socialism for the rich."

It is of interest that the problems caused by continued and excessive subsidization are quite similar to those caused by rent control. In both cases, governmental actions result in artificially low housing expenditures, a misallocation of housing resources, and a bestowal of benefits on the basis of chance rather than need. The main distinction is that, in the case of subsidies, the cause is the government's generosity, whereas in the case of rent control it is an overzealous regulation of private enterprise.

EUROPE IN THE 1970's: THE NEW PATTERN

European countries by the second half of the 1960's were faced with the choice between efficiency and equity. They could opt for efficiency and reduce the subsidy, or they could opt for equity and make more housing subsidies available for lower-income households. The Europeans opted for both. They were able to do so because they made the crucial distinction between housing *production* and housing *assistance*. Efficient production was sought by reforming production programs and greater equity was sought by expanding assistance programs.

Production Programs. The response to the production problem was a streamlining of subsidies. Shallower and shorter-term subsidies have been introduced. These shallower subsidies not only save money, but also bring into balance the social benefits and economic costs.

The German, Dutch, and Danish systems are typical of the new approach. The Dutch system involves an initial markdown of rentals to close to 50 percent of the "economic rent" based on costs. However, the subsidy is annually reduced by six percent (10 percent in the case of homeowner), and therefore entirely phased out in a 10 to 15 year period. The German system involves an initial markdown of a little under 40 percent. The subsidy is, however, reduced by one third every four years, and is entirely eliminated for over-income tenants. The Danish involves an even smaller percentage reduction. At present, the initial reduction is approximately 25 percent—the difference between a 6.5 percent mortgage loan and an 11 percent market loan. The subsidy is, however, reduced to zero at the end of seven years, and the subsidy amount is to be repaid over the next seven years. Such streamlining is possible in these systems since the programs do not pretend to serve the lower-income groups. True, in Denmark a priority is given to families with incomes below the median. The option is meaningless, however, since they cannot afford the rent.

Assistance Programs. On the assistance front, European governments introduced or expanded housing assistance programs for poor people. The primary purpose of these programs is to provide housing dollars to the poor. They, however, also have a number of other important, albeit subsidiary, objectives. One of these is encouraging population growth—a traditional aim of European governments. Another is to encourage the upgrading of housing standards. Payment is often conditioned on residence in units that meet minimum standards of size, facilities, and even age. In Sweden the program was originally limited to units constructed after 1941. In the Netherlands assistance is still limited to units built since 1960.

Housing assistance is also a strategy that is consistent with a policy of disengagement by governments from intervention in the housing market. In Denmark and Germany, the decontrol of rental housing and the introduction of housing allowances went hand in hand. In England, the introduction of an assistance system and the removal of rent regulation are the crucial part of the

Conservative Government's "Fair Deal for Housing." One of the reasons for government disengagement from an active role is a growing realization that bureaucratic hands were no match for the invisible hand of the market place. Rent control and long-term government subsidies left a situation in Europe in which there were serious mismatches. Occupants of rent-controlled or subsidized units were often paying an inordinately small amount for rent and/or using far more space than they needed. An assistance system permits the government to disengage from its role as a resource allocator, and place this function in the hands of a mechanism—the market—far more suited to play that role.

The actual weight given in each nation to these varying objectives, as well as the different conditions from which they begin, results in very different types of systems. They all, however, run into one common obstacle: the heritage of rent control. The key to success for a shallow-subsidy production program and housing allowances for the poor lies in the fluidity of the existing housing market. Unless the government can increase household mobility in the existing stock, a shallow-subsidy program is doomed to failure. If households don't move from old to new housing when the subsidies are large, they certainly won't move when subsidies are small. It therefore becomes essential for the success of a shallow-subsidy strategy to unfreeze rents. But even rent decontrol is often not enough. With a large sector of the housing stock in the hands of local public and nonprofit groups, the decontrol of rent often does not result in a rise in rent. These latter groups, being political creatures, just do not respond in the same manner as the classical "economic man."

The initial step of rent decontrol is a difficult enough decision. Some countries, such as France, have not even approached the matter, while others, such as Sweden, have toyed with the idea, but believing in the maxim that "discretion is the better part of caution," have stepped gingerly away.

The step beyond rent decontrol is the far more difficult one. It involves government intervention to force rents up in existing housing, rather than to keep them down. In spite of the political acrobatics required by such a move, the Netherlands and England, in the name of "harmony and fairness," have decided to take this leap into the unknown.

Just how well this twofold European strategy with regard to housing production assistance will work, it is far too early to say. But one can say this: Were it not for the heritage of rent controls, there would be every reason to expect it to work quite well. And this has a direct bearing upon America's housing problem, since—always excepting New York City—we have no such heritage to get in our way.

BACK TO THE UNITED STATES

The high production totals of American subsidy programs begin to pose many of the same problems as the old-fashioned European programs. The first is the obvious one of budgetary cost. The problem was stated as follows in the Third Annual Report on National Housing Goals submitted by President Nixon to Congress on June 29, 1971:

> In calendar year 1968, the Federal Government subsidized about 10 percent of all new housing units produced; last year, the figure was up to

almost 25 percent and it is scheduled to remain in this range this year and next. It is estimated that subsidized housing units started or projected for the three fiscal years 1970-72 have already obligated the Federal Government to subsidy payments of perhaps $30 billion over the next 30 to 40 years. And assuming the completion of the six million subsidized units for low- and moderate-income families called for in the 10-year housing goals by 1978, present estimates suggest that the Federal Government will by that year be paying out at least $7.5 billion annually in subsidies. Over the life of the mortgages this could amount to the staggering total of more than $200 billion. Any increase in the number of units to be subsidized beyond those called for in the 10-year goal will only add further to the claims on future budgets.

The second problem is the one of equity. This has at least two aspects. The first is that the program does not serve the poor that Congress wished to serve. The incentives of the interest-subsidy programs are such that it is in the developer's interest to build the most expensive project. The result of the high-cost units is high government costs (since the subsidy is a debt service one). Nevertheless, in spite of the high subsidies, the lower-income household which the program was intended to reach is being squeezed out. In the typical case, the household with an income under $5,000 must pay over 30 percent of its income for subsidized housing. With rising operating costs, developments which rely on low-income households will amost certainly default on their mortgages. This is already happening on an ominous scale. The only way for the program to survive is to attract higher-income households. However, in the words of the National Tenants Organization, this would be a "perversion of subsidies from the neediest families."

A classic formulation of the second aspect of the equity problem is the following letter from a concerned constituent to his Congressman:

As a member of the usually silent majority and an ardent supporter of yours I believe that I should bring to your attention some things that, from my point of view, should be corrected. First of all, I am a young man of 25 employed as the personnel supervisor of a growing concern in the area where my wife is also employed. Between us we earn approximately eleven thousand dollars per year and live within our means in a modest three-room apartment in a 40-year-old building. A new [subsidized] housing area . . . is now open for tenants who earn less than six thousand per annum. *These apartments are as large or larger than ours and in beautiful condition, and the rent is actually less than I am paying. Is it possible that this situation can be justified?*

Perhaps there is a way to justify this situation. But if there is, no Congressman has as yet found it.

A NON SEQUITUR AND A MYTH

Two major justifications for deep-subsidy programs to non-poor households have been that these households cannot afford new housing and that the nation is facing a massive housing shortage. The first of these is a non sequitur, the second a myth.

Wallace Smith has summarized and demolished the first justification:

> Housing commentators in the United States are fond of producing data which show that new housing is priced beyond the means of most of the middle-income population as well as the low-income group. It is a non sequitur to conclude that middle-income households require housing subsidies, because this group finds its housing primarily in the *existing* stock of dwellings. Indeed, *the ordinary homebuilder's reason for not trying to build homes for the lower-middle income group is that he cannot compete with the used housing market where such families get substantially more for their housing dollar.* (Emphasis added)

As for the "housing shortage," Frank Kristof, commenting on the 1970 census, has noted:

> The nation's housing problem has little relationship to physical shortages of housing. If anything, the evidence suggests housing surplus rather than housing shortage. *For two decades the nation has produced an average of 1.5 new housing units for each new household added....* Any talk of housing shortage in America constitutes one of the great mythologies of housing discussion. (Emphasis added)

All this is not meant to prove or suggest that there are no areas in the country in which there is a deficiency of standard housing, or that the poor do not face very real housing problems. It is, however, meant to indicate that misjudging the scale and the nature of present housing problems is perhaps the one sure way to bar a solution.

SOME EUROPEAN LESSONS: PRODUCTION

The European experience not only provides a perspective for understanding our problem but also suggests solutions that may be appropriate. On the production side, the European practice of separating production from assistance is helpful in removing many of the seemingly insoluble cost and equity dilemmas. Once it is recognized that the justification for the subsidy is the need of a particular community for additional housing and that the benefits which accrue to private individuals are incidental by-products, the problem of drawing the line on income limits evaporates. It doesn't matter, for this purpose, *who* lives in *what* house or apartment—so long as there are enough houses and apartments for everyone to live in.

The question then becomes one of setting forth the objectives of an efficient production strategy and of designing specific programs. A production strategy in America should have the following objectives: ·

Low Cost per Net Additional Unit. The ideal production program should result in a unit that would not otherwise be produced—and at the lowest possible cost to the federal government. Present HUD programs only partially fulfill this ideal. The subsidy to public housing authorities results in a unit that would otherwise not be built—but at a high cost to the federal government. A program in which most of the benefits go to high-income households achieves a low per-unit cost—but only a fraction of the units subsidized would not have been built otherwise. *The ideal production program would therefore aim at marginal new housing buyers (or renters) in the median-income range.* The *total* subsidy per unit (house or apartment) could be under $1,500; this is less than 10 percent of the projected section 236 costs and less than five percent of the projected cost of apartments in new public housing.

Responsiveness to Local Market Conditions. A well-designed production strategy should take into consideration regional differences in incomes and housing costs. Even more important, programs should be operative only in areas in which there are shortages. One of the great weaknesses of current HUD programs is that they are not attuned to the nation's diversity. Nationwide mortgage limitations result in "lower-income" housing programs producing luxury or middle-income units in some areas of the country while being totally inoperative in other areas. It also often means that high national production totals are achieved by glutting some markets and ignoring areas where a shortage exists.

Market Discipline. A housing production strategy should provide incentives for efficiency. The interest of the producer, the consumer, and the government should all be pulling in the same direction. At present, all of HUD's programs are perversely constructed. The fact that the subsidy is in the form of a debt service means that the highest subsidy in the program goes to households that can afford the most expensive units! Under the section 235 program, the household with an $8,000 income has the same mortgage payment whether it purchases a $14,000 or $24,000 house. The present programs also insulate the builder from market competition for tenants. Thus, a $75 subsidy payment in the section 236 program may represent only a $25 cost saving to the consumer.

Since we are here dealing with a shallow-subsidy program, the European experience is especially valuable. Their subsidy programs involve substantial initial subsidies *but with a phasing out of all subsidies over a period of years.* At the moment, European subsidies are not performing smoothly. These hitches, however, reflect conditions, already mentioned, that seem to be unique to Europe. First, the continued existence of rent control, which results in an artificially high gap between the rents of old and new units, dampens the fires of consumer demand. Second, the substantial portion of the older housing supply in Europe that is subsidized reduces the attractiveness of new units with shallow subsidies, especially at a time when interest rates and construction costs are rising rapidly. Finally, the market for new housing is proportionally much smaller in Europe than in America. Whereas in the United States the cost of constructing a new house is approximately two times median annual income, in Europe the ratio is three and four to one. Given these harsh European conditions the amazing thing is not that production thrives but that it survives. If such a program were transplanted to the fertile soil of America and nurtured by efficient and aggressive homebuilders, the main problem would be to limit its expansion.

A full-scale housing production program following the European model would solve only half the American housing problem, and the lesser half at that. What is, of course, essential is a program that will enable poor households to afford the cost of living in decent housing.

The absence of a large-scale housing assistance program in America has been costly both to the poor and to the nation's housing supply. In order to obtain standard housing, the poor must pay a very high percentage of their income as rent. If the poor are unwilling or are unable to pay, however, they are not the only ones who suffer. To again cite Dr. Kristof:

> Normally, the increasing availability of older housing should lead to a (relative even if not absolute) drop in its price and its readier availability to low-income families. But the fragmentary evidence suggests that the price drop in the housing occupied by low-income minority in-migrants, to the extent that it occurred, in many areas had led to disinvestment and deterioration through decreased maintenance by owners of rental properties . . . As a consequence, large quantities of central cities' housing stock not only filtered down but filtered out of the housing market because owners cut their losses by ceasing to operate their properties—in short, abandonment.

Nor is abandonment a fate reserved for old housing. The costs of the section 236 program are so high that the poor can only live in them if they are willing to pay upwards of 30 percent of their income for housing. Since in many areas the poor are refusing to make this type of bargain, many projects—although they may be no more than one or two years old—are rushing along the road of deterioration and default.

On the public housing side, a ceiling has been imposed on rent by raising the subsidy sky-high. The Brooke Amendment, enacted in 1968, limits the tenant contribution to 25 percent of income. In new high-cost projects the government contribution often exceeds $200 per month for each apartment. Even so, public housing is becoming a less and less appealing alternative even for the poor. In the words of a friendly critic, E.D. Huttman:

> Public housing is perceived as an unhappy, stigmatized environment by tenants and public alike. To the tenant it is a stressful environment created by poor management policies, the unacceptable actions of other tenants, the isolation and size of the projects, and the socially unpleasant aspects of the housing design itself. To a large proportion of the public today, it is viewed negatively as a government repository for socially unfit families. Ironically, a public effort to build decent housing for the poor has produced housing whose reputation is worse than that of the slums.

Even if public and publicly-assisted housing did produce "penthouses for the poor," they would still involve a cruel game of chance for most of the poor. At best, there is fewer than one unit of assisted rental housing for every 10 low-income households. The program of building new houses for the poor can be compared to a program that would allow a select few of the poor to eat in French restaurants while the rest of them are left to scrounge for the remains.

Again, the European experience here has great relevance to America. As in the case of shallow production subsidies, there is no question of the workability of a large-scale housing assistance program. The objectives of the American assistance program would, however, not be the same as those in any particular European country. The absence of a significant housing shortage, and the absence (until quite recently) of rent control, would mean that an American assistance program could concentrate on providing poor households with the means to pay for decent, safe, and sanitary housing in a suitable environment. *Such a program should not be designed to stimulate either directly or indirectly the production of new units.* To the extent these latter programs are necessary, they should be designed for a different income class.

The income class to be served by the assistance program should be primarily those at the poverty line and below, in the particular locality. The program would be aimed at providing these households with the widest possible choice of housing. As a corollary, the government subsidy would vary with the percentage of income the household pays for housing. The higher the percentage, the higher the subsidy. If a family decides that it wishes to spend a small percentage on housing (or to put it more positively, if the family wishes or is required to allocate a higher percentage toward medical or educational expenses) and as a result lives in substandard housing, this becomes a matter of free choice. The government will have fulfilled its obligation to provide the family with the means to pay for decent housing. For the government to go farther and force the family into a rigid expenditure pattern is a remedy which might very well be far more unpleasant than the illness itself.

This argument in favor of greater freedom and dignity for the poor household raises the question: Why not go the complete route and just give the household money to spend as it pleases? In theory, this is a valid objection. However, this is not the choice we face. Although the recipient might be better off with a direct cash payment, it is unlikely that Congress will enact a cash transfer program with a level of payment high enough to enable the poor to pay for standard housing in high-cost areas. The reasons for this include the costs of such a program, regional variations in the cost of living, the disincentives to work for low-paid workers, and Congressional unwillingness to see money "frittered" away for "non-essentials." As James Tobin has written, "The social conscience is more offended by severe inequality in nutrition and basic shelter . . . than by inequality in automobiles, books, clothes, furniture . . . "

The housing assistance program could be piggybacked on to the general assistance program. In areas where low-priced housing is available, or where general assistance has been raised to a level that permits occupancy in standard units without undue pressure on the family budget, no (or very small) housing assistance payments would be made. Finally, although the housing assistance payment has no production function, the payments—by creating an effective demand for well-maintained older properties—will markedly improve the nation's housing stock.

The European experience indicates that, given a minimum of bureaucratic "eptness," the administrative problems of such a program are not too great. Nor is the budgetary problem. The cost of such a program would be in the $5-10 billion range annually (assuming a subsidy reaches approximately 10 million poor households). Is this a lot of money? It certainly isn't, considering that the President's Report indicates we shall be spending $7.8 billion a year in the latter part of the decade if we continue our present programs, which have a proven track record of offering a maximum of aggravation and a minimum of assistance.

NOTES

(1) "Public housing":—This housing is, as a general rule, developed, owned, and administered by local public housing authorities. Projects are financed through the sale of tax-exempt bonds to private investors. The federal government agrees to make annual subsidy payments in sufficient amounts so that rent of the project need cover only the expenses of operation, repair, and maintenance, and a payment (in lieu of taxes) to the locality equal to 10 percent of the shelter rent (rent less utilities). Eligibility for residence, in general, is limited to families in the lowest income group and to low-income households that are either elderly or displaced.

(2) Section 235, homeownership program:—This housing is developed by private builders. Units are financed through private lending institutions and the mortgages are insured by the FHA at a market interest rate. Interest-subsidy payments are paid to the mortgagee sufficient to cover the difference between (a) the cost of debt service (interest plus amortization of principal), taxes, insurance, mortgage insurance, and (b) 20 percent of the household's adjusted income. The maximum amount of the interest-subsidy payment is the difference between debt service at the market rate of interest (plus the mortgage insurance premium) and one percent.

(3) Section 236, rental program:—This housing is developed, owned, and administered by private lending institutions and the mortgages are insured by the FHA at a market interest rate. The mortgagors' interest payments to the mortgagee are made as if the interest rate of the mortgage were equal to one percent. HUD pays the mortgagee the difference between one percent and the market rate. Each tenant must pay the greater of (a) a basic rental (calculated on the basis of a mortgage with a one percent interest rate) or (b) 25 percent of his adjusted income. Rentals collected by the mortgagor in excess of basic charges are returned to HUD.

DISCRIMINATORY ZONING:
LEGAL BATTLEGROUND
OF THE SEVENTIES

Arthur S. Lazerow

Discriminatory zoning—the utilization of zoning codes to exclude undesired residents from a given municipality on the basis of implicit racial and economic criteria—is flourishing today in America.(1) Increased demand for housing, precipitated by the population explosion and migration from city to suburbia, has generated intensive development of farmlands surrounding the cities and has created unexpected demands for municipal services which are disproportionate to the revenue attributable to newcomers. Motivated by fiscal self-defense and suburban snobbery, local governments turned to land-use control measures for relief.

The consequences of discriminatory zoning laws, i.e., larger lot requirements, prohibition of multi-family units, and minimum floor area standards, are to inflate land acquisition and construction costs, make development of low and moderate income housing uneconomical for the builder, and raise rent and purchase price beyond the means of the lower and lower-middle class wage-earner. This effectively locks specific economic groups into the cities. The correlation between lower income levels with racial and ethnic minorities explains the increasingly nonwhite character of the central cities,(2) and housing in these city cores is rapidly becoming substandard.(3) Furthermore, suburban townships are encouraging the relocation of industry (and jobs) out of the cities concomitantly restricting development of housing for clerical and blue-collar workers attracted to these companies. Through the use of discriminatory zoning, nationwide economic and racial segregation of residential opportunities developed.(4)

There are indications that discriminatory zoning will become the issue of the Seventies, comparable in scope to the civil rights issue in the Sixties. The

National Association for the Advancement of Colored People, for instance, has served notice on local governments of its intention to nullify discriminatory zoning practices.(5) Oyster Bay, Long Island, is the first target city in this effort.(6) Located near Grumman Aircraft Company and Republic Aviation Division of Fairchild Hiller, Oyster Bay enacted a zoning code which restricts development of multi-family units, thereby barring industrial workers from migrating along with their jobs into the suburbs of New York City.(7) The NAACP requested that the town rezone twenty percent of its land for multi-family dwellings under threat of federal court action, which elicited a response from the city that a formal zoning petition must be submitted "since new zoning would require expansion of schools, housing, highways, health centers and other facilities."(8) This is the traditional fiscal zoning argument.(9) Oyster Bay is representative of nationwide discriminatory zoning practices which the U.S. Supreme Court has refused to consider.(10)

The NAACP pronouncement neither spearheads nor initiates the struggle to reverse this subtle form of discrimination. Instead the effort has been slowly accelerating into the campaign proclaimed by the NAACP. Developments thus far underscore the complexity and the widespread entrenchment of discriminatory zoning.(11) However, if the latest surge of attention given the problem during the last five years on the regional, state, and federal levels among social action groups, legal commentators and certain pockets of the judiciary is at all indicative, there is indeed a hint of silver lining around an otherwise ominous cloud. This comment will attempt to identify the breadth of the problem and highlight recent events which may facilitate abatement of discriminatory zoning to open opportunities for the construction of low and moderate income suburban housing.

THE INSTITUTION OF DISCRIMINATORY ZONING

Zoning laws were not originally popular,(12) primarily because the courts in the early 1900's upheld the individual's right to the unhampered use of his property.(13) As the cities developed, it became obvious that failure to regulate overcrowding of buildings and unwanted land uses was unwise, and thus the cities carved zoning laws out of the legal doctrines permitting the regulation of nuisances.(14) The principle was to protect property owners from the adverse practices of neighbors. Zoning became popular in the 1920's for regulation of land development, which was then occurring on lot-by-lot basis.(15) The *Standard State Zoning Enabling Act*(16) was a model enabling act written by the U.S. Department of Commerce and established the pattern of zoning regulations. The scheme proposed was to divide the municipality into districts and further subdivide the districts as to permissible uses and the size of buildings which can be placed thereon.(17)

> Indeed, so great was the acceptance of this scheme that the division of the community into specified use districts with defined boundaries has sometimes been regarded synonymous with zoning rather than one method of zoning.(18)

The legal propriety of zoning was settled by the U.S. Supreme Court in 1926 with its decision in *Village of Euclid v. Ambler Realty Co.*,(19) which concluded "it is enough to determine, as we do, that the ordinance in its general scope and dominant features, so far as the provisions are here involved, is a valid exercise of [municipal] authority."(20) This decision occurred contemporaneously with the emerging "home rule" laws(21) and combined to give local municipalities autonomy in the administration and control of land use. At the time *Euclid* was decided, 564 cities had similar zoning ordinances. In 1968, 6,880 municipalities and 2,004 townships had more or less adopted similar zoning ordinances.(22)

PERVERSION OF ZONING

Any paper proposing the diminution of "home rule" zoning must acknowledge the benefits accrued to the cities prior to the onset of suburbanization.(23) The American Society of Planning Officials(24) prefaced its critical analysis of restrictive zoning by saying:

> [z]oning has done much more good than harm; as difficult as the problem of guiding urban development is, the situation is much better than it would have been without zoning. Many millions of families live today under conditions that are the envy of the rest of the world.(25)

The Standard State Enabling Act(26) enumerates these salutary purposes of zoning: (a) to secure safety from fire, panic and other dangers; (b) to promote health and general welfare; (c) to provide adequate light and air; (d) to prevent the overcrowding of land; (e) to avoid undue concentration of population; and (f) to facilitate the adequate provision of transportation, water, sewage, schools and parks, and other public requirements.(27) Unfortunately, to think that these are the only purposes for which zoning is used is euphoric in light of the unbridled economic and racial discrimination promoted by the zoning practices of suburban governments.(28)

The perversion of zoning purposes into an exclusionary vehicle has discouraged orderly development of large tracts of municipal lands.(29) Lot-by-lot procedures have created stereotyped monotony throughout the housing industry.(30) Municipal governments twist zoning ordinances into implicit anti-democratic social stratification according to race and income.(31) Fiscal policies derogate efficient land use.(32) Decisions which foster local needs are often contrary to the overall public interest of the region and impose insoluble burdens on the central city. The National Commission on Urban Problems aptly concluded:

> Today a basic problem results because of the delegation of zoning power from the states to local governments of any size. This often results in a type of balkanization which is intolerable in large urban areas when local government boundaries rarely reflect the true economic and social watersheds.(33)

Exclusion of low income families from suburbia contributes unmistakably to the racial and economic imbalance in American society. The New York Regional Planning Association, for instance, has estimated that a family with an annual income of less than $15,000 cannot afford to live in the suburbs of New York

City, yet ninety percent of New York City residents are in this economic category.(34) Furthermore, new job openings in the New York City Metropolitan area show a seven-to-one ratio in favor of the suburbs.(35) Thus, zoning practices originally intended to permit the local municipality to control its growth patterns became a method to limit the influx of unwanted residents.

IMPLICIT DISCRIMINATION

The persistence of discriminatory zoning is due to its implicit nature. The conversion of zoning from a tool to a weapon required the shift from overt discrimination to more subtle forms of regulation and restriction. Obvious discrimination has been consistently overruled.(36) The U.S. Supreme Court in Buchanan v. Warley(37) invalidated an ordinance of Louisville, Kentucky, which made it unlawful for a Negro to move into a house on any city block where the majority of residents were white. Similar holdings are reported on the state level where racially exclusive zoning ordinances are identified by the courts as such.(38) Likewise, an attempt to segregate specified subdivisions by relating income to housing values has been declared unconstitutional.(39) To circumvent these judicial attitudes, local governments found that zoning ordinances establishing minimum lot sizes, minimum floor areas for housing, and limits on multi-family units would insure the exclusion of unwanted residents. This is not to suggest this movement on the part of local governments toward zoning was purposeful, but the result produced discriminatory effects.(40)

Minimum floor area ordinances were viewed at first as an unreasonable exercise of the police power, because the courts did not correlate the relationship of these restrictions with the promotion of public health, safety, morals or welfare.(41) As the suburban communities' development accelerated after World War II, public considerations became a principal argument of the municipalities.(42) Wayne Township, in defense of its zoning ordinance prescribing minimum living areas of 768 square feet for a one-story house, 1,000 square feet for a two-story house with attached garage, and 1,200 square feet for a two-story house without an attached garage,(43) offered extensive testimony by Dr. C.E.A. Winslow, Professor of Public Health at Yale Medical School, on the health merits of these minimum standards.(44) The New Jersey Supreme Court upheld the zoning ordinance on the grounds of public health and general welfare,(45) and minimum floor area ordinances consequently proliferated.(46)

The prohibition, or at best the limitation, of multi-family housing found judicial support from the argument of density control, an avowed purpose of the *Standard State Zoning Enabling Act*.(47) Babcock and Bosselman made an in depth study of the suburban attitude antagonistic to apartment houses; they lamented:

> These early courts seemed to find a cause and effect relationship between numerous families per structure and the social problems of the occupants of poorer neighborhoods. This cause and effect relationship justified the exclusion of multi-family housing from the better neighborhoods, since the intrusion of multiple housing would produce all the evils associated with the worst tenement neighborhood.(48)

Similarly, minimum lot area regulations were upheld on the basis of control of adequate amounts of air and light.(49) The effect, of course, has been to constrain the total number of housing units which could be built on any given property, thereby raising the price per unit of family housing, which is precisely how these restrictive zoning practices have transformed the exercise of legitimate zoning into de facto racial and economic discrimination.(50)

URBAN CONSEQUENCES

Suburban zoning fences minority citizens into high-density central-city living conditions. There were 228 metropolitan areas(51) in 1967 containing sixty-three percent of the United States population.(52) These 228 areas were served by 20,745 local governments, half of which exercised zoning powers.(53) The San Francisco Metropolitan area contained 100 zoning governments, Philadelphia 200 and New York 500,(54) each instinctively protecting its fiscal and social character. Since the impact of zoning is greatest on undeveloped areas, exclusionary practices of the suburban ring around the metropolitan areas leave only inner city housing affordable by lower income families. Statistical projections to the year 1985 emphasize this segregation.(55) The total population of the United States will expand by 73 million people at the present rates(56) with nonwhite population increasing by an approximate factor of two over white population.(57) Yet the central cities will show a ninety-four percent (9.7 million people) increase in nonwhite residents compared with a five percent (2.4 million people) loss of white residents. The end result is that in 1985:

> . . . three-fourths of all nonwhites in metropolitan areas will still be residing in central cities and only a fourth in the suburbs. In contrast, by reason of maintaining a trend of some duration, seven-tenths of the whites would be residents of the suburban ring and only three-tenths would be residents of the central cities. The prospects vividly portray the geographic fulfillment of the fears expressed by the President's Commission on Civil Disorder—that American society is becoming an apartheid society.(58)

Furthermore, inner-city housing is rapidly becoming substandard. The majority of inner-city row-house tenements were built originally to house poor immigrant workers. One study showed that within nine of twelve selected cities, fifty percent or more of the housing in nonwhite areas was built in 1919 or earlier.(59) The report concluded that the "[a] dvanced age of the buildings, a large percentage of substandard dwellings, and high frequency of crowding are virtually standard characteristics of the housing in areas of nonwhite residence."(60) The high correlation among poverty, substandard housing and minority groups magnifies the malaise of urban life, such as job and school segregation, social disorganization, crime, slums and racial exploitation.(61)

The concentration of low and lower-middle income classes in the cities and the out-migration of more affluent families tightens a financial vise around the cities' resources. There are two aspects to this problem. As the exodus to the suburbs continues, low income families move in. First, this shrinks revenues due to decreasing property values.(62) Second, while the Suburbanite is no longer a contributer, the City Dweller requires greater outlays in the areas of social welfare and education. Thus the newcomer is a financial liability, replacing his predecessor who was a financial asset. The *Hodge* and *Hauser* predictions(63) do not impart confidence in the cities' ability to respond to this challenge.

SELF-SUSTAINING NATURE OF DISCRIMINATORY ZONING

Discriminatory zoning is inherently self-sustaining. Part of this is due to the suburban ethic. The Suburbanite is a first or second generation escapee from the inner city who ignores the fact that he has a cultural, economic, social and political dependency with the city. Instead, it is of paramount importance that the advantages of suburban life, such as low crime rates, enlightened schools, slower pace of life, racial homogeneity, and single-family home ownership, be preserved against encroachment from the late-coming city dweller knocking at his suburban door.(64) The Suburbanite views the approach of the city-dwelling establishments, the apartment complexes, and the high-density single-family housing projects, as synonymous with "rent control, rising taxes, operating and maintenance costs, absentee ownership, deliberate block busting by realtors and local apathy."(65) It has been said that the Suburbanites' participation in zoning hearings "is often more emotional than intellectual."(66) This attitude is inimical to principles of social mobility and economic opportunity which permitted today's Suburbanite to leave the city originally, but this should not be unexpected. "Keeping up with the Joneses" includes residing in an exclusive neighborhood. As Lawrence Sager said:

> 'No man should be unable to live in a neighborhood of his choosing because of his poverty' is simply not a proposition for which one could expect to find nationwide support in 1969. Exclusive neighborhoods, indeed an entire range of neighborhoods, of graduated exclusivity, are commonplace and, unlike racial ghettos, are not even the objects of widespread verbal lament.(67)

While the suburban ethic provides psychological impedance to reforms from within, there are equally imposing political and economic biases which preclude self-imposed easing of discriminatory zoning practices. Home rule municipalities have been granted broad powers of self-governance.(68) Reformers took up the cry for local autonomy, or "home rule," in the 19th Century, and the movement has been an American institution ever since.(69) Home rule was founded on the principles that each community should be self-governing and that the governmental level closest to the problem is most responsive.(70) Yet as municipal problems became more complex, home rule functions diminished to the point that one of the last major home rule powers remaining is the authority to zone.(71) As such, a municipality will not voluntarily attenuate the power over its lands, especially where the exercise of this power maintains the town's residential exclusivity. A recent analysis of the impact of home rule on racial and economic discriminatory zoning explained that local politicians and administrators are "local people responsive to local wants and desires."(72) Local officials thus are subservient to the protectionist and exclusionary attitudes of the suburban ethic discussed above. To be otherwise would be political suicide for locally elected officials.

Historically the governmental distribution of financial responsibilities has required the financing of schools and public services by the municipal government. Local real estate taxes are the primary source of revenues, and it is the widespread belief(73) that major economic advantages accrue from the encouragement of "nonresidential development, expensive housing, and perhaps efficiency apartments"(74) which incur higher taxation with a minimum burden on public services, and the discouragement of multi-family units which requires a greater outlay of revenues for public services but which have lower tax liabilities.(75) This is called "the land use control system [which] provides financial bonuses as a reward for economic discrimination."(76) Corresponding to the tax revenue consideration, condonation of large scale housing projects is accompanied by the need to expand schools, roads, hospital facilities, police and fire departments, recreational facilities and other municipal services, all of which cost substantial sums of municipal funds. Exclusionary zoning practices by suburban communities impose these burdens on the cities.

The judiciary has been generally unresponsive to the issue of discriminatory zoning.(77) First, the courts adhere to the presumption of statutory validity.(78) In order to overcome this presumption, three requirements must be met by a litigant attacking a zoning ordinance. The burden of proof of the unreasonable, arbitrary, or discriminatory nature of the act is on the petitioner.(79) If the validity of the ordinance is debatable, it is upheld.(80) Finally, the court will not substitute its judgment for that of the legislature unless compelled to do so by the unreasonableness of the act.(81) This places the litigant at a severe disadvantage since municipal ordinances and comprehensive plans must comply with the state's enabling act.(82) The argument that a health and welfare ordinance is implicit racial or economic discrimination is difficult to make in the face of the presumption of legislative validity. Where there is no obvious economic and racial discrimination in the zoning ordinance, the presumption is cited and the act is upheld.(83) Although this presumption was intended to promote "the constitutional separation of the legislative, executive and judicial functions and powers,"(84) its application in the area of the de facto discrimination permits implicit accomplishment of discriminatory results that the local government could not perfect explicitly.(85) In deference to the balancing of the police power with private property rights, while ignoring the broader social exigencies found in *Ambler v. Euclid Realty*,(86) the courts have narrowly defined zoning appeals.(87) This judicial hesitancy to move against discriminatory zoning with the same resolution with which the courts have attacked explicit discrimination against minority groups(88) provides encouragement for the continuation of these zoning patterns.

Thus, there are pervasive social, political, economic, and judicial grounds explaining the self-perpetuation of racial and economic discriminatory zoning. The Suburbanite assumes that low or moderate income families will bring the ills of the inner city into his neighborhood. Suburban politicians are dependent upon the electorate and therefore slaves to suburban attitudes. Municipal governments attempt to protect real estate values, on which property taxes are predicated, by limiting the construction of low and moderate income housing. The judiciary has given tacit concurrence to these exclusionary attitudes by reaffirming the presumption of statury validity. Taken together, these are the inherent forces which impede improvement of the housing opportunities for lower income families.

TRENDS TOWARD REVERSAL OF DISCRIMINATORY ZONING

Discriminatory zoning, it has been shown, is the vehicle by which suburban communities exclude low income families from residential areas and employment openings in the suburbs to the social and economic detriment of these families and the central cities. To overcome this form of discrimination requires a reevaluation and readjustment of priorities by balancing each community's interest in a controlled and orderly growth with the metropolitan area's requirement for low income housing and relief from financial and physical deterioration. "Population pressures, technological changes, economic advances and racial reform have demonstrated that what was once a satisfactory instrument to regulate urban growth is no longer adequate to the task."(89) Home rule zoning is today undergoing scrutiny,(90) and leaders on the governmental, judicial, legislative and community levels of society are slowly awakening to this urban-suburban dichotomy and its effects.(91)

FEDERAL CONCERN

Attorney General John M. Mitchell announced that the Nixon Administration plans to issue "a new policy on racial discrimination in suburban housing shortly after the turn of the year."(92) This indicates that federal officials are aware of the debilitating effects of racial and economic zoning. The report of the National Commission of Urban Problems(93) provides an in depth "study of building codes and technology, zoning and land use, federal and local taxes affecting housing and urban growth, housing codes, development standards, and ways to increase the supply of decent housing for low income families."(94)

Although the Commission made specific recommendations, national leaders have been unable to devise an effective substantive approach. Representative William B. Widnall, a member of the House Banking and Currency Committee, concurred with the Commission's finding that discriminatory zoning prevents the development of low income housing but could not imagine appropriate Congressional action.(95) Lack of federal funds is not the only problem.(96) Three housing acts passed between 1964 and 1968 include subsidies to private industry for the construction of low and middle income family housing.(97) Although the Department of Housing and Urban Development planned to subsidize 450,000 units of this type housing in 1970,(98) failure to effectively reduce restrictive zoning has restrained the housing effort.(99)

Two recent cases demonstrate local resistance to federally subsidized low income housing projects. In *South Almdea Spanish Speaking Organization v. City of Union City*,(100) Mexican-American citizens applied to the city council and were granted rezoning for 279 federally subsidized low and moderate income family apartments on a 23.4 acre site. The local residents petitioned the city council for a referendum and subsequently overruled the rezoning decision. The trial court refused to grant a temporary injunction and the U.S. Court of Appeals for the Ninth Circuit affirmed on the grounds that "the fact that discrimination resulted from the referendum, and that Union City has failed to make satisfactory provision for low income housing, is not so clear as to demand preliminary relief."(101) In *DeSimone v. Greater Englewood Housing Corp*(102) however, the New Jersey Supreme Court overruled opposition to a similar town council rezoning action for federally funded housing.(103) The court said:

> Sadly to relate, however, the objectors, despite all the legalisms in which this intense and pervading litigation is couched, in truth are not trying to vindicate the policy of the many statutes they invoke, but rather only to oppose this project. . . .(104)

To circumvent restrictive zoning by local communities, Secretary Romney of the Department of Housing and Urban Development has proposed a law barring the use of zoning, building codes and other municipal powers which interfere with the construction of federally funded low income housing.(105) The penalty that federal officials would invoke would be to withhold federal funds from the local community. This unfortunately sets federal power against municipal power in an area which admittedly requires consideration of a wide range of local matters.(106) However, it would provide exceedingly persuasive leverage for low income housing advocates since local governments are no longer financially self-sufficient.(107)

STATE ACTION

The state governments are sensitive to local community concerns and yet are far enough removed from local parochialism to appreciate regional deficiencies. Consequently, state action appears to be the most direct and most responsive approach to the discriminatory zoning issue.(108) Several reasons explain why the state role in urban affairs will unavoidably increase in this decade: the growth of urban areas throughout each state, mandatory reapportionment of state legislatures giving urban areas legislative muscle, incentives from federal attention to urban problems, and heightened realization of the need to reform the checkerboard array of local governments in urban areas.(109) The traditional state reaction to the discriminatory zoning issue has been to enact a regional planning commission, charged with the responsibility to make comprehensive region-wide plans.(110) Hawaii, Massachusetts and New York have excepted from this pattern by investing a statewide administrative body with power to reverse local zoning decisions.(111)

The Massachusetts legislature established a Housing Appeals Committee(112) within the Department of Community Affairs to review adverse decisions affecting applications to build low and moderate income housing.(113) The review extends over the full spectrum of local regulative powers, including health, subdivision control, planning, building inspectors, and zoning.(114) Low and moderate income housing is defined as:

> any housing subsidized by the federal or state government under any program to assist the construction of low or moderate income housing as defined in the applicable federal or state statute, whether built or operated by any public agency or nonprofit or limited dividend organization.(115)

The Housing Appeals Committee is empowered to vacate the findings of a local zoning board of appeals where the decision is found "unreasonable and not consistent with local needs," or it may modify decisions which made "the building or operation of such housing uneconomic."(116) The act sets definite standards by which the Committee can oversee local actions. "Consistent with local needs" requires consideration of the health, safety and general welfare of the community where 1. there exists low and moderate income housing in excess of ten percent of the town's existing housing units reported in the last decennial census or on sites comprising one and one-half percent or more of the town's total land area, or 2. the application would result in housing starts on sites comprising more than three-tenths of one percent of the town's land area or ten acres in that calendar year.(117)

The builder's time frame for processing his zoning petition and subsequent appeals has been compressed to about five months by limiting the delays at the local boards, the Boards of Zoning Appeals, and Housing Appeals Committee.(118) Upon failure to comply with the specified time allowed, the application is deemed granted.(119) The Housing Appeals Committee, the applicant and any other person aggrieved by a decision at any level are given standing to enforce or appeal enforcement in the Massachusetts Superior Court.(120)

The Massachusetts Housing Appeals Committee Act eases the burden of restrictive regulations on nonprofit corporations, public agencies and private builders but gives no financial encouragement for the improvement of low and moderate income housing opportunities.(121) As such, the Housing Appeals Committee is a stop-gap measure. There is neither land acquisition assistance nor additional state subsidies to stimulate interest in low income housing construction. Also, this act is appended to the provisions dealing with the Massachusetts Regional Planning Commission but does not indicate how the Committee is to associate the application at hand with regional planning goals.(122) Further, membership on the Housing Appeals Committee is composed of five appointees but fails to include a member of any regional commission.(123)

The initiative of the individual builders is determinative of whether or not a town's zoning attitudes will be challenged. Conceivably many prime locations can be ignored because of land prices or other political or economic factors, and the Massachusetts legislative intention would be controverted by default. Nonetheless, this act provides statewide standards and supervision of restrictive zoning decisions of local municipalities.

The New York Legislature created a state corporation, rather than an administrative appeals board, to improve the quality and quantity of low income housing. The New York Urban Development Corporation(124) (NYUDC) is the only state agency of its type in the country with the power to plan, fund and execute housing projects, and if necessary, this can be accomplished over the disapproval of the local community.(125) The voice of "home rule" was strong in opposition; Mayor Lindsay of New York City disparaged the NYUDC Act as "the thinking of twenty years ago."(126) Nevertheless, the breadth and depth of the state corporation's powers suggest this Act signals a new era of state action in the field of low income housing.

The NYUDC has the power to accomplish a great deal. Most striking is the power to ignore local laws, ordinances, zoning codes, and building regulations when "in its discretion, compliance is not feasible or practicable."(127) The same section, however, directs the NYUDC to consider both local and regional goals by working closely with "elected officials and community leaders."(128) The Act confers the power of eminent domain(129) and the right to relocate displacees.(130) The NYUDC is exempt from local property taxes on the increased valuation of land after acquisition but is liable for assessments to fund local improvements.(131) Additional powers include the powers to sue and be sued, to create subsidiaries, lend or give these subsidiaries funds, enter into contracts and issue general revenue bonds.(132)

Thus, the professional staff of the corporation can expedite its plans in a manner atypical of urban renewal projects. In New York City, for instance, the inception-to-completion timespan of an urban renewal project averages thirteen years.(133) The grant of power obviously does not require its authoritarian use. In the first two years of operation, the NYUDC has attempted to play down the "bully with a big stick" image by cooperating with local governments and citizen groups to develop local commitment to each project.(134) NYUDC President Edward Logue has recommended that no more than five percent of a community's housing be low-income housing to reduce the burden on municipal facilities and services.(135) Not all citizens are satisfied with the cautious approach. Recent demonstrations have been held at the NYUDC offices by urban activists charging that the corporation is impeding, rather than promoting, the growth of low income housing by its passive policies.(136)

The most progressive fact about the Urban Development Corporation is its ability to initiate, complete and manage the entire project. It need not be dependent upon private initiative, political or social pressure, or the vagaries of an electorate to pass bond issues. This independence is required if the NYUDC is to fulfill its legislative mandate to combat urban deterioration, social decay and the lack of housing in areas of developing employment.(137) The impact of the corporation on the construction of low income housing will be judged by future events. Nonetheless, there can be no doubt that given its full measure of powers, the New York Urban Development Corporation is a model of state responsiveness to urban problems.

More often than not those low income families excluded from suburbia go unrepresented in zoning litigation. These families are part of the social, political, economic and commercial fabric of the region, but their interests are rarely considered. New Jersey unwittingly corrected this situation by enacting an amendment to its zoning laws entitled " 'Other Interested Party' Persons Included."(138) Newspaper accounts indicate that this was one of several bills passed in the "final hectic moments" of the concluding legislative session of 1969 and that the legislators may have been unaware of the potential impact on local zoning restrictions.(139)

The "Other Interested Party" amendment gives anyone residing within or without the boundaries of the municipality standing to challenge zoning decisions in any court or in an administrative proceeding before a municipal agency if that party's "right to use, acquire, or enjoy property is or may be affected."(140) Furthermore, the right to bring an action is permitted if any other state or federal law would be violated by an action under the zoning laws.(141) The scope of this expression is broad; it theoretically opens proceedings to parties who were previously spectators. This is a small but significant step in the quest for judicial remedy overruling discriminatory zoning.

REGIONAL AND LOCAL DEVELOPMENTS

The home rule philosophy has been previously identified as one of the determinants retarding the abrogation of discriminatory zoning ordinances. Home rule functions, however, are slowly diminishing as problems spill over jurisdictional boundaries and financial resource requirements exceed local revenue. Functions once locally seated are becoming vested at a broader governmental level.

Long range planning has in some states evolved onto the county or state level. The Nassau-Suffolk Regional Planning Board demonstrates the beneficial results from assuming a regional focus. A four-year regional study, completed in 1969, depicted the Long Island area as the "antithesis of rational development patterns."(142) The Long Island Regional Plan is a bi-county attempt to plan the area's environmental, economic, recreational and transportation needs. "Goals have been set to preserve open space, encourage elimination of deterioration and obsolescence, and provide adequate housing linked to jobs."(143) Counteraction has primarily been from zoning commissions since the plan recommends that the Regional Planning Board be made the arbiter of land use and zoning questions. The educational factor of this report is perhaps the long-lasting contribution to the elimination of discriminatory zoning. The various local governments are forced to consider how local myopia has affected the entire range of regional concerns.

Even some local communities have taken the initiative to encourage low and moderate income housing opportunities. Contrapositive to the actions of the citizens of Union City is a citizens' movement in Westport, Connecticut, to remedy the absence of accommodations for newlyweds, parents whose children have grown and moved away, and the town's employees.(144) The first advance in Westport is anticipated in the area of senior citizen housing. A Senior Citizen Housing Committee report in 1969 recommended that between 100 and 200 multi-family units be built and that zoning ordinances restricting the development of apartment houses be amended to permit a Senior Citizen Housing District to be built within pre-existing height and setback regulations.(145) The objective is to provide moderately priced housing "comparable with the neighborhood and surrounding uses so as to protect property values in the neighborhood."(146)

The Westport sympathy for moderate priced housing is meaningful in light of the concern expressed for municipal employees. These are moderate-income people welcomed as workers, but not as neighbors, within the suburban community. To conclude that action must be taken to clear the way for moderate priced housing, the Westport citizens have assumed, perhaps unknowingly, a community responsibility to allow construction of this type housing. The conversion from suburban exclusivity to equal opportunity in housing requires a notion of local responsibility.(147) If this shift coming from within the storm center becomes more widespread, the turmoil bound to be created by legislative or judicial reversal of discriminatory zoning patterns will be mollified.

PROGRESS IN THE COURTS

Judicial decisions have helped to perpetuate discriminatory zoning. Such cases as *Simon v. Town of Needham*(148) and *Lionhead Lake, Inc. v. Wayne Township*(149) arose during the early years of suburbanization and have become ingrained in the judicial mind. This is not to imply that discrimination in local zoning has not been argued. Judge Oliphant dissented forcefully in *Lionshead Lake*, saying:

> ... zoning has its purposes, but as I conceive the effect of the majority opinion it precludes individuals in those income brackets who could not pay between $8,500 and $12,000 for the erection of a house on a lot from even establishing a residence in this community ... A zoning provision that can produce this effect certainly runs afoul of the fundamental principles of our form of government.
> ... They will be relegated to living in the large cities or in multi-family dwellings even though it be against what they consider the welfare of their immediate families.(150)

The state courts' unwillingness to face exclusionary zoning results *inter alia* from the implicit nature of discriminatory zoning, the absence of U.S. Supreme Court direction, and judicial refusal to become super zoning boards.(151) In addition, the state courts have taken a myopic view comparable to that of local governments in ascertaining how zoning restrictions affect the metropolitan area.(152) Decisions invariably relate to the smallest political unit rather than regional needs.(153) However, there have been notable exceptions. Judge Hall's articulate dissent in *Vicers v. Township Committee of Gloucester Township*(154) provided some impetus for these exceptions. In *Vickers*, the New Jersey Supreme Court held valid a municipal zoning ordinance which totally excluded trailer camps to which Judge Hall said:

> I am convinced such a conclusion in this case is manifestly wrong. Of greater concern is the judical process by which it is reached and the breadth of the rationale. The import of the holding gives almost boundless freedom to developing municipalities to erect exclusionary walls on their boundaries, according to local whim or selfish desire and use the zoning power for aims beyond its legitimate purposes.(155)

Those courts which are influenced by the consideration of the regional effects of discriminatory zoning tend to overturn exclusionary restrictions. The courts of New York, Illinois, Missouri and New Jersey have focused on the problem of contiguous municipalities, for instance.(156) This development occurred strictly within the context of traditional zoning problems, such as residential and commercial districts, single-family dwelling restrictions and industrial uses. Only the Supreme Court of Pennsylvania has ruled in a series of cases on exclusionary zoning per se and its consequences in respect to regional needs.

In *National Land & Investment Co. v. Kohn*(157) Easttown Township passed a municipal zoning ordinance which raised a one acre residential lot minimum to four acres. The Township argued that this was necessary to provide proper sewage disposal, provide fire protection over its narrow roads, protect the water supply from pollution, and preserve the character of the community.(158) The Supreme Court of Pennsylvania dismissed these contentions as a camouflage to "prevent the entrance of newcomers in order to avoid future burdens, economic and otherwise, upon the administration of public services and facilities . . . "(159) Justice Roberts, writing for the court, identified the issue as "whether the township can stand in the way of the natural forces which send our growing population into hitherto undeveloped areas in search of a comfortable place to live"(160) and concluded that the township cannot exclude population growth by the use of zoning codes.(161)

In re *Appeal of Joseph Girsh*(162) reaffirmed that factors such as sewage disposal, over-burdened municipal facilities, aesthetics and the character of the community do not warrant exclusionary zoning. The Zoning Code of the township in question, Nether Providence, had no provision for multiple dwellings.(163) Since the topography of the particular tract was unsuitable for single-family homes, Joseph Girsh applied for a building permit to construct a luxury apartment complex. The application was denied on the grounds that the zoning ordinance failed to permit apartment uses.(164) Although the zoning board of adjustment and trial court upheld the zoning board,(165) the Pennsylvania Supreme Court held that the failure to provide for multi-family housing in the township's zoning ordinance was unconstitutional since the ordinance could not reasonably exclude legitimate uses.(166) Although *National Land & Investment Co. v. Kohn*(167) and In re *Appeal of Joseph Girsh* reach the same conclusion, Justice Roberts recognized over-congestion in the cities and the growing job opportunities in the suburbs to support his rejection of exclusionary zoning.(167)

The third case to hold against exclusionary zoning, *Kit-Mar Builders v. Township of Concord*,(170) was decided two weeks after *Girsh*. Justice Roberts wrote the majority opinion, as he had in *National Land* and *Girsh*.(171) Concord Township's zoning ordinance required two acre minimum lots along existing roads and three acre minimums for interior lots.(172) The Pennsylvania Supreme Court was faced with the same arguments in support of the exclusion as in *National Land* and *Girsh* and held that "absent some extraordinary justification, a zoning ordinance with minimum lot sizes such as those in this case is completely unreasonable."(173) But the court went further to express its contempt for defensive zoning:

> Neither Concord Township nor Easttown Township nor any other local governing unit may retreat behind a cover of exclusive zoning. We fully recognize that the overall solution to these problems lies with greater regional planning; but until the time comes that we have such a system we must confront the system as it is. The power currently resides in the hands of each local governing unit, and we will not tolerate their abusing that power in attempting to zone out growth at the expense of neighboring communities.(174)

The significance of these cases is that the highest court of a state discarded those attitudes which have impeded reprobation of exclusionary zoning. The Pennsylvania Supreme Court did not hide behind the presumption of statutory validity but instead agreed to supervise local zoning practices. The three Pennsylvania cases cited above broaden the judicial perspective to include regional as well as local needs. In its search for the out-limits of the general welfare, the Supreme Court of Pennsylvania has determined that "it is clear . . . that the general welfare is not fostered or promoted by the zoning ordinances designed to be exclusive and exclusionary."(175) The majority opinion in *Kit-Mar Builders*,(176) furthermore, cites Sager's article discussing the U.S. Supreme Court's "energized equal protection doctrine" in relationship to exclusionary zoning.(177) Thus, the state court was responsive to the legal commentators who are raising loud dissent against legislative and judicial condonation of exclusionary zoning.(178) Query whether Justice Roberts' opinions invalidating discriminatory zoning will rank with Judge Traynor's fight against anti-miscegenation laws(179) to presage future U.S. Supreme Court direction.

CONCLUSION

A fundamental assumption has been made herein that developments which will eventually contravene the enforcement of racial and economic zoning ordinances have reached a threshold rather than an impasse. The advances described above suggest that this assumption is not unrealistic. Important inroads have occurred. Legal precedent and presumptions have been questioned. Federal officials are genuinely concerned, and several states have enacted legislation intended to improve housing opportunities in the suburbs for low and moderate income families.(180) Also, some local communities are proposing self-imposed measures.(181) These are meager in comparison with the pervasiveness and widespread entrenchment of discriminatory zoning. Nonetheless, these initial efforts are irreversible. Without effective solutions, the disruption and decay of the cities will become more acute, and urban-suburban discord will intensify. Concurrently, the voices calling for reform will press for judicial and legislative leadership to open the suburbs to the full social and economic spectrum of American families. This is the goal, but the tensions present will make discriminatory zoning the legal battleground of the decade.

NOTES

(1) See National Commission on Urban Problems, Building the American City, H.R. Doc. No., 91034, 91st Cong. 1st Sess. (1969) [hereinafter cited as Douglas].
(2) P. Hodge & P. Hauser, The Challenge of American's Metropolitan Outlook—1960 to 1985, at 19 (1968) [hereinafter cited as Hodge & Hauser].
(3) President's Committee on Urban Housing, A Decent Home 8 (1968) [hereinafter cited as A Decent Home].
(4) N.Y. Times, Nov. 7, 1969 at 16, col. 3.
(5) N.Y. Times, Dec. 7, 1969, at 1 col. 1.
(6) Id.

(7) Id.

(8) Id.

(9) Compare the response of this Oyster Bay official with the arguments made in support of exclusionary municipal zoning codes in National Land & Investment Co. v. Kohn, 419 Pa. 504, 215 A.2d 597 (1965), In re Appeal of Joseph Girsh, 437 Pa. 237, 263 A.2d 395 (1970), and Kit-Mar Builders v. Township of Concord, 439 Pa. 466, 268 A.2d 765 (1970).

(10) Flora Realty Inv. Co. v. Ladue, 362 Mo. 1025, 246 S.W.2d 771 (1952), appeal dismissed for want of a substantial federal question, 344 U.S. 802 (1952); Lionshead Lake, Inc. v. Wayne Township, 10 N.J. 165, 89 A.2d 693 (1952), appeal dismissed for want of a substantial federal question, 344 U.S. 919 (1953). In James v. Valtierra, 39 U.S.L.W. 4488 (U.S. April 27, 1971), the U.S. Supreme Court upheld the California Constitutional provision, Calif. Const. art. XXXIV, (1950), which placed city and county public housing decisions under the state's general referendum clause, Calif. Const. art. IV, § 1 (1911). Although the majority called the referendum "[t]his procedure for democratic decision-making." 39 U.S.L.W. at 4490. Mr. Justice Marshall retorted, "It is far too late in the day to contend that the Fourteenth Amendment prohibits only racial discrimination; to me, singling out the poor to bear a burden not placed on any other class of citizen tramples the values that the Fourteenth Amendment was designed to protect." 39 U.S.L.W. at 4490. He had previously noted in a footnote that "only low income housing programs are subject to the mandatory referendum provision of Article 34 even though all of the agencies' (Renewal Area Agencies) programs may receive substantial governmental assistance." 39 U.S.L.W. at 4490.

(11) See generally Douglas, supra note 1, at 17-20.

(12) I. E.C. Yokley, Zoning Law and Practice 5 (3rd ed. 1965) [hereinafter cited as Yokley].

(13) Houlton v. Titcomb, 102 Mc. 272,66 A. 733 (1906).

(14) R.B. Const. Co. v. Jackson, 152 Md. 671, 137 A. 278 (1927), which held that the restricted height limitation was valid to improve air and light.

(15) Yokley, supra note 12, at 66.

(16) Y.S. Dept. of Commerce, A Standard State Zoning Enabling Act (1926).

(17) missing from m/s

(18) missing from m/s

(19) 272 U.S. 365 (1926).

(20) Id. at 397.

(21) Lemaire v. Crockett, 116 Me. 263, 101 A. 302 (1917).

(22) Douglas, supra note 1, at 199.

(23) Schnore & Jones, The Evolution of City-Suburban Types in the Course of a Decade, 4 Urban Affairs Q. 421 (1969).

(24) Research Rep. No. 2. American Society of Planning Officials, Problems of Zoning and Land Use Regulation (1968) [hereinafter cited as ASPO] .

(25) Id. at 5.

(26) U.S. Dept. of Commerce, supra note 15.

(27) Id. at § 2.

(28) See Lionshead Lake v. Wayne Township, 10 N.J. 165, 89 A.2d 693 (1952). (Oliphant, J., dissenting); Douglas, supra note 1, at 19.

(29) Research Rep. No. 15, F. Bosselman, Alternatives to Urban Sprawl: Legal Guidelines for Governmental Action 50 (1968) [hereinafter cited as Urban Sprawl].

(30) Hanke, Planned Unit Development and Land Use Intensity, 114 U. Pa. L. Rev. 16 (1965).

(31) Williams, Planning Law and Democratic Living, 20 Law & Contemp. Prob. 349 (1955) [hereinafter cited as Planning Law].

(32) Am. U.L. Rev.

(33) Id. at 48.

(34) N.Y. Times, Dec. 14, 1969, at 68, col. 3.

(35) The New Republic, Dec. 20, 1969, vol. 161, at 7.

(36) Buchanan v. Warley, 245 U.S. 60 (1917); See also Re Lee Sing, 43 F. 359 (N.D. Cal. 1890); Norwalk CORE v. Norwalk Redevelopment Agency, 395 F.2d 920 (2nd Cir. 1968).

(37) 245 U.S. 60 (1927). The Court applied the fourteenth amendment of the U.S. Consitution as a limitation to the exercise of municipal police power. "The right which the ordinance annulled was the civil right of a white man to dispose of his property if he saw fit to do so to a person of color, and of a colored person to make such disposition to a white person. . . . We think this attempt to prevent the alienation of the property in question to a person of color was not a legitimate exercise of police power of the state, and in direct violation of the fundamental law enacted in the fourteenth amendment preventing state interference with property rights except by due process of law." 245 U.S. at 81, 82.

(38) DeSena v. Gulde, 24 App. Div. 2d 165, 265 N.Y.S.2d 239 (1965); compare Deerfield Park Dist. v. Progress Dev. Corp., 22 Ill.2d 132, 174 N.E.2d 850 (1961), which upheld the condemnation of two open housing subdivisions for use as city parks.

(39) Stein v. Long Beach, 2 N.J. Misc. 121 (Sup. Ct. 1924).

(40) Aloi, Goldberg, & White, Racial and Economic Segregation by Zoning: Death Knell for Home Rule?, I.U. Toledo L. Rev. 65, 68 (1969) [hereinafter cited as Death Knell for Home Rule].

(41) Frischkorn Const. Co. v. Lambert, 315 Mich. 556, 24 N.W.2d 209 (1946); Senefsky v. City of Huntington Woods, 307 Mich. 728, 12 N.W. 2d 387 (1943); Brookdale Homes, Inc. v. Johnson, 123 N.J.L. 602, 10 A.2d 473 (1940), aff'd, 126 N.J.L. 516, 19 A.2d 868 (1941).

(42) Lionshead Lake v. Wayne Township, 10 N.J. 165, 89 A.2d 693 (1952); Thompson v. Carrolton, 211 S.W.2d 970 (Tex. 1948).

(43) Lionshead Lake v. Wayne Township, 10 N.J. 165, 169, 89 A.2d 693, 697 (1952).

(44) Williams & Wacks, Segregation of Residential Areas Along Economic Lines: Lionshead Lake Revisited, 1969 Wisc. L. Rev. 834 n. 19 [hereinafter cited as Lionshead Lake Revisited].

(45) Lionshead Lake v. Wayne Township, 10 N.J. 165, 169, 89 A.2d 693, 697 (1952). See generally Haar, Zoning for Minimum Standards: The Wayne Township Case, 66 Harv. L. Rev. 1051 (1953).

(46) In New Jersey alone, the number of these ordinances increased between 1950 and 1966 from 64 to 292, predominantly in "developing counties." Lionshead Lake Revisited, supra note 43, at 829 n. 5.

84 HOUSING

(47). U.S. Dept. of Commerce, supra note 15.

(48) Babcock & Bosselman, Suburban Zoning and the Apartment Boom, 111 U.Pa.L.Rev. 1040, 1047 (1963) [hereinafter cited as Babcock and Bosselman].

(49) Town of Nichols Hills v. Aderhold, 250 P.2d 36 (Okla. 1952); Smith v. McKee.

(50) See A Decent Home, supra note 3, at 47.

(51) Hodge & Hauser, supra note 2, at 75.

(52) Id.

(53) Douglas, supra note 1, at 199.

(54) Id. at 209.

(55) Hodge & Hauser, supra note 2, assumes that no change will occur in the rate of accelearation of the growth trends identified by their statistical analysis so that population projections are extensions of previous growth patterns.

(56) Hodge & Hauser, supra note 2, at 19, table III-1.

(57) Id.

(58) Id. at 53.

(59) D. McEntire, Race and Residence: Final and Comprehensive Report to the Commission on Race and Housing, 37, Table 7 (1960).

(60) Id. at 36-37.

(61) Death Knell for Home Rule, supra note 39; see also Note, Suburban Ordinances and Building Codes: Their Affect on Low and Moderate Income Housing, 45 Notre Dame Law. 123 (1969).

(62) The city, however, has remained the economic and cultural center of the metropolitan area and must continue to finance police and fire department, water and sewage systems, transportation and numerous other services for the benefit of the entire metropolitan area.

(63) Hodge & Hauser, supra note 2.

(64) See Babcock & Bosselman, supra note 48, at 1061-72; R. Babcock, The Zoning Game 108 (1966).

(65) Washburn, Apartments in the Suburbs, In re Appeal of Joseph Girsh, 74 Dick L. Rev. 640 (1970) [hereinafter cited as Apartments in the Suburbs.]

(66) Death Knell for Home Rule, supra note 39, at 72.

(67) Sager, Tight Little Islands: Exclusionary Zoning, Equal Protection, and the Indigent, 21 Stan. L. Rev. 767, 791 (1969) [hereinafter cited as Tight Little Islands].

(68) The Washington State Constitution, for instance, reads "Any county, city, town, or ownership may make and enforce within its limits all such local police, sanitary and other regulations as are not in conflict with general laws." Wash. Const. art. XI, § 11 (1899).

(69) H. McBain. The Law and Practice of Municipal Home Rule (1916).

(70) Id.

(71) Death Knell for Home Rule, supra note 39, at 72.

(72) Id. at 103. Babcock wrote, "The village has a direct interest in the weight of vehicles which use the residential streets that are paid for, maintained by, and primarily used by local residents. The village has a valid if not exclusive interest in fire protection.... The village may be the logical and sole decision-maker when it comes to identifying those business uses whose presence in the central shopping area will destroy the vitality in that area. To the extent that property in the village pays the school costs, the impact of a proposed land

development on school facilities may be a legitimate consideration."

(73) Lionshead Lake Revisited, supra note 43, at 829, n. 4.

(74) Id. at 829.

(75) Id.

(76) N.Y. Times, Dec. 7, 1969, at 1, col. 1.

(77) Vickers v. Township Comm'n of Gloucester Township, 37 N.J. 232, 181 A. 2d 129 (1962), appeal dismissed, 371 U.S. 233 (1963); Lionshead Lake, Inc. v. Wayne Township, 10 N.J. 165, 89 A. 2d 693 (1952), appeal dismissed for want of a substantial federal question, 344 U.S. 919 (1953); Flora Realty Inv. Co. v. Ladue, 362 Mo. 1025, 246 S.W. 2d 771, appeal dismissed for want of a substantial federal question, 344 U.S. 802 (1952). Contra, Lakewood Homes v. Board of Adjustment of the City of Lima, 52 Ohio Op. 2d 213, 258 N.E. 2d 470 (1969). See also the recent holdings of the Pennsylvania Supreme Court discussed in Section III.E. infra.

(78) See Justice Hall's dissent in Vickers v. Township Comm'n of Gloucester Township, 37 N.J. 232, 234, 181 A.2d 129, 140 (1962), in which the scope of the presumption of legislative validity is explored.

(79) Caires v. Building Comm'r of Hingham, 323 Mass. 589, 83 N.E.2d 550 (1949).

(80) Euclid v. Ambler Realty Co., 272 U.S. 365, 388 (1926); Vickers v. Township Comm'n of Gloucester Township, 373 N.J. 232, 181 A.2d 129 (1962).

(81) Welsh v. Swazey, 214 U.S. 91 (1909); Atkins v. Kansas City, 191 U.S. 207 (1903), Clemons v. City of Los Angeles, 36 Cal. 2d 95, 222 P.2d 439 (1950); City of Idaho Falls v. Grimmett, 63 Idaho 90, 117 P.2d 461 (1941).

(82) C. Rathkopf, The Law of Zoning and Planning, 21-28 (3rd ed. 1962).

(83) Mack v. Cook County, 11 Ill. 310, 142 N.E.2d 785 (1957); State v. Stark, 100 Mort. 365, 32 P.2d 890 (1935).

(84) McAdam v. Sheldon, 153 Conn. 278, 216 A.2d 193, 195 (1965).

(85) Compare Buchanan v. Warley, 245 U.S. 60 (1917) with Vickers v. Township Comm'n of Gloucester Township, 37 N.J. 232, 181 A.2d 129 (1962), appeal dismissed, 371 U.S. 233 (1963).

(86) 272 U.S. 365 (1926); see Douglas, supra note 1, at 217 and Saks & Rabbin, Racial and Religious Discrimination: A Report of Legal Progress, 45 Iowa L. Rev. 488 (1960).

(87) There are several reasons why courts have taken such a narrow focus on zoning appeals: 1. property law is a venerable branch of the common law; 2. the importance of the social issues inherent in discriminatory zoning has only recently emerged; 3. the U.S. Supreme Court has refused to hear a case adjudicating these issues since Nectow v. City of Cambridge, 277 U.S. 183 (1928); 4. there is a definite reluctance to search the motivations of public officials; and 5. the factual material of the litigation often does not disclose the exclusionary effects of the ordinance. Douglas, supra note 1, at 217.

(88) Buchanan v. Warley, 245 U.S. 60 (1917).

(89) ASPO, supra note 23, at 5.

(90) See generally Douglas, supra note 1.

(91) The reforms proposed to overcome racial and economic discriminatory zoning are varied in their scope, as shown by the following enumeration: elimination of zoning, Comment, The Constitutionality of Local Zoning, 79

Yale L. Rev. 896, 924 (1970) [hereinafter cited as The Constitutionality of Local Zoning] ; invalidation of discriminatory zoning ordinance by the courts, Lionshead Lake Revisited, supra note 44, at 779; withholding federal funds from localities which enforce restrictive zoning measure, N.Y. Times, Jan. 3, 1970, at 1, col. 5; creation of regional zoning authorities, Research Rep. No. 18, J. Coke & J. Gargan, Fragmentation in Land Use Planning and Control 75 (1969) [hereinafter cited as Fragmentation]. Douglas, supra note 1, at 236; retraction of the zoning power from local communities by the state, Note, Large Lot Zoning, 78 Yale L. Rev. 1418, 1437-40 (1969); establishment of statewide zoning standards, The Constitutionality of Local Zoning, at 924; regional or statewide administrative review of zoning in terms of metropolitan needs, Id., Fragmentation, at 78; Haar, Regionalism and Realism in Land Use Planning, 105 U. Pa. L. Rev. 515, 530-31 (1957); utilization of zoning variants, such as checkerboard or cluster techniques, Tight Little Islands, supra note 67, at 797, application of corporate pressure precedent to suburban relocation to ensure the availability of low and moderate priced housing for clerical and blue collar workers, N.Y. Times, Nov. 7, 1969, at 16, col. 3; creation of Planned Development Zones (PDZ) for intensive development at prescribed scales, Urban Sprawl, supra note 29, at 11-21; compensatory regulations to reimburse property owners subjected to restrictive zoning, Id. at 27-35; public land assembly by eminent domain for public or private development, Id. at 41-60; extension of standing to sue provisions to include those discriminated against, The Constitutionality of Local Zoning, at 924; formulation of private development incentives by land banks and mortgage guarantees, Fragmentation, at 1-2; the provision for direct federal or state fiscal rewards for the repeal of discriminatory zoning laws and the encouragement of low income housing, Id. at 91.

(92) Washington Post, Dec. 19, 1970, § A, at 7, col. 1.

(93) Douglas, supra note 1.

(94) Fragmentation, supra note 91, "About the Commission," printed inside front cover of the Government Printing Office edition.

(95) N.Y. Times, Jan. 15, 1970, at 71, col. 1.

(96) Although federal and state funds are available, the funds in relation to the needed dollars place absolute limits on the total effect. See Reilly & Schulman, The State Urban Development Corporation: New York's Innovation, 1 Urban Lawyer 129, 145-46 (1969) [hereinafter cited as Reilly & Schulman].

(97) Housing Act of 1961, 12 U.S.C. 17151-d(3) (1964); Housing and Urban Development Act of 1965, 12 U.S.C. 1701s (Supp. IV, 1968); Housing and Urban Development Act of 1968, 12 U.S.C. 17152 (Supp. IV, 1968).

(98) N.Y. Times, May 17, 1970, at 58, col. 1.

(99) The growth of Wayne Township during the twenty years subsequent to Lionshead Lake, demonstrates how restrictive zoning impedes the developments of housing opportunities. Lionshead Lake Revisited, supra note 44, at 841-846.

(100) 424 F.2d 291 (9th Cir. 1970); Compare Ranjel v. City of Lansing, 293 F.Supp. 301 (Mich. 1969), rev'd, 417 F.2d 321 (6th Cir. 1969).

(101) 424 F.2d 291, 296 (9th Cir. 1970).

(102) 56 N.J. 428, 297 A.2d 31 (1970).

(103) Id.

(104) 56 N.J. at 432, 267 A.2d at 35. Blackjack, Missouri, is another example

of community resistance to federally subsidized low income housing. This community, population 3,000, was unincorporated and had no zoning powers. It is located approximately a half-hour drive from central St. Louis, Missouri. When a Methodist Church-sponsored nonprofit corporation announced its plans to build an interracial townhouse development in Blackjack, with federal subsidies, for families with annual earnings of between $6,000 and $10,000, Blackjack incorporated itself under Missouri Law with zoning powers and enacted a zoning code totally excluding multi-family residences. N.Y. Times, Nov. 15, 1970, § IV, at 5, col. 4. On January 8, 1971, the A.C.L.U. filed suit in the federal court on behalf of the nonprofit corporation to challenge Blackjack's zoning code. N.Y. Times, Jan. 8, 1971, at 15, col. 1.

(105) N.Y. Times, June 3, 1970, at 1, col. 5.

(106) Beckman & Ingraham, The States and Urban Areas, Urban Problems and Prospects 68, 81 (1965) [hereinafter cited as The States and Urban Areas].

(107) Id.

(108) Id. at 68.

(109) Id.

(110) Typical state legislation is found in Ill. Ann. Stat. art. 34, § 3001 (Smith-Hurd 1929); Mich. Stats. Ann. § 5.3008 (1945); RCWA § 35.63.070 (1965).

(111) Mass. Acts of 1969, ch. 774, amending Mass. Ann. Laws ch. 40B by adding § § 20-23; New York State Urban Development Corporation Act, N.Y. Unconsolidated Laws ch. 174 (McKinney 1968) [hereinafter cited as NYUDC Act]; Hawaii Rev. Stat. § 98H (Supp. 1963). Due to the uniqueness of the island of Hawaii, its comprehensive land use legislation is not applicable to mainland states. See Fragmentation, supra note 91, at 57.

(112) Mass. Acts of 1969, ch. 774, amending Mass. Ann. Laws ch. 40B by adding § § 20-23.

(113) Id. at § 20.

(114) Id.

(115) Id.

(116) Id. at § 23.

(117) Id. at § 20.

(118) Id. at § § 20, 22.

(119) Id. at § 23.

(120) Id. at § 21.

(121) Compare the Massachusetts Housing Appeals Committee Act with NYUDC Act.

(122) Mass. Ann. Laws, ch. 40B, § § 3-18 (1960).

(123) Mass. Acts of 1969, ch. 774, amending Mass. Ann. Laws ch. 23B by adding § 5A, provides that the Housing Appeals Committee shall have five members, three appointed by the Commissioner of Community Affairs, one of whom must be an employee of that department, and two members appointed by the Governor, one of whom must be a member of a board of selectmen and one a member of a city council.

(124) NYUDC Act.

(125) NYUDC Act § 16(3). See also N.Y. Times, May 17, 1970, at 58, col. 1.

(126) N.Y. Times, Apr. 12, 1970, at 32, col. 1. The mayors of Albany, Syracuse, Binghampton and Auburn, N.Y., supported the bill. N.Y. Times, Mar.

14, 1970, at 37, col. 1.

(127) NYUDC Act § 16(3).

(128) Id. at § 16(1).

(129) Id. at § 5(7).

(130) Id. at § 10(c).

(131) Id. at § 22.

(132) Id. at § 5, 12, 18.

(133) Reilly & Schulman, supra note 96, at 139.

(134) Id. at 139-40.

(135) Look Magazine, Apr. 1, 1969, at 70.

(136) N.Y. Times, May 17, 1970, at 58, col. 1.

(137) NYUDC Act § 2.

(138) N.J. Laws § 40:55-47.1 (1969); see infra, note 139.

(139) N.Y. Times, Jan. 25, 1970, § VIII, at 9, col. 1.

(140) N.J. Laws 40:55-47.1 (1969).

(141) Id.

(142) N.Y. Times, July 13, 1970, § VIII, at 1, col. 1.

(143) Id.

(144) N.Y. Times, May 24, 1970, § VIII, at 1, col. 1. See also News Release of the Suburban Action Institute, dated June 22, 1970, announcing a suit against racial and economic zoning exclusions which are allegedly in violation of the equal protection clause of the fourteenth amendment of the U.S. Constitution. This also is the first "outsider's suit" filed under N.J. Laws § 40:55-47.1. N.Y. Times, June 23, 1970, § L, at 33, col. 5.

(145) N.Y. Times, May 24, 1970, § VIII, at 1, col. 1.

(146) Id.

(147) This is occurring in other communities. In Massachusetts, the enactment of the Housing Appeals Committee has been followed by favorable response to proposals for low and moderate income housing by Lexington, Wellesley, Lincoln, Concord, Needham, Weston, and Westford. Comment, Snob Zoning: Developments in Massachusetts and New Jersey. 7 Harv. J. Legis. 246, 257 n.51. Montgomery County, Md., is holding hearings on an ordinance designed to require all housing projects located within "transit impact zones" surrounding the underground rail transit terminals to contain a fixed percentage of low and moderate income housing. Washington Post, Jan. 3, 1971, § A, at 1, col. 6.

(148) 311 Mass. 560, 42 N.E.2d 516 (1942), which is one of the initial cases to uphold minimum lot size requirements.

(149) 10 N.J. 165, 89 A.2d 693 (1952).

(150) 10 N.J. 165, 174, 89 A.2d 693, 701.

(151) For an example of the frustration experienced by a trial judge in attempting to equitably adjudicate the issues raised in discriminatory zoning litigation, see Lakewood Homes v. Board of Adjustment of the City of Lima, 52 Ohio Op. 2d 213, 258 N.E.2d 470 (Ct. C.P. 1969).

(152) Gross v. Allan, 37 N.J. Super. 262, 264, 117 A.2d 275 (App. Div. 1955), held that "the governing body of Kearney was entitled to ordain a zoning plan upon considerations fairly comprehensive of the statutory zoning desiderata in relation to the municipality to which its jurisdiction was confined, and uniformly applied within its boundaries."

(153) 10 Local Government L Service Letter 12 (1962).

(154) 37 N.J. 232, 181 A.2d 129 (1962).

(155) 37 N.J. 232, 243, 181 A.2d 129, 140.

(156) Chusud Realty Corp. v. Village of Kensington, 40 Misc. 2d 259, 243 N.Y.S. 2d 149 (Sup. Ct. 1963), aff'd. 22 App. Div. 2d 195, 255 N.Y.S.2d 411 (2nd Dept. 1964); Huttig v. City of Richmond Heights, 372 S.W.2d 833 (Mo. 1963); Burrough of Cresskill v. Burrough of Dumont, 28 N.J. Super. 26, 100 A.2d 182 (1953); aff'd, 15 N.J. 238, 104 A.2d 441 (1954); LaSalle Nat'l Bank v. Chicago, 4 Ill.2d 253, 122 N.E.2d 519 (1954); Hannifin Corp. v. City of Berwyn, 1 Ill.2d 28, 115 N.E.2d 315 (1953); Dowsey v. Village of Kensington, 257 N.Y. 221, 177 N.E. 427 (1931).

(157) 419 Pa. 504, 215 A.2d 597 (1965). Compare Bilbar Const. Co. v. Board of Adjustment, 393 Pa. 62, 141 A.2d 851 (1958); In re Volpe's Appeal, 384 Pa. 374, 121 A.2d 97 (1956).

(158) 419 Pa. 504, 215 A.2d 597, 602-03.

(159) 419 Pa. 504, 532, 215 A.2d 597, 612.

(160) Id.

(161) Id.

(162) 437 Pa. 237, 263 A.2d 395 (1970).

(163) 437 Pa. 237, 238, 263 A.2d 395, 396.

(164) Id.

(165) Id.

(166) 437 Pa. 237, 239, 263 A.2d 395, 397.

(167) 419 Pa. 504, 215 A.2d 597 (1965).

(168) 437 Pa. 237, 263 A.2d 395 (1970).

(169) 437 Pa. 237, 240, 263 A.2d 395, 398.

(170) 439 Pa. 466, 268 A.2d 765 (1970).

(171) There are distinct differences of philosophy and viewpoint between Justice Hall's dissent in Vickers v. Township Committee of Gloucester Township, 37 N.U. 232, 181 A.2d 129 (1962), and the three opinions of Justice Roberts. Justice Hall's focus is on the scope of municipal zoning powers and the need for controlled and orderly growth of local communities. He wrote "I suggest only that regulation rather than prohibition is the appropriate technique for attaining a balanced and attractive community." 37 N.J. at 250, 181 A.2d at 147. Then he repeated that a "desirable and balanced community can be realized without destroying the higher values of the privilege of democratic living." Id. Justice Roberts is concerned with the effects of discriminatory zoning on the individual. In Girsh, he discusses the growing number of jobs in suburban areas and the people's search for a "comfortable place to live." 437 Pa. at 240, 263 A.2d at 398. In Kit-Mar Builders, he wrote that the court "will not let the community keep out people rather than make community improvements." 439 Pa. at 469, 268 A.2d at 768.

(172) 439 Pa. 466, 467, 268 A.2d 765, 766.

(173) 439 Pa. 466, 468, 268 A.2d 765, 767.

(174) 439 Pa. 466, 470, 268 A.2d 765, 769.

(175) National Land & Investment Co. v. Kohn, 419 Pa. 504, 521, 215 A.2d 597, 612 (1965).

(176) 439 Pa. 466, 268 A.2d 765 (1970).

(177) In the cited section, the author is questioning the constitutionality of

discriminatory zoning ordinances. He points to each such ordinance as "a governmental act that strongly reinforces the social propensity to form tight little islands of residential exclusivity." Thus, the court has drawn from the heart of Sager's article. Tight Little Islands, supra note 67, at 761.

(178) Tight Little Islands, supra note 67; Apartments in the Suburbs, supra note 65; Lionshead Lake Revisited, supra note 44; Death Knell for Home Rule, supra note 40.

(179) Compare Perez v. Sharp, 32 Cal.2d 711, 198 P.2d 17 (1948) with McLaughlin v. Florida, 379 U.S. 104 (1964) and Loving v. Virginia, 388 U.S. 1 (1967). The scope of this comment does not include consideration of possible constitutional arguments against exclusionary zoning practices. Plaintiffs in James v. Valtierra, 39 U.S.L.W. 4488 (April 26, 1971), argued that the California referendum procedure written into the California Constitution, Calif. Const. art. IV, § 1 (1911) and XXXIV (1950), as applied to low income housing, is in violation of the supremacy clause of the U.S. Constitution, the privileges and immunities clause, and the equal protection clause. 39 U.S.L.W. 4489. The U.S. Supreme Court disagreed with each argument. Consideration of the constitutional questions associated with economic and racial discriminatory zoning is found in Tight Little Islands, supra note 67; Schwartz, Exclusionary Zoning—Suggested Constitutional Attacks, 4 Clearinghouse Rev. 345 (1970); Planning Law, supra note 31, and, The Constitutionality of Local Zoning, supra note 91.

(180) Mass. Acts of 1969, ch. 774, amending Mass. Ann. Laws ch. 40B by adding § § 20-23; NYUDC Act.

(181) See text section III.C., supra.

THE INTERRELATIONSHIP BETWEEN EXCLUSIONARY ZONING AND EXCLUSIONARY SUBDIVISION CONTROL

Robert E. Hirshon

A considerable number of American communities have adopted zoning laws which have had the effect of preventing ethnic and racial minorities as well as the poor from moving into a suburb or a particular section of a city.(1) Yet it is becoming increasingly clear that exclusionary zoning is not the only means available to achieve this end. A second, but less well-known exclusionary practice is subdivision control.

In a city which has enacted both zoning and subdivision control ordinances, a developer of a proposed low-income housing project faces two barriers before his project will be approved. First, he must meet the generally well-defined requirements of the city's zoning law. Second, he must comply with the ill-defined and often completely discretionary requirements of a subdivision control ordinance. For example, although the developer's project might meet the height, minimum lot size, and locational requirements of the zoning law, the planning board or commission which administers the subdivision control ordinance might find that the project will overtax the sewage and drainage capabilities of the area or cause too great an increase in the flow of traffic—highly subjective determinations.

This article will examine both exclusionary zoning and subdivision control with a view toward analyzing the assumptions common to both types of laws. The operative differences between exclusionary zoning and subdivision control may be non-existent. If this is truly the case, the judicial response to each practice should be the same.

THE PROBLEM

Only the areas outside major cities remain available for the construction of low and moderate income housing on a large scale. The supply of vacant land in cities has greatly diminished,(2) and the cost of purchasing land and removing existing structures often raises the cost of housing beyond the means of many persons.(3) Urban renewal, once considered the savior of our inner cities,(4) has forced many city residents to attempt to move away from the central area.(5) Yet, data indicate that only wealthier whites are able to take full advantage of opportunities in the suburbs,(6) while low-income Whites and Blacks have concentrated in ever-increasing numbers in the city. For example in 1950, 34 percent of all Whites and 43 percent of all non-Whites lived in cities;(7) by 1968 the percentage of Whites living in cities had declined to 26 percent and the number of non-Whites had increased to 55 percent. In 1978, it has been projected that 22 percent of all Whites and 61 percent of all Blacks will be living in the city.(8)

The migration of industry to the suburbs has compounded this problem. Job opportunities have moved to suburban areas beyond the reach of poorer inner city inhabitants.(9) Moreover, because of the resulting decrease in the tax base, cities have been forced to reduce the amount and quality of public services.(10)

In order to solve these problems, state and local governments must insure that low-income groups have the opportunity to move into the suburbs and must at the same time discontinue the practice of concentrating low-income housing projects within the already overcrowded and poor core cities. This idea is by no means novel; it has been referred to as "dispersal" or "scattered-site" housing(11) and has recently received favorable comment from the federal government.(12) Nevertheless, exclusionary zoning and subdivision control may be used to impede the use of this approach.

THE HISTORY AND NATURE OF ZONING AND SUBDIVISION CONTROL

Public restrictions on the use of private property originated with the failure of private contractual restrictions to prevent industry from encroaching upon residential sections of our cities.(13) Although these private covenants were incorporated in the contracts of some landowners to satisfy their desire to keep the property residential, it is improbable that restrictive covenants were ever meant to provide a system of comprehensive land use control.(14) In any event, by the early 1900's industrial development had led to instability of property values in many areas and to urban decay,(15) and it had become apparent that public land use control was the only way to preserve the integrity of residential areas.(16)

When zoning, the first means of public land use control,(17) began to receive widespread attention, most legal commentators argued that it was merely an extension of the common law doctrine of nuisance.(18) The only appreciable difference, they argued, was that zoning is a means for the municipality, not the court, to declare that certain land uses are nuisances.(19) The United States Supreme Court formally adopted the extension of the common law nuisance argument in 1926, when it upheld the constitutionality of zoning in *Village of Euclid v. Ambler Realty Co.*,(20) a landmark case which cleared the way for massive acceptance of zoning regulations by municipalities.(21)

While the historical setting from which zoning first evolved is drastically different from the present setting, the nature of zoning has remained unchanged: it is still a tool for selective inclusion and exclusion of certain land use practices.

In recent years, however, zoning has been examined in a new light—a light which focuses on its exclusionary effects.(22) *Exclusionary zoning may be defined as that practice which results in closing the suburban housing market to low and moderate income families.* Although exclusionary zoning takes many forms, it is most often exemplified in minimum lot(23) and floor area(24) requirements and prohibitions against certain types or all forms of multi-family dwellings.(25) Although not discriminatory on their face, these requirements and prohibitions may have discriminatory effects.(26)

From the beginning, then, zoning has been considered a means to promote orderly land use and stabilize property values. Subdivision control on the other hand has different roots. Early laws regarding subdivisions simply called for the recording of plats to prevent uncertainty with respect to land titles.(27) Subdivision control, as we know it today, did not get its major impetus until 1924 when Secretary of Commerce Hoover appointed a committee on city planning and zoning. One of the primary purposes of this committee was to draft a model city planning enabling act which was to embody a comprehensive approach to subdivision control.(28) Four years later this model act was published, and soon was enacted by a large number of municipalities.(29)

The model act designates the city's planning commission as the subdivision control agency.(30) The first task of that agency is to adopt regulations establishing standards of subdivision control,(31) which may provide for the proper arrangement of streets and sewer and water facilities, as well as adequate space for utilities, recreation, light and air, and traffic.(32) Only after these regulations have been adopted may the agency begin approving subdivision plats.(33) Today, most subdivision control agencies still operate under enabling acts similar to the model drafted by the Hoover committee,(34) although each state has attempted to tailor the model to its own particular needs.(35)

Thus, the purpose of subdivision control acts today is no longer limited to an attempt to assure good land titles; rather, like zoning, the acts are concerned with the development of standards for ordered land use. Concommitantly, in deciding whether a subdivision plat meets established standards, the subdivision control agency may have a great deal of discretion—a discretion that can be easily used for exclusionary purposes and that is not easy to reverse.(36)

ZONING OR SUBDIVISION CONTROL: HEADS OR TAILS?

Although both subdivision regulations and zoning ordinances may at times embrace a common goal, they involve two distinct statutory systems.(37) A municipality's subdivision and zoning ordinances frequently differ with respect to the timing of their application to a proposed subdivision. Many city ordinances require that a proposed subdivision meet all zoning regulations before the subdivision control agency is legally bound to decide whether a particular use conforms to subdivision standards.(38) If the proposed subdivision has not met the city's zoning requirements, further inquiry as to whether the plat should be approved by the subdivision control agency is unnecessary. A second difference between zoning and subdivision control is that zoning ordinances are aimed at controlling the type of building or use intended for the property; subdivision control is aimed at controlling the manner in which land is divided and made ready for a building or a particular use.(39)

Nevertheless, upon closer analysis these distinctions tend to disappear. Before an area is *zoned* for a particular use, the zoning board must first ascertain whether that area is physically suited for that use and whether the present or reasonably anticipated level of public services (that is, streets, utilities, fire and police protection, etc.) is adequate to meet successfully the additional demands that full use of the area might entail.(40) Therefore, when an area is originally zoned, the zoning board will thoroughly consider most if not all of the factors later examined by a subdivision control agency. Although it is arguable that subdivision control agencies serve a distinct function in applying these standards to the current state of affairs and therefore in considering changes that may have occurred since the zoning ordinance was adopted, the frequent practice of amending zoning ordinances and granting variances should serve to rebut these arguments.(41)

If, therefore, there are no viable distinctions between zoning and subdivision control, the judicial response to the use of subdivision control for exclusionary purposes should be the same as the judicial response to the exclusionary use of zoning ordinances. One of the earliest challenges to local land use practices involved the application of a municipality's zoning regulations. In *Village of Euclid v. Ambler Realty Co.*(42) the United States Supreme Court relying upon a due process analysis held that zoning ordinances were constitutional unless shown to be "clearly arbitrary and unreasonable, having no substantial relation to the public health, safety, morals, or general welfare."(43) Two basic assumptions were necessarily vital to this holding: 1. zoning is a rational means to effect land use control; and 2. local governments are equipped to judge the appropriateness of such regulations. Since *Euclid*, the Supreme Court has generally refrained from ruling on the constitutionality of zoning ordinances.(44) State and lower federal courts have adopted a similar "hands-off" approach.(45)

Recently, however, challenges to local exclusionary land use practices based upon the equal protection clause of the fourteenth amendment, have become more numerous.(46) Courts have refused to hold that all exclusionary land use practices are unconstitutional.(47) Indeed, the courts have refused to take even the more limited step of striking down exclusionary zoning ordinances that are aimed solely at the poor.(48) These same courts may however, invalidate zoning ordinances which have the effect or purpose of excluding racial minorities.

In *Dailey v. City of Lawton*(49) a nonprofit housing sponsor challenged the Lawton City Council's refusal to rezone a tract of land in a White neighborhood where the sponsor wanted to build a multi-family residential housing project. The district court found for the plaintiff-sponsor, rejecting the city's claim that its refusal to grant a zoning change had been based upon findings which indicated that the change would place an undue burden upon public services.(50) Rather, the court found that the reason for the city's refusal to rezone the area was the opposition of White residents. The court held that the city could not use zoning procedures to effectuate the discriminatory goals of its residents and ordered the rezoning to take place.(51)

On appeal, the United States Court of Appeals for the Tenth Circuit affirmed, stating:

The appellants argue that a finding of discriminatory intent is barred because the project was opposed on the grounds of overcrowding of the neighborhood, the local schools, and the recreational facilities and the overburdening of the local fire fighting capabilities. The testimony in this regard was vague and general. No school, fire recreational, traffic, or other official testified in support of the appellant's claims. The racial prejudice alleged and established by the plaintiffs must be met by something more than bald, conclusory assertions that the action was taken for other than discriminatory reasons.(52)

In *Lawton* the city relied on the alleged burden upon public facilities and services which the low income housing project would create as the grounds for denying the requested zoning charge, not upon a contention that existing statues did not permit the construction of the housing. Thus, the rationale in this case would be equally applicable to a subdivision control agency's decision as to whether a plat should be authorized, since the factors the city relied upon for rejecting the request to rezone are the same as those which a subdivision control agency would examine.

Southern Alameda Spanish Speaking Organization v. City of Union City (SASSO)(53) is a major breakthrough in exclusionary land use litigation. Here the Organization had succeeded in getting the Union City Planning Commission and City Council to pass an ordinance rezoning a tract of land to accommodate a 280-unit medium density housing project. Immediately thereafter the citizens of Union City rejected the ordinance in a referendum. The Organization then brought suit alleging among other things that their right to equal protection of the laws had been violated. The Ninth Circuit held that the Organization, while it could not inquire into the motives of persons voting in the referendum, could state a sufficient claim for relief if it could show that the referendum was discriminatory:

> If the voters' purpose is to be found here, then, it would seem to require far more than a simple application of objective standards. If the true motive is to be ascertained not through speculation but through a probing of the private attitudes of the voters, the inquiry would entail an intolerable invasion of the privacy that must protect an exercise of the franchise. [Citation omitted].
>
> Appellants' equal protection contentions, however, reach beyond purpose. They assert that the effect of the referendum is to deny decent housing and an integrated environment to low-income residents of Union City. If, apart from voter motive, the result of this zoning by referendum is discriminatory in this fashion, in our view a substantial constitutional question is presented.(54)

The importance of *SASSO* is its acceptance of a "discrimination by effect" standard; the court did not focus on zoning but on the effect of this zoning—discrimination. Once a court's attention is directed toward the problem of discrimination, then whether discrimination is caused by zoning or subdivision control practices will become an issue of secondary importance.

In *Kennedy Park Homes Association, Inc. v. City of Lackawanna*(55) the city planning board's refusal to approve a subdivision plat was overturned by the courts. The local Roman Catholic diocese had agreed to sell a tract of land to the Kennedy Park Homes Association, Inc., so that a low-income housing project could be developed. When this agreement became known to the public, a campaign was initiated to prevent the sale from taking place,(56) and a petition carrying the name of the Mayor and President of the City Council was circulated opposing the sale "due to the lack of schools and inadequate sewage facilities." Subsequently, the Lackawanna Zoning Board of Appeals and the Planning and Development Board recommended to the City Council a moratorium on all new subdivisions until such time as the sewage problem was solved. There was also a rezoning of the area to provide for open space and park area.

Lackawanna did have a sewage problem. The city could trace the minutes of its City Council meetings for over a decade to show numerous references to its concern over the sewage problem. Indeed, Lackawanna argued that it was trying to rectify an urgent problem which affected the health and welfare of its citizens. Nevertheless, both the federal district court(57) and the United States Court of Appeals for the Second Circuit rejected the city's arguments. Focusing upon the discriminatory effect of the city's actions, the Second Circuit stated:

> Lackawanna is obligated to deal with its sewer needs without infringing on plaintiffs' rights. Even were we to accept the City's allegation that any discrimination here resulted from thoughtlessness rather than a purposeful scheme, the City may not escape responsibility for placing its black citizens under a severe disadvantage which it cannot justify. [Citations omitted]. The city must provide sewerage facilities to the plaintiffs in conformity with the Equal Protection Clause of the Fourteenth Amendment and provide it [sic] as soon as it does for any other applicant.(58)

Like the Ninth Circuit in *SASSO*, the Second Circuit focused not upon the means used to achieve the discriminatory result, but upon that result itself. Such a rationale should apply irrespective of whether the means used to achieve the discriminatory result are zoning or subdivision controls.

Exclusionary subdivision control practices may become more common when cities discover that zoning ordinances are subject to close scrutiny by the courts. Nevertheless, as the above analysis has attempted to demonstrate, subdivision control practices should have no more success in excluding minority groups than zoning. If the courts focus on the *effect* of the practice rather than the *type* of practice, discrimination however achieved will not be allowed. The fate of exclusionary subdivision control is inevitably tied to the fate of exclusionary zoning.

NOTES

(1) For discussions of exclusionary zoning, see Note, Exclusionary Zoning and Equal Protection, 84 Harv. L. Rev. 1645 (1971): Symposium—Exclusionary Zoning, 22 Syracuse L. Rev. 465 (1971): Legislative Development. Snob Zoning: Developments in Massachusetts and New Jersey, 7 Harv. J. Legis. 246 (1970).

(2) The Report of the President's Committee on Urban Housing, A Decent

Home 139 (The Kaiser Report, 1969) [hereinafter cited as Kaiser Report].

For example, in 1940, 64 percent of the land was vacant in Los Angeles; by 1960 that figure had dropped to 31 percent. Statistics show that in 1955, only 4 percent of all the land in Washington, D.C. was vacant, while in 1954, that figure for Detroit was only 8 percent.

(3) Id. at 140-42.

(4) S. Grier, Urban Renewal and American Cities 13-34 (1965).

(5) H. Gaus, The Failure of Urban Renewal 4 (American Jewish Committee Commentary Report, 1965).

(6) The median income of those Whites living in the central city is approximately $2,000 less than the median income of Whites living in the suburbs. Bureau of Labor Statistics U.S. Dept. of Labor, Statistical Abstract 318 (1971).

(7) Kaiser Report, supra note 2, at 40.

(8) Id. at 40.

(9) An example of the extent of this burden was reported in the New York Times, Jan. 29, 1971, at 1, col. 1. In the Ford assembly plant in Mahwah, New Jersey, the average worker who commutes to work must travel approximately thirty miles to reach the factory. This represents a cost of about $1,000 per year for each commuter, a significant financial burden.

(10) New York Times, Jan. 23, 1971, at 1, col. 7.

(11) New York Times, Sept. 23, 1971, at 1, col. 6.

(12) Id. Scattered site housing received an unexpected boost when the Department of Housing and Urban Development (HUD) recently ruled that a subsidized housing project in Philadelphia which had previously been approved should have been rejected. HUD claimed that the project would increase segregation and compound existing social problems within the city. HUD's ruling was understood to have been based upon new guidelines just formulated within the department.

(13) E. Bassett, Zoning 317 (National Municipal League Technical Pamphlet Series No. 5, 1922).

(14) Id.

(15) R. Babcock, The Zoning Game 3 (1966). It has been suggested that the impetus for modern zoning regulations emanated from New York City's Fifth Avenue merchants, who were afraid that the garment industry would further encroach upon their elegant shopping district.

(16) Id. at 3-18.

(17) E. Bassett, supra note 13, at 318-26.

(18) R. Babcock, supra note 15, at 4. Contra. E. Bassett, Zoning 93 (Russell Sage Foundation, 1940).

(19) R. Babcock, supra note 15, at 3—18.

(20) 272 U.S. 365 (1926).

The Supreme Court pointed out per Justice Sutherland:

Thus the question whether the power exists to forbid the erection of a building of a particular kind or for a particualr use, like the question whether a particular thing is a nuisance, is to be determined, not by an abstract consideration of the building or of the thing considered apart, but by considering it in connection with the circumstances and the locality. [Citations omitted]. A nuisance may be the right thing in the wrong place—like a pig in the parlor instead of the barnyard. [Id. at 388.]

(21) Blair, Is Zoning a Mistake, 14 Zoning Digest 249, 249-250 (1962).

(22) See authorities cited in note 1 supra.

(23) See Becker, Police Power and Minimum Lot Size Zoning—Part I—Method of Analysis, Wash. U.L.Q. 263 (1969); Note, Large Lot Zoning, 78 Yale L.J. 1418 (1969).

(24) See Note, Building Size, Shape and Placement Regulations: Bulk Control Zoning Reexamined, 60 Yale L.J. 506 (1951).

(25) See, e.g., Miller v. Board of Public Works, 195 Cal. 477, 234 P. 381 (1925) (upholding validity of ordinance prohibiting construction of multi-family dwellings); Babcock & Bosselman, Suburban Zoning and the Apartment Boom, 111 U. Pa. L. Rev. 1040 (1963).

(26) See, e.g., Davidoff & Davidoff, Opening the Suburbs Toward Inclusionary Land Use Controls, 22 Syracuse L. Rev. 509, 520-22 (1971), for a brief discussion of discriminatory effects of various exclusionary devices.

(27) Reps. Control of Land Subdivision by Municipal Planning Boards, 40 Cornell L.Q. 258 (1955).

An example of early subdivision legislation is 1 Terr. Laws 816 (1821) which was enacted in the Michigan Territory in 1821. For an excellent examination of public control of land subdivisions in Michigan, see Cunningham, Public Control of Land Subdivision in Michigan: Description and Critique, 66 Mich. L. Rev. 3 (1968). Municipalities have also attempted to use subdivision ordinances to shift part of the cost of developing new public facilities necessitated by residential growth to land developers and ultimately the home purchaser. Johnston, Developments in Land Use Control, 45 Notre Dame Law, 399 (1970).

(28) Reps. supra note 27, at 259.

(29) A survey taken in 1934 points out that 269 boards in 29 states were given power to regulate subdivisions. National Planning Board, Federal Emergency Administration of Public Works, Status of City and Regional Planning in the United States, Appendix H (Eleventh Circular Letter, May 15, 1934), cited in Reps, supra note 27, at 259.

(30) Advisory Committee on City Planning and Zoning, U.S. Dept. of Commerce, A Standard City Planning Enabling Act tit. II., § 12 (1928).

(31) Id. § 14

(32) Id. § 14.

(33) Id. § 12.

(34) Reps. supra note 27, at 259.

(35) Some states require the municipal planning board to submit its regulations and standards to a legislative body for approval. Other states, e.g., Maine, require only that approval be given by the town's planning board, an administrative agency, and that this approval be based upon a subdivision's "compliance with municipal ordinances and its general reasonableness." Me. Rev. Stat. Ann. tit. 30, § 4956 (1964).

(36) Those states which have statutes similar to Maine's allow a planning board to disapprove a plat either because it does not meet good land use requirements or it is generally unreasonable. Because of a lack of a definitive standard as to what constitutes good land use and what is reasonable, a plaintiff is apt to have a difficult time proving that the board abused its discretion.

(37) For a textual discussion of zoning and subdivision control systems, see

D. Webster, Urban Planning and Municipal Public Policy 362-488 (1958).

(38) See e.g., Maine's enabling statute, Me. Rev. Stat. Ann. tit. 30. § 4956 (1964).

(39) D. Webster, supra note 37, at 437-38.

(40) I.R. Anderson, American Law of Zoning 478-80 (1968).

(41) I. R. Anderson, supra note 40, at 590-92.

(42) 272 U.S. 365 (1926).

(43) Id. at 395.

(44) Sager, Tight Little Islands: Exclusionary Zoning, Equal Protection, and the Indigent, 21 Stan. L. Rev. 767, 783 (1969).

(45) Id. at 783-84. An exception to this "hands off" approach has been that taken by the Pennsylvania judiciary. See, e.g., Appeal of Kit Mar. Builders, 439 Pa. 466, 268 A.2d 765 (1970) (township zoning ordinance requiring lots no less than two acres along existing roads and no less than three acres in the interior was unconstitutional); Appeal of Girsh, 437 Pa. 237, 263 A.2d 395 (1970) (township zoning ordinance not providing for apartments was unconsitutional) and 32 U. Pitt. L. Rev. 83 (1970).

(46) One author has concluded that "exclusionary zoning ordinances seem ripe for close consideration in terms of modern equal protection doctrine, and in many instances, may well fail to meet the burden of justification inposed by that doctrine." Sager, supra note 44, at 798. Sager forcefully presents the arguments for and against an equal protection approach to exclusionary zoning, id. at 785-800.

(47) Id. at 784-85.

(48) For an examination of exclusionary zoning and the poor, see Cutler, Legality of Zoning to Exclude the Poor: A Preliminary Analysis of Evolving Law, 37 Brook. L. Rev. 483 (1971).

In James v. Valtierra, 402 U.S. 137 (1971), the United States Supreme Court refused to strike down on equal protection grounds article XXXIV of the California Constitution, which required a majority community vote before low-rent housing could be constructed.

(49) 425 F.2d 1037 (10th Cir. 1970).

(50) 296 F. Supp. 266, 267-68 (W.D. Okla. 1969).

(51) Id. at 269.

(52) 425 F.2d 1037, 1039-40 (10th Cir. 1970).

(53) 424 F.2d 291 (9th Cir. 1970).

(54) Id. at 295.

(55) 436 F.2d 108 (2d Cir. 1970), cert. denied, 401 U.S. 1010 (1971), aff'g 318 F. Supp. 669 (W.D. N.Y. 1970).

(56) 436 F.2d at 111.

(57) 318 F. Supp. at 679-81.

(58) 436 F.2d at 114.

JOBS AND HOUSING:
FINAL SUMMARY REPORT
ON THE HOUSING COMPONENT

National Committee Against
Discrimination in Housing

The two-year inquiry into the growth of employment opportunities outside of central cities in the New York Metropolitan Region and the availability of housing to racial minorities in suburban areas accessible to such job sites was broken down into two broad components: (a) a study of economic growth trends in the suburbs and related manpower needs and transportation access, and (b) a study of the availability of housing within the means of all income groups employed in suburban establishments, including the lowest, and open to all prospective occupants, without regard to race or ethnic background.

Essentially, the housing component of this study sought to identify the constraints upon housing for racial minorities with moderate and low incomes. The effort to identify the constraints upon such housing was directed toward finding answers to two basic questions: What is the extent and nature of constraints on the construction of housing within the means of employees of suburban establishments and what is the extent and nature of discrimination against blacks and Puerto Ricans in the sale and rental of housing in suburban housing markets?

The methodology employed in gathering information to answer these questions was largely of two types: (a) a compilation and analysis of reported data on the behavior of the metropolitan housing market, and (b) field investigations in seven selected counties (Bergen, Essex, and Middlesex in New Jersey; Nassau, Suffolk and Westchester in New York and Fairfield in Connecticut), and community studies in some 30 suburban municipalities to determine local attitudes and practices affecting housing opportunities for low- and moderate-income households, specifically blacks and Puerto Ricans.

The study design was initially based on some 32 hypotheses as to probable reasons for the inadequacy of suburban housing at sale and rental levels within the means of low and moderate income families, and probable reasons for the under-representation of minority persons in the suburban counties of the metropolitan region. As the study progressed, insights developed by emerging findings permitted a re-evaluation of the hypotheses and an assessment as to their relative importance and/or validity in explaining the subject phenomena. Since the publication of an interim report, *Jobs and Housing*, the study was directed more intensively toward a reduced number of key issues judged to be crucial in affecting future trends.

Reduction of the area of inquiry was also facilitated by the rapid spread of public awareness of the essential factors in the city/suburb, white phenomenon. This awareness makes most of the reasons advanced for inquiry in the hypotheses commonplace knowledge today, however moral or legal justifications may differ.

The growth in public awareness has been due, in large part, to the study itself, especially the dissemination of some 3,000 copies of the interim report, resulting in widespread use in the national media. The study's subsequent findings were utilized from time-to-time by numerous urban affairs writers. Suburban housing practices have been brought to public attention also by NCDH through use of the study's findings in its action and public information programs; specifically, NCDH publications, litigation, expert testimony before legislative committees and special commissions, speeches to conferences of trade, professional, labor, business and other groups, and collaboration with government officials to make more effective their respective equal opportunity programs in housing.

Public awareness has also been heightened by front page publicity given to dramatic confrontations in a number of communities over exclusionary practices and/or local protests against interracial housing for low income families. As a result, place names such as Black Jack, San Leandro, Warren, Mahwah, Oyster Bay, Forest Hills, became nationally recognized symbols that stood for the issues involved in NCDH's Jobs/Housing study. The impact of these situations has been heightened by the coverage given to corroborative data released from time-to-time by such official sources as the Bureau of the Census, the Department of Labor, the Department of Housing and Urban Development, the United States Civil Rights Commission, and state and metropolitan planning, housing and civil rights agencies.

The spread of factual information about current housing practices in the suburbs, however, has not sufficed to clarify the issues that are central to improving access to suburban employment and housing for racial minorities. These issues revolve, mainly, around (a) the effort to make a distinction in law enforcement and housing program administration between racial discrimination and economic discrimination and (b) the present reliance in enforcement of open housing laws on minimally-productive, case-by-case processing of individual complaints rather than institution of "pattern and practice" proceedings based on de facto evidence of under-representation of minority residents in specific buildings or municipalities.

The summary report on the study's housing component focuses on the constraints identified by our findings as the major obstacles to enlarging the housing opportunities of racial minority households of low or moderate income. The housing opportunities of such households are affected by both economic and racial discrimination in a manner not experienced by either low income whites or high income blacks. Persons of racial minorities with limited purchasing power in the housing market constitute a large and critical mass whose confinement to expanding ghettos is the essence of the urban problem today. It is the latter that has triggered our Jobs/Housing study, and it is to the extent that the study contributes to an understanding of that problem that its value will be judged. The summary report, therefore, will focus on suburban housing from the point of view of constraints for the vast majority of the minority population, without pursuing the question, so largely speculative, as to whether racial or economic factors predominate in shaping local exclusionary practices.

MAJOR CONSTRAINTS AS IDENTIFIED BY STUDY

Blacks and Puerto Ricans seeking to take advantage of growing employment opportunities in suburban areas by looking for housing in the suburbs must overcome (a) the cost barrier (price of house or rental), and (b) the racial discrimination barrier. The study identified the constraints which contribute most to making each of these barriers effective.

CONSTRAINTS ON CONSTRUCTION

Subsidized housing (Federal and/or State) excluded from all but a handful of suburban municipalities. This is the single, most critical constraint on housing supply for low and moderate income families, because the economics of housing construction price almost all non-subsidized housing beyond the means of most minority buyers or renters.

Multi-family housing is prohibited by zoning in most suburban jurisdictions with a significant amount of vacant land. Efforts by builders to obtain zoning changes by amendment or variance are usually blocked, except in some cases where the limitation on apartment size and design for high rents assures suburban officials that occupancy will be overwhelmingly by middle class whites with a minimal pupil yield.

Excessively large lots are required by zoning to increase arbitrarily the cost of single family houses, thereby resulting in a higher tax assessment for such property, as well as pricing them beyond the reach of most Black and Puerto Rican homeseekers. Though current construction and land cost combined with mortgage and property tax rates would result in a sale price beyond the reach of most wage earners, even if built on relatively small lots, zoning that would permit such construction would add to the total supply of housing, thereby easing the pressures for all homeseekers, regardless of income bracket.

Housing site—Choices of builders and public bodies are confined by factors of zoning, community attitude, land availability and cost, and access to Manhattan, without regard to suburban labor markets and their current and future manpower needs, thus contributing to the mismatch of job locations and work force residence between city and suburb, white collar and blue collar, blacks and whites.

Marketing of new suburban housing, both sales and rentals, fails to supply minority homeseekers with systematic information about housing opportunities as related to employment and skill training opportunities. White homeseekers, with earlier and more reliable information, act quicker in taking advantage of opportunities in a tight and changing housing market. Where this involves publicly-assisted housing, such as 236, in predominantly white neighborhoods or suburban towns, it has the effect of "taking away" subsidized units from the minority community that might have built them in ghettos before current HUD site-selection guidelines prevented it.

Civil rights enforcement mechanisms are closed to victims of racial discrimination when practiced by suburban municipalities in the form of land use controls and building regulations. A building owner who refuses to rent to minority tenants, or a homebuilder who refuses to sell to minority homeseekers, is subject to legal proceedings under Title VIII of the Federal Civil Rights Act and similar state laws. A municipality which excludes blacks and Puerto Ricans by its land use and building policy, enjoys immunity, as of now, from action by civil rights enforcement agencies, even in specific cases of actions that bar proposed housing likely to have considerable numbers of minority occupants by virtue of rental levels and other factors.

The local property tax system gives every type of incentive to property owners to oppose housing for low and moderate income households in their community. By placing school costs so largely upon local resources, together with the local share of county costs for health, welfare and law enforcement, the property tax system makes every property owner consider the possibility of direct and immediate tax consequences of housing families of low and moderate income within his tax jurisdiction. The local property tax serves as a respectable cover for every type of discriminating motivation.

ENFORCEMENT OF LAWS AGAINST RACIAL DISCRIMINATION

Discrimination as a pattern or practice remains largely unaffected by enforcement activities, consisting predominantly of individual complaints by victims of discrimination. Owners of multi-family buildings, renting agents, homebuilders, cooperatives, condominiums, apartment management firms, multiple listing systems and property-owners associations can afford to risk the occasional complaint by an individual who is burdened by pursuing it, subjected to frustrating delays granted at the request of the accused, and settled frequently with a negotiated compromise, long after the complainant has found other accommodations and lost interest in the case. "Pattern and practice" suits are initiated most infrequently, Federal and state enforcement agencies citing budget and staff limitations as a reason for not undertaking more "de facto" actions requiring comprehensive and painstaking compilation of evidence in the form of social, economic and demographic data, and racial occupancy records.

Community exclusion of racial minorities maintained by combining the furtively discriminatory practices of public authority (police, schools, tax assessement, social welfare, health, zoning, building inspection, etc.) and private institutions (real estate firms, banks, employers, landlords, churches, neighborhood and taxpayer associations, PTA's, service clubs, Chamber of Commerce, etc.) to resist by non-cooperation, rebuffs, deception and often harassment the efforts of blacks and other minorities to gain a residential foothold in the community. The census reports are replete with long lists of suburban towns, many with large segments of white blue-collar workers, with less than one percent non-white inhabitants. Such communities, most easily identified in the public's mind with San Leandro, California, and Warren, Michigan, because of concentrated attention from the media (or the less widely-known Clifton, New Jersey, in our study area), are not susceptible to civil rights enforcement procedures designed to operate in the area of individual relations, such as between job applicant and employer, apartment hunter and renting agent, homeseeker and real estate broker, etc. Such communities exude hostility to would-be residents of minority races (or are so viewed by minority members) to an extent that causes non-whites to avoid them in their search for housing.

Dual real estate markets—one for whites and one for blacks, continue to operate with the connivance of both white and black brokers. The exclusion of black brokers from boards of realtors and the informal agreements between many white and black cooperating brokers for referral of white clients to the former and black clients to the latter remains widespread. Real estate advertisements that contain code words or pictures to convey racial implications continue to appear despite efforts by state enforcement agencies and responsible newspapers to curtail the practice. The scandalous handling of 235 sales, both discriminatory and fraudulent, was facilitated by the existence of dual housing markets and segregationist practices by brokers of both races.

Absence of racial occupancy records frustrates pattern and practice complaints. Renting offices hide behind old state statutes forbidding the keeping of racial designation records. This situation is being remedied in New Jersey by a pioneer regulation requiring annual reports on racial occupancy by apartment for buildings of 25 units or more.

Fragmented and underground dissemination of real estate information places minority homeseekers, both buyers and renters, at a disadvantage in areas outside of ghettos, especially in distant suburbs. Unlike the highly centralized stock market, the real estate market is decentralized into scores of local situations with the information strings to each in the hands of a local broker or board of realtors. In a tight housing market it often suffices to find occupants by passing the information of a pending vacancy, or offer to sell, via an "underground" of neighbors, friends, local merchants, etc., with the result that blacks or Puerto Ricans never hear of the opportunity.

HOUSING MARKET BEHAVIOR IN NEW YORK

Housing opportunities for racial minorities, as with all other consumers of shelter, are influenced decisively by demographic trends and housing market behavior in the metropolitan Region.

A metropolitan Region, essentially, is a labor market area, with the housing stock a necessary adjunct to shelter the labor force. In large metropolitan regions, such as New York's, there are actually many overlapping sectional and functional labor markets with somewhat parallel housing markets. Theoretically, labor and housing markets should respond to each other's needs: available jobs should induce residential building and available labor force should induce economic expansion and more jobs. It is the mismatch between employment opportunity and housing opportunity in the New York Metropolitan Region's suburbs that constitutes the central problem investigated by this study.

The growth of employment opportunity is a by-product of the economy's growth; induced in specific localities only partially by the availability of a resident labor supply, since transportation facilities are a relative (or elastic) factor and higher wages can attract employees from longer distances. The growth of housing opportunities is governed by many factors, among which the principal ones are (a) mortgage rates; (b) land and construction costs; (c) effective consumer demand; and (d) local land use (zoning) controls and building regulations. The factors that cause job-location decisions to relate to housing supply and housing-location decisions to relate to job supply are, at best, relatively tenuous when operating under free market conditions that permit economic incentives and consumers' choice maximum effectiveness.

However, the free play of market forces in the New York Metropolitan Region is radically distorted, our studies found, by the double constraints of exclusionary zoning and racial discrimination in sales and rentals. The result has been a serious interference with residential mobility, resulting in demographic trends that are separating the population into vast geographic areas by race, income and occupation. Essentially these trends are segregating blacks and Puerto Ricans in vast ghettos in New York City and other old cities of the Region, and housing whites in rapidly growing suburbs—reducing freedom of choice for everyone and depriving minorities of the residential mobility essential to maximize their opportunities in the Region's labor market.

Rational land use for residential construction and sales and rentals free of racial tests would normalize the housing market, but it would still confront the person of low or moderate income with price barriers that reflect the economics of housing today. The nature of the economic barriers can be seen from the behavior of the housing market during the 1960's, essentially the story of a declining number of housing starts and rising sale prices and rentals.

For the nation as a whole, the decade began with 1.3 million starts in 1961 and ended with 1.4 million in 1970 for a total of 10.3 million dwelling units added (starts minus fires and demolitions) over the 10 year period. This represented an 18% increase in the nation's housing inventory, a poor record compared to the 26% increase registered in the 1950's.

In the New York Metropolitan Region, as defined by the Tri-State Regional Planning Commission, the decade began with 140,300 starts in 1961 and ended with 68,700 starts in 1970. Beginning in 1965, each successive year showed fewer housing starts. Total starts for the decade of the 1960's were about one million, compared to 1.2 million in the 1950's. Since demolition and fire loss removed some 350,000 units during the 1960's, there were only 652,928 dwelling units added to the Region's housing inventory from 1960 to 1970 to accommodate a population increase of almost two million during the decade.

In 1969, three building permits were issued per 1,000 population in the New York SMSA, and two permits per 1,000 population in the Newark SMSA. Comparative figures for other areas were Miami-Fort Lauderdale, 30; Orange County, Cal., 24; Phoenix, 20; San Diego, 19; Atlanta, 17; Dallas, 17; Denver, 14; and Houston, 14. The national average was 7 building permits per 1,000 population.

One result was an extremely "tight" housing market in the New York Metropolitan Region with a vacancy rate under 1%, a factor that placed additional upward pressure on sale prices and rentals, already escalating as part of the inflationary spiral. The average rent for the Region's tenants moved from $86 in 1960 to $118 in 1970, despite rent control in New York City. The average value of single family homes in the existing inventory went up from $19,300 in 1960 to $30,500 in 1970.

Comparing the total increase in dwelling units to the increase in population is a crude measurement that is comparable to deciding the adequacy of the supply of shoes for a given number of people without knowing anything about foot sizes, or whether the shoes were designed for men or women, work or bowling, summer or winter. Housing that fits a particualr family's needs as to number of bedrooms, dependable heat and hot water, access to work, and within the budget becomes increasingly difficult to locate as the vacancy rate declines. The difficulty also increases for families in relation to where they rank on a declining scale of incomes. Vacancy rates are lower for less expensive housing, except for the very worst slum housing affected by abandonment.

The decline in housing starts that began in the middle Sixties is usually attributed to the drying up of money for construction loans and mortgages as a consequence of more attractive earnings in other investments. Builders, who customarily operate with a minimum of their own capital, found it increasingly difficult to get financing. Homebuyers who found that the mortgage rates were escalating from 6% to 7% and on to 8% and 8.5% withdrew from the market in expectation of more favorable rates. Terms became stiffer also as lending institutions demanded a higher value-to-loan ratio and credit criteria for borrowers became stricter. The number of families in a financial position to buy shrank, beginning, as usual, with those whose resources were slimmest, including minority families that had just begun to accumulate savings as a consequence of the increase in employment in the 1960's and the decrease in discrimination pursuant to civil rights legislation.

The shrinking of the home buying market slowed sales and made both builders and banks more cautious. Since builders operate with money borrowed for short terms at high interest rates (9% to 11%), slow sales erode profits and can, if stretched out, prove disastrous. The result was a downward plummeting of one-family starts. From a high of 50,500 in 1964 they decreased annually to 25,200 in 1970 in the New York Region.

Rising money rates were accompanied by increased land costs. Aside from inflationary influences affecting all transactions, land values are subject to unique factors relating to depletion of supply in specific locations; the uses and density permitted by zoning regulations; the probability of negotiating zoning changes; and, finally, the market price (or rentals) of housing in the area.

LAND-DEVELOPMENT ECONOMICS

Based on field surveys by Economic Consultants Organization, consultants to the NCDH study, the following picture of land development economics in selected portions of the New York Metropolitan Region emerged:

Interviews with builders and housing developers indicated that the scarcity of land was one of the major "problems" of the home building industry in the Region. The most usual complaint, especially in the more built up areas, was that land was priced too high and/or not zoned for the type of construction builders had in mind. To the extent that builders feel it necessary to obtain a change in zone, lack of land zoned satisfactorily becomes a barrier. In view of the feelings of builders, especially those involved in multi-family housing, one of the ways in which the overall cost of housing can be reduced is through higher density zoning. One other factor which is significant is the size of the individual land parcel. Builders are predisposed to small-sized parcels, as development costs per housing unit are about equal for similar-sized parcels, but rise as the parcel on which the housing unit is built becomes larger. As a result, a one-acre parcel rarely is twice the price of a half acre parcel. (A one-acre lot is rarely exactly 43,560 square feet or even within 5% or 10% of it. When land is subdivided, the builder is somewhat free to parcelize as he desires, with approval of the local authorities. The builder will make lots as small as possible and with as few front feet as possible to cut down on development costs.) Usually, it is somewhat less, a discount in effect to offset the higher development costs. Running contrary to this trend is the fact that home buyers often view ownership of a one-acre parcel as a status goal. Also one-acre parcels are a common breaking point in zoning ordinances; land is zoned for one-acre development on the basis that the higher cost of the land will insure a higher income owner. The builder also understands this and is willing to go along unless the development cost rises to a point where he will have to argue for a zone change in order to assure himself of sufficient buyers with the ability to pay the higher price. The predominant trend is, the larger the lot, the higher the price and the development cost, but size is not linearly related to cost. (A typical case that illustrates the frustrations encountered to obtain a change in zone is the case of one developer in the Region. This developer owned or had control of 100 acres zoned for single family houses on two acre parcels. The land had good drainage and water and sewer utilities could be provided. Requesting a change of zone to permit greater density of development, the developer found discussions stalled for a long period of time. A tentative agreement for higher density housing, but only for the elderly, was attacked by one local group as disturbing the ecology and discriminatory to younger families. No matter what concessions were made, the developer met a stone wall of opposition, with arguments devised to rebut each possible type of agreement. The land is reported to be for sale at its original two acre density level.) From the perspective of the use of land on a regional basis, the size and cost of the parcel has both positive and negative impacts. The fact of extensive large lot zoning which tends to drive up the price of housing could be considered in the interests of conserving a limited commodity, except that there are a sufficiently large number of households willing to pay the price to use up the commodity. Another negative aspect is to keep the lower income household out. Exhaustion of the land supply is less of a problem if it is used in an efficient economic fashion. Large lot zoning (over ½ or ¾ acre) is not economically efficient. Builders will argue that anything over ¼ acre is inefficient in an area with public water and sewer service: if the area is not provided with utilities, larger lots are needed for septic fields and underground water sources.

Ultimately, the relationship between land costs and construction is a function of the market for the particular units at a given price level. This factor leads to varying levels of land cost for essentially the same type of unit in different areas. For any number of reasons (a good many of them non-economic), prospective purchasers or tenants are willing to pay more for land and housing in some areas than in others.

For example, single family land costs in Fairfield and Westchester Counties are generally similar for the same type of area; land of the same size parcels in suburban towns in both counties costs about the same (Table A). However, different sized single family parcels in these counties are priced at varying levels. Accordingly, an acre building site with water and sewer utilities costs from $15,000 to $20,000; a half-acre or smaller parcel in cities in both counties (also with water and sewers) costs somewhat less than a suburban one acre lot in Westchester County, but more than a one acre parcel in Fairfield County.

Land in Nassau County is scarce; there are few communities on the south shore with land available which is zoned for single-family housing. In some communities (Parkville Center, for example), zoning provides for one-seventh acre plots which sell for $20,000 (Table A). The same size lot is priced at $15,000 in Baldwin, but there are reported to be few lots remaining. Land in the northern part of Nassau (Town of North Hempstead and Oyster Bay) is available, but at very high prices. These are individual single family lots in residential sections. Most areas in Nassau County are served by water and sewer facilities.

Land for single-family development in Suffolk County is generally available; these lots are parcels without water and sewer outlets which sell for $4,000 to $6,000 (Table A). Most of the land is along the southern shore or in the central portion of Suffolk. Generally, land farther east on the island sells for the lower end of the range ($4,000) while land farther west, closer to New York City, sells for more ($6,000). Some parts of Suffolk have both water and sewer facilities; the former is more prevalent than the latter. Accordingly, single-family housing in some areas of the southern and central portions have a public water supply along with septic tanks.

In the New Jersey counties (Bergen, Essex and Middlesex), lot sizes are generally smaller than in Westchester, Fairfiled or Suffolk, but building sites in the more intensely developed towns are usually more expensive than land of roughly the same size in the less built up areas. The eastern sections of Bergen, Essex and Middlesex Counties have more intensive development than the western sections. (Table A). One of the factors accounting for the variation is the general availability of in-ground utilities (water and sewer) in the more developed areas.

Land costs for multi-family structures (garden apartments or town houses, at densities of less than 20 units per acre or high rise buildings of greater than 30 units per acre) are usually much lower than for single-family houses. Most multi-family housing is built on land which is served by public water and sewer facilities and located in the more densely settled parts of the suburban New York Region. Within the multi-family category, land for high-rise units costs less per unit than does land for the less dense garden apartment-town house style construction. Nonetheless, there can be considerable variation in land costs for each type of structure in the same areas as well as between areas.

Comparing garden apartment-town house land costs in New York counties to Fairfield County in Connecticut indicates that costs are higher in the latter county, and that there is a considerable range in costs in particular areas (Table B). Suffolk County, in New York, and Middlesex, in New Jersey, have similar per unit land costs. Fairfield land costs are much higher than in any of the other counties included in this report. The same type of variation observed for the less densely built multi-family units also holds for high-rise developments (Table B). Land costs are highest in Fairfield and Nassau Counties and around White Plains in Westchester County. Costs are more nearly the same in the remaining four counties.

The variation in costs within a particular area can be due to many factors such as the ability of prospective tenants to pay enough rent to support a high land cost, and the availability of sites. In the urban areas, such as Stamford, White Plains and Irvington, costs will tend to be higher than in more suburban locales. However, there is usually very little land available in suburban locations already zoned for multi-family use. While it is not possible to differentiate land zoned for multi-family use prior to construction from that where a special permit or zone change is required, the former situation would normally result in a higher land cost than the latter in both urban and suburban locations.

The availability of land for multi-family housing is not uniform throughout the Region. Land for high-rise structures is mostly located in the cities (or major villages or boroughs) while land zoned for garden apartments and two houses is more likely to be located in village and town areas. Many communities exclude multi-unit housing completely or permit it only on land which is zoned for another use. In other instances, the land zoned for multi-unit housing has been developed and any additional housing of this type must be authorized by local jurisdiction through a zone change or special permit.

Accordingly, land costs for multi-family housing in many instances is not a reflection of the actual land costs. If land zoned for single-family use is purchased and then a zone change for multi-family housing is obtained, the original land cost is indicative of the price structure for land zoned for single-family use. Another situation which causes problems in comparing multi-family land cost is that many projects have been constructed on land purchased from urban renewal agencies. These land costs will generally be much below the going rate for non-urban renewal land.

Communities in all of the study area counties have urban renewal programs or have granted zone changes. Stamford and Bridgeport in Fairfield County, White Plains, Mount Vernon, Yonkers and New Rochelle in Westchester, and many villages in Nassau County have had urban renewal programs involving new housing construction on publicly-owned land. In New Jersey, similar programs have been carried out in Hackensack, Newark and other Essex and Bergen County communities. Zone changes and the granting of special permits is widespread in all counties. The examples cited in attached Tables A, B, C of land costs for multi-family units in the study area counties cannot be considered as necessarily typical. Rather, the land costs should be thought of as specific examples which may not apply to other communities in the same area or even to other multifamily projects in the same community.

In assessing the significance of the land component in relation to overall housing costs, a comparison between the respective average annual rates of increase in land costs and household income was developed. Increases in the price of land (both single and multi-family) for selected areas in the seven county suburban New York Region range from a low of about 5% to a high of over 30% per year (Table C). The majority of the rates of increase in land costs are between 5% and 10% per year.

A comparison between the rises in the costs of residential land to increases in income in the seven counties indicates that the former has generally risen at a faster rate than the latter. The greater increases in land costs compared to income reflect a period of rapidly rising prices (1965 through 1968 or 1969) which was paralleled, but not equalled, by general inflationary increases. On a national basis, family income rose by 8% in 1968 and 9% in 1969. Average annual land cost increases for the Region were about the same order of magnitude. However, data for the New York Region (Table D) showed generally a lower overall rate of increases in family and per capita income than for the nation as a whole. (Lower rates of gain in income in the New York area are partly due to a higher overall level of income compared to other sections of the county.) A partial exception is evident for increase in land prices and income in Essex County where the rate of gain in income is greater than rises in the cost of land in the West Orange-Milburn area (Tables C and D).

The implication of a faster rise in land prices than in incomes is that, by 1970, the cost of housing was requiring a larger share of total income than in the middle 1960's.

In January, 1971, the Bureau of Labor Statistics reported that "between December, 1969 and December, 1970, area housing costs have risen by 9.3%—one of the fastest rising major components of the Consumer Price Index. The index for homeownership costs showed a sharp over-the-year increase of close to 15 percent. In recent months, the area rent index has also begun to register substantial increases. In fact, for the 12 months ending December, 1970, residential rents rose by 6.2 percent—the sharpest over-the-year increase since the February, 1958—February, 1959 period."

The annual decline in housing starts, which began in the middle Sixties, caused construction labor unions to harden their resistance to admitting increased numbers of workers into their respective trades in order to preserve decreasing job opportunities for their members. (Coinciding with the heightened efforts of blacks and Puerto Ricans to enter the construction trades, the stance of the construction unions brought them into bitter conflicts with the civil rights forces.) The effect of the unions' resistance was to increase construction costs by (a) creating local shortages of skills from time-to-time that caused costly delays in completions and (b) improving the bargaining position of the union to enable it to increase wage rates by larger increases than prevailed for wage earners as a whole.

The cost of building materials did not reflect the lessening demand due to declining housing starts in the late Sixties. The wholesale index of construction materials moved upward, sometimes outpacing the rises in the consumer price index. In the Fall of 1971 the construction materials index stood at 123 from a 1967 base of 100. However, materials that represent a large part of single-family home construction were leading the index, with lumber at 142, asphalt roofing at 131 and insulation materials at 134.

THE EFFECT OF PROPERTY TAXES

The New York Metropolitan Region's housing market was also affected sharply by exceptional increases in local property taxes during the latter half of the Sixties. Long identified as an anachronism left over from our agricultural beginnings, the property tax has survived because it is basically a regressive tax, i.e., falling most heavily upon those least able to pay. As with all sales taxes, which it is, in effect, the property tax takes an increasingly larger proportion of a family's income as it stands in lower rank on an income scale.

Most governmental services are provided by the smallest units of government; towns, villages, cities, school districts and special districts provide the multiplicity of services and facilities which make the suburbs so enviable a place of residence in the eyes of many urban dwellers. The outstanding exception is provision of social services (welfare) which is a county function in New York and New Jersey. There are no longer any county governments in Connecticut. Traditionally, one of the major attractions of suburban living was the supposed superior schooling available to residents' children. Accordingly, in the late 1950's, attention focused on this area and many new schools were built, often with supplementary facilities such as swimming pools, elaborate auditoriums, and spacious grounds. The costs of these facilities and the highly trained teachers to man them boosted education costs substantially.

In the three New York counties, annual education costs rose by an average of 11% per year for the period 1964 to 1968. In New Jersey, the average annual increases in the operating costs of schools varied from 8% per year to 9% per year for the 1964 and 1966 period. These increases reflect the rising costs of wages and salaries for teachers and other employees, high costs for teaching materials, and, to some extent, the higher construction costs of the new facilities in the form of interest and debt payments.

Relatively high rates of increase in costs of other services are also evident for the same period for municipal functions such as fire and police protection, the local judicial system, local administration (clerks, secretaries, supervisors, managers, councilmen), highway maintenance and snow removal, local planning and zoning and the many other local functions. In the 1964 to 1968 period, these costs rose by 5% to 8% per year for all towns in New York (except for Suffolk County) and about 6% per year for all villages. In Suffolk County, the annual rate of increase was one percent, but, in this case, the villages are relatively small and have not had large increases in population. In New Jersey municipalities, from 1965 to 1969, the average annual rate of increase for current operating expenditures varied from 6% to 8%. These rates are for cities, boroughs and townships combined, analogous to combining the city, town and village information for New York State municipalities. In spite of the slightly different method of presentation, the average annual increases in the cost of municipal operating expenses appear relatively similar for New York and New Jersey communities.

An average value home of $30,000 that is carried on the assessment rolls at $24,000 (80% of market value) in a suburban municipality with a tax rate of $50 per $1,000 pays $1,200 per year in property taxes or $!00 per month for local services alone. Adding taxes to high mortgage rates and the fact that most buyers of a $30,000 house assume a mortgage of $20,000 to $25,000, results in carrying charges of $300 to $350 per month. This requires an annual income of about $15,000 (with withholding for income taxes compensated for by deductions for local taxes and interest). It is estimated that only about 10% of the Region's households with a head under the age of 35 are in a position to assume housing costs in this dimension. This is a radically different housing market that that of the 1950's when mortgage rates were 4% to 5%, taxes $25 per $1,000, and assessed values tended to run from $6,000 to $12,000. It was quite easy for young families to assume the costs of homeownership under those condiions, which required a much smaller proportion of the household budget to be earmarked for shelter. Not only was it easier statistically, but several million young families proved they could afford it in a vast migration to suburban communities consisting of tract housing on 60x100 foot lots, with quarter-acre sites considered generous. (During this hey-day of the suburban homebuyer, discrimination against blacks and Puerto Ricans was blatant and universal and minority families were effectively excluded.)

THE RISE IN MULTI-FAMILY STARTS

As the behavior of the housing market in the New York Metropolitan Region changed during the 1960's those priced out of the homebuying market remained in apartments and the newly formed young families joined their numbers annually. Elderly couples also sought apartments as this cost of carrying single-family homes went up and as pensions permitted others to maintain households who would otherwise have been institutionalized or living with off-spring. The result was a growing demand for apartments in all parts of the Metropolitan Region, including the suburbs, and a response by the building industry with a rapid escalation in multi-family starts, beginning in the late 1950's when the number of units in multi-family structures built annually began to equal and then exceed new single-family homes. In 1965, as the total number of starts began to decline, apartment units represented 60% of all starts. By 1970, apartment units represented 67% and single-family starts had dropped to 25,200 from the decade's high of $50,200 in 1965.

Most significant was the shift in location of apartment construction activity to the suburbs, where, with few exceptions, county ratios show apartment starts increasing and single-family home starts decreasing. Comparing the first half of the decade (1960-64) to the second half (1965-69) reveals that multi-family units in Bergen County moved from 48.1% of all starts in the first half to 60.8% in the second half; for Middlesex from 46% to 57.7% for Fairfield from 27.2 to 39.2; for Nassau from 31.8 to 47.5; for Suffolk from 8.9 to 14.2%; and for Westchester from 54.7 to 65%. Additionally, single-family starts were offset by losses due to demolition and fires, especially clearance in the older suburbs to create sites for apartment houses, to a greater degree than were multi-family units. In Essex County, for instance, the inventory of single-family homes declined by 2,694 between 1960 and 1970, while in Hudson County the figure for declines was 3,504. Queens, though part of the City of New York, exhibits many of the characteristics of a close-in suburban county; it lost 9,031 single-family homes from its housing stock between 1960 and 1970.

Despite ubiquitous, and often fierce, opposition from local groups, builders managed to squeeze apartments into many suburban communities that had experienced little or no multi-family construction since World War II, mainly in the older suburbs. Of a total of 497,818 dwelling units added in the Region *outside* of New York City between 1960 and 1970, 304,761 units were in multifamily structures.

It is now clear that the projections of the 1950's which saw the wave of single-family construction as the wave of the future, and saw "Levittowns" as the prototype of suburban settlement, were being misled by a temporary phenomenon that was flying in the face of housing economics, the historical behavior of money markets, municipal solvency, and the geometry of space. The housing patterns of large metropolitan areas in the United States are being "Europeanized." Both the 7% interest rate and the predominance of multi-family construction appear to have become facts of life in the New York Metropolitan Region, despite the futile—though dreadfully harmful—antics of entrenched suburban majorities who seek to realize a utopian dream of unrelieved, low density, single-family house development in the face of urban reality. The effort to impose the dream by force of legislative majorities will turn it into a nightmare—a long night of terror that sees race pitted against race, "haves" against "have nots," city against suburb, owner against tenant, taxpayer against welfare recipient, and police-enforced law and order against traditional American liberties. The mundane, at times boring, data set down by the shifts and turns of the housing market in the 1960's have a searing message for the New York Metropolitan Region—the socio-economic format for urban settlement that began emerging in the 1950's is unworkable and should be deliberately restructured, beginning with an immediate reversal of present policies, to avoid catastrophe.

THE SUBURBAN ZONING BARRIER

The zoning barrier that surrounds New York City started innocently enough. Zoning began in New York City in 1961; it might be said, therefore, that the city is being strangled in its own noose. Its origins in New York City were not innocent. It was conceived as a legal device to keep the needle trades shops with their lower class, immigrant workers away from the "carriage trade" retail stores on Fifth Avenue. Zoning would keep separate conflicting land uses and prevent overcrowding, thus saving new suburban areas from the blight and disorder so visible in older cities. However, in that very image lay the seeds of its misuse. A latter day version put the purpose of zoning as "to prevent the Bronxification of Westchester," or "the Brooklynization of Long Island," or "to keep Harlem from coming across the George Washington Bridge." The obejctive of keeping the suburbs from "looking like the city" became confused with keeping the suburbs free from the social problems of the city, most easily achieved, many suburbanites thought, by keeping them free of the races and classes of mankind they considered to be the source of the problems. Such confusion comes readily in a status-conscious, race-conscious culture.

The licit and illicit rules of the "zoning game" as outlined in Richard Babcock's *The Zoning Game* are not difficult to discern and document. The objective is to create a community that is as trouble-free an island as human ingenuity can make it in a troubled urban sea, by regulating land use and building construction to provide homes for those deemed desirable and to exclude homes for those deemed undesirable, and to do it as cheaply as possible by attracting non-residential uses that pay taxes but require few services. This is done by creating an income level filter in the form of housing costs by (a) barring housing built specifically for low-income households (subsidized housing); (b) permitting apartments only if rentals will be high and bedrooms few; and (c) by requiring excessively large lots to increase the cost of each property and to limit the number of inhabitants by "using up" the buildable land.

Our study probed the zoning practices of nearly three dozen suburban communities and interviewed hundreds of their residents: Mayors, planning board members, real estate brokers, League of Women Voters members, Chamber of Commerce officials, opposition political leaders, taxpayer association representatives, fair housing groups, civil rights activists, etc. The dialogue invariably pursued the "choreography" of the "Dance of the Seven Veils," that most apt metaphoric description of suburban rationalization for exclusionary practices coined by Professor George Sternlieb of Rutgers.

The list of veils that emerges as a composite of our community interviews is approximately the following:

Fiscal. "We cannot afford it. Our taxes are sky high and our schools are full. Anyone who wants to live here must be prepared to pay their way."

Interviewer: What if the state paid for your schools, and health and welfare were a Federal obligation?

Ecological. "Increased densities will ruin the environment. We already have water quality problems and the town dump cannot handle any more solid waste."

Interviewer.: Since these problems require adequate treatment facilities to correct, why not design them for more than your present density?

Community Character: "Higher densities would ruin the character of our community. We like it this way and we want to keep it this way."

Interviewer: Since anyone who would come here to live would do so, in part, because they like your community, why not enlist them in your effort to keep it attractive? After all, leading architects and urban designers insist that higher densities need not destroy a community's attractiveness.

Status: "We are not just any town. Our residents are fine people. They came here because they knew that this was a community of fine people. The people who live here have given this community a fine reputation. We want to continue to feel proud of our community."

Interviewer: Would it not be in keeping with America's democratic traditions to have fine people of less income live in your fine community?

Quality Schools: "This is a highly educated community. Most of our residents are college people. We have insisted on the very best schools. Many of our people bought homes here because of the reputation of our school system. We never have trouble in our schools. It's a good learning environment. Bring a different type of kid in and the quality is bound to suffer."

Interviewer: Isn't the insulation of your children from contact with groups that are representative of the American people as a whole a poor preparation for living and working as adults in our cosmopolitan society, beginning in college? Aren't you really cheating them?

Crime: "Everyone knows that poverty breeds crime. The few poor people we have around here have been good people from good stock. But if you get a lot of poor people living together there are bound to be criminal types among them. This is a town where we feel safe on the streets at night and go away without locking our doors. We like it that way. If we didn't we could live in New York."

Interviewer: Since the suburban crime rate is going up and since it is more likely that criminals will be from outside the community, not from within, where they are known, are not you going to be forced to put a wall around your town and check everyone who enters the gates?

Race: "I have nothing aginst Negroes. I think they should have all the rights a white man has. There are good and bad in all groups. But I am not in favor of social experiments. Mixing people of such different backgrounds has never worked and only causes trouble. Not that we would try to prevent a black doctor or professor from living here. But when you put up housing that ordinary blacks can afford you're inviting trouble. We are not going to have it."

Interviewer: Would you not say that this is the really basic issue involved in your zoning and housing policy? In any case, thank you for coming to the point.

Our interviews uncovered everywhere an uneasiness in suburban communities that seemed always on the edge of hysteria when questions seemed to suggest change of local patterns. After the initial bland avowal of broad, altruistic motives in local planning and zoning, community spokesmen tended to tense up when pressed and the veils would start coming off, accompanied by the code words of fear: "high taxes," "overcrowding," "community character," "good schools," "drugs, crime and safety," and vague references to "different kinds of people." The mention of the word "apartments" can fill a high school auditorium with an emotional audience for a public hearing quicker than any other words except perhaps "public housing" and "busing."

Data assembled by the project's consultants (Roy Girard of Economic Consultants, Inc.) for the selected counties studied, shows that a "severe limitation on quantity of land zoned for multi-family use" exists in almost all municipalities having significant amounts of vacant land and that it has reduced the supply of rental housing in the suburbs.

In Connecticut such well-known commuter suburbs as Darien, Greenwich, New Canaan, Weston, Westport and Wilton, either prohibited multi-family construction, or permitted it in areas that represented a minute fraction of the municipality's land area, usually either already built upon or zoned for a wide variety of uses: industry, business, etc. Such multi-use zoning increased land costs and discouraged mortgage commitments to the extent that permission for multi-family use was a meaningless gesture. By contrast, Connecticut's older industrial towns zoned large percentages of their land area for multi-family construction and extensive building of such housing took place during the 1960's, as is evidenced by the number of dwelling units in buildings of 5 or more apartments added in Bridgeport (5,136), Norwalk (1,503), and Stamford (4,903).

The same pattern exists in Westchester County: Towns with significant amounts of vacant buildable land and low-density, large-lot developments zoned tiny fractions or no land for multi-family use, as in Mamaroneck (1.7%), Mount Pleasant (0.2%), New Castle (none), North Castle (0.5%), North Salem (none), Pound Ridge (none), Somers (none), Yorktown (0.4%), Scarsdale (0.2%), and Larchmont (1.7%). In contrast, the densely built up communities zoned extensively for multi-family use provided the land for most of the multi-family units built in Westchester in the 1960's. Examples are Mount Vernon, zoned 44.7% multi-family and 1,759 units added in the 1960's; Yonkers, zoned 27.1% multi-family and 9,024 units added in the '60s; White Plains, zoned 18.1% multi-family and 3,043 units added in the '60s; Ossining, zoned 32.5% multi-family and 1,195 units added; and New Rochelle, 8.1% multifamily and 1,555 units added in the 1960's.

In Nassau County such densely inhabited communities as Long Beach, Freeport, Hempstead (Village) and Mineola accommodated a high percentage of the county's multi-family construction in the 1960's, while the low density communities with much vacant land, zoned to exclude or discourage multi-family use, as in the unincorporated areas of the Town of Oyster Bay and such villages as Sands Point, Brookville, Old Westbury, North Hills, Old Brookville, and Oyster Bay Cove.

In Bergen County, New Jersey, multi-family construction in the 1960's has been concentrated in such relatively high density areas as Hackensack, Fort Lee, Lodi, Ridgefield Park and Wallington, while zoning excluded multi-family building from such familiar commuter towns as Allendale, Alpine, Closter, Cresskill, Demarest, Emerson, Englewood Cliffs, Franklin Lakes, Glen Rock, Harrington Park, Haworth, Ho-ho-Kus, Norwood, Oakland, Old Tappan, Park Ridge, Riverdale, Tenafly, Upper Saddle River, Woodcliff Lake and Wycoff.

Even in such a heavily populated county as Essex, a number of municipalities with considerable amounts of vacant land exclude apartments, as in Essex Fells, Fairfield, Livingston, North Caldwell, West Caldwell and Roseland. Multi-family construction is concentrated largely in Newark, Orange, East Orange, Irvington, Bloomfield, and Belleville, old cities in the process of renewal, and in Caldwell, Montclair, Verona and West Orange where high rental, small unit construction has been permitted, largely in high rise buildings.

Middlesex County contains far fewer examples of extreme limitation placed upon multi-family construction or complete prohibition by local zoning. However, Cranbury, South Plainfield, Spottswood, Monroe and South Brunswick, which fall into this category, represent a total land area of almost 70,000 acres, about half of which is vacant. As a consequence, the relatively high percentage of multi-family units in the county's housing increase in the 1960's is concentrated in the northern portion of Middlesex.

The exclusion and severe limitation of multi-family construction by those suburban communities with large amounts of buildable, vacant land has not only reduced the supply of rental housing in the suburbs but has created an unbalanced distribution of such units, forcing additional apartments into the older, more developed portions. Freedom of choice as to location, especially to facilitate access to employment, or such environmental amenities as open space has been severely curtailed for those who rent.

The inventory of housing in the Metropolitan Region outside of New York City (1970) still consists of an overwhelming proportion of single family houses: 2,002,055 such structures as compared to 1,339,152 dwelling units in multi-family buildings. This reflects the historic pattern of predominantly one-family house construction in New York's suburbs before 1960. During the decade of 1960-70, the inventory of one-family houses grew by 174,341 outside of New York City, an increase of 0.8%. During the same period, the inventory of multi-family units grew by 304,761, an increase of 2.2%. This was in a ratio of almost two apartment units for each one-family unit.

In the face of this performance in the suburban housing markets, almost all suburban municipalities with significant amounts of vacant land zoned it for single-family construction only!

Repeated and persistent efforts to initiate a detailed survey of the zoning designation of vacant, buildable land in the Tri-State Metropolitan Region, involving an effort to bring together for collaborative work HUD, the Tri-State Regional Planning Commission and the state planning offices of Connecticut, New Jersey and New York, were not successful. The only survey that was completed and quanitifed was in New Jersey. Initiated by Paul Ylvisaker, Commissioner of Community Affairs in the Administration of Gov. Richard J. Hughes, the study was carried forward under the direction of Sidney Willis, State Planning Director, with the encouragement of Gov. William T. Cahill as part of his commitment to breaking the housing stalemate in New Jersey. The latter survey provides shocking evidence of the miscarriage of zoning by that State's suburban municipalities.

The New Jersey survey of zoning shows that in Bergen County only 0.5% of vacant, buildable land is zoned for multi-family use, though 80% of all dwelling units built in that county between 1960 and 1970 were in multi-family structures. In Middlesex County, only 0.3% of vacant buildable land is zoned multi-family, though 65% of all dwelling units built between 1960 and 1970 were multifamily. In Monmouth County, 0.3% such land zoned multi-family, though 49% of units built during the same period were multi-family. In Morris County, only 1.1% of such land zoned multi-family, though 53% of all units built during the same period were multi-family. In Passaic County, only 3.4% of all such land is zoned multi-family, though 82% of all units built during same period were multi-family.

In Union County, with 98% of all dwelling units built between 1960 and 1970 in multi-family structures, there are only 332 acres of vacant, buildable land zoned for multi-family use, though some 4,409 acres are zoned for one-family construction only. In Somerset County there is not a single acre zoned for multi-family use though 48% of its dwelling unit additions between 1960 and 1970 were in the multi-family category. Even in densely built-up Essex County, there are 6,343 acres of vacant, buildable land zoned for single-family use and only 68 acres for multi-family use; this in a county that had a *loss* of

2,694 single family structures from its housing inventory between 1960 and 1970, with the result that multi-family construction accounted for 123% of all additions to the inventory.

The same survey reveals that in Morris County, 81.2% of all vacant land zoned for residential use requires minimum lot sizes of two acres or more. The same figure for other counties is Somerset, 85%; Monmouth, 84%; Bergen, 54.8%; Passaic, 42%; and Middlesex, 38.5%.

Many suburban communities zone for minimum floor area in one-family structures to assure sufficient house size to result in a value sufficiently high to screen out families on the basis of income and to assure the municipality a satisfactory tax return. Such a requirement to build to a minimum size is defended on family health grounds though it bears no relationship to crowding since it does not relate to number of members of the household, as do housing ordinances. Thus a couple with no children, whether young or old, are required to build the same Procrustean minimum as a family with two, four, six or eight children. The reference to health and crowding is obviously not valid. The requirement for ample family space stands in stark contrast to zoning ordinance requirements of many of the same municipalities that seek to restrict apartment dwellers in the space they can occupy by requiring builders to limit their units to 80% with one bedroom and 20% with two bedrooms.

A requirement of 1,200 sq. ft. for single family houses is the most common in New Jersey. At the prevailing rate of about $20 per square foot for single-family house construction, this requires an expenditure of $24,000 for construction alone. Site improvement and land costs easily bring the total cost over $30,000.

An interesting question arises from the high percentage of multi-family units built during the decade of 1960 to 1970 and the extreme paucity of vacant land zoned for multi-family use. One possible answer that might suggest itself is that almost all the land zoned for multi-family was used for this purpose in the 1960's. This possibility is countered by Regional Plan Association's findings in 1960, which showed very little land zoned for multi-family use in these same counties. It is also countered by the fact that Somerset County had no vacant land zoned for multi-family during this period, but yet added 7,635 multi-family units.

The answer appears to be in these circumstances: the massive demand for rental housing in the 1960's, swollen by households priced out of the single-family market, sent builders scouting for land with a fine tooth comb and resulted in getting apartment houses on parcels in every possible cranny and crevice, mainly in older suburban communities where land assembly involved some demolition. This is suggested by the disappearance of 2,694 single-family houses from the housing inventory of Essex County. The fact that Union County showed a gain of only 311 single-family homes in 10 years suggests that this is the net gain after many one-family structures were demolished to make way for at least a portion of the 19,828 multi-family units added.

The second explanation is that many of the multi-family units were constructed on land that was zoned for single-family use (or a non-residential use) but rezoned specifically for a given multi-family project. Rezoning for multi-family use by negotiation with the builder has become the prevailing method of getting apartment buildings constructed on vacant land.

Both of these circumstances under which multi-family housing gets built are fraught with evil consequences. The first circumstance, land assembly and demolition in old suburban communities, can contribute to overcrowding and to a stratification by race and income. Thus multi-family construction is concentrated in such communities as New Rochelle, Yonkers, Mount Vernon, East Orange, Hackensack and Hempstead, while thousands of acres of vacant land are locked up by single-family zoning.

The second circumstance, negotiated rezoning of vacant land for multi-family construction, permits the suburban "town fathers" to impose their conditions in back room agreements with the builder (not to speak of the incentives for corruption as evidenced by some indictments).

Conditions sought by suburban officials usually reduce the units per acre, the floors per building, and the bedrooms per apartment, while adding every type of amenity likely to make the construction more expensive and necessitate higher rentals.

RACIAL DISCRIMINATION IN SUBURBAN SALES AND RENTALS

The enactment of a Federal open housing law (Title VIII, Civil Rights Act) in 1968 and of state laws on this subject over a decade ago in New York, New Jersey and Connecticut has not ended widespread discrimination against Blacks and Puerto Ricans in residential property sales and rentals in the suburbs of the New York Metropolitan Region. The findings of the study on racial discrimination were reported in considerable detail in the *Interim Report*, based on a survey of the operation of the real estate market in the suburbs by Anne Montero, civil rights/housing specialist, as consultant to the project. The study's monitoring of enforcement of open housing laws subsequent to this report has served to confirm the interim findings, viz, that open housing laws have driven discrimination "underground," where it operates through more subtle and sophisticated practices that continue to constitute an effective barrier to minority homeseekers who do not limit their search to ghetto areas.

The study's findings indicate that very few significant steps have been taken to make more effective the enforcement of open housing laws. Noteworthy as gains in this period are the following:

> Institution of legal proceedings by NCDH and the United Auto Workers to establish the jurisdiction of the New Jersey Division of Civil Rights in zoning where it has the effect of exclusion of persons from residence in the municipality by race. The Attorney General's opinion that the Division does not have jurisdiction has been appealed to the courts, where it is awaiting trial.

> Hearings have been completed on the first major "pattern and practice" suit in the New York Metropolitan Region, brought by the New Jersey Division of Civil Rights against some 19 apartment projects in Parsippany-Troy Hills. These projects contain some 5,600 apartments, only 30 of which were occupied by Blacks. At this writing, the hearing examiner's decision has not yet been given.

> The New Jersey Division of Civil Rights adopted, after hearings and

publication, a rule that requires owners of multiple dwellings containing 25 units or more to report annually the racial composition of tenants and applicants, as well as information on rental turn-over, recruiting techniques, rental rates and apartment sizes. The rule, challenged by apartment owners, is pending in court.

A U.S. Department of Justice pattern and practice suit was filed against the Lefrak realty organization, managers of 150 buildings with 21,000 apartments, mainly in Queens and Brooklyn. It marked the first such suit by the Department of Justice in the New York area. The suit was based on research and documentation by the New York Urban League's Operation Open City project. To the disappointment of civil rights organizations, the Department of Justice dropped the case on the basis of a negotiated settlement in which Lefrak promised to stop discriminating and to assist 50 Negro and Puerto Rican families living in Lefrak's segregated buildings in moving to buildings occupied by whites. The Urban League characterized the latter offer as "straight tokenism." The ineffectual conclusion of the Lefrak case typified Department of Justice resolution of most of its cases under Title VIII, which numbered little more than 100 for the entire United States by the end of 1971.

A major effort of HUD's Equal Opportunity office has been directed toward a public relations campaign in the Eastern half of the country, designed to alert minority homeseekers to their rights under Title VIII. Television, radio and newspaper announcements furnish them with a toll-free telephone number to make complaints. It is indicative of Federal reliance on the one-by-one complaint-by-complaint process.

The Federal Section 235 Program, which enables low-income families to become homeowners through subsidized mortgage rates of as low as one percent, was implemented throughout the New York Metropolitan Region, with few exceptions, through the dual real estate market. Black and Puerto Rican buyers were sold ghetto property, and white buyers were sold homes in white neighborhoods. This pattern seems to have been national. The sales were also beset with widespread fraud. Blacks and Puerto Ricans were victimized by the sale of deteriorated properties that proved unlivable without major repairs for heating, plumbing and wiring that were beyond the means of the new low-income owners.

Fair housing counselors who worked with miniroty buyers in the 235 Program reported bitterly that most white brokers were uncooperative, that most Black brokers sold overpriced, deteriorated slum property, and that the only ones likely to give a minority buyer good housing for his money were the blockbusting brokers who handled properties sold by panicked whites leaving the area. The ease with which brokers corrupted the 235 Program into a tool for strengthening racial separation indicates how little effect Federal and state laws to curb discrimination by the real estate industry have had. The racist misuse of the 235 Program, in flagrant violation of Federal and state laws, caused no headlines nor orders from Washington to stop the whole program until reformed. The Federal Government acted to remedy the situation only when it became widely known that brokers were also using the 235 Program to line their pockets with fraudulent gains at the expense, ultimately, of American taxpayers.

MAJOR CONCLUSIONS AND RECOMMENDATIONS

When the National Advisory Commission on Civil Disorders observed that "our nation is moving toward two societies, one black, one white—separate and unequal," few realized how far the New York Metropolitan Region already had moved toward such division in the form of white suburbs and increasingly black cities.

It is the conclusion of NCDH, based on the study's findings, that a metropolitan region in which the poor, minorities, and the impoverished elderly will constitute the majority in New York City, and whites at all income levels except the very poor will constitute the overwhelming majority in the suburbs, will prove unworkable.

The economic trends of the 1960's which placed nearly three new jobs in the suburbs for each new job in New York City continue to favor the suburbs, even though the recession has greatly slowed the rate of new job formation. According to the *Regional Labor Statistics Bulletin*, No. 30, December 1971, U.S. Dept. of Labor, Bureau of Labor Statistics, Middle Atlantic Region, "Employment in the New York area's suburbs rose by 8,000 in 1971, in contrast to a 72,000 job decline in New York City and a 20,000 employment drop in the eight Northeastern New Jersey counties. Between 1969 and 1970, employment increases in the New York suburbs totaled 30,000 and 12,000 in the eight-county Northeastern New Jersey, while New York City's job total declined 34,000."

The outmigration of whites from New York City to its suburbs, which has totaled nearly two and a half million since 1950, continues, though slowed by the decline in housing starts.

New York City's relief rolls now exceed 1,100,000; one out of seven residents.

The fragmentation of the suburbs into wasteful mini-jurisdictions, unrelated to municipal resources or needs, all dependent upon local property taxes, has resulted in a fiscal crisis that threatens a breakdown of local services, especially schools.

The trip to work becomes longer, costlier and more uncertain for almost everyone.

Crime rates rise in the suburbs, and lawlessness and social disorganization rooted in central city slum conditions triggers building abandonment and population evacuation.

After studying urban trends, the National Commission on the Causes and Prevention of Violence, chaired by Dr. Milton S. Eisenhower, looked into the future of metropolitan areas in its *Final Report*.: "Between the unsafe, deteriorating central city on the one hand and the network of safe, prosperous areas and sanitized corridors on the other, there will be, not unnaturally, intensifying hatred and deepening division. Violence will increase further, and the defensive response of the affluent will become still more elaborate."

IMMEDIATE ACTION RECOMMENDATIONS:

1. An Executive Order suspending Federal grants and FHA and VA underwriting to all communities that refuse to participate in subsidized housing programs.

2. A declaration of emergency by Governors of Connecticut, New Jersey, and New York, suspending zoning ordinances in all municipalities with less than 10% of vacant land for multi-family use and with less than 25% of all existing dwelling units in multi-family structures. Such a declaration would be justified under emergency powers to protect the public welfare from the effect of the housing crisis.

3. Reduction by 50% in bus and rail fares, by utility commission order, and of bridge and tunnel tolls, by authorities' resolution, for reverse commuters, i.e., those traveling from New York City to outlying jobs in morning and returning in evening.

4. Concentration upon pattern and practice suits in use of Federal and state civil rights/Housing enforcement resources.

5. Adoption in New York and Connecticut of New Jersey's multiple dwelling reporting rule, requiring annual listing with state agency of race of occupants.

ADDITIONAL POLICY RECOMMENDATIONS:

1. That the Federal government act as "houser of last resort" by constructing or sponsoring housing for low- and moderate-income families wherever essential to protect the public welfare, as proposed by Senators Brooke and Mondale.

2. That housing for families of low- and moderate-income be allocated by an overall plan for the New York Metropolitan Region in accordance with a formula based on location of employment, vacant land, and transportation access, as pioneered in the widely-heralded Dayton (Ohio) plan. Such a metropolitan plan should be directed by a governmental commission representative of all groups and strata of the Region's population, as proposed for the San Francisco Bay Area by NCDH's demonstration project.

3. Limitation of local minimum lot-size requirement to ¼ acre, unless by special permit of state board of health, through amendment to state zoning enabling act.

4. State legislation requiring issuance of a certificate of convenience and necessity for each new industrial or commercial building to employ 25 or more persons in suburban counties, certifying the availability of housing at cost levels appropriate to wages and for sale or rent without discrimination.

5. Establishment of a central, computerized listing service capable of supplying upon public request information on houses and rentals by location, size, price, terms, etc., for entire New York Metropolitan Region, cross-referenced with information on local employment opportunities.

6. Amendment of Federal and state open housing laws to specify zoning as a

valid jurisdiction for investigation and action by civil rights enforcement agencies where racial discrimination and segregation is alleged to result.

7. Restructuring of state tax systems to remove responsibility for schools and welfare from municipalities and counties.

8. Investigations and public hearings in communities with *de facto* racial exclusion as per NCDH's pioneering program in San Leandro, California.

9. Legal requirement that offerings of residential property for sale or rental be listed publicly for a minimum number of days before acceptance of deposit from buyer or renter.

TABLE A
EXAMPLES OF SINGLE FAMILY LAND COSTS BY SIZE OF PARCEL
SELECTED COMMUNITIES, NEW YORK SUBURBAN REGION

Community and County	Size of Parcel	$1000.00 Cost per Parcel	Water and Sewer	Remarks
Connecticut:				
Fairfield County				
Bethel-Brookfield	1 or 2 acres	$15.0	No	Small number of ¼ acre lots
New Fairfield-				
Newton-Ridgefield	3 acres	15.0	No	–
Redding	3 to 5 acres	20.0–25.0	No	–
Stamford	½ acre	17.5–21.0	No	–
Danbury (area)	1 or 2 acres	10.0–15.0	No	–
Danbury (area)	1 or 2 acres	15.0–20.0	Yes	
Danbury (city)	50x100 feet	6.5	Yes	Few remaining
Bridgeport	Less than 1 acre	10.0	Yes	Some ¼ and ½ acre
Fairfield-Stratford	¼ acre	12.0	–	Parts have water and sewers
Trumbull	1/3 acre	10.0	No	–
Monroe-Easton	1 acre	10.0-15.0	No	–
New York:				
Westchester County				
Cortlandt-Yorktown	1 acre or less	9.0-14.0	No	Some areas have water
Somers-Bedford-				
New Castle	1 or 2 acres	15.0-20.0	Yes	–
Somers-Bedford-				
New Castle	2 acres or more	12.0	No	–
North Salem-				
Lewistown-				
Pound Ridge	1 to 4 acres	12.0-15.0	No	–
Mount Pleasant-				
North Castle	½ to 1 acre	7.5-12.5	Yes	–
Greenburgh	½ to 1 acre	15.0	Yes	–
White Plains-				
Yonkers	½ acre or less	10.0+	Yes	Few remaining
New Rochelle	½ acre or less	12.0+	Yes	Few remaining
Rye (city & area)	1 acre	20.0+	Yes	–
New York:				
Nassau County				
Baldwin	1/7 acre	15.0	Yes	Few remaining
Rockville Center	1/7 acre	20.0	Yes	–
New York:				
Suffolk County				
Throughout County	1 acre	4.0-6.0	No	–
New Jersey:				
Essex County				
Livingston-Roseland-				$40,000 acre for large parcels
North Caldwell	–	–	–	

TABLE A
EXAMPLES OF SINGLE FAMILY LAND COSTS BY SIZE OF PARCEL
SELECTED COMMUNITIES, NEW YORK SUBURBAN REGION

Community and County	Size of Parcel	$1000.00 Cost per Parcel	Water and Sewer	Remarks
New Jersey:				
Essex County (cont.)				
Millburn-Maplewood-				
South Orange-West				
Orange	1/6 acre	15.0	Yes	–
Scattered throughout				
city	1/6 acre	10.0-25.0	Yes	–
Livingston	3/4 acre	25.0	Yes	–
Livingston	1/3 acre	15.0	Yes	–
New Jersey:				
Bergen County				
South and eastern				individual lots
sections of county	1/6 acre	10.0-15.0	Yes	in built up areas
Englewood-Teaneck	1/6 acre	5.0-10.0	Yes	–
Paramus	1/4 acre	10.0	Yes	–
Harrington Park	1/3 acre	9.0	Yes	–
Upper Saddle River	1 acre	18.0-23.0	No	–
Tenafly	1 acre	4.5	Yes	–
New Jersey:				
Middlesex County				
Throughout County	1 acre	12.0-20.0	No	(raw land available
Throughout County	1 acre	15.0-25.0	Yes	(for development
Throughout County	1/6 acre	7.5-9.0	Yes	(individual lots in
Throughout County	1/4 acre	10.0	No	(built up areas
Sawville	1/4 acre	5.0	Yes	
Metuchen (area)	1 acre	15.0+	Yes	
Metuchen (area)	1 acre	12.0+	No	

SOURCE: Interviews with builders, developers, real estate agents, land appraisers and others, New York Suburban Region, 1970.

TABLE B
EXAMPLES OF MULTI-FAMILY LAND COSTS, BY TYPE OF DEVELOPMENT
SELECTED COMMUNITIES, NEW YORK SUBURBAN REGION
1969-1970

Community and County	Land Cost per Unit (000's)	
	Garden Apartment-Town Houses[1]	High Rise[2]
Fairfield County; Connecticut		
New Canaan	$12.5-16.0	−
Stamford	10.0-16.0	$7.5
Westchester County; New York		
White Plains (area)	5.0	3.0-8.0
Yonkers	3.0-7.0	2.0-5.0
Mount Kisco	−	3.0
Nassau County, New York		
Rockville Center	−	6.0-7.2[3]
Great Neck	7.0-8.0-	
Westbury	5.5	
Suffolk County, New York		
Babylon (area)	2.2-3.8	−
Brookhaven	3.0	−
Islip	2.8-3.5	
Bergen County, New Jersey		
Fort Lee	−	4.0+
Essex County, New Jersey		
Irvington	−	
Middlesex County, New Jersey		
East Brunswick	2.0	−

[1] Generally less than 20 units per acre.

[2] In excess of 20 units per acre.

[3] Based on a square footage cost of $6,000 for a 1,000 to 1,200 foot apartment unit.

Source: Interviews with builders, developers, real estate brokers, and appraisers in New York
Suburban Region, 1970.

TABLE C
AVERAGE ANNUAL RATE OF CHANGE IN COST OF LAND
SELECTED COMMUNITIES, NEW YORK SUBURBAN REGION
1970

Community and County	Period	Average Annual Percentage Change	Type of Land
Fairfield County, Connecticut			
Bridgeport area	1968-1970	5	Single family
New Canaan-Darien-Stamford	1967-1970	28	Multi-family
Westchester County, New York			
Mount Pleasant-New Castle	1943-1967	9	Single family
Croton-on-Hudson	1967-1969	10	Single family
Harrison	1965-1968	8	Single family
North Castle	1968-1970	10	Single family
Nassau County, New York			
Oceanside-Merrick- Valley Stream-Baldwin- Wantaugh-Seaford-Massapequa Rockville Center	1968-1970	5-7	Single family[1]
Throughout County	1968-1970	6	Single family[1]
Throughout County	1967-1970	11	Multi-family
Great Neck	1967-1970	28	Multi-family
Suffolk County, New York			
Centerreach (area)	1967-1970	10	Single family
Throughout County	1968-1970	8-10	Single family
Islip	1967-1970	28	Multi-family
Bergen County, New Jersey			
Harrington Park	1967-1970	18	Multi-family
Fort Lee	1965-1970	33	Multi-family
Western County	1960-1970	7	Single family
Paramus	1960-1970	8	Single family
Tenafly	1960-1970	8	Single family
Essex County, New Jersey			
Livingston	1968-1970	20	Single family
West Orange-Milburn	1960-1970	5	Single family

[1] Few lots remaining

TABLE C (Continued)
AVERAGE ANNUAL RATE OF CHANGE IN COST OF LAND
SELECTED COMMUNITIES, NEW YORK SUBURBAN REGION
1970

Community and County	Period	Average Annual Percentage Change	Type of Land
Middlesex County, New Jersey			
East Brunswick	1968-1970	34	Multi-family
Metuchen (area)	1960-1970	8-9	Single family

Source: Real estate brokers and land appraisers, New York Suburban Region, 1970.

TABLE D
ESTIMATE CHANGES IN INCOME LEVELS
COUNTIES, NEW YORK SUBURBAN REGION
1960-1970

County	Time Period	Percentage Change
Fairfield County	1965-1969	3.0[1]
Westchester County	1960-1970	5.6
Nassau County	1960-1966	4.8
Suffolk County	1960-1966	2.0
Bergen County	1960-1968	5.9
Essex County	1960-1968	7.8
Middlesex County	1960-1968	4.9

[1]Estimated composite for all of Fairfield County, based on income changes in various sub-parts of the county.

Source: Connecticut Division of Community Affairs and various local planning and economic studies for Fairfield County communities; New York Department of Commerce and local planning and economic studies; and Middlesex County Planning Board.

THE DAYTON AREA'S "FAIR SHARE" HOUSING PLAN ENTERS THE IMPLEMENTATION PHASE

Lois Craig

About 50 people came hesitantly into the auditorium of the West Carrollton Junior High School as if uncertain they had come to the right place. Or maybe it was the right place and they were reluctant to be there. The tentativeness was reflected in the scattered seating. Although many greeted the evening's speakers by first names, few chose to sit up front near the panel's table and slide projectors. Warm, stale air; bare, institutional lighting; from off-scene the sound of a school band's desultory version of John Philip Sousa; the faces of the speakers drawn with end-of-the-day fatigue.

A few weeks earlier 300 very angry people had gathered in the same community to confront the same panel on the same issue: a plan to disperse in four years 14,000 units of federally subsidized housing throughout the Dayton, Ohio metropolitan area on a "fair share" basis, computed on the basis of both community needs and capacities—in other words, a plan to build low- and moderate-income housing, including public housing, in white suburbs.

The panel members were from the staff of the Miami Valley Regional Planning Commission, which devised the plan, and this was one of more than 100 MVRPC presentations of it in the past year. The crowds have varied from a few dozen to several hundred and the intensity of the confrontation from reserved inquiry to noisy hostility depending on whether the discussion was about the idea of the plan or a specific project.

In some ways the West Carrollton meeting was typical. the opening slide show and presentation led by MVRPC director Dale Bertsch was professional and seemingly effortless. When it was over, no one could quarrel with the extent of housing needs in the metropolitan area. Since most decent citizens feel uncomfortable to quite say that the need ought to be taken care of in someone else's neighborhood, other objections have to be found, ranging from inadequate public services to crowded schools.

Often, as on this particular evening, there is one person who does not share the general reticence. He states defiantly that he is "a racist, although I have not always been one." Broken windows, crime, community destruction come with subsidized housing for "those people" who are, of course, black. Bertsch deals with the speaker with an angry directness, and one can feel the rest of the audience pulling away from the raw bigotry. According to Bertsch, the public meetings go better if someone unequivocally states the hate position at the beginning so that the staff can work with the confused consciences and often genuine fears of the rest of the group. A local minister closed this debate: "Joe didn't allow anyone to vote on him when he came. West Carrollton shouldn't have the right to vote on other people, poor people. What kind of people are we?"

To complaints about crowding the schools there is a logical reply: There is no control over the yield of children from housing built by the private market, while under the plan for government-sponsored housing the capacity of schools is taken into account so that the additional numbers of kids can be predicted for school board planning purposes. Further, an MVRPC study of an upper-income community found that ',very few, if any, single-family households actually pay their own way" for the costs of public education.

Questions about the size of projects elicit from Ann Shafor, MVRPC housing director, the suggestion that the community find several small sites and manage the housing on them as one project with MVRPC help. It is not, says Ms. Shafor, primarily the economics of building that defeat scattered site location but the economics of management.

There are also questions about the quality of projects, and housing expeditor Bob Bush, who works in the MVRPC offices but whose salary is paid with city and county funds, says that one of his jobs is to see that FHA enforces maintenance standards at existing projects. In practical terms, the MVRPC staff knows, one project must be used to sell the next project. Local councils usually take tours of existing projects, and opposition groups always take them. One broken window can become rampant vandalism at a heated community meeting.

The Dayton plan was unanimously endorsed in September, 1970, by the elected officials serving on the 42-member MVRPC, representing the 32 member-municipalities and five member-counties of the region. MVRPC was formed in 1964 and is the planning agency designated by the federal government as the regional clearinghouse for coordinating the expenditure of federal dollars in the area. Federal money supports the agency's planning costs.

A great deal of national attention has focused on the singular achievement of MVRPC in rallying the support of local elected officials for so controversial an effort as distributing subsidized housing in suburban jurisdictions. In Washington top officials of the Department of Housing and Urban Development point repeatedly to Dayton as the model for local effort on a metropolitan scale. And in Congress, legislation (Title V of HR 9688) has been proposed that would encourage establishment of metropolitan housing agencies as a means of distributing federal housing dollars (and units) on a regional and, it is hoped, more rational basis. The Dayton plan is a model for the legislation.

Adoption of the plan was the culmination of carefully worked out strategy and an educational campaign. MVRPC began compiling information on regional housing needs in 1969 and giving increased technical assistance on housing to all those who requested it. In early 1970 a regionwide housing conference drew more than 300 participants and a lot of publicity. The busy, cramped offices of MVRPC became the place where politicans, citizens, builders, housing sponsors, and managers crossed paths and ideas.

It was easy enough for planners to conclude that there was a shortage of sound low- and moderate-income housing units in the region and to quantify the needs. The difficult part was to determine how to allocate the needed housing to the communities of the region, to arrive at local quotas that were reasonable in planning terms *and* feasible in political terms.

MVRPC's Ann Shafor, writing for the American Institute of Planners, has described the process this way: "The entire region was broken down geographically into 53 'planning units.' . . . Then the needed low- and moderate-income dwelling units were assigned to the planning units using a composite of numbers resulting from six calculation methods: 1. equal share, 2. proportionate share of the county's households 3. proportionate share of the county's households making less than $10,000 annually (or less than $7,000 in the three more rural counties), 4. the inverse of 3, 5. a share based on the assessed valuation per pupil of the school districts covering the planning units, and 6. a share based on the relative overcrowding of the school districts."

Ms. Shafor readily admits that "for the purposes of the initial housing plan, a six-factor allocation method has proven relatively satisfactory, although not perfect." She believes that the important things are: "First, that the distribution was made in hard figures, and second, that the formula reflected enough factors to make it sensitive to a few critical characteristics of the planning units. As 1970 census data is available, the housing needs figures and the distribution will be recalculated," she says. "Ways can then be sought of refining the allocation method."

There is continuing political pressure on the planners to revise the numbers. The emphasis on political feasibility—and flexibility—may be what distinguishes MVRPC from other regional planning agencies, which become mesmerized by computerized formulas and other trappings of apparent exactitude. The admittedly inexact formula is a disarming tactic and useful lightning rod in the heat of conflict: "We know the formula is not perfect and we would appreciate any of your suggestions."

The actual federal tools available to MVRPC for bringing national clout to bear on a specific housing distribution plan were few. There were the Civil Rights Acts of 1964 and 1968, and there was the potentially useful A-95 review process, an intergovernmental administrative device established by the Office of Management and Budget to insure compliance with federal legislation. Under the A-95 review procedure, requests for federal funds for a multitude of programs must go through a regional clearing-house—in this case MVRPC—for "review and comment." The process is intended to assure that federal programs are not unnecessarily duplicating other programs in the area and are not in conflict with regional goals. Housing developments having more than 50 single-family units or 100 multifamily units are subject to such review.

Since 1969 MVRPC has been using the review process to insure compliance with the Civil Rights Act of 1964. In January, 1970, Bertsch announced it would further require the provision of low- and moderate-income housing for favorable review of other funding requests.

Essential to even the initial acceptance of the plan by MVRPC officials was the belief that the philosophy often stated by HUD Secretary George Romney would mean HUD would use its dollars to encourage an open communities policy.

In the weeks preceding the vote of the commission, public hearings were held throughout the area, and the MVRPC staff team made the circuit night after night to describe and defend the plan. A council in Greene County specifically instructed its representative not to vote for the plan as it stood. Councilman Gerald Beeman voted for it anyway, balancing, he said, the voice of the community against its needs and his own conscience.

Bertsch and outspoken commission proponents received threatening phone calls. Compromises were made, the major one the elimination of approval for the staff to seek state legislation authorizing the commission to override local zoning in carrying out the plan.

Many elements came to bear to produce the final unanimous endorsement of the plan by the commission. Those elements were as assorted as the individuals and jurisdictional interests they represented, a gamut of moral and political judgments; conviction, worry about the loss of federal money (open space funds had been delayed for suburban Kettering until an open housing ordinance was passed), belief that the plan was utopian and probably wouldn't get down to working anyway. And the nature of Dayton itself.

Average, medium, moderate, middle are adjectives that come to mind when trying to describe anything about Dayton. Election pundit Richard Scammon gave the image currency in his characterization of the average American voter as the middle-class suburban Dayton housewife. Reporters make the pilgrimage to Dayton in search of a Middletown, U.S.A. But such romanticism grays out the variety and conflict and compelling chauvinism that any visitor to Dayton must acknowlege.

On conventional maps it is about 600 miles from Washington, an hour's flight from the nation's capital to the Action City, Birthplace of Aviation, as a banner in Dayton's airport proclaims. On a social map it seems more frontier than middle-of-anything, and it's a very long way when measured in the distance from a citizens' meeting in suburban West Carrollton to the debates in Washington about Title V of HR 9688, the proposed legislation modeled in part on the Dayton plan. Both are real worlds, but different.

The Miami Valley region is a five-county area in southwest Ohio. At about its center, situated on the confluence of three rivers, is the city of Dayton in Montgomery County. To the east is urbanizing Greene County where Yellow Springs, home of Antioch College, is situated. The other three counties are predominantly rural—to the northwest Darke County, to the west Preble County, and to the north the flat farmland of Miami County bisected by the Great Miami River and Interstate 75. About a third of Dayton's population of 243,000 is black—largely concentrated in the city's west side. The region as a whole has a population of 900,000, 11 percent black.

Although MVRPC in its campaign for acceptance of the plan encountered some of the most virulent prejudice in rural areas, the major struggle over dispersal has occurred in urbanized Montgomery County. In the decade 1960-70 the overall population of Montgomery County increased while the city of Dayton lost population and recorded a 30 percent increase in black residents. At the same time the vacancy rate in the Dayton area declined to 1.6 percent and the average price of a house rose from $17,500 in 1966 to $25,300 in 1969. MVRPC estimated that about 55,000 households in Montgomery County make less than $7,000 and for purposes of determining housing needs defined those households making $10,000 and under as the market for subsidized housing.

Major area industries include Dayton Tire, McCall's printing, the Delco branch of General Motors, National Cash Register, Frigidaire, Monsanto Chemical, and the government contract operations of the Air Force Materials Lab at Wright-Patterson Air Force Base and Defense Electronic Supply Center. Economically the area has an unemployment rate higher than the state average and an uncertain future as the national economy shifts away from "hardware" manufacturing enterprises and defense industries face cutbacks. Recently Frigidaire employees agreed to forego increased salary benefits in an attempt to improve the company's competitive price position.

Visually, Dayton has a typically flat, midwestern grid plan downtown—decimated by parking lots and scarred by the familiar economic malaise of central cities. But downtown renewal has not given up, and the city boasts new buildings by prominent architects Edward Durell Stone and Harry Weese. Among the many civic-achievement trophies on display at city hall is one for cleanliness. Air pollution levels, however, frequently exceed state and federal standards. Symbolically, a major expressway, U.S. 35, dead-ends at the boundary where it crosses into black West Dayton—the result of unresolved conflict between automobile pressures and citizen outrage. The blacks had had enough of the community disruption and displacement that resulted from the building of Interstate 75, a north-south wall which separates the ghetto from the rest of the city.

Past the city limits, commercial strip development follows the crisscross pattern of federally subsidized highways and in-between residential enclaves of affluent and not-so-affluent suburban living—overwhelmingly white except for one black suburb to the west. Beyond are the farms and farmlets of river valley country with a scattering of small towns—again white except for Xenia in Greene County, which has a sizable and stable black population. The area is moderate politically although there are small vocal bastions of the far right represented by the National States Rights Party and George Wallace's American Independent Party.

Dayton itself has a city manager form of government dating from the early part of the century when many American cities threw the rascals out in reaction to the political exposés of the day. In present-day terms this results in a relatively powerless and underpaid mayor and city commissioners elected on a good-guy, bad-guy basis rather than on party platforms.

Montgomery County, on the other hand, has a more usual partisan system with three elected commissioners. Montgomery County commissioner Tom Cloud is president of MVRPC and a leading advocate of the Dayton plan. How risky that advocacy is may be assessed when Cloud stands for re-election in 1972.

A Dayton Metropolitan Housing Authority operates both in the city and in unincorporated parts of Montgomery County. Of the other four counties, only

Greene has a housing authority.

Two major and good newspapers serve metropolitan Dayton: the Journal-Herald and the Dayton Daily News. Daily News editor Jim Fain, schooled in the civil rights struggle of Atlanta in the '50s, and the social journalism of Ralph McGill, has been in the forefront of the struggle for the Dayton housing plan. Some of the letters to the editor indicate there are readers who may believe it's Jim Fain's own personal plan to visit social destruction on suburban lifestyles: "What right does Metro have to dump the scum of a five-county area and the cesspool of Dayton into Miamisburg or any other area? If Jim Fain wants subsidized housing how about putting it in Centerville to where he escaped in order not to put up with what he wants to force onto others?"

Other critics of the plan are quick to judge it a failure because the quotas for low- and moderate-income housing units aren't yet reflected in foundations poured in the white suburbs south of Dayton. There are many ways to play the numbers game in assessing the Dayton plan, depending on the point of view. Particularly in the south suburbs there have been major setbacks in obtaining zoning changes, and required local approval for rent supplements (for families with yearly incomes of around $5,000 or less) in subsidized projects.

Progress has been made. Two years ago there was virtually no subsidized housing outside the city of Dayton. Now outside Dayton, 800 units are completed or under construction (including 50 units of public housing), and 3,550 units are somewhere in the bureaucratic pipeline. This figure includes a commitment between the Dayton Metropolitan Housing Authority and Montgomery County to place 1,050 units of public housing in the county. And it includes projects for the south suburbs of Kettering, Moraine, Miamisburg, Centerville, and West Carrollton.

But the plan must be evaluated in the context of a 1975 first-stage target date—and of a process. The justified admiration for the political endorsement of the Dayton plan by MVRPC has obscured the fact that it was a beginning, not a solution. "The plan is only one element of our strategy," Bertsch explains. And consensus did not mean mandate. Now the struggle is taking place over finding real sites for real housing units. And if emotions did battle with reason in getting the plan accepted, that was only a skirmish compared with the difficulties of implementation.

Not surprisingly, there is resistance in white suburbs. There is also passionate resistance in a middle-income black suburb. There is trouble, too, when MVRPC tries to stop proposed projects.

An early test came when the MVRPC gave a negative review to 456 units of subsidized housing in Madison Township, which is directly in the path of the expansion pressures of West Dayton and is the only suburban area with its 1975 "quota" already filled. FHA supported the negative review, and MVRPC had signaled, according to Bertsch, that builders "would have to take their units and play someplace else."

Some builders have expressed concern about the long-range implications of such negative reviews on housing production. There are threats of possible legal action challenging the validity of the plan.

The local affiliate of the National Association of Home Builders has been on record in support of the plan. From the inception of the commission's housing program its members were included in a Housing Advisory Group. To help builders with high front-end costs of lower-income housing, MVRPC stimulated the creation of two local nonprofit groups and a "seed bank" of $250,000, but only $25,000 has been used so far by local builders.

Ed Rausch, corporate executive and former mayor of Trotwood, a white community in Madison Township, voiced the sentiments of those who see the advantages of the quotas as limits as well as goals: "Without a quota the schools would be swamped." The Trotwood Junior High School is already on double sessions, and the community has rejected repeated bond proposals to finance a second intermediate school. Trotwood is an older, close-in suburb of 30,000 with one or two black families. But West Dayton is next door and it is only a matter of time before expansion pressures sweep comfortable Trotwood into the uncertainties of neighborhood change.

The dispersal plan can be viewed as a way of calling on other suburbs to share some of the pressures of urban growth. Rausch complains that "the communities south of town are not doing their share. If their elected representatives are stampeded by heat they may be good politicians but they are not good public officials." He points out that "if the federal government will cooperate and deny assistance on everything we need if we don't measure up on housing, that is the key. At the moment West Carrollton is waiting for financing for a park, and I hope to hell they don't get it." Rausch has been through the emotional meetings and the telephone threats. But he and his seven fellow-councilmen solidly supported the housing plan because, according to Rausch, it needed to be done since Dayton can't bear the whole thing; it was the only way Trotwood would be assured that it wouldn't take more than its share.

Dayton's major builder, Huber Enterprises, has been through many local battles—and sites—to make the Dayton plan yield actual housing units. The firm was first involved in suburban Moraine when a subsidized project was all set until the city fathers conveniently discovered an old plan that called for a road through the site. Having already met suspiciously costly site requirements, Huber had to abandon the proposal. On another developer's project, the Moraine city council reversed the zoning recommendations of its own planners. This situation has provoked investigation by the equal opportunities division of the HUD regional office in Chicago. State Rep. C.J. McLinn unsuccessfully attempted to get the governor to hold up funds for a highway overpass in retaliation.

Huber joined with nonprofit sponsor Luthern Social Services and MVRPC to try for a much-needed victory in Miamisburg with a 166-unit project including rent supplements. The zoning was in order but local council approval was required for the rent supplements. Miamisburg is a largely blue-collar community with a lot of substandard housing and one of the highest welfare caseloads outside the city of Dayton. Many of the residents are employed by nearby Monsanto Chemical. Also nearby is the Dayton Mall with 107 stores in 1.2 million square feet of shopping mall built in 1967 when 58.7 percent of retail sales in the Dayton SMSA occurred outside the central city.

The census says there are 12 blacks in Miamisburg but, a resident commented, "We don't know where they are." Young people are leaving the community because they can't afford to buy homes there. It was not an auspicious setting for a major integration victory, but the advocates felt they had just enough votes to pull it off. The hearing on the project was attended by 500 people, some armed with American Independent Party pamphlets protesting the scattering of "high-rise slums" by MVRPC which could lead to "crime and vice so rampant" citizens would be "afraid to even open their doors in daylight." A concerned Citizens Committee, formed in the weeks preceding the hearing, distributed more reticent literature emphasizing tax loss to the community, overburdened schools and transportation, and sewer overload. The tumultuous meeting ended in a rout for the Dayton plan.

Said Citizens Committee chairman Ted Kozuszek later: "I have no criticism with the plan. I looked at Fairborn (a contemporary-style project in neighboring Greene County) and could not find any fault with it. There's a need for the type of people *there*. Federal dollars improved the area where it was located." He indicated he would even support a Miamisburg project if it were on a different site "where the project would constitute rehabilitation of the area. Why do you have to pick blue-ribbon real estate for this kind of housing?" He resents the accusation of prejudice: "Affluent people didn't turn anyone away. If the substandard housing in Miamisburg is vacated, more will move in. That housing should be rehabilitated." He admitted other prejudices: "Many who signed petitions think there have been too many federal boondoggles." And renters "don't care about the community. They are bad for real estate values. I don't want to repeat what's heard about them." Kozuszek, like other opponents of government-sponsored housing, is well-versed in the horror stories of federal failures.

Ed Dean, a councilman who voted for the project and was later defeated for reelection, said he would advise MVRPC to "forget, write off the people against the plan and mount a terrific program of education of those in favor to get *them* out and vociferous." Councilman General Beeman from nearby Bellbrook had a similar reflection on the early opposition to the plan: "We have to get to the point where people *against* get quiet." Tom Wolford, head of Lutheran Social Services, continues to be optimistic about the plan. He feels that the key is "getting a good demonstration project going south of Dayton, because the longer it takes the tougher it's going to be to implement the plan as the contagion of resistance spreads."

Jim Fain, editor of the Dayton Daily News, predicted that if the "Dixie suburbs," as he calls them, don't open up "people will start dropping out of the plan and justifiably so." He's pessimistic about education changing people: "Bold political muscle is needed." HUD, he believes, will not ultimately solve the problems because it will give up on the tough projects and shift money elsewhere rather than reduce overall production.

Which may explain some of the MVRPC problems with the FHA insuring office in Cincinnati. A number of rulings from that office have confused and discouraged Dayton planners and housing sponsors. Their fury has reached the HUD area offices in Columbus, the regional office in Chicago, and the undersecretary's office in Washington. From February to August of last year only a slight trickle of funds came through and these were limited to the central city. A high-rise project for the elderly in suburban Kettering, approved locally after much patient effort, was first sent back by the insuring office for a higher bedroom count, then rejected on the grounds there was "no market demand," although a nearby elderly project has a waiting list of 1,500. The project is still in limbo because FHA now has raised objections to the site.

HUD went on record in October: "MVRPC will receive priority processing." Miamisburg project may be funded without rent supplements. If further citizen efforts to block the project develop into a petition for a referendum to change the zoning, the controversy could end in court.

Through all the conflicts in the suburban communities runs the debate about whether the resistance is to black people or more generally to poor people. Councilman Ed Dean is clear that in Miamisburg "the issue was black." In Jefferson Township, a middle-income black suburb, the story was different. The arguments for turning down a zoning request, however, were familiar: overcrowding of schools, added tax and police protection burdens, and the possibility of "the hoodlum element" moving in. County commissioner Tom Cloud confessed he was impressed by the resistance to the Jefferson zoning change and perhaps persuaded that this was a "different" situation.

The white upper-income suburb of Centerville is just as emphatic about preserving its way of life and doing business. A mayoral candidate (later defeated) wrote that the Dayton plan "horribly violates the principles of good land planning. Centerville-Washington Township happens to be the prime area of the Miami Valley for development of fine-quality, single-family homes. There will always be a significant portion of our society who aspire to live in this type of community, in spite of the extra cost. . . . The basic purpose for establishing zoning, in the first place, was to provide the people with a method of controlling the development of their community along the lines they feel are desirable. The argument that Centerville has an obligation to provide zoning for large apartment developments to fill a need is ridiculous. . . . I do feel so strongly that Centerville-Washington Township should be developed as a 'unique' and 'prestigious' community."

The Public Opinion Center (established in Dayton by the Sloane-Kettering Foundation and Gallup Polls to do local polling for the purpose of assisting public decision-making) found 74 percent of Montgomery County residents in favor of scattering apartments for low- and moderate-income families throughout the metropolitan area. The center reported in August: "More blacks (82 percent) than whites (72 percent) were for dispersal. Young adults, those under 30, were more in favor of a balanced regional distribution than those over 60, with 82 percent and 66 percent, respectively, for dispersal." The center also reported the results of a poll on racially mixed housing: "About six out of 10 people throughout Montgomery County feel that their own neighborhoods should have a mixture of people of different races. Throughout the country, blacks were much more likely than whites, and the young people more likely than the older, to favor a mixture of races in their neighborhoods."

MVRPC does not feel the operating presence of quite so much reason. The disparity between the attitudes and actions of citizens, between the support of elected officials serving on MVRPC and their fellow officials' votes on rent-supplement housing, reflects the disparity between what people perceive as right and what they perceive as personally and immediately threatening to their economic investments and life styles. Also frustrating to Dayton plan advocates has been the disparity between policy declaimers in Washington offices and their administrators in the field. HUD declares and FHA insures.

The strains of the struggle have taken a toll in the past year. Some of the plan's supporters were defeated in the November, 1971, elections, but others were reelected. In the one contest in which housing views were explicitly a major issue, councilman Ben Ankney, Kettering's advocate of suburban integration, was unseated.

Two county and 10 municipal jurisdictions have considered secession from MVRPC. A member jurisdiction is allowed to withdraw from the commission after a year's notice, but it continues to be subject to A-95 review procedures. Bertsch has been fighting defections with HUD support. The rural counties of Miami and Darke, which always have been critical of federal intervention, quit MVRPC effective February 1, although the municipalities in the two counties will continue as members. Five localities have given the required year's notice.

In recommending withdrawal from MVRPC, the West Carrollton city manager's office said: "The planning and coordinating functions for which the MVRPC was originally created have been downgraded in favor of social action programs. The Miami Valley region has become a 'test bed' for many federally funded experiments of undetermined merit. In areas such as housing, adverse results of unsuccessful federal experimentation may be painfully permanent."

Jim Fain once wrote about Dayton, "If you look short-term, we aren't much better off than Dresden a week after the fire-bombing." But there's something special out there. The unrelenting energy of Dale Bertsch who believes leadership should "listen to the voice of the community but must not allow the majority to infringe on the rights of others." And his staff, as it regroups after defeats like Moraine and Miamisburg, attends public meeting after public meeting trying to sort the fear from the hate—a staff united by its intelligence and commitment, and often by fatigue. Elected officials who for little money, faint praise, and a lot of flak continue to steer a reasoned course in a sea of citizen needs and emotions. The outsider who pays attention can respect Jim Fain's fierce compliment to this adopted city: "I love this crazy town."

Are there more Daytons in America? The Dayton regional council has accomplished something remarkable, is trying for something even more remarkable. But it is also remarkable that there are 435 other regional councils in America with the same mandate, the same federal funding, the same A-95 review power as MVRPC, and innumerable cities with the same problems and inequities—yet Dayton plans are not springing up all over the nation. A few regional councils are working seriously at specific metropolitanwide plans for the fair-share location of low- and moderate-income housing. The Washington, D.C., COG has voted support for a Dayton-like plan but has yet to face the political turbulence of implementation.

Activist Daytonians welcome the national interest as another lever for achieving the goals of the Dayton plan locally, but Jim Fain observes: "The interest so many people are showing in what we are trying to do here is more a reflection of tragic failure in the rest of the country than of any particular success in Dayton."

JAMES Vs. VALTIERRA:
HOUSING DISCRIMINATION BY
REFERENDUM?

Donna M. Murasky

If the poor want the affluent to provide them with housing, it would seem only reasonable that they should expect and be willing to accept the willing consent of a simple majority of those persons who are expected to help pay. . . .(1)

Wherever the real power in a Government lies, there is the danger of oppression. In our Government the real power lies in the majority of the Community, and the invasion of private rights is chiefly to be apprehended, not from acts of Government contrary to the sense of its constitutents, but from acts in which the Government is the mere instrument of the major number of the constituents. This is a truth of great importance, but not yet sufficiently attended to. . . .(2)

In *James v. Valtierra*(3) the United States Supreme Court upheld the constitutionality of article XXXIV of the California Constitution,(4) which requires a local housing authority's selections of low-income public housing sites to be approved in community referenda.(5)

In its opinion the Court touched upon three primary issues: 1. the nature of referenda provisions and the scope of judicial review over them; 2. almost parenthetically, the effect of the referendum upon the rights of an economic minority—the poor; and 3. the referendum's effect upon the rights of racial minorities. The Court broadly endorsed the referendum and implied that referenda should not be subjected to a stringent standard of judicial scrutiny. The Court found that the record would not support the lower court's finding that the provision, although neutral on its face, imposed increased procedural burdens upon racial minorities.(6) Although it suggested that the referendum procedure might disadvantage some persons in the political process, the Court's majority never explicitly referred to the economic composition of that group which had been singled out for special treatment—low-income persons who apply for public housing. The Court found, however, that the community's interest in determining the level of local governmental expenditure and taxation outweighted whatever disadvantages might be incurred by others through the mandatory referendum procedure.

This comment will focus on the three constitutional issues posed by the *Valtierra* case: 1. whether the standard of judicial scrutiny of referendum legislation and decisions is or should be identical to that which applies to representative legislative enactments; 2. whether explicit classifications based upon wealth are or should be disfavored on new or substantive equal protection grounds; and 3. whether the California provision, although neutral on its face, may have an impermissible racially discriminatory effect—raising the question whether the Court's opinion in this respect is consistent with such decisions as *Reitman v. Mulkey*(7) and *Gautreaux v. Chicago Housing Authority.*(8)

JUDICIAL SCRUTINY OF REFERENDUM LEGISLATION

Initially, it is important to determine whether the presumed validity of challenged legislation is affected by the manner in which it is enacted—by the people themselves or by the people's representatives.(9) The majority of the *Valtierra* Court appear to have believed that referendum legislation and decision making occupy a special place in the political process so as to merit a greater presumption of validity than that which attaches to representative legislation. The Court emphasized that the referendum is a "procedure for democratic decision-making" and that "provisions for referendums demonstrate devotion to democracy, not to bias, discrimination, or prejudice."(10)

As the following discussion shows, such a blanket endorsement is inconsistent not only with standards previously announced by the Court, but also with the fourteenth amendment's protection of minorities against unrestrained majority will.(11)

Perhaps the Court's most instructive statement on referendum legislation came in *Lucas v. Colorado General Assembly.*(12) Two amendments to the Colorado Constitution had been proposed by initiative. The first proposal provided for one-man, one-vote representation in both houses of the state legislature, while the second provided for one-man, one-vote representation in the more numerous house only. The second proposal was approved in a public referendum. Against claims that the measure violated the fourteenth amendment, the district court upheld its constitutionality, explaining that it was precluded from reversing the people's judgment rendered in accordance with Colorado's liberal provisions for citizen participation in the governmental process.(13) Faced with the unusual situation of a majority of the electorate denying itself equal representation in both houses of the state legislature, the Supreme Court disapproved the plan, stating that a majority may not, through a public referendum, infringe upon a citizen's constitutional rights.(14)

Lucas, therefore, appears to stand for the principle that when the people act as a legislative body in a referendum, the Constitution imposes upon them the same responsibilities as it imposes upon a representative legislature, and that voter legislation, even if it does "demonstrate devotion to democracy,"(15) or citizen majority rule, is not given any greater presumption of validity for that reason.

For the *Valtierra* Court to extol in unqualified fashion the virtues of the referendum was thus unnecessary and misleading. Moreover, apart from *Lucas*, it may have cast doubt upon a basic principle of *Hunter v. Erickson*(16)—that "a State may distribute legislative powers as it desires and that the people may retain for themselves the power over certain subjects may generally be true, but [that] these principles furnish no justification for a legislative structure which would otherwise violate the Fourteenth Amendment. Nor does the implementation of this change through popular referendum immunize it."(17)

VALIDITY OF EXPLICIT CLASSIFICATIONS BASED UPON WEALTH

Any discussion of the validity of classifications based upon wealth under the new or substantive equal protection doctrine is difficult and somewhat speculative in the context of *Valtierra* because the Court's opinion failed to address that question. Justice Black ignored not only the points raised by Justice Marshall in his dissent(18) but also those cases in which the Court has stated that classifications based upon wealth, like those based upon race, are "suspect."(19) In view of the exclusive applicability of the California referendum provision to low-income housing projects, an examination of the Court's opinion in terms of both the new and the old equal protection doctrines appears to be warranted.

EQUAL PROTECTION—OLD AND NEW

The old and new equal protection doctrines, the subject of wide debate and discussion in recent years,(20) require only brief summarization. Under the old equal protection, legislative classifications are allowed a strong presumption of validity and are constitutionally permissible if "rationally related to a legitimate governmental objective."(21) The contrast with the new equal protection is striking. In recent years the Court has indicated that the new equal protection encompasses two primary branches, fundamental rights(22) and suspect criteria. While the suspect category was initially limited to racial criteria,(23) the Court's recent decisions have suggested that classifications based upon wealth are also included.(24) When either a suspect criterion has been incorporated into a statute or the exercise of a fundamental right is threatened, the statutory classification must be justified by a "*compelling* governmental interest."(25)

Application of the new equal protection doctrine involves close "judicial scrutiny"(26) imposing upon the state a heavy burden of justification.(27) Concomitantly, the Court has sometimes considered whether there are alternatives available to the state by which it can achieve its legitimate objective without substantial infringement upon fundamental rights or without classification by means of suspect criteria.(28) If the Court finds a "less onerous alternative" by which a state is able to achieve its legitimate objective, the state may not employ a method which, though rationally related to that objective, more substantially infringes upon protected rights.(29)

The majority in *Valtierra*, while noting that classifications based upon race are constitutionally suspect, ignored the Court's previous statements that classifications based upon wealth also fall within the suspect category: "Lines drawn on the basis of wealth, like those of race . . . are traditionally disfavored."(30) "[C]areful examination on our part is especially warranted where lines are drawn on the basis of wealth or race . . . two factors which would *independently* render a classification highly suspect and thereby demand a more exacting judicial scrutiny."(31)

The cases in which the Court has invalidated statutes containing classifications based upon wealth have also involved barriers hindering the indigent in the exercise of certain fundamental rights, sometimes formulated for the first time in those cases.(32) In such decisions the question whether wealth, as a suspect criterion, formed an independent basis for the determination of constitutional invalidity or was merely an ancillary consideration has never been expressly resolved. Justice Harlan indicated, however, that the criterion of wealth may have provided an independent basis for invalidation when he stated that "[t]he criterion of 'wealth' apparently was added to the list of 'suspects' as an alternative justification for the rationale in Harper v. Virginia Bd. of Elections. . . ."(33) On the other hand, it has been forcefully argued that because fundamental rights of voting and access to the judicial process in criminal cases were involved, the finding of a suspect criterion was unnecessary to the decision.(34) Inability to pay a fee had no reasonable relationship to a proper governmental objective and, in addition, a pecuniary burden on the exercise of those fundamental rights might have been invalidated under the due process clause.

McDonald v. Board of Election Commissioners,(35) however, has drawn into question this restrictive explanation of the cases involving the poor. Presented with an equal protection challenge to a state absentee ballot procedure, the Court deferred its discussion of the merits of the case until it determined "how stringent a standard to use in evaluating the classifications made [by the statute] and whether the distinctions must be justified by a compelling state interest."(36) The Court stated that the exacting standards of the new equal protection would be applied if the statute involved a classification "drawn on the basis of wealth or race."(37)

The analytical approach of *McDonald*, under which the standard for testing the classification is determined before the substantive issues in the case are decided, was not followed in *Valtierra*, which the Court decided without specifying which equal protection standard it was applying. The Court thus avoided the question whether a classification based upon wealth, like a racial classification, provides an independent basis for application of the new equal protection. Until *Valtierra*, as noted, the cases afforded sound reason to believe that classifications based upon wealth are within the suspect category. These precedents were emphasized in Justice Marshall's dissenting opinion, but the Court failed to respond to them. Through its silence, the Court obscured the developing clarification of a constitutional principle and thereby invited conflicting lower court interpretations.(38)

Assimilation of a prohibition of classifications based upon wealth to the prohibition of racial classifications cannot be accomplished in an unquestioned fashion, notwithstanding one court's succinct rationale for constructing an analogy between the two criteria. In *Hobson v. Hansen*(39) Judge Wright explained that although the judiciary usually defers to administrative and legislative resolutions of conflicting interests, its faith in the justice of such resolutions is often misplaced when the interests of the poor or racial minority groups are involved. A closer judicial scrutiny of judgments adverse to the interests of these groups is necessary because they "are not always assured of a full and fair hearing through the ordinary political processes, not so much because of outright bias, but because of the abiding danger that the power structure . . . may incline to pay little heed to even the deserving interests of a politically voiceless and invisible minority."(40) There are major obstacles, however, to the assimilation of wealth to race as a suspect criterion: the positive value society places upon distinctions of wealth, the tradition of state-imposed financial prerequisites for the enjoyment of certain services and activities, the belief that poverty is remediable, the difficulty of determining what constitutes poverty, and, finally, the difficulty of defining the limits on the substantive areas to which the new equal protection should apply.(41)

Despite these obstacles, there are reasons why the poor, like racial minorities, should be afforded special judicial treatment under the new equal protection. The poor are increasingly comprised of particular racial and ethnic minority groups,(42) so that economic discrimination may be merely a guise for racial discrimination.(43) Moreover, it is superficial to assume that poverty is easily overcome—particularly by members of racial minority groups, for whom residential segregation is a substantial hindrance. And as affluent Americans migrate to the suburbs, the poor—particularly those of racial minority groups—increasingly inhabit decaying urban centers.(44) The consequent decline in tax receipts in urban areas causes a corresponding decline in the quality of municipal services—particularly education, an important prerequisite to employment. The isolation of the poor is exacerbated by the reduction of employment opportunities caused by the flow to the suburbs of commerical and industrial facilities,(45) a phenomenon which further decreases urban tax receipts and aids in perpetuating a cycle of poverty. While this trend might be counteracted by locating low-income housing in areas of growing employment opportunities and better educational facilities, the referendum provision in *Valtierra* permits wealthy suburban escapees to veto low-income housing on the apparent grounds of minimizing municipal expenditures and taxation. If such housing is to be built at all, it must apparently be located in the decaying central cities.(46)

APPLICATION OF THE SUSPECT CRITERION OF WEALTH

Article XXXIV of the California Constitution makes an explicit, de jure classification based upon wealth;(47) for, as Justice Marshall pointed out, "[p]ublicly assisted housing developments designed to accommodate the aged, veterans, state employees, persons of moderate income, or any class of citizens other than the poor, need not be approved by prior referenda."(48) Although the *Valtierra* Court did not state clearly what standard it applied in determining the validity of article XXXIV, it is instructive to analyze the case first in terms of the new equal protection standard.

Assuming wealth is a suspect criterion, the California referendum could have been upheld only were the state able to demonstrate a compelling interest to justify the provision. In its best light, the referendum may be characterized as a measure directed primarily at minimization of municipal expenditures and taxation. The Supreme Court has held, however, that a state interest in saving money is not compelling when it infringes upon the exercise of fundamental rights. In *Shapiro v. Thompson*(49) the Court invalidated a one-year residence requirement for welfare benefits eligibility because it created an "invidious classification" in violation of the equal protection clause, infringing upon the fundamental right to travel interstate. The state attempted to justify the statutory classifications on the grounds that the residence requirement was "a protective device to preserve the fiscal integrity of state public assistance programs" and "an attempt to distinguish between new and old residents on the basis of the contribution they have made to the community through the payment of taxes."(50) The Court firmly rejected both arguments, finding that such "reasoning would logically permit the State to bar new residents from schools, parks, and libraries, or deprive them of police and fire protection" and "would permit the State to apportion all benefits according to the past tax contributions of its citizens."(51) Although the Court recognized the legitimacy of a state purpose to limit expenditures and taxation, the method chosen was void because "saving of welfare costs cannot justify an otherwise invidious classification."(52)

The arguments of the *Valtierra* appellants are barely distinguishable from those of the *Shapiro* appellants—that indigents should be barred from residing in a particular area because their contributions to its tax base would be insufficient to cover the additional governmental expenditures entailed by such residence. Since a municipality is a branch of the state, it reasonably follows that saving money is not a compelling interest even when a community relies upon it to justify barring indigents from residing therein in public housing.(53) And if such an interest is not compelling under the fundamental right branch of the new equal protection, it is doubtful that it is compelling under the suspect criterion branch.

Moreover, had the "less onerous alternative" doctrine been considered in *Valtierra*, the Court may have found that other methods exist whereby California could achieve its objective of minimizing financial hardships incurred by particular communities through the location of low-income public housing sites. The state legislature could, for example, distribute the present burden on local finances by providing communities that have public housing with state grants equal to the difference between the amount the community would have received through taxation of the project at full value and the amount received under existing statutes, which appropriate ten percent of the project's rental monies to the community.

APPLICATION OF THE OLD EQUAL PROTECTION STANDARD

The remaining question is whether article XXXIV is valid under the old equal protection standard—whether the classification made is "rationally related to a legitimate governmental objective."(54)

First, the purpose of article XXXIV must be shown to be permissible. In *Valtierra*, there is a question as to what the purpose is. While providing local communities with a determinative voice in government spending appears to be a permissible purpose, barring indigents unable to assume their proportionate share of the tax burden appears to be impermissible in the light of *Shapiro*.(55) Second, even if it is assumed that cost minimization is the purpose underlying article XXXIV, the mandatory referendum provision may still not satisfy the rational relation test because the category singled out for prior approval may be underinclusive. As the Supreme Court has indicated, the line between rational and irrational is fine. In *Rinaldi v. Yeager*(56) the Court invalidated a state requirement that an unsuccessful appellant repay the cost of a state-provided transcript. The statute, which applied only to guilty defendants incarcerated after appeal but not to those receiving suspended sentences or probation, was held to constitute an invidious discrimination in violation of the equal protection clause. While the purpose of the statue was to reimburse the state, the Court stated that the equal protection clause "require[s] that, in defining a class subject to legislation, the distinctions that are drawn have 'some relevance to the purpose for which the classification is made.' "(57) Apparently determining that the statutory classification was underinclusive, the Court found that "no defensible interest [was] served by focusing on that distinction as a classifying feature in a reimbursement statute, since it bears no relationship whatever to the purpose of the repayment provision."(58)

Whether the classification in article XXXIV is more relevant to the purpose of the statue than the classification struck down in *Rinaldi* is arguable. The determination of rationality appears to involve two considerations directed to the question of underinclusiveness: the extraordinary character of mandatory referenda and the subject matter of the statute—in this instance, low-income public housing. Despite California's long history of referenda,(59) few subjects have been deemed sufficiently important to require mandatory referenda. Furthermore, no other mandatory referendum provision has singled out a particular economic group to bear its burden.(60) Whether the *Rinaldi* standard requires a determination of irrationality seems to depend upon whether municipal expenditures would have to be increased without commensurate increase of tax revenues from other types of housing developments for which referenda are not required.(61) Thus, if communities permit the construction of other types of housing, or perhaps of other types of land use, which are either exempt from local taxation or which do not make a fair contribution to the tax base, the *Rinaldi* test of rationality may not be met.

Perhpps, as Justice Black warned in the majority opinion, to invalidate article XXXIV would presumably mean that a community could not adopt a referendum procedure on any subject unless it submitted all subjects to referenda.(62) *Valtierra* can be distinguished, however, since the provision challenged in that case singles out a particular economic group which alone has to bear the special procedural burden of a referendum. Of course, it is possible that the referendum provision is not arbitrary because it may reflect a careful determination by the community that the benefits provided by other kinds of tax-exempt land uses and housing uniformly outweigh any additional costs imposed,(63) but no such calculation was demonstrated by the state.

Nevertheless, certain policy considerations may lend support to the Court's decision in *Valtierra*. The construction of low-income public housing compels the community to subsidize the project through the imposition of higher taxes or by a decline in the level of municipal services. Although public housing projects can significantly dilute the tax base, *Shapiro* indicates that apportionment of municipal services in accordance with individual contribution is impermissible. However, because the community's residents must bear an extra financial burden, it may seem only fair to allow them to have an influence in determining whether or not to undertake that burden.

DETERMINATION OF AN IMPLICIT RACIAL CLASSIFICATION

From the time it was determined both judicially and legislatively that race was an impermissible criterion in the wholly private housing market,(64) the question of illegal racial discrimination in housing has become more subtle. The present concern is that exclusion of blacks from white residential areas may be accomplished "by using a criterion which does not mention race but which accomplishes precisely the same result. . . ."(65)

The *Valtierra* Court, in addressing itself to the question whether an implicit racial classification is contained within the "benign" criterion of wealth in article XXXIV, found that "the record here would not support any claim that a law seemingly neutral on its face is in fact aimed at a racial minority,"(66) citing *Gomillion v. Lightfoot.*(67) This finding merits closer consideration.

MOTIVE OR EFFECT

If a statue is "neutral on its face,"(68) the question immediately arises how a court should determine whether the "seemingly innocent criterion"(69) or an impermissible criterion is the real basis of a statutory classification. There are two ways in which a court can make this determination—by focusing on the motives of the persons who made the decision or by focusing on the effect of the decision.

In *Valtierra*, the Court's use of the phrase "aimed at"(70) suggests that it was concerned not with any racially discriminatory effect which article XXXIV might have but rather with the motives of the voters in enacting the referendum provision. This suggestion is fortified by the Court's statement that "[p]rovisions for referendums demonstrate devotion to democracy, not to bias, discrimination, or prejudice."(71) This emphasis on the virtues of referenda raises questions regarding the propriety and wisdom of a motive test, particularly in the contest of community approval of proposed public housing sites.

Among the members of the Court and its critics, there are adherents of the motive test as well as of the effect test.(72) Yet when the Court has been directly confronted with the motive-or-effect distinction in the determination of the constitutional validity of statues, the majority of its members have opted for the effect test. Thus, in *United States v. O'Brien*(73) the Court rejected motive as a possible basis of statutory invalidity and interpreted *Gomillion* as standing "not for the proposition that legislative motive is a proper basis for declaring a statute unconstitutional, but that the inevitable effect of a statute on its face may render it unconstitutional. . . . [T]he purpose of the legislation was irrelevant, because the inevitable effect—the 'necessary scope and operation' . . . —abridged constitutional rights."(74) And in *Norris v. Alabama,*(75) the Court inferred from jury selection data that a racial criterion had been used in the selection procedure. The good motives and good faith to which the administrators testified apparently made no difference. Finally, in *Palmer v. Thompson*,(76) decided shortly after *Valtierra*, the Court again confronted the motive-or-effect distinction. It upheld a city council's decision to close all segregated swimming pools after a federal district court had found that segregated municipal facilities constituted a denial of equal protection. In seeking to have the pools reopened on an integrated basis, the plaintiffs charged that the council's decision to close the pools rather than to integrate them had been motivated by racial animosity. While acknowledging that evidence supported the charge, the Court stated that "no case in this Court has held that a legislative act may violate equal protection solely because of the motivations of the men who voted for it."(77) The Court admitted that language in some of its opinions(78) suggests that motive is a relevant consideration in the determination of constitutionality but added that "the focus in those cases was on the actual effect of the enactments, not upon the motivation which led the States to behave as they did."(79)

Both the *O'Brien* and *Palmer* decisions articulated several reasons for preferring the effect test to the motive test. A judicial determination of motive or a collection of motives would be a difficult, if not impossible, task. Moreover, if the Court did find an impermissible motive and voided a statute on that basis, it would be a Pyrrhic victory because the statute "would presumably be valid as soon as the legislature or relevant governing body repassed it for different reasons."(80) Finally, it would be dysfunctional to void a statute which had a legitimate result simply because of the bad motives of those who enacted it. To these considerations can be added the fact that the legal system is usually concerned about racial discrimination only when it appears that the alleged wrong has actually disadvantaged blacks, not when the complaint consists merely of an awareness that someone is thinking bad thoughts about blacks. That is, "[a]ntidiscrimination prohibitions try to regulate by prohibiting the use of a criterion (race), and generally a violation of the prohibition does not turn on the motives or reason for the choice of the criterion."(81)

The preference for the effect test has not gone unchallenged. Justice White, in his dissent in *Palmer*, argued that the swimming pools should be reopened on an integrated basis because their closing had been racially motivated.(82) The view that motive may be a valid consideration has received support from other critics as well.(83) It has been forcefully argued that the usual guidelines for the determination of constitutional validity are inadequate in certain situations. According to this theory, in certain "discretionary" legislative decisions, notably spending and taxing, a plaintiff alleging racial discrimination must show that he was disadvantaged by the statutory classification and that the decision makers were racially motivated in order to shift the burden of persuasion to the state.(84)

Although it is conceded that a disproportionate racial effect may be the best evidence of motivation, it is not the effect but the inference of motivation which is crucial—this is because the state has no affirmative duty to help blacks but only a duty to be neutral. To discern motivation, it has been suggested that the court might examine four factors: "the terms of the law in issue, those effects which must have been foreseen by the decision makers, the historical context in which the law was passed, and the legislative history and other recorded statements of intention."(85) If the court became convinced of the presence of an impermissible motivation—racial animus, indicating that race was the criterion of selection—the burden would fall upon the state to justify the distinction. If the court detected the presence of other permissible motivations, the impermissible motivation would be controlling. The sole exception to this rule would operate when the court could find that only a minority of the decision makers were motivated by an impermissible criterion.(86)

The application of such a motive test to community referenda on low-income housing site selection in California might prove difficult. Within the *Valtierra* context, for example, the four suggested factors would not have been especially helpful to the plaintiff. First, the terms of article XXXIV are neutral with respect to race. Second, it would have been difficult for a court to make a reasonable decision about what possible racial effect California voters could have foreseen in enacting article XXXIV in 1950. Third, the provision was enacted in response to a state court ruling that California's general, optional referendum law was not applicable to selections of low-income public housing sites. Fourth, public statements made at the time of passage of article XXXIV do not indicate that racial bias played a role in its enactment.(87) Under the proposed motive test, regardless of the results of the referenda, the provision could not have been found unconstitutional.

The proponent of the motive test does, however, suggest one additional factor—the court can look at the impact of the provision, but only for the purpose of determining the permissibility of the motivation. Assume that the result is an intolerable one—low-income public housing is ninety percent black and every site proposed for a white residential area is vetoed while every site proposed for a black one is approved.(88) Assume further that statistics show that a majority of white voters approved sites in black areas but disfavored sites in white ones. Before it could possibly make a finding of invalidity, the court must have found that the white voters, or at least a majority of them, were motivated by racial animus. Within the contest of the hypothetical, an inference of racial animus would, judged in the light of extensive resesearch by social scientists, be speculative at best.(89)

A second problem arising from adoption of a motive test would be the determination of the percentage of impermissibly motivated decision makers required in order for a court to invalidate a measure. It has been suggested that a majority of voters must have had an impermissible motivation.(90) In the hypothetical which has been posed, assume that survey research analysis indicates that thirty percent of the white voters voted against all proposed sites because they feared higher taxes, that thirty percent of the white voters voted against proposed sites in white neighborhoods because they do not like blacks, and that forty percent of the white voters approved all proposed sites because they feel sorry for the poor living in substandard housing. The result is that blacks are completely excluded from white residential neighborhoods. Yet only a minority of voters, albeit a crucial minority, were motivated by racial animus.(91) Thus, the law would be valid under the proposed motive test.

One might argue, however, that it is the crucial racially motivated minority which should be determinative of invalidity—that if the votes of this minority were necessary to the outcome of the referendum, as they were in the hypothetical, the referendum provision should be held invalid; but that if a plurality of the voters would have disapproved the sites after excluding the racially motivated votes, the referendum provision should be upheld. While this standard might seem appealing on first impression, it is subject to the criticisms of ascertainability, futility, and disutility.(92) Furthermore, courts may fear, with some justification, that a willingness to make an inquiry into voter motivations in the referendum context by scientific techniques might compel them to receive such evidence when representative legislation and administrative decisions are challenged as the products of illicit motives.

For several reasons, therefore, the effect test seems to be preferable, at least in the context of public housing referenda. If it is discriminatory effect which should be controlling, the crucial determination to have been made in *Valtierra* was not whether California voters were motivated by racial animus in approving article XXXIV in 1950 or in rejecting and approving housing sites since that time, but whether the provision has actually had a discriminatory effect. To say simply that there is no racial discrimination in article XXXIV because approval is required for all low-income public housing sites, not just for those in which blacks will live, does not answer the question whether the provision, although "neutral on its face,"(93) is discriminatory in effect.

FACIALLY INNOCENT CRITERIA

A statute is "neutral on its face" if it makes no express classification on the basis of an impermissible criterion such as race. It is "fair on its face and impartial in appearance."(94) The concern is the " 'real' basis of the [classification] "—is it the "facially innocent criterion" it seems to be, or is it an impermissible criterion?(95) To determine validity, the court must go beyond the face of the statute, examine its effect, and decide whether or not the "facially innocent criterion" is merely the "functional equivalent"(96) of an impermissible criterion.

In the *Gomillion* decision, for example, the Court invalidated a redistricting statute whose effect was that of "fencing Negro citizens out of town."(97) Residence was the facially innocent criterion which was found to be the functional equivalent of race, the real basis of a statute's classification.

In the context of public housing site selection, the question is whether low income is the functional equivalent of race—whether passing judgment on public housing on the basis of low income is the approximate equivalent of passing judgment on the basis of race. It has been suggested that there are two steps necessary to establish functional equivalence: "a determination that the criterion, like race, has or is likely to have an adverse differential impact on Negroes" and a determination that the criterion is no more justifiable as a basis of classification than is race.(98)

The district court in *Valtierra* made both of these determinations, resting its conclusion upon the theory that low-income public housing is a functional equivalent of minority group housing. Not only did the district court find that the criterion had an adverse differential impact upon racial minorities,(99) but it also found that wealth was not a permissible basis of classification.(100) The two criteria of wealth and race seem inseparable in the Court's opinion.

Although the Supreme Court hinted that article XXXIV might disadvantage some persons, it failed to give more than token acknowledgment to the existence of the wealth criterion on which the provision is based. Thus, it would have been difficult for it to have made a finding of functional equivalence. In the context of low-income public housing site selection, however, a court may not be required to make a determination that the criterion of wealth is no more justifiable than race in order to find that the two criteria are functionally equivalent.(101) This determination of functional equivalence may depend upon two factors. First, it may be found to exist when the number or proportion of racial minority group members living in low-income public housing or on waiting lists reaches such a level that, as a practical matter, low-income public housing becomes minority group housing. It is difficult to set a level of minority occupancy which should trigger the conclusion that low-income housing is minority housing.(102) The Supreme Court did suggest a standard in *Valtierra*, however, when it stated that "[t]he Article requires referendum approval for any low-rent public housing project, not only for projects which will be occupied by a racial minority."(103) But if all or nearly all low-income housing projects are occupied, at least in part, by members of racial minority groups, the prohibited result may have been accomplished, whether intentionally or not, "by using a criterion which does not mention race but which accomplishes precisely the same result. . . ."(104)

This standard may, however, be too facile—something more may be necessary to make a determination of functional equivalence. The court may then determine whether the basis of approval of low-income public housing sites is racial—that is, whether sites are generally approved when located in areas of minority racial concentration and generally disapproved when located in white neighborhoods. This does not mean that motive is relevant. Whatever the motive—racial animosity, concern for property values, or concern about the possibility of higher taxes—the effect may be that members of racial minority groups are excluded from white residential areas, and from this it may be inferred that the basis for approval and disapproval is race.

In *Valtierra*, neither the district court nor the Supreme Court examined the question of the location of housing sites which were approved and disapproved. The district court did find that "only 52% of the referenda submitted to voters have been approved"(105) in California, but its opinion gave no indication that the court examined or compared the racial character of the neighborhoods in which the proposed sites were approved and disapproved. In *Gautreaux v. Chicago Housing Authority*,(106) however, in which a federal district court ordered the Chicago Housing Authority to build most of its future projects in white neighborhoods, such an examination was made. The court found that the proposed sites in white neighborhoods were generally vetoed and that the proposed sites in black neighborhoods were generally approved.

The impact of *Valtierra* on the validity of the district court's ruling in *Gautreaux* is not clear. The cases are similar in many respects. In both, the local housing authority's selection of a public housing site was subject to the veto power of an "outside agency." In *Gautreaux* the veto was exercised by the alderman of the ward in which the proposed site was located, while in *Valtierra* it was exercised by the community in which the proposed site was located. In *Gautreaux* the court found no evidence that either the housing authority or the alderman was motivated by racial animus.(107) Regardless of motive, the effect of the site selection procedure was racially discriminatory: "[N]o criterion, other than race, [could] plausibly explain the veto of over 99½% of the housing units located on the white sites . . . and at the same time the rejection of only 10% or so of the units on Negro sites."(108) This showing was sufficient to bring the aldermanic veto within the prohibition of the equal protection clause.

If these same Chicago communities were to adopt a mandatory referendum on low-income public housing site selection and the same pattern of approval and disapproval of proposed sites were to emerge, there is little doubt that the *Gautreaux* court would invalidate the referendum procedure—it would not permit communities to achieve the same result through the ballot box which was constitutionally impermissible when accomplished by an aldermanic veto. Thus, the crucial difference between *Valtierra* and *Gautreaux* may be merely evidentiary—the proof of effect of the site approval procedure. If the *Valtierra* Court was unconvinced by the district court's finding of a racially discriminatory effect, the best procedure may have been to simply remand for trial on the merits, where additional facts could have been introduced.

REITMAN, HUNTER, AND *VALTIERRA*—ARE THEY CONSISTENT?

The foregoing analysis does not, of course, explain the Supreme Court's disregard of the lower court's findings of racial discrimination, which, according to *Reitman*, are entitled to great weight. It is thus reasonable to inquire whether *Reitman*, although not mentioned by the Court, was implicitly overruled.

The lower court in *Valtierra* found that "[h] ere, as in the *Hunter* case, the impact of the law falls upon minorities."(109) Such a *modus operandi* is contrary to that employed by the Court in *Reitman*. In that case Proposition 14, an initiative constitutional amendment neutral on its face, had been approved in a statewide referendum by nearly a two-to-one margin. The amendment repealed state legislation prohibiting housing discrimination and required that further legislation on the subject be approved in a statewide referendum. In rejecting the petitioners' contention that the amendment was neutral with respect to race, Justice White, writing for the Court, stated that because the Court had been given no persuasive evidence to the contrary, the California Supreme Court's belief that the provision would "significantly encourage and involve the State in private discriminations" would control.(111)

Although the lower court in *Valtierra* made no finding of "encouragement,"(112) apparently the Supreme Court gave no weight to the lower court's finding that the referendum provision would impose a special burden on racial minorities—the constitutional standard for invalidity established in *Hunter v. Erickson.*(113) There a referendum ordinance was passed "amending the city charter to prevent the city council from implementing any ordinance dealing with racial, religious, or ancestral discrimination in housing without approval of the majority of the voters of [the city]."(114) The city argued that the challenged provision was valid under *Reitman* because no finding of "encouragement" had been made by the lower court. The Supreme Court dismissed the argument:

> Here, unlike *Reitman*, there was an explicitly racial classification treating racial housing matters differently from other racial and other housing matters. . . .

... Moreover, *although the law on its face treats Negro and white, Jew and gentile in an identical manner, the reality is that the law's impact falls on the minority*. The majority needs no protection against discrimination and if it did, a referendum might be bothersome but no more than that.... [The ordinance] places special burdens on racial minorities within the governmental process. This is no more permissible than denying them the vote, on an equal basis with others.(115)

The Court concluded that "the State may no more disadvantage any particular group by making it more difficult to enact legislation in its behalf than it may dilute any person's vote or give any group a smaller representation than another of comparable size."(116) It is clear that such a special burden might fall on minority groups whether or not an explicit classification is made. The principle of a statute "neutral on its face" gives express recognition to that possibility. This was the finding of the lower court in *Valtierra*.

It may be possible to distinguish *Reitman* and *Hunter* from *Valtierra* on the ground that the provisions in the former cases repealed substantive rights while the provision in the latter did not. However, several factors preclude such an easy distinction. First, the Supreme Court has never held that states have an obligation to pass fair housing laws. Thus, it can be said that after the passage of Proposition 14 in *Reitman* the state of California assumed the same position with respect to housing discrimination as states which had never passed fair housing legislation at all. Second, immediately preceding the *Hunter* decision, the Civil Rights Act of 1968(117) had been enacted and *Jones v. Mayer*,(118) prohibiting private housing discrimination, had been decided. Either the Act or the *Jones* decision would presumably have given a remedy to the *Hunter* plaintiff. However, the Court dismissed the city's argument that the case had been rendered moot by these events. Third, because public housing projects are probably composed of a racially heterogeneous population, it is difficult to determine whether fair housing laws with respect to these occupants or potential occupants have been repealed by article XXXIV.

It is difficult to reconcile *Valtierra* with *Reitman* and *Hunter*, especially since *Reitman* was not mentioned in the *Valtierra* opinions. It is possible, however, to suggest one theory which would permit these cases to be interpreted in a consistent manner: If a statute is neutral on its face and the lower court finds that it will "encourage" racial discrimination, the Supreme Court will give great weight to this determination and affirm unless persuasive evidence to the contrary is offered.(110) If a statute, although treating racial minorities and whites alike on its face, makes an explicitly racial classification whose impact falls upon minorities by imposing special burdens within the governmental process, the Court will invalidate it without requiring a determination of "encouragement" by the lower court.(120) If, however, a statute is neutral on its face and the lower court makes a determination that the impact of the law falls upon racial minorities, the Supreme Court will give no weight to the lower court's determination. The matter would thus seem to be one of employing the correct key word—if the statute is neutral, the lower court should use "encouragement" language; if the statute makes an explicitly racial classification, although treating everyone alike, the lower court should use "special burden" language. This theory is supported by the Court's language in

Palmer v. Thompson:(121)

> Petitioners also claim that Jackson's closing of the public pools authorizes or encourages private pool owners to discriminate on account of race and that such "encouragement" is prohibited by *Reitman v. Mulkey.* . . .

> . . . This Court there accepted what it designated as the holding of the Supreme Court of California. . . .

> In the first place there are no findings here about any state "encouragement" of discrimination, and it is not clear that any such theory was ever considered by the District Court.(122)

The Supreme Court seems to have implied that had the lower court made a finding of "encouragement" with respect to Jackson's neutral act of closing its pools, a different question would have been presented. Both the elements of "encouragement" and "special burden" were arguably present in both *Reitman* and *Hunter* as well as in *Valtierra*.(123) If the explanation offered for reconciling the cases seems strained, perhaps the only alternative explanation is that they cannot be read together and that *Valtierra* implicitly overruled *Reitman*.(124)

The result reached by the *Valtierra* Court is satisfying because in an era of growing federal bureaucracy it leaves to popular resolution a decision which may vitally affect local communities. Yet the decision is also unsatisfying because it exacerbates the isolation of the poor—especially the minority group poor long subjected to discrimination because of race—within the inner city. In sum, *Valtierra* may be more important for what it failed to say than for what it did say and do. For by ignoring the important questions raised by the plaintiff with respect to evolving doctrines of the equal protection clause, the Court may have signaled a retreat from its formerly expansive interpretations of the fourteenth amendment.

NOTES

(1) Brief for Appellants James et. al. at 17-18, James v. Valtierra, 402 U.S. 137 (1971).
(2) 5 Writings of James Madison 272 (Hunt ed. 1904).
(3) 402 U.S. 137 (1971).
(4) Cal. Const. art. XXXIV, § 1 provides:

> No low rent housing project shall hereafter be developed, constructed, or acquired in any manner by any state public body until, a majority of the qualified electors of the city, town or county, as the case may be, in which it is proposed to develop, construct, or acquire the same, voting upon such issue, approve such project by voting in favor thereof at an election to be held for that purpose, or at any general or special election.

> For the purposes of this article the term "low rent housing project" shall mean any development composed of urban or rural dwellings, apartments

or other living accommodations for persons of low income, financed in whole or in part by the Federal Government or a state public body, or to which the Federal Government or a state public body extends assistance by supplying all or part of the labor, by guaranteeing the payment of liens, or otherwise. . . .

For the purposes of this article only "persons of low income" shall mean persons or families who lack the amount of income which is necessary (as determined by the state public body developing, constructing, or acquiring the housing project) to enable them, without financial assistance, to live in decent, safe and sanitary dwellings, without overcrowding. . . .

Apparently only Virginia has a similar law, which provides that the selection of a low-income public housing site in a city with a population not greater than ninety thousand nor less than seventy thousand shall be subject to a city referendum unless the project is authorized for the purpose of relocating families displaced by urban renewal. Va. Code § 36-19.4 (1950). Alabama law provides that public housing projects may not be alienated by the local governing body unless the decision is approved by referendum. Ala. Code tit. 47, § 62(1) (1958). Wisconsin law provides that a project may be liquidated or disposed of by referendum. Wis. Stat. Ann. § 66.40(25)(a) (1957).

(5) The origins of article XXXIV can be briefly summarized:

The United States Housing Act of 1937 (42 U.S.C.A. §§ 1401-1430) established a federal housing agency authorized to make loans to state agencies for the purpose of slum clearance and low-rent housing projects. The California Legislature made the benefits of the federal act available to the cities and counties of this state by enacting the Housing Authorities Law. . . .

The legislation created in each city and county a public housing authority . . . The exercise of the powers entrusted by the Legislature to these agencies was made subject to the preliminary condition that the local governing body, in each case, must formally resolve that public housing is needed.

Housing Authority v. Superior Court, 35 Cal. 2d 550, 552-53, 219 P.2d 457, 458 (1950). In that case the California Supreme Court held that the determination of the housing authority as to site selection of projects was administrative, not legislative, and thus not subject to the general nonmandatory referendum provision. This decision was overruled by article XXXIV, which was adopted in the same year through initiative and referendum.

(6) 402 U.S. at 141. The lower court opinion is Valtierra v. Housing Authority, 313 F. Supp. 1 (N.D. Cal. 1970). A curious difference in perspective between the two opinions is evident. The lower court opinion seems to indicate that the racial and poverty aspects of the case are inseparable, while the Supreme Court opinion summarily disposes of the racial aspect of the case and completely ignores the poverty issue. Justice Marshall's dissent, on the other hand, focuses on the statute's explicit classification on the basis of wealth but fails to mention

the racial aspect of the case.

The term "race" as used herein includes minority groups other than blacks, including Mexican-Americans, Puerto Ricans, and Indians, all of whom suffer much the same type of discrimination as does the black man. See, e.g., U.S. Comm'n on Civil Rights, Mexican-Americans Education Study 11 (1971): "The Southwest has had a long history of ethnic isolation and segregation of Mexican Americans from the remainder of its society. Although segregation probably never has been required by statute in any of the five Southwestern States, it has been practiced not only in the schools of the region, but in other aspects of life as well."

(7) 387 U.S. 369 (1967).

(8) 296 F. Supp. 907, 304 F. Supp. 736 (N.D. Ill. 1969).

(9) In Housing Authority v. Superior Court, 35 Cal. 2d 550, 219 P.2d 457 (1950), the court held that the decision of the housing authority as to site selection was administrative, not legislative, and thus not subject to the existing referendum provision. The court stated that the California statute setting up local housing authorities "expressly recognizes the existence of slum and substandard living areas and enunciates the government's intent to eliminate them," id. at 553, 219 P.2d at 458, and, quoting Kleiber v. City and County of San Francisco, 18 Cal. 2d 718, 724, 117 P.2d 657, 660 (1941), that " 'the subject matter of the action is of more than local concern,' " id. at 558, 219 P.2d at 461.

(10) 402 U.S. at 141.

(11) See Lucas v. Colorado General Assembly, 377 U.S. 713, 736-37 (1964). Other courts have gone so far as to enjoin the submission of certain proposals to public referenda because the effect of the submission itself was prohibited by the fourteenth amendment. In Holmes v. Leadbetter, 294 F. Supp. 991 (E.D. Mich. 1968), and Otey v. Common Council, 281 F. Supp. 264 (E.D. Wis. 1968), submission of open housing referendum proposals to the electorate was held to be within the "encouragement" prohibition of Reitman v. Mulkey, 387 U.S. 369 (1967). For a discussion of the Reitman decision, see text at notes 109-24 infra.

(12) 377 U.S. 713 (1964).

(13) Lisco v. Love, 219 F. Supp. 922, 932-33 (D. Colo. 1963), rev'd sub nom. Lucas v. Colorado General Assembly, 377 U.S. 713 (1964).

(14) 377 U.S. at 736-37.

(15) 402 U.S. at 141.

(16) 393 U.S. 385 (1969).

(17) Id. at 392.

(18) 402 U.S. at 145. Justice Marshall stated that "[i] t is far too late in the day to contend that the Fourteenth Amendment prohibits only racial discrimination; and to me, singling out the poor to bear a burden not placed on any other class of citizens tramples the values that the Fourteenth Amendment was designed to protect." Justices Brennan and Blackmun concurred in the dissent. Justice Douglas took no part in the case.

(19) See e.g., McDonald v. Board of Election Comm'nrs, 394 U.S. 802, 807 (1969); Harper v. Virginia Bd. of Elections, 383 U.S. 663, 668 (1966); Douglas v. California, 372 U.S. 353, 355-58 (1963).

(20) See, e.g., Black, The Supreme Court, 1966 Term, Foreword: "State Action," Equal Protection and California's Proposition 14, 81 Harv. L. Rev. 69,

96-99 (1967); Karst & Horowitz, Reitman v. Mulkey: A Telophase of Substantive Equal Protection, 1967 Sup. Ct. Rev. 39; Michelman, The Supreme Court, 1968 Term, Foreword: On Protecting the Poor Through the Fourteenth Amendment, 83 Harv. L. Rev. 7 (1969); Sager, Tight Little Islands: Exclusionary Zoning, Equal Protection and the Indigent, 21 Stan. L. Rev. 767 (1969); Developments in the Law—Equal Protection, 82 Harv. L. Rev. 1065 (1969).

(21) Shapiro v. Thompson, 394 U.S. 618, 658 (1969) (Harlan, J., dissenting).

(22) See Shapiro v. Thompson, 394 U.S. 618 (1969); Williams v. Rhodes, 393 U.S. 23 (1968); Carrington v. Rash, 380 U.S. 89 (1965); Reynolds v. Sims, 377 U.S. 533 (1964); Skinner v. Oklahoma, 316 U.S. 535 (1942).

(23) See Loving v. Virginia, 388 U.S. 1 (1967); McLaughlin v. Florida, 379 U.S. 184 (1964); Korematsu v. United States, 323 U.S. 214 (1944).

(24) See cases cited note 19 supra. Justice Harlan's dissent in Shapiro v. Thompson, 394 U.S. 618, 658, succinctly summarized what he perceived to be the trend of the Court's decisions in this area:

> In upholding the equal protection argument, the Court has applied an equal protection doctrine of relatively recent vintage: the rule that statutory classifications which either are based upon certain "suspect" criteria or affect "fundamental rights" will be held to deny equal protection unless justified by a "compelling" governmental interest. The "compelling interest" doctrine, which today is articulated more explicitly than ever before, constitutes an increasingly significant exception to the long-established rule that a statute does not deny equal protection if it is rationally related to a legitimate governmental objective.

Justice Harlan's earlier view of the Court's trend is quite different, as expressed in his dissent in Cardona v. Power, 384 U.S. 672, 660-61 (1966):

> It is suggested that a different and broader equal protection standard applies where "fundamental liberties and rights are threatened," . . . which would require a state to show a need greater than mere rational policy to justify classifications in this area. No such dual-level test has ever been articulated by this Court, and I do not believe any such approach is consistent with . . . the Equal Protection Clause. . . .

(25) Cf. Shapiro v. Thompson, 394 U.S. 618, 634 (1969). See also Sherbert v. Verner, 374 U.S. 398, 406 (1963); Bates v. Little Rock, 361 U.S. 516, 524 (1960); Korematsu v. United States, 323 U.S. 214, 216 (1944); Skinner v. Oklahoma, 316 U.S. 535, 541 (1942).

(26) McDonald v. Board of Election Comm'rs, 394 U.S. 802, 807 (1969). For views regarding the content of the concept of "close judicial scrutiny," the point of departure for application of the new equal protection standard, see Karst & Horowitz, supra note 20; Michelman, supra note 20; Sager, supra note 20.

(27) See cases cited note 25 supra; Michelman, supra note 20, at 20.

(28) See Tate v. Short, 91 S. Ct. 668 (1971); Anders v. California, 386 U.S. 738 (1967); Carrington v. Rash, 380 U.S. 89 (1965).

(29) Cf. Carrington v. Rash, 380 U.S. 89 (1965).

(30) Harper v. Virginia Bd. of Elections, 383 U.S. 663, 668 (1966).

(31) McDonald v. Board of Election Comm'rs, 394 U.S. 802, 807 (1967) (emphasis added).

(32) See Boddie v. Connecticut, 401 U.S. 371 (1971) (access to court for divorce proceedings); Williams v. Illinois, 399 U.S. 235 (1970) (imprisonment for longer than maximum statutory sentence for nonpayment of fine); Roberts v. LaVallee, 389 U.S. 40 (1967) (transcript of preliminary hearing for use at trial); Anders v. California, 386 U.S. 738 (1967) (effective advocacy by court-appointed counsel); Douglas v. California, 372 U.S. 353 (1963) (counsel on first appeal from conviction); Smith v. Bennett, 365 U.S. 708 (1961) (filing fee for application for writ of habeas corpus); Burns v. Ohio, 360 U.S. 252 (1959) (filing fee for motion for leave to appeal); Griffin v. Illinois, 351 U.S. 12 (1956) (trial transcript for appeal).

(33) Shapiro v. Thompson, 394 U.S. 618, 658-59 (1969) (dissenting opinion).

(34) However, even one skeptical of the proposition that such cases make the poor a judicially favored class under the new equal protection admits that "[h]eightened judicial skepticism about statutes which explicitly isolate an economic class for special treatment—i.e., the cases 'where lines are drawn on the basis of wealth'—is . . . obviously justified." Michelman, supra note 20, at 26-27.

(35) 394 U.S. 802 (1969). The Court upheld the validity of an absentee ballot statute which had the effect of preventing inmates awaiting trial in Cook County Jail who were residents of Cook County from obtaining absentee ballots while inmates who were residents of other counties could do so.

(36) Id. at 806.

(37) Id. at 807.

(38) The confusion to which the Valtierra Court has exposed lower courts was apparent in the recent decision of Serrano v. Priest—Cal. 3d—487 P.2d 1241, 96 Cal. Rptr. 601 (1971). There the California Supreme Court held the state school-financing scheme unconstitutional on equal protection grounds.

(39) 269 F. Supp. 401, 507 (D.D.C. 1967).

(40) Id. at 507-08.

(41) See Sager, supra note 20, at 785-87. As Professor Sager notes, race is not a valid consideration in determining access to housing, employment opportunities, and places of public accomodation and amusement. It is a far different matter to suggest, however, that wealth should not be a determinative factor. No man is entitled to a twenty thousand dollar home; to a higher salary; or to free admission to hotels, restaurants, and theaters because he is poor. The state charges all persons equally for use of toll roads and universities; for fishing, hunting, and driver's licenses; and more. Because wealth, in contrast to race, is a relative factor, the income level at which a person is entitled to state-provided services is largely discretionary, although qualifying standards which are particularly arbitrary may be effectively challenged. Finally, because poverty, unlike race, is considered remediable, one might be less concerned with the adverse effects of distinctions drawn on the basis of wealth.

(42) 313 F. Supp. at 5.

In 1967, 41 percent of the nonwhite population was poor, compared with 12 percent of the white population. Nonwhites thus constitute a far larger share of the poverty population (31 percent) than of the American population as a whole (12 percent). Moreover, the nonwhite proportion of the poverty population has been increasing slowly but steadily, since the first racial count was made in 1959; it was 28 percent then, and 32 percent by 1967.

National Comm'n on Urban Problems, Building the American City, H.R. Doc. No. 91-34, 91st Cong., 1st Sess. 45 (1968).

(43) See Fiss, A Theory of Fair Employment Laws, 38 U. Chi. L. Rev. 235, 296 (1970); text at notes 95-96 infra. In his discussion of the theory of functional equivalence, Professor Fiss states:

The question then is whether the reach of the antidiscrimination prohibition has been exhausted, and three factors may justify a second look at the criterion: evasion, unfair treatment, and the impact of the criterion on the equal-achievement goal.

The first factor—evasion—[is rooted in a concern that a person will try] . . . to satisfy his taste for discrimination . . . by using a criterion which does not mention race but which accomplishes precisely the same result. . . .

Second, an attempt to reach the seemingly innocent criterion may be rooted in a concern for fair treatment of Negroes. It is thought just as unfair to judge a Negro on the basis of such a criterion as it is to judge him on the basis of race . . . Of course, it may be unfair to judge anyone, white or black, on the basis of such a criterion; but this does not lessen the unfairness when Negroes are judged by such a criterion. . . .

A third source of concern relates to the goal of improving the relative economic positions of blacks.

(44) See Sloane, Toward Open Adequate Housing: The 1968 Housing Act: Best Yet—But Is It Enough?, 1 Civ. Rights Dig., No. 3, at 1, 4-5 (1968).

(45) The fact is that an ever-increasing number of industrial concerns and businesses are locating plants in suburban areas. The Bureau of Labor Statistics has reported that for the period 1960-1967, sixty-two percent of all industrial buildings and fifty-two percent of all commercial buildings were constructed outside the central cities of metropolitan areas. Moreover, more than fifty percent of all new jobs created in the 1960's in the standard metropolitan areas were outside the central city.

Note, Snob Zoning: Must a Man's Home Be a Castle?, 69 Mich. L. Rev. 339, 340 (1970), citing Bureau of Labor Statistics, U.S. Dep't of Labor, Changes in Urban America 1-5 (BLS Rep. No. 353, 1969).

(46) The U.S. Commission on Civil Rights found last year that of the quarter of a million low-rent housing units that have been built by city public housing authorities in the Nation's 24 largest metropolitan areas, in only one—Cincinnati—has the city housing authority been permitted to build outside the central city. There, the authority has provided a total of 76 low-rent units in

a Negro enclave in the suburbs.

Sloane, supra note 44, at 3.

(47) Most commentators have limited their discussions of the "classifications based upon wealth" standard to de facto classifications, apparently assuming that a de jure classification would be invalid. See, e.g., Michelman, supra note 20; Sager, supra note 20.

(48) 402 U.S. at 144 (Marshall, J., dissenting).

(40) 394 U.S. 618 (1969).

(50) Id. at 627, 632.

(51) Id. at 632-33.

(52) Id. at 633.

(53) In a different context, a lower federal court has held that municipal services must be apportioned equally among members of the community. In Hawkins v. Town of Shaw, 437 F.2d 1286 (5th Cir. 1971), the plaintiffs alleged racial discrimination in the apportionment of municipal benefits and services. Although the court found no evidence that local officials had been racially motivated in the distribution of these services, the fact that nearly all municipal improvements had been made in the wealthier, white sections of town to the neglect of the poorer, black sections was sufficient to bring the conduct within the prohibition of the equal protection clause.

(54) 394 U.S. at 658. (Harlan, J., dissenting).

(55) 394 U.S. at 633. In concluding its analysis of the state's fiscal integrity argument, the Court said that "neither deterrence of indigents from migrating to the State nor limitation of welfare benefits to those ragarded as contributing to the State is a constitutionally permissible state objective."

(56) 384 U.S. 305 (1966).

(57) Id. at 309.

(58) Id.

(59) 402 U.S. at 141. In its discourse about the democratic referendum procedure, the Court added one puzzling suggestion. It implied that the validity of the challenged referendum provision was attributable, in part, to California's long history of referenda. As a constitutional principle this cannot withstand analysis. Should an identical constitutional amendment be enacted in another state lacking California's history of referenda, the absence of previous provisions of a similar nature should not be viewed as grounds for constitutional invalidity. Redress from infringement of important constitutional rights should not turn on such historical accidents.

(60) The Court in Valtierra mentioned four types of referenda. State constitutional amendments are permissible since the constitution is adopted by the voters initially and any changes in it should be subject to their approval. Municipal bond referenda are, under Shapiro, a permissible method of adjusting the level of municipal expenditures as long as the benefit or hardship is evenly distributed. Territorial annexations permit self-determination by persons residing in an area sought to be annexed by a neighboring municipality. And legislation first enacted by voter initiative, unless repealable only by referendum, would be subject to repeal by the state legislature immediately after enactment. The subject matter of each of these provisions, however, is clearly different from that of article XXXIV.

(61) It should be noted that some low-income public housing is not subject to

referenda. The referendum procedure is required only for housing units owned by the local housing authority, not for units leased from private landlords nor for certain types of replacement units for persons displaced by a highway project. 51 Op. Cal. Att'y Gen. 245 (1968); id. at 42; see Note, Racial Discrimination in Public Housing Site Selection, 23 Sta. L. Rev. 63, 66 (1970). In addition, the program authorized by section 23 of the Housing and Urban Development Act of 1965, 42 U.S.C. § 1421b(f) (1970), "does not constitute . . . a 'low-rent housing project,' as that term is used in article XXXIV of the State Constitution," so that no prior approval at an election is required. 47 Op. Cal. Att'y Gen. 17, 18 (1966). It would seem that under section 23, units rented from private landlords by the local housing authority are not tax-exempt as are publicly owned housing projects under 42 U.S.C. § 1410(h) (1970).

Moreover, in California a variety of land uses are exempt from local taxation but are not subject to referenda. See, e.g., Cal. Const. art. XIII, § 1; Cal. Rev. & Tax. Code § 202 (public libraries and free museums); Cal. Const. art. XIII, § 1(a); Cal. Rev. & Tax. Code § § 202-03 (Deering 1958) (colleges, including college housing, and public schools); Cal. Const. art. XIII, § 1(c); Cal. Rev. & Tax. Code § 214 (Deering 1958) (property used exclusively for religious, scientific, hospital, or charitable purposes); Cal. Const. art. XIII, § 1½; Cal. Rev. & Tax. Code § § 206, 206.1 (Deering 1958) (church property); Cal. Const. art. XIII, § 12¾; Cal. Rev. & Tax. Code § 211 (Deering 1958) (land used for young grape vines and fruit- and nut-bearing trees). Many of the foregoing land uses directly impose additional costs upon the community, and all indirectly impose such costs by removal of land from possible uses, such as factories, from which localities could reap high property tax revenues.

(62) 402 U.S. at 142.

(63) 42 U.S.C. § 1410(h) (1970). The public housing authority does give the local community in which a project is located ten percent of its rentals. In addition, the authority must pay for any "municipal services" performed by private parties for which other members of the community must pay a fee. Jersey City Sewerage Authority v. Housing Authority, 40 N.J. 145, 190 A.2d 870 (1963).

(64) Jones v. Mayer Co., 392 U.S. 409 (1968), construing 42 U.S.C. § 1982 (1970), 42 U.S.C. § § 3601-31 (Supp. V, 1969(. The state was earlier forbidden to use race as a criterion in regulating the housing market. See, e.g., Hurd v. Hodge, 334 U.S. 24 (1948); Shelley v. Kraemer, 334 U.S. 1 (1948); City of Richmond v. Deans, 281 U.S. 704 (1930); Harmon v. Tyler, 273 U.S. 668 (1926); Buchanan v. Warley, 245 U.S. 60 (1917). This is not to suggest that the question in Valtierra is one of private discrimination, but rather that the difficulty of detecting discrimination in Valtierra is similar.

(65) Fiss, supra note 43, at 296.

(66) 402 U.S. at 141.

(67) 364 U.S. 339 (1960).

(68) 402 U.S. at 141.

(69) Fiss, The Charlotte-Mecklenberg Case—Its Significance for Northern School Desegregation, 38 U. Chi. L. Rev. 697 (1971).

(70) 402 U.S. at 141.

(71) Id.

(72) In Palmer v. Thompson, 403 U.S. 217 (1971), the most recent case in

which the Court confronted the issue whether motive or effect is the proper test for determining racial discrimination, Chief Justice Burger and Justices Black, Blackmun, Douglas, Harlan, and Stewart favored the effect test while Justices White, Brennan, and Marshall preferred the motive test. For views of other commentators, see notes 43, 69 supra and note 83 infra.

(73) 391 U.S. 367 (1968).

(74) Id. at 384-85.

(75) 294 U.S. 587 (1935). The Court's approach in Norris should be contrasted with that in Yick Wo v. Hopkins, 118 U.S. 356 (1886), in which the Court did not infer from the data presented merely that the basis of classification in the statute's administration was race. Rather, the Court also inferred a motive of racial animus. Although under the particular circumstances of that case the inference may not have been mere speculation, it would have been equally consistent with the effect of the state's actions had the motive been a desire to assist white laundry operators rather than racial animus.

(76) 403 U.S. 217 (1971).

(77) Id. at 224.

(78) The Court mentioned Griffin v. County School Board, 377 U.S. 218 (1964), and Gomillion v. Lightfoot, 364 U.S. 339, 347 (1960).

(79) 403 U.S. at 225.

(80) Id.

(81) Fiss, supra note 43, at 298.

(82) In the O'Brien decision, however, both Justices Brennan and White joined in the Court's holding that effect, not motive, was the proper test. Justice Marshall did not take part in that decision.

(83) E.g., Ely, Legislative and Administrative Motivation in Constitutional Law, 79 Yale L.J. 1205 (1970).

(84) When the new equal protection standard is applicable, the state must demonstrate a compelling governmental interest to justify the distinction made.

(85) Ely, supra note 83, at 1220.

(86) Id. at 1268.

(87) It is apparent from the appellants' and the appellees' briefs that California voters were concerned primarily about imposition by the federal government of costs upon particular localities without the consent of their residents. One pamphlet supporting the passage of article XXXIV stated:

> Time after time within the past year, California communities have had public housing projects forced upon them without regard either to the wishes of the citizens or community needs. This is a particularly critical matter in view of the fact that the long-term, multimillion-dollar public housing contracts call for tax waivers and other forms of local assistance, which the Federal Government says will amount to half the cost of the federal subsidy on the project as long as it exists.

> For government to coerce such additional hidden expense on the voters at a time when taxation and the cost of living have reached an extreme high is a "gift" of debatable value. It should be accepted or rejected by ballot. . . .

... [A] "yes" vote for this proposed amendment will strengthen local self-government and restore to the community the right to determine its own future course.

Brief for Appellees at 14-15.

(88) This hypothetical is based upon the facts found by the district court in Gautreaux v. Chicago Housing Authority, 296 F. Supp. 907, 304 F. Supp. 736 (N.D. Ill. 1969), discussed in text at notes 106-08 infra.

(89) See A. Campbell, P. Converse, W. Miller, & D. Stokes, The American Voter (1960); A. Campbell, P. Converse, W. Miller, & D. Stokes, Elections and the Political Order (1966). In the latter work the authors state: "Typically the line of explication has been 'downward' from the readily visible collective event to the component acts of individuals. As we have observed, this has led to speculative descriptions of the psychological basis of individual behavior, of which many have remained wholly untested and some have been proved by historical events to be untenable." Id. at 5. The authors explain further that "[the] problem is to identify what this motivation is. . . . [A]s long as one has only aggregative data at hand one can only speculate as to what moved the individual members of the collectivity. . . ." Id. at 2.

While the results and conclusions of survey research analysis presently available can reliably aid the court in determining motivation, it is doubtful whether the court would choose to rely on survey research analysis. Courts have not previously measured motivation in this manner and might be reluctant to initiate a precedent of scientific probing into people's minds upon every charge of racial discrimination. Furthermore, it is doubtful whether members of Congress or a state legislature would submit to such an examination of their motives. To limit scientific testing of motives to laws passed by the people themselves would perhaps be artificial if it is the surest way to obtain accuracy.

(90) Ely, supra note 83, at 1268.

(91) Professor Ely, while preferring the motive test in racial discrimination cases, does not refer in his discussion of Reitman to survey research analysis which concluded that racial prejudice played a significant part in the passage of Proposition 14. Wolfinger & Greenstein, The Repeal of Fair Housing in California: An Analysis of Referendum Voting, 62 Am. Pol. Sci. Rev. 753 (1968).

(92) See text at notes 79-81 supra.

(93) 402 U.S. at 141.

(94) 118 U.S. at 373.

(95) Fiss, supra note 43, at 297.

(96) Id. at 299.

(97) 364 U.S. at 341.

(98) Fiss, supra note 43, at 299.

(99) "[T]he impact of the law falls on minorities." 313 F. Supp. at 5.

(100) "It is no longer a permissible legislative objective to contain or exclude persons simply because they are poor." Id. at 4.

(101) In Gomillion the Court found that residence is a permissible redistricting criterion. Removal of the necessity of finding that that wealth is no more justifiable than race as a criterion in order to make a determination of functional equivalence represents a departure from Professor Fiss's theory. See

note 43 supra.

(102) In Chicago, the locus of Gautreaux v. Chicago Housing Authority, 296 F. Supp. 907, 304 F. Supp. 736 (N.D. Ill. 1969), approximately ninety percent of persons in public housing or on waiting lists were members of racial minorities. In areas in which the percentage is not nearly as high, analysis of patterns approval and disapproval in the referenda may be necessary to determine whether the basis of decision was racial. This is not to imply that the Court has not previously faced such difficulties. On the contrary, the achievement of educational integration, a "unitary nonracial school system," poses similar problems. See Fiss, supra note 69.

(103) 402 U.S. at 141.

(104) Fiss, supra note 43, at 296.

(105) 313 F. Supp. at 3.

(106) 296 F. Supp. 907, 304 F. Supp. 736 (N.D. Ill. 1969).

(107) Defendants urge that [Chicago Housing Authority] officials never entertained racist attitudes and that the racial character of the neighborhood has never been a factor in CHA's selection of a suitable site. . . . [T]hese statements are undoubtedly true. It is also true that there is no evidence that the Aldermen who vetoed the white sites were necessarily motivated by racial animus when they followed a policy of keeping Negroes out of white neighborhoods.

296 F. Supp. at 914.

(108) Id. at 912.

(109) 313 F. Supp. at 5.

(110) After noting that the district court had chiefly relied on the Hunter case, the Court stated: "The Court below erred in relying on Hunter to invalidate Article XXXIV. Unlike the case before us, Hunter rested on the conclusion that Akron's referendum law denied equal protection by placing 'special burdens on racial minorities within the governmental process.'" 402 U.S. at 140.

(111) 387 U.S. at 381. The somewhat inscrutable opinion of the Court in Reitman has perhaps been most accurately characterized as a "pas de deux with the California high court." Sager, supra note 20, at 790. Justice Harlan, dissenting in Reitman, argued that the Court's decision was premised upon the assumption that the neutrality of the amendment was a sham, and that "[i]n depicting the provision as tantamount to active State encouragement of discrimination the Court essentially relies on the fact that the California Supreme Court so concluded." 387 U.S. at 389-90. Reitman has meant a number of different things to a number of different persons. See, e.g., Black, supra note 20, at 82:

> The rule which I would propose, then, as a basis for the Reitman decision, is that where a racial group is in a political duel with those who would explicitly discriminate against it as a racial group, and where the regulatory action the racial group wants is of full and undoubted federal constitutionality, the state may not place in the way of the racial minority's attaining its political goal any barriers which, within the state's political system taken as a whole, are especially difficult of surmounting, by comparison with those barriers that normally stand in the way of those who wish to use the political processes to get what they want.

According to Karst & Horowitz, supra note 20, at 51, the Court's opinion "makes clear that it decided the case on the basis of the state's involvement in racial discrimination, and not because of any structural limitation on Negroes' ability to make their influence felt."

(112) The meaning of "encouragement" in the Court's opinion is somewhat ambiguous. However, it is perhaps most consistent with the Court's prior opinions, see e.g., United States v. O'Brien, 391 U.S. 367 (1968), discussed in text at note 73 supra, to adopt the view of Karst & Horowitz, supra note 20, at 47: "[T]o the extent that the California Court did hold that Proposition 14 was an encouragement of private discrimination, it plainly did so, not by reading a declaration of purpose into the text of Proposition 14, but by measuring the conceded effect of the amendment. . . ."

(113) 393 U.S. 385 (1969).

(114) Id. at 386.

(115) Id. at 389, 391 (emphasis added).

(116) Id. at 393.

(117) Pub. L. No. 90-284, 82 Stat. 73 (1968).

(118) 392 U.S. 409 (1968).

(119) 387 U.S. 369 (1967).

(120) 393 U.S. 385 (1969).

(121) 403 U.S. 217 (1971).

(122) Id. at 223.

(123) Proposition 14 clearly imposed "a special burden" upon minorities seeking to pass fair housing legislation. The effect of repealing the fair housing ordinance in Hunter and prohibiting the enactment of future fair housing legislation except by referendum would arguably "encourage" discrimination within the meaning of Reitman, although the Hunter court chose not to rely upon the "encouragement" standard in favor of the more traditional equal protection approach of increased procedural burden.

(124) Another approach is, of course, to limit Reitman or Valtierra to its specific facts—to say that constitutional principles apparently enunciated in either case have no application to any other case.

II.

INNER-CITY
HOUSING

TICKING TIME BOMB:
THE REALITIES OF INNER-CITY
HOUSING COSTS

George Sternlieb
Robert W. Burchell
James W. Hughes

Increased housing costs rapidly are demonstrating the inadequacy of historic means of subsidizing housing for moderate- and low-income groups. Construction costs, money costs, and even more strikingly, tax burdens (particularly in older central cities) severely reduce the "throughput" of governmental efforts. As the material which follows makes clear, unless we are willing to leave the housing of the "less than rich" to the vagaries of the filtering-down process, much more striking and much more costly efforts at subsidization will be called for.

The particular housing developments which are analyzed in the following article are located in Newark, New Jersey. This is a relatively high-cost area; however, when the analysis is paralleled to that of the Kaiser Commission,(1) it is clear that it is far from atypical.

The trade-offs between housing subsidies and equivalent expenditures on other social fronts have attracted very little methodical research. Housing has a strong constituency; it is the epitome of the physical, i.e., it can be seen, and the money expended on it can be measured in reasonably clear-cut terms. A high priority is given to housing as one of the primary elements of the good life.

Less obvious but not least among housing's virtues, from a governmental point of view, is that many of the subsidies involved in housing production can be relatively hidden. Amortization periods which would test the longevity of a reinforced concrete dam can be given to lightly constructed residential structures. Interest rates can benefit from government guarantees without seeming to directly impact governmental budgets; massive amounts of capital expenditures can be made in any one year with comparatively small first-year subsidization of interest rates. Local taxes can be forgone and federal taxes can be offset without deleterious and immediate effect on the fiscal balance of the governmental bodies in question.

Despite these demonstrations of fiscal tightrope walking, the gap between the costs involved in the provision of new housing and the rent-paying capacity of those who are to be housed is glaringly evident. The size of the gap, no matter how well-concealed, is of such magnitude as to raise some questions regarding the conventional wisdom in the subsidized-housing sphere.

The material which follows is an analysis of three different configurations of housing: a rehabilitation project, a low-rise housing project, and a high-rise housing project, all within the same city. The costing elements which are utilized essentially are phrased in terms of the rent dollar.

REHABILITATION (THREE-FAMILY FRAME STRUCTURES)

Amity Village is a ninety-six unit cooperative project which will provide housing for moderate-income black families through the rehabilitation of twenty-seven multifamily frame dwellings in the West Ward of Newark, New Jersey. Its physical location is on the fringe of the city in an area that has traditionally been well-maintained.(2)

The final housing program, with rent levels of $115 for studios, $150 for two-bedroom units, and $173 for three-bedroom units, will serve families whose adjusted family income (total income-irregular sources) is greater than $5,500 to $8,300 for the studio to three-bedroom units, respectively.

NEW CONSTRUCTION (LOW-RISE MASONRY STRUCTURES)

University Court is a 270-unit garden apartment development located with walking distance of Newark's main commercial area. It is a local effort which provides low-rise, cooperative-type housing for moderate-income families. The project is constructed on a cleared urban renewal site in an area of mixed land use (industrial, commercial, and residential) in varying construction stages (construction, demolition, and dormant).

This area is typical of those selected for the general urban renewal project. It is an area of significant deterioration in which the nucleus will be upgraded and, hopefully, restored to its former vitality. In this particular case, the time delay between recognition of the problem, land clearance, and the eventual rejuvenation and disposition of the land to the private market was over eight years. The resulting inaction and misreading of market demand has further contributed to the decay of the local neighborhood. It is now questionable whether the surrounding environs are in suitable condition to derive benefit from a local catalyst, regardless of its individual quality or its particular location.

The concept of housing location which established University Court is quite different from that employed by Amity Village. University Court represents an effort to remain within the core and to attempt to overcome local social and physical decay, rather than to move outside in an effort to escape these problems.

This project's rent levels of $123, $150, and $175 for one-, two-, and three-bedroom units closely approximate both rent-schedule and potential-tenant profiles of the Amity Village program.

NEW CONSTRUCTION (HIGH RISE MASONRY)

Zion Towers is a 265-unit, twenty-eight story high-rise rental housing project sponsored by the Congregation B'nai Zion, a Newark-based organization. As was the case with the Amity Village development, Zion Towers is located in a relatively well-maintained fringe area of Newark, which borders but is not within the core and Model Cities areas. It is, for that reason, substantially free from "core politics" and from the massive physical and social decay that plagues the inner city. The resulting rental levels, however, are somewhat different from the previous two examples. One-, two-, and three-bedroom units cost, respectively, $167, $192, and $214.

THE VARIOUS ELEMENTS OF HOUSING COSTS

The three elements of housing costs that appear below represent the cost necessary to *plan housing, construct housing,* and *occupy housing,* and are defined as follows:

1. *Development Cost:* initial expenses incurred on a project *not directly* related to the construction process. They typically include land acquisition, design and engineering, interim financing, miscellaneous fees, and demolition expenses.

2. *Construction cost:* initial expenses incurred on a project which are *directly* related to the construction process. They include site preparation, utility installation, residential construction, and landscaping and paving. Included in these are on-site wages, building and materials, and construction overhead.

Development Cost + Construction Cost = Total Project Cost

3. *Occupancy Cost:* the recurring monthly carrying expenses, which include not only initial costs but also subsequent operating, maintenance, and replacement costs.

Occupancy Cost = Total Monthly Rental Expense

TABLE I

COMPARATIVE DEVELOPMENT COSTS

	High-Rise (Zion)	Low-Rise (University)	Rehabilitation (Amity)
Developer (development fees)	0.0%*	3.0%	0.5%
Architect and consulting engineer (preliminary and final work)	3.0	2.0	1.0
Land purchase	3.0	7.5	36.5
Demolition	0.5	0	1.5
Interim financing	5.5	9.5	5.5
Miscellaneous fees, administration, and relocation	5.0	4.0	6.5
Total	17.0%	26.0%	51.5%

*Nonprofit developer.

Development costs in the Newark area were found to vary from a high of 51.5 percent in the multifamily rehabilitation to a low of 17 percent in high-rise construction.(3)

Interim financing is such a conventional development cost that many brokers and developers include it on their prepared estimate sheets. It consists of brokerage fees, a financing "charge," and the interest on the construction loan. Characteristically, this expense runs between 5 and 10 percent of total project costs and is usually added as one of the items contributing to the mortgaged principal. In the Newark study, interim financing varied from 5.5 to 9.5 percent of total development costs. These differences may be attributed to the difference between the 6.5 percent market interest rate in 1967 compared with the below-market interest rates of 4.5 percent and 5.5 percent available in 1969 (through the State Finance Agency's tax-free bonds).

Land costs in the Newark study varied from $615 per unit in the high-rise structure to $5,850 per unit in the rehabilitation project. The latter, of course, included the residential structure. Site costs in the high-rise development were low because the land area involved was minimal, i.e., less than three-fourths of an acre for 265 units. In the low-rise example, however, a considerable amount of land (nine acres) was purchased at significantly reduced rates from the local urban renewal authority. This resulted in a four- to five-fold saving over what would normally have been paid at the current market rates, and kept land costs close to the Kaiser figure of 10 percent of project costs.

It must be realized that land costs vary widely from city to city. Newark, as part of the New York metropolitan area, is in one of the fastest rising land-cost areas in the country. The 1967 riots, the abnormal tax rate, and city's large nonwhite population have, however, caused inner-city land values to lag significantly behind land values in other parts of the region.(4)

TABLE II

COMPARATIVE CONSTRUCTION COSTS

	High-Rise (Zion)	Low-Rise (University)	Rehabilitation (Amity)
Foundation, excavation	5.5%	5.0%	1.5%
Structural frame	33.0	24.0	8.0
Interior systems	26.5	16.0	13.0
Interior preparation and appliances	17.5	24.0	24.0
Sitework and landscaping	0.5	5.0	2.0
Total	83.0%	74.0%	48.5%

CONSTRUCTION COSTS

Construction costs in the Newark area varied from 48.5 percent in multifamily rehabilitation to 83 percent in high-rise construction. As is indicated in Table II, the most significant categories of costs are those involved with the structural frame, interior systems, and interior preparation, respectively.

The structural frame, consisting of the frame material (wood, steel, reinforced concrete), roof work, siding installation, and exterior door and window placement, was generally the largest construction item in the two new construction projects. One of the usual goals in rehabilitation is to seek a structure which is basically sound. Thus a relatively small amount of money should be necessary to restore the frame and the exterior shell to desired standards (10 percent). Similarly, in low-rise construction, where the frame is usually wood or relatively lightweight structural steel, the simple framing technique and convenience of constructing two to three stories keeps the structural cost modest (24 percent).

Interior systems, that is, work performed by mechanical subcontractors (heating, plumbing, electrical), generally get more complex as the size of housing form increases. In medium-rise and high-rise units elevators, and in some cases central air conditioning, become a necessary part of this expense. As expected, in Newark these costs varied from 13 percent of the project total for the walk-up rehabilitation model to 26.5 percent for the elevated and air-conditioned high-rise. Interior preparation, including appliances, is characteristically the high percentage item for typical rehabilitation projects.

The same high percentages do not hold true for new construction. The general figure given for interior preparation is 24 percent of total project costs, only a few points below that of the structural frame.

OCCUPANCY COSTS

The occupancy costs, summarized for all three projects in Table III, show only slight variations among the building types. It is well established that the drain of debt service is the largest cost of operation in the building industry. In the three cases examined, debt service accounts for 50 to 60 percent of the total costs. This is a direct expense for the renter and accounts for the greatest element of his monthly rent.

TABLE III

COMPARATIVE OCCUPANCY COSTS

	High-Rise (Zion)	Low-Rise (University)	Rehabilitation (Amity)
Payroll, management, and administration	8.0%	11.0%	4.0%
Fuel and utilities	8.0	9.0	10.5
Decorating, maintenance, and repairs	2.5	2.0	5.5
Taxes	11.5	20.0	14.0
Insurance	1.5	2.0	3.5
Debt service	60.0	50.0	54.0
Vacancies/bad debts	4.0	3.0	5.0
Reserves/profits	4.5	3.0	3.5
Total	100.0%	100.0%	100.0%

The second greatest contributor to occupancy costs is real estate taxes.(5) In the three examples, taxes range from 11.5 to 20 percent of rent costs. The variations among the different projects result from the difference between a "20 percent of gross income" tax payment for university and the other two situations. The specific effects of these tax shelters will be dealt with shortly.

The remaining elements, fuel plus landlord-paid utility costs, expenses for payroll, management, and administration, and miscellaneous other expenses which are self-explanatory, are generally in line with the Kaiser study findings.

EFFECT OF SUBSIDIES

The following two sections discuss two integral subsidized elements of occupancy cost: the in-lieu property tax payment and below-market interest rate financing. Each of these elements was of vital importance in keeping the rents within manageable limits.

PROPERTY TAX SUBSIDY

In each case, the rental without the tax shelter was determined by assuming the total project cost equals the true tax value of the project. Utilizing a county equalization ratio of .89 percent and a tax rate of $7.99 per $100 of assessed valuation, an estimated normal tax payment was determined.(6) This was compared to the presently established tax payments: 15 percent of gross shelter rent for Amity Village and Zion Towers and 20 percent of gross revenue for University Court. The difference between the two determinations comprised the rental difference.

TABLE IV

RENTAL LEVELS—TAX SHELTER EFFECT

	Present Rental (Three-Bedroom)	Rental Without Tax Shelter (Three-Bedroom)	Percent Differences
Amity Village (rehabilitation)	$173	$248	43%
University Court (low-rise)	175	250	43
Zion Tower (high-rise)	214	314	47

Table IV vividly illustrates the significance of tax shelters. Without this form of subsidy, it is difficult to see how any private developer can build anything and keep rental levels remotely near the already high ones of the subsidized projects. In the cases at hand, it would not be feasible for a developer to construct three-bedroom units with a rental level below $250 a month.

Concurrently, an important consideration, which must not be overlooked in attempts to provide housing, is the added financial burden placed on the city of Newark through efforts to maintain some semblance of reasonable rental levels by the use of tax subsidies. While housing normally does not provide a substantial profit in terms of a municipal cost-revenue analysis, the deficit incurred by the city is increased significantly when in-lieu tax payments are permitted. The following estimates of the net deficit incurred for a city like Newark underscore this point.

Net Deficit Per Unit(7)

	Full Taxes	15% of Gross Shelter Rent in Lieu of Taxes
Two-bedroom unit	$ 240-$ 600	$ 600-$ 940
Three-bedroom unit	1120- 1710	1540- 2140

The ranges presented represent variations in taxes due to family size, school children, etc., from a low estimate to a conservatively high estimate. Thus, when housing is considered in the broader context of the total urban situation, provision of suitable lower-cost housing introduces a greater gap between revenues and cost of services. Whether this will lead to a raising of taxes or a decrease in services is a significant question still unanswered.

FINANCE COST SUBSIDY

Low-rate, long-term financing is the second major form of subsidy.

TABLE V

RENTAL LEVEL EFFECT–INTEREST RATE

	Present Monthly Rental (Subsidized– 3-bedroom)	Monthly Rental at Market* Rate Financing (Nonsubsidized)	Percent Difference
Amity Village (rehabilitation)	$173	$205	18.5%
University Court (low-rise)	175	222	26.8
Zion Tower (high-rise)	214	258	21.0

*includes Tax Subsidy and financing at 9.5 percent for fifty years (Amity–thirty-five years).

Nonsubsidized financing of the three study projects, at the rate of 9.5 percent (1969) would have resulted in significantly higher monthly rentals. The figures in Table V indicate the degree to which monthly rentals would escalate were New Jersey Home Financing Authority financing not employed. Without this program, a developer-builder would have to charge, on the average, 22 percent higher rents if he used conventional financing.

THE EFFECT OF BOTH SUBSIDIES

With conventional financing and full tax payments, a shortage of even moderate-income housing is unavoidable. For example, the least expensive three-bedroom unit in any of the case studies discussed could not be offered for significantly less than $300 monthly. However, by using NJHFA low-rate, long-term financing and in-lieu tax payments, the monthly rentals were reduced by 60 to 70 percent.

TABLE VI

RENTAL LEVELS–EFFECT OF TAX SHELTER
AND INTEREST SUBSIDY

	Present Monthly Rental (3-bedroom)	Monthly Rental With Conventional Financing and Full Property Tax	Percent Difference
Amity Village (rehabilitation)	$173	$280	61.5%
University Court (low-rise)	175	295	69.8
Zion Towers (high-rise)	214	358	68.0

The significance of subsidized financing and in-lieu tax payments becomes even more dramatic when compared to the low reduction of monthly rentals if a 25 percent decrease in construction costs were used instead of these two forms of subsidy. (A construction cost reduction of 25 percent is of greater magnitude than that which probably will be achieved in Operation Breakthrough.)

The University Court (low-rise) project serves as a good point of comparison. If the occupancy costs for this project are examined, 50 percent of the total cost (rental level) is a function of debt service. This 50 percent equals the total costs of construction and development plus interest. Since construction costs alone amounts to 75 percent of these total costs, its percentage of the total rental cost (occupancy cost) equals (.75 X .50) 37.5 percent. Thus, construction costs make up 37.5 percent of the total rent. If these costs were reduced by 25 percent, this would result in a 9.4 percent (.25 X .375) reduction in the monthly rental.

TABLE VII

UNIVERSITY COURT

	(Low-Rise) Three-Bedroom Unit	Percent Reduction in Rent
Rental level without subsidy	$295	not applicable
Rental level with interest rate and tax subsidies	175	69.8%
Rental level without subsidy–25 percent reduction in construction cost	267	9.4

Reductions in construction costs, therefore, unless of a very dramatic nature, are relatively unimportant when compared to the impact of tax payments and financing costs. As has been shown, while present subsidies reduce rentals by 69.8 percent, a 25 percent reduction in construction costs could only reduce rentals by 9.4 percent. In comparison, subsidized financing and in-lieu tax payments can reduce monthly rentals to between $175 to $214 for a

three-bedroom apartment from unsubsidized levels that would exceed $300.
The factors which actually play the dominant role in the costs which are
passed on to the housing consumer through his rental payment should be quite
evident. The measure of a planner is not really how he reacts to evidence but
how well he resists purposeful propaganda and visible convenient scapegoats.
*This demonstration of how financing charges and inner-city tax levels affect
rental structures should lay to rest some convenient myths.*

SUMMARY AND CONCLUSIONS

Employing the three case studies, as a base, it is possible to determine the
alternative housing types that can be provided in Newark at the present time.
Also shown are the rental levels that could be obtained through existing federal
programs and the income levels a family would require to maintain such rentals.
Two of the housing types—the rehabilitated and the low-rise—can potentially
serve families with incomes as low as $2,850 per year if rent supplements are
utilized.

To begin, it is desirable to review whom the private market serves or can
serve. Assuming a 25 percent of total income allotment for rents, the
unsubsidized projects would require the following incomes:

Type Unit (Three-Bedroom)	Rent	Income Required
Rehabilitation	$280	$14,500
Low-rise	295	15,300
High-rise	358	19,100

It is recognized that the three-bedroom case, illustrated above, may exhibit a
higher rent than the average unit; nevertheless, a majority of the underhoused
families would undoubtedly require such accommodations. In any case, the
private market can only supply new or rehabilitated housing at rents that would
require an income of approximately $15,000, and this for housing which lacks
frills or luxuries. Since only 4.3 percent of the families in the entire city, and 1.6
percent of those in the inner city, earn approximately $15,000 a year, the
private market, publicly unassisted, can only serve a tiny portion of the Newark
population.(8)

Since the private market has such limited applicability, it is obvious why the
three projects examined had to be financed under NJHFA auspices. The rents
resulting from this program, in which two public (nonfederal) subsidies were
employed—in-lieu tax payment by the City of Newark and long-term,
low-interest, tax-free bonds of NJHFA—require the following income levels:

Type Unit (Three-Bedroom)	Rent	Income Required
Rehabilitation	$173	$ 8,300
Low-rise	175	8,500
High-rise	214	10,300

Yet, only 18 percent of inner-city families and 26 percent of families in the
entire city have an income exceeding $8,500.
Federal assistance is necessary if a substantial number of families in Newark

TABLE VIII

HOUSING POSSIBILITIES IN NEWARK

Building Type (3-Bedroom Units)	State		State and Local		Federal, State, and Local			
	No-Subsidy Rent	NJHFA Financing Rent	NJHFA Financing + In-Lieu Taxes Rent	Minimum Income (Per Yr.)	Section 236* Rent	Section 236* Minimum Income (Per Yr.)	Section 101** Rent	Section 101** Minimum Income (Per Yr.)
Rehabilitation	$280	$248	$173	$8,300	$125	$6,000	$52	$2,850
Low-rise	295	249	175	8,500	126	6,000	53	2,900
High-rise	358	314	214	10,300	150	7,200	64	3,100

*Based on $173 rental. Section 236 is the interest-rate subsidy program of the 1968 Housing Act.
**Based on $173 rental. Section 101 is the federal rent subsidy program.

are to be able to afford standard housing. The last two columns of Table VIII show that it is possible to serve families with incomes as low as $2,850 if the Section 101 rent subsidy of the 1968 Housing Act(9) were available.

Income distribution within the core shows that 78 percent of inner-city residents would be served were such housing assistance available. Out of an inner-city population of approximately 100,000, 22,000 would still not be housed by these attempts. In the city as a whole, there are still 65,000 people (16 percent of the total), or 43,000 in addition to those in the inner city, who would not be affected by this type of program. Assuming an average family size of four, there are 5,500 families in the inner city and 16,500 families in the entire city outside the reach of this program.

Thus, the types of fiscal tightrope walking demonstrated in this article still do not span the gap between the costs of providing new housing and the rent-paying capacity of those who are to be housed. The size of the gap, no matter how it is concealed, is so great that it should engender a fresh inquiry into the conventional wisdoms in the subsidized housing sphere.

NOTES

(1) Kaiser, The Report of the President's Committee on Urban Housing, Vol. II, Technical Studies (U.S. Gov't Printing Office, Washington, D.C., 1968).

(2) The Amity Village concept was originated by the Tri-City Citizens Union for Progress, formed in 1967. This group's espoused purpose was the economic unification of the black subpopulations in the Paterson, Jersey City, and Newark areas through increased participation in activities loosely defined as "black capitalism." Tri-City Citizens Economic Union, Inc., a subgroup of the larger organization, was to direct its attention specifically to housing as a means of simultaneously improving shelter for lower-income people and opening construction employment to local black craftsmen.

(3) The variance in development costs for somewhat similar structures in the Kaiser study was much more limited, 28.5 percent for rehabilitation to 25 percent for medium-rise construction.

(4) As stated by Elsie Eaves: "The major variable [in development cost] is site cost, which includes both the costs of acquiring and those of improving the land." Eaves, "How the Many Costs of Housing Fit Together," in Douglas, The President's Commission on Urban Problems (Research Rep. No. 16, U.S. Gov't Printing Office, Washington, D.C., 1969). The range developed in her study was from $464 to $6,361 per dwelling unit.

The Kaiser study refers to the cost of acquiring the land as the "one unique developmental expense. . . . [T]he value of land in this study amounted to nearly one-tenth of the entire project and was the fastest rising element of all major costs." Kaiser, note 1 supra, at 20.

(5) Newark's effective tax rate in 1969 was $7.99 per $100 of assessed valuation, with a nominal policy of full assessment.

(6) In actuality, some form of capitalization is allowed which reduces this "normal" tax payment. Thus the case may be somewhat overstated.

(7) Human Resources Planning Project, N.J. Dep't of Community Affairs, Housing in New Jersey, 1968, p. 31.

(8) Chernick, Indik & Sternlieb, Newark-New Jersey Population and Labor

Force, Spring 1967 (Institute of Management and Labor Relations, Rutgers—The State University, 1967). The core or inner city refers to twenty-five contiguous census tracts in central Newark which are characterized by the lowest income and the greatest percentage of dilapidated housing.

(9) We are using the 1968 Housing Act terminology in this final analysis.

THE HARD ECONOMICS OF
GHETTO FIRE INSURANCE

Richard F. Syron

During the past decade property and liability insurance in the United States has deteriorated from a service that was taken for granted to a critical problem. The difficulties urban core businessmen and residents have encountered in securing and retaining property insurance for over a decade are now spreading to the suburbs. Schools and colleges are facing the choice of not insuring their properties or paying substantial rate increases. Confronted by skyrocketing automobile insurance rates the insurance industry and state legislatures are exploring alternative systems.

This article examines the difficulties associated with one particular line of insurance, fire, in one particular type of area, the urban core, using the city of Boston as an example. It demonstrates the problems urban core residents and businessmen have had with fire insurance and examines the impact of these problems on core areas. The article concludes that a conflict between the idealized functioning of the fire insurance pricing or rating mechanism and the actual incidence of fire loss is a major contributor to the fire insurance problems of core areas. An examination of fire loss data in the city of Boston for the years 1965, 1966, and 1967 indicates a wide variation in fire loss in sections of the city that pay approximately the same fire insurance rate.

Statistical tests indicate that the preponderance of dilapidated and vacant structures in the core area contributed heavily to its higher fire loss. The current FAIR plan for providing insurance in core areas is described and suggestions are made for improving it. Finally proposals are made for improving core area insurability by reforming fire insurance rating and reducing fire loss.

Fire insurance, simply stated, is a mechanism through which a large group of people share the financial burden of fire damage directly experienced by a few of them. When someone insures, he makes the decision to give up voluntarily a relatively small amount of money rather than take a chance of losing a large amount. The principal reasons for this are that an individual or firm may not want to bear the burden of risk directly or may want to use the insured property as collateral for a loan. When real or personal property is used as collateral for a loan, lenders almost always require that it be insured. For example, fire insurance is usually required for a residential mortgage.(1)

TABLE 1

INSURANCE PROBLEMS OF URBAN CORE RESIDENTS AND BUSINESSMEN

		Percentage of Those With Fire Insurance	
	Number of Respondents	Percentage of Total Without Fire Insurance	Who Had Less Coverage Than Desired	Who Thought They Paid More Than the Standard Rate
Businesses				
Boston—1967	247	35	26	54
1970*	124	32	41	22
Cleveland, Detroit, Newark, St. Louis, Oakland—Average	1,045	17	12	19
Homeowners				
Boston	233	5	25	31
Cleveland, Detroit, Newark, St. Louis, Oakland—Average	1,128	7	16	22

*1970 data from Federal Reserve Bank of Boston survey. All other data from the survey conducted by the President's National Advisory Panel on Insurance in 1967.

The fact that insurance is a prerequisite for financing is particularly relevant to the inner core or ghetto areas of the city. Much of the housing stock in Boston's inner core, as in most large cities, is inadequate or in poor condition.(2) Most efforts to improve the housing situation, whether through building new structures or rehabilitating old ones, will depend on extensive financing with a concurrent need for fire insurance. This will be especially true when projects are privately rather than government sponsored.

Insurance as a prerequisite for financing is also related to the employment problems of the core area. Increasing employment within the core itself is one way of attacking ghetto poverty and unemployment. This may be done by either bringing in outside firms or by developing indigenous enterprises. Utilizing either black capitalism or community development corporations, new enterprises in the ghetto usually require extensive financing with the concomitant need for insurance. Even in the absence of this requirement such firms are particularly vulnerable to insurance non-availability since they are often marginal, undercapitalized ventures and as a result, are particularly unable to absorb the financial loss from an uninsured fire. Inability to obtain insurance also deters outside firms from locating in the core area.

Difficulties in obtaining and retaining fire insurance began to plague urban core residents and businessmen as long as 10 years ago. In the early 1960's insurance companies started directing their underwriters to avoid insuring ghetto areas. The term "redlined area" came into usage from the practice of drawing a red line around these areas on maps in company underwriting departments. Uneasiness over the urban riots of the mid-1960's further aggravated the insurance problems of core areas.

In the fall of 1967 a sub-panel of the Kerner Commission was set up to study the insurance problems of city core areas and to recommend solutions. To determine the nature and extent of these problems, the panel interviewed over 2,500 urban core residents and businesses in Boston, Cleveland, Detroit, Newark, St. Louis, and Oakland. The survey results, summarized in table 1, revealed substantial insurance problems in all of the cities surveyed, and Boston's problems were more severe than average.(3)

The Federal Reserve Bank of Boston conducted its own survey in the spring of 1970 to determine whether the core city insurance situation had improved or deteriorated since the Panel's 1967 survey. In order to obtain maximum comparability of results, the same respondent group covered in 1967 was re-surveyed, rather than selecting a new sample. However, the mobility of the population in the area, combined with the constraints of a telephone survey, made it impossible to contact a large enough proportion of the households surveyed in 1967 to have a reliable sample size. Therefore, only the business sample was covered in the 1970 survey. As the table above indicates, the response pattern for all of the questions asked in 1970 was similar to the pattern in 1967.

A vicious circle may exist with respect to the insurance problems of core areas. One reason insurance is unavailable in the ghetto is that it is blighted and companies are reluctant to insure such areas. However, one reason it is a blighted area is that people cannot obtain insurance and as a result have difficulty securing financing to improve or even maintain their property. Even if financing is not needed, a homeowner or businessman has little incentive to improve or maintain uninsurable property. A general neighborhood deterioration may ensue, with insurance non-availability acting as a catalyst.

INSURANCE COMPANY PROFITABILITY

Insurance company data indicate that during the period 1960-70 fire insurance as a whole was less profitable than other lines of coverage for companies that write most fire insurance. The relationship between insurance companies' losses and expenses on a national scale is expressed by what is called the "combined loss and expense ratio." This ratio is the sum of the ratios of fire loss incurred to premiums earned and of non-loss expenses to premiums written.(4) A combined loss and expense ratio of less than 100 percent indicates that a company had made a profit on its *underwriting* experience while a ratio of more than 100 percent indicates it has suffered a loss on its underwriting ventures.

It is very important to note here that the combined ratio reflects only a company's underwriting experience and does not consider its investment income. Insurance companies are quasi-depository institutions in that a substantial part of their income is generated by investing premiums paid to them and held until paid in aggregate for losses. A company with a combined loss and expense ratio of more than 100 percent for all lines of insurance may still make an overall profit if its investment income more than offsets its underwriting losses.

Companies with a stock form of corporate organization write the vast majority (about 80 percent) of American fire insurance. During the period of 1960-1970 these companies had a combined ratio of 99.8 for all lines of insurance, excluding fire, indicating they just about broke even on their underwriting experience.(5) However, during the same period stock companies had a loss ratio of 101.2 for fire indicating this line generated underwriting losses. Thus, the companies that write most fire insurance had a relatively unprofitable experience with that line on a national level. Since urban core areas were considered a particularly risky segment of the whole fire insurance market companies were naturally inclined to avoid them.

THE RELATIVE PROFITABILITY OF INSURING CORE AREAS

Since insurance company earnings and expense data cannot be geographically disaggregated below the state level, no exact data are available to determine how unprofitable ghetto areas usually are. Insurance companies do have some indication of the profitability of business generated by a particular insurance agency. If an agency generates unprofitable business over a long period of time, it is of course in the company's interest to refuse to accept any more business from that agency. Moreover, there is a high correlation between canceling an agency and redlining an area. However, since an agency writes different types of coverage and does not confine its writing solely to one area, an agency's profitability is not a very accurate indicator of the profitability of writing insurance in a given area. Accordingly, in this study, an attempt was made to determine the relative profitability of providing fire insurance for core area property by contrasting the fire loss experience in different parts of Boston with whatever variation there is in the price or rate paid for fire insurance.

For pricing purposes, insurance companies are treated as quasi-public utilities, their prices being set rather than determined by the free interaction of supply and demand. Insurance companies belong to rating bureaus which, acting as their statistical agencies, prepare rate schedules for them. These rate schedules are then reviewed by the State Insurance Commissioner who may subsequently approve or disapprove them. In Massachusetts, the law requires that rates "should not be excessive, inadequate or unfairly discriminatory."(6) Rates are supposed to discriminate among risks with different probabilities of loss, that is, risks with a lower probability of loss should pay a lower rate than those with a higher one.

While there is tremendous constrast between the complexity of the pricing method for fire insurance for commercial structures and the simplicity of the method for dwellings, neither one gives much weight to a property's location within a city. Dwellings are "manually rated," with one rate applicable to all structures that fall within a relatively broad class; commercial risks, on the other hand, are "specifically rated" with a rate developed for each property. Both manual and specific rates consider the building's usage and construction as well as its proximity to and the quality of the fire department serving the area. The municipal fire protection factor is usually the only element in either rating scheme that specifically considers the risk. However, this factor does not provide for much geographic flexibility. Since the same fire department is used citywide, the quality rating is the same and most buildings in large cities are within 500 feet of a hydrant, the best proximity rating. Boston has a high fire protection rating, and therefore it has some of the lowest fire insurance rates in the state.

There is some slight geographic variation in fire insurance rates for dwellings in Boston because of a "conflagration charge" applied to parts of South Boston, the South End, Roxbury and Dorchester. This charge is either five or 10 cents per $100 of insurance and as such is not a source of substantial geographic rate variation. The charge originated from a fear that the density of buildings in these areas might contribute to a general conflagration. No similar charge is applicable to commercial structures.

Because rates are basically the same for similar structures in all parts of Boston, losses need to be approximately the same if companies are going to write insurance in core sections voluntarily. To determine whether there was in fact a substantial variation in fire losses in different sections of the city, information was collected from the Boston Fire Department on approximately 6,000 fires in occupied buildings in Boston during the years 1965, 1966 and 1967.(7) For each fire, data were collected on the estimated amount of building damage, the building usage and in what section of the city it was located.

For insurance purposes, absolute fire loss figures for an area are not meaningful in themselves. The fact that two areas in the city each have $500,000 worth of building damage in a year obviously does not mean that they are equally poor insurance risks. The same gross amount of damage might represent 2 percent of all building value in one area, and one-fourth of a percent in another area. To make the gross building damage in different sections of the city comparable, a common denominator is needed. The only data available citywide on building value are assessed values of buildings, collected by the City Assessor's office by ward. Since assessed value of buildings is only available by ward, all analysis is done on that basis.

Because the insurable value of property is more likely to be correlated with its real or sales value rather than with its assessed value, some adjustments had to be made. The relationship between sales and assessed value varied widely throughout the city of Boston. "A Study of Assessment-Sales Ratios," by Oliver Oldman and Henry Aaron, reveals that the ratio of assessed value to sales value in Boston varies from 35 percent in West Roxbury, an outlying section of the city, to 74 percent in the sub-standard Roxbury area.(8) Accordingly, the data were adjusted for differences in assessment ratios to approximate the sales value of all structures by ward. The resulting figures approximate the sales value of all structures by ward. These corrected figures were then used as the denominator in constructing a "fire loss index." The numerator of the fire loss index is the sum of the estimated damage to all taxable buildings by fire in a ward in a particular year. To summarize symbolically:

Fire Loss Index for Each Ward in Each Year = FLI

$$FLI = \frac{L}{AV \times \dfrac{SV}{AV}}$$

Where

L = Reported fire damage to taxable structures in each ward in each year.

AV = Assessed value of taxable structures in each ward in each year

$\dfrac{SV}{AV}$ = Oldman-Aaron ratio of sales value to assessed value applicable to each ward

The fire loss index is an estimate of the percentage of structure value in a ward destroyed by fire in a year. It is *not* a valid indication of insurance payouts to that area; rather, it indicates the *relative* magnitude of losses in different parts of the city. Table 2 gives the average value of the fire loss index for the three years for each ward of the city, as an indicator of the fire loss experience of the different wards.

TABLE 2
AVERAGE FIRE LOSS INDEX, 1965-67
CITY OF BOSTON BY WARD

Ward	Fire Loss Index	Rank	Ward	Fire Loss Index	Rank
1	.193	10	12	.507	2
2	.281	6	13	.222	9
3	.235	8	14	.244	7
4	.122	13	15	.193	10
5	.052	20	16	.084	16
6	.087	14	17	.084	16
7	.139	12	18	.047	21
8	.437	3	19	.085	15
9	.971	1	20	.022	22
10	.337	5	21	.084	16
11	.399	4	22	.058	19

Statistical tests indicate that the variation between wards in the fire loss index is highly significant.(9) More important for the core area fire insurance problem is the variation between the indices for the core and noncore wards. For example, the average fire loss index for Ward 9 in Roxbury (core area) is 44 times that for Ward 20, West Roxbury (noncore). The average fire loss index for Wards 8, 9, 11, and 12, an area that roughly coincides with the redline district, is .579 or slightly more than four times the average for the rest of the city.(10)

It does not appear that the variation in fire loss index can be explained by building usage and construction, factors considered in insurance rating. As mentioned above, commercial structures and dwellings are rated differently, and businesses often pay higher rates. Accordingly, it would have been desirable to construct two separate sets of fire loss indices, one for commercial structures and another for residences. However, since an essential input in the fire loss index is the assessed value of buildings in a ward and the city can provide this only in aggregate form and cannot say how much of the assessed building value in a ward is devoted to commercial and how much to residential use, it is only possible to construct a composite fire loss index.(11)

This data constraint does not affect our conclusion on core area profitability since the difference between the fire loss index for the core area and the rest of the city is too great to be explained by a reasonable variation in building type and usage. A detailed examination of the characteristics of individual wards reveals that core and noncore wards with similar building use and construction have widely different fire loss indices.(12)

Similarly, when Wards 8, 9, 11, and 12, the core area, are taken together they provide a good cross-section of the building type and usage found in the city of Boston as a whole. However, their fire loss index was much greater than the rest of the city.

While many have blamed riots for the collapse of the urban core fire insurance market, the one civil disturbance in Boston that occurred during this period contributed little to the area's higher fire loss.(13) Although the threat rather than the occurrence of riots may have been important, the insurance problems of the Boston core area, at least, seem to stem more from the conflict between higher fire losses and an inflexible pricing mechanism.

An overall reform of the fire insurance pricing mechanism would seem to be in order. Since most insurance rating schemes were developed in the pre-computer era, the relative risk of insuring different properties was determined judgmentally rather than empirically. While data are used to raise or lower the overall statewide rate structure, no check is made as to whether its internal rate relationships are still reasonable. For example, no examination is made to determine whether a town with a class three municipal fire protection rating does indeed have higher fire losses than a class two town, although residents and businesses of the class three town pay higher rates on the basis of a past assumption that their losses will be greater.

Although the inflexibility of fire insurance rating contributed heavily to insurance companies' reluctance to writing fire insurance in urban cores, improving the pricing mechanism alone will not solve the urban core fire insurance problem. Because of the area's high fire loss experience, many urban core residents and businessmen would be unable to afford fire insurance at a rate commensurate with risk even if it were available. Accordingly, the area's high fire loss must be reduced, its premiums subsidized, or both.

THE FAIR PLAN

In 1968 as an out-growth of the Kerner Commission, Congress passed legislation encouraging the states to establish FAIR Plans (fair access to insurance requirements).(14) The purpose of these plans is to provide property insurance at an affordable rate to urban core residents and businessmen who have been unable to obtain coverage in the open market. Massachusetts, one of the first states to establish such a plan, requires that all companies participate as a condition of writing insurance in the Commonwealth.

Any company writing fire insurance in a state with a FAIR plan is eligible to purchase a government backup, or re-insurance, for losses the company suffers from riots in that state.(15) This re-insurance is sold at a low premium by the Federal Insurance Administration in the Department of Housing and Urban

Development.

Anyone unable to obtain fire insurance in the normal market in Massachusetts may apply to the FAIR plan for an inspection of his property. The property may be accepted, rejected outright or rejected with the understanding it will be accepted if correctable hazards such as faulty wiring are removed. From its inception to September 30, 1971, the Massachusetts FAIR plan wrote 47,532 policies. In the same period 6,134 risks were conditionally rejected while 297 were declined outright. All risks accepted are insured at standard rates.

Because the FAIR plan insures poorer than normal risks at standard rates, it incurs net underwriting losses. The Massachusetts FAIR plan lost approximately $4 million in its first 3 years.(16) While the idea of subsidizing core area fire insurance may be a good one, there are problems with the way the present system does this. While it may be appropriate to subsidize the high cost of providing insurance to urban core residences and businesses, under the present system this subsidy is hidden and may occasionally be misdirected.

The FAIR plan was designed to deal with breakdowns of core area fire insurance markets on the assumption that these breakdowns are caused principally by riots. Accordingly, the plan provides a direct Federal subsidy only in the case of riot loss and these losses have not been very important in the core area of Boston. The deficit the FAIR plan incurs from non-riot losses in Massachusetts is spread over the entire fire insurance market.

The Massachusetts FAIR plan works through servicing companies, which merely handle the administration of the policy for a servicing fee. The non-riot losses of the plan in excess of earnings are shared by all companies in the state in proportion to their statewide share of the normal fire insurance market. Since they become part of insurance companies' loss experience when filing for a rate adjustment, these losses are ultimately passed on to all insurance consumers in the form of higher premiums. Because premiums are closely related to property value, the incidence of the financial burden of the Massachusetts FAIR plan is similar to a property tax.

Although the FAIR plan was designed to provide fire insurance to urban area residents and businesses who cannot otherwise get it, the plan sometimes insures property owners who are not in these categories. The entire Commonwealth of Massachusetts has been designated an urban area for purposes of the FAIR plan. High value but fire-prone commercial structures outside of the core area have been placed in the FAIR plan even though coverage may be available elsewhere at higher rates. The owners of these properties naturally prefer FAIR to paying higher rates elsewhere.

The plan's present setup also encourages companies to "dump" marginal risks into FAIR. By doing this a company can transfer marginally profitable risks into a statewide pool. As mentioned above, the deficit this pool incurs is shared by all companies in proportion to their share of the normal or non-FAIR fire insurance market. By transferring business from its own books into FAIR, the company also reduces its share of the normal market thereby reducing its share of the pool's deficit.

The FAIR plan was designed to protect urban core residents and businessmen who could not obtain insurance because of their location. Unless some safeguards limit it to this type of property, FAIR will degenerate into a subsidized pool for high risk properties of all types.

FAIR coverage should be limited to areas that meet certain objective criteria. Eligible areas could be as small as a few blocks or as large as a whole section of a city. The criteria used would include factors such as the area having a certain minimal structure density and population concentration. A proven areawide difficulty in obtaining insurance in the private market would also be required. State insurance departments would have to certify that an area meets these or similar objective criteria in order to be eligible for FAIR.

The municipality in which an area eligible for FAIR coverage is located should also be encouraged to take steps to reduce the area's fire loss. The high proportion of run-down structures in the core area of Boston contributed heavily to its high fire loss. Statistical tests indicate a high correlation between the percentage of dilapidated buildings in an area and its fire loss.(17) By requiring a pre-insurance inspection, the FAIR plan has taken the right approach in dealing with the influence of structure condition on fire loss. The FAIR plan's efforts in this direction should be enhanced by generally enforcing building code regulations in areas eligible for coverage.

The profusion of vacant buildings in the core area is also a source of fire hazard. During the period 1965 to 1967, approximately 5.0 percent of the estimate fire losses to occupied buildings in the core area was caused by fire spreading from adjacent vacant structures. The comparable figure for the rest of the city was 0.3 percent. Legal problems often prevent the city from tearing down abandoned structures. However, the evidence on the effect of vacant structures on fire loss indicate that when these buildings are not salvageable, they should be removed as soon as legally possible. These steps would reduce the cost of insuring core area properties as well as help arrest the decline of inner city neighborhoods.

The desirability of reducing fire loss, even if there were no insurance problem, is obvious. Fire insurance just redistribures some of the financial loss from fire, it does not eliminate the loss. Fire also has high non-insurable costs to society, in terms of the human suffering of the victims and the cost of fighting fires.

Insurance by its very nature is an expensive way of paying for property losses. Administrative and other costs cause fire insurance companies to spend $1.50 to redistribute $1.00 in losses. From society's point of view, it would be more efficient to spend $1.25 to eliminate these losses than $1.50 to pay for them.

Greater efficiency could also be gained by changing the Massachusetts FAIR plan's form of organization. Of the 28 states with FAIR Plans, 26 including Massachusetts, work through a servicing carrier arrangement described above in which several specified insurance companies handle the administration of a FAIR Policy for a fixed percentage of the premium. California and Pennsylvania, on the other hand, use a syndicate type of operation in which one facility is set up to handle all FAIR plan business. In Massachusetts agents' commissions and other administrative expenses amount to 35 cents of every FAIR plan dollar, the comparable figure for the syndicate operation states is 25 cents.(18)

The nonavailability of fire insurance in the core area of Boston was the result of a constrained market. The range in the regulated price schedule was not large enough to take into consideration the high fire losses of the core area. As a result, insurance companies for the most part stopped insuring these areas. The fire insurance pricing system should be reformed so that rates more accurately reflect actual loss experience.

The profusion of run-down and vacant buildings in the core area contributed heavily to its higher fire loss, demonstrating the inner-relation of the core area insurance and housing problems. Our data indicate that rehabilitating dilapidated structures and tearing down abandoned buildings when possible would reduce the cost of insuring the core areas as well as help arrest the areas' decline.

The Massachusetts FAIR plan has been successful in providing fire insurance to core area residents and businesses that could not otherwise obtain it. The problem with the plan is not that it does not provide insurance to those for whom it was intended but rather that it also includes risks that should be carried in the private market.

NOTES

(1) Richard F. Syron, An Analysis of the Collapse of the Normal Market for Fire Insurance in Substandard Urban Core Areas. See Research Report No. 49 to Federal Reserve Bank of Boston, pp. 12-17.

(2) For example, the 1960 Census of Housing reported that 43 percent of all housing units in Wards 8, 9, 11, and 12, generally considered to be Boston's Core Area, were either dilapidated or deteriorated as compared with 22 percent for the rest of the city.

(3) The President's National Advisory Panel on Insurance in Riot-Affected Areas, Meeting the Insurance Crisis of our Cities. (Washington: U.S. Government Printing Office, 1968). See pages 126-149.

(4) The combined loss and expense ratio is used by insurance stock analysts to examine the profitability of a company's underwriting experience. The combined ratio method of examining profitability differs from the statutory method used for tax purposes, by prorating certain non-loss expenses (primarily commissions) which are "front end loaded" over the entire policy period rather than writing them off at the beginning of the policy when they are incurred. The simple statutory method understates profits in a company in which premiums written are increasing.

The combined loss and expense ratio equals

$$\frac{\text{Loss Expenses}}{\text{Premiums Earned}} \quad + \quad \frac{\text{Non-Loss Expenses}}{\text{Premiums}}$$

where Premiums Earned equals Premiums Written times the percentage of the policy period which has expired. For example, at the end of the first 6 months of a one year policy a company would have earned $150 of a $300 premium since one-half of the period for which coverage was contracted would have expired.

(5) Over 95 percent of all property and liability insurance in the United States is written by companies with either a stock or mutual form of corporate organization. Stock companies are owned by shareholders who have an equity interest in the company while mutuals are essentially owned by their policyholders.

The table below indicates that mutual companies have generally had lower combined ratios than stock companies. This is largely a reflection of the fact that mutuals pay lower commissions to agents and brokers than stock companies. Paying lower commissions allows mutuals to charge lower rates which in turn permits them to be more selective in accepting risks, further lowering their costs.

Mutual and Stock Companies
Combined Loss and Expense Ratios and Market Share*
1960-1970 Averages

	Mutual Companies	*Stock Companies*
Combined Loss and Expense Ratio—Fire 1960-1970 Average	87.1	101.2
Combined Loss and Expense Ratio—All Lines (excluding fire) 1960-1970 Average	96.4	99.8
Relative Share of Fire Insurance* Premiums Written	17.3	82.7
Relative Share of Premiums Written* All Lines (excluding fire)	28.3	71.7

*These market shares represent the relative shares of the sum of stock and mutual fire and other writings. These insurer types write the vast majority of all fire business.

Source: Best's Aggregates and Averages, 22nd-32nd eds., (Morristown, New Jersey: A.M. Best Company, 1961-1971).

The table indicates that mutuals have had a better underwriting experience with fire than they have had with other lines of insurance. This is just the opposite of the stock company experience. However, the table also indicates that while mutuals write about 28 percent of all property and liability insurance excluding fire, they had only about a 17 percent share of all stock and mutual fire writings.

While no data are available to document it, the greater selectivity of the mutuals makes it unlikely that they write even a 17 percent share of ghetto fire business.

(6) Massachusetts Laws, Chapter 175A, § 5.

(7) Vacant structures were excluded since the standard fire insurance contract has a clause voiding coverage on structures left unoccupied for 60 days or more. See General Laws, Commonwealth of Massachusetts, Chapter 175, section 99.

(8) Oliver Oldman and Henry Aaron, "Assessment-Sales Ratio Under the Boston Property Tax," National Tax Journal, XVIII (March 1965), pp. 36-50.

(9) A two way analysis of variance produces an F-statistic of 11.32 at 21 degrees of freedom, for variation between the wards, and an R^2 of .776. The F-statistic is significant at the .01 level.

(10) Some of this variation may be due to errors in estimates but surely not most of it. A t-test indicates that the variation between the average fire loss index of the core wards and the average for the rest of the city is statistically

significant at the .01 level, with a test statistic of 5.43 at 20 degrees of freedom.

(11) The composite fire loss index F_{ij} is some combination of two different indices:

$$F_{ij} = W_i^r F_{ij}^r + W_i^c F_{ij}^c$$

where F_{ij}^r = Fire loss index for residential structures in Ward i in year j

F_{ij}^c = Fire loss index for commercial structures in Ward i in year j

and W_i^c = Percentage of total sales value of structures in Ward i that are commercial

W_i^r = Percentage of total sales value of structures in Ward i that are residential

In fact the "mix" of fire loss in the core and other wards was quite similar. Seventy percent of fire loss in our data period in the core occurred in residential structures as compared to 56 percent in the rest of the city.

(12) For a detailed examination of this problem, see pp. 131-41 Research Report, No. 49.

(13) If riots played a large part in fire losses we would expect a relatively large increase in the core area's fire loss index from 1965 to 1967 since there was a small core area civil disturbance in Boston in 1967. In fact, the increase in the fire loss index from 1965 to 1967 was 37.8 percent for the core area, compared to 61.5 percent for the rest of the city.

(14) U.S. Department of Housing and Urban Development, Urban Property Protection and Reinsurance Act of 1968 as Amended, Public Laws 90-448, 91-152, and 91-609. December 31, 1970.

(15) Fire and allied lines of insurance are eligible for re-insurance. Ibid.

(16) Measured on an adjusted statutory basis using the combined ratio analysis described above, the Massachusetts plan had a $3,933,000 underwriting loss over the period. On a simple statutory basis the plan lost $4,790,000. U.S. Department of Housing and Urban Development, Federal Insurance Administration, Quarterly State FAIR Plan Report, Massachusetts, quarter ending 9/30/71.

(17) A univariate regression analysis comparing the average fire loss index to the 1960 Census measure of the percentage of structures in a ward considered dilapidated yields the following equation:

Fire loss index = .53 + 3.75 percentage structures dilapidated

(1.29) (5.81) t statistics in parenthesis

$F(1.20) = 33.75$　$R^2 - .609$

The equation is statistically significant, at the .01 percent level, as is the coefficient for the independent variable.

(18) Illinois and New York have switched from servicing carriers to a syndicate operation since these data were submitted to the National Insurance Administration. FAIR plan statistics from unpublished reports to Federal Insurance Administration, U.S. Department of Housing and Urban Development, revised 9/30/71.

EMPTY HOUSES: ABANDONED RESIDENTIAL BUILDINGS IN THE INNER CITY

William T. Nachbaur

> At a time when this Nation's housing supply is falling far short of existing needs and we have not begun to honor the goal of 26 million new units by 1978, we cannot permit the abandonment of usable structures to take place.(1)
>
> —Senator Edward S. Brooke

THE PARADOX OF EMPTY HOUSING

A committee of the District of Columbia City Council reported recently that there is "an extreme shortage of accommodations for low income families in the District and spiraling rents . . . place even inadequate housing beyond the reach of many families." The committee called for the construction of 102,000 new units over the next ten years to replace dilapidated units, relieve overcrowding, and meet expected population growth. It noted that in the past decade new construction and rehabilitation of residential units in the District had barely kept pace with the rate of demolition of existing units.(2) A look at the government sponsored new construction and rehabilitation that has been done in Washington makes clear that it has not produced sufficient housing for those who were displaced by demolition.(3) The same pattern is repeated in our other major cities.

Exacerbating this housing shortage, an estimated 1,500 residential buildings that once housed 20,000 persons in the District of Columbia lie vacant,(4) disowned by their former owners and tenants alike.(5) The paradox of increasing vacancies in the core city and other poor sections of Washington, coinciding with an abnormally low vacancy rate for the metropolitan area as a whole,(6) poses numerous unanswered questions about utilization of the housing stock in the city. The situation raises significant problems for government and social agencies faced with the necessity of housing low income families. The housing shortage is forcing many of these families to double up. It is reported that the problem continues to grow; "more and more units in partly occupied buildings are remaining vacant and becoming uninhabitable as tenants move out," and the Distric government "has become concerned about the problem and has undertaken a study to ascertain its causes."(7)

Washington is not the only city confronted by this paradox. What can and should be done with vacant inner-city residential buildings is a question perplexing government officials in most of our major cities. The problem has recently been recognized by the news media as a national crisis. Thus, the press reports that although the housing shortage nationwide is worsening, and vacancy rates have fallen to a twenty-year low, the problem in our central cities "is of an entirely different order—a lack not of buildings but of neighborhoods deemed fit to live in, even by the poor." It is a problem of "acres of houses and apartment buildings . . . abandoned by their owners and tenants to decay."(8) Cities are awakening to the realization that "the number of slum buildings abandoned by their owners as a bad investment is reaching catastrophic proportions, and the trend has yet to reach its height."(9) Approximately half of the vacancies in the inner-city are not available for rental.(10)

There are 5,000 vacant buildings in Baltimore, and Philadelphia is said to have 20,000. It is estimated that 130,000 buildings have been abandoned in New York City in the past four years.(11) Not only is the number of abandoned buildings large, but the rate of abandonment is increasing. Chicago reports that "140 landlords walk away from their buildings every month," and each year sees New York owners "jetison enough buildings . . . to house the entire population of Jersey City."(12)

This article reports an investigation into the factors which are causing owners to abandon residential buildings in the inner city. This research into causes is to lay a foundation for making recommendations toward a partial solution of the housing shortage through preservation of the inner city housing stock.

The problem of what to do about empty houses and how to halt the processes which remove sound structures from the market is a relatively new one for city officials. Congress took no notice of the problem before the summer of 1970. Because there is a paucity of empirical research on the problem, the initial step in the research for this article was to undertake a study of a twenty-one block area of Washington, D.C. The results of this study are reported along with information relating to other cities. As causes and possible solutions are discussed, it will be seen that the problems which lead to abandonment are interrelated, and only a comprehensive plan directed at each and all of the causes can succeed in halting the spread of abandonment.

The reasons most frequently given for the vacant housing problem range from Absentee Ownership to Zoning. In fact, the causes of the problem can only be discussed in terms of lists: Tight money, rising costs of maintenance, "bad" tenants (and the exodus of good ones), over-zealous code enforcement, years of nonenforcement, condemnations, urban renewal, speculative financing, absentee ownership, obsolete construction, poor management, rising crime, rent control, racial tensions, vandalism, taxes, and zoning—all are factors which lead to deterioration and abandonment of our inner-city housing stock. Before turning to a discussion and evaluation of these factors the problem of abandoned buildings must be placed within the context of the general crisis in housing.

HOUSING STOCK

The problem and the process of abandoned residential structures in deteriorating inner-city neighborhoods is a part of the much-publicized problem of a national shortage of adequate, decent, safe, and sanitary housing. This is often characterized as a shortage of new housing construction. The relationship, often overlooked, between new construction and the maintenance of our old housing stock is implicit in the statement of Senator Brooke which opens this article. Used housing, at any given time, is more important in the housing market than new. The nation's housing supply is increased at an annual rate of only two to three percent.(13) Abnormal losses from the housing stock can cancel gains made by new construction. It does little good to construct new homes if an equal number of accommodations are concurrently taken off the market. Thus, although the housing crisis cannot be resolved without increased housing production, it cannot be considered exclusively a production shortage.

Government housing programs which have concentrated primarily on increasing the supply and quality of new units reach only one side of the problem. These production-oriented programs are certainly necessary, but their effect on existing housing is only indirect. Increased new construction relieves demand pressure on the old housing stock and facilitates the "filtering process" whereby the poor move into homes which filter down to them as those higher on the income ladder purchase new ones. However, the filtering process is, at best, "imperfect."(14) The poor inherit housing that has ceased to be decent, safe, and sanitary.

What is needed in addition to such programs are new programs designed to preserve the existing housing stock and place it within the reach of low-income families. Such new programs must focus on the problems relating to the operation and management of housing for low income people and the provision of adequate services in low income neighborhoods. That is, these programs must focus on "housing services." To the extent that low income families cannot support the cost of these services, they must be underwritten by the government. As a matter of economics, existing housing can be preserved at far lower cost than new housing can be built. Thus, money spent to preserve and improve existing housing should be viewed "as an investment that is going to save us a lot of money in the future."(15)

HOUSING SERVICES

This article on vacant residential buildings is, therefore, concerned with a set of problems unlike those related to housing production. It is only after a building is constructed that the problems which relate to the quality and quantity of housing services arise. Such services go beyond capital investment in building and plant. A building may be structurally sound and have a functional heating system, and still have no heat—or no hot water, or no garbage collection, or no maintenance. These housing services are of immediate concern to poor families in slum neighborhoods. The process of improving their housing by new construction and filtering-down is too slow, but they will get immediate benefits from programs designed to upgrade and preserve the housing they presently occupy.(16)

It will be seen that the buildings which are the focus of this article lacked basic housing services long before they became vacant. Abandonment is thus the end of the line.

> The process of physical abandonment is preceded by psychological and fiscal abandonment. By the time that building comes to the city's attention it is a building which at best has not seen any fresh money for a very long time.(17)

But an abandoned building is also more than an end result; it can infect other nearby structures. It is both cause and effect of a multitude of urban problems.

SHAW AREA STUDY

The area of Washington, D.C. chosen for study was a twenty-one contiguous block area in the Northwest quadrant of the city which lies entirely within the Shaw School Urban Renewal Area. It is a fairly representative Washington inner-city neighborhood of predominately single-family row houses, most of which were built before the turn of the century.(18) Although many of these "neo-Victorian" homes would sell for upwards of $50,000 if transplanted to Georgetown,(19) the area is a slum. It is reported that the area has been a slum since the 1860's.(20)

The author, as a VISTA volunteer lawyer, had clients in the neighborhood. The particular sub-area was chosen for study because it was not included by the Redevelopment Land Agency (RLA), the local renewal agency, in either the first or second year action plans for development of the Shaw Area under the Neighborhood Development Program (NDP). Under NDP, the Shaw Project is planned and carried out on the basis of annual increments. The program allows RLA to rebuild in some areas while still planning the development of others.(21) Thus, except for a very small area, there are no immediate plans to acquire property in this area for any specific urban renewal projects. Therefore, the effects of urban renewal on existing housing by actual government purchase or taking were minimized. Also, except for the predominately commercial frontage along one border, none of the study area was damaged in the 1968 civil disorders that followed the assasination of Martin Luther King, Jr.

After the study area was designated, it was surveyed and a list of abandoned residential buildings was compiled.(22) Vacant lots and vacant commercial structures were not included in the list and no attempt was made to determine the number of partially occupied residential structures. It was felt that these three categories of vacancies presented different problems than the category chosen for study.(23) The list of fifty-three addresses was converted to lot and square numbers to facilitate the rest of the research. Ownership, assessed valuation of land and building, the annual property tax liability, and tax unpaid, if any, was determined for each parcel from the records at the District Department of Finance and Revenue. Dates of acquisition and information regarding the cost of acquisition of some of the properties were obtained through an examination of recorded deeds and deeds of trust at the Office of the Recorder of Deeds. Files in the field office of the Department of Licenses and Inspections were examined to determine whether the existence of outstanding code violations necessitating repairs was a factor in the owner's choosing not to rent (or occupy) his property. Similar records were inspected at the Board of Condemnation of Insanitary Buildings. Census data was examined to discern housing trends in the area over the past three decades. They indicated fewer buildings with each survey. The list of vacant buildings was also compared with the Shaw Joint Venture Building Conditions Survey conducted for the Redevelopment Land Agency in May, 1968, to February, 1969.

Employees of the Redevelopment Land Agency, the Board of Condemnation, the Department of Licenses and Inspections, and others, including residents of the area, were interviewed. Questionnaires were sent to owners at their addresses listed in the tax records. Very few responded. Many of these questionnaires were returned marked "addressee unknown."(24) A few of the owners telephoned me after receiving the questionnaire, but they were uncooperative when they learned that I was not interested in purchasing their property.(25) Time did not permit the gathering of information on all of the buildings in the area so as to make comparisons of the data gathered against similar data for nonvacant buildings. Some of the information gathered in this Shaw study will be referred to as factors in the vacant building problem are discussed.

THE IMPACT OF VACANT HOUSES ON THE NEIGHBORHOOD

There is a strong public interest in preventing owners from abandoning their inner-city properties even aside from the fact that it causes an immediate decrease in the stock of available housing. City officials and others who have commented on the problem agree that the effect of abandonment on the surrounding neighborhood can be devastating. Their use of terms like "infection," "blight," or "cancer" in describing deteriorating housing indicate the effects of such housing on the surrounding environment.(26) George Sternlieb, director of the Urban Studies Center of Rutgers University and Robert Embry, Commissioner of Housing and Community Development in Baltimore(27) have observed that even good housing is abandoned when bad housing is abandoned nearby. Similarly, Neil Hardy, of the Housing and Development Administration in New York City, describes abandonment as "a contagious, self-fulfilling prophecy . . . when bad buildings are vacated, the other owners begin to panic and good houses in the vicinity are abaondoned at the same time."(28) To the remaining owners, abandonment signals the neighborhood's decline. They perceive that repair or renovation in the face of encroaching deterioration is futile and financially disastrous. A vacant building is a daily reminder, a symbol to neighborhood residents of degradation and decay.(29)

Empty houses are a hazard to the physical, as well as psychological, health of nearby residents. They pose the threat of fire damage to adjacent occupied buildings. It is notable that in Boston, 18 percent of all structural fires in 1969 were in vacant buildings.(30) Vacant buildings are invaded by rats and other vermin. They constitute attractive nuisances, "haunted houses," dangerous to neighborhood children.(31) They also attract narcotics addicts and drunks(32) and provide a breeding place for crime which "impels law-abiding ghetto dwellers to flight."(33)

This was demonstrated by a study of Boston's South End, "which has the heaviest concentration of abandoned buildings in the city. . . . [and where] 1,431 arrests were made in and around vacant buildings" in a six month period. Drunkenness accounted for over 1,100 of these arrests,s but there were also 246 narcotics arrests, 25 vice arrests, 26 robbery or larceny arrests, 10 assault and battery arrests and one murder.(34) The existence of such buildings, and the flight of those who can get away from them tends to undermine neighborhood social welfare programs and city services such as schools.(35) Owners of property in the study area blame crime, and the government's inability to control it, for driving "decent people" away.(36)

Vacant buildings do not cause the crime problem even though they worsen it. In fact, crime works as a major cause of abandonment in two ways: by causing people to leave and by making a building uninhabitable after they have left. Buildings are rendered uninhabitable through acts of vandalism. The problem is more than windows broken by neighborhood children. Narcotics addicts and others salvage what they can from empty buildings—fixtures, pipe, wiring—and sell it for scrap. Vandalism is frequently cited as a cause of abandoned buildings by experts in other cities. One official notes that "once a building is abandoned it deteriorates within months—sometimes within weeks—to the point where its housing units are irretrievably lost to the city."(37) Because of this, owners prefer a tenant in default on his rent, or even on rent strike, to no tenant at all.

> You are finding landlords don't press hard for rent any more in some areas, and are very slow to evict unless there is a new tenant ready. They would rather have the house not producing rent, or producing only a part of the rent, than have it empty for the scavengers to strip.(38)

The owner of one of the vacant properties in the area studied by the author attested to the rapidity of the process. His last tenant moved out in June, 1969 and "by July the place was completely vandalized." When the fixtures were removed he decided to forget about re-renting the premises.(39)

Vandalism also increases the cost of rehabilitation if the structures are to be taken over by the local renewal agency or a developer. A step toward a reduction of this vandalism was proposed to the author by a neighborhood organizer in the Shaw Area; he proposed that the junkyards in the neighborhood, within walking distance of the empty structures, be closed down. His theory is that few people will go to the trouble of boarding a bus with a length of copper pipe or a kitchen sink to get to a junkyard.(40) It seems like a simple and effective remedy. More comprehensive remedies, of course, will have to be devised. One should note, however, that since the majority of ghetto criminals are addicts, no anti-crime program that is not aimed at stopping the drug traffic and rehabilitating addicts can really succeed.

Crime is not the only factor causing black families to flee the ghetto, but the combination of the exodus of black families from the inner city and the slowdown of in-migration of other families from the South is itself a cause of abandonment. The Commissioner of Housing in Baltimore, for example, notes that Negro families are moving out in droves, some from areas where they have lived all their lives. The reasons he cites are the increase in crime and poor schools—both of which are largely the responsibility of city government. He also feels that recent immigrants from the South, those left behind in the city, are "people not ready for city living" who "have broken down the fabric of the neighborhood."(41) This explanation is also given with respect to the Distric of Columbia by the Assistant Director of Research for the National Capitol Planning Commission who reports that many black families have fled from the inner-city to Prince Georges' County.(42)

In large part, the phenomenon of out-migration from the central city is merely the re-enactment of an old story. Poor inner city residents, both black and white, have traditionally moved out as they climbed into the middle class. A difference today is that in-migration has slowed drastically. Those who remain behind are the poorest of their group. Landlords face the squeeze of rising operating costs and a dwindling number of families that can afford to pay for minimal housing services. Thus we have the irony that this shift of population is producing a housing shortage in the suburbs without releasing pressure on the inner city housing stock. Neighborhood workers in the Shaw Renewal Area report that there is a shortage of decent housing in the area and that many families are forced to double up. A major reason for this is that as tenants move out, owners are closing up. Low income families seeking decent housing in the inner city find that it is not available.

The natural rate of migration to the suburbs is accelerated by crime and also by the fact that jobs are moving to the suburbs. Both government and private industry are locating new facilities outside the old city core.(43) In addition to the pull of jobs and the push of crime, another factor encouraging residents to leave is a general deterioration of city and commercial services. Dirty streets and inadequate police protection make the neighborhood uncomfortable. The lack of commercial facilities makes the neighborhood inconvenient.

Psychologically, vacant stores are, perhaps, more damaging to a neighborhood than vacant homes because they symbolize to the residents the economic decline of the neighborhood. The Shaw study area, like older areas of other cities, is "overstored," with commercial and commercial-residential structures in every block, and about half of them are empty. This state of affairs is in part due to past zoning practices. It is also due to changing shopping patterns, rising crime, civil disturbances and resultant high insurance costs. The decline of the "Mom and Pop" store has happened everywhere, but to the extent that stores have closed for non-economic reasons, such as crime, the neighborhood has been deprived of commercial services that have not been replaced. Not all of the stores in the area should be reopened, but if the neighborhood is to be rejuvenated, it will need some modern stores.(44)

The city itself must share the blame for the deterioration of slum neighborhoods. Its failure to enforce adequately its housing codes, and its failure to maintain services at the level required as the character of the neighborhood changed, have encouraged owners to neglect their properties. The capital improvements required in these buildings today would not be necessary if owners had been required to keep up the maintenance of their properties. The city government's failure to care about the appearance and the quality of life in certain neighborhoods only reinforces the residents sense of hopelessness about ever improving the situation.

The purpose of this section has been to underscore the fact that any attempt to stop the process of abandonment must take a neighborhood approach to the problem. A building and its environment are inextricably interrelated. Just as private owners now find it uneconomical to rehabilitate a building when its neighbors are deteriorating, the city would find its efforts undermined if it were to concentrate on individual buildings. Nor can neighborhood-wide improvement be limited to upgrading buildings. It must also include such things as street repairs, new street lighting, new community recreational and commercial facilities, and improved municipal services.(45) The idea of a neighborhood approach has been accepted in theory by the federal government in the NDP program discussed above,(46) but in practice, not enough resources have been brought to bear to solve the many aspects of the problem of neighborhood blight.

OPERATING COSTS AND ABANDONMENT

Perhaps the most fundamental reason for the existence of vacant buildings is that for a number of reasons, a private investor cannot provide decent low-cost housing and still get a return on his investment. The cost of maintaining inner city housing is rising. The Rand corporation reports that it costs $24 per room per month to adequately maintain an inner city apartment.(47) Studies in New York have shown operating expenses before depreciation and debt service ranging between 40 and 60 percent of gross income.(48) There is substantial evidence that costs have increased even more in recent years.(49) Owners claim that operating costs have gone up 30 to 40 percent in the last five years. One reason for this, they say, is that tenants are becoming increasingly conscious of their rights and are demanding repairs. Another is that riots and crime have caused insurance rates to double and triple.(50) Thus, they cannot afford to make repairs demanded by code-enforcement officials.(51) Meanwhile, tight money has dried up the landowner's sources of financing causing a virtual stagnation in the slum housing market. Additionally, officials report that "[i] t is increasingly difficult to obtain competent maintenance personnel who will work in the inner city,"(52) but this is partially a factor of how much one is willing to pay. In one dilapidated building familiar to the author, repair work ordered by the city was done by neighborhood drunks recruited from the street corner. Needless to say, the job was not done in a workmanlike manner.

Owners of these buildings are not, however, entirely the innocent victims of economic circumstances. A major reason for high maintenance costs is that much needed maintenance "for a variety of economic reasons" has been deferred for years, and such "poor maintenance accelerates the building's aging process and means that any attempts to improve the building will require a larger capital investment."(53) With respect to maintenance there is a "heads we win, tails you lose" phenomenon. When the market is strong, the owner need not make improvements. When it is weak, he fears for his investment and makes no repairs.(54)

Thus, stepped-up code enforcement and the pressures of a newly sophisticated tenantry are merely forces that have belatedly caught up with years of irresponsible milking of the properties. In many cases, the owners who made the biggest profit on these buildings saw the handwriting on the wall and left the market to others who expected that the old practices could continue,(55) but regardless of who is to blame for the present state of repair of inner city housing, the fact is that private individuals cannot afford to maintain it, much less, rehabilitate it, and continue to provide low income housing at a profit.

Operating expenses for an inner city rowhouse are illustrated by the following table.

Illustrative Cash Flow Statement: Inner-City House Held Free and Clear, Baltimore, 1968

Gross income $76 per month x 12	$912
Less: Vacancies and arrears (13%)	120
Effective income:[1]	
Less:	
Real Estate taxes	125
Liability insurance	75
Fire insurance	[2] 40
Total fixed expenses	240
Operating income	252
Less:	
Maintenance and repairs	240
Water and sewer charges	60
Miscellaneous	10
Total operating expenses	310
Net income before management	242
Less: Management (10% of collected rents)	79
Net income from operations	[3] $163

[1] Assumes assessed value of land and building is $2500.

[2] If ground rent on land valued at $1000 is capitalized at 6 percent, annual payment of lessee would be $60, thus increasing fixed expenses to $300 and reducing net income from operations to $103. Moreover, if property were subject to a $2000, 10-year mortgage at 8 percent, monthly debt service would be $24.26 a month, or $291.12 a year; annual cash loss would be $128.12.

[3] Assuming market value equals assessed value, and that property was purchased at this price, return on the investment is 6.5 percent.

Source: 1970 *Hearings* 799.

If the typical owner of slum property has fixed expenses and gross income similar to this example, and in addition has to make payments on a first and a second mortgage, the only way to wring any net income out of the property is to eliminate expenditures for maintenance and repairs. This, unfortunately, is what is done.

Rent control is cited by its opponents as a reason owners abandon their buildings. They say their expenses exceed their rent-controlled income.(56) But clearly rent control is only a small factor since New York City, where it is in force, is not the only city faced with the problem of abandonment. Owners abandon when "rehabilitation or even maintenance costs are greater than any potential return,"(57) but the ceiling on their return is usually not rent control.

> [T] enants' inability to pay adequate rent is a more important contributor to abandonment than rent control. The fact is that in many of the neighborhoods where abandonment is occurring [in New York], the actual rents being paid by the low income tenants are substantially below the rent control maxima. This means that landlords are charging as much as the traffic will bear . . . [The result] is a rent roll insufficient to maintain property and operate efficiently.(58)

Another outside factor in abandonment is the real estate tax structure which operates as a disincentive to repair. New York officials noted in 1968 that a steep rise in the tax rate resulted in an abrupt increase in abandonments. They found that five percent of the buildings in the city were three or four years tax delinquent.(59)

ABSENTEE OWNERSHIP

As noted above, low income tenants and the city lose when it comes to maintenance of inner city housing regardless of market conditions. Typically, owner-investors will improve real property only "if the cost is equal to or less than the increase in value caused by the change."(60) But owners of low income housing, unlike owners of high income housing, "tend increasingly to take profits out of current rental receipts" rather than out of capital gains or other tax benefits.(61) Thus, in a weak market, the landlord cannot increase rents to recoup repair expenditures, and in a tight market, he can increase rental income without making repairs. Improving the value of the income-producing structure is not a separate goal.

This observation about the attitude of owners toward maintaining their properties highlights one of the major problems of the slums—absentee ownership. As Senator Goodell has noted, "A major deterrent to proper management is the preponderance of absentee landlords whose feeling of responsibility to the property is limited."(62) The attitude of an owner who does not himself live on the premises or even in the neighborhood is far different from that of a resident owner whose own physical well-being is intimately involved with that of his tenants and the neighborhood. This was seen in the study area where parcels which were properly maintained were likely to be resident owned.(63) The absentee owner is immune to the pressures on a resident owner to maintain the premises; he can make his decisions on cold economic grounds alone and make only those repairs where "the cost is equal to or less than the increase in value."

This is not to say that owners of slum property are necessarily evil men. Some are small investors who got into the game without knowing what would happen. What they expected to be a source of extra income turned out instead to be a liability and a headache. They find it increasingly difficult to obtain capital for improvements. Regardless, of their original intentions, it is easy for them to forget their bad investment. They are not on the scene forced to cope with their tenants' day-to-day problems.

Another important fact to consider with respect to absentee ownership is that in the inner city this usually means a white owner with black tenants. Racial tensions complicate the landlord-tenant relationship. Some landlords are afraid to personally supervise their properties, and they collect their rents through the mails.(64)

City housing officials are unanimous in their belief that resident ownership means a higher level of maintenance. George Sternlieb finds the correlation "very clear-cut."(65) "The operating procedures of a resident landlord are much simpler and much less expensive than for absentees."(66) For example, he does not have to pay someone else to do minor repairs or collect the rent. The Commissioner of Housing Inspection in Boston feels that encouraging home ownership is "the one way of conserving housing stock today."(67) "Owner-occupancy of small rental buildings, then is one key to preventing deterioration."(68)

Sternlieb notes there is already a trend toward increased minority-group ownership despite the barriers set up by financial institutions. Thus, although others call for "new ownership vehicles for rental properties that can benefit from economies of scale, can retain fill-time well-trained personnel, and can increase minority control over the areas where they live,"(69) he suggests that the government facilitate the trend to homeownership.(70) This would seem preferable to public or nonprofit ownership. Because of the impersonal, institutional nature of public housing management and nonprofit management, such a change of ownership would not resolve many of the difficulties that now appear in absentee owned properties but are avoided in resident owned buildings. The economies of scale and the expertise that are expected to come from a transfer to nonprofit ownership could be better provided by a nonprofit housing management corporation (HMC)—like those proposed by Senator Goodell—in combination with resident owners. However, in larger buildings, resident ownership may prove to be unfeasible, and, in such cases, nonprofit ownership and management should be tried.

The prevalence of absentee ownership in the inner city is in large part due to the practices and preferences of local banks and savings and loan associations. Many of these institutions refuse to lend directly to black homebuyers or homeowners who cannot meet their discriminatory credit requirements. Some financial institutions regard slum housing as too big a risk, while those who find the risk acceptable seem to prefer white absentee owners.

A study of one area of the Distric of Columbia disclosed that three savings and loans made more than 75 percent of their loans to absentee owners.(71) Thus, the practices of these lending institutions, in effect, allow "poor people to buy property for people of means."(72) They must either rent or buy from the slum speculator who functions as the "middleman" extending credit not available to them from conventional sources. He provides this "service" only at great additional expense.

Many of the mortgage loans given to these absentee owner investors were based on inflated property valuations. Large mortgage debts require owners to

set rents at a level high enough to meet mortgage payments and low enough for
low income residents to afford—"and the only way to do that, given the inflated
mortgage situation is to cut maintenance back to nothing"(73)

MANAGEMENT CAPABILITY

A dwelling cannot provide adequate housing services without a constant
reinvestment of dollars for maintenance. The lack of such investment is painfully
evident in the dilapidated housing in the inner city. Just as important as
investment is management—the process of translating financial resources into
housing services. Broadly defined, management includes owners, tenants, tenant
boards, management firms, and even single family homeowners. The resources
available to these participants in the management process and the way they
choose to convert them to services have an immediate effect on the quality of
housing. Good management can forestall abandonment.(74)

Government programs should be developed which will improve the
management of low income housing by providing subsidies for maintenance and
rehabilitation, by encouraging homeownership, and by assisting and facilitating
certain management functions. Grants and loans now available only in urban
renewal and code enforcement areas should be made available in other low
income neighborhoods threatened with deterioration. Homeownership programs
should be extended to include resident ownership of small apartment buildings.
Management assistance could be provided by housing management corporations
as proposed recently by Senator Goodell in legislation designed to "encourage
and assist in the establishment of community oriented and sponsored nonprofit
organizations to provide at reasonable cost urgently needed management services
for low- and moderate-income housing in declining neighborhoods."(75) His
Housing Management Service Act, which was not reported out of the Senate
Committee on Banking and Currency, would have provided funding for local
housing management corporations

> to provide economical and efficient housing management services for
> public and private low- and moderate-income rental housing (including
> cooperatives and condominiums) situated in areas where such services are
> not otherwise being adequately or economically provided. A corporation
> may also provide technical and consulting services with respect to housing
> management in such areas, and may establish programs for the training of
> housing management personnel to serve area needs.(76)

Housing management services as defined in the bill are

> services required for the effective management and maintenance of
> housing, including without being limited to rent collection, bookkeeping,
> filing of vacancies, hiring of personnel, arranging for insurance and
> necessary repairs, and arranging for purchase of supplies, fixtures, and
> utilities.(77)

Both tenants and owners were to sit on the boards of directors of the
proposed corporations to insure that the interests of both groups were

protected.(78) After an administrative determination that the area which the corporation proposes to serve "contains a high concentration of low- or moderate-income housing . . . substantially characterized by an inadequacy of housing management services" and that there is a reasonable probability that the corporation can provide the needed management services, the Department of Housing and Urban Development would license the corporation.(79) The Department could then provide the corporation with financial and technical assistance.(80) Financial aid would be given by way of periodic payments not to exceed the difference in the amount the corporation received for its services and the corporation's actual costs incurred in providing the services.(81)

The corporation, operating in a whole neighborhood, could take advantage of economies of scale in obtaining materials and fuel and in making repairs with its own full-time repair staff. If abandoned properties were repaired by the city or purchased, written down, and sold by the local renewal agency to a developer or a nonprofit resident owner, management could be the responsibility of a housing management corporation. This would obviate the unwillingness of developers to assume the burden and risk of management after undertaking to rehabilitate such structures. A management corporation would also facilitate transfer of ownership to tenants or tenant groups that presently lack the experience and skill needed for efficient management.(82)

Housing management corporations could be a very important component of any program which seeks to develop and encourage homeownership and resident ownership of the inner city housing stock. Senator Goodell expected his corporations to provide counselling and the economies of large scale operation to single-family homeowners as well as to the multi-unit owners. Counselling would cover repairs, taxes, and government programs.(83)

Another important advantage of the proposed corporations is that they could provide neighborhood residents the opportunity to receive training in the field of housing management. Trainees could be hired by the corporations as permanent staff, and training could provide entry into similar jobs in the private middle- and high-income housing markets.(84) Thus, the program would also indirectly relieve the pressure on the housing stock by increasing the purchasing power of some of the area's residents.

It is unfortunate that this bill was not enacted for it would go a long way toward upgrading the quality of housing in the inner city. Perhaps, similar pilot programs can be set up on an experimental basis by HUD-funded Model Cities Programs or OEO-funded Community Action Agencies.

SPECULATIVE FINANCING

As noted above, if a black low or moderate income person wants to purchase a home, he often cannot go to a bank or a savings and loan association for a loan. Down payment requirements and discriminatory practices force him to buy from a slum housing speculator. A major reason for the abandonment of residential buildings in the District, and probably in other cities as well, is the collapse of the mid-1960's wave of speculation in inner-city housing brought about by the present downturn of the economy. Speculation is inner-city property and its disastrous consequences has been documented in a remarkable series of ten articles in the Washington Post.(85) A year-long investigation disclosed that inner-city speculators working with the financial support of a handful of financial institutions milked enormous profits from black homebuyers who could not deal with reputable banks and real estate brokers because of their race.

> Abandoned, unsaleable houses and unfinished apartment buildings now dot Washington's streets. They are the legacy for the Nation's Capital of a system that turned with a vengeance on some of the financial institutions and speculators who fathered it. Some others escaped with large profit.(86)

The speculation system has three basic variations all of which tend toward the same results. Some speculators were mainly interested in buying property at one price and promptly reselling it to a black family at a far higher price. This is simply a variation of the high credit selling that characterizes the sale of consumer goods in the ghetto. Many speculators chose to hold onto their highly mortgaged rental units and charge high rents to cover payments and profit without cutting into this margin by making repairs. A third sort of speculation was to get large loans for the construction of new apartment buildings, spend only a part of the loan on construction, and pocket the difference.(87) Inflated prices, financed by inflated mortgages, meant that a homebuyer would have little money left over after his payments with which to make necessary repairs.

> Floating along on a stream of borrowed dollars, the speculators could move with the migration of low-income white and Negro families. The speculators were looking for the easy low purchase from somebody who wanted to get out and the easy high sale to somebody who wanted to get in, and who was willing to pay high credit rates for what appeared to be easy terms.(88)

The bubble burst when the Federal Government raised borrowing rates to curtail inflation and the mortgage money, which the speculators needed in a continuing flow, dried up. The squeeze of tight money was further tightened as the city government clamped down on housing code violations.(89) Slum speculation contributed to the existence of many run-down and abandoned residential properties and caused the financial ruin of several speculators.

When the credit squeeze eases off, the cycle will probably begin all over again. A study of land records shows that some of the city's now-respectable financial institutions that today avoid dealing with speculators built their loan business in past decades with loans to speculators. "Generations of speculators have fed on the migrations of low-income white and Negro families from one part of Washington to another."(90) Some speculators are taking advantage of the new availability of FHA insured loans to black homebuyers.(91)

Several of the buildings in the study area appear to have been abandoned as a direct result of the collapse of the speculative market. A search of the land records disclosed many of the names mentioned in the *Post* series and in testimony before the House Subcommittee on Home Financing Practices and Procedures. Some were apparently left holding the bag when the market caved in.

One of the owners of property in the study area stated that he decided not to re-rent his property when it became vacant a year ago because he "cannot possibly meet Bank payments." His plans for the property: "Letting the mortgage holder foreclose."(92)

The most effective control on speculation would be to make conventional, "respectable" financing available to black homebuyers. One drastic way of accomplishing this is to restrict lending institutions to financing only of dwellings that will be owner-occupied.(93) Another is through government insured or financed homeownership plans such as Section 235(94) and Turnkey III housing.(95) Such programs, aided by counselling and mass purchasing services of nonprofit housing management corporations, could rejuvenate the inner-city and provide decent homes for low-income people by drastically reducing operating costs.

THE TENANTS

Slum owners frequently blame tenants for the dilapidation of the premises. One of the owners of property in the study area, who regretted that he did not have time to answer my questions, stated that I would have them answered if I would "purchase anyone [sic] of the houses available in the area . . . and rent the house out."(96) Another owner stated that the neighborhood has deteriorated because of tenant attitudes toward the owner. He also stated that maintenance of the building should be the responsibility of tenants.(97) Landlords claim that some tenants intentionally cause code violations in order to avoid payment of rent.(98) Not enough information was obtained from the questionnaires to evaluate the contribution of tenants to building delapidation, but the lack of maintenance by absentee landlords is attested to by an observation of buildings in the study area. Clearly, tenants are not responsible for repair of structural defects caused not by them but by the age of the building and years of neglect.

There has, however, been a definite change in tenant attitude toward owners. Tenants in recent years, especially in the District of Columbia, have become more sophisticated about their rights as tenants.(99) They refer housing complaints to community workers at the local OEO-funded Community Action Agency (The United Planning Organization), attorneys at Neighborhood Legal Services Offices and employees of the Department of Licenses and Inspections. Such action by tenants, to the extent that it increases pressure on owners to bring their buildings into compliance with the Housing Regulations, is possibly a factor in causing building abandonment. Although the results of the study of field inspection records were inconclusive, it is not believed that code enforcement, whether initiated by tenant complaint or otherwise, is a major factor causing abandonment.

A leading expert on the problem of inner-city housing abandonment believes that there is a certain class of tenants that destroys a building. From the correlation between welfare tenantry and abandonment, he has concluded "that when welfare recipients come into a building they ruin the building." He also notes that when landlords will only rent to welfare tenants, it means they have no other tenants to rent to because the building is already deteriorated.(100) This second observation is the more telling. Welfare rents cannot support the repairs which the buildings require, and a welfare tenantry indicates that the owner has already ceased to provide essential housing services.

Some observers of the vacant building problem believe that concerted tenant action has contributed to it. Senator Brooke, for example, lists rent strikes as one of the causes of building abandonment.(101) However, at least in Washington, D.C., rent strikes are not a significant factor. None of the owners of buildings in the study area who responded to the questionnaire asserted that a rent strike caused him to close down. It is unlikely that there have been rent strikes in any of the abandoned buildings in the study area because there have been relatively few rent strikes in Washington, D.C. Neighborhood attorneys do not believe that any of the rent strikes in the city have forced out an owner who was not about to default on his mortgage anyway. Several of the rent strikes, on the other hand, have been successful in forcing an owner to make repairs.(102) One multi-family building familiar to the author just across the border of the Shaw Renewal Area, was sold at a time when a rent strike was ongoing and the building had been condemned. The new owner has made enough repairs to satisfy the Board of Condemnation and the building is still occupied.(103)

Tenants, assisted by community lawyers, can bring pressure on government agencies to force them to deal with the problem of abandoned buildings. Mandamus actions requiring government-initiated repair are one possibility. Another tactic, apparently not tried in Washington, is the "squat-in." The National Tenants Organization (NTO) characterizes a squat-in as "a move-in, stay-in, and live-in of a poor family aided by a tenants' organization." The technique "can beat the snail paced slum-janitor and housing official in terms of delivering a standard unit now." NTO emphasizes the necessity of carefully choosing a person in an especially bad housing situation to make the move. "Public consternation for recalcitrant public and private authorities is more likely where the families are carefully chosen."(104) The "squat-in" is a tactic "well calculated to force confrontations [threatening] the very foundation of American capitalism."(105) One problem with applying this tactic to abandoned buildings is that because of vandalism few are habitable, and are thus not an improvement over most families' present accommodations, but the "squat-in" would appear to be a valuable device for focusing attention on the problem.

An extension of the "squat-in" tactic would be for families to move into vacant buildings and attempt to become owners, if not by adverse possession, at least by the present owner's fear of adverse publicity. In cases where the building is owned by the FSLIC or the FHA, the agency may be willing to write off outstanding mortgages and negotiate a purchase by the new "homesteader."

More important than any tenant activity such as the destruction of property or the withholding of rent, low income tenants contribute to building abandonment mainly by being poor. As obvious as this may appear, it is sometimes over-looked.

> Poverty is the underlying cause of many current housing problems. Some households simply do not have enough income to pay the rent for reasonably maintained housing as it becomes available . . . To pick a hypothetical but not entirely unrealistic figure, say that a rent of $130 a month, or $1,560 a year, was needed to operate an apartment at a reasonable level for a family of four. Paying this much rent would leave the four-person family at the poverty line with only about $2,183 a year

for all its other basic needs. That works out per person to $545 a year, or less than $11 a week for food, clothing, medicine, transportation and all the rest. Housing would be taking 41 percent of the family's income.(106)

Isler's hypothetical but typical poor family that cannot afford "reasonably maintained housing as it becomes available" has no bargaining power to cause its landlord to upgrade its quarters. The family cannot afford to pay higher rent and the owner will not make extensive repairs that will not increase his rent roll. This "noneffective demand" is a problem shared by about 7.8 million American families, one family in eight cannot find decent housing that does not cost in excess of 20% of its income.(107) Attempts to preserve the supply of low cost housing in the city and prevent the abandonment of sound structures, therefore, cannot simply concentrate on improving the housing stock in the hands of private absentee owners. Safeguards must be built into any programatic solution of the problem that will insure that low income persons will live in the rehabilitated structures. One way to do this would be to impose maximum income limits on tenant eligibility to live in the building that was rehabilitated with government assistance. But such restrictions would inhibit economic integration of inner-city housing and restrict the mobility of low income families. It would be better to supplement these families' income so that they can afford decent housing wherever they choose.

President Nixon's Task Force on Low Income Housing recognized the need to focus on income when it urged a new approach to federal housing assistance. It called for "programs that fit dwellings to family needs, with subsidies scaled to family income, rather than housing programmed to fit income levels."(108) The only current federal programs which reach the very low income families are the Rent Supplement Program(109) and the Public Housing Leasing Program.(110) Both programs provide payments to landlords (nonprofit corporations in one case, private owners in the other) to make up the difference between the fair market rent ($130 in the above example) and what the tenant can afford (20-25% of income). The agency administering the payments is obligated to assure that the accommodations thus subsidized are decent, safe, and sanitary. Although these programs subsidize income, they inhibit mobility insofar as the subsidy is tied to particular structures instead of being paid directly to the under-income family.

Based on similar principles, another program, Housing Allowances, is being tried on an experimental basis by the Model Cities programs of Wilmington, Delaware and Kansas City, Kansas.(111) The allowance is the difference between what the family can afford and the fair market rent. The major difference between the housing allowance and the other programs is that the subsidy is not tied to a specific structure. Instead, the payment is made directly to the family, and the family chooses its own accommodations from those available on the market. As in existing programs the agency dispensing the subsidy inspects the housing to see that it meets minimum housing standards.(112)

A comprehensive program to combat abandonment must include income or rent subsidies such as those discussed above. It should also have a component aimed at increasing employment opportunities for neighborhood residents. This component could include projects for training, for improved transportation to jobs, for attracting businesses back to the inner city, and for the creation of new jobs in the community (for example, in a housing management corporation).

In summary, part of the vacant building problem is traceable to the tenants themselves. It is unlikely that many low income tenants in the inner city maliciously destroy property, but increasingly, tenants are demanding that owners keep their buildings up to code standards, and the government has grown increasingly responsive to their demands. Owners are thus forced to make repairs that they and previous owners unlawfully deferred for years. Rental income is usually insufficient to support such repairs, and the tenants cannot afford to pay higher rents. An owner facing such a situation may be forced to close his building. A government subsidy is required if such buildings are to be saved in private hands. This could take the form of a direct subsidy to the owner while limiting the indirect beneficiaries of the subsidy to low income families, or it could take the form of an income supplement directly to families. The latter form of subsidy would give more leverage and choice to the tenants and assure that owners maintain an adequate level of housing services or lose the tenants to someone else.

GOVERNMENTAL FACTORS

Many sorts of governmental activity bear on the problem of deteriorating and abandoned core city housing. Sometimes programs designed to improve housing have worsened it. In other instances, programs supposed to be neutral with respect to housing are actually part of the problem or its solution. This section examines the way that several governmental activities influence the quality of housing for low income people in the inner-city and offers some suggestions for improvement. Other government policies and programs have been suggested previously, and the possibility of direct government action to repair or maintain inner-city housing will be examined later.

TAXES

Real property and income taxes are commonly thought to contribute to the deterioration of slums and to the abandonment of buildings. Increased property tax appraisals penalize improvement(113) and rapid depreciation allowances and capital gains rates are said to encourage rapid turnover.(114) Turnover and the property tax disincentive discourage maintenance. Deteriorating or abandoned decaying properties lose value and drag down the value of neighboring structures. Decreased value means a lower tax base. Thus, physical deterioration increases the need for government services at the same time it lessens the ability of government to provide them. The government is forced to increase the rate of taxation per dollar of assessed valuation, or curtail services, or both. Increased taxes increase the operating expenses of owners who have maintained their properties and this together with a decrease in services may only accelerate deterioration and abandonment.(115) However, it should be noted that the penalty imposed upon an owner of an unproductive vacant building is small compared to what it would cost him to demolish it, especially if he has no alternative use for it and no income to offset with a loss deduction.

A variation of the property tax has been proposed, which would be a tax on land only without regard to the structure on it. Such a system of site taxation would require valuation to be based on the site's locational advantages and other characteristics such as size, shape, topography, and soil conditions. This type of property tax is neutral with respect to improvements; it does not have the disincentives of the present system. This sort of tax has been objected to in that it would be difficult to administer because of the lack of comparable sales of vacant land for use as benchmarks. It would seem, though, that methods of valuation could easily be established. A stronger objection to site taxation is that it would be regressive, providing greatest benefits to parcels with high building to land value ratios. This objection may be answered partially by zoning laws. The zones should be considered in site valuation, so that larger, more expensive buildings would tend to be on more valuable land. Pittsburgh meets this objection with a graded tax, taxing buildings at 50 percent of the rate for the land.(116)

An adequate solution to the problems of property taxation must include a regional tax policy and a metropolitan tax base so that the core city can recapture some of the tax base that has moved beyond its reach while continuing to use its services tax-free. A reduction of the pressure of the center-city tax base could mean reduced taxes and new investment in center city property.(117)

Another area of taxation relevant to the abandoned building problem is federal income tax deductions for depreciation. Accelerated depreciation is said to have encouraged low maintenance and rapid turnover because successive owners could take depreciation deductions and pay tax on their sale at capital gains rates.(118) However, there is little evidence that depreciation deductions were a major motivating factor in the purchase and sale of housing in the study area. Although 38 of the 53 vacant properties have been purchased in the last ten years, many have been in the same families thirty to forty years, and many of those properties recently purchased had not changed hands for many years previous to purchase.(119) Lengthy tenure of ownership does not necessarily equate with adequate maintenance, but the low turnover rate indicated disputes the prevalance of high depreciation as a tax shield. At any rate, Congress followed the recommendation that depreciation on such buildings be limited to the straight line method, thus, attempting to discourage slum deterioration by eliminating a tax advantage that was apparently not utilized.(120)

Although there are several possible income tax reforms which could encourage maintenance of slum property, tax incentives are less efficient than direct government payments to achieve a specific purpose. An intelligent tax policy can only assist a broader program utilizing other tools designed to house low income persons.(121) One reform to encourage rehabilitation of rental housing would be to allow major repairs in deteriorated buildings to be treated as immediately deductible repairs rather than as capital improvements which must depreciate over the useful life of the building. The present treatment of such major repairs disregards the fact that such "improvements" as rewiring a house to meet housing code requirements do not increase the rental value of the property. What is considered an improvement under present tax law is really long overdue repair of conditions accumulated over years of neglect. Appropriate regulations could restrict this tax treatment to slum dwellings.(122)

Zoning is also a factor in the problem of building abandonment. However, the relationship of zoning to abandonment in the inner city study area, where the pattern of development was established well before the enactment of zoning regulations, is of less importance than in more recently developed areas such as Washington's Far Southeast. In the Far Southeast overzoning for apartments without adequate planning for supporting facilities coupled with shoddy development practices has created an area that is deteriorating far more rapidly than other areas of the city. A glance at the zoning map suggests that zoning played a large role in this process. Over 75% of all residential land in the Far Southeast is zoned for apartments. In the remainder of the city such zoning accounts for less than 20% of residential zoning.(123)

Zoning regulations over the years do not seem to have imposed much of a burden on landowners in the study area. Zones were dictated by the existing land development pattern and the expectation that the area would become more commercial and that such development would follow the established linear pattern. Since 1920 "there has been a narrowing down and filling-in process, or what might be called a consolidation with respect to commercial zones in the Renewal Area."(124) Residential areas that failed to develop into commercial areas have been reclassified as residential.

Zoning probably has exerted little positive control over development in the Shaw Area. The regulations appear to have been loose enough to permit an owner to make almost whatever use of his property he chose. It is possible that the over-zoning for commercial uses encouraged speculative purchases of residential buildings in the area in anticipation of commercial development that never came. Such speculation would have been accompanied by a low level of maintenance that would hasten deterioration. Also, it seems that where commercial development became profitable in an area, the lack of commercial zoning was no roadblock and the area was rezoned.

One would expect that rezoning has played a similarly small role in the development of the core areas of other large American cities where development, for the most part, preceded zoning. However, zoning is a tool that would see more intensive use in the control of blight and the preservation of old neighborhoods. New regulations should be established and enforced which would require amortization of illegal or nonconforming uses.

URBAN RENEWAL

Urban Renewal, "a program which should arrest the process of abandonment, sometimes actually fosters it."(125) Owners who might have made repairs do not because they do not feel that they can recover the cost of improvements. Tenants, expecting to displaced, often move out before the renewal agency takes any action to acquire the property.(126) Others are forced to move because of the landlord's failure to maintain the premises. Tenants who have resorted to a rent strike to protest the deterioration of the premises have found that the owner does not attempt to evict them—at least not by legal process. In effect, the tenants suffer a constructive eviction. So long as they stay, the owner can rely on the tenants to prevent vandalism. When they finally move, he will simply board up the building and wait for the local renewal agency to come bail him out.

The designation of an urban renewal area has an "announcement effect" on maintenance throughout the area. Although acquisition of the property may be ten years away, this is something neither owners nor tenants know. The

Neighborhood Development Program, under which certain projects are designated on a yearly basis, leaves large areas of the total project in limbo. In the Shaw Urban Renewal Area there is a general decrease in maintenance throughout the area, but abandonment is more prevalent in the areas already designated for acquisition. The study area did not, however, offer an example of this phenomenon. I had expected to find a concentration of vacant buildings in a part of the study area where properties are being acquired for the expansion of a school, the only redevelopment activity in the study area. Six vacant buildings were found in this area, but just as many were found on other blocks where no action is planned. However, a look outside of the study area indicates concentrations of vacant buildings where government acquisition is imminent.

An obvious solution to the problem of the announcement effect would be for redevelopment agencies to acquire and begin development for the whole area at once, but this, of course, is an unrealistic proposal given funding levels. Nevertheless, a more systematic and predictable plan of acquisition and renewal would reduce the announcement effect.

A better way for the redevelopment agency to encourage maintenance of residential structures in the renewal area is to penalize owners for allowing their buildings to deteriorate. The use of personal and real property in our private enterprise society is subject to control and limitation by the government. For example, a landowner must develop his property in conformity to local zoning laws and once he has erected a structure, there are numerous legal restrictions on his use of it. He must conform to housing, fire, and safety regulations, obtain licenses and permits, and so forth. For violation of any of these statutorily imposed duties, he is subject to a variety of sanctions. Under the police power, a governmental agency may condemn and destroy property which is used illegally and to the detriment of the community without payment of any compensation for the property so destroyed. Thus, for example, the District Government has the power to condemn and destroy unsafe and unsanitary structures.(127) Indeed, as will be discussed, the government may collect its costs from the owner.

Traditionally,(128) the law has been that police power regulation, without compensation to the owner for the restrictions imposed upon him, cannot be extended so far as to allow the government to take the land as well as destroy the building. A taking of the land requires just compensation as a matter of constitutional law. Logically, however, there is no reason why the principles that justify police power regulation to the point of destruction of property cannot be applied in a situation where the government happens to be interested in acquiring the land. The fact that the government is purchasing the land should not take away from the police powers it would have if it were not purchasing the land. Thus, if a building is in such a state that the government would be justified in ordering its removal at the owner's expense, the government should be able to deduct the cost of removal from the cost of acquisition. This means more than reducing the appraisal value of the building to zero. The cost of demolition might even be deducted from the value of the cleared land, since the worthless structure makes the land less valuable. This result would be no different from a case where a building was condemned as unsafe, destroyed at the owner's expense, and *then* purchased by the redevelopment agency. The agency should have "no obligation to pay for any illegal use; nor does the agency have a duty to pay for a nuisance," when it can show "that the improvements have a market value diminished by the cost of remedying the illegal uses or have value that could be ascribed to the illegal uses of the improvements."(129)

Similarly, the agency should be able to deduct for violations of the Housing Regulations which, although they may not justify demolition under the police power, are illegal uses that reduce the value of the structure. The appraisal value of the structure should be reduced by the amount it would cost to bring it up to standard. The agency should be able to make such deductions whether it was acquiring the property for clearance or rehabilitation. Certainly, if renewal agencies were to adopt a policy like this, owners would have an incentive to maintain their property and repair code violations. It may be necessary to adopt a statute authorizing such a procedure,(130) but it is suggested that the agency and the courts already have the power to apply such a doctrine.(131)

This proposed approach involves a refinement of the notion of "just compensation" which has generally been held to be synonymous with "fair market value."(132) Ordinarily, the hypothetical willing buyer in the market value formula does not deduct for code violations. This has only been because owners have been able to reap a return from their investment despite existing code violations. However, it has been established—at least in the District of Columbia—that an owner has no right or a diminished right to a return (rent) if housing code violations exist in his building.(133) Similarly, he can be denied an occupancy permit if he fails to remedy code violations. Thus, if an owner can be denied the profits of his illegal use in other contexts, he would not be allowed to calculate fair market value on the basis of the same illegal use.

Senator Goodell, in discussing the relationship of urban renewal to vacant housing, seems to adopt this rationale.

> Quite clearly, slumlords should not be rewarded for their negligence by receiving high sale prices from the municipality for their properties. Local housing officials must guard against this practice. When property is deteriorating or abandoned, the value of the property is significantly diminished and the sale price must reflect this decreased market value. The owner should be required to satisfy any building code fines or back taxes from the purchase price. Our municipal officials set the purchase prices and they must take the primary responsibility for assessing a fair but not inflated value for property and land acquisition. Any dispute regarding the value, is of course one that must ultimately be resolved by the courts.(134)

Despite the logic of the view outlined above, apparently such an approach has never been tried. The reason for this appears to be the desire of renewal agencies to avoid long, drawn-out court battles. In order to facilitate the urban renewal process, local agencies have typically been generous to the landowners.(135) It is no wonder that owners choose to stop maintenance and "dead-end" their buildings when they know that urban renewal is coming. They have nothing to lose. It would be far better to appraise every building in the area according to the method outlined above and then file condemnation actions against all of the properties simultaneously with the announcement of urban renewal. Court delays would coincide with the ordinary delays of planning, and owners would maintain their properties and settle out of court when they discover that the courts uphold such an appraisal approach.

A problem with this sort of approach is that it could penalize small homeowners in the area as well as absentee owners. Some of the small homeowners unwittingly purchased deteriorated homes from speculators. They lack the resources to make the repairs required. They should be treated differently from the slum landlord. Unless the law can assess damages against the absentee owners, without hurting the small homeowner, urban renewal will continue to reward unscrupulous absentee "investors."

There is a rational distinction between the landlord and the resident homeowner that justifies separate classification and unequal treatment. The absentee landlord holds himself out to the public by renting out units, as offering decent, safe, and sanitary facilities. Just as in the case of other public undertakings, the government has good reason to hold him to a higher standard than the homeowner—i.e., the protection of the public. It is for this very reason that apartment house owners are required to obtain licenses while single-family homeowners are not.

As I have noted above, the appraisal scheme outlined here is consistent with present law. However, the timid may prefer specific statutory authorization. Therefore, language such as the following could be enacted:

> In determining just compensation for any piece or tract of land to be purchased or condemned by the Government, no value shall be assigned for any illegal use, and if a violation of statute or regulation is found to exist in any building upon any such piece or tract of land to be so acquired (other than building regulations which set standards of construction not in effect at the time of construction of said building), and the owner of the subject real estate has not resided in the building for a period of not less than one year prior to the initiation of negotiations for the acquisition of such property, the [Agency/Court/jury] may consider and deduct the cost of remedying such violation from the value of the piece or tract of land.

CODE ENFORCEMENT

The nonenforcement of housing codes has contributed to abandonment of buildings because it has allowed entire neighborhoods to deteriorate to the point where even well-meaning owners hesitate to make repairs. The prevailing view of housing code enforcement, held by officials and employees of the District's Department of Economic Development, and students of the subject, is that it is an effective tool for the preservation of sound neighborhoods, but it is incapable alone of solving the problem of substandard housing in already deteriorated slums.(136) A lawyer employed in the Department's concentrated code enforcement program in an area not considered a hard-core slum reports that he knows of no cases in that area where code enforcement caused an owner to abandon his building.(137) However, personnel in the Department believe that rigorous code enforcement in more deteriorated slum neighborhoods like the study area would result in abandoned buildings and displaced tenants. Thus, to prevent abandonment, code enforcement is relaxed.(138) It was learned that it is the policy of the Bureau of Licenses and Inspections not to inspect single family dwellings in the study area whether owner occupied or not—unless a complaint is received by the office.(139) This shyness with respect to code enforcement is by no means limited to Washington, D.C.

> In most cities, not only are housing code standards minimal, but enforcement also tends to be sporadic, inconsistent and cautious. These policies proceed, at least in part, from the fear that stronger measures will precipitate abandonment of buildings by owners as the rents required by maintenance to code standards rise beyond the reach of neighborhood residents.(140)

A search of the records at the field office of the Division of Licenses and Inspection showed that almost all of the abandoned buildings in the study area had been inspected at some time or another, but many had not been inspected since 1966. Often the code violation cited related to the building's abandonment, e.g., it was not boarded up or trash had collected around it. It was impossible to determine whether the existence of code violations requiring expensive repair had caused any of the owners to close his building because of the poor recordkeeping system maintained at the field office. Consequently, the thesis that code enforcement will cause abandonment was not proved or disproved. It is not clear wheteer the poor records reflect lax inspection and enforcement practices or lack of manpower for record keeping. Lack of manpower seems definitely to be a problem, but the city council committee reports that inspections made "in response to tenant complaints are often cursory and enforcement does not always follow the discovery of violations."(141)

The committee report states further that routine practices of Licenses and Inspections "generally benefit the landlord and burden the tenant" and landlords are often given extensions of time to make repairs.(142) Conversations with officials at Licenses and Inspections confirm that this is the case. It may be that some of the Department's personnel do favor landlords over tenants, but a major reason for lax enforcement is that the sanctions in the Housing Regulations are obsolescent and counter-productive.

Substantial vacancy rates in the early 1900's when housing codes were first enacted made the order to vacate an effective sanction against owners.(143) But with today's extreme housing shortage the sanction is self-defeating. Perhaps, it is because of the current low vacancy rate that the sanction is rarely used in the District and then only when a building is already vacant. It is reported that the shortage of housing in Chicago caused non-enforcement of "over-ambitious" code regulations.(144) Officials there, when faced with the choice of lax enforcement or displacement of tenants for whom there were no better homes available, chose lax enforcement.(145) The government's policy of lax enforcement in urban renewal areas such as the study area, is reinforced by requirements that individuals displaced by code enforcement be assured of relocation housing.(146)

The sanction favored by Licenses and Inspections to encourage compliance, is denial of licensing to owners of buildings having code violations. Since licensing does not apply to single-family dwellings, even if 200 are owned by one person, this sanction is hardly sufficient.

Fines, as an alternative sanction, if and when they are imposed, are said to be "so small in relation to the cost of rehabilitation that they amount to a licensing fee for code violations."(147) This is not true where cumulative fines can be imposed, but most courts refuse to consider code violations as criminal conduct,(148) viewing themselves rather as the compliance board of last resort and often granting further extensions of time to noncomplying owners. A problem in the District has been that of the few cases referred to the Corporation Counsel far fewer go to court.(149) The only effective court sanction against code violations has arisen in the context of eviction proceedings. The Court has held that code violations existing at the time a tenant enters into the premises or developing thereafter justify nonpayment of rent.(150)

The city has the power to circumvent the criminal sanction process and make repairs an owner refuses to make.(151) This power has never been utilized although the city government has requested $50,000 from Congress for this purpose.(152)

It has been suggested that current practice be codified and housing codes be established on a "zoned basis" with different standards for slum areas than for areas where the goal is to maintain existing values.(153) Such suggestions and the present uneven enforcement of the codes, based on the belief that rigorous enforcement in the face of market pressures will only force landlords to close their buildings and worsen the housing shortage, only underscore the fact that code enforcement is only one of the battery of tools which must be used to rehabilitate slum housing. Stricter code enforcement alone cannot solve the abandoned building problem. It must be used as a tool of urban planning in conjunction with public housing, urban renewal, zoning laws, improved management, mortgage guarantee and loan programs, increased municipal services, and so forth.(154)

On the other hand, if putting absentee owners out of business so that resident homeowners or the government could replace them, is the objective, concentrated code enforcement can be a most valuable tool. Such a program could cause owners to abandon their buildings which could then be condemned and demolished at the owner's expense or be appraised at zero or negative value by the renewal agency thereby greatly reducing the cost of renewal and thus the cost of homeownership programs. Such a scheme requires a policy decision to force slum owners to absorb a large share of the costs and it would temporarily worsen the housing shortage.

Several alternative sanctions for code violations have been proposed in other jurisdictions. For example, a New York statute permitting the withholding of rent if "rent impairing" violations remain uncured for six months has not been applied although it was enacted in 1965.(155) Another suggestion is a summary procedure allowing a tenant to get a court order appointing a receiver to make repairs.(1956) This would be a desirable remedy only if it contemplates immediate repair by the receiver and not that the receiver must first collect enough rent to pay for repairs. If the latter is the case or if rent must be paid for the period between report and repair, such a procedure would be a step backward from recent landmark decisions of the District of Columbia Court of Appeals and would be similar to a proposed amendment to the D.C. Housing Regulations which were rejected this year.(157) The court has quite reasonably held that code violations excuse the duty to pay rent. A renter is entitled to decent, safe, and sanitary housing, and he should not be required to pay for it when he does not get it.(158)

The power to condemn unsafe and unsanitary buildings is related to the power to enforce standards of health and safety under the Housing Regulations. Like code enforcement, it may possibly cause an owner to abandon his building rather than invest in it to bring it up to the standards of the condemning authority. However, if the District of Columbia's actions with respect to the fifty-three already-abandoned buildings in the study area indicates the level of its activities in occupied structures, such a causal relationship is doubtful, to say the least.

In the District of Columbia, the power to cause abandoned or deteriorated "buildings to be put into sanitary condition or to be demolished and removed" is vested in the Board of Condemnation of Unsanitary Buildings.(159) Although the Board is a division of the Department of Economic Development, and it is authorized to delegate ministerial duties and responsibilities to the Division of Licenses and Inspections,(160) it maintains its own staff of inspectors.

The Board is also empowered to shore up, take down or otherwise secure unsafe structures.(161) Inspections to determine whether or not a structure is unsafe are made by the construction staff of the Division of Licenses and Inspections at the request of the Board of Condemnation. Recommendations of the construction office are then referred back to the Board for action.(162) However, personnel at the Board of Condemnation report that they are responsible only for unsanitary conditions and that there is a separate board for the condemnation of unsafe structures. Interestingly, the construction office of Licenses and Inspections has no knowledge of the existence of such a board.(163) Personnel at the Board of Condemnation seem eager to narrowly define their authority and are pleased to be able to tell you that a reported condition is not their responsibility but that of the Division of Licenses and Inspections.(164) The Housing Regulations generally relate to unsafe and unsanitary conditions and there seems to be no justification for the Board's policy of condemning only where buildings are *extremely* unsafe or insanitary. The statute prohibits the Board from requiring a building to be brought "into conformity with the D.C. Building Code and other *building* regulations."(165) There is no such prohibition respecting the Housing Regulations which relate to living conditions and not structural specifications.

The foregoing points up the problem common in most cities, of there being no overall agency responsible for regulation of housing conditions. The multiplicity of agencies leads to a duplication of inspections and recordkeeping, and inadequate communication and coordination of enforcement.(166) It also allows for buck-passing. The placing of Licenses and Inspections and the Board of Condemnation under the Department of Economic Development is a step in the right direction but coordination appears to be far from satisfactory at this stage. While there were some referrals to the Board noted in the records at the Licenses and Inspections field office, there was no record of what action, if any, had been taken by the Board. It appeared that the L&I inspector had simply noted that the Board had posted a sign on a building in his territory.(167)

Despite the mandatory language of the authorizing legislation that where an owner neglects or refuses to cause his building to be made safe, the District government "shall proceed to make such structure or excavation safe or remove the same,"(168) this authority appears to be sparingly used. Some of the buildings in the study are reported to have been vacant for as long as three years,(169) yet they have been neither boarded up nor demolished. They continue to stand open, beckoning arsonists and addicts, and endangering the health and safety of the neighborhood. Of the fifty-three abandoned buildings in the study area only a handful were boarded up. The Board of Condemnation could report that action had been or was being taken with respect to only eleven of the fifty-three buildings. Action taken was often ineffectual. Thus, it was learned, for example, that one building, a windowless hulk adjacent to an occupied and relatively well-maintained structure, was surveyed by an inspector in October, 1969, and seen by a member of the Board in December, 1969, but as of April 22, 1970, no action had been taken by the Board.(170)

In the spring the Acting Executive Secretary of the Board refused to permit me to examine the Board's files to determine what action, if any, had been taken with respect to the buildings on my list. He argued that the files were confidential. However, an appeal to the head of the Department of Economic Development opened the files to me. I discovered that action had been taken against only ten of the 53 buildings I had found vacant (not eleven as I had previously been told). Only nine of the files were available in the office. On the average, twenty months had elapsed since the buildings had first come to the attention of the Board. The files showed an appalling failure of the Board to follow-through on its orders. The Board set deadlines, then took no further action until months later. Extentions were liberally granted. A check on the nine buildings revealed that four of them had not even been boarded up.

In fairness, one should note the possibility that the Board has been concentrating its attentions outside the Urban Renewal Area. One should also note the possibility that some Board actions or negotiations with owners occurred that were not entered in the files. Also, if preservation of the vacant buildings as a housing resource is deemed a reasonable objective, the Board's reluctance to order demolition is fortunate.

The Board may order that a building be boarded up and that the grounds be kept clean, but such orders are regarded as temporary measures to be used only until the owner has shown that he does not intend to repair. When this becomes clear, the Board's ultimate sanction is demolition. Although the Board has statutory authority "to cause all buildings to be put into sanitary condition"(171) and to make unsafe structures safe(172) at the owner's expense, it seems to have limited itself to the remedies of prohibiting occupancy, demolition, and boarding-up.

Demolition has been the traditional response of government to the threat an abandoned building presents to health, safety and morals. The authority to demolish substandard structures was established in equity as part of the power of municipalities to abate public nuisances, and the equity origins of this power still affect the constitutional basis of the law of demolition. Thus, the courts might limit the power to demolish to buildings which are in fact nuisances. Generally, the cases have held that mere dilapidation or age is not enough to justify demolition absent imminent danger. In addition to equity's bias against demolition is its preference for repair as an alternative. Some courts will order repair instead of demolition if the danger can thus be remedied.(173) Cases involving equity restrictions on the power to demolish apparently have not arisen in the District of Columbia, and those cases in other jurisdictions where such restrictions were applied involved owners who were resisting demolition and asking to be allowed to repair. Nevertheless, the existence of such restrictions suggests the possibility of petitioning the court to enjoin demolition of structures that could be economically rehabilitated. However, for those structures for which rehabilitation is not economically feasible, demolition may be the only remedy. Residents in the study area did not seem to have any preference for demolition over boarding-up. Most of those talked to would prefer to see the buildings occupied. Demolition can have unintended, deleterious side effects. For example, when a row house was removed in another part of the Shaw Area, several muggings occurred because a new passageway from the rougher neighborhood on the next block was created.

Other than the fact that no money has been appropriated to this end, there appears to be no reason why the Board cannot order repairs and then have them done by a contractor or by government employees when the owner refuses to make repairs himself. Such action appears to be authorized by the statutory language.(174) The Board could determine that due to the housing shortage, demolition is not in the public interest. It has already determined that mere boarding up is unacceptable as a permanent remedy for the dangers which a vacant building present to the surrounding area. The remaining alternative would be repair. The costs could become a tax lien just as is presently the case with demolition costs.

If more specific statutory authority is desired for such an undertaking by the city, it might also include provisions to 1. prevent city demolition of sound structures and, 2. prohibit an owner from keeping a building unoccupied for a certain length of time when the city vacancy rate is below a certain level. To avoid constitutional objections to this latter provision, the owner might be given the option of selling the building to the city at a price determined in accordance with the scheme outlined in the section on urban renewal.

By way of illustration only, the following amendment to Title 5, Chapter 5, of the D.C. Code is offered:

> Any residential structure that is unoccupied and has remained so for—months, while the vacancy rate for the city is below—percent, is hereby declared to be an unsafe structure because of its blighting influence on the neighborhood and the danger of fire damage it presents to neighboring structures. Mere boarding up of the structure shall not be considered an adequate remedy for such unsafe condition, and such structure shall be ordered either reopened or demolished. Demolition of such structure shall not be ordered if, on inspection, the structure is found to be sound. In such a case the District of Columbia shall order, in accordance with the procedures prescribed by this chapter, that the structure be repaired and reopened. If necessary steps are not taken by the owner in good faith within ten days of the order, the District of Columbia shall itself initiate such steps and the costs shall be assessed against the property and collected in accordance with the procedures established by section 506 of this chapter.

WELFARE

Welfare payments may be an unwitting government measure preventing the abandonment of buildings. The District's Department of Public Welfare has a significant impact on housing in the nation's capital. Each year it subsidizes housing with $8,000,000 in shelter payments to welfare recipients. Twelve thousand five hundred of the 16,000 District families on welfare do not live in public housing. In the District fifty-six and one-half percent of welfare recipients are in poor quality housing. Recipients often pay 40 percent of their welfare payments for housing, and some pay 60 percent.(175) Nationally, one third of all welfare payments are spent on housing, most of which is substandard. This 600 million dollars per year subsidy to slumlords is about equal to President Nixon's request from Congress for the Model Cities program.(176) Welfare payments may be keeping slum owners in business who might otherwise abandon their buildings.

This expenditure of tax dollars buys little for the welfare recipient and does nothing to improve the housing stock. If the money were used instead to finance housing development and rehabilitation, recipients might gain new housing with no increased burden on the taxpayer. Six hundred million dollars could support a six billion dollar investment in low cost housing.(177) However, because of the time lag in construction, the government really could not simply reallocate funds from welfare to housing construction or rehabilitation. At least for the short run, welfare payment would have to coexist with increased production and rehabilitation. And some sort of income subsidy will probably continue to be necessary to assure decent housing for low income families.

Highlighting the fact that one third of all welfare payments are spent on housing is to call attention to the fact that welfare agencies presently have it within their power to better existing housing conditions for welfare recipients. The local welfare department could require that recipients live only in standard units and refuse to pay when a unit becomes substandard through the appearance of housing code violations. This requirement was discussed earlier, with respect to the housing allowance, which is, in effect, simply a more adequate welfare payment. Even at present levels, welfare payments increase the recipient's purchasing power. Ordinarily the landlord will respond to this demand by improving the quality of his property only to the extent that he can expect to increase his economic return. But if he can benefit from this demand only by upgrading his premises, and he has no alternative tenants, he may make certain improvements that do not increase his return. Thus, the support of the local welfare agency can increase the tenants' bargaining power. This support should extend to the provision of legal defense for nonpayment of rent when the payment is withheld.

To better the quality of accommodations for welfare recipients, welfare agencies in New York and Illinois are now refusing shelter payments to occupants of substandard housing.(178) New York codified this practice in 1962.(179) The Cook County Department of Public Aid adopted the practice in 1961 without specific statutory authority.(180) The Department of Public Welfare in the District has no similar program.(181)

In the Cook County Program, there is a housing consultant and staff in each of the Department's offices who have precise knowledge of the quality of housing in their area. Landlords are contacted regarding deteriorated units to persuade them to improve their housing. If this fails, shelter payments are withheld. The Department defends a welfare recipient in any eviction action resulting from the withholding or any other action intended to harass him. Since the inception of the program the Department has withheld $705,371.80 from 2,156 property owners housing 36,431 persons.(182)

Similar coordination of welfare and housing code activities has been recommended for Washington, D.C.(183) Such a program in the welfare department would be an important adjunct to existing code enforcement remedies to prevent housing deterioration. The Cook County program, however, is not quite as good as it sounds insofar as withheld rents are apparently paid over to the owner when he makes repairs without deduction for the period during which the accommodations were substandard.(184) Thus, there is no incentive for the owner to make repairs as soon as possible; the withheld rents are like money in the bank. The program, therefore, has the same shortcomings that were discussed in the section on code enforcement with respect to receivership proposals. A plan should not include return of withheld rents to owners when they make repairs because this would undercut court decisions.(185) Rather, the surplus accumulated should be put into a revolving fund for a housing development corporation or be used in some other way to improve housing or encourage home-ownership by welfare recipients. The fund might be used, for example, to increase housing allowances to recipients to increase the effectiveness of their demand for housing. Or perhaps the welfare department could establish a nonprofit corporation—with welfare recipients on the board of directors—that could sponsor FHA housing projects.

REHABILITATION AND REPAIR

A major purpose of this study, aside from determining the causes of abandonment and possible ways to stem the tide, was to determine whether the empty residential structures which dot inner-city neighborhoods can be considered a resource that can be used to reduce the housing shortage. Can they be rehabilitated under government or private sponsorship? All of the buildings in the Shaw Renewal Area were surveyed and rated as to exterior building condition by a team of architects during the period May 1968 to February 1969. A 20 percent sub-sample was surveyed inside as well as out. Buildings were rated either as "sound," "deficient," or "extremely deficient." Twenty-three of the fifty-three buildings in the study area found to be abandoned, about 44% of the sample, had been rated deficient by the earlier study. Seven of these buildings had interior survey reports; there was one sound, one deficient, and five extremely deficient.(186) These figures indicate that rehabilitation could prove to be a rather expensive process if feasible at all.

Rehabilitation is a controversial subject. Some "seriously question the potential of hard core slum areas for rehabilitation . . . the bulldozer approach to such hard core areas would seem to be the only answer."(187) Others claim that "the most feasible way to eradicate blight in our cities is to rehabilitate, on a large scale, existing deteriorating, but structurally sound housing, particularly for families of low and moderate income."(188)

Part of this difference of opinion must relate to different standards of what constitutes a likely candidate for rehabilitation. Thus, one reads that in Chicago vacant buildings are usually structurally sound(189) while in Boston the buildings are mostly beyond rehabilitation.(190) A building may have a sound structure and still require $12,000 to $14,000 per apartment to rehabilitate.(191) Gut rehabilitation has generally proved to be too expensive, but patchwork methods have succeeded in achieving costs within FHA limits.(192) Cost for rehabilitation of a group of seven townhouses in the Northwest #1 Renewal Area of Washington, D.C. averaged $9,004 for construction alone, and total cost averaged $15,400.(193) On one proposition there is general agreement. Even large private owners will not rehabilitate when they cannot recoup their investment through higher rents because present tenants cannot afford to pay, and higher income tenants usually will not move in unless the whole neighborhood is upgraded.(194) Rehabilitated houses cannot be afforded by low income persons except through federally assisted programs.(195)

An important inhibition on rehabilitation of abandoned buildings is that they are scattered throughout the center city. A program aimed at rehabilitating these structures without at the same time improving the rest of the houses in the neighborhood would be prone to fail. This is the reason for the Redevelopment Land Agency's opposition to scattered site acquisition and rehabilitation. On the other hand rehabilitation of such sites makes good sense when surrounding properties are in good condition since the depressing effects of the vacant building on its surroundings can be removed, and the benefits extend beyond the single structure to the whole neighborhood.(196)

PRIVATE REHABILITATION

Few private absentee owners will rehabilitate their buildings since they cannot get sufficient return on their investment. However, with the aid of FHA programs and Urban Renewal grant and loan programs resident owners and nonprofit sponsors may be able to make rehabilitation work for low income families. Thus, if it is decided to rehabilitate scattered vacant building (perhaps in an area less deteriorated generally than the study area), a program such as Section 235(j)(197) would be one way to do it. This program is for low and moderate income families but would not make homeownership available to families at public housing income levels. A nonprofit sponsor can make *rental* housing available to this latter group in a variety of ways. For example, Section 236(198) rehabilitation could make rental, cooperative or condominium units available to the same income group served by the 235 program, but 40 percent of the units could be rented to persons at the public housing income level through the Rent Supplement Program.(199) An alternative to Rent Supplement would be a variation of the Section 23 Leased Housing Program,(200) but that sort of program requires the cooperation of the local housing authority. It should be kept in mind that these programs can only work if used in conjunction with other activities aimed at improving the quality of the neighborhood.

GOVERNMENT ACTION

Although no program of the Federal Housing Administration can put homeownership within the reach of public housing income persons, various programs administered by the Housing Assistance Administration can. These programs require the participation of the local housing authority, and they are financed in the same way as conventional public housing—the local authority sells bonds and the federal government makes annual contributions to cover the full costs of interest and amortization of principal. These programs could be used to rehabilitate inner city housing.

Turnkey III is a public housing program involving the purchase of housing by the local authority from a private owner. Tenants paying normal public housing rents enter a lease-purchase agreement and gradually accumulate equity in the home. This is made possible because the tenant is responsible for ordinary maintenance and that portion of his rent which would normally be allocated to maintenance expense is set aside in an ownership account. This can also be done under the "Los Angeles" variation of the Section 23 Leasing Program which allows a nonprofit sponsor to contract with the local authority to provide housing for low income families with the difference between the public housing rent paid by the tenant and the market rent paid by the HAA. Where this differs from ordinary Section 23 Leasing is that the sponsor enters a "homebuyer's ownership agreement" with the tenant that makes the program similar to Turnkey III.

Section 23(g) of the Housing Act of 1937 authorizes a local housing authority to purchase private housing in order to resell it to tenants or a tenant's organization for 80 percent of its value. Resale is "subject to such terms and conditions . . . as may be necessary to enable the tenants to make the purchase without undue financial hardship."(201) Thus, for a temporary period, the housing authority could pay all of the buyer's interest payments. This amounts to virtually full payment for a period because payment on an unamortized loan goes mostly to pay the interest during the first few years. These public housing programs could be extremely useful in the prevention of abandonment.

Philadelphia intends to use one of these public housing programs to help solve its abandoned building problem. It is reported that over 5,000 empty houses there have been rehabilitated, mostly for rental to public housing tenants. The city guarantees private developers that if a rehabilitated house cannot be sold to a private buyer, the city will purchase the house, at a fixed price, for use as public housing.(202) Apparently this program has operated only on a very small scale. The Assistant Housing Director there implies that the block to expansion of the program is lack of cooperation between local and federal officials in the FHA and public housing programs.(203) Baltimore intends to use vacant buildings as a resource for scattered site public housing in a program similar to Philadelphia's.(204)

Another way for a city to attack its vacant building problem would be through a receivership arrangement whereby the city would appoint a receiver to take over a building which becomes vacant, make necessary repairs, and rent it out to low income tenants. The owner could receive whatever income there was after repair costs were amortized and current expenses were deducted. Such an arrangement runs counter to the traditional notions of the rights of private owners to do as they wish with their property including closing it down. But the owner's right to use his property as he wishes is already restricted by police power regulations such as zoning ordinances and rent control laws. Persons owning housing which they hold for rental to others are helping to meet the tremendous housing shortage; they are thus helping to meet a public need. Their buildings exist to serve the public's need for housing, just as public transportation exists to serve the public's need for transportation.

The public interest in the provision of housing for citizens should justify much stricter regulation of permissible use or non-use of property than is presently the case. In the often-quoted words of *Munn v. Illinois*

> Property does become clothed with a public interest when used in a manner to make it of public consequence, and affect the community at large. When, therefore, one devotes his property to a use in which the public has an interest, he, in effect, grants to the public an interest in that use, and must submit to be controlled by the public for the common good, to the extent of the interest he has thus created.(205)

In a few states, property so invested with the public interest cannot be abandoned without permission of the state.(206) Thus, a city might prohibit the abandonment of residential buildings without a permit. However, most states take the position that when the owner "is willing to abandon all of the property it has devoted to a public service, it may not be compelled to continue operations at a loss."(207) Even under this view, it would seem that the city could require that the owner either continue operations or legally abandon the building rather than continue to hold the building with no intention to rent it out or otherwise use the housing units. The city could then purchase the abandoned buildings.

REPAIRS BY THE CITY

The District's power to make repairs an owner neglects to make(208) provides it with a method to prevent the deterioration that makes abandonment economically more attractive to an owner than rehabilitation. Unlike the procedures discussed above which make use of theoretically available federal (FHA and HAA) funds, this method must depend on Congressional appropriations to the District government which are rather difficult to obtain. In the District, this power to repair properties which fail to meet standards of health and safety can be based on a number of sections of the District of Columbia Code, including the same sections which authorize the government to demolish unsafe and unsanitary structures.(209) However, the section most frequently cited(210) and the one in which this power is most clearly set out is Section 313 of Title 5. That section authorizes the District government "and all other persons" authorized or directed by the government "to enter . . . inspect . . . and do whatever may be necessary to correct in a good and workmanlike manner, any condition that exists or has arisen . . . in violation of law or of any regulation made by authority of law . . ."(211) The owner is chargeable with the duty to correct the violations.(212) If the owner fails or refuses to correct the condition, and fails to show why he should not be required to correct it, the government

> is authorized to, cause such condition to be corrected, assess the cost of correcting such condition and all expenses incident thereto . . . as a tax against the property . . . and carry such tax on the regular tax rolls of the District, and collect such tax in the same manner as general taxes in said District are collected . . .(213)

This seciton, first enacted in 1906, is and has been, for all practicel purposes, a dead letter. Congress has never appropriated any money for carrying out this power.(214) It may be impossible to establish a revolving fund for repairs even with money from some other source because of the prescribed method of recoupment of repair expenses through taxes. Tax revenue goes into the general fund of the District and may not be spent for purposes not authorized by Congress.(215) The District should seek statutory authority to establish a revolving fund for repairs.(216) Language such as the following might be used.

> Moneys paid to the District of Columbia Government by owners as reimbursement for expenditures by the Government to repair, maintain or demolish structures under Title 5 of this Code, or collected as taxes imposed to obtain reimbursement for such expenditures, shall be deposited with the Treasurer of the United States to the credit of a permanent appropriation account to be known and designated "Housing trust fund deposits, District of Columbia." Necessary advances from said account, which may be used only to finance expenditures to repair, maintain or demolish structures, under Title 5 of this Code, shall be made upon requisition of the Commissioner in the manner set forth in Title 5, Section 311 of this Code.

Some question may be raised as to whether Section 313 was intended to cover violations of the Housing Regulations since it has been codified to a chapter headed "Fire Escapes and Safety Appliances." That this law is not limited to fire and safety regulations is easily demonstrable because sections 301 through 312 of the chapter were separately enacted as secitons 1 through 12 of an act of March 19, 1906. Sections 313 through 315 were enacted on April 14.(217) Furthermore, section 310 of the earlier act authorized the government to provide fire escapes and safety appliances when an owner neglects to do so, and to issue tax lien certificates to the contractor. If sections 313 and 314 only authorized the government to do the same thing, they would be superfluous. The language in Section 313, "in violation of law or of any regulation made by authority of law" clearly includes the Housing Regulations and may arguably include the Building Regulations as well.

THE NEW YORK EMERGENCY REPAIR PROGRAM

An example of what might be done under statutes such as those discussed in the previous section is provided by the emergency repair program of New York City which was instituted(218) under a statute similar to Chapter 5 of Title 5 of the District of Columbia Code.(219) This program does not contemplate the remedying of every housing code violation by city repair. Rather, it "was designed to restore to buildings essential services which in their existing state constitute an immediate and clear health or safety hazard to tenants."(220) The conditions which are regarded as emergencies for purposes of the programs are 1. No running cold and/or hot water, 2. No effective sewage disposal facilities, 3. No electricity, 4. No heat supply, 5. Defective boiler, furnace or distribution facilities, and 6. Other immediate dangerous conditions.(221) Thus, the program is aimed at providing only the most fundamental housing services.

The New York program in operation involves the coordinated efforts of several city agencies. In the first year of the program the Department of Buildings inspected and certified conditions, and the Department of Real Estate made or ordered repairs.(222) Since them, the inspecting and contracting operations were consolidated in one office. The Law Department institutes actions for recovery of repair costs.(223) All monies recovered for repairs, by actions against the owners or by collection of rents from the tenants, are paid into the emergency repair revolving fund.(224) The program corrects about 20,000 hazardous and dangerous code violations each year, but it does not reach the more than 100,000 reported conditions which do not present an immediate hazard although they do endanger or inconvenience tenants.(225) (Thus a distinction is made similar to that drawn by the Board of Condemnation in the District. As was seen previously, it takes rather serious and flagrant violations to arouse that body to action.)

The repairs made under the New York program are paid for from a revolving fund. In the first year, the fund was allocated by the Anti-Poverty Operations Board to meet the crisis of tenants in buildings which owners had virtually abandoned. Tenant groups demanded that the city provide heating fuel and make essential repairs.(226) In subsequent years the fund became a part of the city's capital budget. All monies recovered through actions against landlords or collection of rent are returned to the fund. From the winter of 1964-65 to July 31, 1968, $1,444,000 was expended for emergency repairs. Of this, only $343,000 or less than 24% was recouped and almost half of this amount came from tenants.(227) (It should be noted that if such a program were instituted in the District of Columbia, the amount of rents received by the city as receiver would be a far lower proportion since code violations are a defense to the nonpayment of rent in the District,(228) and the program seeks to abate only those conditions considered to require emergency attention, thus leaving numerous other violations uncorrected.)

The New York program is reported to be effective in quickly eliminating offensive emergency conditions where the owner refuses to do so. However, benefits of the program sometimes prove to be only temporary.(229) The greatest number of emergency repairs were found to have been performed in buildings that were vacated shortly thereafter. The owners of these buildings had already decided to "dead end" their buildings before the city made its repairs. Costs were higher in such buildings, and recoupment from owners occurred in less than five percent of these cases. Thus, a large number of emergency repair orders in a given building may signal that the building is on its way to becoming vacant.(230)

This latter finding indicates the importance of obtaining and maintaining adequate records of buildings and code violations as a means of pinpointing problem buildings in order to take corrective action through a repair program before the buildings are abandoned. The type of repair required is also an important indicator. "An increase in plumbing and plastering repairs can mean that a building is on its way to becoming vacant, and that more than patchwork jobs are needed to remedy the problem."(231) Also, the bunching of repairs within a short period of time will indicate a potential abandonment.(232) In New York it was determined "that there is a more than fifty percent probability that a building which has had five emergency repairs will become vacant within a short time."(233)

These findings indicate that an emergency repair program cannot stave off further deterioration when an owner has already decided to "walk away" from his building. In such cases, the city should take over at least the operation if not the ownership of the building and make full repairs. A study of the emergency repair program in New York by the Mayor's Office of Administration recommended the establishment of a repair program for non-emergency conditions. However, it was recommended that such a program be limited to buildings and types of conditions determined to be amenable to such a program.(234) One would expect that there would be a better chance of obtaining reimbursement against owners in cases of city repair of non-emergency violations where the owner has not walked away from the building and still feels that he has some interest worth protecting from a tax sale. Either sort of repair program should be initiated before a building is on the verge of abandonment. An owner of a building is more likely to repay the government for repairs when he still regards his property as too valuable to lose. The more deteriorated a building is, and the more repairs it requires, the less likely the city will recover its expenses. In New York, recoupment in the case of vacant buildings was negligible.(235)

To summarize, private, unsubsidized rehabilitation is not feasible economically because low income tenants cannot afford the higher rents that would have to be charged. It is also risky because the private owner has no control over the maintenance and repair of other properties in the area. Rehabilitation and the intensive repairs that are required can only be done by the government. In the case of government activity, where there is a will there is a way. The problem is that government has not used the tools at its disposal. Several existing federal housing programs could be used, but most of them are underfunded and conservatively administered. Also, cities could use their powers to make repairs under the police power. But efforts in this area have been minimal, and they require funding at the local level, which in the case of the District, means special Congressional appropriations. The state of housing in the District of Columbia, more than anything else, reflects Congress' lack of concern for low income housing in the District.

RECENTLY PROPOSED FEDERAL LEGISLATION

In the second session of the Ninety-First Congress Senator Brooke introduced a bill co-sponsored with Senators Cranston and Goodell "[t]o address the growing problem of abandoned properties and neighborhoods."(236) The "Abandoned Properties and Neighborhoods Act of 1970," as the bill was called, died in committee, but it deserves discussion here because it constitutes the first official recognition of the problem at the federal level. The hearings which the Senate Subcommittee on Housing and Urban Affairs held in connection with this bill have been frequently cited in this article.

Senator Brooke described the bill as a stop-gap measure. He felt that there should be detailed study into the problems posed by vacant buildings, but that Congress should not postpone action to await the results of definitive studies. Thus, Senate Bill 4087 was designed "to draw on techniques which are presently available" to accomplish four basic purposes:

1. to "hold" neighborhoods where abandonment has not yet occurred, but where deterioration is present or imminent;
2. to rehabilitate declining or abandoned buildings;
3. restore neighborhood service facilities to adequate levels; and
4. to provide sufficient rental income to permit owners of rental properties to maintain them at decent levels of repair, with adequate operating and maintenance services being provided.(237)

The bill would have amended several sections of the nation's housing laws. A new section 119 would have been added to title I (the Urban Renewal title) of the Housing Act of 1949 to provide up to 200 million dollars a year in grants to localities to assist the local governments "to alleviate harmful conditions and prevent deterioration in neighborhoods where abandonment is a problem." The funds would not be limited to urban renewal areas but could be applied "to neighborhoods where the local governing body determines that a substantial number of properties have been abandoned, [or] where the local governing body foresees that the problem of abandonment may arise."(238)

The new section 119 would have provided that a local government unit could receive a federal subsidy of two-thirds (or three-fourths in the case of areas of small population) of the costs of its efforts to eliminate blight in the designated neighborhoods plagued or threatened by abandoned buildings. The locality could use this aid in

> carrying out programs which may include but shall not be limited to: 1. the repair of streets, sidewalks, parks, playgrounds, publicly owned utilities, public buildings to meet needs consistent with continued use of the area, 2. the improvement of private properties held by any city . . . to the extent needed to eliminate harmful effects to public health and safety or the physical or social environment involved, 3. the demolition or closing of structures determined to be structurally unsound or unfit for human habitation or which contribute adversely to the physical or social environment of the locality involved, 4. the establishment of recreational or community facilities including public playgrounds, and 5. the improvement of garbage and trash collection, and street cleaning.(239)

Putting aside the proposed level of funding and the fact that the locality, already hard-pressed for funds, must contribute one-third or one-quarter of the amount needed, the proposed act contemplates fairly comprehensive attack on the problem at a neighborhood level. The Abandoned Properties and Neighborhoods Act and the Housing Management Services Act could have provided the nucleus of a significant program to preserve and improve the existing inner city housing stock and provide the services needed to rejuvenate low income core city neighborhoods.

The proposed abandoned properties law could have been—and to the extent that it is directed at the problems examined in this article it would have been—more than an interim measure. The broad language of the proposed Section 119 provides a framework for locally initiated and developed programs aimed at some of the factors this article has explored. Thus, as more thorough investigation into the vacant housing problem proceeds, any new suggestions for treatment of these factors, based on new information, could be accommodated and incorporated into the framework of this legislation by variation in the detail and emphasis of local programs. One would expect, however, that further research will provide more detailed information about the causes of abandonment rather than discovery of facets of the problem not touched upon in this article.

Thus, it is disappointing that the legislation does not seem to be directed to some of the other factors studied earlier. Essentially, Senator Brooke's bill in the proposed Section 119, emphasizes the improvement of neighborhood municipal services. With the exception of improvement of private properties held by the locality, in receivership for example, all of the possible local government programs listed in the bill relate to city services—street repair, community facilities, garbage collection. However, the bill's list of programs which a local government might undertake is not meant to be exclusive. A city could initiate programs to increase commercial services in the designated neighborhoods, provide property tax relief, make emergency repairs in private buildings, or do numerous other things not mentioned in the bill. Nevertheless, it would have been better if the legislation took notice of some of the other factors of abandonment in order to give more guidance to federal administrators in determining whether a given program qualifies for the subsidy.

The extension of the grant and loan programs to the designated neighborhoods provides a new source of funding for rehabilitation in such neighborhoods.(240) A more comprehensive bill would also have included requirements that the Federal Housing Administration and savings and loan institutions liberalize their definitions of what sort of housing and what sort of homeowner constitute acceptable risks. The federal government should commit itself to insuring higher risk loans and be willing to accept more loss.

Perhaps the most significant aspect of S.4087 is its extention of rent supplements to privately owned housing in abandoned properties neighborhoods. This part of the bill is a recognition that poverty is one of the major causes of the problem. Some program of income subsidy, such as rent supplements or housing allowances, must be a part of any comprehensive attack on the problem. Legislation extending such subsidies to the inner city should also direct that administrative procedures be developed to assure that the units thus subsidized are decent, safe and sanitary.

To summarize, the abandoned properties bill could have provided an important stepping stone to the solution of the problems related to abandoned housing. However, given the information already available concerning the multiple causes of these problems, a more comprehensive bill could have been produced.

SUMMARY AND CONCLUSIONS

Many of the major cities of the United States are experiencing the paradox of a severe housing shortage at the same time that an increasing number of existing residential properties are being withdrawn from the housing market. Owners of these properties are letting their buildings stand empty rather than attempting to maintain them to house low income families. This article examines the factors that are causing owners to behave in this manner and suggests several methods of attacking and reversing the trend. Thus, the focus of this article is on the problems engulfing the stock of low income housing in the inner city and on ways to prevent its deterioration and abandonment. Although many of these inner city buildings are old, they are sound, and if they are rehabilitated and properly maintained, they can provide decent homes for low income families for years to come. Not only is rehabilitation of this old housing less expensive than new construction, but it is also a necessity if we are to meet the goal of a decent home for every American. New construction alone cannot close the gap between the supply and the demand for decent housing in the foreseeable future. Allowing the deterioration of existing housing can only widen the gap.

As part of this exploration into the problem of vacant buildings, the author studied the fifty-three vacant buildings found in a twenty-one block area in Washington, D.C. These blocks in the inner city are in an area which has been designated for eventual urban renewal under the Neighborhood Development Program, but aside from the expansion of a school site no definite urban renewal action is yet planned for these blocks. Examination of public records relating to the fifty-three properties and interviews with owners, area residents, and city officials yielded some first-hand information on the problem for comparison with findings available from other cities. In addition, articles and studies relating to inner city blight and urban renewal provided valuable information relevant to the vacant building problem.

A crucial finding of this article—already recognized, at least in principle, in other federal programs aimed at the inner city—is that only a comprehensive program on a neighborhood scale can reclaim some of the vacant structures and prevent the loss of others. No building can be treated apart from its environment. A deteriorating neighborhood can cause a building to be abandoned and an abandoned building can cause its neighborhood to deteriorate. Owners will not repair a building when people are afraid to move into the neighborhood because of crime and when the lack of city and commercial services makes the neighborhood unattractive to anyone who has a choice as to where he will live.

Just as the fate of each building is intertwined with its neighbors and no single building can be preserved against a wave of deterioration of services throughout the neighborhood, there is no single factor explanation of the cause of the neighborhood's downward spiral. Crime, vandalism, the traditional flight to the suburbs, inflation, taxes and numerous other factors have increased operating costs in the inner city housing market and left the inner city to those least able to afford decent housing. The result of all these factors is abandonment of buildings by owners and overcrowding of the core city poor in the remaining structures.

Neighborhoods and buildings deteriorate as a result of inadequate city and commercial services. But these are not the only services which must be brought back to save these withering neighborhoods. Also very badly needed are increases in the quantity and quality of housing services—the day-to-day services provided by proper management deprive low income families of many of these needed services. Absentee speculators who own buildings only to maximize their return sometimes fail to provide essential services that they could afford. Programs to encourage homeownership, discourage speculation, and provide management assistance are proposed.

Exacerbating the problems of rising costs of maintenance and owner disinterest in providing decent shelter, is the fact that most of the residents of deteriorating inner-city neighborhoods have incomes that are insufficient to pay for the level of housing services required in standard housing adequate to their needs. That is, the poverty of the tenantry is an important factor in the deterioration of their housing. Thus, any program designed to renew and preserve inner-city housing and provide decent homes for low income residents must subsidize their purchasing power. This may be done through the use of existing federal subsidy programs, such as Rent Supplements and Turnkey III public housing homeownership, or, more directly, through a housing allowance program.

Activities and inactivity of local government directly affect the quality of low income inner-city housing—often in ways that are not intended. The level of normal city services in a neighborhood seems to be proportional to the income level of its residents, and this accelerates deterioration. Programs designed to improve housing sometimes make it worse. Thus, for example, the announcement of urban renewal or the commencement of strict housing code enforcement after years of nonenforcement can cause an owner to close his building. Another government activity—taxation—penalizes improvements. Property taxes rise with the value of the building. The income tax law treats the repair of conditions resulting from years of neglect as a nondeductible capital investment rather than as a deductible business expense. Reforms are suggested to neutralize the effects of taxation.

Zoning is a government activity which could have been used as a positive force to keep inner city neighborhoods alive. Instead, it became an *imprimatur* for existing patterns of development which already bore the seeds of the neighborhood's demise. Rather than requiring the compulsory amortization of incompatible land uses, zoning commissions have entertained and granted requests to further damage the fabric of the neighborhood. Zoning controls which require the discontinuance of disruptive uses should be part of a comprehensive program to prevent the abandonment of inner-city housing and neighborhoods.

The announcement effect of urban renewal can be decreased by adopting a method of appraisal for government purchase which penalizes owners of deteriorated buildings. The method suggested would encourage owners to maintain their premises up to the level required by the housing code.

The condemnation of buildings found to be unsafe or unsanitary is not a cause of abandonment in Washington, D.C. Owners of condemned buildings seem to be able to continue operating by making token repairs while buildings which have been abandoned for two years have not been condemned. Since the Board of Condemnation's ultimate sanction is demolition, perhaps its inactivity is a blessing in disguise.

Other programs, such as public welfare, provide income to the owners of substandard housing occupied by recipients. Welfare payments provide the government with a great deal of leverage which could be used to make owners conform to the housing regulations. By withholding rents and defending tenants against eviction, the welfare department could accumulate a fund that could be used to improve housing or the general level of welfare.

One finding of this study is that the abandoned structures themselves cannot be considered as a potential housing resource. Although some of these buildings may be structurally sound, if they have been vacant for any period of time they have probably been so vandalized as to make rehabilitation infeasible. However, rehabilitation of sound buildings that are caught before they become vandalized is feasible and desirable. Few private owners will undertake rehabilitation absent a neighborhood-wide improvement plan, and this usually means a government program is necessary. For example, an area may be designated as an urban renewal rehabilitation area, and grants and loans may be made available to homeowners.

The government may also undertake direct programs of repair under provisions of statutes which have long been on the books but never used. These statutes authorize the government to make repairs when an owner refuses to bring his property up to standards. A rather conservative program, under similar statutes, is in effect in New York City. A difficulty with establishing such a program in Washington, D.C. is that expenses recovered as property taxes could not be put into a revolving fund for such repairs without Congressional action.

Recently proposed federal legislation directed at the abandoned building problem would have provided a nucleus for a program to preserve and upgrade our inner-city housing stock. The language of the proposed abandoned properties act seems broad enough to encompass the suggestions made in this article. However, the level of funding proposed would not have been adequate.

Just as there are numerous causes for the existence of empty residential buildings in the inner-city, there must be a comprehensive, multi-faceted programatic attack on the problem. Any solution of the problem will require a massive infusion of federal funds. No solutions to the abandoned building problem—or any other aspect of the nation's total housing problem—will be possible without a reordering of priorities and a true commitment to the provisions of a decent home for every American.

NOTES

(1) Subcommittee on Housing and Urban Affairs of the Senate Committee on Banking and Currency, 91st Congress, 2d Session, 1 Housing and Urban Development Legislation of 1970 794 (Com. Print 1970). (Hereinafter cited as 1970 Hearings).

(2) Housing and Urban Development Committee, D.C. City Council, Housing Crisis in the District of Columbia, at 7-8 (1969).

(3) Southwest Washington housed 23,000 people before urban renewal. After the area was cleared of deteriorated buildings and poor residents, only 929 units of low cost housing were built in the area. Thurz, Where Are They Now? (a study for the Health and Welfare Council of the National Capital Area-1966).

(4) The article will use the words "abandoned," "vacant" and "empty" interchangeably to describe housing that is vacant and not available for eent. The use of the word "abandon" is not meant to imply that there is no one claiming ownership of the property.

(5) Leonard Downie, Jr., Washington Post, March 7, 1970, p. A-1.

(6) The Department of Housing and Urban Development reports that over-all housing vacancy rates have dropped by one-third since 1965, the lowest levels in over ten years. The rental vacancy rate for all metropolitan areas is 4.4 percent.

In the Northeast, 2.8 percent, in major urban areas about one percent. "Vacant Units Fewer, Washington Post, March 7, 1970, p. D4.

(7) Downie, supra note 5, at A-10. The Office of the Housing Administrator has compiled an inventory of vacant buildings based on surveys conducted by housing inspectors in the spring of 1970. However, for lack of manpower, no analysis of the collected data has been made to officially determine the characteristics of Washington's vacant housing.

(8) "When Landlords Walk Away," Time, March 16, 1970, at 88.

(9) "Hollow Shells," Newsweek, January 12, 1970, at 36.

(10) Sternlieb and Indick, Housing Vacancy Analysis, 45 Land Economics 117, 119 (1969).

(11) Time, supra note 8.

(12) Newsweek, supra note 9.

(13) President's Committee on Urban Housing, A Decent Home 95 (1968).

(14) Id.

(15) Testimony of Senator Goodell, 1 1970 Hearings 839.

(16) Isler, Thinking About Housing 10 (1970).

(17) Testimony of George Sternlieb, Professor of Urban & Regional Planning, Rutgers Univ., 1 1970 Hearings 850.

(18) U.S. Department of Commerce, Bureau of the Census, Census of Housing for Census Tracts by Blocks, (1940).

(19) Ronald Russo, Washington, D.C. provides low income home ownership through nonprofit 221 (h) program, J. Housing, June 1969, at 278.

(20) Dagmar Perman, Historical Review of Census Tracts 46 and 77 (prepared for the Urban League Neighborhood Development Center, Washington, D.C. 1965).

(21) Title I, Section 131, Housing Act of 1949 as amended. U.S. Department of Housing and Urban Development, NDP Handbook, RHA7380.1, ¶ 1.

(22) The list compiled was accurate as of March 5, 1970.

(23) Vacant lots, obviously, could be utilized in solution of the housing shortage as sites for new construction, but the problems relating to new construction differ significantly from those relating to the rehabilitation of vacant existing structures. It was assumed that vacant commercial structures would be unsatisfactory as a housing resource. Partially occupied structures present some of the same problems as abandoned structures and would more likely be subject to rehabilitation, but the difficulty involved in determining the number of such units outweighed the value of the additional information. It should be noted that most of the structures in the area are single-family row houses that have been subdivided, in many cases, for two-family occupancy.

(24) Perhaps, this is some indication of the difficulty a tenant might have in trying to locate his absentee landlord.

(25) I am somewhat consoled by the fact that George Sternlieb reports "a relative paucity of owners of abandoned parcels who could be found" during his exhaustive study of the slums of Newark. George Sternlieb, The Tenement Landlord 39 (New Brunswick: Rutgers-The State University, 1966).

(26) "In the Inner Cities Acres of Abandoned Buildings," U.S. News and World Report, January 26, 1970, at 55.

(27) 1 1970 Hearings 797.

(28) Id. at 807.

(29) Philadelphia Housing Corporation, Third Annual Report 10 (1968).

(30) Testimony of Francis W. Gens, Commissioner of Housing Inspection, Boston, 1 1970 Hearings 880.

(31) Id. at 807, 821, 839.

(32) Id. at 801, 807, 829, 833, 834.

(33) Time, supra note 8; the author spoke with an addict in one of the abandoned buildings on Third Street.

(34) Testimony of Francis W. Gens, 1 1970 Hearings 880.

(35) Testimony of Neil Hardy, Housing & Development Administration, New York City, 1 1970 Hearings 807.

(36) Owner's Questionnaire, Robert Earl Fix.

(37) Testimony of Francis W. Gens, 1 1970 Hearings 880.

(38) U.S. News, supra note 9, at 55; see also, Sternlieb, supra note 25, at 94.

(39) Questionnaire, supra, note 36.

(40) Conversation with Parker Duff, United Planning Organization Neighborhood Development Center Number One.

(41) Robert Embry, Commissioner, Housing & Community Development, Baltimore in U.S. News, supra note 26, at 56.

(42) Robert Gold remarks to Urban & Regional Planning students at Geo. Wash. Univ., Feb. 2, 1970. see Washington Center for Metropolitan Studies, "Study shows all-white neighborhoods disappearing from Washington suburbs," Metropolitan Bulletin, March 1971.

(43) "Between 1954 and 1965 more than half of all new industrial and mercantile buildings constructed in the United States were being built outside central cities." Building the American City; Report of the National Commission on Urban Problems 47, citing Newman, The Decentralization of Jobs, Monthly Labor Rev., May 1967; See, e.g., Burtt, Plant Relocation and the Core City Worker (HUD 1967).

(44) Sternlieb seems to think that even the stores which are in operation, "convenient as they often are for local residents," are "a substantial cornerstone for blight"—especially if the facility is a bar or it provides a loitering area. Sternlieb, supra note 25, at 51. Those who cherish the culture of street-oriented urban neighborhoods would surely disagree with him, but he does point up the fact that the older areas of the city are over-zoned for commercial uses.

(45) See, Testimony of Neil Hardy, 1 1970 Hearings 808.

(46) Supra, note 21.

(47) Newsweek, supra, note 9.

(48) Sternlieb, supra, note 25, at 76.

(49) Id. at 79; Testimony of Neil J. Hardy, 1 1970 Hearings 806, 812.

(50) Testimony of Neil J. Hardy, 1 1970 Hearings 806, 812.

(51) U.S. News, supra; note 26, at 55.

(52) Testimony of Robert Embry, 1 1970 Hearings 791.

(53) Testimony of Neil J. Hardy, Id. at 801, 805.

(54) Sternlieb, Slum Housing: A Functional Analysis, 32 Law and Contemp. Prob. 349, 351 (1967).

(55) Sternlieb, supra, note 25, at 71.

(56) See, 1 1970 Hearings 901 et seq.

(57) Testimony of Francis W. Gens, Id. at 879.

(58) Testimony of Neil J. Hardy, Id. at 806.

(59) See, Id. at 806, 831, 857-878, 880.

(60) Nourse, Impact of a Negative Income Tax on the Number of Substandard Housing Units 5, (1969).

(61) Isler, supra, note 16 at 16.

(62) Testimony of Senator Goodell, 1 1970 Hearings 831.

(63) Accord, Sternlieb, supra note 54 at 352.

(64) Testimony of Robert Embry, 1 1970 Hearings 797, 799.

(65) Testimony of George Sternlieb, Id. at 849.

(66) Id. at 852.

(67) Testimony of Francis W. Gens, Id. at 881.

(68) Id. at 891.

(69) Testimony of Robert Embry, Id. at 799.

(70) Testimony of George Sternlieb, Id. at 849, 853.

(71) Ad Hoc Subcommittee on Home Financing Practices and Procedures of the House Committee on Banking and Currency, 91st Congress, First Session, Financing of Inner-City Housing 84-85 (Comm. Print 1969). Hereinafter cited as 1969 Hearings.

(72) Statement of Channing Phillips, D.C. Democratic National Committee-man, Id. at 24.

(73) Id. at 87; Sternlieb, supra note 25 at 119.

(74) See, Isler, supra note 16 at 28.

(75) Senate Bill 4181, reprinted in 1970 Hearings at 1699.

(76) Id., Section 4(b).

(77) Id., Section 3(2).

(78) Id., Section 4(c)(1).

(79) Id., Section 4(d).

(80) Id., Section 5.

(81) Id., Section 6(b).

(82) Testimony of Senator Goodell, 1 1970 Hearings 836.

(83) Id.

(84) Id. at 837.

(85) Downie, Leonard Jr., & Hoagland, James, Washington Post, January 5, 1969—January 14, 1969. Reprinted in 1969 Hearings, supra, note 71 at 286-332.

(86) 1969 Hearings at 287.

(87) Id.

(88) Id. at 288-289.

(89) Id. at 288.

(90) Id. at 328.

(91) Id.; Kessler, "Patman: FHA Aids Profiteers," Washington Post, July 31, 1970, p. A1.

(92) Owners questionnaire, Quinn.

(93) Channing Phillips, 1969 Hearings at 11.

(94) Section 235, National Housing Act (homeownership interest subsidy).

(95) U.S. Housing Act of 1937 (lease-purchase); Sternlieb, supra, note 25 at 299.

(96) Letter from owner, Bernard Justin Greenfield.

(97) Owner's questionnaire, Calcara.

(98) Testimony of George Sternlieb, 1 1970 Hearings 873.

(99) U.S. News, supra note 26.

(100) Testimony of George Sternlieb, 1 1970 Hearings 849.

(101) Testimony of Senator Brooke, 1 1970 Hearings 794.

(102) Conversation with Florence Roisman, NLSP.

(103) The Board was apparently satisfied with the owner's token efforts. When questioned, the Acting Executive Secretary of the Board responded that the tenants could not expect the place to look like Georgetown.

(104) Ted Parrish, "The Housing Crisis and Squat-Ins," Tenants Outlook, February 1970, p. 4 (Dateline: "Charles Street Jail").

(105) "The Housing Crisis and Squat-Ins" (second installment), Tenants Outlook, March 1970, p. 5.

(106) Isler, supra note 16, at 13.

(107) President's Committee on Urban Housing, supra note 13 at 7, 41.

(108) Presidents Task Force on Low Income Housing, Toward Better Housing for Low Income Families 7 (1970).

(109) Section 101, Housing and Urban Development Act of 1965, as amended.

(110) Section 23, United States Housing Act of 1937, as amended.

(111) A housing allowance program will be funded under section 504 of the Housing & Urban Development Act of 1970, Pub. L. No. 91-609.

(112) Elizabeth Nachbaur, The Proposed National Housing Allowance Program: An Exploratory Analysis, January, 1971 (unpublished master's thesis, George Washington University).

(113) Testimony of Neil Hardy, 1 1970 Hearings 806; Testimony of Senator Goodell, Id. at 830-831.

(114) Sporn, Some Contributions of the Income Tax Law to the Growth and Prevalence of Slums, 59 Colum. L. Rev. 1026, 1037 (1959).

(115) Stickeny, Coming of Age in America: The Need for Property Tax Reform, 21 Admin. L. Rev. 325, 327-328 (1969).

(116) Id. at 336-338.

(117) Id. at 339.

(118) P. Hodge and P. Hauser, The Federal Income Tax in Relation to Housing 104 (1968) (Research Report No. 5, prepared for the consideration of the National Comm. on Urban Problems).

(119) See also, Sternlieb, supra, note 25 at 101.

(120) Note, Depreciation Deduction on Used Residential Housing, Turnover Rates in Slum Housing Ownership, and the Tax Reform Act of 1969, 30 U. Cin. L. Rev. 539, 550 (1969).

(121) Hodge and Hauser, supra, note 118, at 102.

(122) Id. at 105.

(123) A fuller discussion of the problems of the Far Southeast, which is beyond the scope of this article, is provided in Office of Community Renewal Programs, District of Columbia Government, Washington's Far Southeast '70, (1970).

(124) National Capital Planning Commission, (NCPC), Report on Zoning in the Shaw School Urban Renewal Area 17 (1968).

(125) Testimony of Senator Goodell, 1 1970 Hearings 832.

(126) Sternlieb, supra, note 17, at 164.

(127) D.C. Code Ann. § § 5-501 et seq, 5-616 et seq. (1967).

(128) At least two commentators have suggested that there may come a time in the future when the government could simply declare slums to be such nuisances that the renewal agency could "take such property in the exercise of its police power without compensation for the land thereunder." Dagen and Cody, Property et al. v. Nuisance et al., 26 Law and Contemp. Prob. 70, 71 (1961).

(129) Id. at 73.

(130) See Ill. Rev. Stat., c.47, § 9.5 (1959) authorizing admission of evidence "as to 1. unsafe, unsanitary, substandard or other illegal condition, use or occupancy of the property, 2. the effect of such condition on income from the property, and 3. the reasonable costs of causing the property to be placed in a legal condition, use or occupancy. Such evidence is admissible notwithstanding absence of official action taken to require the correction or abatement of any such illegal condition, use, or occupancy. See also, U.S. President's Conference on Home Building and Home Ownership, Vol. 3: Slums, Large-Scale Housing and Decentralization 107 (1932) (Income receivable from uses contrary to the public health or other laws or transfer prices based on expectancy of such use should not be admitted as evidence of land value. Residential buildings declared unfit for human habitation should be evaluated at scrap value less cost of wrecking.); Mandelker, Strategies in English Slum Clearance and Housing Policies, 1969 Wisc. L. Rev. 800 (1969) (Unfit dwelling acquired at value of site.); Note, Condemnation of Slum Land; Illegal Use as Factor Reducing Valuation, 14 U. Chi. L. Rev. 232 (1947).

(131) Another way of conceptualizing this policy is to say not that illegal use has inflated value, but that the community standard as established in the Housing Regulations must be taken as the floor for determining value. The community requires all buildings to be up to its standards, and a building can have no legal value until its deficiencies are remedied. Dagen and Cody, supra note 129 at 75.

(132) Riley v. District of Columbia Redevelopment Land Agency, 246 F.2d 641 (D.C. Cir. 1957).

(133) Javins v. First National Realty Corp., 428 F.2d 1071 (D.C. Cir. 1970).

(134) 1 1970 Hearings 838.

(135) Testimony of George Sternlieb, Id. at 854.

(136) See, e.g. Note, Enforcement of Municipal Housing Codes, 78 Harv. L. Rev. 801 (1965).

(137) It should also be noted that special grants are available for rehabilitation in a concentrated code enforcement area.

(138) Interview with official of Department of Economic Development.

(139) Interview with field inspector. He claims that there is no similar policy with respect to licensed multi-family dwellings.

(140) Isler, supra, note 16 at 31.

(141) Housing and Urban Development Committee, supra, note 2, at 36.

(142) Id.

(143) Gribetz and Grad, Housing Code Enforcement: Sanctions and Remedies, 66 Colum. L. Rev. 1254, 1261 (1966).

(144) Note, Municipal Housing Codes, 69 Harv. L. Rev. 1115, 1117, (1956).

(145) Comment, Building and Housing Codes and the Conservation of Chicago's Housing Supply, 31 U. Chi. L. Rev. 180 (1963).

(146) Section 105(c), Housing Act of 1949.

(147) Comment, supra, note 145.

(148) Dick and Pfarr, Detroit Housing Code Enforcement and City Renewal: A Study in Futility, 3 Prospectus, 61, 64 (1969).

(149) Housing and Urban Development Committee, supra, note 2 at 36.

(150) Brown v. Southhall Realty, 237 A.2d 834 (1968); codified: D.C. Housing Regulation, art. 290 (June 12, 1970).

(151) E.g., D.C. Code Ann. § 5-313 (1967).

(152) Housing and Urban Development supra, note 2 at 37.

(153) Supra, note 144 at 1118.

(154) Supra, note 136 at 860.

(155) Letter from Marcel W. Singer, Chairman, Committee on Housing and Urban Development, The Assn. of the Bar of the City of New York, with regard to N.Y. Multi. Dwelling Law § 302(a).

(156) Dick and Pfarr, supra, note 148 at 86.

(157) "Amendments to Housing Regulations of the District of Columbia" (xeroxed hand-out).

(158) See, supra, note 150.

(159) D.C. Code Ann. § 5-616 et seq. (1967).

(160) Id., part I-E.

(161) D.C. Code Ann. § 5-501 et seq. (1967).

(162) Conversation with employee of Construction Division.

(163) Id.

(164) Interview with Mr. Caciatorre at the Board.

(165) D.C. Code Ann. § 5-620 (1967) (emphasis added).

(166) See supra note 144 at 804.

(167) Interestingly, Licenses and Inspections on their inspection form rates building conditions as "excellent," "good," "fair," "poor," "Board of Condemnation."

(168) D.C. Code Ann. § 5-503 (1967).

(169) Conversations with residents of the study area.

(170) Conversations with employee of the Board of Condemnation.

(171) D.C. Code Ann. § 5-616 (1967).

(172) D.C. Code Ann. § § 501-506 (1967); District of Columbia v. Wentworth, 288 F.2d 421 (D.C. Cir. 1961); Brown v. Tobriner, 312 F.2d 334 (D.C. Cir. 1962).

(173) Mandelker, Housing Codes, Building Demolition, and Just Compensation; A Rationale for the Exercise of Public Powers over Slum Housing, 67 Mich. L. Rev. 636, 640-649 (1969).

(174) See, infra, notes 189, 190.

(175) Housing and Urban Development Committee, supra, note 2 at 16.

(176) J. Bailey and H. Shubert, "One Billion Dollar Subsidy for Slums," Architectural Forum, July-August 1969, p. 56; Governor Rockefeller estimated in 1965 that New York was paying $25,000,000 per year in welfare rents to landlords operating substandard dwellings, quoted in Note, supra, note 136, at 843 n.229.

(177) Bailey and Shubert, supra, note 176.

(178) Note, supra note 136 at 843.

(179) N.Y. Soc. Welf. Law § 143(b) (The Spiegel Law).

(180) Letter from John W. Ballew, Director, Public Assistance, Cook County Department of Public Aid, p. 2. This practice was enacted into law in 1965. See Ill. Rev. Stats. ch. 23, § 11-23 (Smith-Hurd 1969).

(181) Comm. on Housing and Urban Development, supra note 2, p. 17.

(182) Letter, supra, note 180 at 2.

(183) Housing and Urban Development Comm., supra, note 2 at 18.

(184) Testimony of Arthur R. Swanson, 1 1970 Hearings 822, 825.

(185) See supra, note 150.

(186) Letter from Sarah Underwood, District of Columbia Redevelopment Land Agency.

(187) Sternlieb, supra, note 54, at 355.

(188) Losbough, Rehabilitation of Housing: Federal Programs and Private Enterprise, 32 Law and Contemp. Prob. 416, 424 (1967).

(189) Testimony of Judge Franklin Kral, Housing Court, Chicago, 1 1970 Hearings 819.

(190) Testimony of Francis Gens, Id. at 881.

(191) Testimony of Franklin Kral, Id. at 819.

(192) "Urban Rehab., small builders team up to renovate slumps," House and Home, December 1969, p. 74; "Big-time Rehab.: It's man v. machine, and man is winning," House and Home, Sept. 1969, p. 4.

(193) R. Russo, "Washington, D.C. provides low income home ownership through nonprofit 221(h) program," J. of Housing, June 1969, at 293. Breakdown of average cost per building.

Acquisition	$ 2,900
Construction	9,004
Architects' Fee	255
Overhead and Profit	1,319
Financing and Title Fees	1,322
Organizational and marketing fees	500
TOTAL	$15,400

(194) See Levi, Problems in the Rehabilitation of Blighted Areas, 21 Fed. Bar J. 310, 311 (1961).

(195) Russo, supra note 193.

(196) See Slayton, Conservation of Existing Housing, 20 Law and Contemp. Prob. 436 (1955).

(197) Section 235(j), National Housing Act.

(198) Section 236, National Housing Act.

(199) Section 101, Housing and Urban Development Act of 1965.

(200) Section 23, U.S. Housing Act of 1937. ("For the purpose of . . . taking full advantage of vacancies or potential vacancies in the private housing market, each public housing agency shall, to the maximum extent consistent with the achievement of the objectives of this Act, provide low rent housing . . . in private accommodations . . .").

(201) Section 23(g), U.S. Housing Act of 1937.

(202) U.S. News, supra note 26, at 56.

(203) Letter from Ivan B. Gluckman, Assistant Housing Director, City of Philadelphia.

(204) U.S. News, supra note 26, at 56.

(205) Munn v. Illinois, 94 U.S. 113, 126 (1877).

(206) See, e.g., California (minority) position with respect to abandonment of rail service, Re Southern Pacific Company, 28 P.U.R.3d 234 (1959).

(207) Priest, 1 Principles of Public Utility Regulation 380 (1964).

(208) E.g., D.C. Code Ann., § 5-313 (1967).

(209) D.C. Code Ann. § § 5-501 et seq., 5-616 et seq. (1967).

(210) 1969 Hearings, supra, note 71, at 6; Housing and Urban Development Committee, supra, note 2, at 36.

(211) D.C. Code Ann. § 5-313 (1967).

(212) D.C. Code Ann. § § 5-313, 315 (1967).

(213) D.C. Code Ann. § 5-313 (1967).

(214) Interviews with various city employees.

(215) D.C. Code Ann. § 47-105 (1967).

(216) See, e.g., D.C. Code Ann. § 47-137 (1967) (Authorization to establish a working fund for printing, etc.); D.C. Code Ann. § 47-311 (1967) (Miscellaneous Trust Fund Deposits).

(217) See legislative history annotations, D.C. Code Ann. § § 5-301 et seq. (1967).

(218) Resolution of the Board of Health of the Department of Health of the City of New York (March 21, 1968).

(219) Admin. Code § 564-18.0. Mult. Dwell. Law § 309 gives the city similar authority.

(220) Kerchner & Rosenthal, The Emergency Repair Program 4 (1968).

(221) Id. at 9.

(222) Id. at 6.

(223) Id. at 7.

(224) Id. at 8.

(225) Id. at 5.

(226) Id. at 6.

(227) Id. at 32.

(228) See, supra note 150; See also Note, D.C. Housing Regulations, Article 290, Section 2902: Construed Pursuant to Brown v. Southall Realty Co. and Javin v. First National Realty Corp.—A New Say for the Urban Tenant, 16 How. L.J. 366 (1971).

(229) Kerchner & Rosenthal, supra, note 220 at 25.

(230) Id. at 37.

(231) Id. at 39.

(232) Id. at 41.

(233) Id. at 43.

(234) Id. at 52.

(235) Id. at 32.

(236) Senate Bill 4087, 91st Cong., 2d Ses. (1970).

(237) Testimony of Senator Brooke, 1 1970 Hearings 794.

(238) Id.

(239) Proposed § 119(b), Housing Act of 1949, S. 4087, § 2 (91st Cong. 2d Sess.).

(240) Proposed § 119(d), supra, note 239; proposed § 312(a)(D), Housing Act of 1964, S. 4087 § 3 (91st Cong. 2d Sess.).

III.

ECONOMIC ANALYSIS
AND
HOUSING MARKETS

THE DERIVED DEMAND
FOR URBAN RESIDENTIAL LAND

Richard F. Muth

An understanding of the demand for urban residential land is necessary for many problems of city structure and growth and for appraising the effects of certain governmental housing policies. In an earlier work I found it both analytically convenient and empirically fruitful to treat land and built structures as inputs into the production of a commodity called housing (1969). So viewed, the demand function for land is derived from the demand for housing and the supply of built structures. Its parameters depend upon the elasticity of housing demand, the elasticity of supply of structures, the relative importance of land, and the elasticity of substitution of land for structures in producing housing. While plausible inferences could be drawn about the values of the first three of these, I had only very sketchy information upon which to base an estimate of the elasticity of substitution. Furthermore, while the view of land described above lent itself well to interpreting many of my empirical findings, I was unable directly to subject it to an empirical test.

Many other writings on urban land problems, notably Alonso (1964), and Wingo (1961), have treated land as an argument of household utility functions. This treatment, though more general, yields weaker empirical implications. Indeed, in the absence of subsidiary hypotheses, the demand for urban residential land in this view need only obey very general restrictions on consumer demand functions. One widespread subsidiary hypothesis about the demand for urban residential land is that it has a higher income elasticity than the demand for structures (Hoover and Vernon, 1959, pp. 169 and 222). This last hypothesis is frequently held to account for the fact that higher income persons live at the lowest population densities and at greater distances from the central business districts of U.S. cities.

In this paper I make use of data that has recently become available to estimate the demand function for urban residential land. I will also test whether this estimated demand function appears to agree with the notion of land as an input into the production of housing. The data used, which refer to new single-family houses financed by Federal Housing Administration (FHA)-insured mortgages, were first published for 1966. They are the only set of data known to me for which the unit price of land is available along with necessary other data for estimating a demand function for urban residential land. The comparisons were limited to data for new houses for the obvious reason that long-run production relationships will be more closely realised for this group than for existing homes. So far as consumer demand for housing is concerned, though, there is no reason to omit existing homes. The second part of the article presents the derivation of demand relationships for urban residential land and related magnitudes which follow from the treatment of land as an input along with structures into the production of housing. After describing the data used in more detail, my empirical findings are presented in the next section. My major findings are: 1. the coefficients of land price per square foot in the demand functions for land and for structures agree quite closely with the hypothesis that land and structures are inputs into the production of a commodity called housing, 2. the elasticity of substitution of land for structures in producing housing appears to be about 0.5, and 3. if anything, the income elasticity of the demand for residential land appears to be smaller than that for structures rather than the reverse.

Finally, in the last section, I will discuss some of the implications of my findings for problems of city structure and for evaluating certain effects of U.S. governmental housing programmes. First I consider the effect of differences in the elasticity of housing supply per unit of land in different parts of a city, given the tendency for urban populations to become more decentralised as they grow. Using my previous estimate of the elasticity of substitution of land for structures (1969), I concluded that differences in the elasticity of housing supply could account for only about half of the tendency for population densities to decline at relatively slower rates in larger cities. However, using the value calculated here for the substitution elasticity, I find that differences in housing supply elasticities would produce greater decentralisation as city size increases than I actually observed. Next I show how the analysis of this paper can be used to determine the effects of a housing subsidy. I conclude that, even if the supply of residential land were perfectly inelastic, housing subsidies to lower-income families would have little effect upon housing prices. Finally, using a constant elasticity of substitution production function for housing and the parameter values found in this paper, I evaluate the effects on the cost per dwelling of building public housing on cleared slum sites as compared with others. My calculations indicate that a public housing unit built upon slum land costs about 60% more and that the resource cost of the U.S. public housing programme was about 20% greater during the 'fifties than it would have been if all units had been built on non-slum sites.

THE DERIVATION OF DEMAND

Assume that land, L, and built structures, N, are used as inputs into the production of the commodity called housing, Q. Q is measured in terms of capacity to provide a flow of housing services, which may vary from dwelling to dwelling, rather than as a number of dwelling units. The production function $Q = j(L, N)$ describes the maximum quantity of housing that can be produced using given inputs of land and structures with a given technology. Let r and n be the unit prices of land and structures, respectively, and p be the unit price of housing. Assuming that producers of housing are competitive in both product and factor markets, the following conditions must hold if these producers are to maximise their incomes:

$$\frac{\partial Q}{\partial L} = \frac{r}{p} \quad \text{and} \quad \frac{\partial Q}{\partial N} = \frac{n}{p}.$$

To determine the impact of changes in underlying conditions in the market for new houses, the production function and the two marginal conditions for income maximisation above can be differentiated. Letting the superscript * designate the logarithmic differential of the variable so designated (Muth, 1964),

$$Q^* - k_L L^* + k_N N^* = 0 \tag{1}$$

$$-k_N L^* + k_N N^* + \sigma p^* = \sigma r^* \tag{2}$$

$$k_L L^* - k_L N^* + \sigma p^* = \sigma n^*, \tag{3}$$

where σ is the elasticity of substitution of land for structures in producing housing, k_L is the fraction of payments to land in the total value of housing (or site value relative to property value), and k_N is the share of payments for structures in the total value of the house. Here it is assumed that $f(L, N)$ is homogeneous of degree one in L and N so that $k_L + k_N = 1$.

A final condition for determining Q, L, N and p for given values of r and n is the demand function for housing. Where η_p is the price elasticity of housing demand, η_y the income elasticity, and y is income,

$$Q^* - \eta_p p^* = \eta_y y^*. \tag{4}$$

It should be stressed that the data used here refer to housing per family. Hence, there is no need to include a variable describing the existing housing stock, as would be needed if I were examining data on aggregate new building in some place such as a city in a given interval of time. Similarly, the estimated values of η_p and η_y from the per family data refer to stock demand rather than flow demand elasticities.

I solve equations (1)-(4) for rL, nN, and pQ along with p because the basic data used in the next section relate to expenditures for housing and land. The solutions are:

$$(rL)^* = \{1 - (k_N \sigma - k_L \eta_p)\} r^*$$
$$+ k_N (\sigma + \eta_p) n^* + \eta_y y^* \tag{5}$$

$$(nN)^* = k_L (\sigma + \eta_p) r^*$$
$$+ \{1 - (k_L \sigma - k_N \eta_p)\} n^* + \eta_y y^* \tag{6}$$

$$(pQ)^* = k_L (1 + \eta_p) r^* + k_N (1 + \eta_p) n^* + \eta_y y^* \tag{7}$$

$$p^* = k_L r^* + k_N n^*. \tag{8}$$

In (8) the unit price of housing is implicitly defined as an appropriately weighted average of the unit prices of land and structures. Unless the shares of land and structures are fixed, which occurs if and only if $\sigma = 1$, (8) holds only approximately for finite changes in input prices. Making use of (8), (7) reduces essentially to (4) and can be used to estimate the elasticities of housing demand.

From the definition of the elasticity of substitution,

$$\left(\frac{N}{L}\right)^* = \sigma \left(\frac{r}{n}\right)^*,$$

so

$$\left(\frac{rL}{nN}\right)^* = (1-\sigma)\left(\frac{r}{n}\right)^*. \tag{9}$$

Thus, σ may be estimated from a regression analysis of the ratio of site value to structure value on the ratio of land to structure prices. The resulting value of σ together with housing demand elasticities obtained as described in the preceding paragraph may be used along with sample averages of k_L and k_N to infer the coefficients of r^* and n^* in (5) and (6). Comparison of these inferred or expected values with actual regression estimates of them, as presented in Table 3 below, provides evidence for the consistency of the model presented here with real-world behavior.

If $f(L, N)$ has a constant elasticity of substitution, then it may be written as

$$Q = [aL^{-c} + bN^{-c}]^{-1/c}, \tag{10}$$

where a, b, and c are constants and $\sigma = 1/(1 + c)$. The marginal product of land is thus

$$Q_L = aQ^{c+1}L^{-(c+1)},$$

and similarly for structures. Equating the ratio of marginal products to the factor price ratio yields

$$\frac{b}{a}\left(\frac{L}{N}\right)^{c+1} = \frac{n}{r},$$

so

$$\ln\left(\frac{rL}{nN}\right) = -\sigma \ln\left(\frac{b}{a}\right) + (1-\sigma) \ln\left(\frac{r}{n}\right). \tag{11}$$

For a constant elasticity of substitution production function, then, (9) is not merely a first-order approximation but holds exactly. Equation (11) then enables one to estimate the ratio of the distribution parameters, (b/a), from known values of relative factor shares, relative factor prices and the elasticity of substitution.

With the exception of the construction cost index, all of the data used for the analysis in this section were obtained from tabulations of characteristics of new single-family houses financed by FHA-insured mortgages in 1966. The data are averages for all such houses for a given FHA housing area, essentially Standard Metropolitan Statistical Areas, which shall be somewhat loosely termed cities, in what follows. Unless otherwise noted, all variables are measured in dollars, and natural logs of all variables were used in the regression analysis.

Since the sample data refer to FHA-insured homes only, they may be subjected to some limitations. It seems quite likely that, since the FHA imposes a fixed insurance charge regardless of the terms of the loan, some owners who prefer to make higher down-payments and borrow for shorter periods than average, would find conventional mortgages less costly than FHA-insured mortgages. Such borrowers are likely to have higher incomes and greater accumulated non-human wealth than FHA borrowers. This could mean that among buyers of a given average income, those financing home purchases by FHA mortgages would tend to have higher costs of capital and thus purchase less housing. The higher the average income of a group of buyers, the smaller presumably would be the fraction choosing FHA financing and the higher the costs of capital of FHA borrowers relative to the average for the whole group. Closely related to the above is the effect of upper limits on the amount of an FHA-insured mortgage. As such limits become effective, with increases in average income the average expenditures on housing of FHA borrowers would increase less than the average for all borrowers. Thus, it is possible that the income elasticity of housing demand obtained from the FHA data would tend to understate the true value for all new homes. There is no particular reason, however, why this understatement should influence the estimated income elasticity of the demand for land more strongly than the demand for structures or vice-versa. Nor is there any reason to anticipate distorted responses to factor price differentials.

The value of new homes, pQ, is measured by the sales price of single-family owner-occupant homes. This is the amount stated in the sales agreement adjusted to exclude closing costs and non-real estate items which the sales agreement indicated were to be assumed by the seller. Expenditures on land, rL, are the FHA estimated market price of the site including street improvements, utilities, and landscaping. The data thus considerably overestimate, probably by a factor of at least two, the raw land value. In addition, there are probably fewer possibilities for substituting improved land for structures than raw land for non-land capital. Hence, the data probably yield an underestimate of the raw land for non-land capital substitution elasticity. Expenditures on structures, nN, were obtained by subtracting expenditures on land from the sales price of new homes.

The variable hereafter designated simply as net family income or income, y, is that obtained by deducting federal income taxes from what the FHA terms 'total effective income'.(1) The latter is defined as the 'FHA-estimated amount ... that is likely to prevail during approximately the first third of the mortgage term' (FHA, 1967). No details of how the estimates are made were given. Based on my experience with FHA loan applications, however, I suspect that some earnings of the household head from other than his or her principal employment and some income of secondary earners are probably deducted from total family income. As such, some transitory income elements are no doubt eliminated from the income variable, but it is by no means certain that this variable closely approximates to normal or permanent income, upon which housing expenditures are likely to be based. Hence, the estimated income elasticities shown below are likely to be downward biased. In addition, because housing prices tend to be positively correlated with income, the estimated price elasticity is likely to be biased toward zero as well. There is no reason to suspect, though, that the demand for land will be differentially affected as compared with the demand for structures on this account. Neither would one expect distorted responses to land price changes relative to changes in structure prices.

The last variable obtained from the FHA tabulations is the average price of site in dollars per square foot, r. As was indicated earlier, the FHA data are unique in presenting such a measure. This measure showed considerable variation over the sample, ranging from as low as $0.20 in some cities to around $1 or more in the California cities included in the sample. The price of structures, n, was measured by the Boeckh index of brick residential structures, 1926-29 U.S. average = 100. This measure varied considerably less than land prices over the sample, ranging from only about 260 or a little more in some southern cities to about 375 in certain north-eastern ones. The limited variability of the Boeckh index relative to the variation of observed land costs among different cities may be partly responsible for its rather disappointing showing in some of the regression results that follow. Availability of the Boeckh index limited the sample to forty-seven U.S. cities. Since the index is reported for large urban areas, in three cases the same Boeckh index value was used for two FHA housing areas in the same urban area—Chicago and Gary in the Chicago area, for example.

My estimates of the elasticity of substitution of land for structures are given in Table 1. (Throughout the tables, standard errors are shown below the coefficients.) The coefficient of the ratio of land price to construction cost in equation (A) implies an elasticity of substitution of almost exactly 0.5. This value is significantly smaller, both in the statistical sense as indicated by its standard error and in a practical sense as will be indicated later, than my previous estimate (1964, p. 229) based upon very scant data. Like the earlier estimate, the new one implies that with a rise in land prices relative to structure costs, less land in physical units is used relative to structures but more is spent on land relative to expenditures on structures. The factor price ratio alone explains about seven-tenths of the variation in the ratio of expenditure on factors.

In equation (B) the income of home buyers was also used as a determinant of relative expenditures on land and structures. Rather surprisingly the coefficient of income is strongly negative, though its inclusion has little effect upon the goodness-of-fit of the regression. Since I have no explanation for the strongly negative coefficient of income, I prefer simply to accept the null hypothesis that the income elasticities of land and structure demand are the same. Clearly, though, the income coefficient in equation (B) is inconsistent with the notion that the income elasticity of demand for land is higher than that for structures.

Equation (C) shows the results obtained when the number of occupant purchase cases in the FHA-sample in each area for 1966 is used as a weighting factor in the regression. The number of observations varied substantially as among the different cities—from about 70 to 1,000. In principle, the weighted regression results would be preferred, but in this instance I feel the standard regression gives better ones for reasons to be noted soon. Here, though the weighted regression yields a factor price ratio coefficient which is almost identical to that in equation (A). As is to be expected, the goodness-of-fit of the weighted regression is noticeably better. Finally, in equation (D) land price was assumed to be endogenous, and the coefficients were estimated using the method of instrumental variables. This last comparison was made to examine the possibility of least-square bias due to simultaneous determination of land prices and expenditures on land. The results of equation (D) indicate such bias as truly negligible, for an almost identical estimate to that of equation (A) is obtained. Thus, regardless of the method of estimation, a land for structures substitution elasticity of very close to 0.5 is obtained. The results of adding income to either (C) or (D), which are not shown, were also virtually identical to those obtained by adding income to the standard regression.

Table 2 explores the results of relating per family expenditures on housing to measures of housing cost and to net family income. In equation (E) land price and the construction cost index are included as separate variables. In equation (F), however, the two separate factor prices were combined into a single housing price variable using equation (8) and the sample geometric mean of the ratio of site expenditures to sales price, which was about 0.18. Comparing equations (E) and (F), the latter's standard error of estimate is actually a little smaller, the reduction in the explained sum of squares being somewhat more than compensated for by the gain of one residual degree of freedom. Quite similar results were obtained using weighted regression and instrumental variable estimates, not all of which are shown in Table 2. These results are quite consistent, then, with the hypothesis that land and structures are inputs into the production of something called housing, and they provide no support for the notion that an independent demand for land exists.

For all three methods of estimation, the estimated price and income elasticities of demand for housing are substantially smaller than one numerically. (The coefficient of housing price is one minus the price elasticity of housing demand, since the dependent variable is expenditure on housing.) On the basis of other evidence, much of which is noted in my recent book *Cities and Housing* (1969), I would conclude that both elasticities are at least as great as unity in absolute value. The weighted regression estimates, equation (G), yield the smallest elasticities, each about 0.7 numerically, which is why I prefer the standard regression estimates to the weighted ones. The differences, though, are of little practical importance. The small values found here may result from the two factors noted previously in this section, namely the nature of the FHA sample and the failure completely to control for transitory income components in the income variable. The standard regression calculations for the earlier version of this paper (1968), however, yielded price and income elasticities which were insignificantly smaller than unity. These earlier calculations were based upon data for twenty-two cities only, mainly larger ones. Thus, the apparent downward bias in the price and income elasticity estimates here may result from the omission of city size or some factor correlated with it. All the other results of the earlier calculations, though, were essentially identical with the ones presented for the larger number of cities in Tables 1-3.

The FHA data also permit one to estimate separate demand functions for

TABLE 1

RELATION OF RELATIVE INPUT SHARES[a] TO INPUT PRICE RATIO

		Explanatory Variables			
Regression Equation	Constant	Land Price/ Construction Cost Ratio	Net Family Income	Standard Error of Estimate	R^2
Standard Regression:					
Equation (A)	1·92	0·507	–	0·135	0·712
	(0·32)	(0·048)			
Equation (B)	5·65	0·552	−0·381	0·131	0·736
	(1·86)	(0·052)	(0·187)		
Weighted Regression[b]:					
Equation (C)	1·80	0·492	–	1·24	0·797
	(0·24)	(0·037)			
Instrumental Variables[c]:					
Equation (D)	1·91	0·506	–	0·135	–
	(0.47)	(0·070)			

[a] Dependent variable is the land/structure expenditure ratio.

[b] Using number of occupant purchase cases in sample to weight the observations.

[c] Using 1960 SMSA population, 1960 relative to 1950 SMSA population, and 1960 urbanised area median family income as instrumental variables and treating land price as endogenous.

land and for structures, which are shown in Table 3. Only standard regressions equations are presented there, but quite similar results were found using weighted or instrumental variable regressions. In addition to the standard regression equations in full, expected land price and construction cost index coefficients are shown. These were derived from equations (5) and (6) together with the price and substitution elasticity estimates derived from regression equations (F) and (A), respectively, and the mean share of land for the sample as a whole. These expected values, of course, were derived from the same body of data as the regression estimates in Table 3. However, they provide a useful check on the consistency of the unrestricted factor demand estimates with the model presented earlier. Examining Table 3 one sees that the coefficients of land price in both the land and structure demand regressions agree quite closely with those expected if land is an input into the production of housing. Neither estimated coefficient differs by as much as one standard error from its expected value. The coefficients of the construction cost index differ somewhat more, though both by less than two standard errors. Because of the limited variability of the construction cost index, however, the standard errors of the construction cost coefficients are relatively large, and little can be concluded from these coefficients. Finally, note that the estimated income elasticity of land demand is less than half that for structures. As was noted in connection with equation (B), the FHA data certainly provided no evidence that the demand for land rises relatively to that for structures as income increases.

Results such as were obtained earlier can be employed for a variety of purposes. Here only a few are sketched out. Of greatest interest are the

TABLE 2

RELATION OF AVERAGE SALES PRICE[a] TO NET FAMILY INCOME AND HOUSING COSTS

Regression Equation	Constant	Explanatory Variables				Standard Error of Estimate	R^2
		Land Price	Construction Cost Index	Housing Price	Net Family Income		
Standard Regressions							
Equation (E)	2·77 (1·21)	0·0692 (0·0303)	0·100 (0·118)	—	0·722 (0·109)	0·0758	0·689
Equation (F)	1·96 (0·88)	—	—	0·238 (0·084)	0·748 (0·106)	0·0757	0·682
Weighted Regression[b]:							
Equation (G)	2·00 (0·78)	—	—	0·313 (0·088)	0·706 (0·106)	0·0726	0·764
Instrumental Variables[c]:							
Equation (H)	1·97 (0·88)	—	—	0·197 (0·092)	0·768 (0·108)	0·0760	—

[a] Dependent variable is average sales price of one-family owner occupant new homes.

[b], [c] Same as Table 1.

TABLE 3

RELATION OF LAND AND STRUCTURE OUTLAYS TO INPUT PRICES AND INCOME

Regression Equation	Constant	Explanatory Variables			Standard Error of Estimate	R^2
		Land Price	Construction Cost Index	Net Family Income		
Land Outlay[a]:						
Standard Regression:						
Equation (I)	4·79	0·488	0·137	0·328	0·141	0·764
	(2·25)	(0·057)	(0·221)	(0·204)		
Expected Coefficient[c]	—	0·458	−0·220	—	—	—
Structure Outlay[b]:						
Standard Regression:						
Equation (J)	1·90	−0·0388	0·110	0·778	0·0695	0·614
	(1·11)	(0·0278)	(0·108)	(0·100)		
Expected Coefficient[c]	—	−0·0492	0·288	—	—	—

[a] Dependent variable is the average market price of site of one-family new homes.

[b] Dependent variable is sales price minus average market price of site.

[c] Assuming $\eta_{lp} = -0.76$, $\sigma = 0.49$, $K_L = 0.18$.

implications of the elasticity of substitution of land for structures, here estimated at 0:5, for the tendency for cities to spread out as they grow and become richer. In an earlier work on the spatial pattern of residential land use in cities (1969), it was argued that, if the substitution elasticity of land for structures in producing housing is less than unity, the elasticity of housing supply per unit of land would be greater in the outer parts of cities than in their inner zones. Consequently, as the demand for housing in a particular city grows, the output of housing per unit of land and thus population density grows more rapidly in the outer parts of cities. In interpreting my empirical findings, I used a value of the substitution elasticity of 0.75, derived from very limited data. I concluded that differential responsiveness of housing output in different locations was not sufficient to account fully for the tendency for population densities to decline at relatively slower rates with distance from the CBD in larger cities (1969, pp. 317-318). The value found here for the substitution elasticity of land for structures, however, implies a still greater responsiveness of housing output to price changes in the outer parts of cities. This, in itself, would produce a numerically larger elasticity of the population density gradient with respect to city size than I previously observed.

In *Cities and Housing* I argued that the decline in population density with distance from the CBD results largely from the decline in the value of housing produced per unit of land. The relative change in the latter was shown to be equal to what I called the elasticity of value of housing produced per unit of land multiplied by the relative change in housing prices, or the price gradient (Ch. 4, pp. 54-55). If $\sigma = 0.75$, the elasticity of value of housing output per square mile would be about +15, but for $\sigma = 0.5$ it is only about +10.(2) The median density gradient observed for U.S. cities in 1950 was about 0.3; hence the price gradient would be about 3% per mile rather than 2%, and the residential land rental gradient about 0.6 (Ch. 4, p. 52). Likewise, substituting into my expression for the change in the elasticity of housing value produced (Ch. 4, p. 57) for $\sigma = 0.5$ and $(r_k/r) = -0.6$, one finds the elasticity to increase by about 2.8 per mile. The last means in particular that, for a city whose radius is six miles, the elasticity of housing value produced per square mile would be only about 1.5 at the centre but 18.5 at its edge.

With an elasticity of housing value per square mile of about +10, a 10% increase in population and hence housing demand would imply a rise in housing prices everywhere of about 8.3% (Ch. 4, p. 317). Consequently, the value of housing output would grow by about 1.25% at the center and by about 15.4% at the edge of the hypothetical city described above. These values, in turn, imply the density gradient would decline by about 0.022 or about 7% with a 10% population increase. The differential output elasticities alone, then, imply a density gradient elasticity of about -0.7, as compared with -0.27 in my earlier calculations using $\sigma = 0.75$ and an observed elasticity of -0.47.

Thus, rather than having to search for additional decentralizing forces associated with population growth, the problem now appears to be one of explaining why cities, as they grow, apparently don't decentralize as much as anticipated. A possible reason is one which originally led me to anticipate a positive relation between the density gradient and city size, namely that greater traffic congestion in larger cities means marginal transport costs are higher there. It may also be the case, as suggested in the third section, that, because the measure of land used here includes some non-land capital investment in streets, utilities, and landscaping, the substitution elasticity estimate of 0.5 underestimates the one between raw land and non-land capital. If so, the calculated value of the density gradient elasticity with respect to city size which was just presented would be too large numerically. I also note that this revised substitution elasticity estimate implies that the differential output response to increased housing demand and an income elasticity of housing demand of only +1 are sufficient to account for my observed elasticity of the density gradient with respect to income, which was −0.63.

The system of equations (5) through (8) can be used in evaluating the effects of a variety of influences upon housing markets. Of course, to complete the model one would need supply schedules of land and structures to the housing industry. In two important special cases, however, the factor supply schedules may be neglected. First, for studying the immediate impact of changes, the elasticities of supply of land and of structures are zero. In this case, $L* = N* = 0$ (hence by (1), $Q* = 0$), so (5), (6) and (8) yield $r*$, $n*$ and $p*$ as functions of the exogenous changes. Second, and of much greater interest, in the long run, it appears that the supply of structures is highly elastic or n is approximately fixed (Muth, 1969, pp. 57-58). The supply of land to the housing industry undoubtedly has a positive elasticity, both because of conversion of urban land from non-residential uses and because of growth of the city. Bounds on other variables may be obtained, though, by assuming $L* = 0$, so that the model determines $r*$, $N*$, $Q*$ and $p*$. Indeed, because land's share is relatively small, the results of calculations such as are shown two paragraphs below are not very sensitive to the elasticity of residential land supply.

For working through some of the implications of the model presented in the second section, it is useful to substitute approximate numerical estimates of the parameters into equations (5)-(8). I will use the value of the substitution elasticity of land for structures obtained here, namely 0.5. The mean value of the share of land in the value of houses for the cities used here was 0.18, as noted earlier. Since the measure of land includes non-land capital in the form of streets, utilities, and landscaping, which could easily be as much as raw land value itself, 0.1 seems a more reasonable value for K_L. I mentioned in the third section that, in my judgment, the price and income elasticities obtained here are too low, and I will assume instead that both are equal to unity. Making these substitutions into (5)-(8) one finds:

$$L* = -0.55\, r* - 0.45\, n* + y* \tag{12}$$

$$N* = -0.05\, r* - 0.95\, n* + y* \tag{13}$$

$$p* = 0.1\, r* + 0.9\, n* \tag{14}$$

$$Q* = -p* + y*. \tag{15}$$

As an example, consider the impact of a 10% housing price or income subsidy to, say, the lowest 10% of families in the income distribution. Many persons have argued that the impact of such subsidies would tend to be dissipated on higher site value or 'profits' to landlords (Grigsby, 1963, pp. 303-304). This is the case, of course, when rentals have adjusted to the higher demand with a fixed quantity of housing services produced. In the long run, however, it is unlikely to be the case even with a fixed quantity of residential land provided the supply of structures is highly elastic, because land's share in the production of housing is small. With either subsidy, the quantity of housing demanded, by (15), increases by 10% for the lowest income 10% of the families or by less than 1% in the aggregate. If the production function for housing is homogenous of degree one, the quantity of land demanded at given factor prices likewise rises by less than 1%. If the quantity of land available to the housing industry were fixed, then by (12) $0.01 - 0.55\ r^* = 0$ or $r^* = 0.018$. The increase in land prices of less than 2% would, in turn, by (14) result in a housing price increase of less than 0.2%. (With a price subsidy, of course, housing prices would have fallen to the recipients by more than 9.8%.) In either case, however, little of the subsidy would be dissipated through higher site costs.

As a final example of the uses of which the analysis of this paper might be put, consider the U.S. federal public housing program. In his excellent evaluation of the public housing program, Edgar Olsen noted what is an apparent substantial waste in its production of dwellings, amounting to around 40% or more of the average expenditure per dwelling during the 'fifties (Olsen, 1968, pp. 70-71).(3) He pointed to the fact that some public housing units are built on cleared slum land, whose price per square foot is much higher than non-slum land, as one source of waste. His estimate of the waste due to building projects on slum land, however, is simply the additional expenditures on construction as structures are substituted for land.(4)

Properly to evaluate the resource cost of building on slum land, consider the constant elasticity of substitution production function for housing, equation (10). This may be rewritten as

$$L = a^{1/c} Q \left[1 + \frac{b}{a} \left(\frac{N}{L} \right)^{-c} \right]^{1/c}. \tag{16}$$

By equating the ratio of marginal physical products to the ratio of factor prices,

$$\frac{N}{L} = \left(\frac{b}{a} \times \frac{r}{n} \right)^{1/(c+1)}, \tag{17}$$

so substituting (17) into (16) yields

$$\frac{L}{Q} = a^{(\sigma/1-\sigma)} \left[1 + \left(\frac{b}{a} \right)^{\sigma} \left(\frac{r}{n} \right)^{\sigma-1} \right]^{(\sigma/1-\sigma)}. \tag{18}$$

Similarly,

$$\frac{N}{Q} = b^{(\sigma/1-\sigma)} \left[1 + \left(\frac{b}{a} \right)^{-\sigma} \left(\frac{r}{n} \right)^{-(\sigma-1)} \right]^{(\sigma/1-\sigma)}. \tag{19}$$

By making these substitutions, of course, I am assuming that public housing units are built at the minimum resource cost for the prevailing ratio of factor prices. Knowing the amount of land and structure per unit of housing as a function of the factor price ratio, the resource cost per unit of housing may readily be calculated.

Making such calculations, though, requires numerical values of the parameters of the production function. One may normalize or define units by taking $a = 1$ and $n = \$1$. From the FHA data used for the calculations in the third section, the geometric mean for the forty-seven cities used of (rL/nN) was about 0.22; that of r was $0.39 per square foot. Substituting into (11) one finds for $\sigma = 0.5$, $(b/a) = 7.7$ and $(b/a)^\sigma = 2.8$. Hence, (18) and (19) become

$$\frac{L}{Q} = \left[1 + 2 \cdot 8 \times \left(\frac{r}{n} \right)^{-0 \cdot 5} \right] \tag{20}$$

$$\frac{N}{Q} = 7 \cdot 7 \left[1 + 2 \cdot 8^{-1} \times \left(\frac{r}{n} \right)^{0 \cdot 5} \right]. \tag{21}$$

As shown in Table 4, the average square foot prices paid for slum and non-slum land were $1.12 and 0.091, respectively (Table 4). Substituting these values in turn into (20) and (21) and then evaluating the resource cost per unit of housing, one finds it to be $14.7 per unit of housing built upon slum land as compared with only about $9.5 for that built upon non-slum land. The resource cost per unit of public housing would thus be about 55% greater for units built upon cleared slum land. Additional expenditure on structures is about 40% of the excess cost of building on slum land, according to these calculations. Since about 36.5% of all units built during the 'fifties were built upon slum land, the resource cost of the public housing program was about 20% greater than it would have been had all units been built upon non-slum land. Since demolition of slum housing to provide sites for public housing not only leads to displacement of, but also makes housing more costly to lower-income persons, at least in the short run, there is little empirically justifiable rationale for such demolitions.(5)

A comparison of certain other actual characteristics of public housing units built on slum vs. non-slum land are shown in Table 4 along with ratios calculated using equations (20) and (21). The agreement between the actual and calculated ratios is close enough for me to put some confidence in my calculations in the paragraph above but divergent enough to make me suspect some real source of discrepancy exists. In making comparisons it is in effect assumed that public

TABLE 4

SELECTED CHARACTERISTICS OF PUBLIC HOUSING UNITS BUILT IN
THE U.S., 1950-59, UPON SLUM vs. NON-SLUM LAND

Built upon	Land Price per sq. ft. ($s)	Expenditures on Land per Dwelling Unit ($s)	Dwelling Units per Acre
Slum land	1·116	1,945	25·2
Non-slum land	0·091	350	11·3

Source: U.S. Housing and Home Finance Agency Fourteenth Annual Report 1960. Washington D.C.: U.S. Government Printing Office. 1961.

housing units built on slum and non-slum land contain the same number of units of housing per dwelling. While such by no means need be the case, it is not at all clear what kind of differences exist and what effects they might have on the calculations. Second, the production function parameter estimates used in deriving (20) and (21) were based upon data for single-family houses only. Many, if not most, public housing units are in multi-family structures, however. I know of no data which could be used to assess the differences in production possibilities for single- *vs.* multi-family housing directly. In an earlier study (Muth, 1969, pp. 314-316), though, I examined some of the implications of different production functions for different types of structures. The evidence, admittedly indirect, seems clearly to favor the hypothesis that different types of structures reflect different ratios of structure to land combined in accordance with a single production function.

TABLE 5

ACTUAL AND CALCULATED[a] RATIOS OF SELECTED CHARACTERISTICS OF
PUBLIC HOUSING UNITS BUILT UPON SLUM *vs.* NON-SLUM LAND

Characteristic	Actual[b]	Calculated[a]
Cost per dwelling	—	1·6
Dwellings per unit of land	2·2	2·8
Expenditures on land per dwelling	5·6	4·5

[a] Using equations (20) and (21) and assuming comparability in public housing units built upon slum and non-slum land.
[b] From Table 4.

Finally, Table 5 indicates that the intensity of land use on slum sites is lower relative to non-slum sites than anticipated. This observation suggests a third possibility. In building public housing on slum sites, its producers may not have substituted structures for land, or built housing as densely, as private producers of housing would have given the higher relative price of land. Indeed, public producers may have felt that to do so would have produced adverse external effects, either for project residents themselves or upon users of surrounding properties. The calculations made above, while taking into account any lesser desirability of denser housing from its inhabitants' viewpoint, fail to make any allowance for possible external effects. Calculations similar to those made two paragraphs above, however, suggest that the failure of public housing to be built as densely on slum sites as anticipated would have relatively little effect upon my estimate of the relative cost of building public housing on cleared slum sites.(6)

NOTES

(1) The monthly figure reported was multiplied by twelve to convert it to the more usual annual basis.
(2) In the notation used here this elasticity is equal to $[1 + (k_N/K_L)\sigma]$.

(3) Proper measurement of the extent of this waste turns out to be a rather complicated problem. As of now I am inclined to value it higher than Olsen does, but I cannot go into the details of my evaluation here.

(4) Indeed, if the elasticity of substitution of land for structures were large enough, expenditures for land per unit of housing might decline with a rise in land price, as seen by setting $\eta_p = 0$ in equation (5). Building on slum land, though, would still involve a higher resource cost per dwelling unit.

(5) Studies by former students of mine suggest to me that the external effects of public housing and similar redevelopments, while somewhat uncertain, are probably small. See in particular Nourse (1963).

(6) Using (16) one can calculate (N/L) on slum sites as a function of that on non-slum sites, assuming the ratio of housing per unit of land on the two sites is 2.2. Assuming further that housing is produced at minimum cost on non-slum sites determines (N/L) on the former and hence on slum sites. Dividing the ratio of cost per unit of land by that of housing per unit of land on slum relative to non-slum sites then yields a relative cost on slum sites of 1.58, as compared with 1.55 if production on slum sites is also at minimum cost.

REFERENCES

Alonso, W. (1964). Location and Land Use. Cambridge, Mass.: Harvard University Press.

Grigsby, W. G. (1963). Housing Markets and Public Policy. Philadelphia: University of Pennsylvania Press.

Hoover, E.M. and Vernon, R. (1959). Anatomy of a Metropolis. Cambridge, Mass.: Harvard University Press.

Muth, Richard F. (1969). Cities and Housing. Chicago: University of Chicago Press.

Muth, Richard F. (1964). The Derived Demand for a Productive Factor and the Industry Supply Curve. Oxford Economic Papers, July.

Muth, Richard F. (1968). The Demand for Housing and the Demand for Land, in Land as an Element in Housing Costs. Study S-324, Institute for Defense Analyses.

Nourse, Hugh O. (1963). The Effects of Public Housing on Property Values in St. Louis. Land Economics, November.

Olsen, Edgar O. (1968). A Welfare Economic Evaluation of Public Housing. Ph.D. Dissertation, Rice University, May.

U.S. Federal Housing Administration (1967). FHA Homes, 1966. Washington, D.C.: Department of Housing and Urban Development.

U.S. Housing and Home Finance Agency (1961). Fourteenth Annual Report, 1960. Washington, D.C.: U.S. Government Printing Office.

Wingo, L., Jr. (1961). Transportation and Urban Land. Washington, D.C.: Resources for the Future, Inc.

AN ECONOMETRIC ANALYSIS
OF RENT CONTROL

Edgar O. Olsen

> It is perfectly astounding to find that the quantity and quality of
> analytical materials on rent control are wholly incommensurate with the
> social and economic importance of the problem. [Grebler 1952, p. 464]

Rent control has affected patterns of consumption and well-being for at least
fifty years; yet empirical evidence on the economic effects of this form of
government regulation is scanty and crude.(1) The primary purposes of this
paper are to provide a general method for answering certain questions about rent
control and to answer these questions for New York City in 1968.

The following questions will be answered. What difference has rent control
made in the consumption of housing service and nonhousing goods by occupants
of controlled housing? What is the mean benefit of rent control to tenants
occupying rent-controlled apartments? What is the total benefit to all families
living in controlled units? How does the total benefit to these families compare
with their total income? Who bears the cost of rent control, and what is the
magnitude of this cost? Are the occupants of controlled housing poorer than the
occupants of uncontrolled housing? Among the set of families living in
controlled housing, how does the size of tenant benefit vary with household
income, family size, and the age, sex, and race of the head of the household?

THEORETICAL FRAMEWORK

The questions posed will be answered with the help of a simple economic
model. Assume that there are two goods—housing service and nonhousing

goods—and three markets—the controlled market for housing service, the uncontrolled market for housing service, and the market for nonhousing goods. Assume that the latter two markets are perfectly competitive and that we observe both markets in long-run equilibrium. Assume that the long-run supply curves in both markets are perfectly elastic.(2) Assume that the long-run supply price of housing service in the uncontrolled market is the same as it would have been in the absence of rent control.

Before proceeding to use these assumptions to derive formulas for answering the questions posed, it is desirable to define the phrase "housing service" with some care. Housing service is an unobservable good emitted in some quantity by each dwelling unit during each period of time. It is the one and only thing in a dwelling unit to which consumers attach value. Intuitively, the quantity of housing service emitted by a dwelling unit can be thought of as an index of all its attributes, including both space and quality. Since it is assumed that the uncontrolled housing market is perfectly competitive, we know that in equilibrium each unit of housing service sold on this market sells for the same price. Hence, if we observe one apartment renting for $200 per month and another for $100 per month on the uncontrolled housing market, then we say that the first apartment emits twice the quantity of housing service per time period as the second.(3)

Let us now use the assumptions made to derive formulas which, when combined with the available data and predictions based on these data, will yield the answers that we seek. In figure 1, D is the demand curve for housing service of some tenant of a rent-controlled dwelling unit, holding the price of nonhousing goods and money income constant. If the uncontrolled market price of housing service were $P_m{}^h$ and if the tenant were to buy housing service on the uncontrolled market, then he would occupy a dwelling emitting $Q_m{}^h$ units of housing service per time period and pay a "rent" of $P_m{}^h Q_m{}^h$. Finally, let us suppose that under rent control the tenant occupies a dwelling unit emitting $Q_c{}^h$ units of housing service per time period and pays a rent of $P_c{}^h Q_c{}^h$ for this dwelling unit.

The relative magnitudes of the variables depicted in figure 1 do not represent the situation of every occupant of a controlled apartment. For example, a significant minority of the occupants of controlled apartments live in better housing than they would have occupied in the absence of rent control (that is, $Q_c{}^h > Q_m{}^h$). Nevertheless, the empirical evidence will show that the relationships between variables depicted in figure 1 are typical of families living in controlled housing.

It is perhaps not obvious why the occupant of a controlled apartment would consume a smaller quantity of housing service at the lower controlled price. The explanation is as follows. The price-quantity combination $(P_c{}^h, Q_c{}^h)$ is preferred to the tenant's best alternative on the uncontrolled market $(P_m{}^h, Q_m{}^h)$ because it permits a sufficiently greater consumption of nonhousing goods to offset the smaller consumption of housing service. Furthermore, the owner of this controlled apartment has no incentive to increase its flow of services. To do so would increase cost but not revenue. Finally, there is nothing in the operation of the controlled housing market which guarantees that this tenant can find an apartment renting for $P_c{}^h Q_d{}^h$ and yielding $Q_d{}^h$ units of housing service per time period. It is extremely difficult to obtain a controlled apartment, and the tenant might well judge the cost of finding a better bargain on the controlled market to be greater than the gain. If he does search for a better bargain, he has no incentive to limit his search to apartments with price-quantity combinations on his demand curve. In short, there is no theoretical reason to believe that all occupants of controlled apartments are on their demand curves, and the evidence to be presented is inconsistent with this hypothesis.

In the case depicted in figure 1, the tenant consumes

$$100 \left[(P_m^h Q_m^h - P_m^h Q_c^h) / P_m^h Q_m^h \right] \text{ percent} \qquad (1)$$

less housing service than he would have consumed in the absence of rent control.

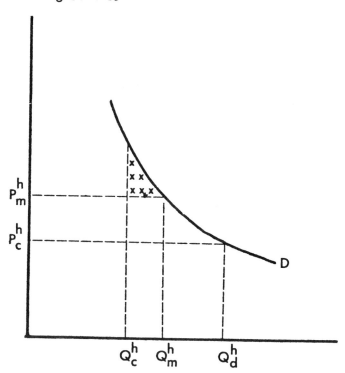

Dollars Per Unit

of

Housing Service

Quantity of Housing Service Per Time Period

Fɪɢ. 1.—The effects of rent control on the occupant of a controlled apartment and his landlord.

On the other hand, he spends

$$P_m{}^h Q_m{}^h - P_c{}^h Q_c{}^h$$

more on nonhousing goods. Hence, as a result of rent control, he consumes a greater quantity of nonhousing goods. To be precise, he consumes

$$100 \left[(P_m{}^n Q_c{}^n - P_m{}^n Q_m{}^n)/P_m{}^n Q_m{}^n \right] \text{ percent} \qquad (2)$$

more nonhousing goods, where $P_m{}^n$ is the market price per unit of non-housing goods, $Q_m{}^n$ is the quantity of nonhousing goods that this consumer would purchase in the absence of rent control, and $Q_c{}^n$ is the quantity of nonhousing goods that he consumes under rent control. Since there are only two goods, everything that the consumer does not spend on housing service is spent on nonhousing goods. Hence,

$$P_m{}^n Q_c{}^n = Y - P_c{}^h Q_c{}^h \qquad (3)$$

and

$$P_m{}^n Q_m{}^n = Y - P_m{}^h Q_m{}^h, \qquad (4)$$

where Y is the tenant's income. Substituting (3) and (4) into (2), we find that the percentage change in the consumption of nonhousing goods by this tenant may be written as

$$100 \left[(P_m{}^h Q_m{}^h - P_c{}^h Q_c{}^h)/(Y - P_m{}^h Q_m{}^h) \right]. \qquad (5)$$

We can calculate the proportional change in the total quantities of housing service and nonhousing goods for a set of families by formulas (6) and (7):

$$\frac{\sum_{i=1}^{k} Q_{c,i}{}^h - \sum_{i=1}^{k} Q_{m,i}{}^h}{\sum_{i=1}^{k} Q_{m,i}{}^h} = \frac{\sum_{i=1}^{k} P_m{}^h Q_{c,i}{}^h - \sum_{i=1}^{k} P_m{}^h Q_{m,i}{}^h}{\sum_{i=1}^{k} P_m{}^h Q_{m,i}{}^h}, \qquad (6)$$

$$\frac{\sum_{i=1}^{k} Q_{c,i}{}^n - \sum_{i=1}^{k} Q_{m,i}{}^n}{\sum_{i=1}^{k} Q_{m,i}{}^n} = \frac{\sum_{i=1}^{k} P_m{}^h Q_{m,i}{}^h - \sum_{i=1}^{k} P_{c,i}{}^h Q_{c,i}{}^h}{\sum_{i=1}^{k} (Y_i - P_m{}^h Q_{m,i}{}^h)}, \qquad (7)$$

where the subscript i indicates the ith family. Notice that the derivation of these formulas requires the use of an implication of our assumptions, namely, that in a competitive market in equilibrium, all consumers pay the same price for the good.

Since the tenant has the option of living in uncontrolled housing, this change in his consumption pattern must make him better off. There is some amount of money B that would make the tenant indifferent to the following two alternatives: remaining in his rent-controlled apartment during some time period, or accepting an unrestricted cash grant of B dollars on the stipulation that he live in an uncontrolled apartment during the time period but could return to his controlled apartment at the end of the time period.(4) If we were to offer the tenant a cash grant of more than B per time period, he would accept. If we were to offer him a cash grant of less than B, he would reject the offer and remain in his controlled apartment. I define B to be the net benefit of rent control to the tenant.

Net tenant benefit is approximately equal to the excess of consumer's surplus at $(Q_c{}^h, P_c{}^h)$ over the consumer's surplus at $(Q_m{}^h, P_m{}^h)$.(5) The consumer's surplus at a point (Q, P) is

$$(\int_0^Q D) - PQ.$$

Therefore, the excess of consumer's surplus at $(Q_c{}^h, P_c{}^h)$ over consumer's surplus at $(Q_m{}^h, P_m{}^h)$ is

$$[(\int_0^{Q_c{}^h} D) - P_c{}^h Q_c{}^h] - [(\int_0^{Q_m{}^h} D) - P_m{}^h Q_m{}^h]$$

$$= P_m{}^h Q_m{}^h - P_c{}^h Q_c{}^h + \int_{Q_m{}^h}^{Q_c{}^h} D \doteq B. \qquad (8)$$

Intuitively, the value of rent control to the tenant whose situation is depicted in figure 1 can be thought of as the sum of two components. First, the tenant benefits because he spends less money on housing service and hence is able to consume more nonhousing goods. The value of this component of net benefit is approximately

$$P_m{}^h Q_m{}^h - P_c{}^h Q_c{}^h, \qquad (9)$$

the excess of housing expenditure in the absence of rent control over housing expenditure under rent control. Second, the tenant loses because he consumes less housing service. The value that the tenant places on a small change in the quantity of housing service consumed is approximately equal to the height of the demand curve times the magnitude of the change in quantity. Consequently, the loss that this tenant incurs by consuming $Q_c{}^h$ rather than $Q_m{}^h$ units of housing service per time period is

$$\int_{Q_m{}^h}^{Q_c{}^h} D, \qquad (10)$$

the negative of the area under the demand curve between $Q_m{}^h$ and $Q_c{}^h$. The sum of (9) and (10) is our approximation of net tenant benefit.

The expression (8) would be of little use in calculating net tenant benefit in the absence of a knowledge of the tenant's demand curve for housing service. Empirical evidence by Muth (1960), Reid (1962, p. 381), Lee (1964), and de Leeuw (1971) on the demand curve holding the price of nonhousing goods and money income constant suggests that the price elasticity of demand is between 0.7 and 1.7. Therefore, it is at least consistent with these empirical findings to assume that each tenant's demand curve for housing service has a constant price elasticity equal to 1.(6) Of all the assumptions about the demand curve for housing service consistent with the empirical evidence, this one is chosen because it leads to a particularly simple formula for calculating net tenant benefit. Specifically, since we assume that each tenant's demand curve is of the form

$$P^h = P_m{}^h Q_m{}^h / Q^h,$$

we will calculate net tenant benefit by the formula

$$P_m{}^h Q_m{}^h - P_c{}^h Q_c{}^h + P_m{}^h Q_m{}^h [\ln P_m{}^h Q_c{}^h - \ln P_m{}^h Q_m{}^h].^7 \quad (11)$$

The mean benefit to a set of families occupying controlled dwellings is obtained by computing the benefit to each family and calculating the mean of these numbers.(8)

In order to provide the tenant with this benefit, someone must bear the cost. The cost is borne primarily by present and past owners of the controlled apartment and by taxpayers who pay for the enforcement of the rent-control law. In the absence of rent control, the owner would receive $P_m{}^h Q_c{}^h$ for his apartment. Under rent control, he receives $P_c{}^h Q_c{}^h$. Hence, he would be willing to pay

$$P_m{}^h Q_c{}^h - P_c{}^h Q_c{}^h \quad (12)$$

per time period to have this apartment decontrolled, provided that he is unable to vary the quantity of housing service emitted by the apartment during this period of time.(9) This is our measure of the cost of rent control during a particular time period to the past and present owners of the controlled apartment. Like the measure of net tenant benefit, it is an approximation.

In principle, we would like to measure the cost incurred by present and past owners during a period of time as follows. We want to compare the situation under rent control with the situation that would have prevailed had rent control never gone into effect. Had rent control never been implemented, this apartment would have yielded its owner some revenue during each period of time and he would have incurred some cost of operating, maintaining, repairing, and altering the apartment. We shall call all of these "operating costs." Under rent control, the owner is likely to obtain some different revenue and to incur some different operating cost during each period of time. Let $Q_a{}^h$ be the quantity of housing service that would have been emitted by this particular apartment during some time period had rent control never gone into effect and O_a be the operating cost that would have been incurred. Let O_c be the operating cost that is actually incurred during the time period. The conceptually correct measure of the cost of rent control during this period of time to the present and past owners of the apartment is

$$(P_m{}^h Q_a{}^h - O_a) - (P_c{}^h Q_c{}^h - O_c),$$

which can be rewritten as

$$(P_m{}^h Q_c{}^h - P_c{}^h Q_c{}^h) + P_m{}^h (Q_a{}^h - Q_c{}^h) - (O_a - O_c).$$

Some operating costs are incurred on activities which affect only the flow of services that will be emitted by the dwelling during the same time period. Other costs are incurred on activities which affect the flow of services in later time periods. It is usually argued that O_a is greater than O_c during each period of time. If this were the case, then Q_a^h would be greater than Q_c^h. Indeed, the difference between Q_a^h and Q_c^h is attributable solely to present and past differences between O_a and O_c. Although P_m^h $(Q_a^h - Q_c^h)$ and $(O_a - O_c)$ tend to cancel each other, they may differ in a particular time period, and hence formula (12) is an approximation to the conceptually correct measure. The conceptually correct measure is not used because the relevant data are not available.

If the only effect of rent control of interest to taxpayers is its administrative cost and if the only people concerned with the redistribution of consumption between a landlord and his tenant are these two people, then rent control must result in waste greater than zero. This waste is the excess of the sum of the loss to the landlord (12) and the cost of administering the program attributable to this particular dwelling unit over the gain to his tenant (11). Therefore,

$$W = P_m^h Q_c^h - P_m^h Q_m^h - P_m^h Q_m^h (\ln P_m^h Q_c^h - \ln P_m^h Q_m^h) + A. \tag{13}$$

In figure 1 the magnitude of the waste, net of administrative cost resulting from regulating the rent of this apartment, is the shaded area. The mean waste for a set of controlled apartments is obtained by computing the waste for each apartment and calculating the mean of these numbers.(10)

Looking back at the formulas derived in this section, we see that if we know each tenant's income, expenditure on housing under rent control, expenditure on housing in the absence of rent control, and the rent of his apartment on the uncontrolled market, then we can answer all of the questions posed in the introduction to this paper.

PREDICTION OF THE HOUSING EXPENDITURES AND MARKET RENTS

The empirical results of this paper are based on data from the 1968 New York City Housing and Vacancy Survey.(11) This survey collected many pieces of information for about 35,000 housing units and their occupants, including whether or not a housing unit is subject to rent control. It should be emphasized that the empirical results are based on data for individual families and housing units rather than on aggregates compiled from individual observations. Since the survey tells us directly the rent paid by the occupants of controlled housing and their income, we need only predict the housing expenditures of the occupants of controlled units in the absence of rent control and the market rents of their dwelling units in order to answer the questions posed earlier. In essence, the method of prediction assumes that a family in a controlled unit would have spent in the absence of rent control the same amount on housing as the average expenditure on housing of families with the same characteristics who actually live in private, uncontrolled rental housing. Similarly, we assume that a controlled unit will rent on the uncontrolled market for the average of uncontrolled units with the same characteristics.

Specifically, assume that the stochastic model explaining differences in housing expenditure by different families occupying uncontrolled rental housing in New York City in 1968 was

$$\ln P_m{}^h Q_m{}^h = a_0 + a_1 \ln Y + a_2 \ln A + a_3 \ln N + a_4 R + a_5 S + u, \tag{14}$$

where Y = annual income of the household, A = age of head of household, N = number of persons in the household, R = 1 if the head of household is nonwhite and 0 if white, S = 1 if the head of household is female and 0 if male, and $u \approx N (0, \sigma^2)$. We also assume that, given a sample of T joint observations $(P_m{}^h Q_m{}^h)_t$, Y_t, A_t, N_t, R_t, and S_t (where $t = 1, \ldots ,T$) produced by the model (14), the successive disturbances $u_t (t = 1, \ldots ,T)$ are mutually independent and that Y_t, A_t, N_t, R_t, and S_t are nonstochastic. Our predictor of how much the occupants of a controlled unit would have spent on housing in the absence of rent control is

$$_e \hat{a}_0 + \hat{a}_1 \ln Y + \hat{a}_2 \ln A + \hat{a}_3 \ln N + \hat{a}_4 R + \hat{a}_5 S, \tag{15}$$

where the a's are least-squares estimators of the a's in (14).(12) Using 4,063 families in uncontrolled housing for whom all of the necessary data were reported, the following results were obtained:(13)

$$\ln P_m{}^h Q_m{}^h = 4.071 + 0.351 \ln Y + 0.055 \ln A - 0.007 \ln N$$
$$\phantom{\ln P_m{}^h Q_m{}^h = 4.071 +} (41.2) \qquad\quad (3.7) \qquad\quad (-0.6)$$

$$\tag{16}$$

$$-0.123R + 0.114S \qquad\qquad R^2 = .32.$$
$$(-7.2) \qquad (7.9) \qquad\qquad\qquad s = .33$$

The t-scores are in parentheses beneath the estimated coefficients. For each of the 5,915 families in the sample occupying controlled housing, the value of the predictor (15) has been calculated.

Assume that the stochastic model explaining differences in the rents of different uncontrolled rental dwelling units in New York City in 1968 was

$$P_m{}^h Q_m{}^h = b_0 + \sum_{i=1}^{31} b_i X_i + u, \quad u \approx N (0, \sigma^2), \tag{17}$$

where the X_i are as defined in table 1. We also assume that, given a sample of T joint observations of the dependent variable and regressors produced by the model (17), the successive disturbances $u_t (t = 1, \ldots ,T)$ are mutually independent and the regressors are nonstochastic. Our predictor of the market rent of an unfurnished controlled apartment is

$$\hat{b}_0 + \sum_{i=1}^{30} \hat{b}_i X_i \tag{18}$$

and of a furnished controlled apartment is

$$(\hat{b}_0 + \sum_{i=1}^{30} \hat{b}_i X_i)/(1 - \hat{b}_{31}), \tag{19}$$

TABLE 1

ESTIMATED RELATIONSHIP BETWEEN MARKET RENT AND HOUSING CHARACTERISTICS

Regressors	Description of Regressors	Coefficients	t-Scores
X_1	Number of bedrooms	426.48	39.05
X_2	Number of other rooms	294.84	19.98
X_3	1 if dwelling sound and 0 if not sound	534.96	6.29
X_4	1 if dwelling deteriorating and 0 if not deteriorating	370.68	4.02
	($X_3 = X_4 = 0$ if dwelling dilapidated)		
X_5	1 if dwelling built in 1967-68 and 0 otherwise	783.60	14.35
X_6	1 if dwelling built in 1960-66 and 0 otherwise	394.04	17.98
X_7	1 if dwelling built in 1947-59 and 0 otherwise	334.80	11.39
	($X_5 = X_6 = X_7 = 0$ if dwelling built prior to 1947)		
X_8	1 if first-story unit in building with elevator and 0 otherwise	−467.04	−10.63
X_9	1 if second-story unit in building with elevator and 0 otherwise	−409.20	−10.86
X_{10}	1 if third-story unit in building with elevator and 0 otherwise	−347.16	−9.39
X_{11}	1 if fourth-story unit in building with elevator and 0 otherwise	−385.68	−10.54
X_{12}	1 if fifth-story unit in building with elevator and 0 otherwise	−316.80	−8.46
X_{13}	1 if sixth-story unit in building with elevator and 0 otherwise	−371.88	−9.93
	($X_8 = \ldots = X_{13} = 0$ if seventh- or higher-story unit in building with elevator)		
X_{14}	1 if first-story unit in building without elevator and 0 otherwise	−722.88	−10.30
X_{15}	1 if second-story unit in building without elevator and 0 otherwise	−826.68	−11.80
X_{16}	1 if third-story unit in building without elevator and 0 otherwise	−922.20	−12.40
X_{17}	1 if fourth-story unit in building without elevator and 0 otherwise	−923.40	−7.23
X_{18}	1 if fifth-story unit in building without elevator and 0 otherwise	−1,304.64	−8.21
X_{19}	1 if sixth-story unit in building without elevator and 0 otherwise	−1,627.08	−6.00
	($X_{14} = \ldots = X_{19} = 0$ if seventh- or higher-story unit in building without elevator)		
X_{20}	1 if located in Manhattan and 0 otherwise	1,174.80	24.00

TABLE 1 (Continued)

Regressors	Description of Regressors	Coefficients	t-Scores
X_{21} ·············	1 if located in Bronx and 0 otherwise	104.40	2.07
X_{22} ·············	1 if located in Brooklyn and 0 otherwise	173.04	3.68
X_{23} ·············	1 if located in Queens and 0 otherwise	233.76	5.05
	($X_{20} = \ldots = X_{23} = 0$ if located in Richmond)		
X_{24} ·············	1 if dwelling is in structure with 1-2 units and 0 otherwise	−234.24	−3.38
X_{25} ·············	1 if dwelling is in structure with 3-4 units and 0 otherwise	−129.49	−1.68
X_{26} ·············	1 if dwelling is in structure with 5-9 units and 0 otherwise	−78.96	−0.88
X_{27} ·············	1 if dwelling is in structure with 10-12 units and 0 otherwise	−129.24	−1.25
X_{28} ·············	1 if dwelling is in structure with 13-19 units and 0 otherwise	−290.52	−2.98
X_{29} ·············	1 if dwelling is in structure with 20-49 units and 0 otherwise	−12.96	−0.29
X_{30} ·············	1 if dwelling is in structure with 50-99 units and 0 otherwise	−122.16	−5.04
	($X_{24} = \ldots = X_{30} = 0$ if dwelling is in structure with more than 99 units)		
X_{32} ·············	Annual contract rent if apartment is furnished and 0 otherwise	0.28	12.81

Note.−Dependent variable is annual contract rent. Constant = −61.44; $R^2 = .58$; $x = 653$.

where the b's are least-squares estimators of the b's in (17).(14) Using 6,449 rental housing units on the uncontrolled market for which all the necessary data were reported, the results in table 1 were obtained.(15) For each of the 5,915 controlled dwelling units in our sample, the value of the predictor of market rent has been calculated.

EMPIRICAL RESULTS

We know the income of and rent paid by a sample of 5,915 families living in private, rental controlled housing, and we have predictions of how much each of these families would spend on housing and how much the dwelling unit that each occupies would rent for in the absence of rent control. The sample means of $P_c{}^h\ Q_c{}^h$, $P_m{}^h\ Q_c{}^h$, $P_m{}^h\ Q_m{}^h$, and Y are \$999, \$1,405, \$1,470, and \$6,229, respectively.

Using formulas (6) and (7), we estimate that as a result of rent control the occupants of controlled units consumed 4.4 percent less housing service in total and 9.9 percent more nonhousing goods.(16) Using formula (11) to estimate net benefit for each family, the mean net benefit to these families is estimated to have been \$213 during 1968. There is considerable variation around each of these estimates of central tendency. Since there were 1,266,829 families living in controlled housing in 1968, the total benefit to all of these families is estimated to have been about \$270 million. On the basis of our sample, the mean income of families occupying rent controlled housing was \$6,229, so we might reasonably say that rent control resulted in a 3.4 (=\$213/\$6,229) percent increase in their real income. The cost of rent control to the landlords of each controlled apartment is calculated using formula (12), and the mean of these costs is multiplied by the number of controlled apartments to obtain the total cost of rent control to landlords in 1968. This cost was about \$514 million.(17) Dreyfuss and Hendrickson (1968, p. 90) report that the cost of administering the rent-control law in 1968 was about \$7 million. The waste of rent control is simply the excess of the costs borne by landlords and taxpayers over the benefits received by tenants. In 1968, this waste is estimated to have been about \$251 million. These are estimates of some aggregative effects of rent control.(18)

Finally, let us consider some of the distributive effects of rent control. Though there are many rich people living in controlled housing and poor people in uncontrolled housing, table 2 clearly indicates that on average the occupants of rent-controlled apartments are poorer than the occupants of uncontrolled housing. The estimates of the standard deviations of the sample means and proportions reported in parentheses in table 2 suggest that the population parameters are extremely close to their estimates and hence that the differences of means and proportions are significant. Surprisingly, there is no significant difference in the mean age of head of household for the two groups.

We can also investigate the variation in benefits among the families in our sample occupying controlled apartments. As a concise way of presenting this variation, we estimate the following statistical relationships by the method of least squares:

$$B = -312.23 - 0.013Y + 8.63A + 68.9N + 44.34R - 29.31S \quad (20)$$
$$ (-6.48)\ (13.48)\ (10.06)\ (1.75)\ (-1.27)$$

$$R^2 = .046$$
$$s = 261$$

and

$$B/Y = -0.079 - 0.0000056Y + 0.003A + 0.0086N + 0.018R + 0.016S$$
$$(-8.19) \quad (13.8) \quad (3.66) \quad (2.06) \quad (2.05)$$
$$(21)$$
$$R^2 = .051.$$
$$s = .261$$

TABLE 2

COMPARISON OF CHARACTERISTICS OF FAMILIES IN CONTROLLED
AND UNCONTROLLED HOUSING

Characteristics	Controlled	Uncontrolled
Mean annual income	$6,223	$9,000
	(68)	(123)
Mean number of members of household	2.5	2.9
	(0.02)	(0.02)
Mean age of head of household	49	49
	(0.22)	(0.24)
Percentage of households headed by a nonwhite	20	17
	(0.005)	(0.006)
Percentage of households headed by a female	33	20
	(0.006)	(0.006)

The numbers in parentheses are t-scores. Under the usual stochastic assumptions, it is clear from (20) that it is quite likely that poorer families receive larger benefits from rent control than richer families, households headed by older persons receive benefits greater than households headed by younger persons, and larger families receive larger benefits than smaller families. Benefits vary less significantly with race and sex of the head of the household. We can be rather certain that blacks receive greater benefits than whites, but we are only moderately confident that households headed by males received larger benefits than households headed by females. A slightly different specification of the stochastic model summarizing the variation in benefit with family characteristics leads to the estimated relationship (21). The same statements can be made about the variation in the percentage increase in real income as were made about the variation in the dollar amount of benefits, except that we can be rather confident that the percentage increases in real income is less for households headed by males than for households headed by females.

Therefore, among the set of families who receive a net benefit from rent control, poorer families receive larger benefits. Furthermore, such families are overrepresented in controlled housing. In these senses, rent control achieves some of the objectives desired by supporters of the program. However, the extremely low coefficients of determination in (20) and (21) suggest a great variance in the distribution of benefits among recipient families who are identical in these five characteristics.(19) There is nothing approaching equal treatment of equals among the beneficiaries of rent control. In this sense, rent control is a very poorly focused redistribution device. Unrestricted cash grants or vouchers for particular goods would permit more equal treatment of equally situated families.

In order to make clear the basic theoretical assumptions, methods of prediction, and empirical results, some potentially important shortcomings of the approach were not mentioned in the preceding sections. The primary purpose of this section is to remedy this defect. In the process, reference will be made to the surprisingly small literature on the economics of rent control.

In this paper it has been assumed that each family is indifferent among all housing units with the same market rent. That is, it has been assumed that all of these dwellings emit the same quantity of housing service per time period. This is an enormously useful simplifying assumption. However, making this assumption precludes considering several of the possibly important sources of inefficiency often attributed to rent control. Specifically, a more detailed theory of the housing market would view housing as a vector of attributes such as space, condition, and location.(20) It has been suggested that the occupants of rent-controlled apartments are not consuming the utility-maximizing combinations of attributes given the market rents of their apartments. In particular, Friedman and Stigler (1946, pp. 15-16), Grampp (1950, pp. 431-33), Grebler (1952, pp. 471-73), and Phelps-Brown and Wiseman (1964, p. 222) argue that most occupants of controlled apartments would prefer less spacious quarters in better condition, while Grampp (1950, pp. 430-31) recognizes that some would prefer lower-quality, larger apartments. Furthermore, it seems likely that many of these families would prefer to live in housing with the same market rent at a different location. As Friedman and Stigler (1946, p. 15), Grampp (1950, pp. 440-41), Paish (1950, p. 7), Turvey (1957, pp. 43-44), and Phelps-Brown and Wiseman (1964, pp. 225-26) point out, rent control creates incentives for people to continue to occupy their controlled apartments even though their places of work change and to reject otherwise preferable jobs far from their present locations. The simple theoretical model of the housing market used in this paper led me to ignore the distorting effect of rent control on the combination of housing characteristics consumed. This is to say that my index of quantity of housing service has the same defect as any index number.(21) As a result, net tenant benefit has probably been overestimated and waste underestimated.

Another source of bias in the same direction stems from the assumption that the controlled rent measures the cost of housing to the occupant of a controlled apartment. In fact, the cost is likely to be higher for several reasons. First, bribes and similar methods are often used by a tenant to gain possession of a controlled apartment (Grampp 1950, p. 437). Although these practices are illegal in New York City (New York Rent and Rehabilitation Administration, 1965), there is reason to believe that they occur with some frequency. Second, the time spent searching for an apartment in New York City is probably greater as a result of rent control not only for people who eventually obtain a controlled apartment but also for those who try without success. Third, as Grampp (1950, p. 438) points out, some occupants of controlled housing will find it advantageous to spend money upgrading their apartments. All of these arguments suggest that many occupants of controlled apartments have less to spend on nonhousing goods than my numbers indicate. Hence, the increase in consumption of nonhousing goods has probably been overestimated and for this reason so has net tenant benefit. Some of the extra housing expenditures are transfer payments and have no effect on my estimate of waste. However, at least the greater search costs are real and imply that my estimate of waste is too low. To the extent that these transfer payments accrue to landlords, the cost of rent control to this group has been overstated.

Let us now consider the effect of rent control on the technical efficiency with which housing service is produced in the controlled sector. Paish (1950, pp. 6-7), Grampp (1950, pp. 438-39), Turvey (1957, p. 44), Phelps-Brown and Wiseman (1964, p. 223), and Needleman (1965, p. 164) suggest that, since the landlord's revenue from his rent-controlled apartment is independent of its condition, landlords will not invest in maintenance. Hence, rent-controlled housing will deteriorate faster than it would in the absence of rent control. These authors fail to draw what in my opinion is a potentially important conclusion from this argument, namely, that the cost of producing a unit of housing service in a controlled apartment will be higher than the cost of producing a unit in the uncontrolled market. The argument is as follows. From the viewpoint of technical efficiency in the production of housing service, there is an optimal path of deterioration for each dwelling. The operation of a competitive housing market results in the attainment of this optimal path. Rent control results in a faster-than-optimal rate of deterioration. Therefore, rent control results in a higher unit cost of producing housing service in the controlled market. In this paper, it has been assumed that the unit cost of production is the same in the controlled and uncontrolled sectors of the housing market. If the conclusion to the preceding argument is correct, then the cost to the landlord has been underestimated as has the waste due to rent control. It should be noted that the rent-control law in New York City (New York Rent and Rehabilitation Administration 1965) contains many penalties and some rewards to induce the landlord to maintain his controlled apartments. Therefore, we cannot say a priori that controlled housing deteriorates more rapidly than it would in the absence of rent control. However, if rent control has any effect on the rate of deterioration, then the preceding argument need be changed only slightly to reach the same conclusion.

In addition, it seems quite likely that the cost of producing housing service in the uncontrolled market is higher than it would have been had rent control been terminated in New York City shortly after the Second World War. The existence of rent control in New York City probably makes the owners of uncontrolled rental housing sensitive to the possibility of changes in the rent-control law which would inflict capital losses on them. Indeed, in 1969 a mild form of rent control was extended to more than half of the then-uncontrolled rental stock. In other housing markets where rent control was terminated fifteen to twenty years earlier, it is doubtful that landlords attach a very high probability to the imposition of rent control. Therefore, it is reasonable to expect that investors in rental housing in New York City will demand and receive a higher-risk premium. If this argument is correct, then contrary to one of the assumptions underlying the empirical results in this paper, the long-run supply price of housing service in the uncontrolled market in 1968 was greater than it would have been had rent control never gone into effect in New York City. This implies that the occupants of uncontrolled housing were worse off than they would have been in the absence of rent control. It also implies that my predictor of the market rent of controlled housing is biased upward. Hence, the reduction in housing consumption is greater than estimated and net tenant benefit has been overestimated. Likewise, the cost of rent control to landlords has been overestimated. The net effect of this shortcoming on the estimate of waste cannot be determined a priori.

All of these omitted considerations lead me to believe that the aggregate reduction in the consumption of housing service was more than 4.4 percent, that the aggregate increase in consumption of nonhousing service was less than 9.9 percent, that mean net tenant benefit was less than $213, that the total cost to landlords was slightly less than $514 million, and that total waste was more than $251 million. Furthermore, it seems reasonable to conclude that rent control has imposed costs on occupants of uncontrolled apartments.

One of the primary arguments used in behalf of rent control is that landlords are richer than tenants and hence rent control has a desirable redistributive effect. However, if rent control applies to all rental housing in a large area, it is doubtful that the landlords are significantly richer than their tenants. In the only empirical study of this question, Johnson (1951, p. 582) concludes, "I do not want to argue that the evidence presented indicates that landlords are poorer than tenants. But the data certainly do not indicate the contrary—that landlords have significantly higher incomes than tenants. Thus, if one of the objectives of rent control is to aid low-income people—and I can find no other important objective that rent control does achieve—it does not achieve that objective. Undoubtedly, there are relatively poor tenants renting from relatively rich landlords, but the converse must also exist." It is more likely that landlords were richer than tenants in New York City in 1968 than throughout the United States during and immediately after the Second World War, because less than half of all dwellings in New York City were subject to rent control in 1968 and the occupants of these dwellings had a mean income significantly less than the mean income of all families in the city. Unfortunately, the New York City Housing and Vacancy Survey did not collect information that would permit one to relate the costs imposed on landlords by rent control to their characteristics.

Finally, my results show that, among equally situated beneficiaries, benefits are far from equally distributed. If we recognize that for any set of family characteristics there were many families living in uncontrolled housing who received no benefits and perhaps incurred slight costs and a few landlords who incurred large losses from rent control, then we must recognize that the variance of net benefits holding family characteristics constant is probably greatly underestimated by the estimated variance of the error terms in the stochastic models underlying (20) and (21). Thus, expanding our consideration of redistributive effects to the entire population of New York City only reinforces our earlier conclusion. That rent control produces a highly random redistribution of wealth has been suggested by Grampp (1950, p. 447), Paish (1950, p. 4), Johnson (1951, p. 569), Phelps-Brown and Wiseman (1964, pp. 224-25), Needleman (1965, pp. 162-63), and Lindbeck (1967, p. 64).

NOTES

(1) To many American economists, rent control is but a dim memory. It had ended in most parts of the United States by 1951. However, in the rest of the world it is still very much alive. For example, rent controls covered about

one-half of privately rented dwellings in Britain in 1964 (Needleman 1965, p. 165), one-third of all dwelling units in Sweden in 1960 and probably a similar proportion in 1965 (Stahl 1967, p. 74), and 18 percent of the population of Mexico City in 1964 (Aaron 1966, pp. 316-17). Even in the United States, there were 1.3 million rent-controlled apartments in New York City in 1968 and only 0.7 million federal public-housing units in the entire country (U.S. Bureau of the Census 1970, p. 682). Furthermore, rent control is making a comeback in the United States. In 1969 Boston and Hartford implemented mild forms of rent control while New York City placed an additional 375,000 apartments under a rent-control law less severe than that applied to previously controlled apartments (Fenton 1969, p. 21; Shipler 1970, p. 35).

(2) This assumption is consistent with the finding of Muth (1960, pp. 42-46), but de Leeuw and Ekanem (1971, p. 814) find price elasticities of long-run supply between 0.3 and 0.7.

(3) Muth (1960) has developed and tested a competitive theory of the housing market using this definition of housing service.

(4) All moving costs are compensated for separately.

(5) The ideal way to estimate net tenant benefit is by reference to an indifference map estimated with data on individual responses to differences in prices and income. This approach is not used in this paper for several reasons. First, there is no published estimate of an indifference map in which the two arguments are housing service and nonhousing goods. Second, it is not possible to infer the parameters of such an indifference map from published estimates of the parameters of demand and expenditure functions in a way which permits the use of available data to estimate benefits. De Salvo (1971) has made such inferences, but his formula for measuring benefits requires a measure of permanent income and my data contain no such information. Third, an indifference map cannot be estimated using my data. Fourth, to produce estimates of the parameters of the desired indifference map using another body of data is to produce another paper. Although we do not have an estimated indifference map, we do have other information about consumer behavior, such as the demand curve D holding money income and the price of nonhousing goods constant. This curve permits the use of Marshallian consumer's surplus analysis to produce a formula for measuring net tenant benefit which is an approximation to the formula that would be obtained from an estimated indifference map. The sense in which it is an approximation has been investigated by a number of economists, including Hicks (1943).

(6) Of course, I realize that these findings refer to aggregate demand curves and that an aggregate demand curve with constant price elasticity equal to 1 does not imply that each family's demand curve has unitary price elasticity. Indeed, I expect otherwise. For this reason, the estimate of the benefit to most families will err. Some estimates will be too high; others too low. Since even my discussion of distribution is only concerned with averages, this source of error is likely to be unimportant.

(7) $\int_{Q_m}^{hQ_c^h} D = \int_{Q_m}^{hQ_c^h} P_m^\lambda Q_m^\lambda / Q^\lambda = P_m^\lambda Q_m^\lambda [\ln Q_c^\lambda - \ln Q_m^\lambda]$

$\qquad = P_m^\lambda Q_m^\lambda [\ln P_m^\lambda Q_c^\lambda - \ln P_m^\lambda Q_m^\lambda].$

(8) This is a consumer's surplus estimator of mean benefit. It differs from a

consumers' surplus estimator obtained by substituting the sample means of $P_m{}^h Q_m{}^h$, $P_c{}^h Q_c{}^h$, and $P_m{}^h Q_c{}^h$ into formula (11). In principle, we want a consumer's surplus estimate, but in practice we must often settle for a consumers' surplus estimate because only aggregate data are available. Fortunately, data on individuals are available for this study.

(9) Even if the controlled rent of an apartment is below its market rent, it does not follow that the present owner has been made worse off by the implementation of the rent-control law. For, suppose that the present owner bought the building in which the apartment is located while rent control was in effect and that at the time of the sale both the present owner and the previous owner correctly foresaw the future course of rent control. In this case, the purchase price of the building must have been just low enough so that the present owner could make a competitive rate of return on his investment. Otherwise, the present owner would have invested his money elsewhere. Thus, the cost calculated by formula (12) which shows up this period was actually incurred by previous owners. Of course, this argument is consistent with the present owner preferring decontrol to a continuation of controls.

(10) Again, this is not the same as substituting the sample means of $P_m{}^h Q_m{}^h$, $P_c{}^h Q_c{}^h$, $P_m{}^h Q_c{}^h$, and A into formula (13) (see n. 8 above).

(11) A description of the sample design and an enumeration schedule containing the questions asked may be obtained from the U.S. Bureau of the Census.

(12) This is not an unbiased predictor of either the conditional mean or the conditional median of the random variable $P_m{}^h Q_m{}^h$. However, because of the large sample size, the mean of the predictor is probably quite close to the conditional median of housing expenditure. The conditional mean of $P_m{}^h Q_m{}^h$ is probably about 6 percent greater than the conditional mean of my predictor. On these elusive matters, see Goldberger (1968).

(13) It has been suggested that my estimate of the income elasticity is extraordinarily low. My estimate is low compared with estimates from studies in which the income variable is permanent income. However, my income variable is current income, and we expect the current income elasticity to be less than the permanent income elasticity.

(14) Larry Orr and James Stucker have pointed out quite correctly that the variable X_{31} is correlated with the error term in (17). As a result, the $\hat{b}$'s are biased estimators of the b's and hence the expected value of the predictor is not equal to the expected value of the random variable. I believe that the bias is small, but superior predictions could be obtained by estimating separate relationships for furnished and unfurnished apartments.

(15) For a more detailed analysis of housing expenditure and market rent functions based on data from the 1968 New York City Housing and Vacancy Survey, see DeSalvo (1970b).

(16) Had an estimate of the conditional mean rather than the conditional median of housing expenditure been used to predict how much each family would have spent on housing in the absence of rent control, the conclusions would have been that occupants of controlled apartments consumed 10.2 percent less housing service in total and 11.7 percent more nonhousing goods (see n. 12 above).

(17) Grampp (1950, p. 436) estimated that the cost of rent control to

landlords throughout the United States in 1947 was roughly $3.87 billion.

(18) The consumers' surplus estimate of mean net tenant benefit is $405, of total benefit is about $513.1 million, and of waste is about $7.9 million. Thus, the use of aggregate data can result in large errors in estimating the benefits and waste from government programs that do not simply reduce the price of a good from some one level to some other level for all subsidized families (see n. 8 above).

(19) This characteristic of rent control was hypothesized two decades ago by Johnson (1951, p. 569), who said, "If rent control has been effective in reducing rents, there has been a transfer of real income from landlords to tenants where rents have been controlled. This transfer has been an indiscriminate one, made without regard to the income position of individual tenants." However, there are at least two other factors which contribute to the low coefficient of determination. First, the functional form selected might be far from the mark. Second, even if all of the original data are measured without error, the derived magnitude, net tenant benefit, contains an error component. Therefore, the error term in the regression of estimated net tenant benefit on family characteristics is the sum of the error term in the underlying relationship between net tenant benefit and family characteristics and the error component in the estimation of net tenant benefit. Hence, the variance of the error term in the underlying relationship has probably been overestimated for this reason.

(20) De Salvo (1970a, pp. 6-12) has elaborated the relationship between such a theory and the theory of this paper.

(21) Muth (1960, p. 32) recognized this index number problem; Baumol (1965, pp. 202-5) lucidly explains the problem in the general case.

REFERENCES

Aaron, Henry. "Rent Controls and Urban Development: A Case Study of Mexico City." Soc. and Econ. Studies 15 (December 1966): 314-28.

Baumol, William J. Economic Theory and Operations Analysis. 2d ed. Englewood Cliffs, N.J.: Prentice-Hall, 1965.

de Leeuw, Frank. "The Demand for Housing: A Review of Cross-Section Evidence." Rev. Econ. and Statis. 53 (February 1971): 1-10.

de Leeuw, Frank, and Ekanem, Nkanta F. "The Supply of Rental Housing." A.E.R. 61 (December 1971): 806-17.

DeSalvo, Joseph S. "A Methodology for Evaluating Housing Programs." P-4364. Santa Monica, Calif.: RAND Corp., 1970. (a)

DeSalvo, Joseph S. "Reforming Rent Control in New York City: Analysis of Housing Expenditures and Market Rentals." Papers and Proc. Regional Sci. Assoc. 27 (1970): 195-227. (b)

DeSalvo, Joseph S. "A Methodology for Evaluating Housing Programs." J. Regional Sci. 11 (August 1971): 173-85.

Dreyfuss, David, and Hendrickson, Joan. A Guide to Government Activities in New York City's Housing Markets. RM-5673-NYC. Santa Monica, Calif.: RAND Corp., 1968.

Fenton, John H. "Boston Returns to Modified Form of Rent Control." New York Times, November 22, 1969, p. 21.

Friedman, Milton, and Stigler, George. Roofs or Ceilings? Irvington-On-Hudson,

N.Y.: Found. Econ. Educ., Inc., 1946.

Goldberger, Arthur S. "The Interpretation and Estimation of Cobb-Douglas Functions." Econometrica 35 (July-October 1968): 464-72.

Grampp, William D. "Some Effects of Rent Control." Southern Econ. J. 16 (April 1950): 425-47.

Grebler, Leo. "Implications of Rent Control—Experience in the United States." Internat. Labour Rev. 65 (April 1952): 462-85.

Hicks, John R. "The Four Consumer Surpluses." Rev. Economic Studies 11 (1943): 31-41.

Johnson, D. Gale. "Rent Control and the Distribution of Income." A.E.R. 41 (May 1951): 569-82.

Lee, Tong Hun. "The Stock Demand Elasticities of Non-Farm Housing." Rev. Econ. and Statis. 46 (February 1964): 82-89.

Lindbeck, Assar. "Rent Control as an Instrument of Housing Policy." In The Economic Problems of Housing, edited by Adela Adam Nevitt. London: Macmillan, 1967.

Muth, Richard F. "The Demand for Non-Farm Housing." In The Demand for Durable Goods, edited by Arnold C. Harberger. Chicago: Univ. Chicago Press, 1960.

Needleman, Lionel. The Economics of Housing. London: Staples, 1965.

New York Rent and Rehabilitation Administration. The New Little Book on Rent Control. New York: New York Rent and Rehabilitation Admin., 1965.

Paish, F.W. "The Economics of Rent Restriction." Lloyd's Bank Rev. 16 (April 1950): 1-17.

Phelps-Brown, E.H., and Wiseman, J. A Course in Applied Economics. 2d ed. London: Pitman & Sons, 1964.

Reid, Margaret G. Housing and Income. Chicago: Univ. Chicago Press, 1962.

Shipler, David K. "Cry for Rent Control Grows." New York Times, January 12, 1970, p. 35.

Stahl, Ingemar. "Some Aspects of a Mixed Housing Market." In The Economic Problems of Housing, edited by Adela Adam Nevitt. London: Macmillan, 1967.

Turvey, Ralph. The Economics of Real Property. London: George Allen & Unwin, 1957.

U.S. Bureau of the Census. Statistical Abstract of the United States: 1970. 91st ed. Washington: Government Printing Office, 1970.

DEMAND AND MARKET FOR HOUSING:
THE BALANCE OF THE DECADE

by James C. Downs, Jr.

Housing is one of the most thoroughly misunderstood, the the most exaggerated and the most deliberately lied-about topics of public discussion in the United States. The common confusion over housing has been contributed to by a wide variety of groups:

By the *government*, in the preambles to a series of landmark legislative actions taken by the Congress beginning with the Housing Act of 1948. These so-called Housing Acts have often been prefaced or followed by Presidential proclamations and departmental pronouncements promising an early solution to the problem by envisaging their prompt implementation. Yet the Congress has seldom backed up its own bills by appropriating sufficient funds to carry out their provisions. The most recent example of this was the Housing and Urban Development Act of 1968, with its reaffirmation of previously adopted goals of "a decent home and suitable environment for every American family" and its determination that this goal could "be substantially achieved within the next decade by the construction or rehabilitation of 26 million housing units—6 million of these for low and moderate income families."

By *social planners*, who for decades have upheld good quality housing units as a cure-all for the nation's social ills, even though the broadening experience with their initial dream (public housing) has exploded it as a cruel myth. The truth is that social planners do not really address themselves to social planning, but instead suffer from the illusion that physical planning will somehow produce beneficial social consequences.

By many of the nation's leading *demographers* whose now revealed miscalculations of the future growth of the U.S. population projected a fabulous quantitative market for housing when the population "explosion" (scheduled to have begun in the mid-sixties) was encountered.

By professional *financial analysts* who seized upon the demographers' forecasts to motivate the broad-scale, over-expectant expansion of corporations into the real estate and housing fields.

By *investment securities underwriters,* who have sold billions of dollars worth of real estate related stocks, trust certificates and limited partnerships to an always-gullible public—an eventuality which may prove in many cases to have been reminiscent of the real estate bond fiasco of the 20's.

By all manner of *political demagogues* who have been quick to seize upon the obvious ideological contradiction between our heralded affluent society and the abject misery of life in an urban or rural slum. Here too we encounter the nonsense notion that our pressing problems of crime, public health, social unrest and national well-being would be solved if every American family were to be provided with a "decent, safe and sanitary housing unit."

Little wonder then that confusion regarding housing reigns in the political arena, in legislative halls, in Administration agencies, in corporate management headquarters, in financial institutions and in the securities marketplace. The overwhelming reason is that we have not faced squarely the complex factors which enter into an understanding of the breadth and depth of the problem.

"DEMAND" AND THE "MARKET"

There are three elements of demand to be considered: the *political* demand, the *demographic* demand and the *"effective"* or *market* demand and each of these requires separate consideration.

In the political demand for housing, reference is made to the broad definition of the word "political" as being "Of, belonging, or pertaining to the state or body of citizens, its government and policy, especially in civil and secular affairs."

As a practical matter, the subject of housing was not *really* of concern to the government of the United States until the great depression of the years 1929-1933. Prior to that time—dating from about the mid-19th century—concerns for public health in certain European countries and in some of the more populous communities and states in our own country had produced collateral interest in housing laws and codes. Avantgarde social planners had embraced the issue of housing and were urging government activity in the field, but their efforts were largely unheeded from the point of view of actual government activity.

Characteristic of its traditional attitudes, it was not socially-motivated, but rather economically-motivated concerns that actually brought the Federal Government into the field of housing. The basic propellant of the U.S. government in its establishment of the Federal Home Loan Bank in 1932, the Home Owners Loan Corporation in 1933, the Public Works Administration housing construction in 1934 and the Federal Housing Administration in 1937 was *purely economic.* The government was interested in two primary objectives: first to rescue real estate from financial collapse and second, to stimulate construction as a recovery measure.

While it is true that broader political objectives were served by the creation of the Veterans Administration and the passage of extensive housing legislation in the period between the depression and the present time, *housing, per se, has not emerged as a really potent national political issue.* In the core cities of a number of our major metropolitan areas one would be led to believe (from the space and time devoted to the subject by the local media) that the issue was "red hot" as a practical political fact. But the truth is that even in these areas, many politicians have been elected through sponsorship of anti-housing measures; few (if any) have been swept into office by the clamor for housing.

There are several reasons why housing is not a major political issue, either on the local or national front. The most significant one is that the *majority* of the electorate in the United States—on both the national and local level—*are housed to their own satisfaction.* A whole host of other issues are assigned *higher priorities* by citizens who are becoming much more conscious of the scarcity of local resources.

Even though many politicians do not realize it, housing when viewed realistically cannot be *isolated* as a significant national problem. Basically, housing is merely *one facet* of the *real* national problem of poverty.

POVERTY IN THE UNITED STATES

The traditional attitude of the average American is that *poverty simply doesn't exist.* Long before John Kenneth Galbraith wrote his famous book on the subject, this average American was convinced that ours was indeed an *Affluent Society.* The "streets of gold" tale which generations of immigrants told their relatives at home is still a part of the lore of the nation. Michael Harrington's significant book on poverty, interestingly titled *The "Other" America,* never hit the best seller list. And in spite of President Johnson's "war on poverty" program and the lugubrious statistics of the government itself, the electorate just doesn't buy the notion of poverty within the U.S.

An added factor in the denial of poverty is to be found in the refusal of virtually everyone (including officials, functionaries and planners) to recognize the nature of our sub-culture of poverty people and the facts of their life styles. It offends our "liberal" sensitivities to admit that our cities contain a hard core of residents who simply do not have the desire and capability to properly inhabit and care for a standard unit of housing. We just do not face up to the fact that these particular hard core poverty families require massive and pervasive social therapy. It should be noted that there are thousands of poor people of all races and nationalities who cannot be included in this hard core group.

Inasmuch as we do not acknowledge both the *facts* and the *inevitability* of poverty (approximately 10% of our potential labor force is incapable of employment; for them poverty is inevitable unless they are supported from some source), it seems obvious that it would somehow be "un-American" to design housing suitable for poverty families. Again we cling to unattainable ideological goals which envisage housing standards that are purely sentimental. Rather than compromise with those completely unattainable objectives, we consign our poor to rat-infested, dangerous and unsafe slums.

Perhaps the most exciting city in the world from the point of view of the housing of the poor is Hong Kong. Here there is no denial of poverty; no lack of awareness of its terrible contrasts; no unwillingness to attack the problem on a practical, meaningful basis. Chinese refugees from mainland China come to Hong Kong penniless. Their initial housing is a miscellany of makeshift shacks—on the hillsides, on roofs as squatters, on rafts in the bay. In spite of the callousness of the fact that there is no public welfare, the government and the people of Hong Kong are deeply conscious of the pressing demand to do something about the housing of the poor. But—unlike Americans—they have not sought to provide units out of *House Beautiful,* nor have they set standards based upon some notion of middle-class mores. Instead, they have designed and built thousands of housing units for families in various stages of poverty. In the first stage these families get one single room, with concrete walls, no private plumbing or cooking accommodations (which are provided in common facilities) and no amenities. But these single rooms are infinitely superior to the shacks from every point of view, and their cost is $3 per week. Moreover, there are more rungs to the ladder of housing progress—still for the poor.

HUMAN REHABILITATION

In the United States this year some 450,000 families will voluntarily buy so-called "mobile" homes without subsidies. The use of the term "mobile" is part of the American housing fiction. In most cases these housing units are hauled to a given location, put on foundations, hooked up to utilities and located permanently. The anomaly is that these houses—by our false official standards—are *not good enough* to be provided for the poor.

At this time there is no evidence that the U.S. will really address itself to the housing of those poverty groups from which the major political pressures arise, i.e., the poor blacks, Chicanos, Puerto Ricans, Indians and Appalachian whites (in mentioning the groups specifically we wish to emphasize that we are referring to a minority of those in each who are victims of the special kind of poverty we have described). It is in the areas occupied by these groups that thousands of buildings have been abandoned, vandalized and burned out. It is in these areas that both public and private agencies have hopefully rehabilitated rundown buildings, only to find them torn up and destroyed or gutted within very short periods. It is these families that present a dilemma to public officials, welfare agencies and police. It is these groups that are being shunted—as a last resort—into public housing where their concentrated presence poses a virtually insoluble prlblem, as it has in St. Louis' famed Pruitt Igoe project, for which there is no apparent solution except demolition. This problem cannot be solved until it is recognized that housing is not an answer in and of itself. Human rehabilitation must take precedence over physical structure rehabilitation.

For example, one of the perils of slum living is the exposure to rat-bite. A massive rodent control project was undertaken as part of Chicago's poverty program. Teams were sent out to exterminate, seal up rat holes and collect garbage, in the process attempting to eliminate everything which might support the presence of the rats, especially exposed food. But it was learned that in the life style of the typical hard-core slum family, when a meal is completed everything is left on the table until it is time for the next meal, a fortuitous practice for rats. Obviously the next step was to undertake a program of housekeeping education for the families involved. On an experimental basis it was found that meaningful results could be obtained only if one social worker was assigned to each two or three families for long periods of time—if habits of a lifetime were to be changed. The program can work, but it requires a greater allocation of resources than our country is willing (or perhaps able) to provide.

"SHELL GAME" SOCIALIZATION

Although the government is as yet unprepared to realistically face up to the problems of housing or rehabilitating the poor, political demands in the housing area are finding response in what might be called "shell game" socialization. For some time it has been predicted that the lowest third of the housing spectrum (from the point of view of the value of premises) will be socialized in the foreseeable future. In other words the government will be directly or indirectly involved in meeting all or part of the occupancy costs of individuals occupying such premises. At present, moves in this direction embrace public housing, unit leasing, rent supplements, artificially low interest rates and other devices in which subsidy to occupants is involved. These factors are referred to as "shell game" socialization measures because they proceed largely without the knowledge of the electorate. Primarily they are responses to minority political pressures of both social and business groups, each of whom seeks special favors.

Nor will the government's activities in housing be confined to the lowest third of the housing spectrum. The current Administration (like those before it since 1932) will be interested in housing construction as a means of stimulating employment and business activity. It will seek continuously to attain its promise of 2,600,000 units a year during the balance of the decade. But its ability to perform this miracle will depend on other elements which will be discussed further on in this text.

THE DEMOGRAPHIC DEMAND FOR HOUSING

It has been observed that, generally speaking, the nation's demographers miscalculated the U.S. population "explosion" on the basis of its long-range implications for the housing industry. However, although they may not be accurate forecasters, they have only moderate problems in enumerating the numbers and ages of people already born. Thus they were quite right in their claim that "war babies" would grow up and be available to consume housing when they reached marriageable age.

Writing in the *National Market Letter* (a publication of Real Estate Research Corporation), of June 1969, Dr. Anthony Downs stated:

> U.S. fertility rates are in the midst of a steep decline from their peak levels, which were reached in 1957. The result has been a sharp drop in the number of births, the birth rate and the overall rate of population growth in the U.S. Future population growth will not be nearly as rapid as many observers have forecast in the past—or even as rapid as the Census Bureau's most conservative present estimates.

Both of these prophecies are squarely on the track of fulfillment.

Years of study indicate that the number of potential housing consumers is, at best, only a marginal clue to housing construction or consumption. The following section will disclose that such data may prove completely irrelevant in their impact on housing demand in a market-oriented society. However, it is agreed, that as socialization creeps up on the scale of the housing spectrum, the simple number of potential consumers will have more influence during the balance of this decade than it has in the past. Reason: if the government picks up the tab, a higher percentage of extant families will be economically capable of actual housing consumption.

It is believed that social mores greatly influence the impact of pure numbers of people and families on the volume and nature of housing consumption. For example, 40 years ago it was generally thought that the number of marriages celebrated in any given year was an important clue to current housing demand. But these changes in mores have invalidated that belief. Prior to 1930 it was reasonable to assume that a marriage was a *permanent* arrangement. The ratio of divorces to marriages was a negligible factor. In recent years divorces in some states are as high as 50% of current nuptials. Studies carried out by the Real Estate Research Corporation show that a higher and higher percentage of current weddings involve people who have been wed before. Given a reasonably stable marriage rate it is obvious from the above that fewer people are getting married at all. Yet—as anyone who manages a volume of urban property can attest—there are other arrangements (unwed couples and homosexual partnerships) under which housing consumers are bulking larger and larger in our society.

A major revolution in family structure is under way. Under the pressures of a materialistic society, children represent a greater and greater economic and social disadvantage as the result of their demands on two scarce resources, i.e., *money* and *time*. At the same time couples in the reproductive ages can more easily and effectively prevent conception without suffering guilt. In consequence, a higher percentage of marriages will be childless and average families will be much smaller. The impact of these trends upon housing is obvious.

The most significant demographic developments in the balance of the decade will relate more closely to *changes* in the population than *gains*. The demands for new housing will arise principally out of social obsolescence of existing accommodations and the relocation of population. Growth will be a declining factor.

"EFFECTIVE" DEMAND AND THE MARKET FOR HOUSING

No one talks about a "food shortage" in the United States, but there is substantial evidence that many people suffer from malnutrition, and some from actual hunger. There are thousands more people who *should* eat well than *do* eat well. No one talks about a "clothing shortage" in our country in spite of the fact that thousands of families are improperly clad and some are virtually in rags. Yet everyone talks about a "housing shortage" as though housing is unique as the only good that is not available in adequate supply to potential occupants.

The fact is that there never was a time in the history of the United States (or any other country, for that matter) when there were as many standard housing units available for occupancy as families requiring shelter. In other words, there has always been a "shortage" of housing in a technical quantitive sense. But it has only been in recent years that a segment of our people has seemingly ignored the fact that, in a market-oriented society, only those who have the purchasing power to acquire goods can become consumers of those goods—whether they be essentials like food and clothing or shelter.

The reason for this apparent anomaly is that the Congress and every recent administration and many governors and mayors have been loose with the truth of their promises. The difference between their veracity in housing and in such essentials as food and clothing is their almost deliberate unwillingness to face the facts of poverty. For example, the preambles to welfare legislation offer the objective of assuring every American family that it will be fed and clothed. But these preambles do not mean that they will be offered a diet or a wardrobe that will be up to the standards of acceptable consumption, even though such goals are far more attainable than standard housing. Instead they offer such poverty fare as is available with food stamps and poverty-standard welfare checks.

QUANTITATIVE DEMAND VERSUS QUALITATIVE RESULTS

When we talk about "effective demand" for housing in the balance of this decade we are seeking to quantify the number of families in the country who will be able to rent or buy housing *at the rentals or prices at which accommodations will be available.*

At this time there are far more families in the United States than there are housing units, yet a growing percentage of these housing units is *vacant.* The obvious reason: because of economically *qualitative* constraints, the *quantitative* demand is prevented from actual satisfaction.

There have been only three periods in this century when economic conditions have created an "actual" (as distinguished from "technical") *shortage* of housing, i.e., when there were some families *economically capable* of consuming a rented or purchased housing unit than there were extant units. These periods were from 1921 through 1927, and from 1941 through 1957 and from 1965 through 1969. These were periods when, from a practical point of view, there was *no vacancy* in the typical U.S. community. In other words, there were more able-to-rent and able-to-buy families than there were available accommodations in the entire category.

Ordinarily, only a war can create such a condition. World War I was responsible for the 1921-1927 shortage of housing, and World War II caused the 1941-1957 scarcity. The 1965-1969 period of virtual 100% residential occupancy was a unique "peacetime" combination of the economic stimulus of the expanding war in Viet Nam, the "guns and butter" Great Society program and the "man on the moon" NASA effort. The impact of these three simultaneous massive spending surges was enough to economically *simulate* a major war.

The prime elements of an "actual" housing shortage are 1. A rapid rise in new jobs to where "full employment" is attained; 2. A sharp increase in urbanization caused by the lure of those jobs, and 3. A cessation or a meaningful decrease in the creation of new housing accommodations.

It is obvious that these three elements were present in the World War I and II periods and in their immediate aftermath. Their respective post-war years saw massive demobilization of millions of men and women whose demand for housing were added to those other millions whose want-satisfactions were thwarted during the years of actual combat. It took until 1927 after World War I and to 1957 after World War II to exhaust these accumulated backlogs. Only then did vacancies reappear.

In the case of the 1965-1969 "shortage," the cutback in the creation of new housing was not as complete as it had been during the two great wars. It was not caused by government regulation or material shortages, but rather resulted from the money crunch of 1965-1967.

Three other factors contributed to its relatively short-term duration: 1. Because the "guns and butter" program did not result in any real accumulation of want-backlog, there was no momentum in the economy when the Viet Nam War wind-down occurred or when the NASA program was cut back; 2. Because Viet Nam was a "limited" war, there was no large, precipitous demobilization, and 3. The 1969-? recession saw a shrinkage in jobs and hence of gross residential demand.

INFLUENTIAL FORCES

There are other significant elements in the 1965-1969 period which have influenced the situation today: 1. The Administration's attempt to control inflation through stringent monetary policy aggravated the recession and frightened the President. He liberalized monetary policy through increased money supply. 2. During the period of the money shortage, an innovative group of securities specialists created machinery to augment mortgage financing through the creation of mortgage REITs—a fact which further increased the money supply at the end of the crunch. 3. In the period of 1963-1969 it became the "style" for profit-and-diversification-hungry corporations to hope to cash in on what appeared (as noted above) to be *the coming real estate boom*. Largely inexperienced in the field, these corporation managers undertook a massive program of investment—in the facilities of housing production, in land and in development companies. To the above money supply, they added billions of dollars. 4. As the recession advanced, the Federal Government augmented its efforts to stimulate the economy by a forced-draft program of pumping credit into the housing industry.

All of these factors produced the phenomenally "active" real estate year of 1971. Both mortgage lending and housing construction recorded not just new highs, but they exceeded all previous records by a *wide margin*.

THE HOUSING MARKET: 1972 AND FORWARD

The conclusions as to the effective housing market outlook at any given point in time are, more than anything else, based upon the raw statistics which measure the relationship of housing *demand* to housing *supply*—at least in what might be called the private sector.

What is it that creates "effective" demand for housing? It is not as has been seen, the mere physical presence of potential consumers in numbers even greater than the number of units of accommodation available. In typical communities, it is rather the number of those *potential* consumers whose current economic status makes it possible for them to become *actual* consumers in consequence of their ability to rent or purchase housing at the *prevailing level* of rents and prices.

With the overwhelming majority of families purchasing power depends on *jobs*. While it is true that an increasing percentage of our population depends upon such income sources as pensions, social security, welfare, disability benefits and the yield of accumulated wealth, these are distinctly a minor segment of the "effective" housing demand.

It has been pointed out above that the number of years of *actual shortages* of housing in this century has been limited to those periods in which the dynamism of the national economy was such as to produce *full employment*. At this time, no such condition exists. Moreover, there is an absence of either war or some unique combination of compulsive circumstances, similar to those which prevailed in the 1965-1969 period and no such condition is in prospect.

CURRENT PROSPECTS

Three facts which are pertinent to the current prospects for housing demand are these: 1. In the 31 years from 1930 to the present there have been only 13 years in which the unemployment ratio averaged less than 4% of the total labor force. These were 1943-1948 (World War II); 1951-1953 (Korean War) and 1966-1969 (Viet Nam War, augmented by the Great Society and NASA programs). 2. In the five years ended in 1969, there was an average of 1,719,000 new jobs per annum. In 1970 the number of new jobs created was 725,000, and in 1971 it appears that there may be as many as 1,000,000. 3. Even at the present level of population growth, it is estimated that the labor force is currently growing at the rate of 1,500,000 persons per year. Until employment grows at least at that rate, unemployment will increase in positive numbers, and quite possibly in rate.

But *demand* is only one side of an equation which determines the housing market. Obviously, the other side is supply, i.e., the net addition to the housing stock. In 1971, new record-level housing construction will see production of something near 2,250,000 housing units, including some 450,000 so-called "mobile" homes, which for the first time have been included in the "official" housing start figures. Of this number, it is estimated that approximately 550,000 units will have been erected on some form of initial or continuing (or both) subsidy. This is not far from our oft-voiced prediction that one-third of the housing market will be "socialized" in the foreseeable future.

In the *purely private* sector of the housing market, there is ample evidence of the fact that the supply of residential space has outrun the demand; that vacancy is increasing; that a substantial percentage of newly-created projects will be unable to support the burden of their financial obligations. This fact will result in a lowering of new housing construction in 1972, principally because lending agencies will back off from their relaxed, "full loan" commitments, so prevalent during the past 18 months.

While it is true that interest rates have declined appreciably in 1971, the costs of construction, operations and taxes have risen sufficiently to absorb the bulk of these savings. Moreover, even before rent control became effecitve, and even if it is liberalized under Phase II of the President's program, the basic markets are not strong enough to support really meaningful rent increases.

THE NET OF IT ALL

There is little likelihood that a housing "boom" of the proportions envisaged by the Government's promise of 26,000,000 units in 10 years will actually take place in the decade of the 70's. A combination of the circumstances described above relating to population growth, the national economy and the local housing markets will probably frustrate this ambition.

It is improbable that the nation will address itself to the solution of the hard core poverty housing problem in a realistic effective way, since such a massive effort (and the human rehabilitation which must accompany it) would require a greater allocation of public funds than the people are prepared to support.

It must be acknowledged that the "normal" conditions in the housing markets of the nation are neither inflationary nor deflationary. Under such "normal" conditions the capacity of the producers of housing is sufficiently great to quickly meet the "effective" demand. The mortgage markets are ample to finance those producers. During these periods there is no real *space scarcity*—the prime ingredient of advancing rents and prices. Instead, we experience what appraisers have always called "normal" vacancy.

If the Viet Nam War is actually concluded and not replaced by another major military involvement, the housing markets in the balance of the 70's will lapse into such a "normal" situation. If the war on inflation is won, there may even be some short-run, traditional deflationary debt liquidation.

James C. Downs, Jr. is founder, Chairman of the Board and Chief Executive Officer of Real Estate Research Corporation, real estate economists and urban analysts. He has been housing consultant to three Mayors of Chicago over a span of more than 25 years and has served as that city's Housing and Redevelopment Coordinator under Mayors Kennelly and Daley. Mr. Downs is presently and has been President of the Chicago Dwellings Association (Chicago's official not-for-profit housing agency) since its founding in 1947. Mr. Downs has written and lectured extensively on the subject of housing before academic, professional, corporate, trade association and government groups.

THE MOBILE HOME MARKET

Shiefman, Werba, and Associates

Very little actual fact has been accumulated about the mobile home market and at present there are only two hard figures in the entire field: the number of mobile home *shipments* (not sales) and the *occupied inventory*. The latter figure is available only every ten years. The following study has resulted in a number of conclusions which appear to be contrary to the generally accepted views regarding the mobile home.

GENERAL INFORMATION

Replacements for units removed from the existing occupied stock account for a large share of mobile home sales. Approximately one-third of 1971 through 1975 sales are expected to come from the replacement market. This is roughly equal to the long-term ratio of replacement market to total market in conventional housing. The average life of a mobile home before removal or conversion to other uses is 15 years. This short life cycle applies to housing uses only while the life span in other uses (e.g., hunting cabins) may be extended.

The depreciation experience of mobile homes is more *favorable* than even most industry sources have claimed. A sampling of the resale prices in the Judy-Berner Blue Book (the industry standard) shows that wholesale values of major brand mobile homes depreciate an average of 10% the first year, 5% the following year, and a total of 45% in eight years. Even after 15 years, when most units will be discarded as year-round housing, mobile homes still retain considerable resale value—between 20% and 35% of original cost. (The rule of thumb which has been accepted by most lenders and dealers is that depreciation is 50% in five years.)

This favorable depreciation trend reflects in part the high rate of inflation of recent years. But even when restated in constant dollars, the trend is more favorable than industry sources have claimed. Blue book prices are conservative. Standard lender practice on sale of used mobile homes is to finance 115% of blue book value.

There is no shortage of existing home parks, except in local and specific cases. On the contrary, many areas are overbuilt and overbuilding seems certain to increase. The overall vacancy rate in new parks is close to 40% and it is over two-thirds in California and Arizona.

The number of park spaces absorbed by the market has never been as high as 25% of the number of mobile home shipments in any one year, nor much over 40% of the net increase in mobile home households in any one year. Only some 55% of the mobile homes occupied as year-round housing are located in parks. And the park share of the occupied stock appears to be declining.

NEW FORMAT: SUBDIVISIONS

Subdivisions represent a growing trend, although still a minute share of all mobile home sites. The mobile homeowner owns his site and puts down permanent footings. The package of mobile home and lot may be purchased with standard mortgage financing and is taxed as real property. Most of these lots are in parks, with a management providing standard park services for a fee.

The mobile homeowner buys a way of life rather than physical housing. He accepts a downgrading in standards of housing and privacy in exchange for involved community living of a kind that is now rare in conventional housing.

The total cost of possession of the average mobile home is somewhat less than for the lowest-rent new apartment and significantly less than the lowest-cost new house available today without subsidy. But there are many areas where mobile homes do not have any price competition because homes and apartments in the lowest price bracket are not available.

Much of the cost advantage mobile homes enjoy is due to their lesser tax burden. In a typical metropolitan area, mobile homes have a $20 a month tax advantage over low-rent apartments and $35 a month over low-price homes. But taxing mobile homes as real property, as now done in Minnesota, Indiana and on mobile home subdivisions in most states, would add less than $5 a month to the average mobile unit's tax load.

Zoning for mobile homes has not opened up in areas where they are taxed as real property, as some industry spokesmen have contended they would.

The measure of effective housing demand in any time period is the net increase in households. The net increase in mobile home households has averaged approximately 19% of the net increase in all households since 1969 and is expected to hold at this level or very slightly higher through 1975.

Other popular comparisons of mobile home and conventional housing production are believed to be less meaningful. These have included the mobile home share of one-family home starts (a high of 34% in 1969, roughly 28% in 1971) and the mobile home share of homes under $15,000 (virtually 100%) and mobile share of homes under $20,000 (roughly 65% in 1969, 60% in 1971).

It is felt that the market for mobile homes will increase gradually over the 470,000 shipments projected for 1971 to possibly 537,000 by 1975. The increase should be related to the growth of the replacement market (that is, the rate of removals) and to the increase in households in the 20-to-35 and 55-to-75 age groups. After 1975, the rate of increase in 20-to-35 age households, which provide nearly 50% of mobile home buyers, will begin to taper off.

Simultaneously, the trend of increasing concentration in mobile home manufacture is expected to continue. In 1970, ten manufacturers accounted for nearly 50% of units shipped, while in 1966, twelve concerns accounted for a slightly smaller share. A parallel trend is increasing vertical integration, with major manufacturers acquiring capabilities to make more and more of their components. Many mobile home manufacturers are now also in modular housing and vice versa.

Other observers have cited a number of factors which they regard as potential stimulants or depressants for the mobile home market. However, within this study it is believed that the factors cited below will *not* significantly affect the market.

Housing Subsidies. Most of the lower-income families eligible for such subsidies consider mobile homes unacceptable and substandard housing, whether in parks or on city lots. This is especially true of black families. At the same time most mobile home owners have incomes too high to be eligible for FHA subsidy programs.

Modular Competition. Mobile homes are being used in many applications: farm and rural housing, vacation homes, mobile home subdivisions—where modular housing would be appropriate. Again, double-wide mobile homes (two 12-wide or 14-wide units which are combined into one unit on the site) have been substituted in a number of urban projects where modular housing was originally contemplated, and have been stacked several stories high.

By the end of the decade, many double-wides and modules may be indistinguishable in manufacturing source, in structure and appearance, except for wheels and hitch.

Despite the increasing overlap it is believed that mobile homes and modules will *not* invade one another's market to any significant degree. In the rural market mobiles still have, and for the foreseeable future will retain, great advantages in cost and mobility. In park communities the appearance of mobility, even if it will never be tested, remains a necessary component of the total complex of mobile home living which rather than a housing unit, is what the buyer pays for.

Double-wides may have one advantage in conventional housing applications. Housing codes which bar modules often permit mobile homes because of the convenient legal fiction that they are vehicles. But this advantage is vanishing as more codes are being revised to permit modules.

OTHER INFLUENTIAL FACTORS: A STANDOFF

Three other factors will have a marginal effect on mobile home demand but will tend to cancel each other out and leave the market still defined by the population and replacement curves: 1. The expected withdrawal of homebuilders (for the second time) from the $20,000-and-under market currently being served by quadrominiums, townhouses and zero lotline developments. 2. The scheduled great increase in Farms Home Administration

TABLE 1

DATA ON MOBILE HOME STOCK

A. Census Data	Occupied Stock	Annual Avg. % Chg.	Shipments	Additions to Vacancies, Dealer Inventories, Removals & Conversions	Net Increase
Census 1950	315,200				
1950-60			966,200	514,800	541,400
Census 1960	766,600	8.3%			
1960-70			2,059,000	977,900	1,081,100
Census 1970	1,847,700	8.3%			

B. Annual Data	Occupied Stock	% Chg.	Estimated Vacancies	Shipments	% Chg.
1959	709,000		25,700	120,500	
1960	766,600	8.1%	27,800	103,700	-13.9%
1961	810,700	5.8%	29,400	90,200	-13.0%
1962	838,700	3.5%	30,400	118,000	30.8%
1963	883,300	5.3%	32,000	150,800	27.8%
1964	955,900	8.2%	34,700	191,300	26.9%
1965	1,061,600	11.1%	38,500	216,500	13.2%
1966	1,182,000	11.3%	42,900	217,300	0
1967	1,291,400	9.3%	46,800	240,400	10.6%
1968	1,412,900	9.4%	51,200	317,900	32.2%
1969	1,592,700	12.7%	57,800	412,700	29.8%
1970	1,847,700	16.0%	67,000	401,200	-2.8%

C. Projected:

	Occupied Stock	% Chg.	Estimated Vacancies	Shipments	% Chg.
1971	2,073,400	12.2%	75,200	447,000	11.4%
1972	2,315,000	11.6%	84,000	478,500	7.0%
1973	2,574,000	11.2%	93,400	495,000	3.4%
1974	2,840,000	10.3%	103,000	517,000	4.4%
1975	3,114,000	9.6%	112,900	536,500	3.8%
1976	3,396,000	9.1%	123,100		

rural housing programs—from 48,000 units in fiscal 1970 to 170,000 in fiscal 1972. 3. The expected inroads of double-wide units on a more affluent market relatively new to mobile homes.

Each factor separately might make a difference in the market of 10,000 to 25,000 units, but the three together are felt to be inconsequential.

The mobile home market is more diversified than is generally realized. Of the 475,000 mobile home shipments which are projected for 1971, approximately 30% will go to increase the stock of mobile homes on farms or on scattered lots in rural areas and small towns. More than half of these will go into the Appalachian region, which is the nation's principal consumer of mobile homes. (In 1969, the 13 Appalachian states received 40% of the nation's mobile home shipments, and mobile home sales were highest in the mountain sections of these states.) In isolated rural areas, such as Appalachia or Maine or the cutover sections of Michigan and Wisconsin, there is no home-building industry and few new homes are built other than mobile homes. For example, a 1969 survey by the Federal Reserve Bank of Boston found that two-thirds of housing "starts" in

TABLE II

ESTIMATED DISTRIBUTION OF MOBILE HOME SHIPMENTS

Census Data	Shipments	Vacancies	Dealer Inventory	% of Shipments	Other Uses	% of Shipments	Removals & Conversions	% of Shipments	Net increase in Mobile Home Households	% of Shipments	Mobile Home Households as % of Total Increase in Households
1950-60	966,200	39,200	41,000	3.9%	159,000	7.8%	737,600	35.8%	451,400	46.7%	4.9%
1960-70	2,059,000								1,081,100	52.5%	10.4%
To:											
1959	120,500	2,100	2,600	3.9%	9,200	7.6%	49,000	40.7%	57,600	47.8%	
1960	103,700	1,600	-3,100	-1.4%	8,400	8.1%	52,700	50.8%	44,100	42.5%	6.2%
1961	90,200	1,000	-1,900	-1.0%	7,800	8.6%	55,300	61.3%	28,000	31.0%	2.5%
1962	118,000	1,600	4,000	4.8%	11,000	9.3%	56,800	48.1%	44,600	37.8%	6.9%
1963	150,800	2,700	4,700	4.9%	10,800	7.2%	60,000	39.8%	72,600	48.1%	9.5%
1964	191,300	3,800	5,800	5.0%	11,000	5.8%	65,000	34.0%	105,700	55.3%	9.0%
1965	216,500	4,400	3,500	3.7%	15,900	7.3%	72,300	33.4%	120,400	55.6%	13.2%
1966	217,300	3,900	100	1.9%	23,200	10.7%	80,700	37.1%	109,400	50.3%	14.2%
1967	240,400	4,400	3,300	3.2%	23,000	9.6%	88,200	36.7%	121,500	50.5%	8.3%
1968	317,900	6,600	11,100	5.6%	23,600	7.4%	96,800	30.4%	179,800	56.6%	12.8%
1969	412,700	9,200	13,500	5.5%	25,200	6.1%	109,800	26.6%	255,000	61.8%	22.8%
1970	401,200	8,200	-1,600	1.6%	41,200	10.3%	127,700	31.8%	225,700	56.2%	15.8%
Projected:											
1971	447,000	8,200	6,000	3.2%	43,000	9.6%	148,200	33.2%	241,600	54.0%	17.7%
1972	478,500	8,800	3,900	2.7%	45,000	9.4%	161,800	33.8%	259,000	54.1%	18.8%
1973	495,000	9,400	2,300	2.4%	47,000	9.5%	170,300	34.4%	266,000	53.7%	19.0%
1974	517,000	9,600	3,000	2.4%	49,000	9.5%	181,400	35.1%	274,000	53.0%	19.2%
1975	536,500	9,900	2,300	2.3%	51,000	9.5%	191,300	35.7%	282,000	52.6%	19.5%
1976		10,200									

For Sources and Methods, see page 310.

Maine were mobile homes. Slightly under 25% will go to increase the stock in mobile home parks. About 10% of the mobile homes will become second homes, temporary housing in disaster areas or go into commercial uses such as mobile units, temporary offices, portable schoolrooms and on-site construction offices. Some manufacturers now make special office models to serve this market. A little over 3% of the mobile homes will either go into dealer's inventories or will offset increased vacancies in the owned or rented stock.

Mobile Home Manufacturers Association (MHMA) reports on dealer inventories (discontinued after 1969) indicate that inventories are in the range of 10% to 15% of sales. Individual observer estimates have placed the ratio even higher, as high as 25% for many smaller dealers.

Mobile home vacancy rates in metropolitan areas, as indicated by local vacancy surveys, range from about 3% to 4%. Vacancies in mobile homes outside metropolitan areas are probably higher and would raise the national average to 4% or more.

Most of the vacancies are probably units offered for sale but some are also in the rental stock.

As noted previously, the largest single category, about one-third of this year's shipments, is the replacement market, offsetting units removed from the year-round housing stock.

PRICE RANGES AND MARKET SEGMENTS

The average price of a new mobile home today is $6,500, but there are many regional variations. In the Appalachian regions, the average price is under $5,000 while in the Midwest, it is $7,500 (but one Michigan observer reports 75% of homes are in the $6,000 range.) On the East Coast of Florida and in California, where the mobile home market includes many retirees, the average is between $9,000 and $10,000.

Prices on *12-wides*, which account for more than 80% of industry shipments, range from $4,500 to $10,000 and on deluxe models may go up to $12,000. *Fourteen-wides*, which are limited by the number of states which permit them to travel on highways, were up to 5% of the market in 1970, their first full year of production. Their price range is $5,500 to $10,500.

Double-wide prices start at $8,000 for a 24 x 47 with two bedrooms and two baths and go up to $15,000 for a standard 28 x 60. Prices on deluxe and custom models go over $25,000. The industry has great hopes for this category. Most of the parks built within the past two years have been designed to accommodate double-wides. Their share of the total mobile home market has grown from 4.8% in 1967 when they were first isolated as a separate category, to 8.5% in first half 1971. But the rate of increase in this share has slowed and it is now less than ½% a year. The further progress of double-wides will depend on development of a new market of relatively affluent households attracted to the mobile home life style.

Three categories, which once dominated the mobile home market, have mainly historical interest today. *Eight-wides*, the original "trailer" back in the 40's, approximates 1% of the market. Ten-wides, which represented more than a third of shipments as recently as 1966, are now under 2%. These widths are rarely used for year-round housing today.

Expandables, units with one or more sections which open out from the basic oblong after it is put in place, once had 15% of the market. Since the introduction of the double-wides, their share has dropped to 2% and the two categories together are less than 11%.

LIVE CYCLE AND REMOVALS

Prior to the 1970 Census, the rate of removals was woefully underestimated by nearly all industry observers. A 1968 MHMA estimate accepted by HUD put the number of mobile home households then at 1,800,000. But this was the number found in the 1970 Census, some 700,000 shipments later.

There is no direct information on the average life-span of a mobile home. (The Census Bureau recently undertook a study of mobile home durability for HUD, but no findings conclusive enough to publish were obtained.) However, almost no industry source estimates the life at higher than 15 years while some estimates are lower. Fifteen years appears to be the highest estimate which would be compatible with the statistics of 1960 through 1970 shipments and the 1960 and 1970 occupied inventory, and constitute the average life expectancy. Homes inside parks hold up better than the average, while those outside succumb faster. It is believed that the newer units and those meeting ANSI (American National Standards Institute) construction standards will have above-average life. The maintenance provided, climatic differences and the size of user family all appear to have some bearing. Some homes in parks are reported in good condition after 25 years.

CHANGE OF USE

Despite the high removal rate among old mobile homes, there is no equivalent of the auto graveyard or of demolition of conventional housing. Usually removal is simply a change of use for after 15 years, a mobile home still has some resale value—approximately 20% to 35% of original value. Worn-out units leave the year-round housing stock to be hauled to lakes for second homes or, if in worse shape, to be turned into sheds, fishing shacks or hunting cabins. And several industry sources report seeing abandoned mobile homes out in the woods or on farms.

There may be a saturation point in the number of old mobile homes that can be disposed of in this fashion but it probably will be several years before it is reached.

DEPRECIATION AND RESALE

The rate of depreciation reflects not only physical wear but considerable produce improvement. Most current models offer more square foot per dollar than eight years ago. Standards of construction and furnishings have risen.

The depreciation rate appears to have been more rapid until quite recently. Several industry sources and articles on financing have cited the rule of thumb that depreciation totals 50% in five years. A sampling of the Judy-Berner Blue Book indicates the true rate of depreciation in actual dollars is about half that. Even when calculated in constant dollars to eliminate effects of inflation, depreciation does not reach 50% until 6½ years.

Blue book prices are compiled from dealer's actual sales prices, which Judy-Berner Company collects on standard forms several times a year. The depreciation rate is then derived by comparing the Blue book wholesale prices with dealer's invoice. Blue book prices are conservative and standard lending practice in resales is 115% of Blue book. As recently as June, 1971, some lenders would go only 100% of Blue book, however they have since fallen into line with the prevailing 115% standard.

Depreciation rates were found rather consistent between the various sizes of mobile homes and the various price ranges. They were very little different between the high end and the low end of a given line. Eight-wides and10-wides, no longer acceptable for new housing, retain their popularity in the used market because their mobility permits them to be hauled without a truck.

The Judy-Berner Blue Book shows resale prices only through the first eight years, a period, the publisher says, which will cover two resales. Extending the depreciation curve of the first eight years provides a means of estimating further depreciation. It indicates that after 15 years the depreciation may still be only 65% to 70%. Financing, however, is rarely available for homes over eight years old, unless the condition is unusually good—and when available is much more conservative.

Resales appear to move rapidly. Some dealers and lenders claim to have never seen a used mobile home on a dealer lot. As with cars, there may be some wholesaling to rural areas of the older and more worn trade-ins.

GRAPH: DEPRECIATION OF MAJOR MOBILE HOMES

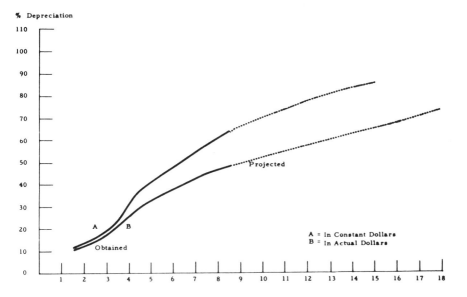

TABLE III

AVERAGE DEPRECIATION OF MAJOR BRAND MOBILE HOMES

A. In Actual Dollars

Type	Age at May, 1971				Depreciation				Projected		
	1½ yrs.	2½	3½	4½	5½	6½	7½	8½	10½	12½	15½
10 foot		12%	16%	30%	34%	38%	45%	47%			
12 foot		14	19	30	35	38	43	47			
Double-Wide		14½	24	29	34	40	44½	48			
Composite	10½%	13½	19	30	34	39	44	47½	53-58	58-65	65-75
Annual Rate (per chart)	10½	3	6	10	5	4½	5	3½	3-5	2½-3½	2½-3½

B. In Constant Dollars

Type	Age at May, 1971				Depreciation				Projected		
	1½ yrs.	2½	3½	4½	5½	6½	7½	8½	10½	12½	15½
10 foot		14%	19%	37%	43%	49%	59%	62½%			
12 foot		16	22½	37	44	49	56	62½			
Double-Wide		16½	28½	35½	43	51½	58	64			
Composite	11½%	15½	23	37	43	50	57½	63	72	78½	85½
Annual Rate (per chart)	11½	4	7½	14	6	7	7½	5½	4½	3	2½

Represents cash value as of May 1, 1971 as a percent of wholesale price when new (recommended selling price less 25%). Each figure above is based on 6 to 28 samples for each year consisting of top- and bottom-of-line samples. Makes covered include Biltmore, Champion, Detroiter, Divco-Wayne, Fleetwood, Great Lakes, Liberty, Magnolia, Nashua, Redman, Skyline and Vagabond. All makes would probably average out at 1 to 3 percent higher depreciation rates.

Source: Mobile Home Market Report and Blue Book, May, 1971, Judy-Berner Co., Maywood, Illinois.

Constant dollars tables are based on standard GNP deflators for 1962 through second quarter of '71. Depreciation of older models is extrapolated from the curve.

It should be noted that the depreciation figures utilized here are probably slightly more favorable than the average. All the sampling of blue book prices focused on major-brand units.

FINANCING

In the area of financing, the mobile home industry still is tied closely to its automotive past. The basic instruments, relationships and lending organizations are outgrowths of, or have their counterparts in, the car finance business.

The standard financing instrument, a conditional sales contract, derives from the auto installment loan and interest is computed on an add-on basis. Finance companies have approximately 50% of the mobile home market. Most of this share is held by 14 national companies who also are leading car lenders. Much of the business by commercial banks and savings and loans is placed through mobile home finance service companies. These are relatively new organizations, the oldest began in 1965, modeled on the precedent of the car credit service companies.

More than 90% of the business comes through dealers. Lenders are expected to floor plan dealers as a condition of getting the retail business. In addition, lenders commonly provide a form of rebate or reserve to dealers, usually 5% of the total financing charges.

A third to a half of all deals involves trade-ins. Roughly 25% of sales, and an even higher proportion in Florida and California, are made for cash. The prevailing interest rate is 7% add-on; 7¼% is the more common rate in the Southeast.

Approximately 65% of the loans are for a seven-year term, while the remainder are about equally divided between 10- and 12-year terms. Most of the 12-year paper is issued by savings & loans that have adopted the longer term as a competitive tool in a new market. But some lenders and insurers are concerned about this procedure and feel the loan balance in the last four or five years will be uncomfortably close to resale value.

All loans must carry physical damage insurance at an annual cost ranging from $1 to $2.40 per $100, depending on the state statutory limitations. About 35 to 40% carry credit life insurance at $.60 to $1 per $100.

FHA and VA, which will insure mobile home loans for terms up to 12 years at true interest rates as low as 7.9%, are infrequently used, for the return available is too small to attract most lenders. For example, in Michigan only one lender, a small savings & loan, will make such loans and it has closed less than a dozen to date. Its interest is not in FHA per se but in learning more about the mobile home business.

LENDING RATIOS

Lending ratios are fairly uniform across the country and on new units, the loan will cover dealer invoice plus 10% plus sales tax plus skirting (the rubber or plastic strip that conceals the wheels and undercarriage). The loan on resales will go 115% of the blue book price. Lenders consider these as 90% loans but dealers are free to obtain a higher downpayment without affecting the loan amount. The HUD 1966 survey found the average purchaser in its sample received 83%

financing.

The repossession rate is high and is heavily concentrated in the first year. The 10-year experience of one service company, which may be more favorable than the average, is 7 to 8 repos per 100.

The majority of business that does not go through service companies involves some form of dealer recourse or dealer buyback. In addition, the standard 5% rebate to dealers is accumulated in a reserve. This reserve must reach a specified minimum balance before any sums can be distributed to the dealer. Credit losses, if any, are deducted from that balance.

A service company solicits dealer business, floor plans the dealer, provides all necessary forms, handles delinquencies and repossessions on retail accounts and in some cases screens the credit of purchasers. The service company also insures the lender against losses, either by obtaining a credit insurance policy at its expense or by depositing a portion of its income from the loans in a cash reserve.

However, the lending institution approves each individual loan. For these functions, the service company receives 1¾% out of the buyer's 7% add-on plus the credit life and physical damage insurance business. In turn (unless the lender has chosen the option of a credit insurance policy), it deposits in a non-interest-bearing account at the lending institution until the reserve reaches the 3% to 7% of outstanding loan balances. This reserve is available to pay any credit losses that may occur. The service company also provides the dealer participation reserve of 5% to 8% of the outstanding balances except in those states (such as Ohio) where this is illegal.

Service company loans, typically, are on a non-recourse basis with the service company providing the entire guarantee. At least five companies now provide mobile home credit insurance, most of which operate on a regional basis only. They prefer to deal through service companies since these will take care of any repossessions, but they also insure loans for direct lenders.

MOBILE HOME PARKS—VACANCIES

At present, the mobile home market is spottily overbuilt and is expected to be seriously overbuilt by the end of 1971. A sharp decline in overall park development appears certain by 1972 and should last for at least three years. It may be 1980 before the national increase approaches the level it reached in 1970 (140,000 new spaces), and it may never come back to the level projected for 1971—180,000 new spaces.

It is estimated that vacancies in rated parks, 77,000 at the end of 1970, will have increased 80% by the end of 1971 to a total of nearly 140,000 spaces, roughly 12% of the total stock. This figure is almost a 15 months supply for the mobile home market projected for 1972. It is believed that the park market will recover strongly until this inventory falls to 75,000 spaces. The maximum the market will absorb in any one year in this decade is expected to be 130,000 spaces.

Over the four years, up to January, 1971, vacancies in rated parks two years old or more have been relatively stable, ranging around 30,000. The great fluctuation has been in vacancies in new parks which rose from 18,000 at the end of 1969 to 47,000 at the end of 1970, constituting a 35% vacancy rate. This category was predicted to exceed 90,000, a 50% vacancy rate, by the end of 1971.

The prevailing wisdom about the mobile home park market is almost the opposite of the reality. Apparently, there is no general awareness of the overbuilding, at least no public acknowledgment. Investors are still flocking into the field believing it a foolproof high return.

Industry spokesmen continue to speak of a shortage of parks and of production of park spaces lagging behind demand. This view seems based on the idea that the number of new park spaces developed in any one year should equal the number of mobile homes shipped in that year. Or perhaps the speakers are not fully aware of the changes in this market since 1968.

There *was* a national shortage of park space or rather a compendium of many local shortages, through the mid-1960's. During this period, steep park entrance fees were common. An upsurge in park development began in 1965, helped by the development of new financing instruments. This kept pace with the tremendous growth of mobile home shipments from 1966 through 1969, at an average rate of three new spaces for ten homes shipped. By the end of 1969, the national market was pretty well in balance.

However, in 1970 park development accelerated while shipments dropped off. Further, the number of pads reported as planned or under construction at year end 1970 was more than double the previous year. Park development will probably grow at a 35% rate in 1971, compared to a 20% growth rate in shipments. The number of new spaces will equal about 38% of shipments, compared to the 23 to 25% the market is capable of absorbing.

Generally, an overbuilt park market can be equated with an overbuilt apartment market. It will not be feasible to reason from the national average to any given local market. The greatest impact will be felt by new parks, by substandard older parks (parks totaling at least 130,000 spaces have been closed in the past four years and this trend should accelerate) and by those with mistakes in location or design. Occupied, well-managed older parks will be less vulnerable, even than apartments in a comparable situation, because of the high cost and difficulty of moving from one park to another.

Some of the markets presently overbuilt include: Atlanta, West Palm Beach in Florida, Jackson, Flint and Western Wayne County in Michigan, and most of California and Arizona. In California, Woodall's reported the vacancy rate in new parks at year end 1970 was over two-thirds and in Arizona it was over 75%.

In Michigan (currently the third largest state in park development) the year end 1970 vacancy rate in new parks was over 50%. A leading park developer and manager estimates a park in a prime location will need 1½ years to fill up, while one in a smaller community will require 2½ years. (But a park at a hot intersection filled up in six months.) This fillup time is for "open" parks where anyone may rent a space. For "closed" parks where spaces are rented as tie-ins to a mobile home purchase, the fillup time is twice as long. A lender reports, "Dealers are crying for people to come in their park." One gives a year's free rent with every mobile home sale.

Much of Florida is considered overbuilt, even though the statewide vacancy rate on new parks is under 25%. One industry spokesman says park development in Florida has almost stopped because so many lots are already zoned for mobile homes.

The majority of today's overbuilding reflects parks that never should have been built, developed by amateurs to the field (many of them large corporations

TABLE IV
MOBILE HOME PARKS MARKET DATA

A. New Park Development

| | 1) Inspected Parks | | | | | | 2) Uninspected Parks | |
| | Parks | | Rebuilding | | Planned or Under Const. | | | |
Completed in Year	Parks (adjusted for overcount)	Spaces	Parks	Spaces	Parks	Spaces	Parks	Spaces
1970	1,120	132,000	106	8,000	434	72,600	149	7,800
1969	919	108,400	132	9,300	223	30,000	123	6,400
1968	892	85,800	151	10,700	158	48,600	119	5,000
1967	995	77,300	190	13,300	248	35,600	133	4,500

B. Vacancy Trends in Rated Parks

| | New Parks | | | Existing Parks | | Total Parks (Adj.) | |
	Vacancies	Adjusted for Est. Overcount	Rate	Vacancies	Rate	Vacancies	Rate
1970	49,789	47,100	36.0%	29,700	3.4%	76,800	7.7%
1969	19,771	18,100	17.0%	28,300	3.7%	46,400	5.4%
1968	11,927	11,300	13.5%	24,700	3.2%	36,000	4.3%
1967	14,958	14,800	19.5%	39,900	5.3%	54,700	6.7%

C. Market Absorption in New and Existing Parks

	Rated Spaces Absorbed	Adjusted for Est. Overcount	Unrated Spaces Absorbed (Est.)	Total Spaces Absorbed (Est.)	Mobile Home Shipments	Sites Absorbed As % of: Shipments	Mobile Home Household Growth
1970	89,800	85,000	7,100	92,100	401,200	23.0%	40.8%
1969	98,300	90,200	6,000	96,200	412,700	23.3%	37.7%
1968	78,400	74,500	4,800	79,300	317,900	24.9%	44.1%
1967E	62,500	62,300	4,200	66,500	240,400	27.7%	54.7%

TABLE IV

MOBILE HOME PARKS MARKET DATA

D. Total Park Space Inventory

	Rated Spaces	Unrated Spaces (Est.)	Total Spaces (Est.)	% of Occupied Mobile Homes	Total Park Spaces Added	Total Park Spaces Closed (Est.)
1/1/71	1,016,200	224,800	1,241,000	56.0%	140,000	(-1,100)
1/1/70	886,400	215,700	1,102,100	53.8%	114,800	(-61,200)
1/1/69	871,200	177,300	1,048,500	61.7%	90,800	(-22,300)
1/1/68	819,800	160,200	980,000	65.7%	81,600	(-46,100)
1/1/67	816,400	128,100	944,500	67.3%		

Source: Park Count and Vacancy Report, Woodall's Publishing Co., Highland Park, Ill., 1967-71 (covers 1966-70). For limitations of data, see Sources of Information, page 28. Market Absorption of park spaces is calculated as the number of new spaces completed during the year, plus or minus the change in total vacancies.

looking for that long land-development profit) without market studies. It may be years before these parks reach profitable levels of occupancy—when the market finally moves out to them or when there are shortages in better locations.

Unlike a new apartment, a new park, however attractive, will not usually fill up by drawing tenants from older parks. The minimum cost to move and hook up a mobile home is $250, the average is $500 and other costs may bring the total to $1,000. This amount cannot be financed, as the original move can. Moreover, older parks tend to have choicer (even if not physically attractive, nearer-in) locations than the new parks.

Local markets where some shortages still exist include Chicago, Indianapolis, Kansas City, Philadelphia and Pittsburgh. In many other markets, there are structural shortages. In other words, the shortages are in areas where zoning codes and land costs make it unlikely that mobile home parks will ever be developed. (E.g., pressed for an example of shortages, one industry spokesman cited near-in Washington and New York.) Whatever parks exist in these areas can command huge entrance fees, sometimes over $1,500, and will continue to do so no matter how much national surplus develops.

Approximately 25% of parks are located outside metropolitan areas, and about 50% in smaller metropolitan areas (e.g., San Bernardino rather than Los Angeles). The other 25% in major markets tend to be located in the outlying sections of the metro area due to zoning restrictions and prohibitive nearer-in land costs. These parks are usually restricted to commercial or industrial districts of metro areas. However, some parks have been successfully developed on land costing $30,000 an acre.

The rents chargeable or, inversely, the amenities required, tend to vary in proportion to the closeness to a major city or major employer. One Midwest developer has two new parks. One park is located in a growing residential suburb of a major market near several major employers and a regional shopping center, has no amenities, not even laundry, 10½ spaces to the acre and rents for $60. The other park, near the extreme edge of the metro area, has only six pads to the acre and a full range of amenities including swimming pool and community house, and rents for $65.

The distribution of mobile homes in and out of parks is largely a regional matter. In Appalachia, probably 65% are on farms or scattered lots. Elsewhere, this proportion is less than 25% and that fraction is almost entirely in rural counties.

Even rural counties are becoming more restrictive in zoning, permitting mobile homes only in approved parks, and eliminating the old farm or rural sidelot parking of mobile units (unless put on a permanent foundation). In many counties, park zoning requirements are approaching residential lot sizes—six, sometimes five units to the acre or pad sizes of 40 x 80 feet. Many local zoning requirements are now stricter than FHA.

Nationally, about 80% of park financing is conventional. Historically, savings and loans and commercial banks have been the principal conventional lenders. However in a few states, notably Michigan, most financing is FHA. Developers now consider FHA procedures and requirements very livable.

Mobile home subdivisions are believed to represent between 3 and 4% of the total inventory of park spaces. In Florida, it is reported they account for 40% of new park spaces. Very simply, these subdivisions are condominium versions of the standard mobile home park. Residents buy a space instead of renting it and put their unit upon permanent foundations. In "closed" subdivisions, mobile home and lot are sold as a package and conventional or FHA mortgage financing is available. In most cases, the park management provides the standard park services and amenities for a fee—about 20% to 25% of a comparable rent. In some cases, residents obtain services through their own association.

Typical lots in the largest Florida subdivision sell for $5,000. Because of their investment, lot owners usually become customers for more expensive mobile homes, most often double-wides. A typical package of lot and mobile home will range between $17,500 and $22,500. Lots in many subdivisions have shown rapid appreciation. Lots in Central Michigan subdivisions which sold for $2,000 in 1963 and 1964 are now reported going for $6,500.

Several large diversified corporations are now active in developing mobile home subdivisions, particularly in Florida. In California, a mobile home manufacturer operates a closed subdivision and custom builds deluxe units to the lot buyer's specifications. The mobile homes in this subdivision have sold for up to $28,000 exclusive of lot.

A second, rarer, type of mobile home subdivision is much more like a residential subdivision. In a typical case, a Midwest land developer platted lots in a rural township at the far edge of a major metropolitan area. In conformity with the State plat act for rural subdivisions, he laid out 12,000 foot lots, three to the acre, and dug foundations. The lots were sold on five, ten or 15-year land contracts and many were bought for cash. No water or sewer facilities were provided, and buyers dug their own well and installed their own septic tank. Nor was there a tie-in with a mobile home dealer.

The mobile homes that buyers placed on their lots ranged from $8,000 to $10,000 and since they were bought separately from the lot, were financed by add-on contract. A year ago the developer started selling the lots for $2,000 and now is selling them at $6,000 and $7,000. This was a case, really, of pure land development with mobile homes figuring simply as the seller's suggestion of a means of instant housing. But it does illustrate the market power of mobile homes in a residential context.

The 1960 Census found that 12% of the occupied mobile home stock was rented, while 1970 figures are not yet available. Renters are usually households seeking instant housing, such as construction workers, military or vacationers.

Rental costs are not greatly higher than effective owning costs. Many park operators rent new or nearly new units (under two years old) for roughly the cost of payments on a seven-year loan plus park rent. There is also some rental of mobile homes on sites outside of parks, in rural areas.

HOUSING COST COMPARISONS

The economics of mobile home ownership are probably more seductive than they should be to an unsophisticated blue-collar worker or newlywed. Imagine, he thinks, owning a home free and clear after making low monthly payments for only seven or ten or twelve years! This view of course is an exaggeration. But it is not an illusion that the cost of possession of the *average* mobile home is significantly lower than the *lowest-cost* conventional new apartment or home

TABLE V
COMPARISON OF HOUSING COSTS
Average Mobile Home vs. Minimum-Cost Home or Apartment

	$6,500 mobile home $6,000 loan, @7% add-on $50/month park rent heat $150/year	$19,000 townhouse $192 monthly payment (FHA 7%; includes $13/month maintenance of common grounds) heat $150/year	Apartment $150/month heat furnished
A. On cost-of-possession basis:			
Costs over 15 years			
move-in cost (downpayment)	$ 1,000	move-in cost (downpayment plus furniture & appliances) $ 1,500	move-in cost (furniture plus security deposit) $ 900
park rent	9,000	mtg. payments 34,560	rent 27,000
heat	2,250	heat 2,250	
maintenance	500	maintenance 1,500	
	$12,750	$39,810	
	1,625		
less, resale value	$11,125		
1. @7-year loan			
loan payments $119/month	9,996	less, buildup of equity 5,000	
less, average tax deduction	580	average tax deduction 5,400	
	$20,541	$29,410	$27,900
Cost differential per year		+$ 592	+$ 491
2. @10-year loan			
loan payments $97/month	$11,640		
less, average tax deduction	830		
	$21,935	$29,410	$27,900

TABLE V (Cont'd)

		$6,500 mobile home $6,000 loan, @7% add-on $50/month park heat $150/year	$19,000 townhouse $192 monthly payment (FHA 7%; includes $13/month maintenance of common grounds) heat $150/year	Apartment $150/month heat furnished
Cost Differential per year			+$ 499	+$ 398
3. @12-year loan	loan payments $87/month	$12,528		
	less, average tax deduction	1,000		
		$22,653	$29,410	$27,900
Cost differential per year			+$ 450	+$ 353
B. On immediate cost basis:				
Move-in cost		$ 1,000	$ 1,500	$ 900
Differential			+$ 500	-$ 100
1. @7-year loan	payment	119 /mo	192 /mo rent	150/mo
	park rent	50 /mo payment		
	heat	12.50/mo heat	12.50/mo rent	
		$ 181.50	$ 204.50	$ 150
Differential per month			+$ 23	-$ 31.50
2. @10-year loan	payment	$ 97		150
	park rent	50		
	heat	12.50		
		$159.50	$204.50	$ 150

TABLE V (Cont'd)

	$6,500 mobile home $6,000 loan, @7% add-on $50/month park heat $150/year	$19,000 townhouse $192 monthly payment (FHA 7%; includes $13/month maintenance of common grounds) heat $150/year	Apartment $150/month heat furnished
Differential per month		+$ 45	−$ 9.50
3. @12-year loan payment park rent heat	$ 87 50 12.50		
	$ 149.50	$204.50	$150
Differential per month		+$ 55	+$ .50

available today without subsidy.

Over the average mobile home's 15-year life span, its cost advantage over the minimum-rent apartment will be $490 a year, and over the cheapest townhouse or quadrominium $590 a year, if bought on a seven-year loan as the great majority of mobile homes are. A ten-year loan will reduce the mobile home edge to $400 and $500 a year and a twelve-year loan to $350 and $450 a year. This is figuring on a cost of possession basis, as economic man would, if such an abstraction existed. But the typical housing consumer does not reason like economic man and is even less likely to if he is young and of modest income. Thus, the more meaningful comparison may be of immediate out-of-pocket costs computed on a monthly rather than yearly basis.

On this basis, a mobile home bought on a twelve-year loan has a $55 a month advantage over the cheapest townhouse or quadrominium, and the advantage grades down to $23 per month for a seven-year loan. The same comparison with a minimum-rent apartment is to the disadvantage of the mobile home. The mobile home owner's immediate costs, including heat, are 50 cents a month lower if his loan is for twelve years, but $31.50 higher if he buys on a seven-year loan. This $31.50 difference may be regarded as one measure of the value that a young family head places on ownership or on the entire complex of mobile home living.

One very important factor is omitted from a pure cost comparison. Low-cost conventional housing is simply not available in many areas. Or where available, it may not be suitable for mobile home families, such as apartments which may refuse to admit children.

TAX ADVANTAGE

In states where mobile homes are taxed as vehicles, they have a typical tax advantage of $20 a month over an apartment with comparable monthly cost and $35 a month over the lowest priced townhouse. If the tax burden were equalized, the cost advantage of the mobile home would be almost halved. However, the low cost and high depreciation of the mobile home almost guarantee that the tax load will never be equalized even if the method of taxation is changed.

In Michigan, for example, the tax burden is $3 a month trailer tax plus an average $2 a month per park space in local property tax. Most other states charge some form of vehicle tax, usually called trailer tax or tag tax. One of the highest is the $125 per year for double-wides in Florida. Several other states and some counties tax mobile homes as personal property which results in a somewhat higher tax load. At least three states tax mobile homes as real property and nearly all areas will similarly tax those that have been put on permanent foundations.

New York imposes its property tax on the original cost of the home, while the mobile home industry considers this unfair. In other states, the property tax is levied on the home's blue book value, after a deduction of up to 20% for the value of the furniture supplied with the unit. The result is that a typical $6,000 unit when four years old, will pay only $5.50 per month in property tax—or less than the trailer or tag tax in many states.

Some of the industry's most astute observers do not consider low taxation of mobile homes an unmixed blessing. An equalized tax load, one park developer said, "would be the best thing that could happen to our industry. Then they'd have to let us into the better locations, into the residential areas."

In practice, however, mobile home subdivisions which pay property tax have in general fared no better in zoning decisions than rental parks where the vehicle tax prevails. Zoning has not improved even in New York.

MOBILE HOME LIVING

The one enduring attraction of the mobile home is the style of living it offers, as commented on by every serious study and virtually every individual observer. The mobile home offers a mixture of informality, gregariousness, visiting back and forth, planned and unplanned shared activity (laundry rooms and bowling leagues). It is fostered by the very shortcomings of mobile home life—the cramped quarters, the density on the land, the lack of privacy—all of which throw people together, and by the many shared facilities and the homogeneity of the population. Many parks tend to be self-selective in their grouping, and people of common needs, incomes and age groups cluster together.

To quote housing economist Robinson Newcomb,

> Parks tend to be real communities rather than aggregations of . . . houses. They offer a break from the impersonal, conventional residential development. They meet certain social as well as financial and physical needs.

And a Macomb County, Michigan planning survey:

> When surveying existing parks, an additional characteristic of mobile home residents was observed. This can best be described as a high degree of social interaction or camaraderie which seems to be present in most parks. Perhaps this is a result of the density within parks and the sharing of park facilities such as laundry rooms and recreation areas. This characteristic may not be true of all parks but it does appear more pronounced in mobile home living than in other forms of residential housing.

Thus, the mobile home life style is a willing exchange of individual amenities in housing for group enjoyments. The life style is a direct reversal of the values that are stressed in most conventional housing reflecting the housing values of an earlier generation and perhaps of a future generation, having something in common with the new communes. From this perspective, the very high first-year repossession rate may be regarded as the drop-out rate of those unable to adjust to the mobile home life style.

It should be noted that the mobile home market is reversing some of the original values of this life style. Homelike privacy is being reintroduced, though still to less than 10% of the market. Many new units include private laundries and extra bathrooms, and new lot sizes and double-wide area sizes approach homelike dimensions.

A component of the life style is the mobile home owner's feeling of independence, derived from the assurance that his home will be free and clear within a short span and that he is not tied to any site, but can pick up his home at will. This viewpoint may not stand up to rational analysis, when one considers the very brief mobile home life remaining after the last payment, the difficulties of moving and the often onerous restrictions of park managements. But one testimony to the strength of this attitude is the number of buyers who pay cash for their mobile homes, or in subdivisions, for mobile home and lot.

SOURCES & METHODS (Table I and Table II)

Occupied stocks from 1950, 1960, and 1970 Census: Annual shipments from Mobile Home Manufacturers Association (MHMA). *Vacancies:* Approximately ½% above rate for conventional housing. (Average finding of FHA-Post Office surveys of vacancies in local markets.) *Dealer Inventory:* 14% of annual increase in shipments. Based on average inventory-to-sales ratio in MHMA surveys (discontinued 1969) and observer reports. *Removals and Conversions:* Based on current 15-year life (consensus of observers; fits with Census data on changes in occupied stock). *Net Increase in Mobile Home Households:* Interpolation between 10-year increase in households and annual shipments. *Other Uses:* A residual, after subtracting all above.

Projections: For mobile home households: based on age group distribution of Census Bureau projections of new households and the HUD 1966 survey of mobile home occupant characteristics. This factor was averaged with projections based on the 1969-70 mobile home share of new households (19.5%). This method yields a projection of 447,000 shipments in 1971. However, as of November 1, 1971, it appears that actual shipments for 1971 will be closer to 470,000. *For removals and conversions:* Based on gradual increase of mobile home life span to 16 years.

A METHODOLOGY FOR EVALUATING
HOUSING PROGRAMS

Joseph S. DeSalvo

This paper presents a methodology for evaluating housing programs that are primarily intended to provide participants with adequate housing at below-market rentals. Of course, for this kind of housing program, which is essentially a transfer in kind to its participants, there may nevertheless be nontenant benefits due to consumption or production externalities. Housing programs also require economic resources, whose cost is generally borne partially by program participants and partially by one or more subsidizers. When these magnitudes—benefits and costs—are known, we can evaluate the program. With respect to economic efficiency, we want to know whether benefits exceed costs. With respect to the transfer goals of the program, we want to know how benefits and costs are distributed by characteristics of the target population, such as income and family size. Sometimes, we may also want to know how much of the cost is borne by tenants and how much by non-tenants.(1)

Before we can hope to measure benefits and costs, we must have precise understanding of what these terms mean in the context of housing programs. This task is performed. A model of consumer choice in the context of a housing program is presented. Later we formulate the following benefit and cost concepts. 1. Net tenant benefits: the amount of additional income the program participant needs to be as well off without the program as with it (a consumer's surplus concept). 2. Gross tenant benefits: the dollar value of the program to the tenant, i.e., net tenant benefits plus the amount he actually pays for the program unit (called project rent). 3. Nontenant benefits: the dollar value of consumption and production externalities created by the program. 4. Total benefits: nontenant benefits plus gross tenant benefits. 5. Total resource cost: cost of the economic factors required to provide a flow of housing services from the program unit. 6. Nontenant contribution: the difference between total resource cost and project rent of the program unit. 7. Tenant subsidy: the difference between market rent and project rent of the program unit.

In conclusion estimable forms are developed for all these concepts except nontenant benefits and, hence, total benefits. However, the minimum amount of nontenant benefits necessary to justify the program on benefit-cost grounds is estimable. Under certain assumptions discussed later, all these quantities can be estimated by knowing only a few variables for each participating household and its program-provided dwelling unit. These variables are: 1. the actual rent of the program unit (project rent), 2. the income of the tenant, 3. the market rent of the program unit (i.e., what it would rent for on the private market), and 4. the tenant's rent-income ratio in the absence of the program (i.e., that fraction of his income he would spend on housing were he not a participant in the program). Of these, the first two could be directly observed for on-going programs, but they would have to be estimated for proposed programs. The last two would require some form of estimation for either on-going programs or proposed programs.

HOUSING PROGRAMS AND CONSUMER CHOICE

The essential feature of most housing programs, from the point of view of the participant, is that they present him with the opportunity of obtaining housing at a lower rental outlay than if he were to purchase the same housing on the open market. Housing programs use a variety of subsidies to achieve this purpose. The question of interest here is how one might characterize these programs in terms of the theory of consumer choice.

First we distinguish two cases. Type I: the participant is permitted free choice in the selection of housing, but he pays less-than-market rental on what he chooses. (He may, of course, pay nothing.) This is a price-subsidy program. Type II: the participant is presented with an all-or-none choice. To participate in the housing program at all, he must live in a housing unit specified by someone else and pay less-than-market rent.

TYPE I HOUSING PROGRAM

The effects of a Type I housing program on the participant may be represented as in Figure 1. The consumer is confronted with the budget constraint given by $y = p_x x + p_h h$ (shown as L_1 in Figure 1), where y is his fixed income, p_x is the fixed price of the composite nonhousing commodity x, p_h is the fixed price of the composite housing good h.[1] Under free market conditions, the consumer maximizes his utility by buying x_1 units of the composite commodity and h_1 of housing, which entails a rent expenditure of $r_1 = p_h h_1$.

Suppose now that the consumer is permitted to participate in a housing program which allows him to obtain housing at less than market rental. In particular, suppose that a housing unit for which the market rent is $r = p_h h$ costs participants in the housing program ar, where $0 < a < 1$. This implies a new budget constraint, $y = p_x x + a p_h h$, and a new optimum consumption of the composite good and housing, indicated by x_2 and h_2 in the figure. The budget line (shown as L_2 in Figure 1) shifts out to the right since a is less than unity.

The consumer is thereby permitted to reach a higher indifference curve, indicated by u_2 in the figure. The quantity h_2 is the number of dollars' worth of housing (in terms of some base point) that the consumer obtains. On the private market he would have to pay $p_h h_2$ in current dollars, but, because of the housing program, he pays only $a p_h h_2$.

TYPE II HOUSING PROGRAM.

In certain housing programs the participant is not given the option of determining the type of housing he wishes. Rather, he is given an all-or-none choice. He either accepts a particular apartment (at the subsidized rental) or does not participate in the program at all.(2) Figure 2 is used to illustrate this type of program. The vertical line at h_2 represents the fixed amount of housing the tenant must purchase under the housing program. He will pay $a p_h h_2$ for it, where, as before $0 < a < 1$. If he were to buy it on the competitive housing market, the consumer would have to pay $p_h h_2$. His preprogram position is indicated by (x_1, h_1) in Figure 2 which has a budget constraint L_1 and a utility level u_1 associated with it. Faced with a fixed income, a fixed price for the composite commodity, and the requirement that $a p_h h_2$ be paid for h_2, the amount of x is determined at x_2. The tenant's choice is therefore (h_2, x_2) in Figure 2 and is associated with a utility level u_2. Notice that if the participant had been given freedom of choice along budget line L_2, he would have chosen point b and achieved a higher level of satisfaction u_0 by trading off some housing for some of the composite good x.

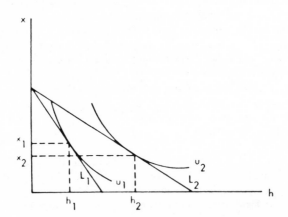

FIGURE 1: Effects of Type 1 Housing Program.

It is, of course, possible that h_2 be chosen such that the participant would be at point b on the indifference curve u_0. The Type II program would correspond to the Type I program in that h_2 is the level of housing he would have chosen anyway. It might also be noted that h_2 could be chosen low enough so that the consumer would prefer to trade off some of the composite good for more housing. It is even conceivable that the all-or-none quantity of housing is so great that the consumer would be worse off as a program participant than as a nonparticipant. Figure 2 illustrates what is probably the more realistic case, i.e.,

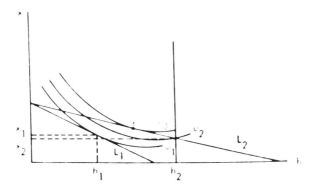

FIGURE 2: Effects of Type 2 Housing Program.

where the participant is required to purchase more housing than he would prefer at prices px and ap_h but not enough to preclude participation.

BENEFITS AND COSTS OF HOUSING PROGRAMS

How might one assess the tenant benefits of housing programs? One way is to find the dollar amount that will make the comsumer as well off without the program as with it. There are several ways to do this, all classed under the rubric "consumer's surplus."(3) Consumer's surplus as used here is the additional money that would have to be given to the consumer to make him as well off as under the program, given that he must pay market prices for the goods he buys and market rental for the housing he consumes.

Referring to Figure 3, assume that an individual who is not a participant in a housing program has a given income and faces given prices of all goods and housing. The solid line in Figure 3 represents the level of his income and relative prices of all goods and housing. The individual would achieve the most satisfaction, under these circumstances, by consuming quantities of the composite nonhousing good x and the composite housing good h indicated by the point a on the indifference curve u_0.

Now, assume that the individual becomes a participant in a housing program and that the quantities of housing and all other goods enjoyed under the

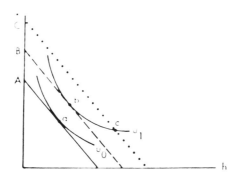

FIGURE 3: Tenant Benefits of Housing Program.

program are indicated by the point c on the indifference curve u_1.(4) Of course, he now pays less-than-market rental for his dwelling unit and enjoys a higher level of satisfaction under the program than without it. If he were to obtain the same level of utility as u_1 but be required to pay market rental for his housing, he would need an income represented by the dashed line in Figure 3 which is tangent to the u_1 indifference curve at the point b. This line is drawn parallel to the initial budget constraint, indicated by the solid line, to reflect the fact that the prices of x and h are the same in both situations. If the income associated with point b is represented by y and the individual's actual income by y_0, then the net tenant benefits of the program are

$$B_t^{\ n} = y - y_0.$$

This is the amount of money which, if added to his income, would lead the consumer to attain a level of satisfaction u_1 equal to that attained under the housing program. This amount can be represented in terms of the nonhousing good by the distance AB in Figure 3.(5)

We define gross tenant benefits to be the sum of net tenant benefits and the project rent, R_p, paid by the tenant, i.e.,

$$B_t^{\ g} = B_t^{\ n} + R_p.$$

It may be noted that $B_t^{\ n}$ (and, hence, $B_t^{\ g}$) is not directly measurable since the income necessary to achieve the level of satisfaction u_1 is not directly observable. However, a method of estimating $B_t^{\ n}$ from observable data will be presented in the next section.

CASH GRANTS AND HOUSING PROGRAMS

Referring again to Figure 3, let the quantities associated with point c be x^c units of the nonhousing good and h^c units of housing. The market value of this combination is given by $p_x x^c + p_h h^c$, which is represented in the figure by the dotted line passing through the point c. Now since the consumer participates in a housing program, he does not pay this amount for the combination (x^c, h^c); rather, he pays $p_x x^c + a p_h h^c$. The difference between these two amounts is the tenant subsidy, S. This subsidy is also the difference between the market rent, R_m, and the project rent, R_p, of the subsidized dwelling unit,

$$(p_x x^c + p_h h^c) - (p_x x^c + \alpha p_h h^c) = p_h h^c - \alpha p_h h^c = R_m - R_p = S.$$

This is obtained by noting that $p_h h^c$ is merely the market rent of h^c units of housing and $a p_h h^c$ is merely the project rent of h^c units of housing. In terms of the nonhousing composite good, S is equal to the distance AC in Figure 3.

Note that the dotted line lies above the dashed line through point b. Or, in terms of the nonhousing composite commodity, the distance AC is greater than the distance AB. This implies the tenant's valuation of the program unit is less than the market's valuation. Moreover, if market prices equal average costs, it would be cheaper to give the consumer a cash transfer equal to net tenant benefits rather than an in-kind transfer equal to the tenant subsidy. Thus, to justify an in-kind transfer, other benefits at least equal to the difference between the tenant subsidy and net tenant benefits must exist.(6)

In general, then, it is more appealing from the point of view of the recipient and may be cheaper for society to give cash grants for purchase of housing and other goods at currently prevailing market prices. Why, then, does society choose to provide subsidized housing in one form or another rather than a cash grant? One reason is that those who provide the benefits are not solely concerned with the satisfactions of the recipients but with their own satisfactions as well. It raises the utility of the provider to see the provided better off, where better off means the recipient lives in "standard" as opposed to "nonstandard" housing. The recipient of a cash grant might not choose to live in standard housing. The housing program is, therefore, a way of imposing "our" will on the participant. Another reason for housing programs is that they are believed to have ramifications on the community well-being beyond those experienced by the participants. These are typically called secondary benefits or spillover effects and encompass such things as elimination of blight and slums, mitigation of poverty, revival of downtown business areas of the central cities, achievement and/or maintenance of an adequate middle-income household component in the central city, etc. Some attempts have been made to incorporate these consumption or production externalities into an economic evaluation of housing programs.(7) However, the conceptually satisfactory schemes are, at this early stage of their development, practically impossible to apply. At the other extreme are ad hoc methods tailored to specific problems. Our analysis provides no conceptual measurement of these nontenant benefits.

With respect to costs, we only wish to observe here that the resource cost, C, of providing subsidized housing can be divided into two parts: 1. that part which is contributed by the program participant himself, which we have called project rent, R_p, and 2. that part contributed by nontenants of program units, which we denote C_{nt}. The identity

$$C = R_p + C_{nt}$$

is an alternative to regarding costs as the sum of component expenditures such as fuel, utilities, payroll, taxes, and so forth. The equation above highlights the size of subsidy involved in providing subsidized housing. Moreover, as will be shown later, under certain circumstances the nontenant contribution and resource cost may be estimated with the same data used to estimate tenant benefits.

ESTIMATING BENEFITS AND COST

One way of estimating net tenant benefits is to estimate the tenant subsidy instead. This has been done before in the evaluation of housing programs,(8) but usually it was not observed, perhaps because it was not realized, that the tenant subsidy and net tenant benefits were not the same thing. In fact, it was shown above that the subsidy will typically be larger than the benefit. Nevertheless, it may be that they are quite close, in which case the tenant subsidy would be a good estimate of net tenant benefits. Usually, of course, one does not know whether these two measures will be close, and treating them as if they are begs the question.

To obtain the theoretically correct measure of tenant benefits, discussed above, we must assume a particular form of the utility function. Let us assume that an individual's utility function is

$$u = h^\beta x^{1-\beta},$$

and that his budget constraint is

$$y = p_x x + \alpha p_h h,$$

where the variables are defined as before and β is the consumer's rent-income ratio.

The assumed utility function implies unitary price and income elasticities for housing and nonhousing. That is, for a given income, expenditures on housing and all other goods remain unchanged as prices change. Also, for given prices, expenditures on both goods increase and decrease in proportion to increases and decreases in income. It is really the restrictions on housing demand and expenditures that are important here, for the nonhousing good is meant to represent all nonhousing consumption. Thus, if it were true that the demand for housing had unitary price and income elasticities, then it would necessarily be true that the same conditions held for the composite nonhousing good. Thus, evidence in favor of unitary price and income elasticities for housing would be evidence in favor of the particular utility function used above (or any other utility function that had the same implications).

DeLeeuw has recently surveyed studies of the demand for housing as well as provided his own analysis. He was primarily concerned with income elasticity since there is more disagreement about it than there is about price elasticity. DeLeeuw concludes that the income elasticity of rental housing ranges from .8 to 1.0. With respect to price elasticity, deLeeuw's own work as well as that of others, such as Muth, indicate an elasticity of unity. Thus, the assumed utility function is consistent with empirical evidence. It is also simple enough to permit the kind of manipulation necessary to obtain a measure of tenant benefits, an exercise we now take up.

The followind demand relations emerge from the maximization of the utility function subject to the budget constraint:

$$h = \frac{\beta y}{\alpha p_h}$$

$$x = \frac{(1 - \beta)y}{p_x}.$$

Now suppose the consumer participates in a housing program (i.e., $a < 1$) and obtains h_1 units of housing and x_1 units of other goods with an income of y_0. The utility level associated with these amounts is, of course,

$$u_1 = h_1^\beta x_1^{1-\beta}.$$

How much income is necessary for the consumer to obtain u_1 when required to pay market rental? This is found by substituting the demand equations (with $a = 1$) into the utility function, setting $u = u_1$, and solving for y; i.e., find the income level that solves

$$\left[\frac{y_0 - \alpha p_h h_1}{p_x}\right]^{1-\beta} [h_1]^{\beta} = \left[\frac{(1-\beta)y}{p_x}\right]^{1-\beta}\left[\frac{\beta y}{p_h}\right]^{\beta}.$$

The solution is

$$y = \left[\frac{h_1 p_h}{\beta}\right]^{\beta}\left[\frac{y_0 - \alpha p_h h_1}{1 - \beta}\right]^{1-\beta}$$

This equation may be expressed in a manner consistent with our earlier notation. Note that

$$p_h h_1 = R_m$$

$$\alpha p_h h_1 = R_p$$

so that(9)

$$y = \left[\frac{R_m}{\beta}\right]^{\beta}\left[\frac{y_0 - R_p}{1 - \beta}\right]^{1-\beta}$$

Then, net tenant benefits are $B_t^n = y - y_0$, where y is given by the last equation above. Gross tenant benefits are, of course, $B_t^g = B_t^n + R_p$.

To obtain an estimate of gross or net tenant benefits, observations or estimates of the following variables are required: 1. the market rent of the unit, 2. the project rent of the unit, 3. the income of the tenant and 4. the parameter β. For an on-going program, the tenant's income and his project rent are observable, but market rent and β are not and must be estimated. For a proposed program or project, we would also need estimates of 2. and 3.

Since the unit is not offered on the private market, its market rent is not observable. However, there are at least two ways one could go about obtaining an estimate of market rent. Perhaps the easiest way is simply to ask someone with knowledge of the housing market in which the program operates to estimate the market rentals of program units.(10) Another approach would be to estimate a rent function (i.e., rent as a function of housing characteristics) and to use it to estimate market rents of program units.(11) There are undoubtedly other approaches as well.

For an on-going program, the tenant's currently observed rent-income ratio cannot be used to estimate β because he will typically be spending differently on housing than he normally would (i.e., than he would as a nonparticipant). One way to estimate the ratio would be to use the average rent-income ratio of people in the private rental housing market. A better way would be to estimate a relation between rent expenditures and family characteristics such as income, family size, etc. Then, this relation could be used to estimate the β for a particular tenant.(12) For a proposed program, it might be possible to obtain the rent-income ratios of prospective tenants, as well as their incomes.(13)

A method for estimating net and gross tenant benefits has been presented. If an estimate of nontenant benefits were also available, then the benefit side of the evaluation of a housing program would be complete. We present no method for estimating nontenant benefits; however, we do show later how to estimate the minimum level of such benefits required to justify the program on benefit-cost grounds.

ESTIMATING COSTS

Resource cost has been defined as the value of resources necessary to provide the flow of services from a housing unit. The direct estimation of the resource cost of a housing program would require extensive cost data on development expenses and subsequent operating expenses. However, under certain circumstances, a simpler method of obtaining an estimate of resource cost may be used.

Economic theory tells us that in the long run under competitive conditions in a market, the market price of a unit of a commodity will equal the average total cost (including normal profit) of providing that unit. Thus, for competitive housing markets, one should expect the market rent of a housing unit to approximate the resource cost of that unit.

It is tempting, therefore, to contend that the market rent of a unit provided by a housing program is equal to the resource cost of that unit. However, this is not true unless an additional condition is met. This condition is that the housing program must provide housing as efficiently as does the private housing market. If the housing is provided less efficiently than that provided by the private market, then the resource cost of a unit is greater than the market rent of that unit.

The condition of efficiency is presumed to be fulfilled in competitive markets. However, since publicly assisted housing is not forced by competition to operate efficiently, one cannot make the same presumption. It has been estimated that the inefficiency associated with one housing program is not insignificant. (See Olsen and Smolensky.) Nevertheless, if one could argue that a housing program provided housing as efficiently as the private market, then the market rent could be used as an estimate of the resource cost. Moreover, even when it cannot be convincingly argued that the program is efficient, using market rent as an estimate of resource cost would provide a lower bound to the true resource cost of program-provided housing and could be used as a check on any alternative cost estimating procedure.

ESTIMATING NONTENANT CONTRIBUTIONS

This same line of reasoning may be extended to provide an estimate of all nontenant contributions where it is impossible or inconvenient to measure these contributions directly. If we assume that the program provides housing as efficiently as the private competitive housing market and we have an estimate of the market rent of program housing, then the tenant subsidy is identical to nontenant contributions.

To see this, recall that resource cost is the sum of project rent (the tenant's contribution— and nontenant contributions, or

$$C = R_p + C_{nt}.$$

But, resource cost equals market rent because of the assumption that the program is as efficient as the private market, so

$$R_m = R_p + C_{nt}.$$

Therefore, nontenant contributions may be measured by the difference between market rent and project rent, i.e.,

$$C_{nt} = R_m - R_p.$$

This is a quantity we have already defined and discussed as the tenant subsidy. It is the amount the tenant would have to pay in excess of his project rent in order to occupy a unit identical to his program unit on the private market. This makes sense as an estimate of nontenant contributions because if the program were efficient, this is exactly the amount which must be contributed by others in order to permit the participant to pay only R_p.

Now it is easy to see why we are concerned if the tenant subsidy is used to estimate net tenant benefits. Under the assumptions that the housing program is as efficient as private housing and that market rent equals resource cost, gross tenant benefits would exactly equal resource cost if the tenant subsidy were used to estimate net tenant benefits. That is, gross tenant benefits and resource cost would both equal the sum of project rent and tenant subsidy and, hence, would be equal by definition.

Since we have shown that net tenant benefits will, in general, be less than the tenant subsidy, gross tenant benefits will consequently be less than resource cost. The difference must be made up by nontenant benefits if the program is to be justified on benefit-cost grounds.

ESTIMATING MINIMUM REQUIRED NONTENANT BENEFITS

If the analyst has an estimate of total resource cost and an estimate of gross tenant benefits, he can obtain an estimate of the minimum amount of nontenant benefits necessary to make total benefits equal total cost. Of course, it would be preferable to have a direct estimate of these nontenant benefits, but an estimate of the minimum necessary may be illuminating to policymakers. If the required benefits are small relative to resource cost or in absolute amount, the housing program would be very much like an unrestricted cash grant (equal to the tenant subsidy) and little indication of nontenant benefits would be required to justify the program. On the other hand, if required nontenant benefits are large, then the justification of the program may be questionable unless some indication of nontenant benefits is found. In any event, the magnitude of minimum required nontenant benefits should give policymakers a good idea of the "price" paid for a housing program versus an unrestricted cash grant. They are then face-to-face with the issue of whether the housing program is worth the price.

SUMMARY

Net tenant benefits for a Type II program may be estimated by using the following expression(14)

$$B_t{}^n = \left[\frac{R_m}{\beta}\right]^\beta \left[\frac{y_0 - R_p}{1 - \beta}\right]^{1-\beta} - y_0$$

Gross tenant benefits may then be estimated as

$$B_t{}^g = B_t{}^n + R_p \,.$$

The tenant subsidy (and, under certain conditions, the nontenant contribution) may be estimated from

$$S = R_m - R_p \,.$$

Under certain conditions resource cost may be estimated by the market rent, i.e.,

$$C = R_m \,.$$

Finally, an estimate of minimum required nontenant benefits is

$$B_{nt}^{\min} = C - B_t{}^g.$$

The variables have the following definitions:

$B_t{}^n$ = net tenant benefits,
$B_t{}^g$ = gross tenant benefits,
$B_{nt}^{\min}$ = minimum required nontenant benefits,
R_m = market rent,
R_p = project rent,
y_0 = tenant income,
β = tenant rent-income ratio,
S = tenant subsidy and
C = resource cost.

With the use of these relationships, economic evaluation of housing programs can be carried out.

NOTES

(1) Think of housing as a bundle of services yielded both by the structure and the land on which it is built. The price per unit of housing is the expenditure needed to obtain a composite bundle of services of land and structure. It is an index of the prices of all those items one generally includes as "housing." A consumer's expenditure on the services of any particular dwelling is the product of the price per unit of housing and the number of units housing the dwelling contains. See Muth [11, pp. 18-19].

(2) The consumer may be given more choice than this. For example, in Federal Public Housing, one is allowed to reject the first two apartments offered before dropping to the bottom of the waiting list. Of course, these apartments are supposed to be equivalent but in fact are different because of age, location, etc.

(3) A good discussion of consumer's surplus may be found in Blaug [pp.

335-345].

(4) From here on the discussion will be in terms of a Type II housing program. Most of the analysis holds unchanged for either type of program. However, an important difference will be noted later.

(5) Some readers will recognize this consumer's surplus measure as the "price equivalent variation." There are at least four other consumer's surplus measures that could have been used. These may be classified as the Hicksian measures (which are in terms of indifference curves) and the Marshallian measure (which is in terms of the demand curve). In principle the Hicksian measures are preferred to the Marshallian in that the former do not require the assumption of a constant marginal utility of income. These measures do differ among themselves and from the Marshallian measure; in particular, the price equivalent variation tends toward the high end of the spectrum. See Hicks and Blaug.

(6) Economists have long been aware, in general, of the basic distinction made here between the tenant subsidy and net tenant benefits. However, this awareness has not always carried over into analyses of housing programs. See, e.g., Bish. Exceptions are Smolensky and Prescott. Friedman presents a clear statement of the distinction although his purpose is to point out the fallacy of composition made by those drawing conclusions concerning the aggregate effects of alternative taxes from analysis of their effects on an individual. The same criticism applies to this page if benefits and costs are aggregated across all program participants, unless the program does not affect the relative costs of housing and other goods in the economy. (Aggregation of benefits also requires the assumption that a dollar to one participant has the same value as a dollar to any other participant.)

The point about nontenant benefits being required to justify in-kind transfers follows from recent discussions of the necessity of transfers for efficient resource use. See Buchanan, Musgrave, Olsen, and Pauly. Hochman and Rogers is relevant although dealing only with cash transfers. Smolensky also appears to recognize the point in the context of housing programs.

(7) For examples relevant to housing, see Nourse, Adams et al., Rothenberg and Olsen.

(8) See, for example, Bish. Ross uses the concept of tenant subsidy as identical to net tenant benefits but does not provide estimates.

(9) This final equation may also be found by minimizing $p_x x + p_h h$ subject to the constraint $u = h_1{}^\beta x_1{}^{1-\beta}$ and solving for the income necessary to attain the minimizing values of x and h. The author is indebted to E. O. Olsen for this point. It can also be shown that this equation is invariant to any positive monotonic transformation of the utility function.

For a Type I program, the requisite income level is obtained either by finding the value of income, which 1. solves

$$\left[\frac{(1-\beta)y_0}{p_x}\right]^{1-\beta}\left[\frac{\beta y_0}{\alpha p_h}\right]^{\beta} = \left[\frac{(1-\beta)y}{p_x}\right]^{1-\beta}\left[\frac{\beta y}{p_h}\right]^{\beta}$$

or 2. minimizes $p_x x + p_h h$ subject to

$$u = \left[\frac{(1-\beta)y_0}{p_x}\right]^{1-\beta}\left[\frac{\beta y_0}{\alpha p_h}\right]^{\beta}$$

The solution is $y = y_0 a^{-\beta}$. Consequently, for a price-subsidy housing program

$$B_t^n = y_0 \alpha^{-\beta} - y_0 = \left[\left(\frac{R_p}{R_m} \right)^{-\beta} - 1 \right] y_0.$$

The net tenant benefit formulas for the two types of housing programs yield the same answer when the all-or-none housing quantity is exactly what the tenant would have chosen under an equivalent price subsidy.

(10)DeSalvo has used this method in his analysis of New York City's Mitchell-Lama program.

(11)Olsen has used this approach in his analysis of New York City rent control.

(12)DeSalvo and Olsen have used this approach.

(13)In the case of a Type I or price-subsidy housing program, since the tenant will be on his housing demand curve both before and after he becomes a participant and since by assumption his housing demand is of unitary price elasticity, β can be observed for each actual or prospective tenant. He will have the same rent-income ratio both as a participant and as a nonparticipant in the program.

(14)For a Type I program $B_t^n = [(R_p/R_m)^{-\beta} - 1] \, y_0$.

REFERENCES

Adams, F.G., G. Milgram, E. W. Green and C. Mansfield. "Underdeveloped Land Prices during Urbanization: A Micro-Empirical Study over Time," Review of Economics and Statistics, 50 (1968), 248-258.

Bish, R. L. "Public Housing: The Magnitude and Distribution of Direct Benefits and Effects of Housing Consumption," Journal of Regional Science, 9 (1969), 425-438.

Blaug, M. Economic Theory in Retrospect. Homewood, Ill.: Richard D. Irwin, Inc., 1962.

Buchanan, J. M. The Demand and Supply of Public Goods. Chicago: Rand McNally and Co., 1968.

deLeeuw, F. "The Demand for Housing: A Review of Cross-Section Evidence," Review of Economics and Statistics, 53 (1971), 1-10.

DeSalvo, J. S. "An Economic Analysis of New York City's Mitchell-Lama Housing Program," unpublished paper presented at Econometric Society Meetings, December 1970.

Friedman, M. "The 'Welfare' Effects of an Income Tax and an Excise Tax," in Essays in Positive Economics. Chicago: University of Chicago Press, 1966.

Hicks, J. R. A Revision of Demand Theory. Oxford: Clarendon Press, 1956.

Hochman, H. M. and J. D. Rogers. "Pareto Optimal Redistribution," American Economic Review, 59 (1969), 542-557.

Musgrave, R. A. "Provision for Social Goods," in J. Margolis and H. Guitton (eds.), Public Economics. New York: St. Martin's Press, 1969.

Muth, R. F. Cities and Housing. Chicago: University of Chicago Press, 1969.

Muth, R. F. "The Demand for Non-Farm Housing," in A. C. Harberger (ed.), The Demand for Durable Goods. Chicago: University of Chicago Press, 1960.

Nourse, H. O. "The Effect of Public Housing on Property Values in St. Louis,"

Land Economics, 39 (1963), 433-441.

Olsen, E. O. "An Econometric Analysis of Rent Control in New York City in 1968." unpublished paper presented at Econometric Society Meetings, December 1970.

Olsen, E. O. "A Normative Theory of Transfers," Public Choice, 5 (1968), 39-58.

Olsen, E. O. "A Theorem in the Theory of Efficient Transfers," Journal of Political Economy, 79 (1971), 166-176.

Olsen, E. O. "A Welfare Economic Evaluation of Public Housing," unpublished Ph.D. dissertation, Rice University, 1968.

Olsen, E. O. "Subsidized Housing in a Competitive Market: Reply," American Economic Review, 61 (1971), 220-224.

Pauly, M. V. "Mixed Public and Private Financing of Education: Efficiency and Feasibility," American Economic Review, 57 (1967), 120-130.

Prescott, J. R. "Rental Formation in Federally Supported Public Housing," Land Economics, 43 (1967), 341-345.

Ross, W. B. "A Proposed Methodology for Comparing Federally Assisted Housing Programs," American Economic Review, 57 (1967), 91-100.

Rothenberg, J. Economic Evaluation of Urban Renewal: Conceptual Foundations of Benefit-Cost Analysis. Washington: Brookings Institution, 1967.

Smolensky, E. "Public Housing or Income Supplements—The Economics of Housing for the Poor," Journal of the American Institute of Planners, 34 (1968), 94-101.

IV.

**RACE
AND
HOUSING**

RESIDENTIAL MOBILITY OF BLACKS AND WHITES: A NATIONAL LONGITUDINAL SURVEY

Ronald J. McAllister

Edward J. Kaiser

Edgar W. Butler

Spatial mobility has been a subject of interest to sociologists, demographers, and geographers for generations. There is an extensive literature on migration in the United States (Mangalam 1968), and a smaller literature describing intrametropolitan residential moves (Simmons 1968). Yet there is a paucity of information about race differentials in both migration and intrametropolitan residential mobility. Given the current extensive theoretical and practical concern about racial segregation within metropolitan centers in the United States, and the growing interest in a national urbanization and growth policy, there is a need to focus more sharply on racial differences for both longer- and shorter-distance moves than previously published aggregate data have permitted. It is the purpose of this paper to shed new light on this relatively untouched area by identifying important black and white differentials and similarities in residential movements and to relate them to current explanations of mobility.

What empirical work has been done is consistent only if one notes the distance of moves being discussed. For example, Tilly (1968, p. 125) points out that "America's racial minorities have generally done less long-distance migrating than whites." Similarly, Lansing and Mueller (1968, p. 263), examining intermetropolitan or county mobility, state that at the "present time geographic mobility is considerably lower among Negro than among white families in the U.S." In contrast, Straits, examining house-to-house movement in Chicago, reports that Negroes had higher average rates of mobility than whites (Straits 1968, p. 575). Although not entirely clear, a double hypothesis appears to emerge: 1. blacks are more likely than whites to make a change of residence (regardless of distance or type); and 2. black moves are more likely to be of short distances than are white moves. Such hypotheses are consistent with findings from analyses of more highly aggregated data reported in recent Current Population Reports published by the Bureau of the Census (see U.S. Department of Commerce 1971 for a recent example).

Unexplored so far is why such differences prevail. Because the data reported here need not be aggregated it is possible to make a more detailed inquiry than was possible in earlier studies forced to rely on census data. With such aggregated data sets it is generally impossible to get below the level of intracounty moves. In the present study, we have the distinct advantage of being able to examine several types of moves which take place within metropolitan areas, thus enabling us to examine moves of relatively short distances such as intraneighborhood changes of residence. In addition, because ours is an interview survey, we can examine respondents' reasons for moving in an effort to explain as well as to describe observed differences.

We utilize data from a two-wave national survey of residential mobility patterns and residential preferences in U.S. metropolitan areas (Butler et al. 1969). Interviews with 1,476 households in forty-three metropolitan areas across the country were conducted in the fall of 1966, using a standard multistage probability sample to the level of small areas containing one or more city blocks. At the block level, quota sampling was used to obtain a representative proportion of respondents by age, employment status, and race, and by head/spouse relationship to household. The sample design specifications assured the correct proportional representation for each of four major census regions, each of three Standard Metropolitan Statistical Area (SMSA) size classes, and equal numbers of interviews in central cities and in the remainder of each SMSA. During the fall of 1969 interviews were again carried out with original respondent households—movers and nonmovers—as well as with all new households that had moved into dwelling units vacated by 1966 respondent-residents. In all cases attempts were made to reinterview original respondents; where this was not possible, spouses were interviewed; where this was not possible, interviews were conducted with some other adult member of the household. The total number of respondents in this second-wave survey was 1,561. If every possible interview had been completed, there would have been over 2,000 interviews. However, approximately 150 potential respondents refused to be reinterviewed in 1969; about 100 "out-mover" households could not be located; and approximately 100 "in-mover" interviews were lost because dwelling units were vacant or had been converted to business or destroyed; finally, another 100 potential cases were never realized for such miscellaneous reasons as death, emigration, language difficulties, and so forth. As might be expected, the racial distribution of these "noninterviews" was not exactly proportional (for a discussion of the impact of this situation, see n. *, table 3).

The data allow several approaches to testing hypotheses. First of all, we can examine the respondent's last move as reported by him regardless of when it was made—retrospective moves; second, we can examine observed staying/moving behavior for the three-year period between the 1966 and the 1969 waves of the survey—subsequent moves; or, finally, we can examine moving plans for the future—prospective moves. There is sufficient precedent for each of these approaches to justify their use (Shryock 1964; Rossi 1955; Butler, Sabagh, and Van Arsdol 1964). In order to present as thorough a view as possible, some attention will be given to all three approaches.

Moves between the first wave of interviews in 1966 and the second wave in 1969 provide data on the most current, actually observed, behavior. Households were placed in one of three categories: 1. no move; 2. local move, a category containing all moves within the same city or town irrespective of actual distance or size of community; and 3. migratory moves containing all moves out of the city or town. This classification of movers agrees conceptually with Bogue's "local moves" and "moves of migration" (Bogue 1959).

TABLE 1

MOVING BEHAVIOR (1966-69) BY RACE

	Race	
Type of Move	Black (%)	White (%)
No move	47.6	57.2
Local move	48.0	25.5
Migratory move	4.4	17.3
Total	100.0 (273)	(100.0 (1,275)

Note.—In this and following tables, if percentages do not total 100.0 percent, it is a result of rounding error; the size of the sample also varies from table to table because of variation in the number of nonresponses to particular questions; x^2 = 67.3 with 2 df (P = .01); figures in parentheses are N's.

Table 1 tests the hypotheses concerning both the greater overall mobility of blacks and the less migratory character of their moves. It can be seen that approximately 10 percent more blacks than whites were movers during the period between surveys. Over one-half of the black households changed their places of residence between 1966 and 1969. However, all but 4.4 percent of blacks remained within the same city or town, as compared with 17.3 percent of whites.

RETROSPECTIVE MOBILITY

More detailed examination of the last previous moves of respondents reveals, further, that over 90 percent of the blacks' previous places of residence were within the same city or town, as compared with less than 60 percent of those of whites. Thus, while the rate of mobility is slightly higher with blacks, their amount of long-distance change in location is substantially less. Examining only migratory moves we find that about half of the approximately 10 percent of black and half of the approximately 40 percent of white migrants were within the metropolitan area, and half of each were outside of it. Of the last local moves, 41 percent of the blacks were within the neighborhood (where neighborhood was defined by the respondent) while 36 percent of the whites were intraneighborhood. Thus the proportional breakdowns within the local move and migratory move categories were similar for both blacks and whites. The principal difference is between, rather than within, mobility categories.

TABLE 2

PLANS TO MOVE EVENTUALLY BY RACE

	Race	
Type of Planned Move	Black (%)	White (%)
No move planned	41.1	41.8
Intraneighborhood	10.2	7.0
Intracity/town	30.9	15.7
Other (migratory)...............	17.7	35.5
Total......................	99.9 (265)	100.0 (1,220)

Note.$-x^2$ = 51.5 with 3 df (P = .01).

PROSPECTIVE MOBILITY

When we change the time orientation to the future and consider prospective or planned moves we continue to find support for the hypothesis. Examining one-year prospective behavior we find that blacks are more potentially mobile than whites. Approximately 19 percent of whites have immediate moving plans, compared with 34 percent of blacks who have plans. In the short run, then, blacks are more likely than whites to be residentially mobile. In addition, we extended future considerations beyond one year by asking respondents if they ever planned to move. As shown in table 2, a disproportionate number of black respondents plan on being locally mobile (41.1 percent as compared with 22.7 percent of the whites), while twice the proportion of whites (36 percent) over blacks (18 percent) plan on making moves out of their present cities or towns. However, there is no support here for that part of the hypotheses which holds that blacks tend to move more than whites. There are nearly identical proportions of members of each racial group who plan never to move from their present places of residence. This would indicate that blacks do not appear any more prospectively mobile than whites, at least not in terms of long-run plans, unless those blacks who do plan to move, move more frequently than whites who plan on moving.

In previous studies of moving plans (Rossi 1955; Butler et al. 1964; Butler et al. 1969) the question has been phrased for one year following the interview. Here, by extending the time limits in an open-ended manner, the meaning of the prospective behavior apparently is changed (McAllister 1970). This similarity among racial groups in terms of open-ended staying behavior (namely, those who plan never to move) may be due to other factors such as "cumulative inertia" among certain population categories in both races (McGinnis 1968; Morrison 1967, 1969) or to class differences such as orientation to the future (Banfield 1970).

The analyses thus far generally support both parts of the hypothesis. However, the support is weaker and more inconsistent for the hypothesis of a higher black rate of mobility. Support is much stronger and more consistent for the hypothesis that black movers both plan and actualize more local moves than whites—while clearly being less migratory than whites. Whether this is entirely due to the racial character of these two groups, however, is another question. Are these mobility differences attributable to race or to other economic, social, or demographic factors with which race may be associated? Are respondents' reasons for moving different between races?

EXPLAINING BLACK-WHITE DIFFERENTIALS

Since it seems to make little difference which of several measures of mobility is used for the analysis, it is advantageous to deal with only one measure. In addition, there are several reasons which justify concentrating on subsequent mobility, namely, mobility between the first interview in 1966 and the second one in 1969. This measure is actual (current), and, unlike measures of retrospective and prospective behavior, it deals with a uniform time period of three years. It also is less subject to measurement error, since it is measured by actual observation rather than by a respondent's recalled or anticipated behavior.

In an effort to identify the dynamics of black-white mobility differences, we shall control for twelve variables which other studies have shown to have some affect on moving behavior. These controls are: age, education, family size, SES (Duncan socioeconomic index), duration of residence, tenure (ownership/rentership), dwelling unit and neighborhood satisfaction, family income, location (city, suburbs), family type (full and extended families, and other groupings; see Butler et al. 1969, p. 51, for a discussion of family type and residential mobility), and social mobility commitment (utilizing a series of questions patterned after the scale developed by Westoff, Bressler, and Sagi 1960).

RATE OF MOBILITY

Rosenberg's method of "test factor standardization" was used to examine the effect of these control variables on the association between race and mobility/stability (Rosenberg 1962). Of the twelve control variables examined, tenure is the only one with an impact which is statistically significant[1].

The remaining variables, however, had little or no effect on the black/white differences. For six of the remaining eleven control variables cited above, the differences between black and white mobility rates were decreased very slightly by this method of control. This indicates that only a small amount of the differences between blacks and whites can be attributed to the tendency for black families to have lower occupational status, shorter duration of residence, lower level of satisfaction with dwelling unit and neighborhood, lower income, and a higher social mobility commitment. Four other controls had even less effect on the differences between black and white rates of mobility. Thus the fact that black families are more likely to have younger heads and to live in the central city, more likely to have larger families, and less likely to be full family types does not help explain mobility rate differentials. Controlling for education of the family head, on the other hand, does have a limited impact. While the white mobility rate rises predictably with educational attainment, black mobility rates tend not to vary[2]. Thus, while education facilitates white mobility, it is not strong enough to appreciably affect black mobility.

The comparison between uncontrolled and controlled percentages in table 3 shows the impact of tenure status. The statistically controlled portion of the table shows what the relationship between race and mobility would be if the effect of tenure were removed. Here it will be noted that the black households are actually less mobile than the whites; that is, the pattern shown in the uncontrolled portion is actually reversed once the two groups are equalized in terms of tenure.

TABLE 3

MOBILITY DIFFERENCES BETWEEN RACES: CONTROLLED IN TWO WAYS TO SHOW THE EFFECT OF TENURE*

A. STATISTICAL CONTROL (TEST FACTOR STANDARDIZATION)

Moving Behavior	Uncontrolled Percentages*		Percentages After Statistical Control**	
	Black (%)	White (%)	Black (%)	White (%)
Stayed	48.7	58.6	58.4	55.9
Moved	51.3	41.4	41.6	44.1
Total	100.0	100.0	100.0	100.0

B. CONTROL BY GROUPING

Moving Behavior	Owners***		Renters****	
	Black (%)	White (%)	Black (%)	White (%)
Stayed	76.8	79.8	35.9	26.6
Moved	23.2	20.2	64.1	73.4
Total	100.0	100.0	100.0	100.0
	(82)	(738)	(181)	(488)

Note.—Figure in parentheses are N's.

* Because of their greater mobility and generally lower SES, blacks account for a disproportionate share of uncompleted cases. However, the rate of noncompletion for blacks was only about 6.2 percent higher than for whites. Combining these uncompleted cases with completed ones and recalculating the lower half of this table, for example, results in no significant changes. In fact, black and white owners tend to become even more alike, with nearly 17 percent moving in each case. Renters, too, become less divergent; with 58.8 percent of blacks and 64.4 percent of whites moving between 1966 and 1969.

*$\gamma = -.20$ $(P = .01)$.
**$\gamma = .11$ (N.S.).
***$\gamma = .21$ $(P = .05)$.

The lower half of this table shows that black renters are clearly less mobile than white renters and that, while black owners are slightly more mobile than white owners, the difference is slight and statistically insignificant. The higher apparent rate of mobility among blacks results only from the fact that most blacks are renters and renters are more mobile than homeowners. Indeed, blacks are fully 30 percent more likely than whites to be renters (69 percent to 39 percent); and of all 1966 renter respondents, nearly 70 percent moved before the fall of 1969, while only 25 percent of those owning or buying a home did so. The conclusion reached from testing the hypotheses using these twelve control variables is clear: the slightly greater mobility of blacks is a result of their tenure status rather than of racial, demographic, socioeconomic, or attitudinal differences(3).

DIFFERENCES IN REASONS FOR MOVING

Looking at social, demographic, and attitudinal correlates of mobility is only one way of identifying the factors which underlie behavioral differences. It is also informative to examine the reasons given by movers for their last moves between 1966 and 1969. In table 4, there are some striking differences in the reasons for moving given by different racial groups. Nearly 21 percent of moves made by blacks were "forced," as compared with only 5.9 percent for white respondents. Furthermore, while this category of involuntary mobility—resulting from dwelling unit destruction, eviction, land taken by eminent domain, etc.—is the reason most frequently cited by blacks, it is the reason least cited by whites.

TABLE 4

REASONS FOR MOVES (1966-69) BY RACIAL GROUPS

Reason	%	Reason	%
Blacks:		Whites:	
Forced to move	20.8	Space	15.0
Seeking a better place	16.0	Job changes.............	12.0
Had been sharing a residence .	14.6	Tenure	11.8
Cost-related	11.1	Seeking a better place	10.2
Space	11.1	Cost-related	8.2
Miscellaneous reasons	7.6	Accessibility	8.2
Formation of new household		Miscellaneous reasons	8.2
or retirement	6.3	Formation of new household	
Other neighborhood related		or retirement	7.6
reasons..............	5.6	Had been sharing a residence .	6.8
Tenure	4.2	Other neighborhood-related	
Accessibility	2.1	reasons..............	6.3
Job changes.............	0.7	Forced to move	5.9
Total	100.1	Total	100.2
	(144)		(527)

Note.—Reasons are listed in order of frequency; numbers in parentheses are *N*s.

These involuntary moves may shed some light on differences which were observed between open-ended moving prospects and moving plans for the next year. It will be remembered that, for the short run, blacks were more mobile;

but that in the long run there was virtually no difference in moving propensity between races. If past behavior is any indication of future patterns, it may be that differences in the short run can be accounted for by "situational" factors. Forced moves and the like could not naturally be anticipated for the open-ended future, but their impact would likely be perceived during the relatively short period of a year.

Reasons given by respondents, furthermore, may be indicative of rather different life-styles. Thus, for example, 14.6 percent of all black families reinterviewed say they moved because they were sharing a place and wanted a place of their own; only 6.8 percent of the whites so answered. Job-related moves tell us a great deal about the relationship between occupation and mobility; only one black respondent moved as a result of a job change, compared with 12 percent of all white household moves for that reason. This may reflect differences in career orientation (for a discussion of careerism as a life-style see Bell 1958). Black households can also be seen to move less often in order to obtain a house or home ownership. Combined with the findings above regarding rentership and mobility, this would indicate the probability of continued high mobility for blacks regardless of longer-term expectations.

Outside of forced moves, the most frequently cited reason for voluntary moving among blacks is "seeking a better place"; if we combine this with "costs" and "space" as impetus for changing residence, we can account for 38.2 percent of all moves made by black households, and for 33.4 percent of those made by white. This clearly implies the role of dwelling unit dissatisfaction in moving behavior of both blacks and whites (Rossi 1955). Yet general dissatisfaction is more often reported by blacks; of those who were reinterviewed in 1969, approximately 28 percent of the blacks were dissatisfied with their neighborhoods and/or houses in 1966, whereas only 10 percent of the whites were dissatisfied.

It is rather clear from table 4 that relatively little correspondence exists between the sets of specific reasons given by each group. This further emphasizes the importance of various reasons in explaining mobility differentials observed by race. Not only do different racial categories move differently, as previously reported; they also do so for apparently different reasons.

DISCUSSION

Understanding the role of dissatisfaction, job changes, forced moves, and tenure should shed some light on which families move and why they do, although it does not fully explain the patterns which emerge for different races, namely, why blacks move more locally, while whites make more migrations. There are a number of factors which—operating separately or in conjunction—could effect these patterns. Some of these are: limited capital on the part of blacks, inability of poor people to secure sufficient loans, the general unavailability of housing for sale on the open market, the failure of new construction to "filter" black households (Lansing, Clifton, and Morgan 1969), prejudice of sellers and lessors, and the "limited social space" (Brown and Moore 1970) in which deprived minorities often exist. Since identification of the crucial factors in this process is a broad issue which itself deserves considerable attention, we shall not speculate on it here. However, at present we are engaged in efforts to elaborate the role which the last item, "social space," plays in this process, since there is reason to believe that it could be the critical issue (Liebow 1967; Hannerz 1969; Suttles 1968).

At the present time, then, we can only say that black households move more often and more locally than white households; and, furthermore, that this is related to the fact that blacks more often rent than own their homes. Further, their reasons for moving are different. In addition, from a practical standpoint, the consequences of these patterns in terms of racial segregation within metropolitan centers and in terms of a national urbanization and growth policy make this question of differential residential mobility one which clearly deserves continued study.

NOTES

(1) It is possible that the cumulative effect of the control variables could be significant even though, individually, they are not significant. A multivariate control analysis, however, was not practical with our data.

(2) Bogue (1969, p. 769) reports similar, although not identical, results in using 1960 census data. The rise in migration rates for nonwhites, while reasonably consistent, is less dramatic than that for whites.

(3) Some argument also could be made for considering (anticipated) mobility as a cause rather than a result of tenure status. Under this reverse thesis, because more blacks are anticipating moving more often they logically choose to rent rather than to buy their homes. This argument, however, leaves more questions unanswered than it resolves; foremost among these, of course, is why blacks anticipate moving so often to begin with. Given what has been shown here in terms of the relative ineffectiveness of variables of life-style, social class, and so forth, it seems unlikely that this hypothesis could be verified. However, it is not unreasonable to suggest that whites who rent are more likely to do so by choice because they anticipate a future move, while blacks who rent are likely to do so more as a result of the biased housing market than by choice. These arguments, while unverified, clearly are worthy of consideration.

REFERENCES

Banfield, Edward. 1970. The Unheavenly City. New York: Little, Brown.

Bell, Wendell. 1958. "Social Class, Life Styles, and Suburban Residence." In The Suburban Community, edited by William M. Dobriner. New York: Putnam's.

Bogue, Donald J. 1959. "Internal Migration." In The Study of Population: An Inventory and Appraisal, edited by Philip M. Hauser and Otis D. Duncan. Chicago: University of Chicago Press.

Bogue, Donald J. 1969. Principles of Demography. New York: Wiley.

Brown, Lawrence A., and Eric G. Moore. 1970. "The Intra-Urban Migration Process: A Perspective." Geografiska Annaler, ser. B, vol. 52, no. 1.

Butler, Edgar W., F. Stuart Chapin, Jr., George C. Hemmens, Edward J. Kaiser, Michael A. Stegman, and Shirley F. Weiss. 1969. Moving Behavior and Residential Choice: A National Survey. National Cooperative Highway Research Program Report 81, Highway Research Board. Washington, D.C.: National Academy of Sciences.

Butler, Edgar, W., Georges Sabagh, and Maurice D. Van Arsdol, Jr. 1964. "Demographic and Social Psychological Factors in Residential Mobility." Sociology and Social Research 48:138-54.

Hannerz, Ulf. 1969. Soulside. New York: Columbia University Press.

Lansing, John B., C. W. Clifton, and J. N. Morgan. 1969. New Homes and Poor People. Ann Arbor, Mich.: Institute for Social Research.

Lansing, John B., and Eva Mueller. 1968. The Geographic Mobility of Labor. Ann Arbor, Mich.: Institute for Social Research.

Liebow, Elliot. 1967. Tally's Corner. Boston: Little, Brown.

McAllister, Ronald J. 1970. Neighborhood Integration and Prospective Residential Mobility. Chapel Hill, N.C.: Center for Urban and Regional Studies.

McGinnis, Robert. 1968. "A Stochastic Model of Social Mobility." American Sociological Review 33 (October): 712-22.

Mangalam, J. J. (with the assistance of Cornelia Morgan). 1968. Human Migration: A Guide to Migration Literature in English. Lexington: University of Kentucky Press.

Morrison, Peter A. 1967. "Duration of Residence and Prospective Migration: The Evaluation of a Stochastic Model." Demography 4 (2):553-61.

Morrison, Peter A. 1969. "Theoretical Issues in the Design of Population Mobility Models." Paper presented at the 64th Annual Meeting of the American Sociological Association, San Francisco, September.

Rosenberg, Morris. 1962. "Test Factor Standardization as a Method of Interpretation." Social Forces 41:53-61.

Rossi, Peter A. 1955. Why Families Move: A Study in the Social Psychology of Urban Residential Mobility. Glencoe, Ill.: Free Press.

Shryock, Henry, Jr. 1964. Population Mobility within the United States. Chicago: Community and Family Study Center.

Simmons, James W. 1968. "Changing Residence in the City: A Review of Intra-Urban Mobility." Geographical Review 58 (4):622-51.

Straits, Bruce C. 1968. "Residential Movement among Negroes and Whites in Chicago." Social Science Quarterly (December): 573-92.

Suttles, Gerald. 1968. The Social Order of the Slum. Chicago: University of Chicago Press.

Tilly, Charles. 1968. "Race and Migration to the American City." In The Metropolitan Enigma, edited by James Q. Wilson. Cambridge, Mass.: Harvard University Press.

U.S. Department of Commerce, Bureau of the Census. 1971. Current Publication Reports, Ser. P-20, no. 210 (January 15). Washington, D.C.: Government Printing Office.

Westoff, Charles F., Marvin Bressler, and Philip G. Sagi. 1960. "The Concept of Social Mobility." American Sociological Review 25:375-85.

DO BLACKS PAY MORE FOR HOUSING?

Victoria Lapham

Many people believe that discrimination against blacks in housing markets is widespread. In general, they have in mind that blacks must pay more than whites for housing of a given quality. In this paper I report on a study undertaken to test this hypothesis and conclude that there is no statistically significant difference in black-white housing costs.

The traditional definition of discrimination is based on identical products being sold for different prices. Since housing units are not identical, some modification of this definition is necessary.

To compare the prices of differentiated goods, it is helpful to view goods as bundles of characteristics.(1) By identifying the prices of characteristics possessed by goods, we can compare the prices of common characteristics to see if they are priced differently to different buyers. This, in effect, defines discrimination in the framework of the traditional analysis: there is discrimination if the same characteristics are priced differently.(2) There is, of course, no reason for the goods themselves which possess different characteristics to have the same price.

This points up one of the difficulties of identifying discrimination in housing markets by looking at the price of the individual units. If there is some characteristic peculiar to housing bought by either blacks or whites, then its price cannot be compared with the price of any other characteristic, and as suggested above, given different characteristics there is no reason for goods to have the same price. The characteristic ordinarily peculiar to housing bought by whites is that it is located in white neighborhoods and similarly, housing bought by blacks is located in black neighborhoods. This segregation of blacks and whites could be caused either by the preference of whites to live near whites (prejudice against blacks) and the preference of blacks to live near blacks (prejudice against whites), or by latent discrimination, that is, the refusal of whites (blacks) to sell to blacks (whites) except at a higher price than they would sell to whites (blacks) and at a price sufficiently high that blacks (whites) choose not to buy. For housing units identical in every way except that one is located in a white neighborhood and one in a black neighborhood, a difference in price is not evidence of discrimination. If P_b is the price of a house located in a black neighborhood identical in every way to a house located in a white neighborhood whose price is P_w, then $P_b > P_w$ could be due to blacks preferring black neighborhoods or to white discrimination or both. If $P_b = P_w$, it is impossible to rule out the possiblity of discrimination for the same reason. Whites and blacks may discriminate, but transactions would occur (and we would be able to observe discrimination) only if members of either race preferred to buy from members of the other. Similarly, if $P_w > P_b$, whites may or may not discriminate. The only implication of this is that whites are willing to pay a premium to buy from whites (perhaps because they prefer white neighborhoods).(3) In summary, it is possible to compare only the prices of common characteristics. By comparing the prices of common characteristics, we may be able to identify discrimination. It cannot be identified by comparing the price of equivalent housing in black and white neighborhoods.

From this, it is evident that segregated neighborhoods not only fail to give conclusive evidence of discrimination, but, in addition, segregated neighborhoods prevent the direct comparison of housing prices to identify discrimination.

Despite these difficulties in identifying discrimination, a first step can be made by identifying differences in prices paid for common characteristics.

DESCRIPTION OF DATA

To identify differences in prices paid by blacks and whites, 650 observations of housing units sold in Dallas in 1960 were obtained from real estate brokers.(4) Of these, 185 were located in predominantly black neighborhoods. The sample houses were located in eighty of the 174 census tracts in the city, but these eighty tracts contain 60 percent of the city's housing units. The tracts represented are scattered throughout the city's area. When a unit is listed with a broker, he records descriptive information on the unit as well as the asking price. When it is sold, the selling price is recorded. The test scheme was to relate price to characteristics and then to compare the prices of characteristics bought by both blacks and whites.

The characteristics listed were: price, square footage of the house, square footage of the lot, front footage of the lot, location (address), age, number of bedrooms, number of bathrooms, type of heating, type of cooling, type of garage, type of facing and whether the unit was fenced or carpeted, whether the unit had a dishwasher or garbage disposal unit, refrigerator or stove, fireplace, or workshop. Table 1 shows summary statistics for the black and white samples. For characteristics 9-27, the mean represents the fraction of total units which possess a given characteristic.

Although the information is fairly detailed, it is incomplete. There are other characteristics of the unit about which no information is available. For example, there is no information about the maintenance of the house or the nature of the lot (number of trees and shrubs). If the excluded variables are independent of those included, ordinary least-square estimators will be unbiased. If they are not independent, then the estimators will be biased. Since the aim is to predict the price of a house with given characteristics, this would not be a serious obstacle if the black and white estimators are similarly biased.

TABLE 1

SUMMARY STATISTICS FOR SAMPLE

Characteristics	White Subsample Mean	Black Subsample Mean
1. Price	11,220.0	9,953.0
2. Square footage of house	994.6	887.9
3. Square footage of lot	8,290.0	8,125.0
4. Front footage of lot	59.35	57.75
5. Minutes to downtown	29.86	26.97
6. Age	13.06	9.77
7. Number of bathrooms.............	1.15	1.03
8. Number of bedrooms	2.46	2.23
9. Central heat	0.3134	0.0540
10. Wall heaters or floor furnaces	0.4776	0.7189
11. Gas jet......................	0.2345	0.2270
12. Central air	0.0171	0.0054
13. Window units	0.3817	0.1838
14. Attic fan	0.2942	0.1622
15. 1 garage.....................	0.6439	0.8108
16. 2 garages	0.2580	0.1081
17. Carport	0.0490	0.0054
18. Fence	0.7719	0.3784
19. Carpet......................	0.4691	0.2108
20. Dishwasher	0.0554	0.0162
21. Garbage disposal	0.0618	0.0216
22. Wood-burning fireplace	0.1258	0.0864
23. Refrigerator and stove	0.0213	0.0216
24. Frame	0.3646	0.4376
25. Brick veneer	0.1151	0.3784
26. Brick or stone	0.5203	0.1838
27. Workshop	0.0448	0.0324

Information about the race of the buyer and seller is not recorded. The only information which permits determining race is location. Units located in white neighborhoods are assumed to have a white buyer and seller; units located in black neighborhoods are assumed to have a black buyer and seller.

Another problem is that the information available does not include a description of the neighborhood in which the unit is located. We generally believe that the quality of housing within a neighborhood is a good proxy for the quality of the neighborhood itself. Since neighborhoods tend toward a fairly high degree of homogeneity (it is this homogeneity which is sometimes used to define a neighborhood), one might expect to find housing in the neighborhood to be similar to the observed unit. If this is the case, the problem is not a serious one. Furthermore, since the study is confined to the city of Dallas, neighborhood desirability does not depend on differences in the level of city services and tax rates except as the city itself discriminates against its various parts. But the possibility remains that in neglecting to measure the desirability of neighborhoods, we are failing to account for a systematic difference between black and white neighborhoods which is not reflected in the characteristics of the housing units. If physically equivalent units are located in "desirable" neighborhoods which are white and "undesirable" neighborhoods which are also black, then by considering only the unit we could find that physically equivalent units bought by blacks and whites sold for the same price, and we would conclude that there is no evidence of a price difference when in actuality blacks would be paying more for equivalent quality of housing where housing includes both the unit and the neighborhood. On the other hand, neighborhood desirability is not easy to define, much less measure. Even if complete information on neighborhood characteristics were available the problem would not be solved. The reason is that variables used as proxies for neighborhood quality, such as median number years of schooling completed in the neighborhood or crime indexes for the neighborhood, are difficult to interpret.

Suppose a black and white neighborhood are identical in every way except the black neighborhood's residents have completed fewer years of schooling. Should we expect to find the price of housing lower in that neighborhood? Only if we believe it is inferior to the white neighborhood. This would seem to be a matter of individual preference. We can only conclude that the effect of including a variable representing the median number of years of schooling depends entirely upon the interpretation given it; that is, we could find a price difference or not depending on the interpretation of this variable.

While a crime index may appear to be a more straightforward measure of neighborhood quality, it, too, is plagued with difficulties. The first difficulty is the creation of such an index, given the problem of weighting various kinds of crime and the generally acknowledged existence of underreporting. The second is the problem of interpreting the effects of crime on housing prices. If a crime index were independent of the nature of housing in a neighborhood and the racial characteristics of the neighborhood, then the coefficient on the index would indicate the variation in the price of housing for differential crime rates. If, however, a crime index were not independent of the racial characteristics of the neighborhood, and if blacks or whites are prejudiced, we would be unable to distinguish between the effects of differential crime rates and the quality of housing.

Given these difficulties, a crime index was not included as an independent variable. It was assumed that a crime index would be independent of the racial characteristics of the neighborhood but not independent of the housing characteristics. In this event, the estimates of the characteristic's implicit prices will be biased, but they should be similarly biased for the black and white samples so that comparison may not suffer.

Two neighborhoods which contain equivalent housing could differ because of the previously mentioned difference in the provision of public services. If there is discrimination in public services in Dallas, then in the absence of discrimination in housing markets we would expect to find the price of equivalent housing lower in black neighborhoods. Housing market discrimination could mask this difference, of course.

The dependent variable used was stated selling price of the house. In the usual case, the seller and the mortgager of a house are different individuals, so that discrimination in credit markets cannot be confused with discrimination in housing markets. A sample of the observations was checked for seller financing. From this, it appeared that the selling price does not vary as a fraction of the asking price depending on whether there is some part of the selling price which is seller financed. From this, I concluded that the stated selling price is not subject to observation error.

I was unable to find a satisfactory way to quantify the location variable and thus to estimate an implicit price for it. Initially, I assumed that location would determine the amount of time a family spent traveling to work, school, and shopping areas. Assuming that the trip to work is most important and that employment opportunities are concentrated in the center of the city, locations near the center would reduce travel time to work and thus be more desirable, *ceteris paribus*.(5) In order to check this hypothesis, the location of each unit was represented by the bus travel time necessary to get to the center of the city. This representation was selected instead of distance because it allowed for the presence of freeways or thoroughfares which could make locations of greater distance more accessible to downtown than locations closer to the city where these are absent. This representation did not contribute to accounting for variations in the price of houses. The correlation of time from center and lot size appears to account for the impossibility of separately identifying their influence on price.

THE TESTING PROCEDURE

The procedure used to test for a difference in the price paid for housing by blacks and whites was to estimate implicit prices of characteristics bought by the two groups.(6) If the functional relationship between the price of housing and its characteristics were known, then it would have only been necessary to estimate the parameters of the function using the black and white data and test to see if the estimates were equal.

Since the relationship was unknown, it was necessary to adopt a procedure to hypothesize relationships between price and characteristics. However, it is well known that if a hypothesis is chosen to conform to a data set, inferences about the distribution of random variables cannot be made. This made it necessary to separate the sample, reserving part of it for hypothesis testing.

The procedure adopted was the following: 1. Hypothesize relationship between price and characteristics using half the randomly partitioned white sample (the search sample). 2. Test these hypotheses on the remaining half of the white sample (the test sample). 3. If the structural parameters are the same in the search and test samples for any of the hypothesized relationships, pool the samples and estimate white structural parameters. 4. Use the hypothesized relationships satisfying 3. To estimate structural parameters for the black sample. 5. Test the hypothesis that the structural parameters are the same for the white and black samples.

Using half the white sample (230 observations), various relationships between price and characteristics were hypothesized. The price of a house was assumed to be a linear function of its characteristics implying that the price of a house is the sum of the values of its characteristics. Different combinations of variables were tried, and the independent variables were represented in alternative forms. Eventually four functions were chosen as reasonable representations of the relationship between price and characteristics. Each accounted for between 75 and 80 percent of the variation in price of houses in this search sample(7)

These four functions were used to estimate structural parameters (implicit prices) for the test sample (the remaining half of the white sample). The question to be answered was whether the structural parameters under any of the hypothesized relationships were the same for the two sets of data. If the parameters were statistically different, it would indicate that the hypothesized relationship was peculiar to the search sample and that the relationship was not a general one. If the parameters were not statistically different, it would imply that the hypothesized relationship could be confronted with a second set of data and yield similar results indicating that the hypothesized relationship was not peculiar to the sample from which it was formulated.

An F-test of the hypothesis that the structural parameters in the two sets of data for the various relationships were the same was performed. For one of the relationships, the hypothesis that the structural parameters for the two sets were the same could not be rejected. On this basis, the search and test samples were pooled. This model was able to account for over 75 percent of the variation in the price of housing in the white sample.

The next step was to use this model to estimate structural parameters in the black samples and test the hypothesis that the structural parameters for the black sample were equal to those for the white sample. An F-test of the hypothesis that the structural parameters in the two samples were the same was performed. The hypothesis was rejected.(8)

Columns 1 and 2 in table 2 show the structural parameters estimated from the white sample and the black sample, respectively. The price differences for some characteristics are large, but the differences are statistically significant only for two variables, floor furnaces and brick veneer facing.

Our test indicated that the structural parameters estimated for the black and white samples are different. Since some of the parameter estimates are larger in the white sample and some are larger in the black sample, we can go one step farther and ask if there is a significant direction to the difference.

This requires that we adopt some scheme to weigh the importance of each of the structural parameters. The scheme developed was to create two indexes. One index uses as a base a black unit with the average of all characteristics in the black sample valued at the implicit prices estimated from the black sample. This is compared with the same bundle priced at the implicit price estimated from the white sample. The index is

$$(\hat{a}_w \bar{X}_b)/(\hat{a}_b \bar{X}_b) = \hat{\bar{P}}_{bw}/\hat{\bar{P}}_{bb},$$

where $\hat{a}_w$ and $\hat{a}_b$ are the vectors of implicit prices estimated from the white and black samples, respectively, and X_b is the vector of the average characteristics of the black sample. Table 2 shows, in addition to the estimated implicit prices, the means of characteristics in the black sample in column 3; in column 4, the contribution that each characteristic makes to the price of the unit based on the white parameters (1×3); and similarly in column 5, based on the black parameters (2 × 3). Summing 4 and 5 and finding the difference indicates that the price predicted by the white coefficients is \$387, or about 3.9 percent greater than the price predicted by the black coefficients. The hypothesis that the two prices were equal could not be rejected by a t-test at the 5 percent level of confidence.(9)

For the second index, the base is a white unit with the average of all characteristics in the white sample priced at the implicit prices estimated from the white sample. It is compared with the price of the same bundle when the characteristics are valued at the implicit prices estimated from the black sample. This index is

$$(\hat{a}_b \overline{X}_w) / (\hat{a}_w \overline{X}_w) = \hat{P}_{wb} / \hat{P}_{ww},$$

where the a's are the same as above and X_w is a vector of the means of characteristics in the white sample.

Table 3 shows that on the basis of this index, the price of a black unit is \$30.90, or about 0.3 percent greater than the price of a white unit. The hypothesis that the two prices were equal could not be rejected by a t-test at the 5 percent level of confidence.(10)

CONCLUSION

This study represents an effort to identify a difference in the prices paid by blacks and whites for housing by identifying differences in the price paid for common characteristics. The estimation of implicit prices resulted in the prices of some characteristics being higher in the white sample, some higher in the black sample. Two indexes were created, one using black housing characteristics as a base, one using white housing characteristics as a base. For the former, we found the price of white housing to be 4 percent higher. For the latter, we found the price of black housing to be 0.3 percent higher. Neither difference was statistically significant.

The results obtained are, of course, peculiar to Dallas. It may be of interest to compare the population characteristics of Dallas with other cities. The nonwhite population of Dallas in 1960 was 19 percent of the total population. This may be compared with a 14 percent nonwhite population of New York and 23.6 nonwhite population for Chicago. The nonwhite population of the Dallas SMSA grew by 56 percent (as compared with 44 percent for the white population) during the period from 1950 to 1960. (Figures for the city lack some meaning because of the incorporation of new areas into the city.) This increase was greater than that for Saint Louis (36 percent) or Washington D.C. (44 percent) but less than that for Chicago (66 percent). While it is difficult to draw conclusions about housing demand from population growth, the relatively large increase in the black population during this period makes it less likely that the failure to identify price differences can be attributed to a stagnant demand for housing by blacks.

The conclusion of this study must also be qualified because of the failure to account for all factors which could cause housing prices to vary between black and white neighborhoods. If white neighborhoods which contain housing physically equivalent to black neighborhoods are more desirable, then blacks

TABLE 2

AVERAGE PRICE AS PREDICTED BY WHITE AND BLACK COEFFICIENTS, BLACK BASE, MODEL (1)

Characteristic	$\hat{a}_w$ (1)	$\hat{a}_b$ (2)	$\overline{X}_b$ (3)	$\overline{P}_{bw}=$ $\hat{a}_w\overline{X}_b$ (4)	$\overline{P}_{bb}=$ $\hat{a}_b\overline{X}_b$ (5)
Square footage of house	3.2811 (0.3310)	3.3633 (0.8136)	887.9	2,913.29	2,986.27
Square footage of lot ..	0.0245 (0.0285)	0.0076 (0.039)	8,125.0	199.02	61.65
Ln age	−461.03 (124.50)	−546.41 (149.9)	1.723	−794.35	−941.46
Central heat	1,477.8 (217.02)	1,842.77 (641.04)	0.05405	79.88	99.60
Floor furnace	1,333.3 (155.08)	650.92 (289.2)	0.7189	958.51	467.95
Central air	145.91 (429.14)	588.57 (1,181.1)	0.0054	0.79	3.18
Attic fan	473.37 (124.81)	408.83 (85.13)	0.1622	76.78	66.31
1 garage	394.2 (192.14)	738.09 (378.7)	0.8108	319.62	598.44
2 garages	1,107.6 (213.09)	1,442.02 (453.9)	0.1081	119.73	155.88
Fence	258.53 (137.69)	295.43 (251.5)	0.3784	97.83	111.79
Carpet	404.16 (119.61)	198.10 (280.5)	0.2108	85.20	41.76
Dishwasher	(569.32 (259.30)	431.03 (1,690.6)	0.0162	9.23	6.99
Garbage disposal	−32.47 (247.55)	−495.09 (1,603.6)	0.0216	0.70	−10.70
Fireplace	452.89 (174.57)	126.76 (406.3)	0.0865	39.17	−10.96
Refrigerator and stove	893.09 (413.80)	1,442.98 (912.1)	0.0216	19.31	31.20
Brick-veneer facing	1,657.5 (205.64)	303.1 (349.8)	0.3784	627.20	114.69
Brick or stone facing ..	2,526.9 (139.89)	2,507.68 (373.1)	0.1838	464.44	460.91
Workshop	−40.75 (269.56)	849.99 (506.7)	0.032	1.51	31.45
1½ or 2 baths	500.64 (164.28)	91.46 (601.4)	0.0108	5.41	0.99
3 or more bedrooms ...	235.15 (135.46)	293.36 (297.0)	0.2108	49.57	61.84
Intercept	5,067.77	5,615.34	1.0	5,068.77	5,615.34
	...	...	...	10,340.21	9,953.13
	...	...	...	9,953.13	...
Difference	...	...	...	387.08	...

Note.—R^2 = .7779; standard errors are shown in parentheses.

TABLE 3

AVERAGE PRICE AS PREDICTED BY WHITE AND BLACK COEFFICIENTS, WHITE BASE, MODEL (1)

Characteristics	$\hat{a}_w$ (1)	$\hat{a}_b$ (2)	$\overline{X}_w$ (3)	$\hat{\overline{P}}_{ww}=$ $\hat{a}_w\overline{X}_w$ (4)	$\hat{\overline{P}}_{wb}=$ $\hat{a}_b\overline{X}_w$ (5)
Square footage of house	3.2811	3.3633	994.6	3,263.38	3,345.14
Square footage of lot ..	0.0245	0.0076	8,290.0	203.11	63.00
Ln age	−461.03	−546.41	2.329	−1,073.74	−1,272.59
Central heat	1,477.8	1,842.77	0.3134	463.14	577.52
Floor furance	1,333.3	650.92	0.4776	636.78	310.88
Central air	145.91	588.57	0.0171	2.49	10.06
Attic fan	473.37	408.83	0.2942	139.27	120.28
1 garage	394.2	738.09	0.6439	253.83	475.26
2 garages	1,107.6	1,442.02	0.2580	285.76	372.04
Carpet	404.16	198.10	0.4691	189.59	92.93
Dishwasher..........	569.32	431.03	0.0554	31.54	23.88
Fence	258.53	295.43	0.7719	199.56	228.04
Garbage disposal	−32.47	−495.09	0.0618	−2.01	−30.60
Fireplace	452.89	−126.76	0.1258	56.97	−15.95
Refrigerator and stove	893.09	1,442.98	0.0213	19.02	30.74
Brick-veneer facing	1,657.5	303.1	0.1151	190.78	34.89
Brick or stone facing ..	2,526.9	2,507.68	0.5203	1,314.75	1,304.75
Workshop...........	−40.75	849.99	0.0448	−1.83	38.08
1½ or 2 baths	500.64	91.46	0.189	94.62	17.29
3 or more bedrooms...	235.15	293.36	0.4416	103.84	129.55
Intercept	5,068.77	5,615.34	1.0	5,068.77	5,615.34
	...	...	...	11,439.63	11,470.53
	...	...	...	11,470.53	...
Difference........	...	...	...	30.90	...

Note.$-R^2 = .7779$.

may be paying more for equivalent housing. It should also be noted that the absence of a price difference does not rule out the possibility of discrimination.

NOTES

(1) This concept was developed by Kelvin Lancaster (1966).

(2) Let Z represent a vector of characteristics of a good x. Suppose $P_x = aZ$ where a is a vector of the implicit prices of the characteristics. Consider two units of x, $x(1)$ and $x(2)$, which possess some characteristics in common. Then $P_{x(1)} = a_1Z_1 + a_2Z_2$, and $P_{x(2)} = b_1Z_1 + b_2Z_3$ where the b's are implicit prices of characteristics possessed by $x(2)$. If $a_1 \neq b_1$, then the common characteristics (Z_1) are priced differently, that is, there is discrimination.

(3) In this discussion, it has been assumed that the observed prices in each market are equilibrium prices. This may not be true, of course. Moreover, there is much to suggest that there is at least some interaction between the two markets and that the resulting adjustment may be difficult. For example, with

black prejudice and white discrimination, the price in the black market may rise high enough to cause blacks to demand housing from whites. The result if whites are prejudiced could be the exodus of whites from neighborhoods which blacks are entering. If this is the case, we might expect a certain amount of price fluctuations reflecting changes in demand and supply conditions in both markets. This suggests that prejudice could complicate observing discrimination even if it were possible to observe the prices paid by blacks and whites in the same neighborhoods.

(4) The data were obtained through visits to the offices of real estate brokers and through a multiple listing service to which many brokers subscribe.

(5) See Mooney (1969), who reports that employment tends to be concentrated in central cities in the South, particularly in Dallas, Houston, and Atlanta.

(6) The technique of estimating implicit price was introduced by Griliches (1961, pp. 173-96). An early effort to apply multiple-regression techniques to housing prices and characteristics can be found in Brown (1964), whose results, while using similar techniques, cannot easily be compared with the result of this study since his national sample consisted only of new houses, and because much of his effort was directed toward accounting for national price variations due to climatic differences, location with respect to SMSA, and differences in housing styles.

(7) See the Appendix for a description of the models and the implicit prices estimated by them.

(8) The calculated F-statistic was 1.70, $F_{.05} = 1.60$. For a discussion of this test, see Johnston (1963 p. 136).

(9) The calculated t-statistic was 1.82, $t_{.05} = 1.96$ (see Johnston 1963, p. 37).

(10) The calculated t-statistic was 0.168.

APPENDIX

In developing relationships between economic variables, one ordinarily hypothesizes those that are suggested by economic theory or by a priori evidence. While the relationship between the characteristics of housing and its value initially seems simple, it is possible to come up with several different relationships which seem plausible.

Let X represent the vector of characteristics of housing units. Many of the elements of X can be represented as dummy variables because the nature of the characteristic is such that the only concern is whether the unit possesses the characteristic or not. For example, X_j may indicate whether the unit had a two-car garage ($X_j = 1$) or not ($X_j = 0$). In the case of some other elements of X, the variables are continuous. If the variable is continuous, it may be represented in many different forms, that is, the continuous variable X_k could enter the equation as log X_k or $X_k{}^2$. Further complexities are introduced when the possibility of interactions between variables are considered. For example, the level effect of a continuous variable may depend on the value of a dummy variable.

For these reasons, many different relationships between prices and characteristics were considered. Four relationships were finally selected from a search process in half the white sample. The initial (and the most simple) relationship hypothesized and the one that proved statistically acceptable for the testing procedure was that the price of a house is a linear function of its characteristics. This can be stated as

$$P = aX + \epsilon, \tag{1}$$

where p is the price of the unit and X is the vector of characteristics. While this relationship does allow the continuous variables to be represented in different forms there is no interaction between the variables, and it is assumed that the price of the house is the sum of the values of its characteristics. In the case of (1), all the continuous variables were represented in their natural form except age, which entered the equation in logarithmic form.

The second relationship was selected on the basis of the assumption that the effects of age depend on the nature of the unit, and particularly on the kind of exterior facing (frame, brick veneer, brick, or stone) that characterizes the unit. This relationship can be represented as

$$p = a_1 A^* X_1 + a_2 X_2 + \epsilon, \tag{2}$$

where A^* is the logarithm of the age of the unit, X_1 is a set of dummy variables representing the different kinds of exterior facing, and X_2 is a vector of the remaining characteristics.

The third relationship hypothesized was selected to represent explicitly the depreciation of a unit with increased age. This can be represented as

$$p = a_1(e^{-\rho A} X_1 Z) + a_2 X_2 + \varepsilon, \tag{3}$$

where X_1 and X_2 are defined as in (1) and (2), A is the age of the unit, and ρ is a depreciation rate depending on the nature of the unit. If ρ were known for different kinds of facing, then $E^{-\rho A} X_1$ would show the depreciation of each unit as a function of its age and facing. Since ρ was unknown and could not be estimated directly with linear regression techniques, an iterative procedure was used to choose the values of ρ which maximized the coefficient of determination in (3). This technique yielded a depreciation rate of 0.0445 for frame houses and 0.01 for brick houses.

Equation (3) does not account for the fact that the total amount of depreciation would presumably vary not only with the age and exterior facing of the unit but with other characteristics as well. In equation (4), total depreciation was allowed to vary with the size of the unit as represented by

$$\rho = a_1(e^{-\rho A} X_1 Z) + a_2 X_2 + \varepsilon, \tag{4}$$

where Z is the square footage of the unit.

The hypothesized relationships were applied to the remaining half of the white sample. Table A1 shows parameters estimated in the data used in the search for each of the four relationships. As indicated in the text, the model represented by equation (1) allowed me to accept the hypothesis that the same structure existed for the two data sets. The F-statistics calculated for each relationship were (1) 1.68, $F_{.01} = 1.84$, (2) 1.76, $F_{.01} = 1.84$, (3) 1.99,

TABLE A1

IMPLICIT PRICES ESTIMATED FOR MODELS (1)–(4)

Variable Number	Model (1) ($R^2 = .7757$)	Model (2) ($R^2 = .7891$)	Model (3) ($R^2 = 7861$)	Model (4) ($R^2 = .8000$)
X_0	4,018.65	5,910.55	52.84	3,976.44
X_1	3.49	3.36	3.9594	...
	(0.5974)	(0.5824)	(0.5608)	
X_2	−499.40	...	...	...
	(193.62)			
X_3	1,439.3	...	...	...
	(352.94)			
X_4	2,365.5	...	...	...
	(233.35)			
X_5	0.1054	0.0938	0.0748	0.0883
	(0.0486)	(0.0472)	(0.0474)	(0.0458)
X_6	1,464.9	1,438.4	1,120.9	1,159.0
	(341.34)	(331.06)	(328.86)	(292.29)
X_7	1,161.1	917.96	748.01	750.61
	(253.77)	(247.55)	(259.04)	(228.81)
X_8	576.78	580.18	640.68	881.49
	(561.44)	(544.39)	(544.31)	(526.94)
X_9	577.25	556.27	467.13	455.46
	(207.98)	(201.59)	(201.72)	(196.37)
X_{10}	461.23	478.88	532.23	575.35
	(269.00)	(260.49)	(260.36)	(252.99)
X_{11}	1,046.5	1,089.7	1,235.6	1,168.5
	(325.86)	(315.17)	(316.61)	(301.18)
X_{12}	−198.31	−589.21	−641.6	−303.88
	(849.08)	(832.71)	(821.11)	(760.09)
X_{13}	525.59	482.03	449.61	547.20
	(227.76)	(220.43)	(221.26)	(212.82)
X_{14}	361.59	580.06	508.99	438.11
	(260.98)	(251.90)	(244.52)	(235.90)
X_{15}	314.85	230.36	·184.88	141.49
	(237.37)	(240.37)	(233.24)	(225.30)
X_{16}	374.71	372.67	346.89	325.08
	(196.49)	(189.94)	(191.02)	(185.90)
X_{17}	791.39	801.76	686.90	759.27
	(429.06)	(415.77)	(413.83)	(398.28)
X_{18}	390.22	402.69	215.60	358.34
	(343.34)	(333.30)	(331.12)	(323.33)
X_{19}	323.86	319.25	361.88	403.04
	(307.31)	(297.99)	(298.23)	(280.57)
X_{20}	1,584.9	1,388.9	1,641.6	1,443.9
	(703.32)	(682.30)	(679.97)	(658.41)
X_{21}	98.02	149.54	265.27	273.74
	(421.77)	(408.49)	(410.49)	(394.68)
X_{22}	...	−555.73	...	...
		(219.69)		
X_{23}	...	−116.46	...	...
		(194.12)		

TABLE A1 (Cont'd)

Variable Number	Model (1) ($R^2 = .7757$)	Model (2) ($R^2 = .7891$)	Model (3) ($R^2 = .7869$)	Model (4) ($R^2 = .8000$)
X_{24}	...	−1,114.7 (193.44)	...	...
X_{25}	...	...	5,014.2 (968.25)	...
X_{26}	...	...	5,897.2 (687.57)	...
X_{27}	...	...	...	4.7240 (0.7567)
X_{28}	...	...	...	5.0627 (0.6382)
X_{29}	...	...	...	5.9796 (0.4982)

Note.—X_0 = intercept; X_1 = square footage of house; X_2 = logarithm of age; X_3 = brick-veneer facing; X_4 = brick or stone facing; X_5 = square footage of lot; X_6 = central heat; X_7 = wall heaters; X_8 = central air; X_9 = attic fan; X_{10} = 1 garage; X_{11} = 2 garages; X_{12} = 1 bedroom; X_{13} = 3, 4 bedrooms; X_{14} = 1, 1/2, 2 baths; X_{15} = fence; X_{16} = carpet; X_{17} = dishwasher; X_{18} = garbage disposal; X_{19} = fireplace; X_{20} = refrigerator and stove; X_{21} = workshop; X_{22} = brick veneer and brick depreciated at 0.01; X_{27} = frame square footage depreciated; X_{28} = brick veneer square footage depreciated; X_{29} = brick square footage depreciated. Standard errors are shown in parenthesis.

$F_{.01}$ = 1.92, and (4) 2.44, $F_{.01}$ = 1.92. While the model represented by equation (2) is acceptable on the above grounds, it was rejected as a model for final testing because one of the coefficients estimated for a variable which distinguishes it from (1) was of the wrong sign.

REFERENCES

Brown, S. D. "Price Variation in New Houses, 1959-1961." U.S. Department of Commerce, Bureau of the Census, Staff Working Paper in Economics and Statistics no. 6, May 1964.

Griliches, Zvi. "Hedonic Price Indexes for Automobiles: An Econometric Analysis of Quality Change." In U.S. Congress Joint Economic Committee. Hearing on Government Price Statistics. 87th Cong., 1st sess., 1961.

Johnston, J. Econometric Methods. New York: McGraw-Hill, 1963.

Lancaster, Kelvin. "A New Approach to Consumer Theory." J.P.E. 74 (April 1966): 132-57.

Mooney, Joseph D. "Housing Segregation, Negro Employment, and Metropolitan Decentralization." Q.J.E. 83 (May 1969): 299-314.

HOUSING MARKET DISCRIMINATION, HOMEOWNERSHIP, AND SAVINGS BEHAVIOR

John F. Kain and John M. Quigley

The question of whether discrimination in the housing market forces Negro households to pay more than white households for identical bundles of residential services has been studied extensively. Still it remains a controversial subject. Those who claim that discrimination markups exist in urban housing markets rely principally on a series of empirical studies which conclude that blacks pay more than whites for comparable housing or that housing in the ghetto is more expensive than otherwise identical housing located outside the ghetto. (See B. Duncan and P. Hauser, R. Haugen and A. James Heins, Kain and Quigley (1970b), D. McEntire, Richard Muth, C. Rapkin, Rapkin and W. Grigsby, Ronald Ridker and John Henning, and M. Stengel.) Those who argue that price discrimination does not exist contend that studies which purport to find evidence of a discrimination markup fail to standardize completely for differences in the bundles of residential services consumed by black and white households (see Martin Bailey (1959, 1966), Richard Muth, and Anthony Pascal).(1) Evaluation of the diverse empirical studies leads us to conclude that blacks may pay between 5 and 10 percent more than whites in most urban areas for comparable housing. Our own analyses of a 1967 sample of nearly 1,200 dwelling units in St. Louis, Missouri suggests a discrimination markup in that city on the order of 7 percent.(2)

Differentials of this magnitude would represent a significant loss in Negro welfare. However, we contend that researchers, in their concern about estimating the magnitude of price discrimination, have overlooked a far more serious consequence of housing market discrimination. In asking whether blacks pay more than whites for the same kind of housing, they have failed to consider adequately the way in which housing discrimination has affected the kinds of housing consumed by Negro households.

There is a great deal of qualitative evidence that nonwhites have difficulty in obtaining housing outside the ghetto (see James Hecht, Kain (1969), McEntire, and Karl and Alma Taeuber). Persistence, a thick skin, and a willingness to spend enormous amounts of time house-hunting are minimum requirements for nonwhites who wish to move into white neighborhoods. These psychic and transaction costs may be far more significant than out-of-pocket costs to Negroes considering a move out of the ghetto. Most blacks limit their search for housing to the ghetto; this limitation is more than geographic. There is less variety of housing services available inside the ghetto at any price. This limited range of housing services within the ghetto almost certainly influences the pattern of Negro housing consumption. A full discussion and evaluation of the many ways in which discrimination may modify the housing-consumption behavior of Negro households is beyond the scope of this paper. However, the general principle can be illustrated by the differential propensities of Negro and white households to own and to purchase their homes.

Two statistical analyses of the probability of homeownership follow. The first is a detailed analysis of the probability of ownership and purchase for a sample of St. Louis households. It indicates there is a substantial difference in the probability of Negro and white homeownership and purchase even after accounting for most of the important differences in the socioeconomic characteristics of Negro and white households. We hypothesize that this difference results from restrictions on the location and types of housing available to Negro households. This "supply restriction" hypothesis cannot be adequately tested for a single metropolitan area. Therefore, we present a second statistical analysis of the differences in actual and expected rates of Negro homeownership among eighteen large metropolitan areas. Finally, the paper examines the implications of the apparent limitations on Negro homeownership on their housing costs and capital accumulation.

HOMEOWNERSHIP AND PURCHASE BY ST. LOUIS HOUSEHOLDS

To investigate Negro-white differences in homeownership, we developed models relating the probability of homeownership to the socioeconomic characteristics of a sample of 1,185 households in the St. Louis metropolitan area (401 black and 784 white households). Subsequently, we examined the decision to purchase or to rent for a subsample of 466 households which had changed residence in the preceding three years.

The analysis employs the regression of a binary dependent variable indicating tenure status (1 = own, 0 = rent) on several explanatory variables reflecting family size, family composition, employment status, household income, and race. Many previous studies have emphasized the importance of the family life cycle to household consumption patterns (see Martin David; John Lansing and L. Kish; Lansing, Kish, and James Morgan; Sherman Maisel; and Morgan). The life cycle hypothesis includes the combined influences of several household characteristics, which we represent by a series of family type/age interaction variables: 1. single person (living alone or in groups) under forty-five years of age; 2. singles over forty-five years of age; 3. couples without children with heads under forty-five years of age; 4. couples without children with heads over

TABLE 1–MODELS OF HOMEOWNERSHIP AND PURCHASE EQUATIONS 1, 2, AND 3 FOR ENTIRE SAMPLE

	Probability of Ownership		Probability of Purchase Given Move			
	Equation 1		Equation 2		Equation 3	
	Coef.	t-Ratio	Coef.	t-Ratio	Coef.	t-Ratio
Race (= black, 0 = white)	-0.088	-2.644	-0.124	-4.550	-0.091	-3.720
Income (thousands of dollars)	0.026	8.351	0.017	3.795	0.013	3.751
Years of education (head of household)	-0.006	-1.190	0.011	2.414	0.003	0.759
Years of current job (head of household)	0.002	1.908	0.001	0.624	0.002	1.365
Retired (1 = yes, 0 = no)	0.231	4.746	-0.070	-1.493	0.065	1.530
No household member employed (1 = yes, 0 = no)	-0.011	-0.277	-0.031	-0.868	-0.014	-0.362
More than one member employed (1 = yes, 0 = no)	0.171	6.130	-0.012	-0.438	0.002	0.102
Household Types						
Single females under 45 years (1 = yes, 0 = no)	-0.403	-5.596	-0.324	-3.665	-0.191	-2.075
Single females over 45 years	-0.295	-5.278	-0.051	-0.569	-0.183	-2.033
Single males under 45 years	-0.277	-2.577	-0.283	-2.864	-0.124	-1.170
Single males over 45 years	-0.108	-1.207	-0.057	-0.539	-0.196	-1.799
Married couples under 45 years	-0.213	-3.407	-0.290	-3.406	-0.095	-1.106
Married couples over 45 years	-0.004	-0.070	-0.124	-1,385	-0.111	-1.159
Families						
Age of head of household	0.002	2.108	0.004	2.212	0.011	2.527
$(Age)^2$ of head of household					-0.000	-2.621
Number of persons (natural logarithm)	-0.156	-3.769	-0.138	-3.342	-0.113	-3.226
Number of school-age children	-0.013	-0.986	0.032	2.626	0.018	1.518
Family headed by female under 45 years (1 = yes, 0 = no)	-0.007	-0.148	-0.145	-3.116	-0.188	-3.712
Family headed by female over 45 years (1 = yes, 0 = no)	-0.192	-2.561	-0.241	-3.663	-0.206	-3.850

TABLE 1 (Continued)

	Probability of Ownership		Probability of Purchase Given Move			
	Equation 1		Equation 2		Equation 3	
	Coef.	t-Ratio	Coef.	t-Ratio	Coef.	t-Ratio
Prior Tenure						
Prior owner (1 = yes, 0 = no)					0.267	4.323
Prior renter (1 = yes, 0 = no)					0.037	1.315
New household (1 = yes, 0 = no)					−0.146	−3.945
Intercept	0.409	5.747	0.126	1.354	0.122	1.212
Degrees of freedom	1166		447		443	
R^2	0.826		0.301		0.445	

forty-five years of age; and 5. typical families (individuals or married couples with children).

Typical families were further described in terms of age of head, family size, number of school-age children, and by dummy variables for: female head of less than forty-five years of age; and female head of more than forty-five years of age. Income, years of schooling (of head), and number of years at present job (for head), were included as explanatory variables for all households. Race was indicated by a dummy variable (1 = Negro, 0 = white).

The probability of ownership equation, obtained by the method of generalized lease squares is summarized by equation 1 (Table 1).(3) All the coefficients of equation 1 have the anticipated signs and are reasonable in magnitude, and twelve are highly significant statistically using conventional criteria. The results indicate that old couples are more likely to be homeowners than young couples, and old singles are more likely to be homeowners than their younger counterparts. None are as likely to be homeowners as male-headed families. Female-headed families are also less likely to be homeowners than male-headed families. Income and employment are positively related to homeownership. Family size is negatively related to homeownership, but only after adjusting for the different homeowning propensities of families with school-age children and with additional workers. The probability of ownership increases as the head of household gets older, and the introduction of a squared age term yields no evidence of any significant nonlinearity.

Of primary importance to this discussion is the coefficient of the race dummy variable. It indicates that, after accounting for differences in life cycle, income, education, and employment status, Negro households have a probability of ownership .09 less than that of whites. Thirty-two percent of Negro households in the sample owned their homes; if they were white, 41 percent would be homeowners.

There are some indications that the barriers to Negro occupancy in white neighborhoods are gradually declining. Thus, it could be argued that current ownership patterns primarily reflect historical discrimination and provide a misleading view of current conditions. To test this hypothesis, we estimated probability-of-purchase (1 = purchase, 0 = rent) equations for those sample households which changed their residence within the past three years. Equation 2 presents the results for the probability-of-purchase analysis (Table 1). The explanatory variables are identical to those included in equation 1. The coefficients of the dummy variables representing household type and age differ in magnitude for recent movers. Aside from these contrasts, the largest differences were obtained for the income and race variables.(4) The coefficient of the race dummy indicates that a Negro mover has a probability of purchase .12 lower than an otherwise identical white. Only 8 percent of Negro movers purchased homes; had they been white 20 percent would have been home-buyers.

Previous levels of housing discrimination may affect Negro households in at least one important way that is not reflected in equation 2. Because of past discrimination, Negro movers are less likely than white movers to have been homeowners in the past. This is important because when homeowners change their residence they are more likely to buy than to rent and, conversely, when renters move they are more likely to move from one rental property to another.

In large part the association between past and present, or present and future tenure arises because renters and owners tend to differ in terms of income, family size and composition, age, and other measured characteristics. Still, prior tenure itself may have an independent influence on subsequent tenure decisions. Therefore, probability-of-purchase equations were estimated with the addition of dummy variables for prior owner, prior renter, and new households. A fourth category "prior tenure unreported," is reflected in the intercept. Equation 3 in Table (1) illustrates these estimates.

Both the prior owner and new household variables have large and highly significant coefficients. Previous ownership raises the probability of purchase by .27. New households are .15 less likely to buy than are established households of the same age, income, and family characteristics.

Accounting for the effects of prior tenure reduces the coefficient of the race variables. Of course, the influence of housing market discrimination is reflected in prior tenure. In the sample of recent movers, only 2 percent of Negro households had previously been homeowners as compared to 17 percent of white households. Yet, even after controlling for the differences in prior tenure, Negro households are .09 less likely to become homeowners than white households in today's "open housing" market.(5)

Several studies of the demand for housing services have concluded that housing expenditures are more strongly related to permanent than to annual income. By extension it might be anticipated that the probabilities of homeownership and purchase would depend more on permanent than annual income. If this were true, all or part of the measured difference in the probabilities of ownership and purchase of white and nonwhite households in equations 1-3 might be attributable to unmeasured white/nonwhite differences in permanent incomes.

As a test of the permanent income hypothesis, we followed the convention suggested by several authors and replaced the annual income term in equations 1-3 by the mean incomes of the sample households stratified by the race and by the years of education of the head of the household (see R. Ramanathan). Presumably, this averaging process reduces the transitory component of income and thereby provides an improved estimate of permanent income. The ordinary least squares estimates of the race coefficient for all three equations are consistently larger than those obtained for the current income models as are the GLS estimates for the purchase model. The GLS estimate of the race coefficient in the ownership equation using the estimated permanent income is more than twice as large as the race coefficient obtained using annual income, and the GLS coefficients in the purchase models using permanent income are also larger than those obtained from the equations including annual income (see equation 1, Table 2).

An alternative and more dubious (both statistically and theoretically) test of the permanent income hypothesis used an estimate of housing expenditures as a surrogate for permanent income.(6) The most obvious statistical problem arises because the estimate of housing expenditures for homeowners must be imputed from housing value using a gross rent multiplier. The use of different variables (monthly rent for renters and market value for owners) transformed by a constant divisor in a regression on owner/renter may produce a spurious correlation. The coefficients of this housing expenditure variable in the

TABLE 2–COEFFICIENTS AND *t*-RATIOS OF RACE VARIABLE FOR ALTERNATIVE SPECIFICATIONS OF INCOME: *OLS* AND *GLS*

	Probability of Ownership Equation 1		Probability of Purchase without Prior Tenure Equation 2		Probability of Purchase with Prior Tenure Equation 3	
	OLS	*GLS*	*OLS*	*GLS*	*OLS*	*GLS*
Current Annual Income	−.150 (5.06)	−.088 (2.64)	−.154 (3.94)	−.124 (4.55)	−.114 (2.96)	−.091 (3.72)
Permanent Income	−.163 (5.23)	−.194 (6.33)	−.199 (3.65)	−.223 (4.73)	−.138 (2.58)	−.103 (2.69)
Housing Expenditure	−.048 (1.99)	−.035 (2.33)	−.077 (2.68)	−.048 (2.76)	−.069 (2.35)	−.029 (1.63)

ownership and purchase equations vary between 20 and 45 times their standard errors; this increases our suspicion that the relation is to a significant extent spurious and arises by construction.(7)

On theoretical grounds, moreover, there is reason to suspect that even an adequate estimate of housing expenditures would not provide permanent income measures which are neutral between Negroes and whites or between homeowners and renters. If price discrimination exists in the housing market, only a demand elasticity of one for housing would prevent housing expenditures from being a biased estimate of the permanent incomes of black households. If housing demand is price elastic for blacks (see Muth), price discrimination would bias this measure of permanent income downward for blacks and would reduce the race coefficient when the ownership and purchase equations are estimated. This bias is accentuated if housing market discrimination reduces Negro homeownership and if homeowners spend more for housing than renters of the same incomes for any reasons. Nevertheless, the race coefficients obtained from models using this estimate of housing expenditure as an explanatory variable are summarized in Table 2, which presents the race coefficients for all three alternative specifications. Also included in Table 2 are the coefficients of the racial dummy obtained by ordinary least squares.

In addition to the equations reported in Table 2, estimates were obtained employing several alternative specifications of the life cycle and age variables; tests for nonlinearity in the education and income terms were also performed with negative results. For all these specifications, the magnitude and significance of the race coefficients for equations 1, 2, and 3 were virtually unchanged.(8)

Taken together the estimates summarized in Table 2 and the alternatives mentioned strongly indicate that Negro households are substantially less likely to be homeowners or buyers than white households of similar characteristics. It does not "prove" that this is the result of discriminatory practices in urban housing markets; and there remain several competing explanations for these results. These alternative hypotheses may be grouped into three broad categories: 1. Differences in the "taste" for homeownership between whites and blacks; 2. Differences in the household asset and wealth positions of white and black families; and 3. Racial discrimination in the housing market as the result either of simple price discrimination in the owner and renter markets or of a more pervasive restriction on the supply of owner-occupied housing available to blacks. "Supply restrictions" could be supplemented or enforced by simple capital market discrimination or by an unwillingness on the part of banks and other mortgage lenders to finance home purchases by blacks outside the ghetto.

While it is most difficult to prove that the much lower probability of homeownership of black households is not due to differences in the taste for homeownership, many of the more commonly believed determinants of the tastes of housing consumers are included as independent variables. Furthermore, stratification by race for all of the three equations discloses no statistically significant differences. We thus conclude that the "differences in tastes" hypothesis is not an important explanation for the observed differences in market behavior between races.(9)

Differences in the asset or wealth positions of Negro and white households may account for part of the differences in white and nonwhite ownership and purchase probabilities. Unfortunately, the sample used in this research shares the deficiency of most other surveys in not including information on household assets and wealth. Therefore, no direct test of the asset hypothesis is possible using these data. However, for several reasons, we doubt that much of the white-Negro differences in ownership and purchase are the result of an unmeasured difference in wealth. All three equations include income, years-on-job, and life cycle variables, which may account for much of the white-black differences in assets. For most households, black and white, equity in owner-occupied housing is itself the largest component of net worth.(10) Therefore, in the probability of purchase model (equation 3) prior tenure may account for much of the remaining differences in wealth. Down payment requirements are a major reason why assets might be expected to affect the decision to purchase a home. However, FHA and VA down payment requirements, especially for small single family homes purchased more than ten years ago, were small or nonexistent.

Housing market discrimination is the third, and to us, the most plausible hypothesis explaining the regression results in Table 1. The exact mechanism is hard to specify. Differential price "markups" in the owner and rental submarkets do not explain these differences in Negro and white purchase and homeownership probabilities.(11) We are forced to conclude that "supply restrictions" on Negro residential choice and on the kinds of housing available to black households may be largely responsible for the wide discrepancy between ownership rates for otherwise identical black and white households.

Further support for this position is provided by data on the average increase in the market value of Negro- and white-owned single family units in St. Louis, For this sample, the units owned by white central city residents have increased in value at a compound annual rate of 5.2 percent per year as contrasted to a 7.2 percent annual increase for the central city properties owned by Negro households. If this is interpreted as a difference in the net appreciation of ghetto and nonghetto properties, the findings of equations 1-3 become even more difficult to explain. Rather than a difference in the net appreciation of black and white owned properties, however, this finding appears to be still another manifestation of limitations on Negro residential choice. White households wishing to improve their housing can buy newer or larger houses in better neighborhoods. Negro homeowners are much less able to improve their housing in this way; as a result we hypothesize that black homeowners spend more for renovation and repair than white households of similar characteristics. An annual increase in suburban white-owned properties of 4.1 percent provides some evidence for these inferences.

DIFFERENCES AMONG METROPOLITAN AREAS

A complete test of the supply restriction hypothesis cannot be accomplished from an analysis of a single metropolitan area. A more powerful test of the effect of supply restrictions can be obtained by analyzing differences in black homeownership among cities. Metropolitan areas and their ghettos differ in terms of the characteristics of their housing stocks, and, therefore, in the extent to which a limitation on being able to reside outside the ghetto is an effective restriction on the supply of ownership-type housing available to blacks. For example, supply restrictions should be much less important in Los Angeles, where a large portion of the ghetto housing supply consists of single family units, than in Chicago, where ghetto neighborhoods are predominantly multi-family. We analyzed the difference between "expected" and actual black ownership rates in several metropolitan areas. Expected black ownership rates were computed by multiplying a matrix of white ownership rates (stratified into income and family size groups) by the income and family size distribution of black households. Table 3 presents this measure in 1960 for all eighteen metropolitan areas for which the necessary census data are published.(12) The difference between the actual black ownership rate and the expected black

TABLE 3–ACTUAL AND EXPECTED OWNERSHIP RATES OF NEGRO HOUSEHOLDS BY METROPOLITAN AREA

City	Actual	Expected
Atlanta	.31	.52
Boston	.21	.43
Chicago	.18	.47
Cleveland	.30	.58
Dallas	.39	.54
Detroit	.41	.67
Los Angeles/Long Beach	.41	.51
Newark	.24	.50
Philadelphia	.45	.66
St. Louis	.34	.55
Baltimore	.36	.61
Birmingham	.44	.56
Houston	.46	.56
Indianapolis	.45	.58
Memphis	.37	.50
New Orleans	.28	.40
Pittsburgh	.35	.59
San Francisco/Oakland	.37	.51

ownership rate for each SMSA is identical in principle to the difference in the probability of ownership attributed to race in equation 1 for St. Louis in 1967. (For St. Louis this more primitive technique yields −21.0 in 1960 as compared to an OLS estimate of −15.0 and a GLS estimate from equation 1 of −8.8 in 1967.)

As a test of the supply restriction hypothesis we then regressed these estimated differences upon 1. the proportion of central city dwelling units that are single family, a proxy for the proportion of the ghetto housing stock that is single family; 2. the proportion of the SMSA black population living in the central city, a measure of the extent of suburbanization of the black population; and 3. the actual rate of white ownership in the SMSA.(13) The first two variables measure the extent of the supply restrictions among the eighteen metropolitan areas, while the latter measures any differences in the level of both white and Negro homeownership that might be attributable to such factors as intermetropolitan variation in the relative cost of owner-occupied and renter-occupied housing or differences in the timing of urban development. Equation 4 presents the regression in difference form (expected black ownership rate minus actual black ownership rate), while equation 5 presents the same equation in ratio form (expected black ownership rate−actual black ownership rate). The t-ratios are in parentheses under the coefficients.

Equation 4:

$$(O_B^* - O_B) = -0.24 + 0.82O_w$$
$$\quad\quad\quad\quad\quad (2.36) \quad (4.64)$$

$$-0.36S_c + 0.12B_c$$
$$(6.49) \quad\quad (2.03)$$

$$R^2 = .76$$

Equation 5:

$$(O_B^*/O_B) = 0.89 + 1.52O_w$$
$$\quad\quad\quad\quad\quad (1.52) \quad (1.47)$$

$$-1.74S_c + 0.90B_c$$
$$(5.34) \quad\quad (2.52)$$

$$R^2 = .74$$

where,

$O_{B_i}^* =$ Expected black ownership rate in the ith SMSA

$$\left[\sum_k \alpha_{wk_i} \cdot H_{bk_i} \right] \Bigg/ \sum_k H_{bk_i}$$

$O_{B_i} =$ Actual black ownership rate in the ith SMSA

$$\left[\sum_k \alpha_{bk_i} \cdot H_{bk_i} \right] \Bigg/ \sum_k H_{bk_i}$$

$O_{w_i} =$ Actual white ownership rate in the ith SMSA

$$\left[\sum_k \alpha_{wk_i} \cdot H_{wk_i} \right] \Big/ \sum_k H_{wk_i}$$

and

$\alpha_{wk_i} =$ Proportion of whites in the kth income/family size category who are homeowners in the ith SMSA.

$H_{bk_i} =$ Number of black households in the kth income/family size category in the ith SMSA.

$S_c =$ Proportion of central city housing that is single family (Number of central city dwelling units that are single family ÷ total central city dwelling units)

$B_c =$ Proportion of metropolitan Negro households residing in central city (Number of Negro households in central city ÷ number of Negro households in SMSA.

The means and standard deviations of the variables used in equations 4 and 5 are shown in Table 4. The average expected homeownership rate for black households is .54 and the mean actual black ownership rate is .35. The actual white rate for these eighteen metropolitan areas in 1960 averages .65. Of the .30

TABLE 4–MEANS AND STANDARD DEVIATIONS OF
VARIABLES USED IN INTER-CITY REGRESSION

	Mean	SD
$O^*_B - O_B$	0.19	0.06
O^*_B / O_B	1.61	0.36
O_W	0.65	0.07
O_B	0.35	0.08
O^*_B	0.54	0.07
S_C	0.55	0.22
B_C	0.78	0.14

difference between actual white and black ownership rates in these eighteen metropolitan areas Negro-white differences in family size and income account for .11; the residual difference, .19, must be attributed to other factors, including the differences in supply restrictions among the areas.

Both equations strongly support the hypothesis that the differences between observed and expected black ownership rates are small: 1. when the ghetto housing supply includes a larger proportion of single-family units; 2. when blacks have more access to the suburban housing market, with its preponderance of owner-occupied units. As the statistics in Table 3 show, the difference between the actual and expected homeownership rate of black households is relatively small for cities like Houston and Los Angeles, where the central city and its black ghetto include more single-family housing, and is relatively large for cities like Chicago, where the ghetto is predominantly multi-family and where blacks are effectively excluded from the suburbs.

The extent of black suburbanization also appears to have a significant, though small, influence on the gap between actual and expected black homeownership.

In all U.S. metropolitan areas, black households are heavily concentrated in the central cities. The mean proportion of blacks residing in the central city for the sample metropolitan areas is .78 and the standard deviation is only .14. Equation 4 indicates that a city which is one standard deviation above the mean in terms of this characteristic (92 percent of metropolitan area blacks live in the central city) would have a gap .034 larger than one which is one standard deviation below the mean (64 percent of blacks live in the central city).

The findings presented in equations 4 and 5 provide further support for the view that housing market discrimination limits Negro homeownership.(14) Specifically, these results indicate that a limited supply of housing suitable for homeownership in the ghetto and restrictions on Negro purchase outside the ghetto strongly affect the tenure-type of the housing consumed by Negro households as well as its location.

HOMEOWNERSHIP, HOUSING COSTS, AND CAPITAL ACCUMULATION

Limitations on homeownership have significant effects on Negro housing costs, income, and welfare. As is illustrated in the Appendix, an effective limitation on homeownership can increase Negro housing costs by over 30 percent, assuming no price appreciation.

Much of the savings from homeownership results from favorable treatment accorded homeowners under the federal income tax. These tax provisions favoring homeowners are widely recognized and well documented (see Henry Aaron and Shelton). Our findings suggest that Negro households at all income levels are impeded by housing market discrimination from purchasing and owning single family homes. As a consequence, Negro households are prevented from taking full advantage of these tax benefits. Since tax savings from homeownership increase with income, this aspect of discriminatory housing markets cuts most sharply against middle and upper income black households.

Limitations on homeownership also rob Negro households of an important inflation hedge available to other low and middle income households. Calculations presented in the Appendix show that under reasonable assumptions about the appreciation of single family homes, a Negro household prevented from buying a home since 1950 would have out-of-pocket housing costs in 1970 more than twice as high as the costs which would have been incurred if the family could have purchased a home twenty years earlier.

Negro households at every income level have less wealth than white households. Current and historical limitations on homeownership may be an important reason. The importance of this method of capital accumulation among low and middle income households is apparent from a typical example. The average house purchased with an FHA 203 mortgage in 1949 had a value of $8,286 and a mortgage of $7,101 (see U.S. Federal Housing Administration). Assuming that this house was purchased with a twenty-year mortgage by a thirty-year old household head, the owner of this unit would have saved more than $7,000 and would own his home free and clear by his fiftieth birthday. Thus, if his home neither appreciated or depreciated, at age fifty he would own assets worth at least $8,000. However, the postwar years have hardly been characterized by price neutrality. Although difficult to estimate, the average appreciation of single-family houses during the past twenty years most certainly exceeded the 100 percent increase in the Boeck composite cost index for small residential structures (see U.S. Federal Housing Administration).(15) This conservative 100 percent increase in value would mean that the typical FHA-financed homeowner by age fifty would have accumulated assets worth at least $16,000, a considerable sum that he could use to reduce his housing costs, to borrow against for the college education of his children, or simply to hold for his retirement. Perspective on this hypothetical example is obtained when it is recognized that the mean wealth accumulation of white households in 1966 was only $20,000 (see Henry Terrell). Of course, the situation would have been different if the postwar period had been one of a general decline in the price of urban real estate. But it was not.

Homeownership is clearly the most important method of wealth accumulation used by low- and middle-income families in the postwar period. Equities in single-family, owner-occupied structures account for nearly one-half of all the wealth of the lowest income group. As family income increases, the relative importance of home equities decreases. Still, home equities accounted for more than one-third of the wealth of all U.S. households earning between $10-15,000 in 1962 (see D. S. Projector et al.).

The dominant position of home equities in the asset portfolios of low and middle income households is not difficult to understand. Other forms of investment, such as the stock market, require far more knowledge, sophistication and discipline. In addition, low- and middle-income households have more leverage available in the real estate than in other investment markets.

Much of the savings imbedded in home ownership, especially among low- and middle-income households, is more or less involuntary or at least unconscious. Discipline is maintained by linking the investment (saving) decision to monthly payments for the provision of a necessity, with heavy penalties (foreclosure) imposed for failure to invest regularly.(16) Moreover, because of federal mortgage insurance and special advantages provided to thrift institutions, the low- and middle-income home buyer is able to borrow 90 percent or more of the purchase price of a new home. This may amount to $15,000 or more of capital at moderate interest rates. By comparison, in the stock market he can borrow 30 percent, a ratio which he must maintain even with price declines.

If, as our findings suggest, discrimination in urban housing markets has reduced Negro opportunities for homeownership, this limitation is an important explanation of the smaller quantity of assets owned by Negro households at each income level.

APPENDIX:
OWNING AND SAVING VS. RENTING AND CONSUMING

In an analysis of the relative costs of owning and renting a home, Shelton concludes that owning is usually cheaper than renting, as long as the household expects to live at the same location for more than three and one half years. The three and one-half year cut-off is obtained by dividing a 2 percent per year annual savings into a nonrecurring transfer cost for owner-occupied units of about 7 percent of their value.

The nonrecurring transfer cost consists of realtor commissions plus an allowance for certain fixed costs. The annual savings from homeownership include tax differences, management costs, vacancy allowances, and savings in annual maintenance expenditures for homeowners (who are able to maintain the same level of quality for about one-half percent of market value less per year). For homeowners, the total annual housing costs include: maintenance, obsolescence, property taxes, interest on mortgage, opportunity cost of money plus (discounted) transfer cost. For renters, annual rent equals landlord costs plus return on investment: maintenance, obsolescence, property taxes, vacancy allowance, management, interest on mortgage, plus return on investment.

Much of the savings from homeownership results from favorable tax provisions, i.e., from the ability to deduct interest payments and property taxes and especially from the absence of any tax on imputed rent. Therefore, the magnitude of the savings in monthly housing costs varies somewhat according to family circumstances, the size of the mortgage and the amount amortized, and the assumed opportunity costs of the family's equity.

Shelton develops an example which suggests the magnitude of the yearly savings in housing costs obtained through ownership. This exmaple assumes that a family may choose to buy its dwelling for $20,000 or to rent it for $167 per month. (This represents a gross rent of $2,000 per year, based on a widely used gross rent/value ratio). To purchase the unit, the prospective homeowner invests $4,000 as a down payment on the house and assumes a 6 percent mortgage.

As compared to the $2,000 yearly rental costs, Shelton estimates that purchase would mean yearly expenses before taxes of $1,590. Property tax and interest payments create tax shields that reduce the true costs of these two items by an amount which depends on the homeowner's tax bracket. He concludes that a conservative estimate of the tax savings created by homeownership would be $200, yielding yearly after tax costs of ownership of $1,390. This represents a saving of $610 or a 15.2 percent return (after taxes) on the $4,000 invested in homeownership, as compared to an assumed stock market return of 9 percent before taxes. Since stock market earnings are taxable, the comparable before tax return on homeownership is 18 percent. The relative return on a homeownership investment declines as the mortgage is amortized. The investment return is larger, however, if down payments are smaller or if the opportunity cost of equity capital is lower. Thus, 18 percent is likely to be a low estimate.

The savings from homeownership can also be expressed as a percentage of the costs of renting. From this viewpoint a limitation on homeownership would increase housing costs beyond three and a half years by 30 percent, assuming no price appreciation ($610 savings ÷ $2,000 annual rent). As with the rate of return analysis, the savings are larger if a smaller down payment or a lower opportunity cost of capital is assumed.

Aaron obtains even larger estimates of the tax subisdy to homeowners. He presents an example, similar to the one just discussed but with a more valuable house ($25,000) and a larger equity ($10,000), which yields a $342 tax saving (as contrasted to the $200 saving computed by Shelton) and an after tax return on a $10,000 equity of 7.4 percent (as contrasted with a before tax return of 4 percent on other assets). However, Aaron implicitly assumes that the real price of owner- and renter-occupied housing is the same. Shelton, in contrast, contends that there is an equilibrium price difference, excluding tax differences, favoring owner-occupied housing by 1.4 percent of value. If Shelton's analysis of the comparative costs of homeownership and renting is correct in this respect, the savings to homeownership based on Aaron's example would amount to 28 percent of monthly rent computed as [$342 + .014 ($25,000 in housing value)] /($2,500 annual rent).

The substantial divergence in housing costs noted above is in addition to any discriminatory pricing which may exist. Moreover, it must still be regarded as a lower bound estimate of the economic cost of an effective limitation on homeownership during the postwar period, since it fails to incorporate the effects of inflation on housing costs and does not admit to the special position of homeownership in the savings behavior and capital accumulation of low- and middle-income households.

A spending unit's equity in its home can be divided into three components: the initial equity or down payment, the amortization of the mortgage (savings), and any appreciation or depreciation of the property as a result of general or particular price changes (capital gains or losses). The last two items form the important link between homeownership and capital accumulation.

Although it is technically correct to view an increase in the value of an owned home as an increase in the household's wealth and to consider the opportunity cost of the equity capital as part of the spending unit's monthly housing costs, there are indications that many households do not view the matter in precisely this way. Out-of-pocket costs appear to be more important considerations for many low- and middle-income families, and it seems many view the savings in the home as a bonus to homeownership. Thus, it is of more than passing interest to compare the current out-of-pocket costs of a St. Louis family who purchased an $8,000 FHA or VA home on a twenty-year mortgage in 1949 with an otherwise identical family who rented throughout the entire period.

Assuming a conservative capital appreciation of 100 percent over the twenty-year period, the value of this house in 1969 would be $16,000. Since the mortgage has been paid off, the homeowner has only insurance, real estate taxes, heating and utilities, and maintenance and repairs as out-of-pocket costs. These would total roughly $64 per month for a St. Louis home of this value in 1969.(17) By comparison, a renter would have to pay somewhat more than twice this amount ($133-160 per month) to rent a dwelling unit of this value.(18)

The preceding comparisons may help to explain the recent findings of the Survey of Economic Opportunity which indicate that at every level of current income, black families have fewer assets than whites, but that housing equity represents a larger proportion of the net worth of black households than of white households.(19) In fact, limitations on homeownership over several generations may be an important part of the explanations of the smaller quantity of assets owned by Negro households at each income level.

NOTES

(1) The only empirical study known to us which fails to find evidence of higher prices in the ghetto is by Baily who concludes, "there is no indication that Negroes, as such, pay more for housing than do other people of similar density of occupation" (1966, p. 218.) A detailed presentation of the argument against the existence of a ghetto markup (price discrimination) is contained in Muth. Muth's own empirical research on the South Side of Chicago, indicates

that "Negroes may pay housing prices that are from 2 to 5 percent greater" than whites pay, p. 239. However, he argues that these measured differences, and presumably those obtained in many other empirical studies, are due to cost differences (higher operating costs for housing in Negro neighborhoods) and do not represent a discriminatory markup.

(2) This study, based on a 1967 sample of 629 renter observations and 438 observations on single-family detached housing of the city of St. Louis, goes further than any previous study in attempting to "standardize" the bundles of residential services consumed by whites and blacks. Contract rent or market value (for owner-occupied, single-family homes) was regressed upon a detailed set of qualitative and quantitative attributes of the bundles of housing services. In addition to variables used in previous studies, such as the number of rooms and floor area, our regressions included as explanatory variables an elaborate set of quality evaluations for the dwelling unit, the structure, the adjacent structures, and the immediate neighborhood, as well as indexes of the quality of the neighborhood public school and of the level of criminal activity. Also included was a variable measuring the racial composition of the census tract in 1967. These models are discussed in some detail in Kain and Quigley (1970b).

(3) The generalized least squares regression estimates are obtained by weighting each observation by $[1/P(1-P)]$ where P is the value of the probability predicted by ordinary lease squares. It can be shown that this procedure provides more efficient estimates of a linear probability function.

(4) As with the ownership models, separate Negro and white equations were estimated for the probability of purchase. Except for their intercepts they were identical, and a covariance test indicated no statistically different relationship.

(5) A similar difference in Negro-white probabilities of home purchase was obtained by Daniel Fredland for Philadelphia. Fredland's model differed in a number of respects from equation 3 in Table 1. It included a somewhat different set of explanatory variables, was for married households only, and was estimated by ordinary least squares. Even so, he obtained a coefficient of $-.16$ for a minority dummy (nonwhite or Puerto Rican) and a coefficient of .27 for the prior-owner dummy.

(6) This technique was suggested by the anonymous referee. We report it, in spite of strong statistical and theoretical reservations.

(7) The housing expenditure models reported in Table 2 use housing value $\div$ 100 as an estimate of homeowners' monthly expenditure (see Muth). This gross rent multiplier, as well as the 1-to-120 rule (see John Shelton), is widely used in housing market analysis to make market value roughly commensurate with monthly rent. In addition to the results reported, we estimated equations using gross rent multipliers of 1/185 and 1/164. These ratios were derived by regressing monthly rent and value upon a detailed set of the individual characteristics of rental and owner-occupied units and thus deriving estimates of the equivalent value of the average rental unit (164 x rent) and the average rental fee for the characteristics of owner-occupied units (value/185). The race coefficients were indistinguishable from those presented. Details of the specification and implications of these relationships may be found in Kain and Quigley (1970a and 1970b).

(8) As a further test of the influence of housing market discrimination, separate Negro and white equations of the same form as equation 1 were

estimated; a covariance test indicated no statistically significant difference between them ($F = 1.32$). In addition separate models for equation 1 were estimated for each of four household types described above: single persons; couples; female-headed families; and male-headed families. In each case, the coefficient of the race variable was highly significant and varied in magnitude between $-.13$ and $-.16$. When similar analyses were performed for the probability of home purchase, the sample sizes became uncomfortably small for some subgroups.

(9) Household expectations about moving frequency may be the only important excluded taste variable. (As will be discussed subsequently, mobility also affects the economics of homeownership.) However, a fairly extensive analysis of the mobility rates of the households in this sample indicates no important differences in the frequency of moves between white and Negro households after accounting for other socioeconomic factors.

(10) For example, recent Survey of Economic Opportunity tabulation indicates that for lower-middle income ($5,000-$7,000 per annum) families, housing equity alone represents 40 percent of the net worth of white households and an even larger proportion of the net worth of black households. See the Appendix for further details.

(11) Price markups were estimated for owner and renter occupied structures using the St. Louis sample for three alternative specifications (see Kain and Quigley (1970b)). Of the three specifications, two indicate a smaller percentage markup in the owner market. Even if the markup were smaller for rental than for owner-occupied properties, it would require an extremely large price-elasticity-of-choice to reduce the probability of black ownership by 10 percentage points.

(12) These 18 SMSA's consisted of all those for which the data on black and white ownership rates by income and family size classes were published. The expected black ownership rate was obtained by applying the ownership proportions for white households by income and family size for each SMSA to the income and family size distribution of black households (see U.S. Bureau of the Census (1960a, Table B3)) and summing.

(13) The percent of single family housing in the central city for SMSA was obtained from U.S. Bureau of the Census (1960a, Table B-7). The percent of SMSA blacks residing in the central city was obtained from U.S. Bureau of the Census (1960b, Table 13).

(14) At the minimum, it would take a peculiar spatial distribution of tastes for homeownership or of asset differences to explain these findings.

(15) Our sample suggests an annual rate of increase in value of white-owned properties of 4.7 percent during the 5-10 year period prior to 1966.

(16) As long ago as 1953, James Duesenberry argued persuasively that levels of savings and asset accumulation are heavily dependent upon the form in which savings is maintained. Citing specifically the high proportion of savings invested in assets associated with the reason for saving (e.g., housing equity, pension and insurance reserves, and investment in unincorporated businesses), he suggests a close connection between the motives for saving and the form which the saving takes. Thus, although we cannot deduce that because people invested in some particular asset, they would not have saved if that type of asset had not been available, there appears to be a strong association.

If Duesenberry's insight is valid, then even if capital markets were perfect in every sense of the word, we would expect to find substantially fewer assets for households denied certain forms of saving (i.e., those forms associated with the reason for saving) such as home ownership, pension and insurance investment, and unincorporated business investment.

(17) The $64 per month out-of-pocket costs is based on estimated homeownership costs for existing (used) FHA insured homes in St. Louis in 1967. These totaled $58.02 for the median home in 1967 (valued at the difference in median value $14,597 vs. $16,000) plus increases in costs between 1967 and 1969. If the homeowner still itemizes his tax return (less likely without interest payments), he can deduct $26 per month of these expenses. This would produce tax savings of between $5 and $10 per month depending on his tax bracket. These expense data were obtained from U.S. Federal Housing Administration.

(18) The $133 ($160) per month rent is again based on the same widely used rent to value ratio 1 to 120 (1 to 100). There is reason to believe the above calculations understate the extent of asset accumulation by the average homeowner. Many homeowners increase the value of their structures by improvements and additions. These outlays, of course, represent further savings and capital accumulation. Others trade up by using their accumulated equity as a down payment on a larger or better quality house, thus maintaining an even higher savings rate.

(19) Recent tabulations from the Survey of Economic Opportunity on the asset and liability position of Negro and white families by income group show that home equities account for an even greater share of Negro than white wealth. For example, these data indicate that white families with incomes between $5,000 and $7,499 have a net worth of $12,556 as compared with a net worth of $3,636 for Negro families in the same income class. Despite the fact that Negroes at each income level are less likely to be homeowners, housing equity represents 67 percent of this smaller Negro net worth as compared to 40 percent of that of white families.

Although the mean housing equity of Negro homeowners is smaller than that of white homeowners, $7,344 vs. $11,753, the difference in Negro net worth is not to any significant degree attributable to this difference. Rather, it results from the fact that at each income level a smaller proportion of Negroes than whites are homeowners and even more importantly from the fact that the discrepancy in Negro and white ownership of other assets is even larger than the discrepancy in homeownership. Thus, if the Survey of Economic Opportunity data on assets are to be believed, Negroes in the income class $5,000-$7,499 have net worth in nonhousing assets equal to only 16 percent of that of white households in the same income level, and all Negroes have net worth in nonhousing assets equal to only 9 percent of that of all whites. Of course, these results can be considered as suggestive only. The weaknesses of savings and wealth data are notorious, and the interpretation of these differences, if real, would require a complete theory of Negro and white savings behavior, which encompasses the manner in which discrimination or lack of opportunity in the various markets affects the savings behavior of Negro households. The authors wish to thank Andrew Brimmer and Henry S. Terrell for making these unpublished tabulations available to them.

REFERENCES

H. Aaron, "Income Taxes and Housing," Amer. Econ. Rev., Dec. 1970, 60, 789-806.

M. J. Bailey, "Note on the Economics of Residential Zoning and Urban Renewal," Land Econ., Aug. 1959, 33, 288-92.

M. J. Bailey, "Effects of Race and Other Demographic Factors on the Values of Single-Family Homes," Land Econ., May 1966, 40, 215-20.

G. S. Becker, The Economics of Discrimination, Chicago 1957.

M. H. David, Family Composition and Consumption, Amsterdam 1962.

J. S. Duesenberry, "The Determinants of Savings Behavior: A Summary," in W. W. Heller, F. M. Boddy, and C. L. Nelson, eds., Savings in the Modern Economy, Minneapolis 1953.

B. Duncan and P. Hauser, Housing a Metropolis—Chicago, Glencoe 1960.

D. Fredland, "Residential Mobility and Choice of Tenure," unpublished doctoral dissertation, Harvard Univ. 1970.

R. A. Haugen and A. J. Heins, "A Market Separation Theory of Rent Differentials in Metropolitan Areas," Quart. J. Econ., Nov. 1969, 83, 660-72.

J. L. Hecht, Because It's Right: Integration in Housing, Boston 1970.

J. F. Kain, "The Commuting and Residential Decisions of Central Business District Workers," in Transportation Economics, Universities-Nat. Bur. Econ. Res. conference series, New York 1965, pp. 245-74.

J. F. Kain, "Effect of Housing Market Segregation on Urban Development," Savings and Residential Financing, 1969 Conference Proceedings, Chicago 1969, pp. 88-113.

J. F. Kain, and J. M. Quigley, (1970a) "Evaluating the Quality of the Residential Environment," Environment & Planning, Jan. 1970, 2, 23-32.

J. F. Kain, and J. M. Quigley, (1970b) "Measuring the Value of Housing Quality," J. Amer. Statist. Ass., June 1970, 65, 532-48.

J. B. Lansing and L. Kish, "Family Life Cycle as an Independent Variable," Amer. Soc. Rev., 1957, 22, 512-19.

J. B. Lansing and L. Kish, and J. N. Morgan, "Consumer Finances over the Life Cycle," in L. Clark, ed., Consumer Behavior: The Life Cycle and Consumer Behavior, 2, New York 1955, pp. 36-52.

D. McEntire, Residence and Race, Berkeley 1960.

S. J. Maisel, "Rates of Ownership, Mobility, and Purchase," in Essays in Urban Land Economics, Los Angeles 1966, pp. 76-108.

J. N. Morgan, "Factors Related to Consumer Savings When it is Defined as a Net-Worth Concept," in L. R. Klein, ed., Contributions of Survey Methods to Economics, New York 1954.

R. F. Muth, Cities and Housing: The Spatial Pattern of Urban Residential Land Use, Chicago 1969.

A. H. Pascal, The Analysis of Residential Segregation, The RAND Corporation, P-4234, Oct. 1969.

D. S. Projector et al, "Survey of Changes in Family Finances," Federal Reserve Tech. Paper, Washington 1968.

C. Rapkin, "Price Discrimination Against Negroes in the Rental Housing Market," in Essays in Urban Land Economics, Los Angeles 1966, pp. 333-45.

C. Rapkin and W. Grigsby, The Demand for Housing in Racially Mixed Areas,

Berkeley 1960.

R. Ramanathan, "Measuring the Permanent Income of a Household: An Experiment in Methodology," J. Polit. Econ., Jan. 1971, 79, 177-85.

M. G. Reid, Housing and Income, Chicago 1962.

R. G. Ridker and J. A. Henning, "The Determinants of Residential Property Values with Special Reference to Air Pollution," Rev. Econ. Statis., May 1967, 49, 246-57.

J. P. Shelton, "The Cost of Renting Versus Owning a Home," Land Econ., Feb. 1968, 42, 59-72.

M. Stengel, "Price Discrimination in the Urban Rental Housing Market," unpublished doctoral dissertation, Harvard Univ., May 1970.

K. and A. Taeuber, Negroes in Cities, Chicago 1965.

H. S. Terrell, "Wealth Accumulation of Black and White Families: The Empirical Evidence," paper presented before a joint session of the Amer. Econ. Assoc. and the Amer. Fin. Assoc., Detroit, Michigan, Dec. 28, 1970, mimeo.

Survey Research Center, Institute for Social Research, Univ. Michigan, 1960 Survey of Consumer Finances, Ann Arbor 1961.

U.S. Bureau of the Census, Statistical Abstract of the United States: 1967, 88th ed., Washington 1967.

U.S. Bureau of the Census, U.S. Census of Housing: 1960, vol. II, Metropolitan Housing, Washington 1963.

U.S. Bureau of the Census, U.S. Census of Population: 1960, vol. I., Characteristics of Population, Washington 1963.

U.S. Federal Housing Administration, FHA Homes, 1967; Data for States and Selected Areas on Characteristics of FHA Operations undre Section 203, Washington 1967.

HOME OWNERSHIP AND THE
WEALTH POSITION OF BLACK AND
WHITE AMERICANS

Howard Birnbaum and Rafael Weston

Most economic research on differences between black and white Americans has concentrated on income, employment, and prices, and their relationship to discrimination in the labor and housing markets, and has ignored wealth considerations. Two recent papers by Henry Terrell(1) and by John F. Kain and John Quigley(2) are important exceptions. Both demonstrate the importance of including wealth considerations in evaluating the economic situation of blacks.

In the first section of this paper, we provide a more complete description of the wealth position of blacks, by expanding Terrell's analysis of their investment portfolios, using the same data source, the Survey of Economic Opportunity. We present tabulations for various wealth categories to provide an overview of their investment behavior and to provide a foundation for the remainder of this paper. Our analysis indicates that blacks and whites follow fundamentally different patterns of investment: at the same levels of both income and wealth, blacks consistently invest more in consumer durables, especially housing, than do whites.

We then examine these differences in investment behavior in the context suggested by Kain and Quigley. They find that blacks have a substantially lower probability of home ownership, a result they attribute to housing market discrimination. They speculate that this impediment to home ownership may explain, at least in part, the lower levels of black wealth accumulation at every income level.

Our findings suggest, however, that the Kain and Quigley result may be due to their specification of the model. A somewhat different specification, with at least an equally strong basis in theory and econometrics, suggests that it is quite possible that blacks have a higher probability of owning a home than do "equivalent" whites. While all such "conclusions" must remain tentative, for reasons discussed in the final portion of this paper, we suggest that these investment differences are not solely due to the income and wealth position of blacks. Rather, these investment differences with black "overinvestment" in housing, relative to whites, may be due to a smaller set of investment opportunities which has been institutionally fostered by an information gap created by the forces of discrimination.

PORTFOLIOS OF BLACKS AND WHITES

To summarize distributional inequalities, Terrell's work emphasized Geni Coefficients. However, in order to gain a better understanding of the processes behind these distributions, it is necessary to disaggregate this summary statistic. Thus, a set of tabulations was computed. In this section we first summarize these tabulations, and then discuss the clear pattern which emerges. The appendix describes our data.

Tabulations displayed in Table 1 reveal the relatively well known fact that wealth is much less evenly distributed than income among both blacks and whites. This result holds for every category of wealth, except home equity and car equity, which are distributed quite similarly to income. In addition income appears to be more evenly distributed among whites than among blacks, although the difference is not large.(3) Within each classification of wealth, and overall, much the same pattern of inequality occurs when looking at the distribution of wealth by income class. In total wealth and in each of its components, the top 5 percent of households (by income) hold disproportionally large amounts of most assets, as does the top 20 percent and to some degree, the next 20 percent. Car and home equity are the least unequally distributed while stocks and business equity are the most unequal. This is especially pronounced in the case of blacks, where virtually no business or stock is held outside the top 20 percent and most of that is held by the top 5 percent. Home equity is less unequally distributed for blacks than for whites while the opposite is true of most other equity. Also, in every income group, blacks have net debt in the "other" category (which includes unpaid bills, loans to others, etc.). Further, the greatest proportion of this debt is held by the middle and upper income classes; for whites, only the middle income classes have net debt in this category.

The tabulations in Table 2 are meant to provide some perspective on the absolute amounts involved in these comparisons. On average, whites hold approximately 4.5 times as much wealth as blacks, compared to only 1.5 times as much income. This result holds within each income class, where whites hold from 2.5 to 4.5 times the wealth of blacks, at least up to incomes of $15,000. At incomes above $15,000 there were so few observations that the results are not very meaningful.

The portfolio composition for black and white households is displayed in Table 3. No monotonic relationship exists between income and the percentage of wealth held in the various assets. For some assets, such as farm and other real equity, business equity, and stocks, a positive relationship is apparent. For car and home equity, an inverted U-shape seems more likely. Most important, however, Table 3 gives the initial suggestion that blacks and whites differ fundamentally in their investment patterns with blacks investing more in assets

TABLE 1
DISTRIBUTION OF ASSETS AMONG INCOME CLASSES BY RACE*

Percent

	Bottom 1-20	20-40	40-60	60-80	80-100	Top 95-100
White						
Farm & Other	4.2	10.1	5.9	41.7	38.1	18.1
Real Estate	6.7	2.3	10.8	16.9	63.3	42.4
Business Equity	9.4	12.5	17.2	24.3	36.6	10.3
Car Equity	10.9	10.0	16.1	20.8	42.2	14.6
Money	9.8	6.4	8.6	21.7	53.5	35.4
Bonds	3.4	2.3	5.0	30.5	58.8	48.9
Stocks	8.4	10.6	14.9	26.2	39.9	12.8
Home Equity	4.3	(7.3)	(4.8)	37.5	70.3	47.0
Other	6.8	7.9	10.5	29.4	45.4	22.8
Total Wealth	6.6	13.2	18.3	23.4	38.5	14.4
Income						
Black						
Farm & Other	1.6	8.7	5.6	10.5	73.6	46.7
Real Estate	0.0	0.9	2.4	1.0	95.7	82.8
Business Equity	6.0	7.5	20.7	24.3	41.5	11.4
Car Equity	0.9	11.4	10.0	17.3	60.4	27.0
Money	0.4	5.0	12.9	33.9	47.8	20.0
Bonds	0.0	0.0	1.7	6.4	91.9	74.0
Stocks	0.0	0.0				
Home Equity	13.1	12.1	18.3	24.1	32.4	8.5
Other	(4.7)	(10.8)	(43.1)	(25.1)	(16.3)	(0.1)
Total Wealth	9.8	10.3	11.8	20.2	47.9	21.9
Income	5.9	11.6	18.1	25.6	38.8	12.6

Income Bounds on Percentiles

	1-20	20-40	40-60	60-80	80-100	95-100
White	(-4,300)-5,000	5,000-7,340	7,400-9,300	9,320-12,500	12,520-82,550	17,360-82,550
Black	60 -2,770	2,800-4,600	4,690-6,660	6,660- 9,080	9,100-24,160	12,950-24,160

* Table I shows what percentile of income hold what percent of each asset (rows sum to 100 in table). All categories are net equity = asset value − debt owed. Wealth is the sum of the eight preceding asset categories. Parentheses note negative net equities.

TABLE 2
MEAN HOLDING OF EACH ASSET BY INCOME GROUP AND RACE
AND PROBABILITY OF OWNERSHIP

	0-2,500	2,500-5,000	5,000-7,500	7,500-10,000	10,000-15,000	15,000-20,000	Over 20,000	All
White								
Farm & Other Real Estate	353	1,185	2,109	2,127	7,820	12,860	13,936	4,436
Business Equity	4	619	127	903	660	4,558	10,321	1,164
Car Equity	441	530	665	936	1,479	1,954	2,571	1,051
Money	1,615	1,564	1,353	2,077	3,819	5,499	12,281	2,805
Bonds	22	176	86	237	168	310	3,150	255
Stocks	273	700	339	767	4,738	2,004	51,729	3,073
Home Equity	5,812	1,578	3,726	5,852	11,371	12,609	23,564	7,195
Other	-110	416	-385	-120	2,148	1,417	14,359	947
Total Wealth	8,408	6,768	8,021	12,779	32,201	41,213	131,910	20,925
Income	1,401	3,854	6,070	8,651	12,053	16,627	32,616	9,139
Black								
Farm & Other Real Estate	58	175	297	500	1,748	5,086	1,500	550
Business Equity	0	10	30	16	273	13,907	0	294
Car Equity	160	198	586	674	1,066	1,429	1,365	513
Money	21	151	236	342	850	4,694	300	360
Bonds	0	11	46	134	99	329	25	56
Stocks	0	0	5	69	27	2,571	250	63
Home Equity	2,181	1,984	3,587	4,587	4,113	6,929	11,500	3,266
Other	-129	-325	-1,242	-555	-710	1,853	-2,250	-580
Total Wealth	2,290	2,204	3,544	5,766	7,466	36,797	12,690	4,520
Income	1,616	3,578	6,182	8,628	11,734	16,634	22,585	6,196
Probability of Ownership for Whites	.441	.222	.415	.642	.824	.860	.857	.594
Probability of Ownership for Blacks	.177	.236	.433	.537	.636	.571	1.00	.390

yielding consumption services. Indeed, 72 percent of all black wealth is held in home equity, while whites invest only 35 percent of their wealth there. Yet only 39 percent of blacks own their homes as compared to 59 percent of whites. One possible explanation for the concentration of black wealth in home equity is that blacks are forced to buy consumption goods because of their much lower income position. However, most black wealth is in consumer durables, even among the highest income blacks. The top 20 percent of blacks by income have a higher percentage, 49 percent, invested in home equity than does any white

TABLE 3
PERCENT OF TOTAL WEALTH IN EACH ASSET CLASS
BY INCOME GROUP AND RACE*

	Bottom					Top	
	1-20	20-40	40-60	60-80	80-100	95-100	All
White							
Farm & Other							
Real Estate	12.0	26.3	10.9	30.5	18.0	16.8	21.1
Business Equity	5.4	1.6	5.7	3.2	7.7	10.3	5.5
Car Equity	6.9	7.9	8.2	4.1	4.0	2.2	5.0
Money	21.4	17.0	20.5	9.5	12.4	8.6	13.5
Bonds	1.7	0.9	0.9	0.9	1.5	1.9	1.3
Stocks	7.4	4.4	7.0	15.3	19.1	31.5	14.7
Home Equity	42.1	46.0	48.9	30.7	30.3	19.4	34.4
Other	3.1	(4.1)	(2.1)	5.8	7.0	9.3	4.5
	100.0	100.0	100.0	100.0	100.0	100.0	100.0
Black							
Farm & Other							
Real Estate	2.0	10.3	5.7	6.3	18.7	25.8	12.1
Business Equity	0.0	0.5	1.3	0.2	12.9	24.4	6.4
Car Equity	6.9	8.2	19.8	13.6	9.8	5.9	11.3
Money	0.7	8.8	6.7	6.8	10.0	9.7	8.0
Bonds	0.0	0.6	1.3	2.1	1.2	1.2	1.3
Stocks	0.0	0.0	0.2	0.5	2.7	4.7	1.4
Home Equity	96.5	85.0	111.3	86.4	49.0	28.3	72.3
Other	(6.1)	(13.4)	(46.3)	(15.9)	(4.3)	0.0	(12.8)

* Table 3 shows the portfolio distribution by income group; that is, what percent of total wealth is held in each asset (columns sum to 100).

income class. At every income level, blacks consistently invest a larger percent of wealth both in home and car equity, than do whites. Comparing similar income groups: the top 20 percent of blacks (income range $9100-$24,160) invested approximately 60 percent of their wealth in cars and housing, while the 60-80 percent income group of whites (income range $9300-$12,500) invested only 35 percent of their wealth in those durable consumption goods. Thus it seems clear that there is a reason other than pure economic necessity for the large relative "overinvestment" by blacks in home and car equity.

One possibility is that the presentation of the data in Tables 1-3 by income class obscures a fundamental wealth relationship. It may be that a smaller

TABLE 4
PERCENT OF TOTAL WEALTH IN EACH ASSET CLASS BY WEALTH GROUP AND RACE

	0-2,500	2,500-5,000	5,000-10,000	10,000-15,000	15,000-20,000	20,000-30,000
White						
Farm & Other Real Estate	6.9	8.2	5.1	13.2	7.9	7.1
Business Equity	0.0	7.9	2.0	2.6	2.2	1.2
Car Equity	65.4	26.3	12.8	8.1	6.6	6.5
Money	32.2	18.8	15.4	16.9	10.8	17.4
Bonds	1.2	1.1	1.1	1.0	0.4	2.3
Stocks	0.5	1.2	3.0	2.2	1.3	7.1
Home Equity	30.4	61.1	63.1	57.0	71.7	53.0
Other	(36.6)	(17.5)	(2.8)	(1.0)	(0.8)	(5.4)
	100.0	100.0	100.0	100.0	100.0	100.0
Black						
Farm & Other Real Estate	0.5	7.5	9.0	11.1	2.0	1.3
Business Equity	3.7	0.1	0.7	0.0	1.0	0.0
Car Equity	65.0	21.4	9.9	6.1	11.3	6.1
Money	20.5	13.1	3.2	7.0	3.5	11.7
Bonds	8.7	0.8	1.3	0.9	1.1	0.5
Stocks	1.2	0.1	0.0	0.9	0.2	0.7
Home Equity	46.2	70.6	85.1	78.1	84.9	81.3
Other	(46.0)	(13.7)	(9.2)	(4.1)	(4.1)	(1.5)
	100.0	100.0	100.0	100.0	100.0	100.0

percentage of that wealth is put into investments such as home equity as wealth rises. Since it has already been shown that whites have more wealth than do blacks at every income level (by a factor of 2.5-4.5), it would be quite reasonable for blacks to put a larger fraction of their smaller portfolios into housing.

This possible wealth explanation is considered in Table 4, which shows comparative portfolio distributions for blacks and whites by absolute wealth level. No significant negative relationship between level of wealth and the proportion invested in home equity is apparent. Further, blacks put a far larger share of their wealth into home equity than do whites at every level of wealth. Whites tend to invest more in car equity, but the difference is much smaller than in the case of housing. Again the finding indicates that blacks of similar wealth "overinvest" in durable consumption goods relative to whites of similar wealth. No tabulations are given for those families with negative wealth or wealth over $30,000 because the number of observations were too few.

What explains these differences in the behavior of black and white households? Two possibilities, not unrelated, immediately come to mind: discrimination and lack of sophistication about investment opportunities. Discrimination is usually thought of in terms of the housing market, but it may well exist in the markets for these other assets also. If the barriers in these other investment markets are greater than in the housing market, blacks may, for lack of an alternative, be forced to invest in housing. Moreover, the fact that blacks tend to put more of their wealth into housing than do whites is not, by itself, evidence against the existence of housing market discrimination. For example, Kain and Quigley have elsewhere found that blacks pay approximately 8 percent more than whites for similar housing bundles, a result which may be taken as evidence of price discrimination.(4)

Blacks may be less familiar with the usual means of obtaining investment information that is available to the well educated and upper classes. This lack of information could result from a combination of educational achievement and social class background. Because of discrimination and other environmental considerations, blacks may not know how to evaluate the information they do have. A good deal of information on investment possibilities comes from friends and business associates. Because of housing market and job discrimination, middle class blacks are limited in the extent of their informal contacts with middle class whites.

It is tempting to conclude that blacks make fewer "correct" investment decisions than whites, and that blacks thereby earn lower rates of return, and have lower rates of capital accumulation. A satisfactory test of this hypothesis, however, would require information on alternative rates of return, which is unavailable. Therefore, we can merely conclude that blacks, for a number of reasons, invest differently than whites and, relative to whites, "overinvest" in consumer durables. This "overinvestment" in consumer durables is of considerable interest. In particular, the tendency of blacks to invest more than whites in housing merits further inspection, given the extensive literature on housing market discrimination.

Since 72 percent of black wealth is in housing, achieving an understanding of black investment in home equity is central to an explanation of black wealth accumulation. Our tabulations of the SEO demonstrate that whites are far more likely to own their homes (59 percent vs. 39 percent for blacks). It is differences such as these that can lead to arguments of discrimination in housing markets. A fairly large body of literature has been built up investigating the question of whether blacks, due to discrimination, pay more than whites for housing of a given quality. While the issue is not thoroughly resolved, the consensus is that blacks pay considerably more.(5) However, this Becker-type of price discrimination may not be the only, or even the most important form of housing market discrimination. It may be that, rather than having to pay a higher price for any given type of housing, blacks are simply less able to buy houses under any circumstances. Moreover, housing bundles in certain locations are totally unavailable to blacks.

In a recent paper John Kain and John Quigley consider this second type of housing market discrimination.(6) Gross figures on black and white ownership rates, such as those cited earlier, are deceptive since on average blacks have lower

TABLE 5
OLS AND GLS ESTIMATES OF
THE PROBABILITY OF HOME OWNERSHIP

Variables	OLS	GLS
Race	$-.150^a$	$-.088^a$
Income	$.013^a$	$.026^a$
Education	$.005^d$	$-.006^d$
Yrs. current job	$.009^a$	$.002^c$
Retired	$.241^a$	$.231^a$
None employed	$-.035$	$-.011$
More than one employed	$.041^d$	$.171^a$
Families		
Age	$.033^b$	$.002^b$
Number of persons	$-.136^a$	$-.156^a$
Number of children	$.045^a$	$-.013$
Female head $<$ 45 yrs.	$-.270^a$	$-.007$
Female head $>$ 45 yrs.	$-.188^b$	$-.192^b$
Household types		
Single female $<$ 45 yrs.	$-.312^a$	$-.403^a$
Single female $>$ 45 yrs.	$-.147^a$	$-.295^a$
Single male $<$ 45 yrs.	$-.172^c$	$-.277^b$
Single male $>$ 45 yrs.	$-.040$	$-.108^d$
Couple $<$ 45 yrs.	$-.306^a$	$-.213^a$
Couple $>$ 45 yrs.	$.032$	$-.004$
Constant	$.302^a$	$.409^a$
R^2	$.213$	$.826$

Significance of t ratios for coefficients

    a $>$ .01
    b $>$ .05
    c $>$ .10
    d   t ratio greater than 1.0

incomes and less education than whites, attributes which have been shown to be positively correlated with home ownership.(7) Kain and Quigley attempt to show that even after correcting for "all" relevant socio-economic characteristics, blacks still have a significantly lower probability of owning a home than do whites.

Kain and Quigley apply regression analysis to a large body of detailed information collected from households in the St. Louis area. The dependent variable is a dummy variable, 1 if the household owns a house, 0 if it does not. The independent variables included most relevant socio-economic characteristics of the household, including race. The calculated value of the dependent variable in such a regression may be interpreted as the conditional probability of home ownerhsip for given values of the socioeconomic characteristics. The coefficient of the race variable then may be interpreted as the difference in the probability of ownerhsip between blacks and whites, after correcting for all of the other measured household characteristics.

The results of the Kain and Quigley regression are reproduced in Table 5. Of primary interest to our analysis is the race coefficient, which they interpret as indicating that blacks have an 8.8 percent lower probability of home ownership than whites, holding all other relevant characteristics equal.

Kain and Quigley offer three possible explanations for this difference: 1. tastes, 2. wealth considerations, 3. discrimination. After considering all three, they conclude that discrimination is the explanation and that "supply restrictions" on black residential choice and the types of housing available are the most likely mechanisms at work. These "supply restrictions," they assert, mean blacks are less able to take advantage of favorable income tax provisions available to home owners and the lower long run costs of owning. This impairment, they argue, may reduce black savings rates and impede capital accumulation.

While this analysis is an interesting approach to the problem, it, in turn, raises other problems. Kain and Quigley conclude that blacks are less likely to own their homes than whites even after black-white differences in pertinent socioeconomic characteristics are considered. Yet, we find that blacks invest a significantly larger proportion of their wealth in housing. While these two results are not necessarily inconsistent, they do need to be reconciled.

Two problems with the Kain and Quigley work are apparent. First, their statistical models do not include measures of the household's wealth, because these data were not available. This suggests all relevant characteristics may not have been held equal. Second, our analysis indicates that the investment behavior of blacks and whites are quite different. This leads us to question Kain and Quigley's use of a single equation with a racial dummy variable. It may be that two separate equations should be estimated for blacks and whites. Kain and Quigley tested this hypothesis and rejected it using their different data. However, our analysis suggests that the question should be re-examined using the SEO data.

As a first step, we estimated an equation similar to Kain and Quigley's (Table 6). While the equation is not precisely the same (there were, for example, no data in the SEO on the number of years on the job), the results are quite similar to those of Kain and Quigley. The race coefficient is somewhat smaller, but it is still substantial and significant. Then we estimated a second equation using wealth as an additional variable (Table 6). Both equations are estimated by Generalized Least Squares, following the Kain and Quigley procedure.(8) Wealth is defined as the sum of net equity in home, farm and other real estate, business, car, money, bonds, stocks, and a residual we have called "other." When the wealth variable is added, the coefficient on race decreased in absolute value and

TABLE 6
PROBABILITY OF HOME OWNERSHIP, SEO DATA

		Probability of Ownership Without Wealth		Probability of Ownership With Wealth	
		Coefficient	t Ratio	Coefficient	t Ratio
R:	Race (1 = black, 0 = white)	−0.093	2.60	−0.059	1.78
T:	Retired (1 = yes, 0 = no)	−0.10	1.13	−0.099	1.13
E:	Years Education	−0.017	3.28	−0.0046	0.94
Y:	Income (10's of dollars)	0.00026	7.14	0.00018	4.54
A:	Age	0.011	5.79	0.0084	4.80
N:	Natural log of number of persons	0.29	6.72	0.19	4.81
CP:	Children present (1 = yes, 0 = no)	−0.062	1.35	−0.0048	0.11
W:	Wealth (10's of dollars)	−	−	0.000021	5.22
X_1	At least 1 worker (1 = yes, 0 = no)	−0.16	4.18	−0.016	0.39
X_2	More than one worker (1 = yes, 0 = no)	0.94	2.48	0.10	3.17
X_3	Single female over 45 (1 = yes, 0 = no)	−0.33	4.12	−0.077	1.03
X_4	Single male under 45 (1 = yes, 0 = no)	−0.41	2.05	−0.18	0.97
X_5	Single male over 45 (1 = yes, 0 = no)	−0.24	1.63	0.061	0.45
X_6	Married couple under 45 (1 = yes, 0 = no)	−0.11	2.69	0.077	1.83
X_7	Married couple over 45 (1 = yes, 0 = no)	−0.19	2.79	0.027	0.41
Intercept		−0.0095	0.086	−0.27	2.57
R^2		0.32	−	−	0.47

its t ratio fell from 2.6 to 1.8. The coefficient of wealth is positive, with a t ratio of 5.2. The employment and family variables $(X_1−X_7)$ have low t ratios, but they were retained to keep the equation similar to the Kain and Quigley one, and while the individual t ratios are small, when groups of the variables were tested together, the F statistic was significant. These regression results confirmed our view that differences in wealth cannot be neglected in any analysis of the economic behavior of black and white Americans.

We now consider our second objection to the Kain and Quigley model—their use of a single equation. Since blacks and whites invest differently, separate equations should be estimated. Therefore, the sample was stratified and Chow tests were performed for the separate equation both with and without wealth. For the specification without wealth, the F-statistic is $F(14,872) = 2.59$; for the specified with wealth, the F statistic is higher, $F(15,870) = 4.52$. The critical value, at the .01 level is 2.02. In both cases, therefore, the null hypothesis that blacks and whites behave the same was rejected. The separate equations, including wealth, are shown in Table 7.

TABLE 7

PROBABILITY OF HOME OWNERSHIP FOR BLACK AND WHITE HOUSEHOLDS

	Blacks		Whites	
	Coefficient	t Ratio	Coefficient	t Ratio
T	0.021	0.19	0.0058	0.57
E	−0.0056	0.91	0.0029	0.49
Y	0.00022	3.73	0.00010	2.43
A	0.013	5.26	0.0071	3.02
N	0.075	1.87	0.29	4.87
CP	0.079	1.70	0.0051	0.085
W	0.00019	8.20	0.000016	3.64
X_1	0.019	0.49	0.10	1.61
X_2	0.082	1.87	−0.0065	0.16
X_3	−0.24	3.67	0.27	2.19
X_4	−0.13	0.67	−0.0070	0.25
X_5	−0.39	2.63	0.54	3.81
X_6	0.036	0.83	0.28	3.90
X_7	0.0061	0.77	0.28	3.09
Intercept	−0.47	3.90	−0.61	4.67
R^2	0.58		0.51	

Kain and Quigley clearly demonstrate that there are important differences among cities. Therefore our data for several cities may obscure some of these differences. These same equations were re-estimated using a sample of 172 observations from St. Louis, the city which Kain and Quigley used. No important changes have taken place (Table 8). The smaller t ratios reflect the reduction in sample size. The St. Louis results confirm the findings based on national data and demonstrates that the inability to pool the two equations is not an accident of the data used.

Given these two separate equations for blacks and whites, in order to test the results concerning probability of ownership, we calculated predicted mean probabilities by inserting mean values of the variables into the equations. A comparison of these probabilities serves the same purpose as the racial dummy variable in the single equation model. Three different sets of mean values—entire sample means, black means and white means—were inserted into the equations, both including and excluding wealth, Table 9. Interpreting the estimated equations as describing the behavioral patterns of blacks and whites, and the means as average socioeconomic characteristics of each group, a number of

TABLE 8

PROBABILITY OF HOME OWNERSHIP, FROM SEO DATA, FOR ST. LOUIS

	Race Dummy–No Wealth		Race Dummy–With Wealth		Black Equation With Wealth		White Equation With Wealth	
	Coefficient	t Ratio	Coefficient	t Ratio	Coefficient	t Ratio	Coefficient	t Ratio
R	−0.10	1.22	−0.03	0.40	—	—	—	—
T	0.49	3.50	−0.07	0.43	−0.10	0.67	−0.32	1.06
E	−0.01	1.11	−0.027	2.27	0.029	2.83	−0.030	1.74
Y	0.00015	1.81	0.00028	2.26	0.00032	2.94	0.00046	0.54
A	0.0044	1.07	0.0096	2.45	0.0074	1.88	0.012	1.89
N	0.085	0.81	0.043	0.42	0.039	0.67	0.061	0.35
CP	0.19	1.75	0.17	1.70	0.11	1.38	0.16	1.05
X_1	0.16	2.12	0.19	2.12	0.024	1.37	−0.027	0.17
X_2	0.19	2.48	0.12	1.45	−0.065	0.97	0.909	0.76
X_3	0.33	1.75	−0.14	0.85	0.55	3.74	0.071	0.23
X_4	0.091	0.36	0.0036	0.15	−0.52	0.46	0.36	0.89
X_5*	—	—	—	—	—	—	—	—
X_6	0.020	0.21	0.011	0.11	0.045	0.70	0.25	1.48
X_7	0.14	0.88	0.081	0.57	0.44	3.54	0.11	0.45
W	—	—	0.000043	1.35	0.00036	3.98	0.00010	3.23
Intercept	−0.28	1.21	−0.32	1.34	−0.75	3.12	−0.17	0.50
R^2	.49		.51		.74		.61	

Chow Tests: No Wealth: $F(13, 146) = 2.51$
With Wealth: $F(14, 144) = 4.98$
Critical .01 Value = 2.21

* Limitations of the St. Louis sample made it impossible to include X_5 in these equations.

interesting hypothetical comparisons can be made.

In all three cases without a wealth term, we found that whites have a higher probability of owning a home. However, when we inserted the means into the equations containing a wealth term, contradictions began to appear. In two of the three cases, we found that blacks appear to have a higher probability of ownership than do whites. Using entire sample means, blacks have a higher probability than whites, .62-.53; using white means, blacks again were higher, .80-.59. However, using black means in the wealth equations, whites have a higher probability, .47-.39. The same procedures yielded similar results with the St. Louis data, Table 10.

TABLE 9
PREDICTED MEAN PROBABILITIES OF HOME OWNERSHIP
FOR NATIONAL SAMPLE

Means Inserted	Without Wealth		With Wealth	
	Black Equation	White Equation	Black Equation	White Equation
Total Sample	.393	.533	.618	.533
Black Sample	.390	.482	.390	.474
White Sample	.406	.592	.797	.592

TABLE 10
PREDICTED MEAN PROBABILITIES OF HOME OWNERSHIP
FOR ST. LOUIS SAMPLE

Means Inserted	Without Wealth		With Wealth	
	Black Equation	White Equation	Black Equation	White Equation
Total Sample	.464	.510	.624	.528
Black Sample	.368	.457	.368	.470
White Sample	.580	.597	.895	.597

The following interpretation may be given to this last set of results. Overall, we predict a higher probability of ownership for the average person in our sample, using the black behavioral equation. However, the average black in our sample would have a higher expected probability of owning a home if he behaved as a white in a white world, while the average white would have a higher probability if he behaved as a black in a black world. While America today is more closely approximated by the white world hypothesis, it is still the ambiguity of these results which stands out. Without wealth considerations, whites do appear to have a higher probability of home ownership. When we allow for the effect of wealth, however, we become aware that the results are quite dependent on the exact formulation of the model. Thus, it is clear that the problem is more complicated than it initially appears. Both the specification of our model and Kain's and Quigley's are inadequate.

THE SIMULTANEITY PROBLEM

Since home equity comprises the largest single portion of total wealth, there is a serious simultaneity problem. The relative magnitudes of the coefficients are symptomatic of this. As expected, income, age, and family size are important for both blacks and whites. However, blacks have a much larger coefficient on wealth. Further, a computed Beta-coefficient on wealth was overwhelmingly high for blacks, but not for whites. There is no theoretical justification for this divergence if wealth is simply a behavioral determinant of home ownership. While we have been viewing wealth as a determinant of home ownership, the causal chain also runs the other way. Thus, for blacks, wealth plays the role of a dummy variable in our equation, positive if blacks own a home and zero if they do not. What we are left with is very close to an identity. One solution to this problem is to develop and estimate a complete simultaneous model.

Since other research has found the demand for housing to be correlated with the level of educational attainment, note that education rarely enters significantly in our model. Part of the problem may be a trade-off which exists between receiving from one's parents either education which would increase wealth indirectly in the long run, or an inheritance which would directly enter into wealth. Unfortunately, no data on inheritance were available. In addition, the simultaneous relationship of income and wealth is clear. What is ultimately needed, then, is a model which begins with inheritance, education and a better set of life cycle variables. These would then enter into a grand model which simultaneously determines wealth (perhaps broken down into its component parts), home ownership and income.

While such a model is beyond our present capabilities, it was possible to make a crude correction by redefining the wealth variable so as to purge it of that portion causing the simultaneity. Using other definitions of wealth, all of which excluded home equity, all equations were re-estimated and predicted probabilities re-calculated. In some of these formulations, the results changed, while in others they remained the same. No consistent pattern was apparent. This can be seen in Table 11 which shows, as an example, sets of race coefficients and t ratios for three possible definitions of wealth. Any final conclusions on the question of probability of ownership must await further research.

While it is quite possible then that blacks do have a higher probability of ownership than whites, even a situation in which blacks have a lower probability of ownership and yet put a larger portion of their wealth into housing is paradoxical. Two related hypotheses are plausible. The first revolves around the notion of discrimination. Due to discrimination in the financial markets, when blacks buy a home, they are forced to make larger down-payments. Further, because of housing market discrimination, blacks tend to move less often than whites. Thus, they do not continually re-finance as whites tend to do. Rather they concentrate on repairing and improving their existing housing. All of these factors would cause blacks to put more of their wealth into housing. In addition, while there may be discrimination in the housing market, it may be worse elsewhere—for example, the business community. Hence, even with discrimination, housing may be the only market available for investment.

TABLE 11
COEFFICIENTS ON RACE,
UNDER VARYING DEFINITIONS OF WEALTH

	Coefficient	t Ratio
Wealth = W	−.059	1.78
Wealth = W-HE	−.061	1.39
Wealth = W-HE-FOE-BE ..	−.082	2.64
Without Wealth	−.093	2.60

Where:
> W = Wealth as defined previously as the sum of Farm and Other Real Estate, Home Equity, Business Equity, Car Equity, Money, Bonds, Stocks, and "Other."

> HE = Home Equity.

> FOE = Farm and Other Real Equity.

> BE = Business Equity.

The other explanation is taste, broadly defined as due to something in the sociological-historical background of blacks. For a variety of reasons, blacks may view owning a house as more important than do whites. It may, for example, be seen as something of a status symbol. Or, having no reason to trust the white capital structure, blacks may view a house as a more secure investment. Finally, as mentioned earlier, blacks tend to have different kinds of personal contacts as a result of past business and residential segregation. In his conversations, a black is less likely to have any financial discussions and is likely to remain ignorant of many possibilities. In any case, the discrimination and taste hypotheses are not independent, and both no doubt play an important role in this problem of wealth accumulation of black and white Americans.

CONCLUSION

Most previous studies of the black economic position have concentrated on current flow variables, largely because good micro-data on stocks of assets and liabilities have not been available. It is hoped that our work with the Survey of Economic Opportunity will help fill this void.

Our tabulations give an overall view and lay the foundation for the remainder of the work. Perhaps most important from this section is the conclusion that blacks and whites tend to invest their wealth differently, with blacks putting relatively more into consumer durables, especially housing. This led into the work on housing market discrimination in general and the Kain and Quigley work in particular. In this regard, at least some doubt has been cast on previous results and some insight into the effect of wealth considerations has been gained.

Further research could take many forms. Comparisons between regions (especially North-South) and central city versus suburbs would be interesting.

Non-linearities definitely deserve to be investigated. While rates of return are beyond the scope of the present paper they should be investigated in any future comprehensive research. Finally, as mentioned earlier, the logical extension of this study would be the formulation of a complete simultaneous model. This paper has shown that wealth considerations are quite important, and their omission can lead to deceptive results. Our approach should provide a useful framework for future analysis.

APPENDIX

The 1967 Survey of Economic Opportunity is the data source for this paper. In 1966 and 1967, SEO's were conducted for the Office of Economic Opportunity by the Bureau of the Census. The SEO contains much of the information collected in the annual February-March Current Population Survey (CPS) plus other financial and demographic information usually obtained only in the decennial census years. Most important, for the purposes of this paper, it also included a relatively detailed breakdown of family assets and liabilities.

The SEO sample of 30,000 households consists of two parts. The first is a national self-weighting sample of 18,000 households, drawn in the same way as the CPS. In addition, in order to obtain better information concerning the poor, especially blacks, 12,000 other households were drawn from areas with large non-white populations. Essentially the same households were interviewed and the same questions asked in both survey years. A household, in the Survey, consists of an address. Within each household, there may be many interview units, which are essentially families; the interview unit was the basic unit of observation in this paper. The data used here was taken from the 1967 tape of the entire 30,000 observations. Nine hundred observations, 400 blacks and 500 whites, were drawn randomly from among those residing in SMSA's. Those units which did not report one or more of the categories of their assets or iiabilities were eliminated from our sample, since no imputations were made in the Survey.

NOTES:

(1) Henry Terrell, "Wealth Accumulation of Black and White Families: The Empirical Evidence," paper presented at the American Economic Association—American Finance Association Convention (Detroit: December, 1970).

(2) John F. Kain and John M. Quigley, "Housing Market Discrimination, Home Ownership, and Savings Behavior," American Economic Review (June 1972).

(3) Some of the differences in our results and those reported by Terrell can be explained by differences in methodology. Terrell computes two sets of Geni Coefficients; both computations yield lower coefficients for whites than for blacks (lower coefficients imply greater equality). The first set, based on all observations, imputes a zero figure for total wealth to those people who do not report any of certain categories of wealth. The information is coded in this form in the Survey. The second set is based on a sample in which "no responses" and households who reported zero wealth were both eliminated. In Table 1 "no responses" are excluded, but actual zeros are included, a procedure made

possible by other information in the Survey.

(4) John F. Kain and John M. Quigley, "Measuring the Quality and Cost of Housing Services," Journal of the American Statistical Association (June 1970).

(5) For a listing of sources, see Kain and Quigley, "Housing Market Discrimination," p. 1.

(6) Kain and Quigley, "Housing Market Discrimination."

(7) James N. Morgan, "Housing and Ability to Pay," Econometrica (April 1965).

(8) Arthur S. Goldberger, Econometric Theory, Wiley and Sons, New York, 1964. Goldberger (p. 249) has shown that when the dependent variable is dichotomous [(0.1) in this case], the classical assumption of homoskedastic disturbances is untenable. Therefore we used a two-stage procedure. First, we estimated the equation by Ordinary Least Squares, and calculated fitted values, $\hat{p}$. Second, we performed a weighted regression, using $[1/p(1-p)1/2$ as weights.

V.

HOUSING
FINANCE

THE "NEW SYSTEM" OF RESIDENTIAL MORTGAGE FINANCE

Leo Grebler

Major reforms of a nation's financial system are rarely, if ever, initiated without crisis. It is not enough to demonstrate that institutional arrangements stand in need of improvement. More often than not, it takes some kind of emergency to overcome the inertia of legislators and regulators, as well as the status quo bias prevailing among institutional managers. Thus, most of the innovations in the residential mortgage market during the past generation originated in the Great Depression, with the Federal Home Loan Bank System, the Federal Housing Administration, and the Federal National Mortgage Association being the most obvious examples.

However, there has been a more recent and significant change in the structure of residential mortgage finance, also induced by crisis or near-crisis conditions: the fuller development of intermediaries providing the housing sector with access to the securities market. Here, reform of institutional arrangements may be safely associated with the emergencies of 1966 and 1969, and can be summed up in terms of massive "disintermediation," sharp curtailment of mortgage lending by savings institutions, and the attendant effects on residential building.

Under pressure from these conditions, Congress has established new federally sponsored credit agencies which can transmit funds from the securities market into residential mortgage investment, and has enlarged the scope of operations of existing agencies performing this transformation function. The links between the securities market and housing finance have been greatly strengthened, so much so that an astute analyst has been led to speak of "the new mortgage finance system."(1)

Of course, the system is not new in a literal sense. The first links between the housing sector and the securities market were forged a generation ago with the

FHLB System and the forerunners of FNMA. Both of these agencies have obtained the bulk of their funds from the sale of their obligations and have used the proceeds to support the residential mortgage market, through advances to savings and loan associations or through purchase of government-underwritten loans. However, their operations before 1966 were for the most part marginal, relative to total net residential mortgage lending.

Only in two years of the 1955-1965 period did the amount of funds supplied by FNMA and the FHLB System account for more than 10% of the annual net increase in total lending; these were the "tight money" episodes of 1957 and 1959-1960 (see Table 1). In other years, the agencies accounted for zero to 5% of the total.(2) In much of the 1966-1970 period, their operations were far more significant. In 1968, they represented an unprecedented 23% of total net lending cushioning, but not offsetting, a sharp decline in net mortgage investment by primary lenders. Their share of the market reached a new peak of 41% in 1969, and it was only due to these "second-layer" intermediaries(3) that total net lending exceeded the 1968 volume. Even in 1970, when the flow of savings deposits began to increase and the lending capacity of traditional mortgage investment institutions improved, funds supplied by FNMA and the FHLB System equalled nearly one-third of the total.(4)

INTERMEDIARIES TAPPING THE SECURITIES MARKET

Although mortgage bankers are familiar with the ingredients of the "new system," a brief summary is warranted. The potentials for mortgage financing through securities have been augmented in recent years by the following legislative and other developments:

1. *The Federal Home Loan Mortgage Corporation* was established in 1970 to buy and sell conventional as well as government-underwritten residential mortgages. Operating under the FHLB Board, the Corporation obtained its initial capital stock of $100 million from the FHLBanks. The FHLMC may obtain additional funds through issuance of its obligations or by borrowing from the FHLBanks which, in turn, can sell securities to finance the FHLMC, as well as their traditional operations. The FHLMC began in 1970 to buy FHA and VA loans and participations in conventional loans.

2. The previous mandate of the *Federal National Mortgage Association* to buy and sell government-underwritten loans was extended in 1970 to conventional loans. This action broadens FNMA's scope of operations on the asset side and adds to the amount of funds it needs to raise through sale of securities.

3. *The Government National Mortgage Association*, in late 1969, began to implement its authority to guaranty mortgage-backed securities granted in 1968. Under two plans, these securities can be offered by a variety of private and semi-public issuers. Through mid-1971, about $1.6 billion of GNMA-guaranteed securities of the "bond type" had been issued, mainly by FNMA and FHLMC, and $2.3 billion of the "pass-through" type had been placed by others, notably mortgage companies. Only government-underwritten mortgages are eligible for the program.

TABLE 1
ANNUAL NET CHANGES IN FNMA-GNMA MORTGAGE HOLDINGS AND
IN FHLB ADVANCES OUTSTANDING COMPARED WITH NET CHANGES IN
TOTAL RESIDENTIAL MORTGAGE DEBT, 1955-1970.

Year	FNMA & GNMA Holdings[a] (Millions) (1)	FHA-VA Debt[b] (Billions) (2)	Clm. 1 as % of Clm. 2 (3)	FHLB Advances[c] (Millions) (4)	Conven. Debt[b] (Billions) (5)	Clm. 4 as % of Clm. 5 (6)	Sum of Clms. 1 and 4 (Millions) (7)	Sum of Clms. 2 and 5 (Billions) (8)	Clm. 7 as % of Clm. 8 (9)
1955	$ 180	$6.8	2.6%	$ 549	$ 6.6	8.3%	$ 729	$13.4	5.4%
6	430	4.9	8.8	-189	6.4	-2.9	241	11.3	2.1
7	926	3.8	24.4	37	5.2	0.7	963	9.0	10.8
8	-73	3.6	-2.0	33	8.0	*	-40	11.6	*
9	1,643	4.0	41.1	836	11.0	7.6	2,479	15.0	16.5
1960	759	3.1	24.5	-153	9.0	-1.7	606	12.1	5.0
1	-80	3.3	-2.4	681	10.9	6.2	601	14.2	4.2
2	-184	3.9	-4.7	817	12.5	6.5	633	16.4	3.9
3	-1,304	4.0	-32.6	1,305	14.9	8.8	1	18.9	*
4	-265	3.8	-7.0	541	16.1	3.4	276	19.9	1.4
1965	-42	4.0	-1.0	672	15.0	4.5	630	19.0	3.3
6	2,232	2.9	77.0	938	10.6	8.8	3,170	13.5	23.5
7	1,807	4.1	44.1	-2,549	12.0	-21.2	-742	16.1	-4.6
8	2,517	4.6	54.7	873	14.1	6.2	3,390	18.7	18.1
9	4,383	7.4	59.2	4,030	13.0	31.0	8,413	20.4	41.1
1970	4,916	7.0	70.2	1,326	12.2	10.9	6,242	19.2	32.5

* Less than 0.5%.

a For the purpose of this table, segregation of FNMA and GNMA holdings is immaterial. It should be noted, however, that the text, for the sake of simplicity, refers to FNMA holdings (although this label is not entirely accurate after 1968, following the transfer of special assistance, management, and liquidation functions from FNMA to GNMA). Source: Statistical Yearbooks of the U.S. Department of Housing and Urban Development and Federal Reserve Bulletin.

b Source: Economic Reports of the President and Federal Reserve Bulletin.

c Source: Federal Home Loan Bank Board.

4. An increasing number of *state agencies* have been authorized to make or acquire mortgages and to finance this activity by sale of obligations. By October 1970, 13 states had adopted legislation permitting such operations, usually for the benefit of moderate- and low-income housing.(5)

5. In the private sector, *Real Estate Investment Trusts* have been proliferating in recent years. After an inauspicious start in the early 1960s, REITs issued nearly $1 billion of equity and debt securities in 1969 and a similar amount in 1970. The potentials of these companies are difficult to gauge at this time. The viability of some REITs, especially those not sponsored by large financial institutions, is yet untested. Also, most of them concentrated on short-term construction lending in 1969-1970. Ultimately, however, they may become more significant mortgage, as well as equity, investors in housing and other real estate.

Even if some of the recent developments turn out to be transitory, it is clear that the access of the housing sector to the securities market has been substantially broadened. This change in our system of housing finance has two important implications. It can moderate the cyclical instability in residential mortgage lending and housing to the extent that instability is related to the supply of funds; and it can augment the supply of mortgage loans in the long run.

MODERATING CYCLICAL INSTABILITY

Net mortgage lending by intermediaries holding savings deposits or contractual savings tends to contract sharply under conditions of credit stringency. This is true, especially for specialized savings institutions which commit all or most of their funds to the mortgage market. Average returns on their long-term mortgage portfolios lag substantially behind current interest rates when the latter are rising. Consequently, savings and loan associations and mutual savings banks are unable to offer returns on deposits that are competitive with those on other financial assets, especially open market securities.(6) Net savings inflows are reduced as investors shift from deposits to market instruments.

The curtailment of savings flows in the tight-money periods of 1966-1970 may have been aggravated by the general savings rate control in effect since 1966. However, it is highly questionable whether the net earnings of savings institutions would have permitted them to pay substantially greater returns to savers if rates had not been regulated. Deposit institutions have attempted to combat investors' shifts to market instruments by offering longer-term, minimum-balance savings accounts earning higher returns than ordinary passbook accounts. The associated diversion of passbook savings to special accounts has dampened the resulting net gain in savings, and this must be expected to repeat itself under similar conditions. Hence, further changes in the "savings product mix" will make only a moderate contribution to the mortgage lending capacity of deposit institutions in future tight-money situations.

Intermediaries obtaining funds through the issuance of securities are not subject to the same constraints that curtail the mortgage investment by savings institutions in periods of credit stringency. They share with other lenders the problems of being "locked in" with long-term investments yielding fixed interest rates, and, as will be shown later, the conversion of credit market instruments into mortgages entails problems of its own. Nevertheless, intermediaries using securities as a source of mortgage funds have one important advantage over other lenders: They can more easily engage in "marginal funding" when interest rates are rising—that is, pay high market rates on security issues so long as they can invest the proceeds in acceptable high-yield mortgages providing a sufficient spread between the cost of new borrowings and the return on new loans.

As rates increase, the intermediaries issuing securities are immune to actions by holders of previously sold obligations until the latter mature. The holders may sell securities in the secondary market, but they cannot claim redemption. Because deposit institutions are less immune to depositors' actions, they operate under greater restraints on marginal funding under similar circumstances. They cannot pay higher rates on new savings than on old savings without inviting futile account transfers, except for the limited flexibility afforded by the previously mentioned special accounts. In contrast to the issuer of securities, the deposit institution incurs the risk of withdrawals of funds already invested, or committed to be invested, in mortgages. Hence, its capacity for new lending is seriously reduced. Under conditions of credit stringency, then, the going market yields offered on securities can coax out a supply of mortgage funds that would otherwise not be available.

INCREASING THE LONG-RUN SUPPLY OF MORTGAGES

Improved access to the securities market can benefit the housing sector in the long run as well. For example, efforts to interest private and public pension funds in direct residential mortgage investment, spanning two decades, have had relatively meager results. Mortgage loans account for only 6% of their combined financial assets. By offering these funds mortgage-backed paper that conforms to their requirements, practices, and preferences with regard to type, size, and marketability, as well as yield, additional moneys can be drawn into the mortgage market. The same is true for bank-administered personal trusts, which are ill-equipped to acquire mortgage loans directly.

Life insurance companies, which have curtailed their net residential mortgage lending in recent years, may also be induced to buy mortgage-backed securities if these meet their investment requirements for bonds and similar obligations. Even if substitutions between direct mortgage acquisition and the purchase of mortgage-related obligations are taken into account, the net gain could be substantial. For example, should private and public pension funds over a period of years buy mortgage-backed securities equal to 5% of their present assets, $8 billion would be added to the supply of mortgages. Should personal trusts and nonprofit organizations do likewise, at least another $6 billion would be supplied.(7) If Real Estate Investment Trusts develop into a significant, growing, and permanent component of the industry, the long-run potentials for transmitting funds from the securities market to housing will be further increased.

Mortgage financing through the sale of securities would become especially crucial if this country, as some analysts argue, faced a chronic "capital shortage." Of course, mortgage lending through securities would not relieve the overall capital shortage. However, the supply of residential mortgage funds from the traditional sources would be relatively scarce under such conditions, as the yields on market instruments would exceed the rates on savings deposits more frequently. Hence, intermediaries capable of tapping the securities market could cushion the impact of general capital shortage on housing, even though the extent of their market support would vary with the short-term fluctuations of interest rates around a high average level of rates.

While broader access of the housing sector to the securities market promises distinct benefits, the use of this source of funds is not devoid of problems. The main issues are discussed below:

Effects on the securities market. So long as the net demands on the market by housing credit agencies were marginal, their effects on other issuers of securities in terms of cost and availability of funds could be more or less ignored. In recent years, however, obligations issued on behalf of housing reached such major proportions that the assumption of a minimal impact on the aggregate market could no longer be maintained. In 1966, the $2.6 billion net issued by FNMA and the FHLB System accounted for 10.5% of a reasonable "proxy" for the total net increase in debt securities.(8) In 1969, the net increase of $7.7 billion in obligations sold by the two agencies equalled 27.5% of the total. With the injection of such large amounts of mortgage-related securities into the market, the yields to be offered by sellers of all types of securities must increase under conditions of fairly inelastic supplies of funds, and some potential sellers are rationed out of the market.

The postponements of issues planned by corporations and state and local governments in 1966, and especially in 1969, testified to these consequences. It is impossible, however, to estimate the expense to other sectors in the critical periods of 1966 and 1969, or in future situations of this kind. Among other things, an estimate would involve the unreasonable assumption that the total volume of security issues during a given period would be reduced correspondingly if no mortgage-related obligations were sold. In fact, other borrowers would enter the market or would increase their security offerings.

Effects on the savings deposit market. The issuance of housing-related securities at high yields relative to rates on savings deposits results in additional disintermediation, which reduces the capacity of deposit institutions to make or commit mortgage loans. At the extreme, the process has been characterized as "self-defeating" or as a mere "recycling" of savings that would have been available for mortgage lending in any case. Of course, the shifts involved in the process are part of the general rechanneling of funds in response to yield differentials. Whether investors are induced to buy mortgage-related or other securities makes no difference in principle. In its simplest form, the "recycling" argument seems to assume that in the absence of security issues for mortgage financing, the demands made by other sectors of the economy on the securities market in 1966 or 1969 would have been no higher; i.e., that disintermediation would have been correspondingly lessened. This assumption is wholly unrealistic.

The issue, then, is reduced to the question how much additional disintermediation may be generated by housing-related security issues. Stated in these terms, the diversion of actual or potential savings deposits can be viewed as a "leakage." For example, the amount of funds supplied by FNMA and the

FHLB System in the tight-money periods of 1966-1970 did not represent the net contribution of these agencies to the mortgage and housing markets. To arrive at such a net figure, the funds which the agencies' security issues diverted from savings deposits must be taken into account.

"LEAKAGES" IN SAVINGS DEPOSITS—ESTIMATES

In the absence of direct data,(9) the author has prepared estimates of the "leakages" in savings deposits and residential mortgage lending that may have been attributable to FNMA and FHLB obligations in recent years. The estimates pertain to the household sector; the disintermediation involved in the leakage argument relates mainly to household savings and not to the negotiable CDs issued by commercial banks in large denominations to nonhouseholds. The estimates are necessarily based on a number of assumptions and indicate ranges rather than single magnitudes.(10)

Briefly, the most probably results show that about 10 to 20% of the shortfall in household savings in commercial banks, mutual savings banks, and savings and loan associations in 1966, 1968, and 1969 was attributable to the purchase of FNMA and FHLB System obligations by households. (1967 is omitted because it was a year of reintermediation, and combined retirements of FNMA and FHLB obligations exceeded combined new issues.) Marginal disintermediation was in the neighborhood of 50%.

Another set of estimates shows the residential loans which the institutions might have made had they not experienced the savings shortfall attributable to household purchases of FNMA and FHLB System obligations. Again, taking the most likely result, the "mortgage lending leakage" is estimated at 16 to 22% of the net increase in FNMA mortgage holdings and FHLB advances in 1966, 4 to 6% in 1968, and 21 to 22% in 1969. In other words, the net contribution of FNMA and the FHLB System to the residential mortgage market in the two crucial years 1966 and 1969 was about 80% of their gross contribution. In absolute amounts, the residential mortgage market was better off to the tune of about $2.5 billion (net) in 1966, $3 billion in 1968, and $6.6 billion in 1969. These were substantial net gains for housing.

With the growing importance of intermediaries issuing mortgage-related securities, it becomes imperative to adapt the maturity structure of liabilities more closely to the actual repayment pattern of the mortgage assets. In principle, the risks of failure to balance the maturity structures are two-fold. One is described by the familiar "borrowing short to lend long," which has caused so many problems in the recent years of sharply rising interest rates. The other is borrowing too long relative to the actual repayment period of mortgage loans. This risk is pronounced when interest rates are falling. In such periods, the intermediary will face accelerated repayments of principal due to refinancing by existing borrowers and/or more frequent property transfers; and the declining revenues from mortgage holdings and from the reinvestment of prepayments in new loans may not support the interest on long-term obligations issued at a time of high levels of rates. The second type of risk can be minimized by appropriate call or redemption arrangements for long-term debt instruments. The first type can be minimized by avoiding heavy concentration on short-term financing; this kind of risk became quite apparent in FNMA operations during the latter part of the 1960's.(11)

The pattern of mortgage repayments from regular amortization, prepayment of principal, and complete terminations, of course, is influenced by many factors such as changes in interest rates, real estate market activity and the attendant prepayment by supersession, and defaults and foreclosures. Hence, past experience cannot be projected with absolute certainty. Nevertheless, it can be useful for projection. Yet, no comprehensive record is available of the repayment patterns of cohorts of loans made at various times and representative of nationwide performance. Such a record should be promptly generated.

TABLE 2
CUMULATIVE PERCENTAGES OF PRINCIPAL REDUCTION FOR 25-YEAR
MORTGAGE LOANS AT VARIOUS INTEREST RATES
FHA EXPERIENCE COMPARED WITH SCHEDULED AMORTIZATION

At end of	Derived from FHA Sec. 203 Experience			Scheduled Amortization		
	5¼%	6½%	8.0%	5¼%	6½%	8.0%
3 years	13.2%	12.3%	11.4%	6.3%	5.3%	4.3%
5 years	27.8	26.5	25.1	11.1	9.4	7.7
10 years	61.2	59.7	58.0	25.5	22.5	19.2
15 years	81.8	80.6	79.3	44.1	40.5	36.4
18 years	89.5	88.7	87.8	57.9	54.5	50.5
20 years	93.6	93.0	92.3	68.4	65.6	61.9

NOTE: The use of FHA data involves a number of assumptions.

The aggregative termination record of FHA (1968 Statistical Yearbook of the U.S. Department of Housing and Urban Development, FHA Table 75, p. 165) pertains to mortgages insured through 1966 and made at various interest rates generally far below those prevailing in recent years. The termination experience of loans made at higher rates may differ from those included in the FHA record, especially if interest rates should decline. In the absence of data, the termination experience of FHA loans, perhaps averaging 5.5% interest, has been granted on the contractual principal payments for loans of 6.5 and 8.0%. Further, the FHA grafted data show only the *number* of loans terminated or surviving. Hence, the figures assume that loans terminated in a given year according to FHA experience had the same average balances relative to original principal as the surviving loans. Finally, the FHA loan terminations include foreclosures in addition to prepayments in full, prepayments by supersession, and other minor items. To this extent, implied principal reductions or cash flows are overstated, especially in the early years.

In its absence, Table 2 has been constructed from data for FHA home mortgages to indicate how much the principal reductions and the corresponding cash flows tend to exceed scheduled amortization, especially in the early years of mortgage loans. The problems in using the data for our purpose are stated in the notes to the table. In terms of security issues, the results suggest that about one-fifth to one-quarter of a given total could be retired within the first five years, an additional one-third after another five years, and most of the remainder within 10 to 20 years after the date of issue. Of course, these specifications may need to be modified to meet the requirements and preferences of investors in securities under varying conditions in the market(12) and in light of anticipated sales of mortgages by the intermediary.

Obligations of the FHLB System represent a special case. Their maturities and redemption patterns are not related to mortgage repayments, but, rather, to the terms for FHLB advances and the freedom with which the borrowing S&L associations can renew short-term advances or prepay long-term advances. In the past, the borrowers' degree of freedom was quite large, and the distinction between short-term advances (up to 1 year) and long-term advances at the time of borrowing not as meaningful as it may appear. Because of this condition, and the resulting uncertainties in planning the cash requirements of the FHLBanks, the System until recently rarely ventured into the issuance of longer-term obligations. The policy was changed in 1969-1970.

Concurrently with the conversion of short-term advances into longer-term advances, the System issued a larger proportion of longer-term obligations. The average maturity of obligations marketed in 1970 was 31 months as against about 12 months in earlier years. Still, the liabilities management of the FHLBanks will remain subject to the uncertainties of their members' net demand for advances, which in turn is related, among other things, to the cost of advances relative to the cost of savings accounts.(13)

EVALUATION

On the whole, the developments described in this article can be viewed as a desirable reform of the institutional framework for the financing of housing. Their significance becomes clear when one recalls that mortgage investment in this country has traditionally drawn upon two principal sources of funds: (a) savings deposits, and (b) the contractual savings accumulated in life insurance reserves and, more recently and to a limited extent, pension fund reserves. Reliance on these sources has been a function of our instituional arrangements rather than a constraint dictated by economic logic. There is no economic reason why the housing sector should be barred from the securities market while the business and government sectors can obtain funds through the issuance of obligations as well as other means. Indeed, the mortgage-financing systems of most countries on the European Continent have for a long time included intermediaries which sell market securities (mortgage bonds) as well as institutions which channel savings deposits and contractual savings into mortgages.

The potential benefits of tapping the securities market for housing in the United States appear to be substantial in terms of greater cyclical stability of the housing sector and its long-term growth. The problems in transforming market securities into mortgage loans are manageable, as in the case of more balanced maturity structures, or they suggest caution and restraint so as to minimize adverse effects of security issues on the savings deposit market. Both of these problems indicate the need for a greater admixture of long-term obligations; short-term paper seems to be a closer substitute for savings deposits than are long-term securities.

CREDIT AGENCIES—A MULTIPLICITY

True, the "new system" is awkward. It operates largely through second-layer institutions and therefore involves multiple transaction costs. A multiplicity of federally sponsored credit agencies competes for funds in the securities market. The complexity is most obvious in the GNMA program, while piles a guaranty of market instruments on the government insurance of FHA and VA loans which back these instruments; when FNMA and FHLMC are the issuers of GNMA-guaranteed obligations, the program invokes practically the whole gamut of federally sponsored housing credit agencies. Surely, a simpler and neater structure could be devised if a housing finance system were designed *de novo*. But such a design is out of the question; we cannot start from scratch. Instead, the recent innovations build upon existing arrangements in a manner consistent with the present financial system. In this perspective, for example, the GNMA guaranty appears justified to make the relatively novel mortgage-backed securities more acceptable to investors; and the multiplicity of agencies reflects the fact that each of them operates mainly with its own constituency of primary lenders (mortgage companies in the case of FNMA, and S&L associations in the case of the FHLB System and the FHLMC).

To assure effective operation, however, coordination of the agencies tapping the securities market will become a paramount necessity. Such coordination must extend beyond the customary clearance of security issues by the U.S. Treasury Department, which serves primarily the purpose of consistency with federal debt management. Coordination will also be required to avoid the bidding up of prices for comparable mortgage loans acquired or committed by FNMA and FHLMC, and to maintain compatible commitment and similar fees. Competition between government-sponsored intermediaries may be wholesome by offering mortgage sellers (or buyers) a choice. But it can become hazardous if it results in adverse selection of loans accepted for purchase, or if policies are influenced by rivalry for preeminence in the galaxy of intermediaries and eagerness to cater to the special constituencies attached to each of them.

Further, the mandate of the federally sponsored second-layer instituions to operate in a contra-cyclical manner relative to housing cycles, now implicit, must be made explicit through appropriate legislation. This means reduction or withdrawal of market support when the funds available from primary lenders are sufficient to meet sustainable demand in periods of rising or high levels of residential construction, as well as intensified support under opposite conditions.

CONTRA-CYCLICAL OPERATION

In the 1966-1970 period FNMA and the FHLB System acted in a broadly contra-cyclical manner relative to the mortgage investment and housing cycle. From the present vantage point, it seems highly questionable whether federal housing credit policy was conducted in a similar manner in 1971. At a time when savings flows into mortgage lending institutions were more than ample, and housing starts increased to new peak levels, FNMA stepped up its commitments sharply. In August, a massive FNMA-GNMA Tandem Plan was initiated, and FHLMC raised its price for FHA loan purchases.

These measures, together with a reduction of minimum liquidity requirements for S&L associations and permission for the associations to make 95% home loans, were clearly expansionary when the mortgage and housing markets did not need stimulation. Rather, it appears that the policy was at least in part designed to keep the interest rate on government-underwritten loans at the submarket level of 7% and to restrain the rate increase for conventional loans. But the expansionary posture is likely to lead to over-stimulation, which will become visible in higher vacancy rates and a greater volume of unsold homes, and will eventually result in greater market instability. Thus, while the increased array and scope of federal housing credit agencies means that they are better equipped to moderate the cycle, such an outcome is not assured unless the agencies adopt the principle of contra-cyclical operation.

A comment is in order on two more general objections to the "new system." One of these pertains to the rapid growth of federal credit agencies, which is partly the result of increased housing agency activities. By "de-budgeting" these operations, it is argued, they have been placed outside the control of the federal budget.(14) However, the de-budgeting is related to the fact that the federal budget fails to distinguish between expenditures for the acquisition of capital assets, such as mortgage loans, and operating expenditures. This has become an increasingly serious defect since the functions of the federal government were broadened to include a large variety of credit and investment activities. Also, the flexibility needed for the performance of credit functions would be sacrificed and uncertainty over the availability of funds greatly increased if federal agency operations were reincorporated in the budget.

MONETARY POLICY

The other objection concerns the effectiveness of monetary policy. The support of the housing sector through agencies tapping the securities market in periods of credit restraint, it is claimed, reduces the potency of monetary policy as an instrument of general economic stabilization. "Under the present system, the largest and fastest impact of monetary policy is on residential construction, and this impact is to a considerable extent attributable to changes in mortgage credit availability. If the availability effects on housing were eliminated, monetary policy would . . . be significantly weakened."(15) This is true, even if the function of the federally sponsored agencies is interpreted as cushioning rather than eliminating the effects of credit availability on housing. However, the above statement is an explicit admission that the effectiveness of monetary policy in the past has rested largely on its disproportionate impact on one sector of the economy. The question is whether such an allocative effect, intentional or not, is justified, especially when it bears down on a sector endowed with substantial public interest. We believe it is not. The highly uneven impact of monetary policy is one of the reasons for advocating a stronger dose of fiscal policy as an instrument of economic stabilization.

Further, the "new system" need not be viewed as an exclusive solution of the problems of housing finance, or a cure-all. For example, if the much discussed variable mortgage interest rates should turn out to be practicable, accepted by large groups of lenders and borrowers, and sanctioned by FHA and VA, the difficulties of savings institutions in meeting the yield competition of market instruments during periods of credit stringency might be eased, and their mortgage lending capacity might be better maintained. If so, the need for financing housing through the securities market would be lessened. However, widespread adoption of variable mortgage interest rates in this country is still an "iffy" proposition. In contrast, the "new system" of residential mortgage finance is available, has demonstrated reasonable effectiveness, and can be improved to make it a viable supplement to the traditional methods of financial intermediation.

CONCLUSION

The "new system" is certainly preferable to alternative proposals designed to broaden the sources of funds for housing finance. One of these would require pension funds and other intermediaries with special income tax status to invest a prescribed minimum percentage of their assets in residential mortgage loans—a coercive method of dubious effectiveness as the same preference could be claimed for the growing number of other "social priority" investments. Another plan would reduce the cash reserve requirements of Federal Reserve member banks holding specified proportions of their assets in mortgages and mortgage-backed securities—an "arm-twisting" approach again inviting extension to other socially desired investments, as well as offsetting changes in the use of funds by nonbank lenders.

A third proposal calls for investment in residential mortgages of Social Security reserves and similar federal trust funds, such as National Service Life Insurance. In this case, the amounts allocated to mortgage investment would result in an equal reduction of U.S. obligations now held by the federal trust funds. The U.S. obligations not placed with the trust funds would need to be absorbed by the private sector, with the result that the supply of other funds by private sources would be reduced correspondingly.(16) Under yet another suggested program, general credit controls would be imposed to help allocate funds in favor of housing and other priority sectors of the economy.(17) Here, one must ask whether the nation's housing condition is indeed so desperate as to warrant such a radical measure. The results of the Housing Census of 1970 demonstrate again that this is not the case. Other, less drastic, methods are available to improve the flow of funds for housing generally and to help solve the problem of low-income families.

Considered in the light of these alternatives, and others too numerous to discuss here, the new and old intermediaries tapping the securities market represent the most promising policy instruments for cushioning the impact of credit stringency on the housing sector, and for augmenting the flow of mortgage funds in the long run. The further development and improvement of these instruments meets several desiderata. The "new system" is reasonably consistent with the existing financial structure. It builds upon techniques already tested instead of attempting innovations of unpredictable effectiveness. Although it represents a greater degree of "Federalization" of residential mortgage investment, the implicit federal involvement is in the nature of potential contingent liabilities rather than in the form of substantial budget impacts. It affords a flexibility of operations difficult, if not impossible, to achieve in direct government activities. In relation to private institutions, it relies on incentives and opportunities rather than on coercion. Hence, the federally sponsored intermediaries should be given a chance to demonstrate their potentials over a span of years before the need for other arrangements is examined.

NOTES

(1) Warren L. Smith, "The Role of Government Intermediaries," Proceedings of the Monetary Conference, sponsored by the Federal Reserve Bank of Boston, Melvin Village, N.H., October 1970.

(2) FNMA's support of the government-underwritten mortgage market in periods of net loan acquisition by FNMA was generally greater than the FHLB System's support of the market served by S&Ls. See columns 3 and 6 of Table 1.

(3) This term is used to denote intermediaries transacting with primary lenders, but not with the borrowing public.

(4) Relating net FNMA purchases of FHA and VA loans to total net increases in FHA and VA loans outstanding is a simple and straightforward procedure. Relating net advances of the FHL Banks to total net increases in conventional residential loans outstanding is conceptually more complex. FHLB advances may be made to strengthen the liquidity of S&Ls and to replace savings outflow, as well as to increase their mortgage lending potential. It is always questionable whether a specific source of funds can be related to a specific use in institutional operations, especially when source and use are treated on a net change basis. Nevertheless, one can support our procedure by reasoning that the total funds available to S&Ls for mortgage lending from net savings, loan repayments, FHLB borrowings, etc., would have been correspondingly lower if they had not received a given net amount of FHLB advances. Conversely, the total funds available to associations for mortgage lending would be correspondingly higher if they had not repaid a given amount of such advances. However, the interrelationships are not as straightforward as in the case of FNMA vis-a-vis the government-underwritten sector.

(5) U.S. Department of Housing and Urban Development, State Housing Finance Authorities (revised, October 1970). The securities authorized by the various state laws range from general obligation bonds to revenue bonds, with provision in some cases for budget appropriations to meet any deficiency in revenue-bond financing. Concerning the tax exemption of state obligations involving "interest arbitrage," see the temporary regulations of the Internal Revenue Service in the Federal Register, Vol. 35, No. 221, November 13, 1970, pp. 17406-17408.

(6) This condition is aggravated by changes in the yield curve usually associated with increasing levels of interest rates, with short-term rates high relative to long-term rates, which is unfavorable for intermediaries borrowing short and lending long.

(7) The assets of private pension funds and state and local government employee retirement funds totaled about $155 billion at the end of 1969. Those of bank-administered personal trusts and estates totaled $119 billion, of which less than 2% were held in mortgages (Trust Assets of Insured Commercial Banks—1969, issued by the Board of Governors of the Federal Reserve System, Federal Deposit Insurance Corporation, and the Office of the Comptroller of the Currency). The net additions to the mortgage supply after the initial period would probably be smaller than indicated above, depending on the growth of total assets and investment portfolio policy.

(8) The proxy includes direct U.S. government obligations exclusive of savings bonds, federal budget agency and federally sponsored credit agency

issues, state and local government obligations, corporate bonds of nonfinancial issuers including foreign bonds, and finanace company issues.

(9) Although a few savings institutions have attempted to trace the intended use of funds withdrawn from their accounts, this information does not lend itself to generalizations. Moreover, there is no way of estimating directly the savings deposits which would have been made in the absence of more attractive yields on securities. The Treasury data on ownership of U.S. and federal agency obligations are too deficient for tracing shifts from deposits to market instruments. As a standard footnote to the "Survey of Ownership" in the Treasury Bulletin indicates, the data understate institutional ownership and overstate the holdings of "other investors" who otherwise might be considered as a proxy for households, which hold the bulk of savings deposits.

(10) For a full account of the procedures and estimates, see Appendix G of the author's paper for the Board of Governors of the Federal Reserve System. The set of Federal Reserve papers is expected to be published shortly.

(11) The weighted average maturity of FNMA obligations outstanding declined steadily from 5 years, 5 months in 1964 to 1 year, 3 months in 1969. During much of the period, interest rates were rising, and FNMA had to pay higher rates for refinancing as well as new money. The result was a severe erosion of net earnings. In 1970 and 1971, FNMA issued longer-term securities which were beginning to restore a better balance in the maturity structure of its assets and liabilities; FNMA earnings were increasing.

(12) The mortgage repayment flows, in principle, may suggest the issuance of serial bonds. These types of bonds, used by municipal and similar government units and sometimes for special equipment obligations, appeal to different maturity segments of the market. However, their acceptance is limited partly because each series has a relatively small secondary market, and they are generally more costly to the issuer. GNMA is reported to have approved at least one serial issue.

(13) Thus, FHLB advances outstanding declined by $3.4 billion in the first 6 months of 1971 as savings flows into S&L associations increased. The average cost of advances, which were financed by earlier security issues of the System at relatively high yields, exceeded substantially the average cost of savings accounts.

(14) For a statement of both objections discussed in these paragraphs, see Henry Kaufman's discussion of the paper by Warren L. Smith, "Role of Governmental Intermediaries."

(15) Warren L. Smith, ibid.

(16) The proposal is sometimes supported by reference to Latin-American countries in which social-security institutions do make loans for housing, mostly "social housing." However, the analogy is faulty. The social-security institutions in these countries are divorced from the central government and its financing so as to provide greater assurance of availability of benefit payments. They make a large variety of investments in the private and public sectors of the economy, including mortgage loans, in a manner akin to life insurance companies in the United States. Their semi-autonomous status, and the reasons for it, have no parallel in this country.

(17) "The Residential Mortgage Financing Problem," by Henry B. Schechter, Senior Housing Specialist in Congressional Research of the Library of Congress, Committee Print of the House Committee on Banking and Currency, 92nd Congress, First Session, September 1971.

REAL ESTATE INVESTMENT TRUSTS
IN AN ERA OF INNOVATION

Peter A. Schulkin

Real estate investment trusts (REITs), with assets currently in excess of $10 billion, are rapidly becoming a major participant in real estate and mortgage markets. Operations of this new financial intermediary were extensively described by the author at year-end 1970.(1) Since then, total REIT assets have grown substantially and conditions in the real estate and mortgage markets have changed markedly. The focus of this article is on the strong growth of REIT assets during 1971, and the incentives to organize new trusts in the current market.

The modern history of REITs begins with the 1961 Real Estate Investment Trust Act and may be divided into three phases: the early phase (1961-1968), the tight-money phase (1969-1970), and the phase of competition and innovation (1971 to the present). Although this article deals mainly with the third phase, the historical origin of REITs and the first two phases will be briefly recounted.

REIT HISTORY THROUGH 1970

REITs had their origin in an old Massachusetts law that prohibited a corporation from owning real property other than that incidental to its business.(2) This law led to the development during the nineteenth century of Massachusetts real estate trusts with transferable shares which were purchased by the general public, often by small investors. When prospective returns from local properties were relatively low, these trusts invested in properties outside of Massachusetts.

When federal corporate income taxes were introduced by constitutional amendment in 1917, the real estate trust form of organization was considered exempt. An unfavorable 1936 federal court ruling removed this exemption. When the corporate tax rate soared after the start of World War II, the small number of existing REITs began a long fight to obtain the same tax benefits that had been afforded mutual funds by the Investment Company Acts of 1938 and 1940. Their efforts helped create the Real Estate Investment Trust Act of September 1960. This Act exempted REITs from federal corporate income taxes provided they met certain requirements designed to insure that a REIT is essentially a real estate and mortgage mutual fund.(3)

From 1961, when the Real Estate Investment Trust Act became effective, through 1967, about $350 million of REIT securities were sold to the public. About one-half of this total was sold in 1961 and 1962 alone.(4) Most of the early REITs specialized in investment in real properties and became known as equity REITs. Coexisting with the early equity REITs were three small REITs which specialized in making construction and development (C&D) loans.

In the years following 1961, the equity REITs grew very slowly in terms of assets, earnings per share, and share prices, in part because the investing public was not familiar with real estate operations, in which much of ownership reward is derived from appreciation of property values and in which cash flow is protected to a considerable extent by depreciation write-offs. Since the depreciation reduced reported net income and since real property on the REIT books could not be revalued until it was sold, it seems likely that the shares of equity REITs failed to command as high a market price as they could have if investors were more knowledgeable.(5) In addition, the equity REITs usually acquired ownership interests in existing properties, thereby avoiding the developer's risk but missing the opportunity to earn the developer's substantial profit. These factors, combined with very conservative managements, contributed to a lackluster earnings and stock market performance for equity REITs.

In contrast, the early C&D REITs proved to be growth stocks. Those REITs found that they could obtain short-term bank loans at rates sufficiently below the REITs lending rate to afford them an attractive profit margin and enable them to leverage earnings per share. The REITs also found that by selling new shares at an earnings-to-price ratio lower than the yield the new money could earn, they could further leverage their earnings per share. Finally, C&D REITs were able to benefit their shareholders by selling some low-rate, long-term debt accompanied by "sweeteners." As a consequence of all these factors, the best performer of the three early C&D REITs, Continental Mortgage Investors, showed an earnings-per-share growth of about 20 percent per year through 1971, while its assets grew from an initial offering amount of $25 million in 1962 to over $400 million in 1971.

The profit potential of C&D REITs did not attract new participants until 1968, when three new trusts were organized. (The first was founded by a former employee of Continental Mortgage Investors.) Then, as Wall Street was discovering this new investment form, the 1969-1970 tight-money period began, greatly increasing REIT lending opportunities. Tight money led many institutions to consider sponsoring C&D and other types of REITs. Before the end of 1970 such pillars of finance as the Chase Manhattan Bank and Connecticut General Life Insurance Company each had organized a major (i.e.,

TABLE 1
AGGREGATE BALANCE SHEET FIGURES FOR REITs BY QUARTERS 1969-1971
(MILLIONS OF DOLLARS)

	1969				1970				1971				
	I	II	III	IV	I	II	III	IV	I	II	III	IV	IV*
C&D Loans	260	388	539	848	1254	1560	2005	2576	2960	3383	3833	4254	
FHA & VA Mortgages	94	115	135	148	155	150	145	142	161	140	131	175	
Long-Term Mortgages	26	26	24	26	36	40	50	97	183	328	481	569	
Other Mortgages	3	46	69	85	140	198	263	404	511	546	568	765	
Real Property	553	565	610	702	722	763	880	949	1006	1115	1214	1353	
Mortgage Liabilities	357	368	378	430	433	448	520	546	582	616	633	680	
Short-Term Debt	90	124	181	231	258	358	513	797	1164	1458	1770	2238	
Net Worth	465	663	857	1237	1739	2069	2529	3186	3420	3803	4098	4432	4845
Total Assets	1034	1284	1549	2031	2583	3037	3737	4726	5389	6107	6833	7723	8136

Explanatory Note: The data in this table was obtained from REIT quarterly financial statements. The components of any one quarter are not strictly comparable since they could be as of any of three month-end dates, i.e., not all REITs were on the March, June, September, December reporting cycle. In a limited number of instances the full breakdown of the REIT balance sheet was only available in the annual report. In that event whatever information was not available in the quarterly reports was estimated. The last column of data, 1971 IV*, includes in the assets and net worth totals the value of securities sold by REITs which made initial offerings during the fourth quarter of 1971 (financial statements for 1971 IV were unavailable), plus the value of the securities sold by one large private REIT which would not provide balance-sheet data for this study. As new REITs reported balance-sheet data for the first time, they were added to the tabulation. The 1971 IV column, for which all data is tabulated, represents the balance-sheet totals of 127 REITs. Several small REITs, with less than $3 million in total assets, were excluded because adequate data could not be obtained. This study did confirm the existence of 145 REITs at year-end 1971, but it is likely that a small number of very small local REITs were not identified.

The category Other Mortgages covers principally junior mortgage loans, including "wrap around" mortgages, and intermediate-term mortgages on completed properties. A careful attempt was made to insure that the C&D Loans category did not include amounts that should have been included in the Other Mortgages category. Land loans were included in the C&D Loans category. Mortgage Liabilities refers to the mortgages on real property owned by REITs. Short-Term Debt includes both bank loans and commercial paper. It is estimated that at least three-quarters of the total is in commercial paper. Convertible long-term debt was considered part of net worth. Since only a handful of REITs had issued nonconvertible long-term debt, long-term debt was not included in any category.

initial securities offering in excess of $100 million) REIT, and total REIT assets grew from $1 billion at the start of 1969 to almost $5 billion by the end of 1970.

REIT GROWTH in 1971

During easy-money 1971 (when commercial banks and other traditional lenders began rebuilding depleted real estate loan portfolios), the growth of total trust assets continued to be very impressive. Assets increased 63 percent from year-end 1970 to year-end 1971, or about $3 billion in absolute terms. This substantial asset growth was made possible by moneys tapped from three major sources: an increase in the amount of REIT short-term debt outstanding of $1.4 billion (principally commercial paper); initial public offerings by new REITs of over $900 million; and public offerings by existing REITs of over $600 million.

Where did REITs invest the $3 billion of funds that they raised in 1971? Table 1 indicates that of the four major REIT investment categories, construction and development (C&D) loans showed by far the biggest increase during 1971—about $1.7 billion. In contrast, long-term mortgages and investments in real property each increased by only about $500 million, and "other" mortgages increased by about $350 million.

How were REITs able to increase their loans so rapidly during 1971, a year when the traditional real estate lenders found themselves flush with money to lend? One factor was that in their competition with other lenders, REITs were able to exploit fully their lending and investing flexibility. In addition, many REITs began making types of loans and investments that were not normally

TABLE 2
OUTSTANDING CONSTRUCTION LOANS BY QUARTERS 1970-1971
(MILLIONS OF DOLLARS)

	1970		1971			
	III	IV	I	II	III	IV
Commercial banks	13,864	14,280	13,915	14,580	16,111	16,846
Major lenders*	20,207	21,335	21,616	23,836	26,156	27,122
REITs	2,005	2,576	2,960	3,383	3,833	4,254
Estimated total for all lenders	24,200	25,900	26,600	29,200	32,000	33,400
REITs as a percent of estimated total	8.3%	10.0%	11.2%	11.6%	12.0%	12.8%
REITs as a percent of commercial banks	14.4%	18.0%	21.4%	22.9%	23.7%	25.2%

Source: For commercial banks and major lenders: news releases of the Department of Housing and Urban Development (the information on outstanding construction loans is not available prior to 1970 III); for REITs: quarterly financial statements (see Explanatory Note to Table 1); for estimated total for all lenders: rough estimate designed to take into account mortgage bankers, finance companies, and other minor construction lenders as well as the major lenders and REITs.

* A category employed by HUD in its statistical releases. It contains commercial banks, federal credit agencies, life insurance companies, mutual savings banks, private noninsured pension funds, savings and loan associations, and state and local retirement funds.

made by the traditional real estate lenders. Still another factor was that the value of new construction activity in 1971 showed the largest year-to-year increase in the recent past, making it possible for both REITs *and* their competitors to show large increases in outstanding loans and investments.

A useful way to obtain a more detailed analysis of REIT activities during 1971 is to examine developments in each of the four major REIT loan and investment categories. The recent trends in these categories—construction and development (C&D) loans, other mortgages, long-term mortgages, and real property investments—are discussed next.

C&D LOANS

As noted earlier, most of the REIT asset growth in 1971 showed up as an increase in outstanding C&D loans. Indeed, as Table 1 indicates, most of the funds raised by REITs since 1969 have been invested in C&D loans. This is an interesting development since the C&D REIT operates much like a real estate finance company in its function as an intermediary. The C&D REIT borrows substantial amounts of short-term money (up to twice the amount of shareholders' equity), largely through commercial paper sales, and uses almost all of the proceeds to make construction loans—high-yielding short-term assets.

The recent success of the C&D REITs may be attributed to the fact that they could obtain low-cost funds by selling large amounts of commercial paper at the prime commercial paper rate, and the fact that C&D REITs enjoy a number of nonrate advantages over commercial banks, their largest competitor (see Table 2).(6) Generally, the specialized and streamlined REIT orgnaizational framework can offer better service to borrowers than can the more cumbersome administrative apparatus of a large bank. Moreover, REITs are subject to none of the business restrictions that sometimes hamper banks.(7) These include geographic limitations, ceilings on the rates that can be paid for funds, and prohibitions on certain types of real estate loans and investments.

The growth of C&D REITs was further enhanced by the decisions of many banks (or bank holding companies) to market their lending expertise by establishing a REIT. Bank-affiliated REITs accounted for more than one-third of all outstanding construction loans in the fourth quarter of 1971. And there is little doubt that some of the C&D loans made by these bank-affiliated REITs would have been made by the sponsoring bank if it did not manage a REIT.(8)

During 1971 the competition among all construction lenders was strong. Consequently, those REITs which once made C&D loans exclusively began to make use of the flexibility of REIT lending powers to move into other types of mortgages and real property investments. This permitted them to maintain their growth and to decrease their dependence on one type of mortgage loan. At the same time, due in part to low long-term mortgage rates, many of the REITs which had been formed during 1969-1970 to invest primarily in long-term mortgages began moving heavily into C&D and other mortgage loans as well as into real property investments. Thus, competitive pressures both from within the REIT industry and from other lenders have forced REITs to diversity and have blurred the distinctions that in the past have enabled a REIT to be classified easily, according to its lending specialty.

As construction lending became increasingly competitive in 1971, REITs began to make increasing amounts of innovative mortgages which offered attractive yields and virtually no competition from the large institutional lenders. Consequently, the "other mortgage" category showed a 90 percent increase from the fourth quarter of 1970 to the fourth quarter of 1971. This increase consisted of junior mortgage loans, many of which were "wrap around" mortgages, and intermediate-term mortgages on completed income properties.(9)

A wrap-around mortgage may be sought by a property owner who wishes to refinance a property in order to raise more capital, but does not want to pay off the existing first mortgage because its interest rate is below current long-term rates or because the first mortgage contains prepayment penalties or restrictions. Thus, to retain some advantage from his existing first mortgage or bypass its restrictive provisions, the owner decides to obtain second mortgage financing in order to raise additional capital. If the second mortgage is set up as a wrap-around, the owner signs a new mortgage note to the wrap-around lender for the amount of the existing first mortgage plus the amount of the new second mortgage, and the wrap-around lender assumes the responsibility for making the first mortgage payments. For example, suppose the existing first mortgage, at 5 percent, has a $2 million balance, and current long-term rates are 8 percent. The owner may be able to negotiate a $3.5 million wrap-around mortgage at 7.25 percent. The wrap-around lender will advance the owner $1.5 million and take over the payments on the 5 percent first mortgage. Since the wrap-around lender receives 7.25 percent on the entire $3.5 million and pays 5 percent on $2 million, his effective yield on the $1.5 million he has invested is considerably higher than 7.25 percent.

The intermediate-term mortgage on a completed property is for a term of less than ten years with little or no amortization. Because the intermediate-term mortgage offers no promise of substantial amortization in its later years and because new financing is needed to pay off the lender, it is usually considered slightly more risky than a long-term mortgage and consequently, may command a somewhat higher rate of interest. However, since projects with a successful operating history can get significantly better financing from long-term lenders than projects with no operating history, it may well prove advantageous for a developer to use intermediate-term financing until his project is a proven success. Moreover, intermediate-term financing may be the developer's best alternative when long-term rates are high and long-term mortgage terms preclude prepayment for many years.

The intermediate-term mortgage is very often negotiated at a rate which is tied to the prime commercial loan rate, thereby protecting the lender against a rise in interest rates.

LONG-TERM MORTGAGES

During the 1969-1970 tight-money period, a number of REITs (particularly those created by life insurance companies) were organized with a stated primary investment objective of long-term first mortgages on income properties. These mortgages were especially attractive during 1969-1970 because the lender could usually get a "sweetener" in addition to a relatively high mortgage rate.(10) This sweetener almost always took the form of some percentage of gross rentals on the mortgaged property or some percentage of rentals in excess of a stated amount. If the percentage was based on gross rentals, it was usually 2 or 3 percent. If the percentage was based on the increase in rental income, it was usually 10 to 15 percent of the income in excess of the base. These sweeteners were especially attractive since the borrower was usually locked into the mortgage for at least ten years and since the total yield on the mortgage could reach very high levels as mortgage principal was paid down.

As money became more readily available in 1970 and 1971, insurance companies, savings and loans, and other lenders became more active in the income property long-term mortgage area. Rates declined and sweeteners became rare. Yield on long-term mortgages fell to levels which were generally unacceptable for the long-term mortgage REITs, and new commitments dropped sharply.(11) To improve earnings these long-term mortgage REITs turned to equity investments and to short- and intermediate-term mortgage loans which could be financed with low-cost commercial paper.

REAL PROPERTY INVESTMENTS

Our historical survey indicated that almost all of the early REITs invested only in real property. And for the reasons cited, these REITs offered their shareholders a lackluster performance over the years. Nevertheless, during the past two years a number of very large ($60 to $100 million initial offering) REITs were organized with the primary objective of acquiring income properties. Almost all of these large equity REITs are currently selling below their issue price (as are many of the *older* equity REITs).

The real property statistics in Table 1 represent for the most part an ownership interest in income property which is usually, but not always, subject to a mortgage. Also included in this total, however, is land acquired in purchase-leaseback transactions, which have characteristics considerably different from those of the ownership positions in income properties.

Purchase-leaseback transactions usually arise because the developer of the property wants to lease the land rather than own it, in order to minimize his cash investment in the project. The lessor (purchaser) in the transaction usually subordinates his interest to that of the mortgagee in order to help the developer negotiate first-mortgage financing. To compensate for the relatively high risk of his subordinated interest, the lessor usually requires 1. a return of about 1½ percentage points more than the first mortgage rate, plus 2. a share of the increase in the gross receipts of the property. The high yield on this type of real property investment has attracted many REITs, which see purchase-leasebacks as a way to improve earnings and avoid competition from most institutional lenders.

INCENTIVES TO ORGANIZE AND MANAGE A REIT

We indicated earlier that there are some very strong incentives for a company, institution, or one or more individuals to organize a REIT and act as its adviser. Although the Real Estate Investment Trust Act of 1960 permits an adviser to own nearly 50 percent of a REIT's shares, most advisers own very few shares of their REITs. Thus, the motivation must be sought in reasons other than the prospect of share price appreciation. As the following discussion indicates, those reasons are the REIT management fee and other sources of income.

MANAGEMENT FEES

The REIT management fee is almost always set as some percentage of invested assets. That the assets be invested in mortgage or real property in order for the adviser to collect a fee is not a burdensome requirement, since the adviser presumably can always find investments for its REIT, although severe competition might force it to accept low-yielding alternatives. Since REITs are closed-end, the only way a REIT can lose assets is through write-downs in the value of its investments, and such write-downs are almost never significant. Thus, a REIT adviser can look to its management fee as a very steady continuing source of revenue.

Most REITs set a management-fee ceiling of 1.5 percent of invested assets, with a 1.2 percent floor. The adviser must pay for all of its operating expenses out of its management fee, and these usually amount to less than 0.75 percent, depending upon the individual REIT circumstances such as size, type of investments, and allocation of expenses between the adviser and the REIT. Consequently, as long as the REIT is larger than some minimum size, the adviser can only lose money if its operating expenses are extremely high for some unforeseen reason.

To establish a REIT and secure its management-fee income the adviser need risk very little in terms of investment capital. The principal risk is that there will be insufficient investor interest to permit a share offering of a profitable size. Should this be the case, the REIT probably never gets off the drawing boards, and the prospective adviser must bear whatever organizational expenses have been incurred. Once the REIT makes a successful share offering, however, the organizational expenses are charged to the REIT. Thus, the REIT management fee offers the adviser a handsome return on a negligible capital investment.

In the cases of virtually all existing REITs, the adviser or an affiliate was already operating a real estate-related business before the REIT was formed. Consequently, REITs usually both complement some of the adviser's existing operations and compete with them. Where the adviser's portfolio objectives overlap with those of its REIT, the adviser probably organized its REIT in the belief that the adviser was generating and would continue to generate more real estate investment opportunities than the adviser or its affiliates could finance by themselves. By sending some of its excess supply of investment opportunities to its REIT, the adviser is able to earn a percentage on them through the advisory fee.

In addition to the management fee, there are a number of ways an advisor can obtain direct financial benefits from REIT management. Most of these arise from the meshing of the REIT's activities with the adviser's other real estate operations. For example, many advisers or their affiliates are in the mortgage banking or related businesses, and they collect substantial fees from real estate developers for arranging financing for their projects. By choosing its own REIT to finance the developer, the adviser not only collects a placement fee that otherwise might be lost but it receives additional compensation in the form of the REIT management fee, which is based on the amount of invested assets.

Other indirect sources of adviser income from REIT management include mortgage servicing fees, property management fees, and (for advisers which are banks) income from various banking services. In a few cases, REITs have purchased or financed real estate projects of the adviser, affiliate, or franchisee. It is difficult to determine in these situations whether the adviser has given itself better terms than it could have obtained in the market. However, even if the adviser does not profit from exceptional terms, the REIT represents a complementary business and a reliable source of financing. An example of a REIT and adviser which falls into this category is the Hotel Investors REIT and both Hilton Hotels Corporation and Marriott Corporation (which owns shares of the adviser).(12)

UTILIZATION OF ADVISER'S PERSONNEL

The employees of many REIT advisers are often required to divide their time between REIT affairs and the real estate affairs of the adviser or affiliates. Thus, managing its REIT often gives the adviser an opportunity to offer more responsibility and higher salaries to its employees than would be possible otherwise. The adviser consequently is more likely to retain its best people and attract highly qualified personnel—to the benefit of both the REIT and the non-REIT real estate operations.

Adviser working conditions may be improved in other ways by REIT management. For example, a commercial bank or life insurance company is likely to find that its real estate staff is largely idle during tight-money periods, with much of their activity at such times consisting of rejecting loan applications. This situation can be eliminated if the staff is also employed in REIT management.

LEGAL ADVANTAGES

If the adviser is a commercial bank or a savings and loan association, its own real estate operations are subject to various legal restrictions which apply to the liability side of the balance sheet as well as to the asset side. For instance, banks and savings and loan associations are subject to ceilings on the rates that they can pay for funds, and prohibitions and restrictions on how their funds may be invested in real estate and mortgages. By managing a REIT, the institution is able to offer a wider range of services and better accommodate its real estate customers. The fact that there are no restrictions on the rates or ways in which REITs can raise funds also makes it possible for these institutions to supply their customers with all the funds they need during tight-money periods and thus avoid the loss of clientele.

Similarly, by being able to make all types of real estate loans through its REIT, the adviser can accommodate its regular customers and earn income where it would otherwise earn none.

MARKETING NEW REITs

While the incentives to organize a REIT are strong, a constraint on the volume of new REIT offerings is the problem of selling the shares.(13) Among the important factors that influence the marketability of shares are 1. the name and reputation of the sponsor, 2. the recent performance of new REIT offerings, and 3. the expected returns from an investment in REIT shares.

The name and reputation of the sponsor are extremely important in determining the success of a new offering because the REIT itself has no track record. Those sponsors with the best reputations are able to capitalize on them by offering as many shares as the market will bear. Thus, REITs sponsored by such institutions as Chase Manhattan Bank, Connecticut General Life Insurance Company, and the Continental Illinois National Bank have been able to raise more than $100 million each in their initial public share offerings.

There is a limit to the number of sponsors with the reputation and expertise necessary to assure a successful initial offering of over $50 million. However, little-known sponsors have been able to have REITs underwritten with initial offerings of $10 million to $40 million. Moreover, the number of banks and insurance companies with well-known names is quite large, making up a reservoir of possible REIT sponsors that could be tapped for years to come. In addition, nothing limits REIT sponsors to only a single REIT. Examples of companies that are advising two REITs are Conill Corporation (Continental Illinois National Bank and Trust Company of Chicago), which advises Continental Illinois Properties and Continental Illinois Realty, and CNA Financial Corporation, which advises Larwin Mortgage Investors and Larwin Realty and Mortgage Trust.

Despite the continued marketing of new REITs during 1971, REIT share prices were enjoying relatively strong investor demand until November 1971, when one of the oldest and largest REITs, Continental Mortgage Investors, announced that it was about to encounter its first earnings decline.(14) This unexpected development shocked analysts and investors into reassessing the future of REITs, and caused substantial decline in REIT share prices. Although many REIT share prices subsequently recovered, investors have generally anticipated a slower growth of REIT earnings per share and have become less receptive to new REIT issues.

COMMERCIAL BANK REITs

In mid-1972, twenty-nine REITs had advisers at least partially owned by a commercial bank, bank holding company, or a corporation controlling a bank holding company. Twenty-four of the twenty-nine make up the set of REITs identified as commercial bank affiliates in Table 3. The total includes two REITs which had operated for some time with a nonbank adviser before a subsidiary of a bank holding company became the adviser. The total does not include either the single REIT having as an adviser a subsidiary of a savings and loan holding company (which includes a commercial bank), or the single REIT having as an adviser a subsidiary of a mutual savings bank holding company (which also includes a commercial bank).

As Table 3 indicates, most bank-affiliated REITs have construction and development loans as their principal portfolio holdings. Several hold substantial amounts of long-term mortgage loans, and two are building up a portfolio of real property investments.

Bank-affiliated REITs may enjoy some competitive advantage over other REITs but are subject to more possible conflicts of interest. In addition, banks

TABLE 3
AGGREGATE BALANCE SHEET FIGURES FOR
24 COMMERCIAL BANK-AFFILIATED REITs AS OF
THE FOURTH QUARTER OF 1971
(MILLIONS OF DOLLARS)

Construction and development loans	$1537
Long-term mortgages	43
Other mortgages	241
Real property	113
Total investment assets	1934
Cash and miscellaneous assets	37
Total assets	$2071
Mortgage liabilities	$ 37
Other liabilities	972
Net worth	1062
Liabilities and net worth	$2071

Explanatory Note: This study identified twenty-nine commercial bank-affiliated REITs as of June 1, 1972. Of these REITs, financial reports for the fourth quarter of 1971 were available only for the twenty-four included in Table 3. The data for these twenty-four REITs is subject to the explanatory note for Table 1.

(or bank holding company subsidiaries) which advise REITs often have more opportunities to generate income from REIT management than do most other advisers. Banks derive very little income from *owning* shares in their REITs because they, like nonbank advisers, typically hold an insignificant amount of shares.

ADVANTAGES ENJOYED BY BANK REITs

Organizing a REIT allows a bank to capitalize on its reputation. A REIT run by a large bank with a good reputation undoubtedly creates a favorable image in the minds of investors. Justified or not, the feeling may also exist that if the REIT runs into difficulties, the bank will stand behind it, rather than jeopardize the bank's name.

The sponsoring bank's reputation and business connections also give the bank-affiliated REIT better access to credit, possibly at lower rates than could be obtained by nonbank REITs. And many banks extend lines of credit to their own REIT, while a few guarantee for a fee the commercial paper issued by their REIT.

DO BANK SHAREHOLDERS BENEFIT FROM A REIT?

There is no clear-cut answer to the question whether bank (or bank holding company) shareholders benefit if their bank chooses to organize and advise a REIT. If the REIT limits itself to loans and investments that would not otherwise have been made by the bank, then the REIT management fee represents an extra source of bank income and the shareholders are better off except in the unlikely situation of the bank incurring expenses in excess of its management fee. If the REIT does take real estate loans and investments away from the bank, then the outcome for bank shareholders depends on whether the bank makes a higher return on the alternative use of its funds (together with the management fee that it earns).

The foregoing analysis assumes that the REIT shareholders are separate from the bank shareholders. It is possible to have a situation where the bank spins off its real estate lending operation to its shareholders in the form of REIT shares. In this case the bank shareholders clearly would come out ahead under the present tax schedules. The income earned on the bank's real estate operation would no longer be subject to double taxation from the shareholders' point of view, since such income would not be taxed to the REIT. This advantage is somewhat offset (the extent of the offset depending upon the shareholders' income tax brakcets) by the fact that the REIT cannot retain its earnings as the bank can do, and thereby convert some income into shareholder capital gains.

In the final analysis other factors, some of which are not readily quantifiable, must also be taken into account. For example, the REIT's operations are likely to directly and indirectly generate significant income for the bank or bank holding company through the sale of banking, mortgage banking, and other services. Another factor might be that by becoming an adviser to a REIT a bank may be better able to attract and retain competent real estate personnel. These factors and others may well be of critical importance in determining whether or not a bank should start a REIT.

THE REIT AS A SOURCE OF INCOME TO THE SPONSORING BANK

Banks can derive revenue from their own REITs in more ways than other REIT advisers. Examples of possible areas of profit which are unique to bank advisers are 1. acting as depository for its REIT's bank accounts; 2. acting as depository for the bank accounts of its REIT's customers; 3. acting as its REIT's transfer agent and registrar; 4. acting as its REIT's dividend agent; and 5. making loans and extending lines of credit to its REIT or guaranteeing the REIT's short-term debt. In addition to these sources of indirect income, banks, of course, obtain management fees and other extra income just as do nonbank advisers.

CONFLICTS OF INTEREST

Bank-affiliated REITs are perhaps more vulnerable than any other type to possible conflict-of-interest charges. These possible conflicts arise because the bank's loan or trust department may make the same types of loans or investments as its REIT (and also because the bank performs a variety of services for its REIT). Conflict-of-interest complaints could be lodged either by the bank shareholders or the REIT shareholders. For example, the former might complain that the REIT's construction loans are depriving the bank of profitable business. The latter could argue that the bank is charging too much for its banking services or requiring the REIT to purchase banking services it does not need.

On the whole, conflict-of-interest complaints are more likely to come from REIT shareholders, since bank shareholders may be persuaded that any action taken to favor the REIT will benefit the bank. In any event, bank advisers, like other REIT advisers, take precautions to guard against possible conflicts. An example of a standard precaution is to require that a majority of the REIT's trustees having no connection with the bank approve any REIT dealings that involve the bank.

IMPLICATIONS FOR MONETARY POLICY

Currently, REITs which are advised by commercial banks or by subsidiaries of bank holding companies account for upwards of 25 percent of all REIT assets. These bank-affiliated REITs may enable banks to mitigate the effects of interest-rate ceilings during tight-money periods by providing banks with access to an unregulated source of funds with which to satisfy the real estate loan demands of their customers. In the same way, *all* REITs act, in a sense, to frustrate monetary policy during tight-money periods. Developers who cannot obtain financing from the traditional real estate lenders can turn to REITs, which have been able to raise large amounts of equity and borrowed funds during tight-money periods. The net effect of REIT activity is to cause monetary policy to have more of an impact through rate rationing and less through credit rationing. REITs are not subject to Regulation Q interest rate ceilings, nor to outflows of savings account money in search of the highest rates available or life insurance policy loans. But REITs must pay the market rate for the funds that they do obtain, and they must charge their customers a still higher rate to make the transaction profitable.

As REITs become a larger factor in the mortgage markets and as multifamily structures account for an increasing proportion of housing units, the unregulated access of REITs to the capital markets should mean that the real estate sector of the economy need no longer bear the brunt of monetary policy, as it has in the past.

CONCLUSION

REITs have grown rapidly in the past three years from about $1 billion in assets at the start of 1969 to over $8 billion in assets by the end of 1971. Since REITs must earn a rate of return high enough to attract and compensate their shareholders, they must commit most of their funds to relatively high-yielding mortgage loans or real estate equity investments. These high-yielding mortgage loans consist principally of C&D loans and to a small extent include junior mortgages and intermediate-term mortgages.

Over 55 percent of REIT assets are currently in construction and development loans, and as can be seen in Table 2, REITs have gradually increased their share of the construction-loan market to almost 13 percent by the end of 1971. The main competitors of REITs in construction lending are commercial banks and S&Ls, both of which are subject to the vicissitudes of monetary policy.

Single-family-home mortgage loans and long-term first-mortgage loans on income properties do not ordinarily provide sufficient yield, after the typical REIT operating expenses of 1.5 percent of invested assets, to make them attractive REIT investments. During past tight-money periods, however, income property first-mortgage yields (including sweeteners) have reached attractive levels. Moreover, it is probable that many property owners will seek intermediate-term mortgages from REITs during future tight-money periods rather than lock themselves into high-rate long-term mortgages.

Thus, both in the longer-term first-mortgage area and in the construction-loan area, REITs serve as a safety valve during tight-money periods. It is likely, then, that REITs with their new sources of real estate capital will significantly lessen the impact of future tight-money policy on the real estate sector and generally improve the flow of funds into that sector.

In periods of easy money REITs will probably grow less rapidly, pursuing the higher-yielding mortgage and equity investments while leaving the lower-yielding mortgages to the traditional real estate lenders.

NOTES

(1) See "Real Estate Investment Trusts: A New Financial Intermediary," New England Economic Review, pp. 1-14 (Nov.-Dec. 1970). Copies are available on request from Research Department, Federal Reserve Bank of Boston, Boston, Mass. 02106.

(2) The 1970 Annual Report of Real Estate Investment Trust of America, the oldest operating REIT (its history goes back to 1886), was the source for the pre-1960 history of REITs.

(3) For a list of these requirements and for a more detailed institutional treatment of REITs, see the author's article cited in note 1 supra.

(4) Smith & Jacobson, "Real Estate Investment Trusts: In the Money and Here to Stay," Real Estate Forum, p. 28 (Oct. 1970).

(5) Equity REITs can either retain depreciation or pay it out to shareholders. If it is paid to shareholders it is considered return of capital and it is not taxable income for the shareholders. However, the shareholders must reduce the cost basis of their share purchases by the amount of depreciation when computing capital gains or losses on the sale of the shares.

(6) See the author's article, "Construction Lending REITs Are Giving Banks a Run for Their Money," Journal of Commercial Bank Lending, pp. 23-28 (June 1971).

(7) REITs do have some constraints of their own in the form of various Internal Revenue Code requirements that they must meet in order to qualify for their federal corporate income tax exemption. And in connection with publicly held shares, REITs, like ordinary corporations, must comply with state and federal securities regulations.

(8) Many banks offer the REIT they manage the right to participate in construction loans made by the bank as a way of limiting conflicts of interest. When the REIT's trustees exercise this participation right the REIT may well be increasing its construction loan portfolio at the expense of the bank's portfolio.

(9) In addition, some REITs began making more risky C&D loans and long-term mortgages in order to obtain higher yields and in order to induce customers away from other lenders. Such increased risk may, for example, take the form of higher loan-to-value ratios on low-risk properties or standard loans on high-risk properties.

(10) There is no generally accepted series on the rates for commercial and

multifamily mortgages. One reason is that each property is relatively unique, another, that owner's credit is an important factor in rate determination. Sweeteners will further confound anyone who attempts to make a consistent series of mortgage rates because their impact on the mortgage yield is unknown at the time the mortgage is closed.

(11) Given that their operating expenses including management fee were approximately 1½ percent of invested assets per annum, an 8 percent income property long-term mortgage would net a REIT 6.5 percent. Since long-term mortgages could only be safely financed with relatively expensive shareholders' equity or long-term debt, this net yield was not satisfactory. For these reasons, single-family-home mortgages, which have lower yields than income property mortgages, have never been attractive investments for REITs.

(12) A highly critical assessment of such conflict-of-interest situations is made by Abraham Briloff in his article in Real Estate Review, Fall 1972.

(13) Only a handful of advisers have purchased more than a token amount of their REIT shares.

(14) The market for REIT shares may have been buoyed by imposition of dividend controls under the economic stabilization program (from which REITs are exempt). REITs also benefited from the absence of controls over interest rates charged for loans and over rents charged to commercial and industrial tenants.

CAVEAT EMPTOR IN REAL ESTATE EQUITIES

Samuel L. Hayes III

Leonard M. Harlan

In the past five years there has been a remarkable growth in the involvement of corporations and high-income individual investors in large-scale real estate development. While both groups are usually thought of as sophisticated, there is reason to question whether their understanding extends to this less familiar area.

On the basis of a study over several years focusing on real estate development and financing and involving interviews with business executives, entrepreneurs, and Wall Street financiers, it is concluded that many corporate developers and individual investors are insufficiently aware of all the ramifications of their real estate decisions.

The main reason for their shortsightedness is the emphasis that the real estate industry and Wall Street place on the tax-shield benefits of investment in this field. Unless the responsible industry leaders and investment advisers rededicate themselves to selling the genuine elements of value in projects rather than selling the often-illusory tax shields, a collapse of confidence in real estate investment similar to that of the 1950's is in the offing. This will, in turn, speed the exodus of important corporate and personal financing resources from the field.

THE NEW BOOM

The recent entry of an impressive array of industrial and financial corporations into real estate development came in response to the expectation of a dramatic growth in housing demand during the 1970's and the profit prospects from it. However, even during this short time span, the nature of the market has changed, which has led to shifts in corporate strategy. Among the companies that have altered their objectives are American Standard, International Paper,

International Telephone & Telegraph, and CNA Financial.

The drive for year-to-year gains in reported profits that often grips managements of publicly held companies initially spurred many new corporate entrants to bid for large, successful single-family home builders. These tract builders have a short cycle of construction and sale of their product which has permitted operating results to be reflected quickly in their parent companies' earnings statements.

Then, when housing demand shifted in the direction of multifamily housing units, these corporate entrants faced a dilemma: How could they cater to the growing demand for apartments but avoid the operating book losses that usually accompany long construction periods? In view of the commensurate reported losses (largely from depreciation) and operating management responsibility, should they modify the traditional policy of holding and managing the building complexes once they begin renting?

Obviously, postponement of recognition of gains by retaining the property was inconsistent with management's commitment to increasing near-term reported earnings—even when analysis indicated that considerable additional value would accrue to shareowners from holding and "seasoning" the property for some time. Many companies shifted their thinking from the sales value of assembled bricks and mortar in a single home to the idea of the capitalized value of an income stream in a multiunit building.

ENTER THE PACKAGER

Clearly, the solution to the problem was to find someone to whom the units could be sold, so that the profit could be "booked" immediately. Fortunately for the corporate developers, an important segment of the investing public was ripe for this role. The favorable outlook for real estate development also had aroused the interest of many individuals who earlier had not considered such equities as a feasible investment.

Of even greater importance was an increasing preoccupation of high-income persons with saving tax dollars, securing a reliable hedge against inflation, and a growing disillusionment with other forms of tax shelter—particularly oil, gas, and cattle investments. The tax law of 1969 further focused investors' attention on real estate construction by preserving its tax advantages while reducing those on some other favored tax-shelter investments. The law singled out residential development for favorable treatment, especially government-backed, low-income housing projects.

But the corporate real estate developer usually has not generated this investor interest on his own because he lacked many investor contacts, felt inexpert in this area, and wanted third-party insulation from legal and public relations problems. Many developers have therefore contracted the function of raising equity capital to outsiders and, in the process, have fostered a new group in the real estate industry—the financial packager-distributors.

The real estate financial packager is analogous to the securities underwriter; he assembles the project in an appealing way to high tax-bracket individuals and then markets it in investment units to a variety of potential investors. In fact, the packager often is a securities underwriter. Because the real estate industry has become the "darling" of Wall Street, a growing number of investment-banking houses have established real estate departments. They compete with many more specialized intermediaries scattered around the country, including commercial banks, mortgage bankers, and real estate brokers and other entrepreneurs.

Being a "professional" in the capital markets, the financial packager knows the underlying preoccupations of both investors and corporate developers and caters to them with sometimes complex and sophisticated packages rivaling anything concocted during the merger boom of the 1960's. His success in generating demand for these syndicate participations has created something akin to a "new issue" bull market in this form of investment.

In essence, the real estate industry has "gone public," using the limited-partnership medium for project ownership and common stock for the development companies. (The limited partnership has become standard as the mechanism to limit the investors' financial liability to the cash invested. But the tax-shelter aspect of partnerships provides them with a pass-through of any reported losses.) Although limited partnerships are increasingly treated as public offerings and registered with the Securities and Exchange Commission, in the past most have been private placements to a small number of investors and therefore not subject to SEC registration rules.

The syndicators' packaging skills have brought such good prices for their projects that some long-established development firms, not so concerned with earnings per share because they typically are privately held, have substituted their traditional policy of construct and hold to one of presell and then construct. This drift toward higher prices deserves closer analysis.

INDIFFERENCE OVER PRICE

Business logic dictates that the buyers should bargain vigorously for a lower price while the developer-seller presses for a higher one. In this type of real estate deal, however, hard bargaining is not focused on price, so the purchasers of the property may pay a relatively high sum. The investors' pliancy is usually attributable to an obsession with the tax implications at the expense of the long-run economics.

To them, each extra dollar they pay only adds to the depreciable base of the project. Depreciation of the project at an accelerated rate for tax purposes accents the investors' tax shelter during the early years of operations. When the project is sold, the reported income will be taxed at the capital gains rate (unless it is sold during the early years, in which case the gain is taxed as ordinary income).

In other words, each incremental dollar paid for a project represents for the 50% tax-bracket person 50 cents of tax saving through depreciation writeoffs. At the time of sale for the same incremental dollar, he pays a capital-gain tax of 35 cents, "making" 15 cents on the transaction as well as having an interest-free loan from the government for the entire 50 cents.

The financial packager can usually show that the yield on the project, as calculated using discounted cash flow, is often enhanced by the higher depreciable base. Since the higher price need not entail an additional cash payment (the seller often takes back a second mortgage or similar seller financing instrument), few investors put up resistance to a higher price tag.

(Fees the packager receives which are not identified as part of the selling expense, but which may represent a significant portion of the investor's equity ante, sometimes help escalate the price. These fees have absorbed as much as 35% of the cash contributed by the investors.)

The buyer focuses primarily on the amount of cash investment and how rapidly it can be repaid in cash generated by the project and, more important, by the "soft" dollars (excess tax losses) applicable against his income from other sources. Most investors consider the tax shelter a near certainty, dependent only on their ability to earn enough to push them into a high marginal bracket.

SHORT-RUN ECONOMICS

Whether this elaborate packaging creates any additional economic value is an important question. Another is whether, in spite of the impressive internal rate of return calculation (discounted cash flows), the project is really viable. To examine these questions, one must separate the considerations into short-run and long-run viewpoints.

The corporate developer who sells the project for a substantial book profit, but for little cash, risks a liquidity squeeze. The extent to which present-day "generally accepted accounting principles" can misrepresent the true cash impact of such a transaction is clearly revealed in reviewing the sale of an apartment project.

Assume that construction costs are $3 million and the developer has been able to secure a typical first mortgage of $2.6 million. If he sells the project for $3.4 million, he has made a $400,000 pretax profit.

But if, as often happens, the buyer is willing (or able) to put up only a portion of the money—say, $350,000 in this case—to consummate the sale, the seller will be forced to take back a $450,000 second mortgage on the property. The second mortgage can be disguised in several ways, such as a "wrap around" first mortgage or a subordinated land lease. Since the project cost $3 million and the seller received only $2.95 million in cash and a note for $450,000, he is $50,000 out of pocket although he has reported a $400,000 profit.

Financing instruments created to facilitate a sale, such as the second mortgage, are usually structured to minimize debt-service payments and provide maximum tax benefits by emphasizing the interest portion and minimizing amortization. These seller instruments may appear at first glance to be acceptable financing vehicles, but for the most part they cannot be sold at face value in the money market. The aim of minimizing the annual debt-service burden is accomplished, but their interest coupons and amortization schedules usually do not reflect the risks associated with their repayment.

A shortage of cash at the time of sale is a problem for the small, independent real estate developer whose capital resources are thinly spread. But even large corporate developers can feel the impact of this situation too. It was a contributing factor in the collapse of the Penn Central Transportation Company, whose majority-owned subsidiary, Great Southwest Corporation, was generating a substantial portion of the parent's reported earnings during the two years preceding the bankruptcy. But it was producing almost no cash; property sales had been made on a "note" basis.

The project itself may encounter a liquidity bind and become insolvent. The inflated price typically is reflected in seller financings such as a second mortgage. Its carrying charges, while written to minimize the additional debt burden, can nevertheless substantially increase the "financial" risk (on top of the "operating" risk, which is a function of the rent receipts and operating costs). What might have been a break-even point of 75% to 80% of capacity or occupancy on a lower total price, requiring only a conventional first mortgage, can easily rise to 90% or more of anticipated gross rents when the seller's secondary financing is added.

Sometimes the investors are protected by guarantees built into the purchase arrangements. The good packager will see to it on his own initiative that such safeguards are included, and smart investors will insist on them if they are absent. The most common safeguard is the developer's guarantee of completion.

The risks of construction are normally borne by the developer either directly or through bonding insurance, and therefore are not a factor in this discussion. The risks of the "rent up" period are another matter altogether. Significant uncertainties exist in the timing of achieving the rental goals, not to mention reaching them at all. The variables are both the rent per unit and the number of units rented.

Some investors, eager to believe in the certainty of a proposal, will read the packagers' projections of operating cash flow as though there were already a five-year operating history. But the fact is that each project is essentially a new enterprise with all the risks which that implies. While forecasts for certain types of real estate ventures can be made with somewhat greater confidence than is typical for, say a new manufacturing business, the investors still face considerable uncertainty. An unscrupulous developer can often change the investors' anticipated return out of an apartment complex from mediocre to very appealing simply by raising his projection of monthly rentals by only $10 per unit.

Even after the rent-up period has been weathered, many subsequent operating uncertainties still must be resolved. Property taxes, the rate of lease renewals, the market rate for rents, and certain operating expenses (such as the fixture replacements) are subject to variation before they finally stabilize. To sell a deal, financial packagers have sometimes resorted to programming of increases in anticipation of hikes in rents on competing projects by the time of project completion.

The rent schedule of a typical financial projection or pro-forma cash flow analysis also assumes a 3% to 5% vacancy rate. On the assumption that recent national and regional vacancy rates will continue to prevail, this range would be a more than adequate anticipation of performance. Unfortunately, however, national or even regional experience is a poor basis for prediction. Degree of vacancy risk is peculiar to a limited geographical market, which in turn may be so fractionalized that a forecast can apply only to the project site itself.

Within a limited regional market, moreover, developers can overbuild causing a temporary glut that exacerbates fluctuations in the variables we referred to. For example, developers in the Seattle area, building to meet a market demand, saw the demand evaporate when a local depression came in 1970. Soon they were faced with vacancy rates of 15% to 20%—at a time when the national average was less than 5%.

Unexpectedly high vacancies may force a downward adjustment in rents which could cause a shortfall in the revenue forecasts for the foreseeable future. In regard to the risks of raising the break-even point, we suggest that the combination of only modest shortfalls in both rent levels *and* occupancy could have serious effects on a highly leveraged project.

It should now be clear that even a modest variance from estimate in several uncertainty factors can dramatically reduce the return to investors and, more seriously, throw the project into a cash deficiency condition—perhaps even insolvency. In that event, the project may revert to the holder of the second mortgage or even be defaulted to the first mortgage holder.

It is questionable whether these risky syndicated projects, because of their high cash break-even points, can survive the variety of possible short-term swings we have referred to. If disaster forced the projects into liquidation, what would be the implications for each of the parties involved?

TAX IMPACT ON THE PROJECT

The greatest risk is the possibility of default during the project's early years when the investors have received a major portion of the tax losses, which are disproportionate to the cash distributions from operations of the project. Since the income statement differs so radically from the cash flow, an investor could virtually go broke while making an "audited profit" because he does not have the cash to pay his tax bill. For investors, forfeiture of a project is construed for tax purposes as a sale, and a tax becomes immediately payable on the recapture of the tax shield carried up to that point. (See the results of the investment sequences in the Appendix.)

New construction can be depreciated at an accelerated rate significantly greater than "straight line." The recapture provision of the tax law substantially penalizes the seller of property in the early years. Tax-accounting treatment for individuals can create a tax liability at ordinary income rates. In effect the recapture provision tends to "lock in" the investor to his position for 10 or more years, which places even greater emphasis on assessing a project's long-run economic outlook.

The law says that the cumulative difference at the time of sale between the book value under straight-line depreciation and the book value of a project using accelerated depreciation is subject to taxation at the ordinary rate. Only the gain in excess of the difference is accorded the more favorable capital gains tax rate. The percentage of the difference subject to recapture decreases 1% per month after the one hundredth month—except for low-income housing, where the decrease begins after the twentieth month.

In a tax-oriented deal, book value is always less than the value of the mortgages beyond the first few years of project life. The difference between the two constitutes the taxable gain or "profit" without regard for the fact that the investors have received no cash. In such a forfeiture, all future cash flows are lost, as is the capital already paid to amortize the mortgage. Recovery of even a modest amount of cash through the liquidation is unlikely, since a forced sale in what is typically an illiquid market must be expected to suffer a substantial discount from fair market value.

Investors in a problem project can provide the additional cash to keep it afloat, but generally they assume their cash obligations to be confined to that stipulated in the limited-partnership agreement. If the financial packager is working in the investors' interest, he has already shifted responsibility for the financial staying power to the developer, at least during the early years while the project "seasons." In some instances the developer commits himself to lend the partnership funds to cover any cash deficits. In other cases packagers have attempted to construct a lower cash break-even point for the project by obtaining one or more of these concessions from him in the agreement: 1. Subordination of the annual project management fee to other operating expenses and all financing charges. 2. Subordination of the second mortgage and deferral of the amortization and/or the interest payments, or 3. Waiver or deferral of lease payments in cases where he retains ownership of the land and leases it to the buyer. But the value of these guarantees and subordinations is arguable. Can they be enforced in a way to provide the cash when it is most needed?

If the developer has made such concessions, there is a question whether the paper he has taken back as payment for his equity in the project may not actually be worth the value at which he entered it in his earnings statement.

This leads to the question whether the developer has sold the project or is in fact a continuing partner. The accounting entry recording the sale suggests a clean break from the project, which is not usually the case. The accounting profession, which only recently has begun to examine this question, should consider two points: 1. The developer may have been forced to leave a net investment of cash in the project (as distinct from the profit taken back as a second mortgage) and 2. Through all the subordinations granted and guarantees made, he may be bound to the risks of the project far into the future. The seller and his accountants must concern themselves with the long-range prospects of the project and the soundness of its operating management in order to get assurance of the realization of profits through the subordinated financing instruments. If the seller has any doubts, he is actually a de facto partner with the limited partners in the syndicate, and he should stand ready to assume management of the project if the designated managing agents should falter.

LONG-RUN ECONOMICS

Disposition of the property some years hence could create another type of cash problem for the investors. Investors and developers sometimes mistakenly assume that a project's residual value will generate sufficient cash to satisfy whatever tax is incurred on the implicit capital gain. But as the example in the Appendix shows, a project sold in default has the potential for cash squeezes as a consequence of profits.

In the long run the chances are better that even a high-priced project—if it survives the early threats to reaching the cash break-even point—will be a sound investment, though it may take tax savings and continued inflation to do it.

The investors' conviction that they will have ample taxable dollars to shelter seems reasonable. While federal tax *rates* may have reached a peak and may even decline modestly, rising personal income is pushing more people into marginally higher tax brackets. The result is that the federal tax bite on individuals will be maintained, if not increased, into the foreseeable future.

Moreover, state and municipal income taxes have been mushrooming and in some cases have risen to a sizable percentage of the federal tax bill. In 1971, income tax levies edged out sales taxes as the largest single source of state revenue. The fact that tax-deductible expenses for real estate investments apply to local and state taxes (in New York and many other states), as well as to federal income taxes, further whets investors' appetites for real estate equities offering tax shelter.

The other factor that may "bail out" seemingly overpriced real estate projects is persistent inflation. Many persons in the industry expect inflationary increases in rent rolls to outpace increases in operating expenses, particularly if the projects are financed by long-term, fixed-interest mortgages. They foresee an ever-widening cushion of net cash flow as inflation rises over the years, with a resulting decline in the cash break-even occupancy rate and an accompanying decrease in project risk.

Many marginal projects constructed during the early 1960's became huge successes as a result of inflation and an acute space shortage during that period. But corporate developers' reliance on their ability to sell new projects, with scant concern for market demand, is already creating an oversupply of some types of real estate in certain markets—such as office buildings in New York City and Chicago, and apartment projects in Dallas and southern California. Continued pressure in this direction could create chronic oversupply and negate the bailout possibilities we spoke of.

Furthermore, lenders are increasingly demanding and getting a share of inflationary rent increases (often buried in the fine print). Continued inflationary pressures on interest rates could also influence lenders to stop writing long-term loans and opt instead for shorter-term, periodic refinancings. Amortization schedules may still be based on 25- to 30-year terms, but mortgages will be more likely to have 10- to 15-year lives with large balloon payments at the end that require refinancing.

Finally, subordinated notes purchased by the original developers to lower the investors' required cash investment could reduce or even eliminate the cash that investors expect to receive at the time of sale. Thus, while inflation may help them on balance, investors must not blindly assume that if can be counted on to rescue their project.

WHO DOES THE ANALYSIS?

Obviously, both the seller and buyer have a vital stake not only in the final price but also in the terms of a real estate transaction. While every deal should, of course, be subjected to the same type of analysis described here, it is not always certain just who, if anyone, is doing it. Consider each participant:

The investor—The investigation indicates that investors are not usually doing it for themselves; most of the new wave of investors are relatively unsophisticated in real estate. But even if they were analyzing each property, in many deals the investors are too numerous and too dispersed to exert much influence on the complex development of the project proposal. They are limited to simply accepting or rejecting the finished package.

Moreover, investors tend to infer a stamp of approval on a proposal which bears the name of a well-known developer, lender, or packager. Interviews with a large sample of investors indicate that the more recongizable the name of the "sponsor," the more sophisticated the financial analysis they assume he has made.

The developer—He is not always doing a detailed analysis either. He often relies on the first-mortgage lender to signal the attractiveness of a proposed project by his decision on whether to advance the mortgage money and, if he decides to, by the amount as related to the project cost. Further, the developer is more frequently "leaning on" the financial packager to indicate to him the amount for which the finished project can be resold. On the basis of these assurances from lender and packager, the developer may feel he has eliminated most of his market risk and with this "closed transaction" can dispense with further economic and market analysis.

This may be shortsighted, however, because even if the loan is granted and the packager successfully syndicates the deal, the developer is likely to remain economically tied up in the project after the "sale" in one or more of the forms we mentioned earlier. At the very least, his reputation is riding on the outcome.

The lender—If the basis for developing the project is the approval of the capital sources, is the prospective lender doing the analysis? Interviews indicate he is doing *an* analysis, but it is not one an investor should act on since it seldom identifies for the equity investor what *his* risks are. The lender focuses on the prospective operating performance of the business, against which he measures the exposure of his first-mortgage money.

But the lender's and the investors' occupancy break-even points are not the same. The former's is perhaps 75% to 80% of capacity and the latter's is perhaps 90% of capacity where seller financing has been employed. Equity investors must carefully examine their own break-even points and exposure to the variability of the cash flows available to service their requirements. These variations are a function of the additional layers of financing burden beyond the first-mortgage lender's exposure.

Incidentally, since lenders are increasingly taking equity positions in conjunction with their mortgage loan extensions, they too should be analyzing the equity investors' financing risks. Their frequent failure to do it may be attributable to the notion that equity participation is a "free ride," so detailed risk analysis of that additional position is unnecessary.

The packager—If neither the developer nor the lender typically analyzes the project from the investors' viewpoint, is the financial packager performing this service? This should, of course, be his first step. Conscientious analysis would position him to negotiate with the seller on firm ground—instead of reacting to the price and other terms established by the developer. If he did the analysis, he would serve the investors' interest as well as his own.

However, the incentives, the economic environment, and human nature combine to influence the packager to act merely as a broker between investors and developer, thus earning his immediate commission. For the packager with questionable integrity the great current interest in real estate tax shelter is ideal. The nature of the investment delays adequate assessment of the quality of a project for two to four years. This creates ripe conditions for packagers to exploit the investor euphoria, make their money, and leave the business—to be replaced by a new wave of middlemen.

Unlike the stock market, where "performance" is quickly measured, real estate requires time for the project to be constructed (12 to 18 months), rented (6 to

12 months), and then stabilized. During this period a packager motivated strictly by the commission dollars (typically received when the outside investors contribute their cash) can often operate very profitably without being called to account. Few packagers remain tied to the project over the life of the investment.

CONCLUSION

Real estate development undoubtedly will continue in strong demand during the balance of the 1970's. It offers an attractive opportunity to developers, including corporations that have entered the field only recently. But this is not an area in which the boom momentum will bail everyone out of his mistakes.

Companies' preoccupation with the near-term earnings impact of their real estate activities may cause them to forget the longer-term economics of their projects. This oversight can blind management to the potential liabilities and the impact on individual investors' decisions which their endorsement precipitates. Already there are signs of overbuilding by developers who have not had to justify their new construction economically. Conscientious use of analytical tools such as simulation, statistical measurements of risk, and comprehensive market studies can expose a project's weaknesses and save the company the embarrassment of surprise financial liabilities.

The dangers are far reaching for real estate development in this decade. An unhappy experience with real estate development threatens to (and is beginning to) drive recent industrial and financial entrants away and deprive the real estate industry of the financial and managerial support it so badly needs.

Of equal importance is the possible impact that a series of unsuccessful syndicated deals could have on the investing public. After the bottom fell out of the last real estate syndicate boom in the late 1950's, investor confidence did not recover for a decade. If investor confidence dries up, thus choking off the important sources of financing that it represents, real estate developement would suffer a serious setback.

The real estate industry has plenty of incentive to police itself since obviously everyone would be damaged by disenchantment among recent corporate entrants and syndicate investors. But the inevitable pressures on packagers to sell everything in which they can interest investors make it doubtful that the job can be left to the industry. Then who can and should be overseeing this new industry?

The most effective way to build credibility in real estate syndication is to make changes at the public-policy level. Public policy guidelines can be separated into incentives and regulation.

To date, incentives have centered on tax avoidance. Wittingly or unwittingly, fiscal policy has focused investors' attention so single-mindedly on the tax-saving opportunities in real estate development that investors tend to neglect the basic project economics. The epitome of this attitude is the current rage for new low-income housing.

Although tax incentives are very desirable, gauging their true value in the context of an investment proposal requires a high level of sophistication. To further responsible investment analysis, public policy should encourage the employment of professional counsel either on an individual basis or through establishment of professionally managed limited partnerships. Only recently have such large, publicly registered real estate investment "funds" begun to appear. A marked increase in the number and size of these equity investment funds as the industry becomes more institutionalized is expected.

But before this trend represents a real advancement of investors' interest, a way must be found to sort out the roles of packager and fund manager. Should the manager also be permitted to act as a packager and take substantial front-end fees for deals he obtains for the fund, regardless of the eventual fate of the projects involved? A way must be found to make the packager-manager's remuneration contingent on the long-run success of the fund.

As for regulation, government protection of the investor is unfortunately lacking in many of these syndicated deals. As already noted, few of them are registered with the SEC. While these offerings are usually registered with state securities departments, only a few state agencies—including New York and California—subject them to close scrutiny or strict regulation.

REGULATORY GUIDELINES

It is suggested that future regulatory guidelines be addressed to:

1. A set of uniform standards of disclosure to buyers describing the risks, the economics and break-even implications of the project, and the impact of the available tax shelter. Since federal and state "blue sky" commissions habitually view real estate registrations within a framework of corporate securities, the packager is not allowed to include financial projections in the prospectus. But in real estate investment, projections under varying assumed conditions, with their underlying assumptions, are vital for adequate appraisal of the investment. Adequate disclosure can be made without putting the regulatory body in the apparent position of passing on the quality of the investment.

2. A standard format for describing the profit attraction of a project and a uniform definition of return on investment, both directed toward the residual owners of the property.

3. A revised set of accounting rules for companies involved in real estate development that more adequately reflect the realities of the various levels of financing. The accounting profession has begun to attack this area, but more work is needed.

The first two suggestions could be implemented by the real estate industry without imposition of elaborate governmental regulatory machinery. If important portions of the industry persist in adopting a short-run attitude toward syndication, however, some form of regulation may become inevitable. Governmental attention can more usefully focus on the long-run implications of the incentives legislated so as to spur certain forms of real estate development.

Awareness of the pitfalls on the part of individual and corporate developers, packagers, investors, and regulators can contribute stability to the real estate equity as it becomes a popular and widely accepted investment. The coming years should see a marked institutionalization of the industry which, if properly handled, will help satisfy the huge real estate equity capital requirements.

APPENDIX: PROJECT ECONOMICS, START TO FINISH

This appendix is designed to show the impact of construction losses on the investment, the effects of leveraging through a second mortgage, and the consequences for investors of sale of the project. There is no attempt to analyze the rate of return.

Assume that an investor is offered the opportunity to purchase the equity position in a to-be-constructed 260-unit, middle-income apartment complex. As *Table A* shows, he pays $1,200,000 cash above a $3,500,000 first mortgage, so the seller receives $4,700,000. If the construction period is one year, the losses for tax purposes are expected to amount to $400,000.

Therefore, a 50% tax-bracket person can consider his investment at the time

TABLE A
INITIAL AND OPERATING ECONOMICS OF PROJECT
CARRYING A SINGLE MORTGAGE

Purchase
Cash payment $1,200,000
First mortgage (8½%, 27 years)................................. 3,500,000

    Total $4,700,000

Losses during construction
Interest .... $ 195,000
Taxes   50,000
Prepaid fees..   35,000
Financing charges   120,000

    Total .... $ 400,000

Operation
Pro-forma cash flow (stabilized)
Gross rentals .... $ 720,000
Commercial fees and rents   20,000

Gross revenue .... $ 740,000
Less 5% vacancy   37,000

Effective gross rent .... $ 703,000
Less operating and management costs   260,000

Net free and clear .... $ 443,000
Less interest and amortization   331,000

Cash flow available to investors .... $ 112,000
Return on investment
Full cash investment:
$$\frac{\$112,000}{\$1,200,000} = 9.3\%$$
After construction losses:
$$\frac{\$112,000}{\$1,200,000 - [.50(\$400,000)]} = 11.2\%$$
Occupancy break-even point:
$$\frac{\text{Operating cost} + \text{debt service}}{\text{Gross revenue}} = \frac{\$260,000 + \$331,000}{\$740,000} = 80\%$$

of rent-up not as $1,200,000 but, rather, that amount less the cash value of the losses (50% of $400,000). So his investment is $1,000,000. The value of the construction losses is diluted if the construction period is very long and his entire cash investment was made at the beginning. But often the cash investment is spread over the construction period.

TABLE B
INITIAL AND OPERATING ECONOMICS OF PROJECT
CARRYING TWO MORTGAGES

Purchase
Cash Payment . . . . $ 550,000
First mortgage 3,500,000
Second mortgage (7%, 27 years)   800,000

Total $4,850,000

Operation
Pro-forma cash flow (stabilized)
Net free and clear . . . . $ 443,000
Less first mortgage debt service   331,000
Less second mortgage debt service   66,000

Cash flow to investors . . . . $ 46,000
Return on investment
Full cash investment:

$$\frac{\$46,000}{\$550,000} = 8.3\%$$

After construction losses:

$$\frac{\$46,000}{\$550,000 - [.50(\$400,000)]} = 13.1\%$$

Occupancy break-even point:

$$\frac{\text{Operating-cost} + \text{debt service}}{\text{Gross revenue}} = \frac{\$260,000 + \$331,000 + \$66,000}{\$740,000} = 89\%$$

The anticipated cash return on his net investment is 11.2%, after construction losses are taken into account (this is a simple, not discounted, rate of return), which is well in excess of the anticipated 9.3% cash return on the full $1,200,000 investment. The cash flow break-even point is anticipated to be 80% of the projected gross rentals (often mistakenly cited as a 20% vacancy rate).

The investor and seller may agree to a higher price for the project, with the seller assuming a second mortgage, as shown in *Table B*. The purchase price is increased by $150,000 while the cash payment is reduced by $650,000. Despite a "higher" price, the return on net investment increases from 11.2% to 13.1%. By inserting such leverage, the sale is improved for both the buyer and seller. The former receives a higher projected return on his investment, while the latter expects to receive $150,000 more for the project. But the cash flow break-even point, one measure of project risk, has been increased from 80% to 89%, and the cash return on total cash investment is reduced from 9.3% to 8.3%.

Comparison of the sale of the one-mortgage and two-mortgage examples at the end of 10 years demonstrates the liquidity requirement, a hidden liability in most real estate transactions. In *Table C* and *D*, a sale is assumed at the outstanding balance of the mortgages. (The project is given to the mortgage lender.) In each instance the project's book value is substantially below the

TABLE C
SALE AFTER TEN YEARS OF PROJECT CARRYING A SINGLE MORTGAGE

Book value at time of sale	
Original building	$3,900,000
Less depreciation (double-declining balance, 30-year life)	1,950,000
Building, depreciated	$1,950,000
Land	400,000
Depreciated project book value	$2,350,000
Mortgage balance at time of sale	
Original	$3,500,000
Less amortization	550,000
Balance	$2,950,000
Gross profit (sold for mortgage value)	
Mortgage balance	$2,950,000
Less book value	2,350,000
Gross profit	$ 600,000
Federal tax liability*	
Income tax recapture	
Accelerated depreciation	$1,950,000
Less straight-line depreciation	1,300,000
Cululative difference	$ 650,000
Times recapture percentage	.80
Profit subject to recapture	$ 520,000
Taxes to be paid	
Gross profit	$ 600,000
Less profit subject to ordinary income tax	520,000
Profit subject to capital gains tax	$ 80,000
Ordinary income tax ($520,000 X 50%)	$ 260,000
Capital gains tax ($80,000 X 35%)	28,000
Tax liability	$ 288,000

* This calculation slightly simplified for purposes of clarity

mortgage balance. The differences of $600,000 and $1,180,000 represent the reported profits and the profit subject to federal and, where applicable, state taxes. Note that although the addition of the second mortgage appears initially to favor both buyer and seller, as shown in *Table D*, the tax exposure is increased by $206,000.

(How the recapture-of-tax rate is determined is worth some explanation. In all cases except low-income housing projects, the rate drops by 1% a month after the first 100 months of the life of the project. In this case the development was sold after 120 months, so the recapture rate is 100% − 20% = 80%.)

TABLE D
SALE AFTER TEN YEARS OF PROJECT CARRYING TWO MORTGAGES

Book value at time of sale
    Original building $4,050,000
    Less depreciation (double-declining balance, 30-year life) 2,025,000

    Building, depreciated ....$ 2,025,000
    Land 400,000

    Depreciated project book value................................. $2,425,000
Mortgage balance at time of sale
    Original... 4,300,000
    Less amortization 695,000

    Balance $3,605,000
Gross profit (sold for mortgage value)
    Mortgage balance $3,605,000
    Less book value.. 2,425,000

    Gross profit.. $1,180,000
Federal tax liability*
    Income tax recapture
        Accelerated depreciation $2,025,000
        Less straight-line depreciation 1,350,000

        Cumulative difference .... $ 675,000
        Times recapture percentage .... .80

        Profit subject to recapture .... $ 540,000
    Taxes to be paid
        Gross profit $1,180,000
        Less profit subject to ordinary income tax 540,000

        Profit subject to capital gains tax............................ $ 640,000
        Ordinary income tax ($540,000 X 50%) .... $ 270,000
        Capital gains tax ($640,000 X 35%) 224,000

        Tax liability .... $ 494,000

* This calculation slightly simplified for purposes of clarity.

The seller receives no cash in these transactions as described, but with recapture at the ordinary income rate and the remainder at the capital gains rate (which beginning this year is effectively 35%), the seller will have a federal tax liability of either $288,000 or $494,000, while registering a profit of $600,000 or $1,180,000. *Before* the sale, the investor must be prepared to provide the cash necessary to meet the tax bill. The knowledgeable investor, however, will have set aside a portion of the earlier cash and tax-shelter "profits" as a reserve to meet this tax liability.

REAL ESTATE INVESTMENT TRUSTS: IMPACT ON MORTGAGE CREDIT

Leon Krobow

Richard J. Gelson

The rapid growth of Real Estate Investment Trusts (REITs) during 1968-70 provides another illustration of the ability of financial institutions and markets to make adaptive changes in the face of severe liquidity pressures and credit scarcities. These investment companies operate under the Real Estate Investment Act of 1960, which exempts the trusts from corporate income and capital gains taxation, provided they pay out nearly all their income. A fundamental objective of the legislation is to facilitate real estate investment by granting trusts the same tax advantages enjoyed by regulated investment companies, such as mutual funds, which invest mainly in corporate equities and bonds. The legislation also encourages REITs to seek wide ownership of their shares, thus promoting broad-based participation in the ownership of real estate assets.

Tax advantages alone, however, do not explain the recent flurry of activity in the formation of trusts or the growing interest in the sponsorship of new trusts by banks, life insurance companies and mortgage companies. Why these trusts have met with such recent success in a market where the major financial intermediaries have had long experience can be explained by a variety of institutional, regulatory and economic factors.

The increasing participation of REITs as specialized lenders and investors in the real estate industry can best be understood in the context of the particularly adverse impact that financial stringencies have had on mortgage markets. The intense liquidity strains of 1969 and 1970 created new opportunities for profitable intermediation by these trusts which face no restrictions on the interest rates they can pay on borrowings and therefore, are able to compete more effectively for funds than other institutional lenders. Frequently their funds have been obtained at high cost, but the trusts have been in a position to select the most promising investments while their favored tax status facilitates the payment of an attractive after-tax yield.

The REITs' improved opportunities arose in part because commercial banks curtailed sharply the dollar growth of their mortgage assets (see chart) in response to heavy demand for business loans. In view of the increased difficulties the banks faced in obtaining funds from both deposit and nondeposit sources, it was not surprising that many of them either shifted prospective mortgage customers to REITs with which they had working relationships or sold the trusts a part of their mortgage loans. The sales provided the banks with new funds and helped meed REIT needs for portfolio assets. Bank sponsorship of new trusts facilitated such timely transactions. In addition, attractive fees and service charges became available through the advisory relationship that often accompanied sponsorship. Such income at times may have reflected REIT profits on investments that could not have been made by the banks directly because of various regulations.

The portfolio preferences of life insurance companies, which typically hold long-term assets also were changing during this period. Investment in home mortgages was handicapped in part, by state-imposed interest rate ceilings and by the limits specified in Federal home-loan-guarantee programs, although "points" or fees and service charges helped boost effective rates. Consequently, life insurance companies restructured their total mortgage assets to meet the substantial demand for conventional mortgages on multifamily and commercial properties. These types of mortgages generally represent borrowing by business firms, and in many states such borrowing is subject to less severe regulation of interest charges compared with regulation of rates on home mortgages. Moreover, life insurance companies like the banks, were alert to the possibility of expanding profitable operations without financial strain through sponsorship of REITs. Thrift institutions have also evidenced some interest in trusts, regarding them as a potential device for improving their competitive position in the mortgage market.

During 1968-70, most of the growth in REIT assets reflected proliferation of new trusts that absorbed sizable amounts of existing mortgage debt from other lenders. Consequently, it is impossible to regard the entire increase in REIT holdings of mortgages as a net addition to the overall increase in such outstanding debt. Moreover, it is argued below that the trusts' use of market borrowings to finance the acquisition of debt on commercial and multifamily properties, on balance, probably contributed to a diversion of funds away from home mortgates.

LEGAL AND REGULATORY STATUS OF REITs

To qualify for special tax treatment, REITs must distribute at least 90% of their ordinary income to their shareholders, derive not less than 75% of their gross income from real estate transactions (e.g., rents, interest on mortgages, and sales or property) and hold at least 75% of their assets in the form of real estate loans and property, cash, and Government securities. The shares of a REIT must be issued to no fewer than one hundred persons, and the holdings of five or fewer individuals cannot exceed 50% of the total.(1) In addition, REITs must function as investors in, rather than managers of, real estate and they may not hold property primarily for resale.(2) When the trusts so qualify, the income and capital gains they distribute are taxed only when received by their shareholders. These provisions permit the trusts to offer returns that are attractive to investors in the low to moderate income-tax brackets.

REITs face relatively few restrictions by Federal regulatory authorities. In fact, the Board of Governors of the Federal Reserve System has included the advising of REITs among those activities which are appropriate for a bank holding company.(3) Thus, commercial bank sponsorship of a REIT appears to be on firm ground.

The REITs have wide latitude in the issuance of equity or debt instruments (except, of course, that they cannot accept deposits). Moreover, the existence of

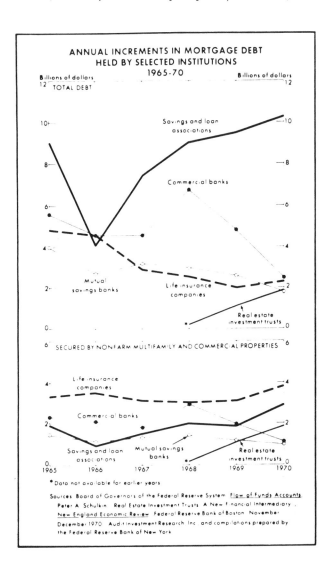

ANNUAL INCREMENTS IN MORTGAGE DEBT HELD BY SELECTED INSTITUTIONS 1965-70

*Data not available for earlier years

Sources: Board of Governors of the Federal Reserve System, Flow of Funds Accounts; Peter A. Schulkin, Real Estate Investment Trusts: A New Financial Intermediary, New England Economic Review, Federal Reserve Bank of Boston, November-December 1970; Audit Investment Research Inc. and compilations prepared by the Federal Reserve Bank of New York

an advisory relationship between a commercial bank and a REIT has not constituted affiliation for purposes of Regulation D. Consequently, borrowing by REITs through the commercial paper market has not been subject to reserve requirements even when the proceeds are used to purchase an asset from the bank adviser (see appendix). The trusts must observe local usury laws, but they are not inhibited by regulations concerning the geographic areas in which they may operate, the size of the loan to a particular borrower or its quality. However, some states have imposed very tight restrictions on the sale of shares by a REIT. These regulations appear to have discouraged the marketing of REIT shares in these areas, although it is not clear that they are an effective hindrance to REIT lending.

The conditional tax exemption granted REITs by the 1960 legislation has tended to inspire caution on the part of trust managers to avoid transactions that might lead to an adverse Treasury ruling on a trust's tax status. The proliferation of new trusts suggests, however, that the legal qualifications are not a significant roadblock. On the other hand, the rapid growth of REIT activity has led interested observers to express concern over the price a trust might pay should it fail to qualify for tax exemption in a particular year. The question has arisen, for example, whether a REIT's tax-exempt status might be jeopardized by sales of participations in mortgage loans originated by the trust or by sales of property received through foreclosure. Critics of the REIT Industry cite potential conflicts of interest between trust and sponsor, especially where the latter is a bank, as the basis for more stringent official regulation. It seems likely, however, that the various doubts over the ability of REITs to serve their shareholders' interests and meet the requirements and objectives of the 1960 act will be resolved gradually without the need for further legislation.(4)

PROFILE OF THE INDUSTRY

The newer REITs, such as the trusts sponsored or advised by commercial banks, life insurance companies, or mortgage companies, largely hold mortgage debt (both short and long term). However, many trusts have invested a sizable amount in direct ownership of real properties. The overwhelming preference of the newer trusts for mortgages partly reflects the financial orientation of the sponsors, who may wish to avoid the actual or potential risks and problems associated with direct ownership of real property.

The flurry of activity in REITs between 1968 and 1970 added more than 100 new institutions to the 61 trusts already operating. At the end of 1970, the assets of a group of 114 trusts whose dollar volume is believed to account for over 90% of the industry total, amounted to $4.3 billion (see Table I).(5) Close to $2.5 billion of this amount reflected the assets of institutions formed during 1969 and 1970. Commercial-bank-sponsored REITs bulked the largest among the newer trusts. Such institutions held nearly $850 million of assets, or almost 20% of the $4.3 billion total. Another $600 million, or about 14%, was accounted for by trusts sponsored by life insurance companies, and a further $400 million, or around 10%, by REITs that are advised by mortgage companies. The remaining 57% consisted of the assets of trusts which are not closely linked to banks, insurance companies, or mortgage companies.

REITs have resorted to public offerings of both debt and equity instruments for initial capital. They have attempted to appeal simultaneously to investors who may be attracted either by a high current yield or by the prospect of capital appreciation. Consequently, the offerings frequently have taken the form of units that consist of shares of beneficial interest coupled with either warrants or convertible debentures. Very often the price of the unit is low enough to attract investors holding relatively small amounts of funds.

TABLE 1
ASSETS OF 114 REAL ESTATE INVESTMENT TRUSTS
DECEMBER 31, 1970

| | | Assets | |
| | | Dollar volume | Share of total |
Type of Trust	Number	(in millions)	(in percent)
Independent trusts	59	1,780	41.3
Trusts sponsored or advised by:			
Commercial banks	22	847	19.7
Life insurance companies	8	596	13.8
Mortgage companies	13	415	9.6
Financial conglomerates	12	672	15.6
Total	114	4,310	100.0

Source: Peter A. Schulkin, "Real Estate Investment Trusts: A New Financial Intermediary," *New England Economic Review* (Federal Reserve Bank of Boston: November-December 1970), pages 4-5.

The success with which REITs have been able to draw funds from the capital markets is suggested by the upsurge of their securities flotations during the years 1968-70 (see Table II). Only six issues, amounting to $91 million, were offered in the three years 1961-63 and none in the next four years. The pace began to accelerate in 1968, however. In both the equity and longer term debt markets, REIT offerings absorbed increased shares of the new issues market. By 1970, REIT equity issues constituted almost 11% of the total offered, compared with 1% in 1961. Debt issues accounted for 2.4% in 1970, compared with none nine years earlier. This growth was remarkable in view of the keen competition for funds and very high borrowing costs in recent years.

Although capital issues remain a source of funds for expansion, REIT managers have been alert to the possibilities of short-term borrowing, particularly from banks. Bank lines of credit are perhaps equally important as a prerequisite for the issuance of commercial paper. Examination of the prospectuses of many newly formed REITs indicated that bank credit totaling several hundred million dollars was arranged, partly to provide coverage for prospective commercial paper issues. In some cases, sponsoring organizations agreed to guarantee a specific amount of commercial paper issued by a REIT, and it is clear that several bank holding companies have increased their issuance of commercial paper to finance the real estate operations of nonbank subsidiaries or affiliates. It is likely that the sales of such paper may well become

TABLE II
CAPITAL ISSUES OF REAL ESTATE INVESTMENT TRUSTS*

Period	Equity			Debt		
	Number of issues	Dollar volume (in millions)	Share of public offerings of all new corporate issues (in percent)	Number of issues	Dollar volume (in millions)	Share of public offerings of all new corporate issues (in percent)
1961	3	39.3	1.0	0	0	0
1962	2	40.5	2.3	0	0	0
1963	1	11.4	0.8	0	0	0
1964-67	†	†	†	†	†	†
1968	4	69.3	1.5	2	27.5	0.3
1969	30	899.9	10.7	2	70.0	0.5
1970	29	938.8	10.8	21	611.7	2.4

* Publicly underwritten issues of $10 million or more.

† None issued.

Sources: William B. Smith and Benjamin R. Jacobson, "Real Estate Investment Trusts: In the Money and Here to Stay," *Real Estate Forum* (October 1970), page 27; Audit Investment Research, Inc. *Realty Trust Review* (February 1971), page 11; and *Federal Reserve Bulletin*.

TABLE III
ANNUAL INCREMENTS IN PRIVATE FINANCIAL INSTITUTIONS'
HOLDINGS OF TOTAL MORTGAGE DEBT AND OF MORTGAGE
DEBT SECURED BY NONFARM MULTIFAMILY AND
COMMERCIAL PROPERTIES
(IN BILLIONS OF DOLLARS)

Holdings of mortgage debt	1968	1969	1970	Amount outstanding December 31, 1970
Total mortgage debt in the United States:				
All types	27.4	28.6	27.0	453.6
Multifamily and commercial	10.1	11.2	12.3	142.7
All private financial institutions' holdings:				
Total	22.4	21.5	20.5	377.9
Multifamily and commercial	9.9	9.7	12.0	125.3
Real estate investment trusts:				
Multifamily and commercial*	0.2	1.1	1.9	3.8
Trusts sponsored or advised by:				
Commercial banks†	0.0	0.1	0.8	0.9
Life insurance companies†	0.0	0.1	0.5	0.6
Mortgage companies†	0.0	0.2	0.2	0.4
Other	0.2	0.7	0.4	1.9
Commercial banks:				
Total	6.7	4.8	2.5	72.5
Multifamily and commercial	2.9	2.0	1.1	26.2
Life insurance companies:				
Total	2.5	2.0	2.3	74.3
Multifamily and commercial	3.0	3.1	3.8	42.1
Savings and loan associations:				
Total	9.0	9.5	10.3	150.6
Multifamily and commercial	2.0	1.9	2.9	25.3
Mutual savings banks:				
Total	3.0	2.6	1.8	57.9
Multifamily and commercial	1.4	1.2	1.0	20.5
Other private financial:‡				
Total	1.0	1.5	1.7	18.8
Multifamily and commercial	0.4	0.4	1.3	7.4

Note: Because of rounding, figures do not necessarily add to totals.

* The figures shown are those for total trust mortgage assets, but it is believed that virtually all trust mortgages are secured by multifamily and commercial properties.

† No such trusts were believed operating in 1968.

‡ Includes credit unions, private pension funds, state and local government retirement funds, nonlife insurance companies, mortgage companies, and banks in territories and possessions.

Sources: Flow-of-Funds Accounts data, adjusted to allow fully for the estimated mortgage holdings of real estate investment trusts. The latter figures were obtained from the Federal Reserve Bank of Boston's *New England Economic Review* (November-December 1970) and from unpublished estimates of Audit Investment Research, Inc. Where no asset data were available, the dollar values of capital issues were used as approximations. All data are as of the year-end.

a model for future REIT financing patterns.

During the three years ended December 1970, when total mortgage debt increased by about $83 billion, REITs added an estimated $3.2 billion to their holdings of mortgage debt. This increase raised the level of the trusts' mortgage assets to an estimated $3.8 billion (see Table III). By the end of 1970 commercial-bank-sponsored trusts held about $900 million, those sponsored by life insurance companies about $600 million, mortgage-company-sponsored trusts some $400 million and other REITs about $1.9 billion. These estimates clearly indicate that aggregate REIT mortgage assets holdings are very small in relation to the total stock of mortgage debt. However, the trusts added increasing amounts of mortgage debt to their portfolios during 1968-70, whereas commercial banks and mutual savings banks curtailed their mortgage lending and life insurance companies' acquisitions steadied.

By 1970, the annual growth of REITs' mortgage assets increased to $1.9 billion. In contrast, the absolute increase in commercial bank holdings of mortgage debt slowed markedly to $2.5 billion, the growth at mutual savings banks slipped to $1.8 billion, and life insurance companies added a relatively stable $2.3 billion. Only savings and loan associations increased the pace of their mortgage investments, adding $10.3 billion. Inasmuch as the available information strongly indicates that the REITs' mortgage assets are virtually all secured by multifamily and commercial properties (nonhome), it is obvious that their impact was greatest in that sector. In 1970, the trusts' estimated total acquisition of nonhome mortgage debt far exceeded the increments in such assets reported by commercial banks ($1.1 billion) and mutual savings banks ($1.0 billion). However, it was well below the amounts added by life insurance companies ($3.8 billion) and by savings and loan associations ($2.9 billion).

Although REITs' mortgage lending obviously was becoming increasingly important relative to other mortgage lenders during the last few years, the trusts' loans probably, at least in part, simply reallocated the existing supply of mortgage credit. A study of the behavior of private financial institutions' shares of mortgage obligations during the recent period of heightened REIT activity sheds some light on this matter. The market share of aggregate mortgage debt and of debt on multifamily and commercial properties held by various types of financial institutions is shown in Table IV for the years 1968-70.

It is significant that the portion of aggregate mortgage debt held by private financial institutions declined from 84.4% at the end of 1968 to 83.3% two years later, despite the increasing pace of REIT activity. In contrast, the share of debt on commercial and multifamily properties rose from 86.9% to 87.8%.(6) REITs increased their share of lending in this latter sector even more, from 0.7% at the end of 1968 to 2.7% by the end of last year. The failure of private financial institutions' share of total debt to rise suggests that the growth of REIT assets did not entirely represent a net contribution to the growth of aggregate mortgage debt.

IMPACT ON MORTGAGE LENDERS

Although a REIT may engage in portfolio transactions with an institution other than its adviser, a rough approximation of the impact of trust operations on each of the major types of mortgage lenders may be obtained by viewing

TABLE IV
PRIVATE FINANCIAL INSTITUTIONS' SHARES OF TOTAL MORTGAGE DEBT AND OF MORTGAGE DEBT SECURED BY NONFARM MULTIFAMILY AND COMMERCIAL PROPERTIES

Holdings of mortgage debt	1968	1969	1970
	Amount outstanding (in billions of dollars)		
Total mortgage debt in the United States:			
All Types	398.0	426.6	453.6
Multifamily and commercial	119.2	130.4	142.7
	Share of totals (in percent)		
All private financial institutions' holdings:			
Total	84.4	83.8	83.3
Multifamily and commercial	86.9	86.9	87.8
Real estate investment trusts:			
Multifamily and commercial §	0.7	1.5	2.7
Trusts sponsored or advised by:			
Commercial banks	0.0	0.1	0.6
Life insurance companies	0.0	0.1	0.4
Mortgage companies	0.0	0.2	0.3
Other	0.7	1.1	1.3
Commercial banks:			
Total	16.4	16.4	16.0
Multifamily and commercial	19.4	19.2	18.4
Life insurance companies:			
Total	17.6	16.9	16.4
Multifamily anc commercial	29.5	29.4	29.5
Savings and loan associations:			
Total	32.9	32.9	33.2
Multifamily and commercial	17.2	17.2	17.7
Mutual savings banks:			
Total	13.4	13.2	12.8
Multifamily and commercial	15.4	15.0	14.4
Other private financial:			
Total	3.9	4.0	4.1
Multifamily and commercial	4.8	4.7	5.2

Note: See Table III for sources and other footnote references.

§ As a share of all types of mortgage debt in the United States, the REITs' holdings accounted for 0.2 percent in 1968, 0.4 percent in 1969, and 0.8 percent in 1970.

jointly the mortgage debt held by the trust and its sponsor or adviser. For example, pooling the mortgage-lending activity of banks and bank-sponsored trusts in the nonhome sector indicates that the combined share declined from 19.4% at the end of 1968 to 19.0% by the end of 1970. Similarly, commercial banks' portion of total mortgage debt decreased from 16.4% to 16.2% if the lending by bank-sponsored trusts is included. It is clear that commercial banks used the funds obtained from REITs and other nondeposit sources primarily for pusposes other than to finance mortgage loans.

Life insurance companies' share of nonhome debt was little changed between 1969 and 1970. Moreover, the portion of such assets held by these companies and their sponsored trusts rose from 29.5% to 29.9% during that period. In contrast, the life insurance companies' share of total mortgage debt dropped from 17.6% to 16.4%, the decline resulting mainly from a reduction in home mortgage lending.

Insufficient data preclude a similar analysis of the effect of REIT activities on lending by mortgage companies, which function largely as mortgage brokers but also may invest in such assets. However, mortgage companies account for only a very small part of total mortgage debt and for that reason are included in the category "other private financial" institutions in Tables III and IV.

Not many thrift institutions have acted as sponsors to or advisers of REITs and, so far as is known, they have not engaged in any significant volume of portfolio transactions with REITs. The availability of funds from the Federal Home Loan Bank Board enabled savings and loan associations to increase their portion of nonhome debt from 17.2% at the end of 1968 to 17.7% two years later and to raise their share of total mortgage debt from 32.9% to 33.2%. Without recourse to such funds, mutual savings banks sustained a decline in their portion of nonhome mortgages from 15.4% to 14.4% and in total mortgage debt from 13.4% to 12.8%.(7) These reduced shares were substantially the result of the adverse deposit flows the mutual savings banks experienced as rising market rates of interest placed thrift deposits at an increasing competitive disadvantage, although in part the decline also reflected a portfolio shift by these institutions in favor of higher yielding corporate securities.

The data on which these various shares are based leave much to be desired. They do suggest, however, that REITs probably helped to insulate the market for nonhome mortgages, to some extent, from the adverse impact of the recent monetary stringency. Principally, this insulation resulted from the REITs' use of funds obtained in the capital markets to acquire mortgages secured by multifamily and commercial properties. Interest on such instruments was subject, as noted earlier, to much less restriction, compared with the usury limits on conventional home mortgages in many states and on debt issued under Federal home-loan-guarantee programs. Moreover, the REITs' demand for mortgage assets enhanced the marketability of nonhome debt held in the portfolios of other mortgage lenders. To some degree, however, the REIT sales of debt and equity instruments probably contributed to the diversion of funds from thrift institutions and from mortgage markets.

FUTURE PROSPECTS

During the relatively short period of their activity, REITs have demonstrated their skill at intermediating profitably between mortgage borrowers and lenders of funds in a highly strained monetary environment that tended to discourage the participation of some of the major mortgage lenders. It is to be expected that the recent renewal of heavy deposit flows to thrift institutions and the greatly improved liquidity position of other mortgage lenders will increase the competitive pressures on REITs. However, the trusts, which generally tend to be high-cost operations, will concurrently benefit from the greatly improved availability of bank credit and market sources of funds.

The improved liquidity situation may well delay the implementation of any latent plans by thrift institutions to enter the field of sponsors of REITs. Recently, only one REIT of substantial size was sponsored by a savings institution. However, thrift industry spokesmen have recognized the possibilities for widening the base of their operations through sponsorship of REITs.

Despite changing monetary conditions, the trusts are likely to remain attractive vehicles for real estate and mortgage investments. Commercial banks, in particular, may well continue to regard a relationship with a REIT as potentially rewarding over the longer term. Not the least of the advantages afforded by sponsorship of a trust are the opportunities for bank portfolio adjustments to be financed indirectly by REIT borrowings through open market instruments. Other substantial advantages follow from the advisory fees a bank may earn, the possibility of providing a customer indirectly with a larger loan than the bank itself could extent because of regulatory limits on the size of any one loan, and the capacity to meet demands which the bank alone could not fill because of restrictions on acceptable collateral or other regulatory limitations. Bank sponsorship of trusts may be viewed, therefore, as a further and undoubtedly viable development in the trend toward increased activity by banking organizations over a widening range of financial services.

APPENDIX: THE EFFECT OF REITs ON BANK CREDIT STATISTICS

The trusts' borrowing operations and portfolio transactions can present problems in the measurement of bank credit similar to those created by commercial banks' resort to other nondeposit sources of funds in 1969-70. During that period, the effective impact of Regulation Q ceilings prevented banks from competing for funds through deposit instruments. Consequently, many banks initially turned to the Euro-dollar market and then to affiliated institutions or parent organizations that had access to market sources of funds without being subject to interest rate ceilings (or reserve requirements) on borrowed funds. A foreign branch of a United States bank thus was able to borrow in the Euro-dollar market and pass the money to the head office, or the bank's affiliate could issue commercial paper, without encountering any such restrictions. The proceeds of the commercial paper were used largely for acquiring loans from the bank; in this way, outstanding bank credit was shifted to the books of the affiliate while freeing bank resources to finance new loans.

BANK INCENTIVES

Banks' incentives to make further use of such non-deposit sources of funds have been reduced, following the imposition of marginal reserve requirements on banks' Euro-dollar borrowings in October 1969 and the placing of reserve requirements in September 1970 on the proceeds to the bank from commercial paper issued by bank affiliates.(8) As noted earlier, transactions by commercial-bank-sponsored REITs are not subject to these regulations, even though a REIT's purchase of a mortgage asset from a bank may be financed in much the same way (*i.e.*, through commercial paper sales) as a purchase of a bank loan by a bank affiliate, and has much the same effect on a bank's lending capacity as an affiliate's purchase. Of course, it may be argued that a commercial bank sale to a REIT with which the former has no explicit relationship is hardly different from any market sale of an asset by a bank. However, when the transaction involves a trust that the bank has sponsored, or with which the latter has an advisory relationship, the sale may hold more significance within a broadened definition of the banking system.

BANK-SPONSORED TRUSTS

Nonetheless, because bank-sponsored trusts are not considered affiliated institutions, few attempts have been made to gather data on their credit-creating activities. Such credit creation is not covered by the adjustments incorporated in member bank data to obtain accurate current estimates of bank credit growth. One measure used to obtain such estimates is the "adjusted bank credit proxy," which encompasses the credit extended by the bank as well as the credit generated by affiliated institutions.(9)

At present, the adjusted proxy estimates the total volume of loans extended by banks and their affiliates by adding to the original bank data the total amount of commercial paper issued by the parent organization or affiliate of a bank. These commercial paper issues have come to be known as a bank-related paper. If the proceeds of such paper are used by the affiliate to purchase a loan from the bank, and the issue of paper was for less than thirty days, the bank must meet demand deposit reserve requirements against these proceeds. The bank must meet time deposit requirements against funds obtained from longer term issues. (No reserve requirements are applicable to commercial paper proceeds which are not shifted to the bank but are used instead to finance the operations of a parent organization's non-bank subsidiaries.) Because the proxy includes both reservable and nonreservable bank-related paper, it reflects the associated outright loan sales concluded between parent organization and affiliated bank plus the credit-creating activities of the parent organization through its nonbank affiliates.

The failure of the indicators of bank credit to blanket those REITs that are sponsored by banks can have adverse short-term effects on these indicators inasmuch as bank sales to trusts can amount to several hundred million dollars. In fact, data on nondeposit sources of funds filed by weekly reporting banks with federal Reserve Banks suggest the total outstanding volume of bank sales of real estate debt to REITs may amount to as much as $1 billion.

NOTES

(1) See Public Law 86-779, Section 10, September 14, 1960, which added Sections 856-58 to Chapter 1, Subchapter M, of the Internal Revenue Code of 1954.

(2) For a detailed description of the operations of various types of trusts, see Peter A. Schulkin, "Real Estate Investment Trusts: A New Financial Intermediary," New England Economic Review (Federal Reserve Bank of Boston: November-December 1970).

(3) Acting under the authority of the Bank Holding Company Act

Amendments of 1970, the Board of Governors has amended Regulation Y (applicable to bank holding companies' interests in non-banking activities) and has determined that it is proper for a bank holding company to act as, or to retain or acquire an interest in a company which acts as, an investment or financial adviser to a REIT. See Board of Governors of the Federal Reserve System, Bank Holding Companies, Amendments to Regulation Y, Section 222.4 (Nonbanking Activities).

(4) For example, the Comptroller of the Currency recently ruled that a national bank's trust department may not make investments in a REIT when the bank is the investment adviser or sponsor, or has other relationships that may possess elements of a conflict of interest.

(5) Information on the number of trusts in existence is obtained largely from announcements of new issues. Moreover, no time series is published for assets and liabilities of REITs. Data for a subset of 114 institutions have been compiled at the Federal Reserve Bank of Boston by Schulkin, "Real Estate Investment Trusts," pages 4-5.

(6) The cited behavior of the share of mortgage debt held by private financial institutions fully reflects the upward adjustment made in the Flow-of-Funds data to include REIT mortgage lending in the debt totals held by private financial institutions.

(7) Although mutual savings banks are eligible for membership in the Federal Home Loan Bank System, only a small number of such banks have chosen to be members and the amount of funds advanced to these institutions has not been large.

(8) Board of Governors of the Federal Reserve System, Amendment to Regulation M, Section 213.7 (Reserves Against Foreign Branch Deposits); Federal Reserve Bank of New York, Circular No. 6593, August 21, 1970 (Regulation D: Amendment, Supplement, and Interpretation, including Part 204 on commercial paper of bank affiliates).

(9) For a definition of the adjusted bank credit proxy, see this Review, page 178, Chart I; see also Federal Reserve Bank of Cleveland, "Bank Credit Proxy," Economic Review (February 1971), pages 3-10.

VI.

POLICY
CONSIDERATIONS

WAYS TO MODERATE FLUCTUATIONS
IN THE CONSTRUCTION OF HOUSING

Board of Governors,
Federal Reserve System

Recently the staff of the Board of Governors completed an extensive study of short-term cycles in housing production, of their relation to general credit conditions and monetary policy, and of means by which these fluctuations might be moderated. The individual study papers were submitted to the Congress last fall. Since then, the Board has considered what its recommendations in this area should be.

In order to provide the background needed for assessing public policy, this report on ways to moderate fluctuations in the construction of housing begins with a brief review of the salient facts about the problem of short-run variability in housing production.

SHORT-RUN VARIABILITY IN HOUSING CONSTRUCTION

Wide variations in the rate of homebuilding have occurred throughout the postwar period. These fluctuations have characterized all major classes of permanent dwelling units: multifamily dwellings and single-family homes alike, housing units financed by Federally-backed mortgages, as well as those that are conventionally financed.

Production of mobile homes, on the other hand, has been relatively stable. This category of home construction is less responsive to variations in general credit conditions. The terms of finance and the sources of funds for mobile homes differ considerably from those for traditional dwellings. Also, statutory and regulatory restraints on lending are less stringent for mobile homes.

There is no evidence that short-term fluctuations in traditional types of residential construction are moderating with the passage of time. One of the sharpest postwar declines occurred from the first quarter of 1966 to the first quarter of 1967, when residential construction expenditures fell by about one-fifth. In that period, the Nation's savings and loan associations experienced a marked decline in net deposit inflows. Another sharp reduction in their deposit inflows occurred in 1969. Housing activity during that year did not contract as much as it had in 1966-67, however, because of the greater underlying strength of housing demand, and the large-scale intervention by Federally-sponsored credit agencies to help stabilize the supply of mortgage funds.

Instability in residential construction is not confined to the United States. In Canada and the industrialized countries of Western Europe, downturns in private housing production have occurred repeatedly during periods of credit restraint in recent decades. There is evidence, also, that instability in residential construction afflicts the socialized economies of Eastern Europe—where the allocation of resources is determined through central planning.

Thus, instability of housing construction has been a problem practically everywhere. No quick or easy solution is in sight. Wide-ranging, persistent, and well-considered efforts will be needed to limit the swings in housing construction without compromising our national economic stabilization objectives.

RELATION TO AGGREGATE ECONOMIC ACTIVITY

Short-term swings in our Nation's housing production are related closely to fluctuations in the pace of aggregate economic activity. Housing has provided a balance wheel for the rest of the economy—tending to boom during periods of slack in the economy and to turn down when activity in most other lines was rising briskly. These variations in housing production have helped to temper inflationary pressures in periods of excess aggregate demand and to support economic activity during recessions, thus serving to even out fluctuations in total output and employment.

The tendency for housing production to vary inversely with general economic activity is at times identified as a response of residential construction to changes in monetary policy. There is some truth to this. In the very short run, restrictive monetary policies do result in reduced availability of credit and higher interest rates, just as expansive monetary policies produce a temporary easing in general credit conditions. The experience of recent years indicates, however, that these effects of monetary policy on credit markets are transitory. The more lasting effects on the cost and availability of credit come from the demands for loanable funds, particularly as these demands are influenced by the expected rate of inflation.

Funds for housing typically are in short supply when demands for credit from other sectors rise rapidly—as they did in 1966 and again in 1969. Competition faced by the housing industry for a limited volume of loanable funds may stem from a variety of sources, including Federal deficit financing. The strongest competition, however, usually comes from the business sector. When retained earnings of business firms rise less than the planned increase in their investments in fixed capital and inventories, they must depend more on external sources of finance. The share of total available funds absorbed by businesses then tends to rise, while the share available for housing falls.

The housing industry is not the only economic sector that responsds sensitively to changes in general credit conditions. Repeatedly in recent years, State and local governments have been subject to financial constraints when interest rates have risen. Numerous small business firms, too, have had difficulty coping with cyclical changes in the cost and availability of credit. It appears, however, that variations in general credit conditions have had a much larger effect on the rate of residential construction than on other major economic activities.

One basic reason for this special effect on the housing industry is the dependence of this industry on nonbank thrift institutions for long-term mortgage funds. Over the past 15 years, savings and loan associations and mutual savings banks have supplied nearly two-thirds of the increase in the Nation's outstanding residential mortgage credit. These institutions depend almost exclusively on consumer-type time and savings deposits as a source of funds, and they make the bulk of these funds available for home financing. As a consequence, when deposit inflows to these institutions shrink, the aggregate supply of residential mortgage credit from private lenders also declines.

Deposit inflows to savings and loan associations and mutual savings banks have become increasingly volatile over the past two decades. In years when interest rates in the open market have risen, the flow of consumer savings has been diverted away from depository institutions, which pay interest rates that are relatively inflexible, and has moved instead towards market instruments. Conversely, in years when yields on market securities have fallen relative to those paid on deposits, inflows to the depositary institutions have risen.

These swings in deposit flows have of late been on a massive scale. With market interest rates rising rapidly, the increase in total deposits at savings banks fell by more than half between 1967 and 1969. In 1970, short-term market interest rates fell substantially, and the net deposit inflow doubled—regaining its 1967 level—and then more than doubled again in 1971. Such alternations of feast and famine are bound to create instability in mortgage credit supplies and in home-building.

The asymmetry of the assets and liabilities of the nonbank financial intermediaries needs to be carefully noted. These intermediaries provide highly liquid assets for individuals to hold—assets that are close substitutes for short-term market securities on which yields are highly variable. But these intermediaries specialize in mortgage lending, and thus pile up assets with a long average life. Since the average yield on their earning assets changes little in response to variations in current market rates of interest, the nonbank depositary institutions are in a poor position to compete for consumers' savings, and to maintain their mortgage lending, when yields on market securities become more attractive.

Thus, by their very nature, these institutions are ill equipped to cope with widely fluctuating market interest rates. Moreover, this problem has been aggravated by the ceilings on rates of interest that depositary institutions may pay to attract consumer savings. The legislative extension of these ceiling rates in 1966 to cover savings and loan associations and mutual savings banks has reduced competition among financial institutions, and it may therefore have spared some individual institutions from a drain of funds to a nearby competitor. But the ceilings have interfered with the ability of all depositary institutions to compete effectively with market securities in periods of rising yields.

There are numerous legal and regulatory obstacles that discourage or prevent lenders from acquiring residential mortgages, thereby contributing to the uneven flow of mortgage credit. Chief among these are the ceilings imposed on the interest rate paid on conventional mortgages by State usury laws and on FHA-insured and VA-guaranteed loans by Federal regulations. At times, these ceiling rates have gotten so far out of touch with market realities that mortgage funds—in certain regions of the country or for certain classes of loans—have literally vanished. Such laws and regulations were originally designed with the purpose of providing borrowers with funds at reasonable rates of interest, but their effect has often been to limit or to prevent the access of borrowers to mortgage credit.

There are other laws and regulations that also prevent funds from moving freely into mortgages. Federally-chartered savings and loan associations, and mutual savings banks in some States, face rather stringent geographical restrictions on lending. The terms on which national banks may make funds available for conventional real estate loans are limited by statute, and their total investment in such assets is also restricted. Many State-chartered commercial banks face statutory restrictions similar to those applicable to national banks. And the Federal Reserve Act discriminates against mortgage loans at the discount window: such loans are eligible as collateral for member bank borrowing only at a penalty rate of interest.

These imperfections of financial markets are not the only source of instability in the housing industry. Some categories of spending respond much more than others to changes in interest rates. Variations in the cost of credit tend to lead to particularly large changes in spending when the asset acquired is very durable, when the purchase is postponable, when there is heavy dependence on external financing, and when interest costs bulk large relative to the buyer's total expenditure. For all these reasons, the demand for housing is highly sensitive to changes in interest rates.

THE COURSE FOR PUBLIC POLICY

Given the factors responsible for the sensitivity of housing to changes in general credit conditions, public policy actions on several fronts are needed to moderate fluctuations in residential building. Legal and regulatory obstacles to the flow of mortgage money need to be removed or reduced. Ways need to be devised for reducing the instability of deposit flows to savings and loan associations and to mutual savings banks. And some significant changes will be required in the character of our Nation's economic stabilization policies.

The most important single contribution that could be made to stability of housing production would be to obtain better control over the forces of inflation. Housing activity in the postwar period has declined whenever our Nation has failed to adopt promptly the policies of restraint needed to avert excess aggregate demand. Improvements in the use of all of our instruments of stabilization policy are clearly needed. But avoidance of sharp fluctuations in interest rates and credit conditions will require heavier reliance on fiscal tools, and less reliance upon monetary policy, to achieve our national economic stabilization objectives. Once variations in general credit conditions are lessened, both the supply of mortgage credit and the rate of housing construction will become more stable.

In considering the proper scope and direction of public policy, it is important to recognize that complete elimination of fluctuations in housing production is not a feasible objective. From time to time, excess aggregate demand will reemerge, and then it will become necessary to curb demand in order to reduce, if not prevent, inflationary pressures. At such times, some curtailment in residential construction need not be against the national interest. During brief periods of excess demand, reduced output of highly durable assets, such as houses, would permit the achievement of restraint in the use of real resources without much sacrifice of current standards of consumption and, in the process, would contribute to holding down inflation. Since the stock of houses is very large, a moderate decline in the rate of new production for several months or a year would have negligible effects on the quantity and quality of the total housing available for use by the public.

In the past, however, credit-induced declines in housing construction have often gone beyond the point of tolerance, creating unnecessary hardships for construction workers, contractors, and those employed in associated industries. These declines have also interfered with improvements in the efficiency of resource use in residential construction—improvements that could lead to lower housing costs if fluctuations in the rate of housing production were moderated. Economic policy, therefore, should seek to redress the balance of restraint during periods of excess aggregate demand—by imposing more restraint on categories of durable goods output other than housing and, in the process, reducing the burden to be borne by the residential construction industry.

In recent years, a number of significant steps have been taken to reduce the severity of short-term declines in housing construction. Federally-sponsored agencies concerned with housing credit or related fields have focused more insistently on the problem; new agencies and programs for dealing with the problem have been established by the Congress; and the powers of existing Federal agencies have been expanded.

The present network of Federally-sponsored credit agencies has demonstrated its capability of contributing powerfully to bolstering the supply of mortgage credit during periods of general credit stringency. During 1969, these agencies supplied directly, or indirectly through loans by the Federal home loan banks to savings and loan associations, over 40 percent of the net funds borrowed to finance housing. In the absence of these massive operations, a much more precipitous decline in housing construction would have occurred in 1969.

Undoubtedly, additional improvements could be made in Federal credit programs to assist the housing industry when private mortgage funds are in short supply. But it would be unwise to rely entirely on this approach to solve the housing finance problem. The main thrust of new initiatives should strike directly at the sources of fluctuation in housing construction.

The Board recommends that the Congress eliminate all interest rate restrictions on FHA-insured and VA-guaranteed loans. Rates on these loans then would reflect market conditions and permit a larger flow of funds into residential construction than would otherwise occur at a time of credit stringency. Legislation enacted in 1968, putting responsibility for determining ceiling rates in the Department of Housing and Urban Development and in the

Veterans Administration, was a step forward. More flexible adjustments in ceiling rates are now possible than was the case when these rates were established by congressional statute.

Under present arrangements, however, decisions to change these ceiling rates can never be free from political constraints. There are likely to be recurring periods, therefore, when mortgage discounts rise again to levels that severely limit or actually deny the access of borrowers to this type of credit.

Such troubles can be avoided by abolishing the ceilings. Alternatively, the Congress might instruct HUD and the VA to adopt a mechanical rule that ties the ceiling rate to a market-determined interest rate.

State governments should also be encouraged to remove their usury ceilings, or to raise them to levels at which they would no longer block the flow of funds into mortgages. There is a growing awareness of the damage that usury ceilings have done, as is evidenced by the fact that numerous States in recent years have raised their usury ceilings—some of them only temporarily, however. Action by the Congress in dispensing with ceiling rates on Federally-backed mortgages would encourage State governments to take similar actions.

Several changes in Federal banking laws are needed to remove impediments to investment in residential mortgages by commercial banks. First, the Federal Reserve Act should be modified to permit the Federal Reserve Banks to lend to member banks on the basis of sound mortgage collateral at the regular discount rate. The Board has recommended this action on prior occasions. Second, quantitative limits on acquisitions by national banks of conventional, and some types of FHA-insured, real estate loans should be abolished. These loans presently may not exceed the capital stock and surplus of a bank, or 70 percent of its time and savings deposits, whichever is greater. Although mortgage acquisitions at present are probably not being limited significantly by this provision, its retention seems unnecessary. Third, the Board recommends rescinding the requirement that conventional real estate loans of national banks may not exceed 90 percent of the appraised value of the property mortgaged, nor exceed 30 years in maturity. Removal of the maximum maturity provision would be essential to investment by national banks in variable-rate mortgages with variable maturities, as discussed later in this report.

Once these provisions were dropped, investment by national banks in conventional mortgages would be governed principally by considerations of safety and soundness, to be tested by bank examinations, as is the case with most other types of loans. The Board believes, however, that it would be prudent to authorize the Comptroller of the Currency to establish safeguards through such regulations as may prove necessary.

Many State banking laws applying to investment in conventional mortgages by State-chartered banks are similar to national banking laws and regulations. Here, too, action by the Congress in liberalizing the mortgage provisions of the national banking laws would provide guidelines that the States could follow.

Especially stringent geographical restrictions on mortgage lending by depositary institutions are found in regulations applying to conventional mortgage loans of Federal savings and loan associations. Though liberalized about a year ago, these regulations still impose rather narrow limits on the geographical mobility of mortgage funds. It is doubtful whether limits of this kind are needed to protect the soundness of individual associations. In our judgment it would be helpful to drop these restrictions, so that funds of savings and loan associations could be loaned out wherever the need seems greatest.

Such action might prompt States in which mutual savings banks operate to reconsider geographical restrictions on conventional mortgage lending by those institutions.

Elimination of these legal and regulatory constraints on mortgage lending would augment the long-run supply of mortgage funds, as well as lessen short-term fluctuations in mortgage credit supplies.

IMPROVEMENTS IN THE FUNCTIONING OF DEPOSITARY INSTITUTIONS

Let us next consider ways of improving the capability of depositary institutions to compete more effectively for consumer savings during periods of rising market interest rates, and thereby to provide a more even flow of funds to the mortgage market.

The problem that nonbank financial intermediaries face, as noted earlier, stems from their nature as specialized financial institutions that lend chiefly in the mortgage market. These institutions would function better in a world of fluctuating market interest rates if the average life of their earning assets were shortened. This objective could be accomplished by diverting a substantial part of their loanable funds to assets other than residential mortgages. Such a solution, however, could well affect adversely the long-run supply of residential mortgage credit and thus raise the average cost of mortgage borrowing.

There is no fully satisfactory solution to this dilemma. The Board believes, nonetheless, that courses of action are available that will improve the ability of nonbank thrift institutions to stabilize their deposit flows and their mortgage lending, while avoiding an undue reduction in the long-run supply of residential mortgage funds.

In the near term, there are good prospects for reducing the asymmetry of the assets and liabilities of nonbank intermediaries by measures to encourage lengthening in the average maturity of deposits and a reduction in deposit turnover rates. Progress in this direction already has been made in recent years, but further steps could be taken. For example, ceiling rates of interest on deposits established by the supervisory authorities could be modified to provide for greater differentiation of accounts by maturity classes, and to permit higher interest rates to be paid on longer-term deposits. The Board intends to pursue these matters with the other regulatory agencies.

Some benefits also can be gained by encouraging the specialized mortgage lending institutions to put a modest proportion of their earning assets into consumer loans—perhaps a maximum of 10 percent. Over the long run, this may tend to reduce somewhat the flow of funds from these institutions to the mortgage market. However, since the average effective life of consumer loans is much shorter than that of mortgages, the average yield on earning assets would respond better to changing market interest rates over a period of several years. This would enhance the ability of nonbank depositary institutions to increase their interest rates on deposits at times when market yields were rising and thus at least partially reduce the tendency of consumer savings to shift to market instruments.

Another step well worth considering would be enabling all depositary institutions to offer mortgages with variable interest rates and attendant safeguards, side by side with the traditional fixed-rate mortgage, as a means of home financing. Depositary institutions holding variable-rate mortgages would experience more flexible average earnings rates. Since they could then change deposit interest rates in response to variations in yields on market securities, deposit inflows should be more stable. Short-term fluctuations in mortgage credit supplies would thereby be reduced, so that home buyers could reasonably expect to find mortgage funds available even during times of general credit restriction. This greater cyclical stability of mortgage credit availability could be achieved, moreover, without affecting adversely the long-run supply of mortgage funds.

There are, of course, some problems associated with rate provisions that would involve the absorption by borrowers of some of the risks of interest rate fluctuations. This would be a complicating element in the budgeting and financial planning of a homeowner carrying a mortgage. It would be wrong, however, to assume that he has no capacity at all to absorb such risks. Variation in interest rates are to a significant degree attributable to changes in the rate of inflation. Increases in the interest rate on a variable-rate mortgage, consequently, would generally be accompanied by a rise in the average borrower's income and his debt service capacity. And, of course, there would be times when borrowers would enjoy a decline in their mortgage interest rate, since a variable-rate mortgage contract would need to provide for reductions in the contract rate when market yields moved down, as well as for increases when market yields rose.

In negotiations over this kind of rate provision, professional lenders would have significant bargaining advantages over relatively unsophisticated homeowner borrowers. If such advantages were exploited, an undue share of the burden of interest rate adjustment could be shifted to homeowners. Accordingly, variable-rate mortgages should have protective features to safeguard the interests of borrowers.

For example, it would be wise for public policy to limit the degree to which any individual borrower is subjected to changes in his mortgage interest rate. This could be done by designing a mortgage instrument on which the possible fluctuation in interest rates is restricted to a moderate range. Furthermore, lenders could be required to provide prospective borrowers with data showing the differences in costs that could result over the life of the contract under alternative assumptions as to interest rate movements. Also, the fixed monthly payment form of the variable-rate mortgage would need to be given particular encouragement. In such a mortgage contract, the variation in interest rates under most circumstances would take the form of a lengthening or shortening of the term to maturity rather than a change in the monthly payment. This would be more suitable for borrowers than the variable monthly payment form, since adjustments in other expenditures would then not be required to accommodate changes in outlays for debt service.

The Federal Government could help prepare the way for use of variable-rate mortgages as an instrument in home financing. Thus, HUD and the VA might authorize variable rates on FHA-insured and VA-guaranteed mortgage loans, and the Federal National Mortgage Association and Federal Home Loan Mortgage Corporation could include such mortgages in their secondary market operations.

Also, assistance might be given to the community of mortgage lenders in developing a standard contract for variable-rate mortgages, and to the States in developing model legislation to provide mortgage borrowers with adequate safeguards against possible abuses by lenders.

It should be emphasized that the proper role of variable-rate mortgages is additional and complementary to the traditional fixed-rate mortgage contract. Borrowers should have the option of choosing freely between these instruments. Unless a potential borrower expected interest rates to decline, he would usually prefer to finance his home purchase with a fixed-rate mortgage—thereby avoiding the uncertainty inherent in a variable interest rate. In view of this normal preference of borrowers, lenders would probably need to make the initial interest rate and other contract terms more attractive than those on a fixed-rate mortgage.

If promptly implemented, it would probably still take a decade or longer for variable-rate mortgages to reach a sizable fraction of the portfolios of the Nation's depositary institutions. In time, however, this financial innovation might be of substantial help in moderating swings in the availability of mortgage credit and in residential construction.

Steps discussed in this section to strengthen our depositary institutions, if implemented, should speed the day when ceiling rates of interest on consumer time and savings deposits would no longer be needed. Removal of the ceilings would permit savers to be rewarded more fully; it would increase efficiency of financial markets and it would enable each depositary institution to compete with market securities to the maximum extent permitted by its own earnings position.

Although it would be wise to leave standby authority in the hands of the regulatory agencies to impose interest rate ceilings on consumer time and savings deposits in the event of unforeseen contingencies, the Board believes that it is time to begin planning for gradual withdrawal of ceiling rates as an instrument of financial regulation. The Board again recommends, therefore, that the Congress make permanent the authority—which was granted to the regulatory authorities in the fall of 1966 and extended since then on several occasions—to differentiate between kinds of deposits for purposes of deposit rate regulation and to suspend interest rate maxima when it is judged appropriate to do so. It would also be constructive if the Congress saw fit to indicate a desire to have the regulatory authorities formulate, and begin implementation of, a long-range plan for step-by-step removal of effective ceilings.

IMPROVEMENTS IN THE USE OF FISCAL POLICY

Some years will pass before the above recommendations for reform of the depositary institutions and for the removal of legal and regulatory barriers to mortgage fund flows can have their full beneficial effects in stabilizing housing construction. In the short run, the principal hope for lessening the variability of home-building lies in gaining a fuller measure of control over inflation—and particularly in improving the use of fiscal policies, so that lesser reliance would need to be placed on changes in credit conditions to stabilize aggregate economic activity. Indeed, as students of the housing problem have long recognized, increased reliance on fiscal policies to stabilize aggregate economic activity has a permanent role to play in any well-conceived prorgram to lessen the instability of housing construction.

Such a course has a number of related advantages. If we succeed in establishing a financial environment conducive to less volatile flows of mortgage credit, other sectors that are sensitive to fluctuations in credit market conditions will also benefit. State and local governments, for example, will not be confronted with such pronounced variations in financing costs, and smaller business firms will experience less difficulty in securing funds when business is booming. Furthermore, greater stability in residential construction will be achieved without sacrificing the broader objectives of stability in aggregate employment, production, and prices. By resorting to a more flexible use of fiscal tools, sectors of the economy in which spending is influenced relatively little by monetary policies could thus be made to bear their share of restraint during periods of excess demand.

A variety of fiscal tools could be used to stimulate or restrict spending in one or more sectors other than housing. However, suggestions for flexibly administered fiscal policies previously set forth by academic economists and others have not been viewed by the Congress with much enthusiasm. The Congress has been understandably reluctant to take steps that might interfere with efforts to rationalize tax policy, or result in manipulating private spending incentives capriciously, or give the Executive Branch excessive control over Federal expenditures or tax rates. It may be possible, however, to overcome these objections with a systematic approach that minimizes the threat of undermining either tax policy or budget policy.

A promising approach is to use fiscal policy to control changes in the rate of business investment. Outlays by business firms on machinery and equipment are large and cyclically volatile. Clearly, greater stability in such purchases would foster a more steady growth rate of aggregate production and employment. These expenditures, furthermore, are relatively insensitive to monetary policy, particularly in the short run. During periods of credit restraint, the business sector has repeatedly drawn on financial and real resources that would otherwise have probably gone into the housing industry.

One instrument of tax policy, the investment tax credit, has in recent years been employed to influence business investment decisions. By now the investment tax credit is well understood by the business community, by the Congress, and by the general public. Its effects on the rate of business fixed investment have been demonstrated in actual experience.

The investment tax credit was originally thought of as a device for providing additional stimulus to business capital expenditures over the long run. However, successive congressional measures dealing with this tax credit since 1966 have suggested that the credit might also be used flexibly to even out the behavior of business investment spending over the course of the business cycle. Thus, the magnitude of the tax credit could be lowered when excess aggregate demand threatened to generate inflationary pressures, or it would be raised when the economy was in need of stimulus. If the tax credit were adjusted in this fashion, variations in business external financing demands would tend to be reduced, fluctuations in market interest rates would tend to diminish, and these developments could contribute to stabilizing the flow of mortgage credit and housing construction.

A flexible use of the investment tax credit would require orderly procedures for adjustment of the rate of credit. Experience suggests that, if timely adjustments are to be made, the Congress would need to assign responsibility to another body for determining when a change in the rate of tax credit should be effected. However, this could be accomplished in ways that protected and preserved the ultimate responsibility of the Congress to determine tax policy and that avoided subjecting the business community to capricious changes in taxes.

For example, the Congress might grant to the President authority to vary the investment tax credit within prescribed limits—say, from zero to 10 or 15 percent. Once a change in the rate of tax credit was announced by the Executive, it would go into effect 60 days hence, retroactive to the date of the announcement, unless the Senate or the House of Representatives disapproved of the rate change in the intervening period. The Congress might, if it so chose, stipulate that the President could act only after a public recommendation had been made by an advisory body, such as the Council of Economic Advisers.

Under such a system, timely adjustments of the investment tax credit could be achieved, but there would also be ample time for careful deliberation by the Congress to determine whether the proposed fiscal action was in the national interest.

CONCLUDING COMMENTS

The Board recommends that priority consideration be given to establishment of the machinery for a variable investment tax credit. This is the most important single contribution that could be made to easing the plight of the housing industry in recurring periods of credit restriction. The Board also suggests consideration of actions to enable the use of variable-rate mortgages to finance residential structures.

Other recommendations set forth in this report, though less significant individually, would in the aggregate also serve to reduce materially the instability of credit flows to the housing industry.

At present, the residential construction industry is not suffering from any want of credit. Housing activity has been rising rapidly for over a year and a half, with starts reaching a new peak in January of this year. Even now, mortgage interest rates are falling, while inflows of time and savings deposits at commercial banks and nonbank thrift institutions continue at unusually high levels.

These recent developments do not imply that the cyclical problems of housing and housing finance are behind us. On the contrary, they illustrate that the supply of mortgage credit and the rate of housing production are still highly sensitive to changes in general credit conditions.

This is a good time for the Congress to consider carefully the most appropriate steps to help stabilize supplies of mortgage credit. In the course of its deliberations, the Congress will no doubt wish to obtain the judgments of a number of governmental agencies, of consumer groups, of representatives of industry and finance, and of recognized scholars in the housing field.

The Board would urge the Congress to take the opportunity afforded by present conditions in the mortgage credit and housing fields to move forward and put in place the machinery that will be needed for moderating fluctuations in residential construction in the years ahead.

FEDERAL HOUSING POLICIES:
SUBSIDIZED PRODUCTION, FILTRATION
AND OBJECTIVES

Frank S. Kristof

The level of federally subsidized housing production has reached over 500,000 units annually over the two years, 1970-1971. This output nearly doubled the amount of subsidized housing produced in the first thirty-five years since federal legislation was enacted (1934). A host of questions about the costs and the effectiveness of this output in meeting the nation's housing goal—as set forth in the Housing Act of 1949 and re-affirmed in the Housing Act of 1968—of a "decent home and suitable living environment for every American family" has gained momentum and the breadth and depth of these concerns create fundamental issues about federal housing policies. Between April 1950 and April 1970, some 96 percent of the nation's total housing production was built for ownership by the private sector. Substantial improvement in housing conditions was recorded during this period even though only a small proportion of total production was oriented toward "housing-poor" families. This fact raises basic concerns. How great was the progress recorded during the 1950-1970 period? To what was this progress attributable? To what extent did housing filtration successfully operate to improve the nation's housing status?

The history of federal influence upon housing policy in the United States may be conceptually divided into three periods—1934 to 1961; 1961 to 1968; and 1968 to date. The initial period was characterized by the first groping efforts toward realization of a national housing policy of a "decent home . . . for every American family." Except during the World War II period of controls, the tools essentially took the form of indirect intervention in the housing market—the creation of conditions that would encourage new private housing construction. These included the Federal Housing Administration mortgage insurance system (National Housing Act of 1934), liberalized mortgage terms, slum clearance and urban renewal, initial attempts to create a secondary mortgage market and a modestly financed low-rent public housing program. Only two per cent of total housing output was directly supported by explicit federal subsidy in this period.

The second period was characterized by: 1. growing disaffection with the rate of improvement in housing conditions in the nation's urban centers as contrasted with the suburbs; 2. new experiments with direct federal assistance to housing production; 3. substantial increase in efforts to create a secondary mortgage finance system; and 4. initial experiments in family rent allowances that could be used in existing as well as new housing. During this period national housing starts aided by direct federal assistance rose from 3 per cent in 1961 to 12 per cent in 1968.

The third period was marked by passage of the Housing Act of 1968, which established as a national housing goal the production of 26 million housing units in ten years, of which six million were to be federally subsidized. Passage of the 1968 Housing Act represented the culmination of disaffection with progress made in achieving the nation's housing policy. Again, this disaffection was rooted in urban centers, particularly in the older central cities.

COSTS AND EFFECTS SINCE 1968

The 1968 Act created formidable housing programs to implement subsidized housing output. These, in essence, embody the principle that the federal government subsidize the mortgage interest cost of new or rehabilitated housing for moderate-income families from the market rate down to an interest rate of one per cent, effectively cutting monthly housing costs by one-third to nearly one-half when partial tax exemption from real estate taxes under state and local programs is included.

As indicated earlier, in 1970 and 1971 nearly one million federally assisted housing units were placed in construction.(1) This unprecedented performance vitually achieved the rate of subsidized production called for in the Housing Act of 1968. Even more startling is the cost this effort thus far entails: some thirty billion dollars over the next 30 or 40 years.(2) At this rate, the federal government's direct budget commitment will grow to $7.5 billion annually for the forty-year mortgage life of housing being aided by federal programs.(3) In terms of legal eligibility for housing assistance, nearly half of the nation's population can qualify under one or another of the direct housing assistance programs.

The sharp increase in federally assisted housing output from about six per cent of total starts in the early 1960's to one-quarter of the total in 1970 has been accompanied by alarmed reactions about both the costs and the effectiveness of this housing production. The complaints cover a wide range: the housing is being built in the wrong places for the wrong persons; much of it is shoddily built and over-priced, enriching careless or unscrupulous builders and real estate dealers at the expense of buyers or renters—and winds up repossessed by the Department of Housing and Urban Development (hereinafter referred to as HUD) through mortgage defaults; it is being produced in deteriorating central city areas and other unmarketable locations where the customers are too poor to pay the necessary rents; thus vacancies, rent delinquencies and mortgage defaults follow.

At the other extreme, when such housing is developed in better neighborhoods, are charges that families of substantially similar incomes are paying full housing costs while their more fortunate economic peers receive the benefits of federal subsidies. This raises political as well as equity questions about the allocation of housing assistance.

Another and different expression of concern about the location of new subsidized housing production is that it is not going to places where it is most needed—suburban areas of employment growth where employees in intermediate pay scales ($3.00 to $4.50 per hour) are demanded in large numbers but cannot afford new housing at conventional rents or prices. It is in such growth areas that available housing at modest costs also tends to be in short supply. It is argued that some aid to housing would provide a needed balance in these locations where higher cost, conventionally-financed housing normally represents the only additions to the supply. On the cost sides, the annual direct and indirect subsidies per family for housing produced under the 1968 Housing Act range from $500 to $5,000 per family per year depending upon location, programs involved, and whether low- or moderate-income families are being aided.(4)

Another serious charge is that a large proportion of these high costs do not go to the intended beneficiaries but are lost to private and governmental intermediaries in the assisted housing production process. These include promoters, builders, realtors, investors, local housing authorities, other local governmental agencies, and the Department of Housing and Urban Development. One estimate, dealing with the federal public housing and rent supplement programs, is that between one-fifth and one-half of the total federal subsidies do not reach the residents but are lost in the form of "federal and local administrative expenses and for tax benefits to investors."(5) Another contribution to subsidy waste is the padding of cost bids by developers of government-subsidized housing. This is attributed to the higher costs of construction experienced by developers in contending with the inefficiencies and delays in dealing with government agencies. These excess costs are borne both by the taxpayer through unnecessarily higher subsidies and by the occupants in the form of higher rents. Possibly the most serious criticism of recent subsidized housing production is that most of it is not reaching housing-poor families—those living in substandard or otherwise inadequate housing and whose incomes are too low to afford even existing standard housing.

Finally, basic questions are being raised about the nation's housing production goals. Is too much emphasis being placed upon production of new housing to the neglect of maintenance of existing housing and neighborhoods? This question has come to the fore since the latter part of the 1960's when a wave of housing abandonments began to hit virtually every major city in the nation as well as hundreds of smaller communities. For the first time, concern with housing standards has shifted from concentration upon the provision of the capital good (the house or apartment) to consideration of the flow of services from that good and what it is that keeps it flowing to provide satisfactory services to the consumer.(6)

The critical question for national housing policy is how the most rapid and efficient rate of improvement in the nation's housing standards may be achieved within a defined level of allocation of national resources. The latter requirement is a crucial component of the discussion since, if resource allocations are pushed sharply upward as in 1970-1971, we are faced with an additional question: what sacrifices have to be made to achieve a given improvement in housing standards and are the benefits gained worth the costs incurred?

Framed in the context outlined above, the experience of the two decades 1950 to 1970 becomes highly relevant. Early 1970 Housing Census data provide a bewildering disparity between usual perceptions of the nation's lack of housing progress and the facts. After five years of soaring construction costs, rising interest rates and a dampened level of conventional new construction, the salient conclusion that emerges from examination of the 1970 Housing Census results is that the nation has for the most part maintained the rate of progress realized since 1950.

With only minor shifts, the 1970 housing needs of the nation, as defined in the Douglas Commission Research Report #10, declined virtually as projected in December 1967:

> Since the goals established by the Housing Act of 1949 were set, the Nation has made steady and unremitting progress in meeting its housing needs in the context of commonly accepted criteria of that day. In those terms, housing needs were reduced from a 1950 level of 20.5 million units, or 44 per cent of the total housing supply, to 15.4 million units in 1960, or 26 per cent of the total housing supply; and to a projected total of 10.8 million units in 1970, which will constitute about 16 per cent of the housing supply at that time.(7)

As shown in Table I (line 26), preliminary 1970 Census data indicate that housing needs in 1970 declined to about 10.4 million units or 15.1 per cent of the nation's 1970 housing inventory.(8) Despite the fall-off of new, private construction during the latter years of the decade, overall housing progress nevertheless was maintained by the intervention of two influences: 1. Continued increases in federally-financed or assisted new housing output over the 1960's—particularly FHA Section 221-(d)(3) and its successor programs, Sections 235 and 236. Approximately 300,000 new units enumerated in the 1970 Census were contributed by federal programs in the two years prior to the Census. The decade total from this source (including the low-rent public housing programs) was slightly in excess of one million units. 2. A sharp upward jump in occupancy of mobile units. The inventory of this form of occupied housing more than doubled in the 1960's, contributing 1.1 million units toward the decade's net income of 10.4 million housing units. These two influences prevented the nation's 1960-1970 rate of progress from falling off relative to the rate of improvement recorded during the years 1950-1960.

It is worth tracing the components of change shown in Table I to note the similarities in housing trends of the 1950's and 1960's despite the above-noted mixture of positive and negative influences during the past decade. The relatively low rate of household formation in the early 1960's was abruptly and sharply reversed in 1968 and 1969 when persons from age groups with a high propensity to form households (the baby boom of the late 1940's) entered the housing market in large numbers. A nearly doubled rate of household formation in these two years contributed to an increase of a million more households than were

TABLE 1–ESTIMATES OF COMPONENTS OF INVENTORY CHANGE
AND CHANGES IN HOUSING NEEDS FOR THE UNITED STATES: 1950-1969
(IN THOUSANDS OF UNITS)

Subject	Actual 1950-59	Estimate 1960-69	Actual 1960-69
1. Total housing inventory at beginning of the decade	46,137	58,468	58,326a
Components of Inventory Change			
2. Units added to housing inventory	16,861	16,900	17,114b
3. New construction	15,003	15,300	15,514b
4. Units added by conversion	807	600	600b
5. Units added through other sources	1,050	1,000	1,000b
6. Units lost from housing inventory	−4,530	−5,900	−6,761b
7. Units removed through demolition	−1,933	−2,700	n.a.
8. Units lost through mergers	−815	−700	n.a.
9. Units lost through other means	−1,783	−2,500	n.a.
10. Net change accounted for by:	12,331	11,000	10,353a
11. Increase in number of households	9,986	9,400	10,426a
12. Change in vacancies:	2,345	1,600	−73a
13. Available for sale or rent	1,412	300	158a
14. Other vacancies	933	1,300	−231a
Changes in Housing Needs			
15. Housing needs at beginning of decade	20,530	15,364	15,364
16. Substandard units to be removed	17,007	11,407	11,407
17. Crowded households in standard units	2,682	3,957	3,957
18. Increase in standard available vacancies	841	–	–
19. Changes in housing need during decade	−5,166	−4,577	−4,998
20. Change in number of substandard units:	−5,600	−4,524	−5,334c
21. Demolitions, mergers, other losses	−3,446	−3,885	n.a.
22. Substandard units added during decade	1,886	1,551	n.a.
23. Upgrading in existing inventory	−4,040	−2,190	n.a.
24. Change in crowding in standard units	1,275	−53	312b
25. Change in standard available vacancies	−841	–	24b
26. Housing need at end of decade	15,364	10,787	10,366
27. Substandard units to be removed	11,407	6,883	6,073
28. Crowded households in standard units	3,957	3,904	4,269
29. Increase in standard available vacancies	–	–	24

Sources: Frank S. Kristof, Urban Housing Needs Through the 1980's, The National Commission on Urban Problems, 1968, p. 6. The figures in column two are estimated as of December, 1967.

a U.S. Bureau of the Census, 1960 and 1970 Census of Housing. U.S. Summary.

b Estimated.

c 1960 and 1970 Census of Housing, adjusted to include an estimate for dilapidated units not enumerated in 1970.

TABLE II–GENERAL HOUSING AND OCCUPANCY CHARACTERISTICS, UNITED STATES: 1970, 1960, 1950

Subject	1970	1960	1950	Percent change (1960-70)	Percent change (1950-60)
Tenure, Race and Vacancy Status					
All housing units	68,679	58,326	45,983	17.8	26.8
Occupied	63,450	53,024	42,826	19.7	23.8
Vacant	5,229	5,302	3,157	−1.4	67.9
Available (year-round)	2,133	1,975	732	8.0	169.8
For sale	477	522	215	−8.6	142.8
For rent	1,655	1,453	517	13.9	181.0
Not available	3,096	3,327	2,425	−7.0	37.2
Owner occupied	39,885	32,797	23,560	21.6	39.2
White	36,979	30,823	22,241	20.0	38.6
Non-white	2,906	1,974	1,319	47.2	49.7
Renter occupied	23,565	20,227	19,266	16.5	5.0
White	19,551	17,057	16,803	14.6	1.5
Non-white	4,014	3,171	2,463	26.6	28.7
Conditions and Plumbing Facilities					
Occupied units	63,450	53,024	42,826	19.7	23.8
Not dilapidated, with all plumbing facilities	59,159	44,550	27,632	32.8	61.2
White	54,220	41,438	n.a.	30.8	n.a.
1.01+ persons per room	3,979	4,658	n.a.	−14.6	n.a.
Non-white	4,939	3,112	n.a.	58.7	n.a.
1.01+ persons per room	1,232	1,456	n.a.	−15.4	n.a.
Dilapidated or lacking plumbing facilities	4,291	8,474	15,194	−49.4	−44.2
White	3,050	6,442	n.a.	−52.7	n.a.
Non-white	1,241	2,032	n.a.	−39.0	n.a.
Rooms (Occupied)					
Total	63,450	53,024	42,826	19.7	23.8
1	1,108	1,221	1,103	−9.3	10.7
2	2,132	2,146	2,997	−0.7	−28.4
3	6,758	6,007	6,205	12.5	−3.2
4	12,977	11,162	9,304	16.3	20.0
5	16,007	13,355	9,258	19.9	44.3
6	13,008	10,578	7,435	23.0	42.3
7	6,185	4,749	3,226	30.2	47.2
8+	5,276	3,805	3,295	38.7	15.5
Median	5.0	4.9	4.7	2.0	4.2
Persons					
Occupied housing units	63,450	53,024	42,826	19.7	23.8
1	11,146	7,075	3,993	57.5	77.2
2	18,781	14,859	12,023	26.4	23.6
3	10,909	10,008	9,763	9.0	2.5
4	9,803	9,130	7,878	7.4	15.9
5	6,199	5,878	4,466	5.5	31.6
6	3,360	3,129	2,258	7.4	38.6
7+	3,252	2,945	2,445	10.4	20.4
Median	2.7	3.0	3.1	−10.0	−3.2

TABLE II—Continued

Subject	1970	1960	1950	Percent change (1960-70)	Percent change (1950-60)
Space Utilization					
Total persons in housing units	197,400	175,263	145,031	12.6	20.8
Total occupied rooms	325,376	265,913	205,612	22.4	29.3
Total rooms per person	1.65	1.52	1.42	8.6	7.0
Total persons per occupied housing unit	3.11	3.31	3.39	−6.1	−2.4
Persons per Room					
1.00 or less	58,238	46,910	36,092	24.1	30.0
1.01 to 1.50	3,802	4,211	4,084	−9.7	3.1
1.50 or more	1,408	1,903	2,650	−26.0	−28.2
Financial					
Median value (occupied one-family units)	$17,000	$11,900	$7,354	42.9	61.8
Median contract rent (occupied units)	$89	$58	$36	53.4	61.1
Median income (families)	$9,856	$5,660	$3,073	74.1	84.2
Median gross rent as a % of income	n.a.	19.2	17.4	n.a.	10.3

Sources: U.S. Bureau of the Census, 1950, 1960 and 1970 Census of Housing.

a Includes vacant seasonal and migratory units, units rented or sold, awaiting occupancy, held for occasional use, and other vacant.

b To permit comparability an estimate was made for dilapidated units (not enumerated in 1970) using 1968 data of Bureau of the Census' Housing Characteristics report, Series H-121, No. 17, February 1970.

projected for the decade in Table I (line 11).

Nevertheless, the gross addition of 17.1 million housing units estimated for the 1960's (line 2 of Table I) appeared sufficient to absorb a high rate of housing losses (6.8 million units, line 6) while total household formation exceeded that of the 1950's. The decade-end surge of household formation created pressures upon the vacant housing supply—the overall available vacancy rate in 1970 fell relative to that in 1960 (3.1 per cent versus 3.6 per cent). On balance, the nation's housing status during the 1960's remained at reasonable equilibrium even with the appearance of new trends—a high rate of housing additions contributed by mobile units and publicly assisted housing as well as an acceleration of housing losses.

Advances in the nation's housing status in the 1960's matched or exceeded those of the previous decade. The overall decrease in "housing need" in the 1960's (line 19, Table I) was almost as great as that projected in 1967. The decrease in substandard units was 18 per cent greater than projected (line 20) but this was partially offset by slight increases in crowding in standard units (line 24) and in vacancy "requirements" (line 25). On balance, the improvement in housing conditions over the decades 1950-1970 has been impressive.

Specific aspects of the 1950-1970 improvements may be traced in data in Table II. Average number of persons per household fell from 3.39 to 3.11 while the median number of rooms per housing unit increased from 4.7 to 5.0. As a result, the nation's households in 1970 occupied more space per person than ever before—an average of 1.65 rooms per person compared to the 1950 figure of 1.42.

Another contribution to housing improvement was the decrease in 1- and 2-room units while increases were recorded in each category of housing units with 3 to 8+ rooms. Since most older 1- and 2-room units are conversions with shared bathroom facilities, their decrease correlates closely with the reduction in substandard units (dilapidated or lacking plumbing facilities). The latter category experienced sharp decreases of 49 and 44 per cent over the past two decades.

Another reflection of improvement in housing standards over the two decades was the ability of individuals to establish or maintain households. One-person households increased by 7.1 million, nearly trebling between 1950 to 1970; in this short time-period they increased from 9.7 per cent to 17.6 per cent of all households—the fastest growing category in the nation. At the other extreme, households of 8 persons or more decreased from 2.8 to 2.5 per cent of the total while 6 and 7 person households fell from 9.4 to 8 per cent. The combination of smaller households with slightly more rooms per unit also led to a decrease in crowding: 5.2 million households had more than 1.01 persons per room in 1970 (8.2 per cent) compared with 6.7 million households (15.7 per cent) in 1950.

These housing gains were accompanied by, and in large part were attributable to, advances in family income. Only rising incomes whose rate of increase equaled or exceeded rent and house price rises could sustain the high volume of new construction experienced over most of the past two decades. Median family income rose 84 per cent between 1949 and 1959 and 74 per cent in the following decade. Rents and prices of single-family homes increased at a slower rate (Table II). Rent-income ratios increased only slightly indicating that the improvements in housing standards purchased over the past twenty years did not create excessive drains on consumer budgets.

HOUSING IMPROVEMENT AND THE FILTRATION PROCESS

Up to this point we have defined the nature of unprecedented progress in housing standards over the two decades 1950-1970 which produced the most sustained period of high-level housing construction in the nation's history—30.5 million new housing units—while the net addition of households numbered 20.4 million. The aggregate number of substandard units fell by 70 per cent—from 17 million to 5 million. Space standards per person reached new highs while crowding reached new lows. Given the fact that increased federal housing assistance has become effective in only recent years, the question arises about the extent to which the observed improvement was traceable to the effective functioning of the filtration process. What are the requirements for ascertaining the effective functioning of the filtration process? A search of the literature develops some parameters that are accepted by most analysts: 1. New construction must be greater than the rate necessary to house normal growth, i.e., an excess of housing supply over demand at the point from which filtering is to originate. 2. New construction exerts a downward pressure on rents and prices of existing housing; permitting lower income families to obtain better housing bargains relative to their existing quarters. 3. Exogenous factors are held constant, including the general level of incomes and rent-income ratios.(9) 4.

Decline in quality is not necessarily forced by reduction in maintenance and repair expenditures to the extent that rents and prices are forced downward. 5. A mechanism must exist to remove the worst housing from the market without adversely affecting rents and prices of housing at the lowest level.

The above basically represents Richard Ratcliff's exposition with modifications suggested by Grebler, Winnick and Fisher to permit more precise measurement of the process as distinct from its effects. Ratcliff and subsequently, Ira Lowry concluded that, as a means of improving housing quality, filtering essentially is a self defeating process. Ratcliff puts it as follows:

> Filtering . . . is not a controllable device. The end production of filtering, at the bottom of the chain reaction, is substandard housing; thus filtering produces the very blight which we seek to remedy. Filtering cannot increase in effectiveness without the removal of housing as it sinks below minimum standards. And if by some drastic change in conditions the rate of filtering were accelerated to the point of adequacy, the cost to property owners through the concomitant depreciation in the value of their properties would be tremendous.(10)

Thus a loss in value sufficient to drive rents and prices to such a low level that only standard quality housing can be found at the bottom of the rent-price ladder might have the perverse effect of driving rents and prices of the entire housing spectrum to the point that new construction would come to a halt, prices and rents would again rise and doubling-up or excessive conversion of housing at the low end of the scale would once again dilute housing quality as well as occupancy standards.

Not only would the process be unsuccessful in the end but there would be great costs on the way. If market price were to decline so that successively lower-income groups can afford the housing while removing substandard housing within a reasonable time period, society would have to pay a high price in accelerated loss in value of the housing stock. This position is strongly supported by Ira Lowry who demonstrates, in his filtering model, that the actual and logical response of property owners to declines in value or rent will be a policy of undermaintenance of property so that, in addition to normal deterioration that occurs over time, the deterioration caused by disinvestment will lead to far more rapid declines in quality of housing than otherwise might occur. As a result, it is extremely unlikely that downward filtered dwellings will, in fact, provide satisfactory housing to occupants who obtain them at low rents or prices.(11)

Only one question remains open in this exposition: if value decline is accelerated through a large and consistent influx of new construction that persistently clears the market year in and year out, is it not possible for the rate of value-decline to outstrip quality decline, with a resulting improvement in housing standards? Lowry would argue that this is not possible within the framework of the "pure" filtering theory and that the 1950-1970 improvement in housing standards in the nation occurred within a framework of filtration reinforced by exogenous variables such as rising incomes. To put it in his own words:

> The reason why it is important to distinguish the effects on housing

standards produced by 'exogenous' factors such as rising real incomes from the effects produced by new construction through filtering (as I have defined it) is that confusing the two can lead to mistaken policies. Thus, if it were strictly true that quality of a housing unit changed promptly and proportionately in response to changes in its market rent (because the owner would change his maintenance policy), the special public measures (such as subsidies) to encourage new construction might result in a chain of moves, but would not result in better housing at the bottom of the chain—unless the families last in line paid higher rents to support better maintenance than previously. On the other hand, if measures (such as rent assistance) were taken to increase the real incomes of these families, thus enabling them to spend more for housing, its quality would rise without the need for special encouragement of new construction.(12)

The discussion can at this point be summarized. When filtration is defined in the manner posited by Lowry, "a change in the real value (price in constant dollars) of an existing dwelling unit" for the purpose of ascertaining whether the value declines of housing that occur in the filtering process can result in providing sound housing for low-income families, it remains seriously questionable whether the filtering process by itself can be credited with the observed improvement in housing standards that occurred in the decades 1950-1970. Nothing in the position taken by others who have discussed filtration theory (Grebler, Winnick, Fisher, Grigsby) necessarily contradicts Lowry's position since the only difference in their position is to allow the influence of exogenous variables to be incorporated in analysis of the effects of filtration, a position that Lowry explicitly rejects. Thus, whether filtration works or does not work to improve the housing supply depends upon whose definition is used.

Some empirical evidence on the subject may be gleaned from information made available by the Census Bureau's 1950-1959 components of inventory change which permits analysis of the path by which substandard housing left the housing inventory during that period (Table III). This information provides little support for the traditional conception of filtration. The first point of note is that eight per cent of the new housing added during the 1950's was classified as substandard—it had nowhere to filter—but up.(13) In fact, the augmentation of the substandard supply from new construction (1,235,000 units) was even greater than the one million substandard units added by deterioration in the existing housing supply ("same" units). In the same time period, 5 million substandard units of 1950 had been upgraded to standard status by 1959. The result was a net improvement of 4 million units in the existing housing inventory that substantially exceeded the 2.65 million substandard units that were demolished or removed by "other means." It is important to note the outcome of these complex changes: despite the addition of 1.2 million substandard units through new construction and 2.5 per cent annual rate of deterioration in the existing housing inventory that created an additional one million substandard units, the upgrading of 5 million existing substandard units to standard status overwhelmed the negative influences on the housing inventory.

Other changes, through conversions and mergers, in the quality of housing existing in 1950 resulted in a further net reduction of more than one-half million

TABLE III—DECREASE IN SUBSTANDARD HOUSING FOR
THE UNITED STATES: 1950-1959
(IN THOUSANDS OF UNITS)

Item	Number	Percent of 1950 Total
Net Decrease in Substandard Units	5,600	33
Substandard Units, 1950	17,007	100
Increase in Substandard Units,		
1950-1959:	2,886	17
Among new units added during		
decade	1,235	7
Among units added through		
conversion	234	1
Among units added through		
other means	417	2
Through deterioration of		
"same" units	1,000	6
Decrease in Substandard Units,		
1950-1959:	8,486	50
Among units demolished	1,382	8
Among units removed through		
merger	790	5
Among units removed through		
other means	1,274	7
Through rehabilitation or im-		
provement of "same" units	5,040	30
Substandard Units, 1959	11,407	67

Source: U.S. Census of Housing: 1960, Vol. IV, Components of Inventory Change, HC(4), Part 1A, No. 1.

substandard units. The foregoing leaves questions about whether the housing inventory filtered up, down or in both directions—and whether traditional views of filtering are either useful or relevant in attempting to explain the link between new construction and the improvement of the housing inventory.

It is abundantly clear that no explanation for the marked improvements in the nation's housing status can be ascertained without examination of the factors referred to by Lowry as "exogenous variables." Once this course is undertaken another major responsibility must be assumed. Only glancing reference has been made here so far to dissident trends in the nation's central cities that cast a cloud over the bright historic housing progress that has been made on a national level. The last four years have been difficult ones on the housing front in many ways. For example, an advancing rate of deterioration and widespread abandonment of housing in the central cities has created wholly new sets of problems. Thus, no conclusion about the larger picture is warranted until the relevant exogenous factors are thoroughly explored.

NOTES

(1) The President's Third Annual Report on National Housing Goals, June 1971, Table 2, p. 8.

(2) Ibid., p. 22. This figure includes financing of 113,000 rehabilitated units in addition to 945,000 new units.

(3) Ibid.

(4) A single housing unit conceivably can be aided by some or all of the following programs, each of which has a specific measurable cost: urban renewal land writedown, FHA Section 236 1-per cent interest subsidy rent supplements, real estate tax exemptions, lost federal (and state) taxes on tax-exempt bonds (for state and municipally-financed programs) and through tax benefits to limited partner equity investors.

(5) Bernard J. Frieden, "Improving Federal Housing Subsidies: Summary Report," Papers submitted to Subcommittee on Housing Panels, Part 2, Committee on Banking and Currency, House of Representatives, 92nd Congress, First Session, p. 473.

(6) This distinction was made cogently by Morton L. Isler in "The Goals of Housing Subsidy Programs," in Part 2, Papers submitted to Subcommittee on Housing Panels, Committee on Banking and Currency, House of Representatives, 92nd Congress, First Session, June 1971, pp. 419ff.

(7) F. S. Kristof, Urban Housing Needs Through the 1980's: an Analysis and Projection, Washington, D.C., The National Commission on Urban Problems, Research Report #10, 1968, p. xi.

(8) Because the "condition of housing" item was dropped from the 1970 Census enumeration, a small component of the 1970 needs figure (about 10 percent) had to be estimated. When the 1970 components of change data become available, this figure can be confirmed or corrected. The margin of error is likely to be under 500,000.

(9) There is some question about this point: William Grigsby would incorporate exogenous factors as a part of the filtering process whereas Ira Lowry bars such an approach as analytically confusing.

(10) R. U. Ratcliff, Urban Land Economics (New York: McGraw Hill Book Co., Inc., 1949), pp. 333, 334.

(11) Cf., Ira S. Lowry, "Filtering and Housing Standards," Land Economics, November 1960, p. 362 ff.

(12) Letter, Ira S. Lowry to F. S. Kristof, April 7, 1971.

(13) Of the 15 million housing units constructed between 1950 and 1959, 945,000 were recorded as lacking some or all plumbing facilities and 290,000 were enumerated as dilapidated. Three-quarters of these substandard units were built outside of SMSA's, mostly in non building permit areas, where they constituted a surprising 18 per cent of all new construction. It may be surmised that the great bulk of these were "do-it-yourself" houses, some of which were little more than "jerry-built" shacks as indicated by the fact that 272,000 of these substandard units (29 per cent) consisted of 1 or 2 rooms. A possible explanation for the larger units without plumbing facilities is that they were built over a period of years by families with limited resources. Full plumbing facilities (when installed) usually represent a final luxury for such families.

TAX INCENTIVES FOR
REHABILITATING RENTAL HOUSING

John D. Heinberg

Emil M. Sunley, Jr.

The Tax Reform Act of 1969, while tightening up on a number of tax preferences, added a new one for real estate by providing a five-year write-off for qualified expenditures for the rehabilitation of low and moderate income housing. In this paper the basic mechanism of the new tax incentive is described, and certain administrative problems are discussed. The magnitude of the tax incentive is measured by computing the reduction in the rental cost of capital. The two major issues examined in the paper are the flowthrough of the tax benefits from the landlords to the tenants and the distribution of the tax benefits among tenants. These issues are examined under the assumption that the tax incentive works independently of other subsidized housing programs and under the assumption that the tax incentive is coordinated with the Section 236 subsidy program sponsored by the Department of Housing and Urban Development. It is concluded that the new tax incentive probably will provide to lower income tenants benefits which are marginal rather than substantial.

ESSENTIAL FEATURES OF THE FIVE-YEAR WRITE-OFF

Under the new Section 176(k) of the Internal Revenue Code, a taxpayer may elect to compute his depreciation deduction with respect to qualified rehabilitation expenditures using a special five-year useful life, the straight-line method of depreciation, and no salvage value. In order to qualify for the five-year write-off, a taxpayer must spend at least $3,000 per dwelling unit for rehabilitation during a two-year period. In addition, not more than $15,000 in expenditures per dwelling unit will qualify for the accelerated depreciation. The threshold limitation is designed to assure that the rehabilitation is a substantial one, not just a painting and general fix-up; and the ceiling limitation is designed to deny the benefit beyond what is needed to do an adequate job for low and moderate income tenants.

The special rehabilitation write-off is available only with respect to "low-income rental housing," which the statute defines as "any building the dwelling units in which are held for occupancy on a rental basis by families and individuals of low or moderate income, as defined by the Secretary (of the Treasury) . . . in a manner consistent with the policies of the Housing and Urban Development Act of 1968 . . ."

The five-year amortization is available only with respect to expenditures incurred after July 24, 1969, and before January 1, 1975. The termination date will require Congress, the Treasury, the Department of Housing and Urban Development, and the recipients of the tax benefits to examine the effectiveness of the tax incentive in 1974.

In a related provision, the Tax Reform Act provides for "recapture" as ordinary income (instead of as capital gain) of any part of the gain on the sale of rehabilitated property attributable to "additional depreciation"—that is, taken in excess of the straight-line depreciation that would otherwise be allowable in the absence of the special rehabilitation incentive. If, however, the property is held for longer than 100 months, the recapture as ordinary income of "additional depreciation" is gradually phased out at the rate of one percentage point per month.(2) Thus, if the property is held for 200 months, there is no recapture, and the entire gain on the sale is taxed at the preferential capital gains rates. This recapture rule is essentially the same as that provided for new housing other than publicly assisted housing which qualifies for a phase-out rule beginning after 20 months.

The Tax Reform Act of 1969 also provides for a minimum income tax equal to 10 percent of the sum of certain specified tax preferences less the taxpayer's regular income tax and less a $30,000 exemption. By making the rehabilitation write-off a tax preference item subject to the minimum income tax, Congress in effect simultaneously created and partially withdrew this tax preference. In the examples in this paper, it is assumed that an investor has sufficient regular income tax so that the minimum income tax does not apply.

ADMINISTRATIVE INTERPRETATION OF THE STATUTE

One of the alleged advantages of tax subsidies as compared to direct government expenditures is that the former involve less government red tape. Tax subsidies do not require the setting up of a new bureaucracy. Any individual or firm that rehabilitates low income housing is eligible for the subsidy. It is as simple as that.

In actual practice, it is more complicated. After Congress enacted and the President signed the Tax Reform Act in late December, 1969, it became the responsibility of the Treasury Department to issue regulations interpreting and clarifying the statute. Proposed regulations implementing Section 167(k) were published on August 4, 1970,(3) and public testimony was received on November 23, 1970. Final regulations are pending.(4)

The most important issue to be resolved by the regulations is the definition of "low and moderate income." The decision on this issue determines the population group which the subsidy will directly benefit, the revenue loss to the Treasury, and the type of rehabilitation encouraged.

The proposed regulations defined "low and moderate income" as gross family income (reduced by the amount of any trade or business expenses allowed as a deduction under the tax law) not in excess of 150 percent of the maximum income eligibility levels for public housing in local areas. This definition followed the usual income tax definition of income and would have simplified the administration of this housing program by the Internal Revenue Service. While in many respects this definition is comparable to the definition of income used for current FHA programs, there are significant differences. Under the FHA Section 236 program, a family qualifies if its "adjusted income" does not exceed 135 percent of the local income eligibility limits for public housing. However, FHA allows a deduction of 5 percent of total income plus $300 for each minor. Also, income earned by minors is not taken into account. As a result, it would be possible for a family to qualify under the 135 percent FHA standard and fail under the 150 percent standard contained in the proposed regulations. In addition, the Section 236 program has an "exception" income limit equal to 90 percent of the income limits under the FHA Section 221(d)(3) housing program.(5)

Table I gives the income limits for a family of four for New Orleans, New York, and Washington, D.C.. Under the proposed regulations, a four-person family in New Orleans with income of less than $7,200 per year would have been considered as a family of low or moderate income. In contrast, the 135

TABLE I—HUD INCOME LIMITS, APRIL 1971
(FOUR PERSON FAMILY)

City	135 Percent of Public Housing Income Limit	150 Percent of Public Housing Income Limit	90 Percent of Section 221(d)(3) Income Limit
New Orleans	$6,480	$7,200	$7,400
New York City	8,555	9,506	10,800
Washington, D.C.	6,885	7,650	8,950

SOURCE: Department of Housing and Urban Development.

percent standard would imply an income limit of $6,480, and the Section 236 exception limit would permit eligibility up to $7,400.

Witnesses at the hearings on the proposed regulations stressed the importance of conforming the income limits under the regulations with the income limits established for HUD programs. After consideration of this testimony, the Treasury Department decided that the taxpayer should be given an option. The final regulations will define low or moderate income as "adjusted income" not in excess of 90 percent of the Section 221(d)(3) income limits. The taxpayer may compute the adjusted income of a family under either the tax law concept contained in the proposed regulations or the income concept used for the Section 236 program. The taxpayer must use the same method of computing adjusted income with respect to each occupant of a dwelling unit during the taxable year, but may use one method with respect to the occupants of one dwelling unit and the other method with respect to the occupants of another dwelling unit.

Other issues which must be resolved by the regulations include whether the five-year write-off may be claimed by an investor who first places the rehabilitated property in service but did not own the property when it was rehabilitated; whether the five-year write-off may be claimed by an investor who leases rehabilitated units to a public housing authority which subleases to qualified tenants; how costs should be allocated which are attributable to more than one dwelling unit or partly attributable to commerical units; and whether costs to provide parking qualify for the five-year write-off. Until these kinds of issues can be resolved by final regulations, there is investor uncertainty whether particular expenditures will qualify for the rehabilitated incentive.

REDUCTION IN THE RENTAL COST OF CAPITAL

The significance of an acceleration in the allowable depreciation deductions can be gauged by computing the reduction in the rental cost of capital, which is the price an investor must pay (or impute to himself) for the use of capital assets. The rental cost of capital is the price for the use of physical capital, just as the wage rate is the price for the use of labor services. It includes an amount for capital recovery, a net after-tax return on the amount invested, and the tax on this income. If the tax "bite" is large, the corresponding capital cost is also large. An acceleration of tax depreciation reduces the tax bite and thus reduces the rental cost of capital.

The rental cost of capital is the underpinning of recent empirical work to determine the influence of tax incentives on investment. The underlying model assumes that a reduction in the cost of capital increases the desired capital stock. Investment then depends on a lagged relationship between the desired and actual capital stock. Though data are not available to permit a measurement of the impact of the new tax incentive on the amount of rehabilitation, we can indicate the magnitude of the reduction in the cost of capital.

The derivation of the cost of capital in models of investment in machinery and equipment generally assumes an infinite time horizon and continuous replacement.(6) In adapting the cost of capital concept to real estate investments, it is probably better to assume that the investor is considering the purchase of one building and planning to hold it for "n" years. The building is a desirable investment only if the discounted value of the future cash flow is greater than or equal to the initial outlay. The neoclassical theory of capital accumulation assumes that investment will occur until the discounted cash flow is equal to the initial outlay. Using this equilibrium assumption, the rental cost is determined as follows:

$$K_0 = \sum_{t=1}^{n} (R_t - T_t)(1 + r)^{-t} + (S_n - RT_n - GT_n)(1 + r)^{-n}$$

where,

K_0 = initial purchase price
R_t = rental income, net of operating costs

T_t = income taxes, except on sale
S_n = sale price at end of year "n"
RT_n = recapture taxes in year "n"
GT_n = capital gains taxes in year "n"
r = discount rate.

However,

$$T_t = m(R_t - D_t)$$

where,

m = marginal tax rate
D_t = depreciation deduction.

Thus,

$$K_o = (1 - m) \sum_{t=1}^{n} R_t (1 + r)^{-t} + m \sum_{t=1}^{n} D_t(1 + r)^{-t} + (S_n - RT_n - GT_n)(1 + r)^{-n}$$

Letting PV ( ) equal the present value of the variable in parentheses, $PV(R_t)$ must equal:

$$PV(R_t) = \frac{K_o - mPV(D_t) - PV(S_n) + PV(RT_n) + PV(GT_n)}{1 - m}$$

The last equation above indicates that an investor is only willing to invest in real estate if the present value of the future rents net of operating costs is equal to the expression on the right hand side of the equation, which includes an amount for capital recovery, a net after-tax rate of return on the amount invested, and the tax on this income. A liberalization of tax depreciation will affect not only the depreciation deductions but also the recapture and capital gains taxes. If variables designated by an asterisk indicate the value of these variables after a liberalization of tax depreciation, the percentage reduction in the rental cost is equal to 100 times:

$$1 - \frac{PV(R_t)^*}{PV(R_t)} =$$

$$\frac{m[PV(D_t)^* - PV(D_t)] - [PV(RT_n)^* - PV(RT_n)] - [PV(GT_n)^* - PV(GT_n)]}{K_o - mPV(D_t) - PV(S_n) + PV(RT_n) + PV(GT_n)}$$

Before computing the percentage reduction in the rental cost due to the rehabilitation incentive, two caveats should be made about this last equation. First, no allowance is made for debt financing. As a result, the discount rate is the required after-tax rate of return on both the debt and the equity portions of the investment. It would be possible to define the rental cost of capital so the cash flows include all the cash flows of the debt financing associated with the investment. Then the discount rate becomes the required after-tax rate of return on the equity portion of the investment.

Second, the results are sensitive to the assumption concerning the sales price. Since little is known about how the sales price varies with the holding period, the analysis does not permit much to be said about the optimal holding period.

TABLE 2
PERCENTAGE REDUCTION IN THE RENTAL COST OF CAPITAL(9)

| Holding | Discount Rate | |
period	10 percent	15 percent
Sale price = adjusted basis of property under straight-line depreciation with a 20-year useful life.		
10 years	15.7%	15.3%
20 years	14.5	15.0
Sale price = original cost		
10 years	20.5	17.6
20 years	17.2	15.9

Table 2 gives the percentage reductions in the rental cost of capital due to the five-year write-off for rehabilitation expenditures for discount rates of 10 and 15 percent and holding periods of 10 and 20 years. It is assumed that the investor is in the 50 percent tax bracket and that the alternative to the five-year write-off is SYD depreciation(7) with a 20-year useful life. Two alternative assumptions are made concerning the sales price. First, the sales price is equal to the adjusted basis of the property if the property had been depreciated under the straight-line method of depreciation with a 20-year useful life. Second, the sales price is equal to the original cost.

Under the first sales price assumption, the reduction in the rental cost is approximately 15 percent for an investor using either a 10 or 15 percent discount rate and planning to hold the property 10 or 20 years. Under the second sales price assumption, the reduction in the rental cost is somewhat greater, especially for the lower discount rate and the shorter holding period. These reductions in the rental cost are considerably greater than the reductions resulting from the 7 percent investment tax credit available for new investments in machinery and equipment.(8)

Put another way, the rehabilitation incentive could reduce significantly the rent per unit of housing service which must be charged tenants of rehabilitated buildings.(10) Indeed the primary rationale for the incentive is cast in these terms: a better pattern of distribution of real income through improvements in the housing of certain tenant households. We now turn to the probable character and extent of these benefits.

THE INCENTIVE AS A MECHANISM FOR PROVIDING BENEFITS

Two basic areas of inquiry can be identified. The first we will term "program efficiency": Of the tax revenue forgone when accelerated depreciation is allowed, how much actually flows through to tenants? Second, how are the benefits which do flow through distributed among tenants? To amplify, what income levels of renters are likely to receive assistance? And among households receiving assistance, do they receive basically the same amount of benefit, or is there a variance in subsidy by measure of need? In appraising these questions, we will examine the incentive both in terms of program independence and of program coordination. Under the latter assumption, the incentive is employed in conjunction with direct programs for rehabilitation sponsored by HUD (or the Department of Agriculture).

It is worth stating here the judgment that, if the rehabilitation incentive is to become a major housing program, it will have to work independently of direct subsidies. If the incentive finds its predominant use as a coordinated program, the incremental aggregate benefits which it makes available to tenants will be small. This is so because major HUD programs involving assistance for the rehabilitation of privately owned rental housing all provide subsidies for new construction as well as rehabilitation. If the overall demand for expenditure subsidies under these programs exceeds the funds appropriated by Congress—as is likely to be the case for the foreseeable future(11)—any increments to rehabilitated housing will not represent net benefits to tenants as a group. Rather, they will represent primarily the substitution of subsidized rehabilitated units for subsidized new units. We will develop the more detailed implications of this point later.

THE REHABILITATION INCENTIVE AS AN INDEPENDENT POLICY

Our analysis of the probable effects of the incentive as an independent policy results in the following hypotheses which should be tested empirically as the incentive is in fact elected by investors. The first is that relatively few renter households within the range of "low-to-moderate incomes" which Congress intended to assist will receive benefits from independent use of the incentive. The second is that the households which do benefit will tend to be those of "moderate incomes," clustered close to the maximum permitted income limits. The second hypothesis stems from the profitability aspects of the incentive, and we will discuss it first.

From the landlord's viewpoint, the requirement under the incentive that units be occupied by low or moderate income households is a constraint, not an objective. Any household which can barely be shoehorned in under the income limits makes the investor eligible to take just as large a depreciation allowance as if he rented the unit to a household with zero income.(12) On general economic grounds, landlords are likely to prefer higher income tenants. Such tenants are clearly able to pay higher rents for a given level of service. In addition, the costs of providing a given level of service over time to higher income households may be lower.(13) For example, they may cause less wear and tear on the property, thus extending its useful life and/or enabling a reduction in expenditures on maintenance. There is also a smaller likelihood of rent delinquency and non-payment.

The basic point is that the tax incentive fails to provide any positive inducement to landlords to rent rehabilitated units to households who are more than marginally below the income maximums or have other specific household characteristics, e.g., only one parent present, large numbers of minors per adult, etc., which may increase operating costs and affect profitability.

Even if landlords are less than singleminded in trying to attract and hold tenants of the highest possible incomes and the most favorable behavioral characteristics which will still allow them to elect the incentive, it will not in general be feasible for them to elect the incentive if their tenants are low in the range of incomes potentially eligible. It is the first hypothesis which we stated earlier—that of benefits being provided to relatively few renter households—which is primarily a function of feasibility rather than profitability of independent use of the incentive.

In this context, it is the effect on rents following rehabilitation of the threshold level of $3,000 in expenditures that is of crucial importance. Although, as we have shown in Section III, the availability of the incentive enables landlords to charge rents lower than they would otherwise charge, they will not, in general, invest in a minimum of $3,000 in rehabilitation unless the absolute level of rents they charge increases substantially.

One commonly used rule of thumb in real estate is that the monthly gross rent must be equal to approximately one percent of capital value to justify investment in housing. But studies of specific housing markets which actually serve low income tenants—the older core areas of Oakland and Newark—indicate that multifamily rental property is traded at multiples of gross annual rent which generally do not exceed four and may be even lower,(14) implying monthly gross rent equal to approximately two percent of capital value. This in turn implies a monthly rent increase of slightly over $60 following $3000 of rehabilitation.

One offsetting factor relating to rehabilitation must be mentioned. The rule of thumb relationships between gross rent and capital value typically allow for costs to the owner of paying for heat and other utilities and carrying out routine maintenance and repairs. These expenses vary, but tend to run roughly 25 percent of the rent or monthly housing expense of units serving the lower segment of the market.(15) Expenditures on rehabilitation do not in any obvious way increase and may decrease utility and maintenance costs, assuming tenants of the same market level are served.

We set forth, therefore, the tentative judgment that landlords would require monthly rent increases of roughly 1.5 percent of the amount spent on rehabilitation. It is perhaps suggestive that this is the same relationship between rent increases and rehabilitation costs as the allowable maximum during the recently concluded wage-price freeze and under current Phase II rent stabilization regulations.(16) For the $3000 threshold level of expenditures, monthly rents would have to increase by about $45 per unit.

As we have previously shown, however, use of the rehabilitation incentive by a taxpayer in the 50 percent bracket lowers the rental cost of capital by approximately 15 percent. This would enable the minimum rent increase to be cut from $45 to about $38.

It we assume that landlords will have difficulty obtaining rent increases of more than 25 percent from their current tenants—even for units providing higher levels of service—the minimum pre-rehabilitation rent for occupied units would be approximately $150. The rent following rehabilitation would then increase to $188. If we make the further assumption that households should pay no more than 25 percent of income for rent—the normal maximum cost for residents of Federally subsidized housing—the minimum annual income required would be approximately $9,000 ($188 x 4 x 12). Referring to Table I, this implied minimum income is higher than the maximum income limits in New Orleans for a four-person family, approximately the same as the maximum in Washington,

D.C., and clearly lower only for New York City.

This reasoning points to a more general characteristic of the incentive. The threshold effect on rent increases, and the implied minimum income of households who could benefit does not vary by household size or housing market area. In contrast, maximum income limits are lower for smaller households and for areas of lower housing cost. Therefore, smaller households and households in lower cost areas, at a given level of income, have a much lower probability of receiving assistance than do large households and households in higher cost areas. Indeed, it seems highly unlikely that any benefits at all under the incentive will be provided to one- and two-person households. Put another way, in high cost areas, $3,000 of rehabilitation implies a smaller amount of real rehabilitation, and as a result the threshold limit is less of a constraint.

The way in which the minimum income cutoff was constructed admittedly involves a chain of assumptions which can introduce considerable cumulative error. We simply do not know enough about the range of tenant and landlord behavior under the incentive to provide a compelling, precise estimate. Specifically, landlords might find it feasible to rehabilitate units for households below our specified cutoff because of some combination of the following: the landlord may feel the possibility of capital gains is excellent for a particular structure; he may view the behavioral characteristics of particular tenants as excellent in terms of prompt rent payment and minimum wear and tear on the structure; and financing may be available on particularly favorable terms.

Notwithstanding possible variance in outcomes, however, the existence and importance of a threshold effect in terms of the minimum incomes of households which can typically be served under the incentive seem clear. A landlord in the 50 percent bracket with occupied units would tend to elect the incentive only if he felt that (a) current tenants were eligible under the income limits and were able and willing to pay monthly rent increases of roughly $38 or more, or (b) he could fairly easily attract new tenants with higher incomes—and rent-paying ability—that would still be below the maximums.

Under the second assumption, the landlord replaces tenants who make the rehabilitation unfeasible, because they cannot afford the indicated rent increases. In this case, however, the incentive reduces the housing choice of the lower income tenants required to move. The rehabilitated units are then rented to households that are already relatively better off. This seems a perverse outcome for a desirable public policy; indeed it is parallel to an often criticized distributional effect of urban renewal projects.(17)

There are at least two other possible situations which would permit benefits to a wider range of eligible tenants. First, some landlords may have accumulated so much deferred maintenance that expenditures on rehabilitation may be required simply to maintain present rent levels. In these cases, taxpayers may carry out the rehabilitation, elect the incentive, and increase rents very little, if at all. One must be extremely cautious, however, in attributing this rehabilitation expenditure to the existence of the incentive. If they were truly necessary to assure a continued flow of income, many of these enpenditures would take place in the normal course of events.

A second set of circumstances where the incentive is claimed and may clearly be of benefit to lower income tenants is when a building is vacant. In these circumstances, however, sufficient rent will have to be charged to earn a return on the pre-rehabilitation value of the property, the expenditure on rehabilitation, and the current costs of maintenance and operation, including local property taxes. The ability of the incentive to reduce rents applies only to the portion of those costs attributable to rehabilitation. And, as we have indicated, even for those costs the effect is limited—approximately 15 percent for a taxpayer in the 50 percent bracket.

Although acknowledging these other possibilities, our overall judgment is that the rehabilitation incentive operating as an independent program will not make possible rehabilitation in the lower portions of the eligible range of incomes.

We will now attempt to summarize the probable nature and character of benefits to tenants under the assumption of program independence. The first question which we posed was that of "program efficiency"—the extent to which benefits paid to the taxpayer are shifted to the tenant. It is not easy to give a clear answer to this question. In a sense, the question is irrelevant since the maximum percentage reduction in the rental costs of capital is so small that landlords typically will not be able to obtain the minimum absolute rent increase necessary from eligible tenants to make the threshold level of rehabilitation feasible. Under circumstances where rehabilitation is feasible, however, our judgment is that benefits will be shifted in substantial part to tenants. This margin of feasibility is so narrow that landlords must flow through benefits to tenants in order to persuade the latter to agree to the necessary rent increases.

The second issue is how those benefits to tenants are distributed. The probable answer to this question is, as we have seen, more clearcut. The incentive provides no additional inducement to select tenants with incomes more than marginally below the maximum necessary to qualify. It is, therefore, neither as profitable nor as feasible to rehabilitate for tenants with incomes much below the eligibility limits. It also will be difficult in terms of feasibility to rehabilitate for very small households (one and two persons) since the per-unit expenditures required are the same as for larger households, but the maximum income limits are lower. A similar pattern applies in the case of low cost and high cost geographic areas.

THE REHABILITATION INCENTIVE AS A COORDINATED PROGRAM

As we have indicated, the rehabilitation incentive operating independently is not likely to provide benefits for low income tenants, although it may provide assistance to some moderate income households. There are, however, subsidy programs operated by HUD which can be used for rehabilitation of rental housing and which have a much greater capacity to reduce rents than does the tax incentive acting independently. In this section, we will describe one such program and examine the probable effects if the tax incentive is corrdinated with it.

In terms of currently available contract authority, the major HUD program which can be used to subsidize rents in privately owned rental housing which has been rehabilitated is Section 236.(18) The basic vehicle for subsidy is interest reduction. It enables the lowering of mortgage payments from an amount required to amortize a "market rate" FHA mortgage—including payment of the annual mortgage insurance premium—down to an amount that would be required for principal and interest if the mortgage bore an interest rate of one percent with no mortgage insurance premium payment.

One illustrative analysis of the maximum rent-reducing effect of this subsidy shows that the monthly market rent that would have to be charged for an "average" unit in a typical privately owned rehabilitation project with an FHA-guaranteed mortgage is $170. If HUD pays the interest subsidy available under Section 236 on behalf of the owner to the mortgage holder, rent could be reduced to $115, a 32.5 percent decrease.(19) At a rent of $115 and assuming a maximum rent-income ratio of 25 percent, tenants with incomes as low as $5,500 could be served.(20)

One feature of all HUD expenditure programs is that they contain mechanisms to provide "program efficiency." That is, the subsidies are designed explicitly to translate into lower rents for tenants. Under Section 236, program efficiency is handled by the device of computing "fair market rents." The rents are established—at least theoretically—at a level which allows limited-dividend owners of projects at 6 percent return before taxes on their equity investment. In view of the general rates of return demanded by real estate investors, it is evident that they would not be willing to invest at all in such projects were it not for the other obvious source of "income:" the tax shelter provided by the depreciation allowances.(21) Since the normal subsidized housing project is 90 percent debt-financed while depreciation is a function of the total cost of a real estate investment, the allowable depreciation—assuming the 200 percent declining balance or sum of the year's-digits method—is quite large in relation to the equity investment. Depending on the precise assumptions surrounding the circumstances of the sale of the project, the value of the tax shelter on new construction housing under Section 236 can bring the after-tax yield on equity to an investor in the 50 percent bracket in the range of 15 percent.(22)

If the explicit cash return on the equity and the implicit benefit from the tax shelter afforded by generous depreciation allowances provide a sufficient return to investors so that a Section 236 project is feasible, the benefits provided by expenditure subsidies translate into equivalent rent reductions to tenants. In the case of Section 236, the interest reduction payments do not increase the return to the owner but simply enable him to lower the rents charged tenants below what they would otherwise be. In addition, the amount of expenditure subsidy paid to a project—up to a maximum—is larger the lower are the incomes of tenant households. This enables distribution of benefits to tenants over a range of income levels.

As we have indicated above, HUD expenditure subsidies for the rehabilitation of rental housing under Section 236 make available a potential for rent reductions to tenants which substantially exceeds that provided by the rehabilitation incentive alone. If this is true, why provide a tax incentive on top of the existing program? One obvious reason might be that this would induce private owners to charge even lower rents. In turn, this would permit better housing to be made available to households of lower incomes than would otherwise be possible.

In analyzing whether this will in fact happen, we must distinguish between two possible ways in which use of the incentive might lower rents. The first we will term the direct effect. Owners of subsidized housing claim rehabilitation would simply reduce the rents they charge to tenants in order to reflect—at least in part—the tax benefits they receive.

It is highly unlikely that this will happen under the Section 236 program as it is currently being operated. As we have indicated, the method of establishing "fair market rents" and the cash return on equity by profit-motivated investors under this program take no account of that portion of the investor's return provided by the tax shelter. If, therefore, the value of the tax shelter is increased through election of the five-year write-off, nothing in the Section 236 program would require, or even encourage owners to lower the rents they charge. And since expenditure subsidies already permit owners to offer units to tenants at below-market rents, it is doubtful that, if the tax incentive were elected, market pressures would cause further rent reductions.

Thus, under present legislation and institutional arrangements, the direct effect of the rehabilitation incentive as coordinated with Section 236 programs will be zero "program efficiency"—the entire benefit of the incentive will accrue to the investor. Indeed, at least two examinations of the incentive have been based implicitly on this assumption.

One illustrative analysis, carried out by Arnold H. Diamond and John Dickie, indicates that election of the rehabilitation incentive in coordination with a section 236 project makes available to investors in the 50 percent bracket annual after-tax discounted rates of return on equity ranging from 34 to 56 percent.(23)

Another appraisal by James E. Wallace explicitly separates the function of the developer and investor, approaching the issue under the assumption of "tax shelter syndication."(24) This institutional approach is used because the developer of a limited-dividend Section 236 project typically does not have sufficient other income to take maximum advantage of the tax shelter created. A limited partnership is therefore formed. The developer is the general partner, retaining control over basic business decisions relating to the project. The limited partners are primarily passive investors. Their involvement consists of capital investment in return for which they receive a share of the project—basically a share of the tax shelter which they can use to offset other taxable income.

In this analysis, it is assumed that the limited partners require a 25% after tax return on their equity investment in Section 236 rehabilitation projects. Based on Wallace's assumption about sales price and calculation of optimal holding period, the present value of the tax shelter plus the annual 6 percent dividend is such that an investor or investors in the 50% bracket could pay a capital contribution or "development fee" to the general partner equal to 18 percent of the mortgage amount.(25) Wallace estimates that the expected returns both to the developer and passive investors are considerably higher than for a comparable new construction project under Section 236. Clearly, investment in rehabilitation appears to be a very attractive proposition.

The attractiveness of the incentive to housing developers and investors may shift the mix of subsidized housing toward rehabilitation and away from new construction. This may result in benefits to tenants through what we will call the indirect effect. Rehabilitation is generally thought to be less expensive than new construction, in many instances, as a way of making available a set of housing services of acceptable quality. It is difficult to document this assertion; at present neither an adequate conceptual framework nor a body of data on comparable projects exists to carry out a definitive analysis. There is, however, some evidence which leads to the tentative judgment that rehabilitation can produce units with rents or monthly housing expenses approximately 20 percent lower than for comparable new construction.(26)

Since the minimum rents which can be charged to tenants under the subsidy formula for Section 236 are a fraction of the monthly occupancy cost (or rent) for units assuming no interest subsidy, and since this fraction does not differ significantly for the two forms of construction, the minimum rents for rehabilitated units can be lower. Specifically, if we assume that unsubsidized occupancy costs for rehabilitation are 20 percent lower, then subsidized rents can also be about 20 percent lower.(27)

If the owners of Section 236 rehabilitation projects respond by renting to tenants requiring the maximum interest subsidy, then an equal number of tenants with incomes 20 percent lower can be served than with new construction. Alternatively, owners of rehabilitation projects can respond by renting units to tenants with the same incomes as those in comparable new construction projects. Under this assumption, smaller amounts of per-unit subsidy are required with rehabilitation, and somewhere between 20 and 25 percent more housing units could receive assistance.(28)

The actual aggregate response will probably include some of both—more units and more lower income tenants. As is the case with independent use of the incentive, the economic returns to owners do not increase if they rent to tenants of the lowest possible incomes. Indeed, these returns may be lower if maintenance and operating costs increase for such tenants. Unlike independent use of the incentive, however, the fact that the amount of expenditure subsidy increases as tenant incomes decrease makes extension of benefits feasible. Owners in certain market circumstances, moreover, may have to rent to tenants over a reasonably wide range of incomes to keep their projects fully occupied. They may also be under pressure from HUD and local community groups to make benefits available to tenants of the lowest possible incomes.

We can now evaluate the probable effects of coordinated use of the incentive. It will not, as we have seen, lead to any tenant benefits through direct rent reductions. Benefits to tenants in the form of lower rents and net additional units subsidized will only occur indirectly as rehabilitation is substituted for new construction that would otherwise have taken place.

It is not at all clear how much substitution there will be. If significant cost advantages to the use of rehabilitation under Section 236 are truly present, one could argue that it is not necessary to have a tax incentive in order to achieve substantial use of rehabilitation. Existing HUD procedures for the allocation of contract authority for subsidy payments among proposed housing projects might be expected to take the lower comparative costs of rehabilitation into account. Yet despite their supposed cost advantage, projects involving rehabilitation amount only to approximately 5 percent of the housing units started under Section 236.(29)

It is only within the last two years, however, that HUD has really organized to make a serious and concerted effort to produce rehabilitated rental housing under its subsidized programs. The November 1969 reorganization which divided the responsibility for housing production and housing management within HUD involved the establishment of an Office of Assistant Commissioner for Rehabilitation. This provided a previously lacking focus for rehabilitation efforts within the Department. That office is currently concentrating on Project Rehab, a major effort to stimulate relatively large scale rehabilitation of rental property. Project Rehab is currently operating actively in 20 cities with an initial goal of renovating approximately 37,500 dwelling units within a two-year period.(30)

Given the past lack of success in the achievement of a significant volume of rehabilitated rental housing under HUD programs, making Project Rehab succeed is not going to be easy. The availability of a tax incentive to encourage participation by developers and investors is surely welcome to those at HUD trying to run the program—it is an additional "carrot" they can offer.

It is difficult to predict precisely how the availability of the incentive and the implementation of Project Rehab will lead to changes in the process by which developers request and HUD grants subsidies for the rehabilitation of rental housing. The rehabilitation share of the units assisted under Section 236 will not increase significantly unless such changes take place.

What can be said is that there are a variety of barriers to the achievement of a larger volume of rehabilitation under Section 236. Further, the parameters of the tax incentive do not relate in any clearcut way to these problems. Previous efforts to rehabilitate—both by nonprofit and profit-motivated developers—have often floundered on the shoals of: government red tape and lack of coordination among different government agencies (e.g., the Federal Housing Administration, local urban renewal authorities, local code enforcement agencies); community participation in the planning, execution, and the management and operation of rehabilitation projects; the provision of opportunities for contractors, employment and manpower training for minority groups; and relocation of families unable to afford rents following rehabilitation.(31)

It seems clear that the rehabilitation incentive was not designed to deal in any precise way with the problems which have plagued rehabilitation under HUD-subsidized programs in the past. The intent of Section 167(k)—to the extent that we have been able to determine it—was to act as a rather general encourager of rehabilitation which could be administered relatively simply within the broad framework of the Internal Revenue Code. It is extremely unlikely, therefore, that it would turn out to be precisely the sort of incentive that would mesh smoothly and efficiently with HUD programs providing expenditure subsidies.

Although the process of carrying out rehabilitation of rental housing under Section 236 is subject to uncertainties which are relatively uninfluenced by the incentive (thus making any statement about the inducement of a greater volume of rehabilitation problematical), even under extreme assumptions about this induced effect, the incremental benefits to tenants stemming from it are not likely to be large.

Three factors are of crucial importance in this regard. First, as we noted previously, the demand for expenditure subsidies for rental housing exceeds the available supply, and this relationship is likely to continue to hold. Rehabilitated housing, therefore, must essentially be considered a substitute for, rather than an addition to, newly constructed housing under Section 236.

Second, there are limits in the degree to which rehabilitation can and will be substituted for new construction. For example, Federal programs will want to subsidize new housing in specific locations, e.g., developing suburbs, where use of rehabilitation simply may not be possible. Finally, we have previously estimated that the cost in expenditure subsidies of making available a substantially rehabilitated unit is at least 80 percent of the cost of a newly constructed unit.

The share of total housing units (started with Section 236 assistance) that are rehabilitated is currently, as we have indicated, about 5 percent. If this fraction were to double to ten percent, based on our estimate of comparative costs, this could at most add one percent to the incremental number of subsidized housing units provided. This assumes that landlords rent to tenants at the same income levels as those served by new construction under Section 236. Alternatively, the additional number of subsidized units could remain the same, but about 5 percent more of the households assisted could have incomes as much as 20 percent lower. As we have indicated, however, project owners lack any positive inducement to respond in the latter fashion. The precise distribution of incremental benefits to tenants is clearly uncertain. It can only be determined by a careful empirical study structured in light of these possible alternative responses.

Even small aggregate benefits of this character and magnitude may be judged worthwhile, but they must be evaluated in terms of the administrative complexity and costs of using the incentive and also in terms of alternative ways of accomplishing the same results. One obvious alternative is to provide a fee to developers through an increase in direct expenditure subsidies to Section 236 rehabilitation projects. One could ask why the Treasury Department should, in effect, be in the business of mailing out subsidy checks to developers and investors at the same time HUD is mailing out similar checks to tenants.(32)

CONCLUSION

If the probable effects of the rehabilitation incentive as set forth in this analysis prove to be valid, the tax incentive will result in benefits to lower income tenants which are marginal rather than substantial. Since the incentive is only now being implemented administratively, however, this paper can only be termed a first step—a structuring of certain hypotheses concerning its operation.

The Policy Committee of the AREUEA, in a statement to be submitted to the Association this year, urges the membership to study and evaluate programs affecting housing and the urban environment. One such program is the rehabilitation tax incentive which will expire at the end of 1974 unless Congress extends it. We believe that any Congressional action in 1974 should be based on careful empirical evidence concerning the extent of benefits to lower income households stemming from the incentive, the distribution of those benefits among households of different incomes and other demographic characteristics, and the costs in foregone tax revenues of producing those benefits. This evaluation should also explore thoroughly alternatives for providing improved housing services to those households whom Congress determines should receive government assistance. We hope that our initial efforts will encourage others to focus their research on the usefulness of the rehabilitation tax incentive.

NOTES

(1) Section 167(k)(3)(B) of the Internal Revenue Code of 1954.
(2) If the property is sold during the first year, the entire gain is ordinary

income to the extent of any prior depreciation.

(3) Federal Register, XXXV (August 4, 1970), pp. 12400-04.

(4) The delay in promulgating final regulations is due mainly to the involvement of the Treasury and IRS staff with the new regulations for the depreciation of machinery and equipment. The substance of the final regulations was outlined by Assistant Secretary Cohen in a speech before the Tax Section of the New York Bar Association. See Treasury Department Press Release K-S75, January 28, 1971.

(5) Nationally, up to 20 percent of subsidies authorized under Section 236 may be made available for projects occupied during the initial rent-up period by tenants with incomes above the 135 percent limit, as long as their incomes do not exceed the exception limits.

(6) See, for example, R.E. Hall and D.W. Jorgenson, "Tax Policy and Investment Behavior," The American Economic Review, LVII (June, 1967), pp. 391-414.

(7) Absent the rehabilitation incentive, investment in rehabilitating a structure would be treated as "new housing" for tax purposes and thus be eligible for the double-declining balance or sum of the year's-digits methods of depreciation.

(8) Since the investment tax credit does not require a basis adjustment, the reduction in the rental cost as a result of the credit is greater than 7 percent.

(9) Assumes that the alternative to the five-year write-off is SYD depreciation with a 20-year useful life. The investor is in the 50 percent tax bracket.

(10) Note, however, that the reduction in rental cost as presented above is net of operating cost.

(11) On the likelihood of incremental commitments to pay expenditure subsidies under current HUD programs being held roughly to existing levels in future years, see Housing Affairs Letter 71-13 (April 2, 1971), p. 1; Third Annual Report on National Housing Goals, 92nd Congress, 1st Session, House Document 92-136 (June 29, 1971), pp. 22-24.

(12) Even this income constraint might be termed loose since the proposed regulations provide that any increases in income of continuing tenants subsequent to initial certification have no effect on the ability of the taxpayer to elect the accelerated depreciation. Landlords, therefore, have an inducement to search out upwardly-mobile tenants (those whose current incomes are less than their "normal" or "permanent" incomes).

(13) George Sternlieb discusses the relation of household characteristics to care and maintenance costs, although he does so primarily in the context of race and household composition rather than income alone. The Tenement Landlord (New Brunswick, N.J. 1966), pp. 73-75.

(14) For the discussion of income multipliers, see A.H. Schaaf, Economic Aspects of Urban Renewal: Theory, Policy, and Area Analysis (Berkeley, 1960), pp. 26-27 and Sternlieb, Tenement Landlord, pp. 103-104. Both these studies are somewhat dated as guides to current conditions. Schaaf's work was done about 1957-58 and Sternlieb's mainly in 1965. If anything, however, these studies probably understate the relation of rent to capital value which investors in these submarkets demand today. Several factors point to this conclusion. First, general interest rates were lower during these earlier periods than is true currently. Second, operating and maintenance costs as a percentage of gross

rents were also probably lower than is the case today. Finally, the risk and uncertainty of operating real estate in portions of the lower income sectors of the housing market have probably increased due to concern over urban riots, increased militancy on the part of tenants, possible adverse effects of housing code enforcement on profitability, etc.. For a more recent paper by Sternlieb, based substantially on an empirical study in New York City, which confirms the growing weakness in the low income market and lender reluctance, see "Abandonment and Rehabilitation: What Is To Be Done?" Papers Submitted to Subcommittee on Housing Panels, House Committee on Banking and Currency, Part I (June, 1971), pp. 315-372.

(15) On rental housing, see Sternlieb, Tenement Landlord, pp. 77-78. For similar data on single-family houses with low market value, see F. de Leeuw, "The Demand for Housing: A Review of Cross-Section Evidence," Review of Economics and Statistics, LIII (February, 1971), p. 2.

(16) For the latter, see Federal Register, XXXVI (December 30, 1971), p. 25389. An alternative way of expressing this percentage is to say that landlords will demand a rent increase equal to two percent of capital value times the 75 percent portion of rent not earmarked to cover maintenance and utilities cost.

(17) See Jerome Rothenberg, Economic Evaluation of Urban Renewal (Washington, 1967), Chapter IX, for an excellent discussion of this point.

(18) Virtually all discussion of coordinated use of the incentive at the oral hearings on the proposed regulations and in the literature has been in terms of Section 236. Other programs which seem capable of coordination are the Rent Supplement program and the Section 23 Leased Housing program. They are not discussed here due to space limitations and their lesser quantitative importance. We might note that the analysis presented for Section 236 holds substantially for rent supplements as well; indeed, these programs can be used in tandem in certain circumstances.

(19) R.P. O'Block and R.H. Kuehn, Jr., An Economic Analysis of the Housing and Urban Development Act of 1968 (Boston, 1970), p. 13.

(20) Actual data on operations of the Section 236 program indicate that households of even lower incomes are receiving assistance. The latest reported median income families in Section 236 projects is $5,303. See D.D. Kummerfeld, "The Housing Subsidy System," Papers Submitted to Subcommittee on Housing Panels . . ., Part 2, p. 469.

(21) The subsidized project typically throws off negative taxable income in the early years. These tax losses can be used to shield income which otherwise would be subject to tax. The resulting tax savings then increase the after-tax cash flow from the project.

(22) For a discussion of how tax factors affect the profitability of investment in federally subsidized housing, see A Decent Home, The Report of the President's Committee on Urban Housing (Washington, 1968), pp. 82-85.

(23) See A.H. Diamond, "Tax Incentives and Disincentives: Impressions, Impact, and Implications," Proceedings of the Sixty-third Annual Conference of the National Tax Association (1970), pp. 197-98. The results presented are based on specific assumptions about sales price and holding period. The range of results stems from differing assumptions about the precise amount of equity held by investors and the ability to use the new tax provision providing for tax-free sales of Federally assisted housing under certain circumstances.

(24) "The Role of Federal Income Tax Incentives in the Development and Operation of Low and Moderate Income Housing" (Unpublished paper, 1971). Mr. Wallace is a Ph.D. candidate, Department of Urban Studies and Planning, MIT.

(25) Dividing the "fee" by the mortgage amount is simply a convenient way of scaling it to the magnitude of the project. This fee is gross of some cash expenses the developer must incur; its basic economic function is to provide an entrepreneurial return for "putting the project together."

(26) The only well documented comparative cost study of rehabilitation and new construction based on data for individual projects is that by R. Burchell, J. Hughes, and G. Sternlieb, Housing Costs and Housing Restraints: Newark, New Jersey (New Brunswick, N.J., 1970). By adjusting the data presented there to enable a valid comparison, we estimated that the monthly cost of a rehabilitated unit was about 21 percent lower than for comparable new units. Even here it is not strictly correct to assume that a substantially rehabilitated unit provides the same increment to housing services as a new unit. Some adjustment should probably be made for the amount of housing services which a "substandard" unit would yield if it were not rehabilitated. This is particularly true if rehabilitation involves the relocation of an existing tenant.

(27) The reduction is actually less than 20 percent, since an interest subsidy is a function of capital costs only, and rehabilitated units have a lower ratio of capital related costs to monthly housing expense than does new construction.

(28) It will be less than 25 percent for the same reason given in the preceding footnote.

(29) This estimate is constructed from data in FHA Monthly Report of Operations—Part I, "Project Mortgage Programs" (August, 1971; December, 1970; and December, 1969). There is no upward trend in 1971.

(30) Project Rehab was announced officially in July 1970. Since this administrative restructuring is being implemented simultaneously and in tandem with the rehabilitation incentive, it is going to be extremely difficult to disentangle their separate effects in inducing additional rehabilitation.

(31) These generalizations can be documented by completed research on specific rehabilitation projects. For a comprehensive and illuminating case study of the largest scale rehabilitation effort to date, Boston's BURP program, see L.C. Keyes, Jr., The Boston Rehabilitation Program: An Independent Analysis (Cambridge, 1970).

(32) For one exploratory discussion of how direct fees to developers might be implemented, see Wallace, "Roles of Federal Income Tax Incentives," pp. 24-27.

DEATH OF THE AMERICAN DREAM HOUSE

George Sternlieb

The private house in America is the focal point of the myth/dream/reality of the good life for its middle classes as well as the aspirants to those annointed ranks. The automobile has lost much of its glamour: the boat, the trailer, the vacation to Europe are separately and together becoming powerful symbols, but their use—and excursions involving their use—begins with the house.

To current blue-collar workers, moreover, the private house is what the old postal savings system or employer-automatic wage deductions for the purchase of Liberty Bonds or Savings Bonds or War Bonds were to previous generations—a form of relatively painless savings. For all but the more affluent in our society, a house is not only a home, it is typically a major repository of capital investment and stored equity. As any imaginative architect will testify, houses are purchased to be sold, not to be lived in. Their ultimate sale represents the edge which makes Social Security and Old Age pensions endurable. Possession of a house makes a man a full citizen of the work group.

In this last generation, workingmen of America have moved from being renters to owners. The ramifications of this past shift are far from fully explored, but more important to understand now are the present facts and future realities of the housing stock for American workers. Who builds it? For whom? How? Why? And where?

THE NEW HOME BUSINESS

About 90 percent of all the new private one-family housing under $15,000 built in the United States in 1971, for example, was in the form of mobile home units. This type of configuration will yield approximately 450,000 out of the anticipated 1971 total of two million or so units. Another 400,000 units will be divided nearly evenly between single family homes and multiple family residences supported by government mortgage subsidies under the 235-236 Programs which, depending upon income levels, may bring interest rates down to the 1 percent level. These particular programs are now the primary form of direct federal subsidization of the housing market. (Left out of this discussion are the interminable squabbles on government subsidization of private ownership through preferential tax treatment. Rarely considered are the changes in rents—and possible tax rates—if these nominal windfalls were rectified.)

During the 1930s simple government guarantees of mortgages under the earlier FHA (Federal Housing Administration) programs were sufficient to inspire developers. In more recent years the inflated amounts of government guaranteed indentures, as a function of federal deficits, has increased the interest rate which these bear to the point of making the guarantees in themselves of little use in providing housing. States and municipalities have used the tax-exempt status of their securities with increasing abandon in stepping into the gap. Substantial amounts of housing have been generated under such programs. About a quarter of the states, for example, currently have housing authorities which are financing middle-class housing using tax-exempt securities—and their number is being added to. Again, however, the enormous amount of such tax-exempt securites—windfalls for the rich though they may appear to be—has created a market situation in which the interest rates required to market them is too substantial to permit housing for anything approximating the blue-collar group. In New York City, for example, the Mitchell-Lama Program, which involves tax-exempt 50-year mortgages and local tax exemption up to the 85 percent mark, yields a housing unit renting currently for $90 per month per room. We will come back to why this should be, but for the moment let us accept the case, even though involving perhaps the national high spot in the providing of public housing, as all to characteristic of what has occurred under tax-exempt financing.

In the last decade, the federal government substantially exhausted the potential of even below-market interest rates, which under the 221-d3 Program for example, brought interest rates down to the 3 to 3½ percent level. This too lost its charm and so the 235-236 Programs at the 1 percent level.

Even with these subsidies, however, the absolute costs of amortization involve cash flow requirements of enormous magnitude. Even stretched out over more than lifetime expectancies (50 years with Mitchell-Lama, the 48 years of New Jersey Housing Finance Agency and the like), together with steep rises in local taxation and operating costs, they increasingly leave the working classes out of the spectrum of housing groups that can be accommodated within the present state of the art. In Trenton, New Jersey, for example, 400 units under the 236 Program were just completed at costs of $33,000 per unit. The rents with the full subsidy package approximate $200 a month for two-bedroom units. Since there is an income limit under the 235-236 Program of 135 percent of public-housing admission standards for people who will be subsidized by the program, the answer was to raise the local public-housing limits so that people with incomes of $10,000 and more are presently being housed by a program which was dedicated in its inception to the needs of blue-collar America.

There is a growing body of opinion which holds that the very intervention of governmental subsidy mechanisms into the housing market has served to engender additional increases in the housing costs which they were intended to resolve.

Residential construction costs in America over the last twenty years have never been forced to meet the test of the market. When housing starts to slow down, when land speculators begin to be worried about the inflated values of their holdings, when building-trade workers start shading their prices, the cry comes up that something must be done about housing and a new stimulant is added to the market. This is all in good cause and good conscience. The result, however, is that private conventional housing in much of the Northeast has substantially disappeared at anything under the $25,000 mark; indeed in many of the more affluent suburbs one would have to add another $10,000 to the cost.

In many cases the blue-collar worker finds himself too poor to compete in the unaided market and too rich or sometimes too poor to take advantage of the current forms of government subsidy. There is little in the way of technological innovation which would seem to alter this picture. The answer presently being implemented, in any case, is the lessening of housing quality, size of structure and general lowering of standards; and all of these efforts succeed only at best in momentarily stabilizing prices.

The new private house may be the dream of blue-collar America; its reality, however, is drifting away.

THE SUBURBAN SQUEEZE PLAY

The question of where new housing is to be built is one of the most publicized elements in the current dilemma. It has been highlighted not only in terms of the provision of housing but also for securing a variety of public ends.

There has been a significant upgrading of land use requirements in most suburbs. In the northern half of New Jersey, for example, more than half of all the vacant land zoned for residential purposes requires lots of one or more acres. And this, to any good, concerned citizen is prima facie evidence of the wickedness and sinfulness of the suburbanite. To paraphrase Berthold Brecht: the rich (and the middle-class and the blue-collar worker) may love the poor, but they hate living near them. This is particularly true when their skin color or languages may be different from the mainstream.

Without minimizing the role that prejudice undoubtedly plays in suburban freezeout, one should also not disregard the old-fashioned role of economics. The poor cost more. To use very rough numbers, if one assumes that local realty taxes (which are the main source of revenue for community expenditures) represent at most 25 percent of the rent dollar (and in public housing typically the payments in lieu of local tax are only 10 percent of the gross shelter rent) it becomes very evident that typical local revenues derived from poor families are inadequate to provide the schooling of even one child. This is without attention being paid to any of the other increments in cost generated by the addition of a family. And the same holds true for the blue-collar worker at typical incomes.

In some unique, highly affluent suburbs, liberal forces are at work to crack the suburban barrier. In Princeton, New Jersey, for example, there are presently under consideration more than 500 units of public and low-income housing. The resistance to this addition comes not so much from the affluent of the community as it does from the lingering remnants of blue-collar workers and low-level municipal employees—from the policemen making $10,000 a year and paying 10 percent of it in local taxes, from the maintenance working working in the local RCA plant and third generation in the community, owning a house and feeling it slipping from his fingers as local taxes increase at a 10 percent-a-year, compounded annually, rate.

The great bulk of government programs which intervene in the municipal sphere at best supply subsidies for capital grants; at worst they tend to involve the community, practically willy-nilly, in greater levels of operating cost. Until, and unless, there is some fiscal packaging of the local costs generated by the additions of moderate and low-income families to the community, the political reality—"cracking zoning is suicide"—will hold. The recent California court decision, Serrano et al. v. Ivy Baker Priest, which declared that substantial dependence on local property taxes violated the equal protection clause of the Fourteenth Amendment, may have much more in the way of positive results in opening up the suburbs than all of the efforts at intervention based upon racial equity.

In the meantime, however, the blue-collar workers, particularly those who reside in the older suburbs, guard the walls as best they can from the middle-class aspirants who are fleeing the central city. Certainly this is in substantial part because of prejudice but even more through economic fear.

Racial factors cloak basic economic elements and keep us from coming to political grips with them at great general cost. And for proof that these fears within the parameters of present societal organization are not merely fantasies, the suburban blue collars have only to look at the plight of those of their fellows who remain in the central city.

TRAPPED IN THE CITY

There are many profundities that have been exchanged on the subject of the relatively poor interface between older ethnic minorities, particularly those in the blue-collar occupations/income levels and the black and Puerto Rican populations within central cities. Perhaps so obvious as to be beneath intellectualizing are the impacts of the basic economic elements.

Newark, as in so many other areas, is a clear-cut prototype. The current tax rate is approximately 8 percent of real value. The worker residing in the city—perhaps in one of its white enclaves—or for that matter, since skin color is irrelevant here, the new minority-group homebuyers find that the house, that may have been purchased a dozen years ago and which was looked forward to as the essential cushion for the Florida retirement or as the cash with which to make the down payment on a more desirably sited residence, is instead a dead end. The man that can afford a $1,600 tax bill on a modest $20,000 house doesn't want to live in Newark; the man who can only afford $20,000 for a house can't afford the tax bill. And in neither case is there a bank to grant a mortgage or an insurance company to give essential coverage. The blue-collar worker in Newark is joined by his equivalent on the police department or the fire department in a strong resentment against those who he feels have occasioned this impasse.

There is an interesting variation in owner attitudes towards the central city's problems. In a recent survey of Newark absentee owners, typically of multiple tenancies, viewed their tenants as their prime problem. Resident owners, on the other hand, ranked taxes and tax increases as the premier difficulty and this is a response which is substantially independent of race. Whether in the central city or in some of the older suburbs that are open for mixed occupancy, there are an increasing number of black home-owners typically recruited either from the ranks of the better paid blue-collar workers or equivalent income levels of white-collar and governmental operations. Their attitudes and responses, at least to our surveys, are much more in accord with the economic frame of reference, regardless of their skin color, than they are of any racial element.

THE MYTH OF HOME-OWNERSHIP

For the first time since the Second World War the level of multiple-tenancy housing starts will exceed that of private one-family houses. In part this is a tribute to the characteristics of our new household formation; the post-war baby boom is rapidly coming to fruition; the children of 1946, 1947, 1948, 1949 are forming the new households of 1971 and must be housed. Typically this takes on the form of the garden apartment house or its equivalent. But these accommodations, in turn, at least according to folklore and for that matter much reality of the recent past, are viewed by consumers as essentially way stations on the life cycle, serving as a temporary abode until (with one-and-a-half children) the migration is made to the one-family tract development. There is increasing evidence that at least for the blue-collar workers in America and for all others of equivalent income this may no longer be a tenable mode.

As pointed out earlier, the well of housing subsidies is beginning to run dry; its effects no longer, at least in the higher-cost areas of the country, adequate in providing modest one-family developments in conventional settings. Again the response in earlier years has been to increase the level of subsidies in one form or another. The question may well be asked, given the political pressures that are so virile in housing, as to whether this process may be repeated in the future.

WORLD COMPETITION AND AMERICAN LABOR

There is a substantial question, however, as to whether Americans still have their old options open to them to choose internal domestic policy on housing as well as other areas. The current economic difficulties of the United States will continue after Vietnam; they will continue regardless of the political complexion of the administration. They might not have occurred quite so quickly with more foresighted economic policies, but it is my thesis that they would have occurred nevertheless.

The gap in wage scales of American production workers as compared with those in hitherto less fortunate parts of the world is not new. In previous years, however, it was buffered by relatively high transportation costs and time lags affecting the foreign competitor. Further, American wage scales for blue-collar employment, particularly, were supported by a level of unparalleled capital intensification and managerial and technological expertise. Now both of these conditions are rapidly dissipating. Japan, Italy and Formosa dominate the Sears

Roebuck catalogue.

The development of great supertankers and container ships is being paralleled in terms of dry cargo. The manufacture of labor-intensive products such as brassieres, for example, first shifted to Puerto Rico and now with the minimum wages there moved further afield to Formosa, to Hong Kong, to Singapore. This will be happening to more and more goods.

Other than agricultural products and a few very high cost, high technology items which the United States scale of market and financing have supported (computers and airplanes are cases in point) there are very few things that the United States does so singularly well as to support production workers' wage levels which are at least double those of the competition.

Both American technological innovation and American housing have been supported by the relative cheapness of financing in the United States. In France, for example, housing mortgages of more than 15 years are very rare indeed and conventionally they have been for no more than half the face value of the property. Even our close neighbor Canada until fairly recently has had no financing mechanisms for housing that come even close to matching those available in private United States markets, to say nothing of the government-supported efforts.

But these may be things of the past. We have already seen in the space of not much more than 20 months a very Republican president forced into a series of economic postures earlier antithetical both to his party and to himself. They are probably too little and too late. Over the next five to ten years the basic outer shell of total resources available for domestic programs will be determined much more abroad than they are in Washington. The range of priorities which can be met internally will therefore be shortened.

The sad facts of England indicate that current consumption and large levels of social input supported at the cost of capital investment in crucial industries and economic growth are self-defeating. The Galbraithian thesis, that the pie of American affluence is so very large that the basic requirement is merely a redistribution of the pieces, is an obvious fallacy, if for no other reason than the substantial increase in our labor force resulting from the high birth rate for the post-World War II days.

Where wil the jobs come from? Who is going to pay for them? What is going to make their products competitive? The grand cure-all of automation displacement—the growth in service occupations—may run into the same basic problem. Who is going to pay the bill?

Much of the wealth which we have enjoyed has been the product of the exploitation of native raw material and resources, and many of them are exhausted. Their replacements historically, for any of a variety of political reasons, were relatively cheap. But the days of dollar-a-barrel oil, of sheikdoms for a handful of Cadillacs, of bottomless copper mines worked by dollar-a-day labor are over.

In the new operating sheet of the future, the role and the amenities of the blue-collar worker will be subject to very intensive re-evaluation. Home-ownership will be a critical issue, among others, for its day-to-day impact on the working-class family as well as its symbolic meaning. The bitterness between the older blue-collar elements truly sold on affluent America, on the life styles promulgated so victoriously by the mass media, and minority groups striving for economic advance are accentuated by a relatively closed economic universe. It is amazing how much tolerace is generated by a gross national product that increased 5 or 6 percent a year—and how much bigotry is engendered by one that does not.

.